HOW TO RESTORE YOUR
DATSUN Z-CAR

WICK HUMBLE

FISHER BOOKS

Dedication

I lovingly dedicate this book to my wife,
Benita,
without whose unfailing support
it would still be just a daydream.

Publishers: Bill Fisher
Helen Fisher
Howard Fisher
J. McCrary

Editor: Tom Monroe. P.E.

Production: Karen McGraw

Art Director: Josh Young

Cover Design: Gary D. Smith, Performance Design
Cover Photos: ©1997 Nissan, North America, Gardena, CA
   Datsun 240Z Restoration Project,
   Photographer Hal Thomas
   ©1997 Pierre'Z by Hal Thomas

Published by Fisher Books, LLC
5225 W. Massingale Road
Tucson, AZ 84743-8416
(520) 744-6110

© 1990 Fisher Books
All rights reserved. No part of this book may be reproduced or transmitted in any form or by any means, electronic or mechanical, including photocopy, recording or any information storage or retrieval system without written permission from the publisher, except by a reviewer who may quote brief passages.

**Library of Congress
Cataloging-in-Publication Data**
Humble, Wick, 1945-
   How to restore your Datsun Z-Car / by Wick Humble.
      p.   cm.
   ISBN 1-55561-208-3 : $19.95
   1. Datsun automobile—Conservation and restoration. I. Title.
TL215.D35H85   1989
629.28'722dc20   89-17171
                                                                  CIP

Printed in U.S.A.
Printing 10 9 8 7 6

Notice: *The information contained in this book is true and complete to the best of our knowledge. All recommendations on parts and procedure are made without any guarantees on the part of the author or Fisher Books. Because the quality of parts, procedures and methods are beyond our control, author and publisher disclaim all liability incurred in connection with the use of this information.*

Table of Contents

Foreword 4
Introduction 5
   What is Restoration? 6
   How to Use This Book 7
Chapter 1—Procedures & Tips 9
   Planning Your Project 10
   Storage 12
   Restoration, Over-Restoration or Modification 14
   Frame-Up Versus Staged Restoration 16
   Used Parts 17
Chapter 2—Engine & Transmission Removal . . 21
   Engine Check 21
   Transmission Check 22
Chapter 3—Body Exterior Teardown 29
   Remove Fuel Tank 31
   Body Dissassembly 32
Chapter 4—Body Repair & Paint 37
   Engine-Compartment Preparation 37
   Prepping New Body Panels 39
   Rust Damage 43
   Trial Fitting of Body Parts 50
   Body & Paint 50
Chapter 5—Interior Trim & Component Removal 61
   Interior Dissassembly 62
   Remove Hatch 71
   Remove Instrument Panel 75
Chapter 6—Front Suspension & Brakes 81
   Remove Front Suspension, Steering & Brakes 81
   Remove & Recondition Brakes 85
   Recondition Front Suspension & Steering . . 87
   Install Front Suspension, Steering & Brakes . 90
   Remove & Recondition Steering Column . . 93
   Fasteners 96
   Install Steering Column 98
Chapter 7—Rear Suspension,
   Differential & Brakes 99
   Remove Rear Suspension,
      Differential & Brakes 99

Restore & Assemble Rear Suspension 106
Install Rear Suspension, Differential & Brakes 110
Recondition Halfshafts & Drive Shaft 112
Recondition Rear Brakes 112
Brake Fluid 113
Chapter 8—Electrical Components & Wiring . 115
   Restore Wiring Harness 116
   Electrical Parts Suppliers 117
   Install Wiring Harness 117
Chapter 9—Interior Assembly 121
   Restore Instrument Panel 121
   Restore Interior 126
   Install Glass 130
   Insulators 137
   Install Brake & Clutch Pedals
      & Master Cylinders 138
   Install Instrument Panel 144
   Restore & Install Console 143
   Restore Seats 147
   Restore & Install Taillights 152
   Restore & Install Radio Antenna 153
   Standard Bolt-Torque Specifications . . . 158
Chapter 10—Body Exterior
   & Driveline Assembly 159
   Restore & Install Doors 159
   Restore & Install Hatch 167
   Install Engine & Transmission 170
   Restore & Install Fuel System 170
   Bleed Hydraulic Systems 185
   Install Body Front End 186
Chapter 11—Technical Bulletins,
   Hi-Lights & Recalls 193
Chapter 12—Insuring Your Z-Car 201
Chapter 13—Z-Car Identification & Codes . . . 203
Parts & Services 204
Parts Illustrations 205
Metric Conversion Chart 237
Index 238

Thanks

I acknowledge the support and confidence of George Sinner, Karen Armor, Ida Grace Armor, Scott and Teri Humble, Ross and Anita Bullen, Brian Humble and many unnamed friends and relatives.

"Hands-on" helpers include Jerry Brooks, Ruben Mendivel, Cameron Olson and, of course, Holly and Cordy Humble.

Thanks to Denis Miller; Greg Smith of Motorsport Auto, Inc.; John Richmond of John's Foreign Car Repair; David Daigh of Daigh's Vintage Auto; Rod Taylor and Ray Postal of Chico Nissan Parts/Service Department; Greg Smith of Motorsport Auto, Inc.; Mike Castano and Howard Tarter at Chico Auto Parts Paint Department; Bob Hess of Auto Rust Doctors; Tim Donovan of Tabco; Joe Goldblatt of g-Machine, Inc.; Joe Triolo of Z Club of America, Bathurst, Inc.; and Bob Salz.

Special thanks to Janet Leiker, Frank Honsowetz, Neil MacKenzie and the helpful people at Nissan Motors in U.S.A. Also, to Eddie Korkes of the Z Club of America.

Extra special thanks to my friend and illustrator extraordinaire, Yoshihiro Inomoto, for allowing me to grace page 9 with one of his superlative phantom drawings of a Z-car.

Also to Tom Monroe, who—besides setting high technical and editorial standards—must have discovered new depths of patience and forbearance within himself while being my editor!

Foreword

How to use this book: I strongly recommend that if you are attempting a serious restoration, do your *homework*. By that I mean a good restoration—one that produces the maximum positive result with a minimum of anguish and expense. Accomplishing your goal requires not only adequate tools, skills and materials, it also requires knowledge. Such knowledge only comes from research combined with comprehension.

My own background is teaching, not preaching, as some readers might tend to surmise. I wrote this book using my own research, filtered through my own experience and powers of comprehension—not to mention the combined resources of my mentors listed in the Acknowledgements—to facilitate that experience.

But one book, or even several books, can be of little use if you don't utilize them fully. Please read each step through carefully *before* you attempt to carry it out. I, too, am tempted to look first at the illustrations in a manual, then read their captions and finally plow though the text itself.

I enjoyed writing this book almost as much as I enjoyed restoring our faithful Z-car. I hope you share that experience.

Use your Authorized Service Manual for all the information it contains—much of which both of us must rely on to do a correct restoration. I only give torque values on some major fasteners—the service manual should be your source of information for the rest, as it was mine. I filled in many of the gaps Datsun left and provided some steps that might not be approved of at a dealership, but are accepted by restorers. As for other publications, those I mention in the text are unbeatable for their content and readability. They belong on the shelf of any true Z afficionado.

Obtain catalogs from reliable suppliers such as those listed at the end of the book—Motorsport Auto, ZAP Automotive, Bob Sharp and others are worth the cost—just as resource materials. Use other books on Zs, magazine articles and Datsun advertising materials as research, just as you would if you were restoring a Cord or early T-Bird. Restoration can be a great hobby. Done correctly, it saves rather than costs money!

Though Fisher Books and I have given *How To Restore Your Datsun Z-Car* our best shot, errors or omissions may have crept in. Because you have agreed to read the text *and* look at the pictures, you may find them. Please inform me of any discrepancies you may find by writing the publisher. And if you find the book helpful, we'd like to know that, too!

Thank you!

Introduction

July, 1970, Brooke Army Medical Center, Texas. Fresh off the boat, back when Z-car owners actually waved when they met on the highway. In most respects, our project 240Z is in better condition today than it was then.

Congratulations! You've made two very good decisions:

One—because you are reading this book, you probably own a Datsun 240Z, 260Z or 280Z. That indicates you have good taste, a strong sense of value and, of course, the ability to enjoy driving more than the average car owner.

Two—because you've selected this Fisher Book to be your restoration reference, you can be assured that *How to Restore Your Datsun Z-car* has the information you will need to do a top-notch restoration of the body, chassis and interior of your Z.

Because of space limitations this book does not include engine, transmission or differential rebuilding, just detailing. These are so complex that a separate manual would be required for each.

Of course, if you wish or need to rebuild your Z-car's engine or merely want to gain a better familiarity with it, I highly recommend *How to Rebuild Your Nissan/Datsun OHC Engine* by Tom Monroe, Fisher Books' Publisher. Also available is *How to Modify Your Nissan/Datsun OHC Engine* by Frank Honsowetz, of Nissan Motorsports. In addition to these I strongly advise that you also familiarize yourself with the factory service manual for your car. These are available for Datsun/Nissan products from:

Dyment Distributing Service
20770 Westwood Drive
Strongsville, OH 44136
(800) 247-5321

The cost is reasonable and, along with this book, the factory manual will be indispensable during the course of your restoration.

Factory Authorized Service Manuals—you can't do without one. I've been using the two-book set since 1970.

Z-Car History—Whether or not you consciously considered it, many of the qualities that attracted you to your Z-car are the same ones that will assure the first-series Zs—pre-ZX—their special niche among modern automobiles. Also, for better or occasionally worse, they've already had a marked effect on the relative values of the various 240Z, 260Z, 280Z and derived 2+2 models.

What your Z-car is actually *worth*, other than sentimental value, is determined by good old supply and demand. As a Z-car fan from the beginning, I must say that the only thing standing between inflated values on an original Z is that Z-car sales in the United States have always been excellent. It is, in fact, the all-time best-selling sports car ever! Over 542,000 units were sold worldwide, according to Datsun. In other words, there are a lot of them out there . . . but demand is growing.

The original 240Z was a whole new kind of quality and performance machine for that manufacturer and really the Japanese auto industry as a whole. Sales were better than even the builder ever expected. And the Z spearheaded the Japanese auto industry's ultimately successful invasion of the American market. As such, the Z-car will always be significant in automotive history. The enthusiastic reception it received should provide that a relatively plentiful supply will continue to be available.

Logically, this in itself will preclude any real strong rarity factor, such as might occur with less well-received cars. The good news is the Z-car appreciates in value over time. And because of their high numbers, parts availability will be good.

What Is Restoration?
Let's look at what I mean by the word *restoration*. Webster defines restore as: "To bring back to a former or normal condition, as by repairing, rebuilding, altering, etc." In this book I take a rather strict interpretation of the term *alter* to mean *alter back to original condition, as-manufactured specifications and appearance if modifications were made*. It is not within the format of this book to detail non-factory modifications, although I may allude to approved retrofits, recall modifications, competition or heavy-usage applications that might be considered original.

To some people, the word *restore* has become as hackneyed as *rebuild*. Pick up *How to Rebuild Your Nissan/Datsun OHC Engine* to see what is correctly meant by *rebuild*. And in the same sense, this book will define restore as it applies to the Z-car. Not that any product of the hand of humankind is too perfect to improve upon—but more than enough literature exists on the various and plentiful modifications that a Z may or may not benefit from. This book provides a baseline. The rest is between your wallet, your skills and your Z-car.

What Do You Have to Restore?
The original 240Z, built from late 1969 through the 1973 model year, was hailed by drivers and the motoring press as a near-miracle of style, performance, comfort and value. Some 135,905 units—Datsun's model HSL30—were sold in the United States. Only 9977 were registered as 1970s; 26,733 as '71s; 46,537 as '72s; and 52,556 as '73s.

A number of detail changes took place on the 240Z series, such as the ventilator outlets moved from the hatch to the C-pillar, differential mounting moved rearward slightly to decrease axle angularity and, for the 1973 year, a more protruding bumper. Engine displacement remained at 2393cc (146 cubic inches). These first three years of Z-cars are generally acknowledged to be the most sporting performers in stock trim.

Though the 240Zs are far from the lowest in total production numbers, their age and their use in competition has contributed to a high degree of rarity. Along with obvious antiquity, all Zs have a fatal susceptibility to premature rust out—not a good factor, especially with a unit-body car. More on this later!

Few 1970 Zs were sold at or near their much-publicized suggested price of $3671. The reason was dealers realized their strong demand early on and added many price-inflating options. Due to their very low total production, a good unrusted, untrashed '70 example is the rarest Z of all. If pricing trends are any indication, the more refined '72—even with a 5:1 sales margin—has assumed a preeminence in the hearts of Z-car buyers. On the other hand, any sound original 1970—72 Z doesn't depreciate!

More changes were made on the 1973 240Z due to pressure from both government for decreased exhaust emissions and the buying public to maintain levels of performance and economy. Consequently, a revised induction system was adopted. In an uncharacteristic lapse of Japanese technology, the new Hitachi/SU carburetion immediately hurt drivability on later 240Zs and ensuing 260Zs in 1974.

A displacement increase to 2565cc (156 cubic inches) was initiated for the type GSL30 to compensate for performance-stealing weight from structural and equipment additions. Some 45,160 units, including 9499 of the longer 1974 2+2 version, were sold in the US—an appreciable slip from the previous year's total. An entirely new instrument panel/console design was incorporated on the 260Z, as well as other interior changes. These, combined with a one-year-only model run, make the 260Z the second-rarest Z. Interestingly, early-year '74s retained the previous year's bumper with shock mounts, but a mid-year switch to what would become the 1975 280Zs energy-absorbing bumpers tends to stigmatize the 260Z as a stopgap model.

Some car publications deplored what they thought was a softening of the original Z-car's sporting tendencies and the steady increase in sticker price. But the new-for-'75 280Z—now at 2753cc (168 cubic inches)—found 50,213 buyers in the U.S. This increased to 54,838 in 1976 and a high of 69,516 in '77. Because the all-new on the outside 280ZX appeared in 1978, some 41,842 (worldwide) 280Zs finished the original Z-car model run.

It is true, along with a steady escalation of the list price, Datsun's dealers took every advantage to load showroom Zs with as many approved options and aftermarket glitz as possible. Many buyers from about the late '70s onward never laid eyes on the steel wheels or hubcaps originally installed on their cars. Much like the two-seat Thunderbirds, the flashier, rowdier early Zs established the marque's mystique, but the luxurious, less-athletic later versions with the greatest market penetration made the most profit.

By the time the 280Z was supplanted, it had indeed become a plush grand tourer. The relative value of these Zs has suffered little if any on

Original Datsun advertising literature is fun to collect for your year and model Z-car. Be aware such material was often published well in advance of vehicle introduction, so it may not represent the final production car. Early accessory brochure is interesting in this respect.

the used-car market, meaning that valuations are sure to increase. Now, of course, early Zs have begun to be recognized on established collector's value guides.

The Datsun Z seems to have offered something for most every sports-car buyer—except a convertible—and the later series don't need any rarity factor to preserve their value. Features such as air conditioning, choice of 5-speed or automatic transmissions and optional 4-place seating combine to make the 280Z a capstone to what is essentially the most successful sports/GT car ever. These options are enhanced by power assists and, best of, all the efficient and responsive Bosch L-Jetronic fuel-injection.

From the beginning, Datsun Zs have been successfully campaigned in races and rallies. And they have always won high marks for styling and engineering. Z-cars have proved to be consistently well-constructed and durable. They respond to owner's repair and maintenance efforts and benefit from a still growing aftermarket-parts market.

It's no wonder, then, that you and I—along with over half-a-million driving enthusiasts from Japan to the Netherlands—find the Z-car worth owning, driving and now restoring.

Collector-car publications as early as the Zs second season adroitly predicted that Datsun had built a true modern classic—the first Japanese car ever to so aspire. And I will stick my neck out to state that the 240-260-280Z will probably remain the most historically important of that nation's automobiles.

So—again, congratulations! And welcome to what I hope will be a rewarding and satisfying experience in restoring your Datsun Z-car.

Tips On How To Use This Book

Some Things Come In Pairs—There are more than a few automobile components that there are *two* of—seats, doors, headlights and so on. Therefore, if I provide step-by-step instructions on how to dismantle, restore and reassemble a brake caliper, assume the process applies to *both* calipers. Do two, even if the book doesn't remind you to do so.

Datsun Nomenclature—I am alternately charmed and confounded by some of the names the factory folk use for many of the parts and operations related to the Z-car in both

Service Manuals and Parts Manuals. Because these tend to be confusing, I substituted common Americanized names for clarification.

Organization—Chapters of this book are arranged in order for a *frame-up* restoration. As with an engine teardown/buildup text, I follow the particular sequence as it occurred during the restoration of my project car.

I have always disliked how-to-do-it instructions that tell me to "Install (or reassemble) in the reverse order of removal (or disassembly)." In restoration, much more thought and effort—to say nothing of expense—goes into a reassembly or reinstallation than would otherwise occur in a routine dealer-type repair.

Sidebars—Please don't skip the information contained in the "boxed-in" sections. Sidebars aren't necessarily less important or accurate in any respect. They merely provide a convenient way to present related material.

Early & Late—You will find many references to *early* and *late* types. The premier series Z-car was built from late 1969 through early 1978. During that period Datsun made a number of changes in what was basically the same automobile . . . and not all at the same time, either. So there are early and late Zs within one model year, too.

Series Designations—240Z, 260Z and 280Z—reflect only an approximation of engine displacement and not necessarily anything else. As examples, there were distinctly different (early/late) steerings, instrument panels, turn signals, taillights and finishers, seats, door latches, induction systems and floorpan designs. Also, there are three different styles of consoles, interior vinyl, seat-belt systems, bumper systems, hub caps and more! Add transmission options, automatic or standard (4- or 5-speed) and a larger four-passenger body style—you get the picture.

At first glance this could seem like too much diversity to include under one heading. And if you're just reading for pleasure, it might be. But I assume that you already have a specific Z-car and know which one it is. Thus, when the text refers to an *early* cardboard glove-box liner or a *late* plastic glove-box liner, the information to follow will be obvious if you can distinguish one material from the other. Looking at it another way, an early 240Z and a late 280Z—eight years apart in age—probably have more in common than a 1955 Chevy and a 1957 Chevy of the same body style.

Help!—In a number of places I mention that a helper, or at least another hand, will be beneficial. Some assistance at your beck and call is a nice luxury, but you can perform many procedures on a Z restoration by yourself. Not that I won't accept a little help when I can get it, but I did most of the work on my project car alone—including the photography! Just be sure, as I do, that you don't jeopardize your health by attempting risky jobs or using unsafe practices in your shop.

Safety—Heed any cautions or warnings I give. When that "writer guy" says to be careful, take precautions and think through iffy situations. Do it for your Z, if not for yourself!

What's in a Name—You won't be surprised to find that Datsun-Nissan didn't make every single part of your car in their own factory. No manufacturer does! Here are some trademarks that can be found on Z parts: Bridgestone, Toyo, Iki, Fuji, Kiko, Clarion, Sumitomo, Nippon Denso, Jeco, Tokiko, Hitachi, Nabco, NGK, Amco and some that are undoubtedly in Japanese—to name a few. And these are all original-equipment manufacturers (OEM). So don't hesitate to use parts or accessories that have other than the Datsun-Nissan name or trademark on them. Just know your supplier—and be sure HE has confidence in the parts he has for your car.

I have strived to write as clearly as possible, but a few definitions are in order before we begin.

When I say *Z* or *Z-car,* I mean the first series 240, 260 and 280Z, without the X.

When I say *Datsun,* I mean the name of the company in the USA back when it sold the Z-car—all were registered as *Datsun.*

When I say *Nissan,* I mean the same company as of the time this book was written, after its name change. Nissan was always the parent company in Japan.

And, when I say *He* or *She,* I mean she or he—because both genders were and are fans of the fabulous Datsun Z! I hope that these distinctions provide clarity and not further confusion.

1 Restoration Procedures & Tips

Phantom 240Z: Datsun commissioned a series of illustrations to be done for the initial Z-car introduction. This cutaway drawing by Yoshihiro Inomoto and a red non-phantom version were issued to dealers as a poster. They are collectors' items now. Courtesy Nissan.

Rule number-one: During disassembly, don't trust your memory! You *will* forget, or "mis-remember," after a surprisingly short time.

Few humans have the kind of photographic memory that can recall every detail of an assembly sequence. Experts who study the human-thinking process generally agree that the problem is less forgetfulness than the *overlayment* of new thoughts and information on previous ones. The same result occurs in any event.

The problem in disassembling and reassembling a mechanism is that even a simple sequence becomes blurred by each succeeding step. In other words, what seems obvious while you are doing it may become a total blank even a few moments later. It is altogether too easy to assume that some detail is so obvious that you couldn't forget even if you tried. But if you're like me, anything can blur enough of that supposedly "indelibly imprinted" thought to make reassembly with absolute confidence impossible. This can be caused by a subsequent disassembly procedure, an interruption like a call to the telephone or even dropping a tool.

What Should I Do?—Because memory is so unreliable, take precautions. Do whatever it takes to jog your recall to prevent those frustrating mistakes. Of course, when I'm authoring a book, I make copious notes and take lots of photos—only a portion of which see print. Following are some techniques I've used that you might find helpful:

Use a sensible, standardized storage system. Techniques suggested in this book not only keep bits and pieces safe, they also go a long way toward keeping you organized. Your memory has a fighting chance of being helpful if it is relieved of the task of keeping tabs on every little nut and clip.

Keep a sharp, soft-lead (HB or #2) pencil or two handy. Keep a notebook, preferably with graph-ruled paper (grid of little squares) close to your work area. Even if you aren't an artist, don't worry. You aren't producing for anyone but yourself. Out of necessity, develop a method of sketching that will provide you with the kind of detailed information you can't entrust to memory. Don't forget, that is *most of the information!*

The Nissan Authorized Service Manual is as good as anyone's, but most always seem to take for granted just the detail or sequence that is desperately needed. Not only are Service Manuals valuable for the information they provide, they have another benefit—if you don't mind writing in them.

Use that sharp pencil to draw on the illustrations or make your own notes in the margins. Use Post-it® notes on the pages, paper clip your sketches or exploded drawings in the appropriate section or stick a manila envelope to the "service journal" or "bulletin reference" pages. I keep all paperwork that comes with replacement parts handy, even if the text is in Japanese. Better a slick restoration and a messy service manual. After all, it's your book!

I include a number of exploded drawings of body and chassis assemblies from obsolete Datsun parts books. These are not included in technical manuals, having been committed to microfiche by the manufacturer. They are available here courtesy of Nissan and the Z Club of America. Space limitations prohibit listing all parts numbers originally keyed to these. Old Datsun parts books occasionally turn up for sale at swap meets, but copies with Z information are hoarded like First Editions of Shakespeare!

Photos—Sure, though this is expensive. A Polaroid snapshot makes the most sense because you can tell almost immediately if the information you need actually shows up. Black-and-white pictures are adequate, but color film and processing for instant cameras and even the little Instamatic variety are cheaper than black-and-white. Adequate lighting is a must if prints are to be truly useful. A photograph is invaluable if your memory needs jogged!

The advent of the personal video recorder opens up a whole new dimension to memory-jogging. It is still theoretical in my shop. I'm interested to know if you have tried it!

Self-Control—Leave subassemblies together until you really need to tear them down. Only a novice will dismantle every bit of every mechanism at once. It's asking for trouble later on. I remove all components necessary to begin my restoration. Then I take on the repair and restoration of each component or assembly in a logical sequence.

The master cylinder, for instance, waits until it is nearly time to put it back on the restored firewall before I spread the many parts over the bench. If I farmed out the rebuilding or bought a rebuilt unit that required an exchange core, that's different. Then I wouldn't be tearing it down at all. I allow enough lead time to assess any damage or deterioration. Then I order all the parts needed to rebuild an assembly.

Talk To Yourself—When you tear down a part, make notes regarding parts that you think you will need. Use these notes to keep tabs on what is received and what may be back-ordered and so forth. If you need to remove some part from an assembly, note this as well. This is especially true if you suspect you have lost or broken any items during the disassembly. I even keep stripped screws, torn rubber parts and—within reason—corroded or worn-out pieces until I have the exact replacements on hand. That way I know what the deficient part looked like in case the exact replacement isn't available. I can make a serviceable substitution that still looks right in most cases.

When you work with obsolete vehicles, it doesn't take long to learn the hard way—obsolete parts are in short supply.

Some Hard-Learned Tips
One For the Pot—If you lose fasteners, make a note and be sure you replace them before reassembly time. Nothing is more frustrating than to come up one nut short. Seriously, I usually buy one extra fastener each time I replace a set. The cost is usually minimal and the peace of mind is worth it!

Inventory—If you must send out small parts of any kind, such as for replating, make an inventory. Identify screws and nuts by size and thread. Keep this list with the assembly until the parts are safely in hand. I have nothing against plating shops, but you can expect to come up short one piece or another.

You should appreciate what a plater goes through in accounting for the many small but vital parts he routinely checks in and out. By carefully organizing them, you can help the shop manager and assure that a maximum amount of expensive bits and pieces are returned to your custody.

Consider taking in a limited number of parts to be plated—especially fasteners—every time the previous batch is done. This might be easier on the budget, also.

Planning Your Project
Plan Ahead—Not a joke! If this is not your first restoration, you know what I mean and how valid it is. Many diverse factors can affect a restoration during its course. The quality, cost and degree of satisfaction you enjoy at its completion are directly influenced by the extent of your planning.

Even though this may be your first restoration, you should be optimistic because you bought this book. But don't delude yourself. Use all the resources at your disposal to prepare for and schedule your project realistically. Whether you opt for the "frame-up" or "staged" restoration or something in between, the last thing you should derive from the experience is that "Never again . . ." feeling at some point!

Only you—and your family—know what things will bear most heavily on your "born-again" Z-car. Capital outlay—"What's this all going to cost?"—is frequently the biggest hurdle.

My long-suffering wife Benita has endured six or seven restorations in our married life. She confided that she usually adds about 30% to my most-pessimistic estimates of project costs! Fortunately, we have acquired the skills and facilities to do the largest part of our projects on our own. Saving on labor really increases your ability to afford a complete restoration.

What Work Can You Do Yourself?—While we're on the subject, ask yourself what, if anything, can you tackle on your Z-project? What you attempt will depend heavily on the resources you have or can borrow. A good set of hand tools is imperative, including metric end wrenches and sockets. Engine rebuilding is

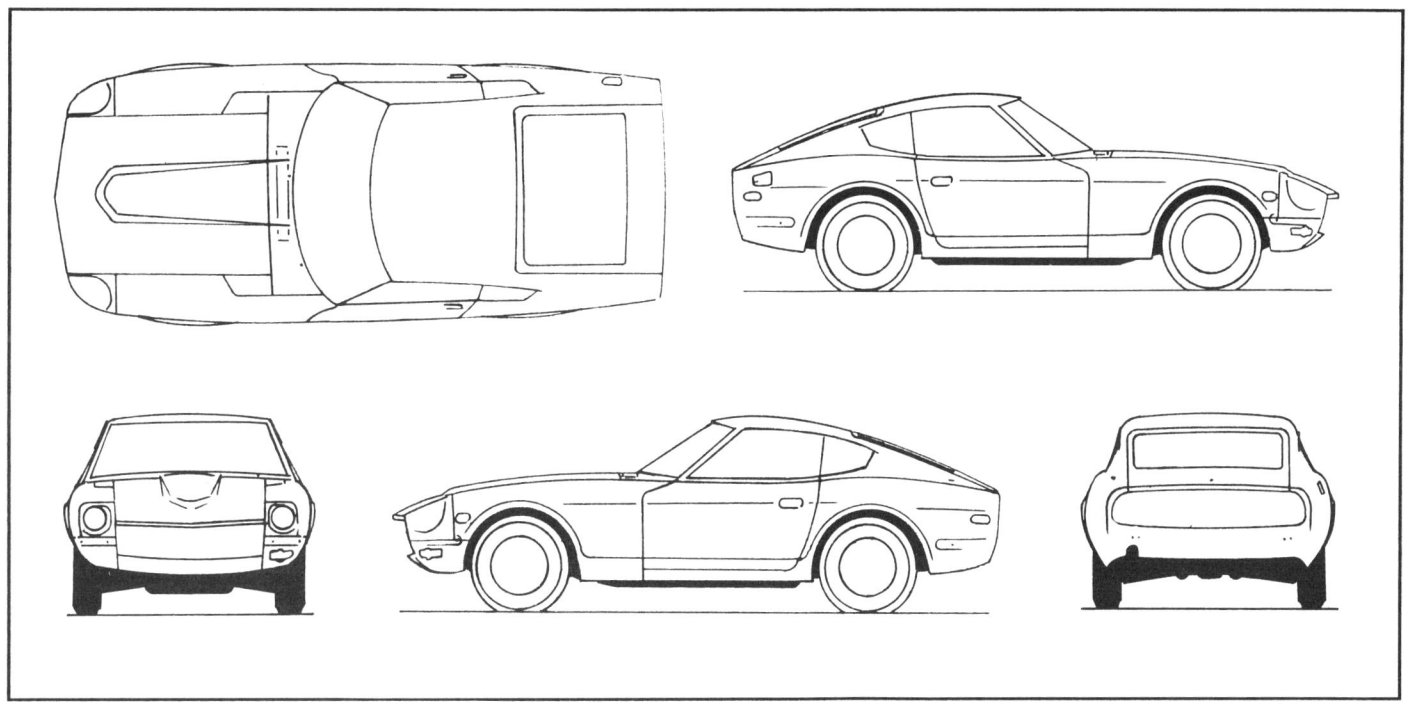

Use these views to inventory dents, scratches and rust on your Z project. Use my code, page 12, and write on the page. After all, it's your book!

within the realm of the nonprofessional, if information and services of a quality machine shop are available.

Information is already available. Tom Monroe authored *How to Rebuild Your Nissan/Datsun OHC Engine*. This definitive manual for the L-24, L-26 and L-28 Datsun six-cylinder engine is written in concise "American" and has over 500 illustrations! Fisher Books publishes it.

Also, if modifying your engine is in order, refer to *How to Modify Your OHC Nissan/Datsun* by Frank Honsewetz, Nissan Competition Director. You will be surprised at what can be done with Nissan Competition parts—while remaining fairly "original." Fisher Books publishes it.

If you do the painting, HPBooks publishes Don Taylor & Larry Hofer's Paint & Body Handbook, which will tell even the novice all he or she needs to know. This book includes much that is specific to the Z-car breed. Refer to it for basic body-repair and paint information, which is beyond the scope of this book.

Upholstery & Trim Work—Much of this work is within the realm of the shadetree restoration enterprise, particularly if you have Don Taylor's *Auto Upholstery Handbook*, published by Fisher Books.

Beyond a commercial "walking-foot" sewing machine, which you may be able to rent, trimming can largely be accomplished with simple, easily acquired tools. Being a meticulous seamstress, Benita found that one college extension class and the aforementioned tools were enough to enable her do virtually all interior work . . . with excellent results!

A good variety of presewn kits are available, most of which are authentic in appearance and as serviceable as the original. I show how to install a replacement seat-cover kit as well as a headliner and other trim.

Parts and supply costs will depend largely on how much work your example of *genus* Z needs to bring it to the condition that satisfies you. The more you can do yourself, the more of your budget you'll have for these expenses. This may mean a better, more thorough job and less downtime and sooner enjoyment of your pride-and-joy.

Before You Start

Take Inventory—We've discussed planning your restoration to some degree. Now you should take a good look at your raw material. As a TV series of the '60s opened: "There are 500,000 stories in Z-city . . . this is one of them." Maybe that wasn't it. But every one of the surviving half-million-plus Z-cars sold worldwide has by now lived at least one car's normal lifetime, although each life was different. What you must do in restoring yours depends on what it "tells" you it needs.

Ultimately, the sweat, worry and money you expend also depends on the quality and completeness you demand in a restoration. I believe that a job worth doing is worth doing right—to repeat a cliché. A basic strategy I endorse is taking inventory of the needs a car shows outwardly. Body sheet metal is a case in point and a good place to begin.

Before you remove anything from your car, take a series of photographs; one each from the side, then front and rear. A high-angle shot or two is invaluable, especially of the hood and fenders. These are not to grace your family album, though before and after shots are great for "oohs" and "aahs" from folks later on. You'll use them for an inventory of body damage, establishing just where and what is there before the pounding and sanding begins. As an alternative, use accurate line drawings.

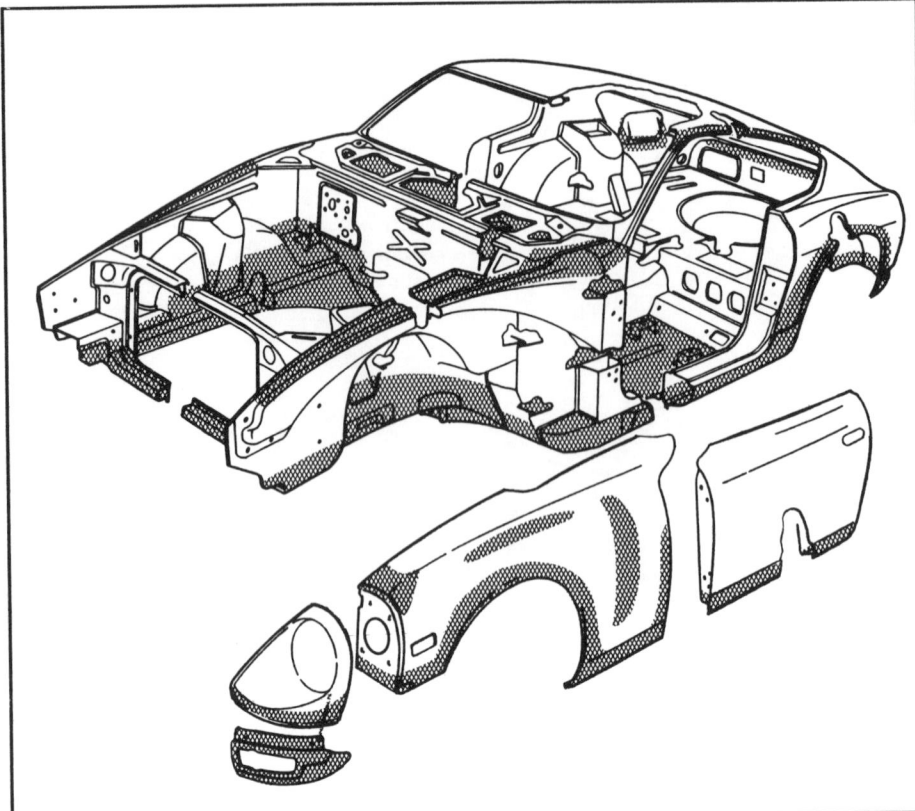
Shaded areas on drawing indicate those most likely to rust. Courtesy Nissan.

For clarity's sake, the larger the prints, the better. Adopt a set of symbols to indicate what the problem is as well as where it is. My code is simple: An **X** shows high areas, places where impacts or stresses have caused the metal to be displaced *upwards* from the original plane. In cases of a crease, I mark a line along the ridge with a small **x** at each end.

For the more common dents, an **O** or some distortion of that shape to delineate where the metal has been displaced *downwards* relative to the original plane. Because most dents and dings are not round, I draw lots of ovals and amoeba-shaped forms!

Just Extra Work?—It might seem superfluous to do all that marking on a photo, where you may very well be able to see the damage well enough. But obvious distortions are not the crucial ones. What you're after are the subtle dings and wrinkles that suddenly become invisible after the gloss is gone from the old paint.

Just knowing were a problem exists beforehand is more important in rectifying it. This is true even if you *guide-coat* and block-sand a panel. Where there was once a distortion there will still be a distortion until you fix it!

Take care of these problems in an orderly manner, using the appropriate methods in a sensible sequence. What could be more frustrating than to have a panel that appears to be completely smooth, then find a major ripple over the crown that will require torch, grinder and dolly work to correct it?

Equally frustrating is a parking-lot ding you missed because it was close to a bigger dent. You discover it after your thousand-dollar paint job has gone on! Referring back to your photo-inventory of problems just once before the final finish goes on can save a lot of embarrassing, frustrating glitches in the final finish.

I refer to my prints at guide-coating time, well before it is too late to do a little filling and blocking. You can't go wrong with this method. Using drawings or photos of other than your car might provide a good frame of reference as well. But it seems more relevant to look at your own project, if possible.

Suspected Rust—I use cross-hatching on photos to indicate areas that may be rusted. Because of its insidious nature, rust becomes *more* evident as the overlying paint comes off. Really advanced rust-out gives more than adequate outer signs: blistering paint, perforations, discoloration. Less-advanced rust may only show pinhole or freckled evidence. I cover rust detection and elimination in more detail in Chapter 4.

If your Z is like most other cars, most rust damage will be out of sight. Be aware, however, of missing small rust infestations in your preoccupation with the grosser areas. These inevitably grow, even under new paint.

File your photo inventory near your work area. It will be of little help tucked in with last year's tax forms!

Storage

Dealing With Your Needs—An often underestimated concern in a restoration project is adequate storage. You need storage for your Z-car, plus all the many bits and pieces that will be removed from it.

It seems that at least one standard garage space is minimum for a standard-size sports car. I say minimum because I have seen quality restorations done in no more room than an automobile is expected to occupy. The Z is not a large car. The average suburban garage accommodates a complete, *intact* Z-car nicely.

The problem, however, is the space that same car requires when stripped for the work to be performed on its various areas. The old rule about "the whole is more than the sum of its parts" is inverted in a frame-up restoration—a dismantled Z easily occupies over twice its assembled volume! Even if you are careful and efficient to a fault, you will be most comfortable having the absolute maximum space to work in.

My Place, or Yours?—Of course, if you are having your car done in a commercial shop, your storage problem may be solved. Just make sure you are guaranteed where it will be and what steps are taken to protect it during the restoration. Usually, but not always, a good inspection of the shop will reassure you as to the management's procedures and capacity. Don't take anything for granted. Some years back I found a project car that I had stripped to bare metal sitting in the rain behind the body shop that was to give it a deluxe refinish job! The ensuing scene was not a pretty one and was what prompted me to do my own paint and bodywork!

Additionally, if your restoration plan is to be done in stages, considerably less space at any given time may be required. However, don't expect a driveway or carport to be satisfactory, for security reasons, if nothing else. Give yourself every advantage and overestimate space needs.

Storage of large parts and assemblies needn't take too much room until those pieces are rebuilt and refinished. This is especially true in the case of a frame-up project. Many components may be painted separately from the body-chassis. But they must be protected until the time comes to reinstall them. Crowding your beautifully painted front fenders, doors, hood and other sheet-metal parts into your work area is running the risk of damaging your laboriously perfected surfaces.

Maximize What Is Available—Don't squander usable space. Secure, dry indoor-storage volume is premium. Attics can be used in many cases to stash parts that aren't overly heavy or bulky. The average two-car garage potentially has cubic yards of dry, out of the way storage among its rafters. Even a truss-built roof can accommodate fairly large sheet-metal parts, if they are placed right.

Then there are the garage walls, which shelving can be placed against. Nothing is more space efficient for storage. Buy them or build them, but make sure shelving is secure and can't fall over. Just imagine a shelf loaded with a steering gear, brakes, suspension parts and similar components falling over on your newly painted Z. So fasten the shelves to the wall if that's what it takes.

The old restorer's gag about hiding windows or rechromed bumpers under the bed has basis in reality. Storing car parts in your house requires cooperation from your family. If they are well wrapped or boxed and out of sight, this may help your cause . . . and it will ease shop overcrowding. Just assure your house-mates that it is only temporary!

Use Common Sense—I hate to indulge in more "Don't's," but wedging upholstered panels behind a water heater may not only ruin the upholstery, it may also create a fire hazard. Don't stack parts haphazardly or obstruct pathways. Develop a plan of attack, taking into consideration various factors that influence your particular project.

Small-Parts Storage—Few things can be more frustrating than knowing you have all the parts to reassemble your project, but are unable to put your hands on whatever you need to do it! The antidote for this plague is a *methodical* disassembly and a carefully *organized* parts-storage system.

Small parts—bushings, capscrews, washers, nuts and other fasteners especially—look a lot alike after a while. While some may be interchanged without ill effect—washers, for instance—the majority were designed and spec'd for just where they originally fit in an assembly.

Equally frustrating is not being able to find a particular component you need, even if it is only a correctly graded capscrew. Imagine having your engine swaying over the spotlessly refinished engine compartment and not being able to find the bolts needed to attach it to its mounts. Or having a coil spring compressed and in place on its strut assembly just to discover that you're short the exact nylock nut needed to secure it to the shock rod. Such occurrences show poor planning and take a lot of fun out of a restoration.

As Tom Monroe aptly put it, "Most people have an inherent knack for taking things apart." Most of us have the "ghost" of some mechanical gadget disassembled with no hope of reassembly. This often happens because we trust our frail memory to accomplish the reverse process. Unless you are blessed with a photographic memory, reassembling in reverse order of disassembly is at best a formidable challenge. Never mind what some manuals suggest.

What Works?—Besides plenty of technical information readily at hand, I find that careful and categorical parts storage works best when something has to go back together—right! There are as many ways to organize and keep all those bits and pieces as there are restorers. I'll tell you what works best for me, then you decide what will work best for your project.

In the Bag—How small is the part? My all-time favorite storage helper is the zip-lock plastic bag. Marketed under different brand names, they have many advantages. First, you can see what's inside and whether or not you have cleaned and refinished it. An adhesive label can be stuck on the outside or notes can be included inside with the part. They are moistureproof, protecting bare metal from corrosion or clean areas from dirty parts. A good-size box stores them conveniently and is very economical.

Zip-lock bags come in a variety of sizes. I use dozens of the sandwich size to sort small parts. That is the biggest advantage—convenience in identifying specific parts during disassembly. I don't usually trust them to hold really big, heavy parts. But being able to put two little screws and washers in a bag by themselves is a plus if I need to remember exactly where they go. Another advantage is they can be reused providing they are clean. The main disadvantage of zip-lock bags is their vulnerability to "hot" solvents such as lacquer thinner.

A cousin of zip-lock bags is the trash-can liner. These are also inexpensive and come in a variety of sizes and gauges. While most bulky parts and assemblies are too heavy for the average garbage bag, they are quite effective in protecting these from moisture or soil. Paint masking can be done with trash bags, too.

Twist-ties like those that come with garbage bags can also be used to organize parts. I keep a spool of twist-ties handy for just this purpose. Occasionally, the more glamorous tie-wrap is handy for the same thing, but costs too much for temporary duty.

Wired—Similarly, a spool of soft mechanic's wire is inexpensive and much stronger. I keep some handy for dipping parts into cleaning solvents and suspending them while painting. Old coat hangers can also be used.

Something that is very handy is old-fashioned single-strand household electrical wire. This wire is mostly obsolete and, thereby, cheap! Electrical wiring has a vinyl insulation,

14 How to Restore Your Datsun Z-Car

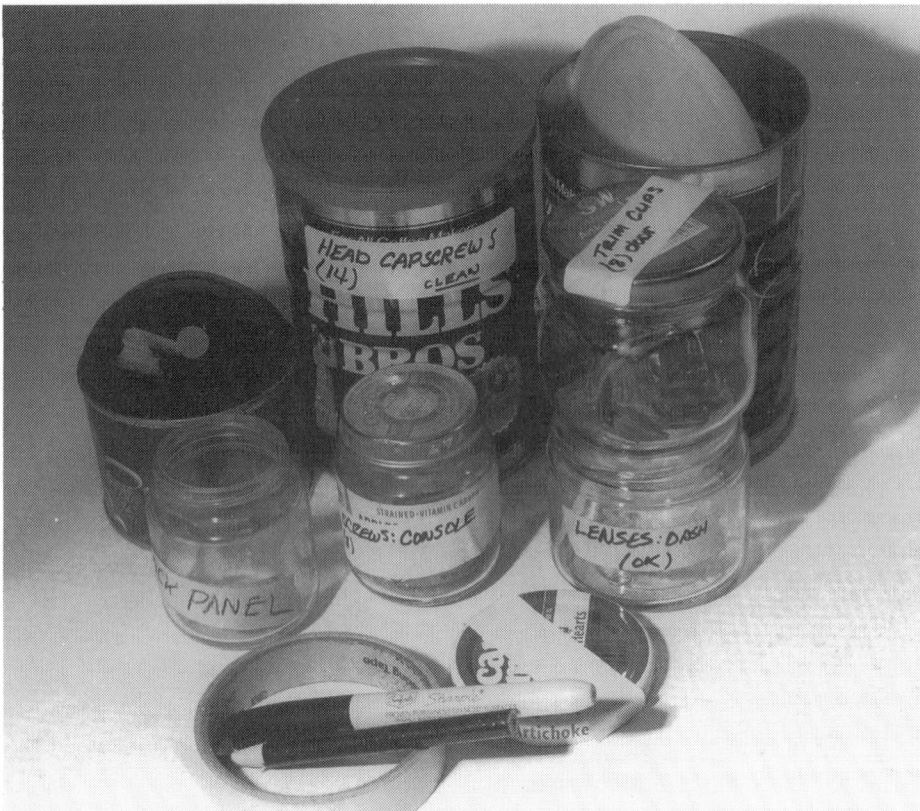

Storage containers and markers: Zip-lock bags are great for small-parts storage. Sharpie pens and China-marker grease pencils are moisture-proof.

which protects painted surfaces. I keep it on hand for holding components I'll paint separately.

Sealable Containers—Another classic is the coffee can with a reusable plastic top, which comes in various sizes. Put out the word to your coffee-drinking friends and you'll accumulate a good stock in no time. When I'm painting, I never seem to have enough clean coffee cans.

Baby-food jars can be used for storage, but those currently available usually don't have metal-lug seals. And there's always the problem of breakage. Although plastic medicine bottles usually aren't transparent, as are glass jars, and have a small mouth, they are durable and seal well. Also, you can write on them with a permanent felt-marker pen. Plastic or metal 35mm film cans are super for storing teeny parts.

Boxes—All kinds of boxes are handy. I keep a bunch of the kind that holds four six-packs in broken-down form, ready to be taped into shape for holding big items.

A convenient box-storage system can be made from the flat, narrow carton that fluorescent shop-light fixtures come in. Simply tape both ends shut securely, then slice the box on a diagonal 6—10 inches up. This gives two file-type containers used by parts houses for each carton, and they are very convenient when lined up on a shelf. Paper-supply outlets sell all kinds and sizes of cardboard cartons, but they aren't cheap. Be creative and save!

Identification—Big and small parts alike must be identified.

Caution: Avoid sticking anything to a restored part. For instance, many mechanics like to use masking tape to tag parts. Don't! I repeat, *don't use masking tape* to identify parts, particularly if you must leave it on for more than a few days.

Masking tape was not meant for permanent use. If exposed to direct sunlight, it turns crisp and brittle. The adhesive that chemists at 3M worked so hard to make removable when "fresh" is maddeningly hard to get off when dried out. Ironically, this is especially true if it is stuck to a freshly painted surface! And don't use silver duct tape, commonly called *racers tape*, either.

I recommend the old-fashioned pasteboard tag secured by whatever you choose: soft wire, string, fish line, twist-tie or whatever. If laminated with a layer of clear-plastic tape, it will survive even a steam-cleaning.

Labels for your zip-locks, coffee cans or cartons are another story. Masking tape is fine for this, especially wide varieties. Be aware that there are two qualities of masking tape. Brand name body-shop masking variety—3M, Behr-Norton and others your paint-and-body-shop supplier sells are fine. The bargain kind typically sells two-for-a-buck at discount stores. Although OK for labels, get the "good stuff" for masking. For legibility, a better alternative is self-sticking mailing labels. Available at office-supply stores, they come in various sizes and in colors—which can be used to code different component classifications. Another possibility is old video-cassette labels.

I keep several *Sharpie*-type permanent flow-tip pens in my tool box, breaking in a new one when the old one starts to make a fat line. They will even mark directly on parts or photos if the need should arise. The ink dries fast and won't rub off. If you mark a photo with a ball-point pen, the ink never dries. It just rubs off on the next photo in the pile and eventually blurs out so you can't see what was there in the first place. Sharpies come in black, blue and red.

Restoration, Over-Restoration or Modification

As I mentioned in the Introduction, the scope of this Fisher Book is the process of how to restore a Datsun Z-car to a condition no better or worse than it was when it came off the assembly line. To me, this describes an honest-to-goodness *restored* car.

Many restorers, in their zealous appreciation of their favorite car, tend to take the "nothing-is-too-good" attitude. This simply leads to what is known as "over-restoration."

I can't disagree that hand-rubbed lacquer gives a deeper luster than the original synthetic-enamel finish, for instance. Or that "trick" acrylic urethanes to protect suspension components are a more durable substitute

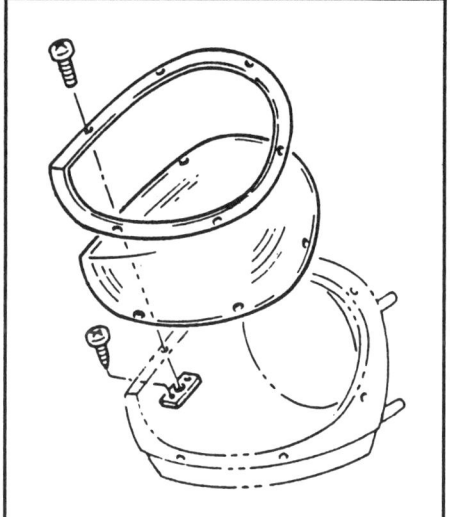

Plexiglass headlight cover was original Datsun dealer-installed option. Versions from aftermarket suppliers may vary. Courtesy Nissan.

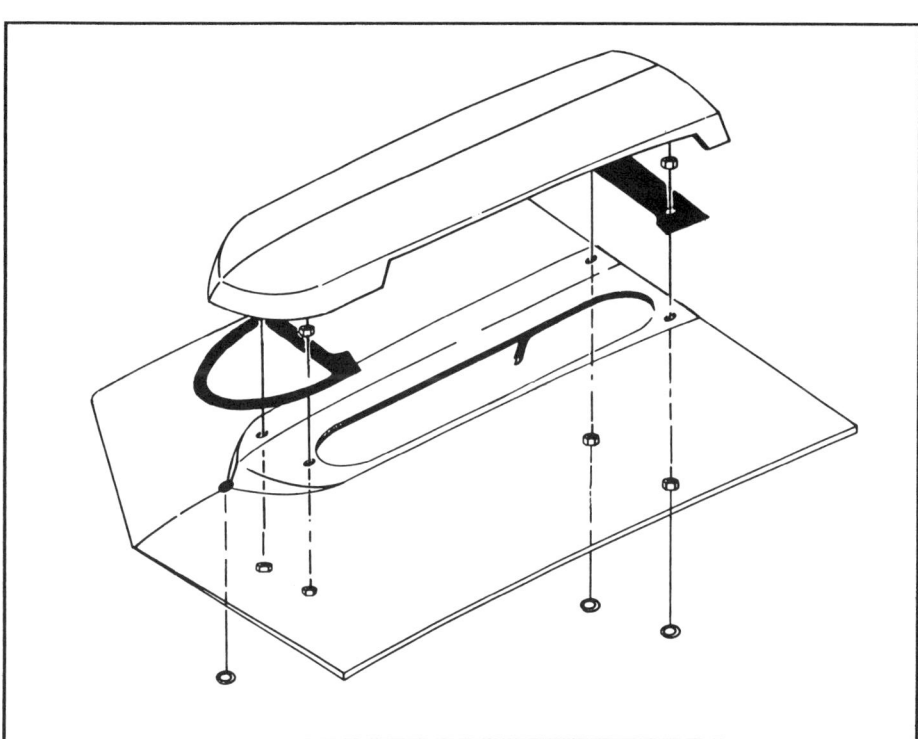

Hood vent was another part with official blessing from Datsun. Ostensibly for competition, it was a stopgap to reduce underhood temperatures. (Later 240Zs and all 260Zs had notorious vapor-lock problems.) Courtesy Nissan.

for the factory's semi-gloss enamel dip process. Real leather for the seats and interior looks—and smells—a lot better than the original vinyl/leather imitation. And chrome outshines the utilitarian zinc plating on underhood hardware. These options remain for you as the proud owner to decide.

But if you ever want to show your restoration in a class for *original cars*—as-built, factory-stock—you can lose competition points despite how perfectly the work was done. This is particularly true if a car yours is competing against was restored in total Datsun orthodoxy. In concours d'elegance competition, an incorrectly restored component—not as originally built and supplied on that car—can void all points for the entire judging area it falls under. Consequently, it's possible for a less well-restored competitor to handily out-point a better prepared, but UN-original car.

This stricture will only apply to a certain class of show car. Obviously, not everyone will opt to restore his or her Z to totally concours-variety originality. But you should know that you could wind up showing in a class with highly modified street machines, one where a nearly stock Z might not be particularly outstanding to the judges, so keep these factors in mind.

Modification—I don't mean to be judgmental on you or your car, but you must agree that a restoration book per se should serve as a baseline reference as much as possible. In that sense, I don't include information on Chevy, Ford or MoPar V8 engine swaps. Nor do I discuss suspension modifications for autocrossing. It only makes sense for me to address the Z-car as it was minted by Datsun back in the '70s, including improvements and upgrades that Yokahama chose to do itself. You can take your individual restoration from there. Many revisions Datsun made improve an early Z—but not all!

On the other hand, if your car is to be modified anyway, let your good taste and your bankroll be your guide. One of the most salient aspects of this type of automobile is expression of its owner's individuality. Often, the mark of a truly great car is in its adaptability to various uses . . . and the degree of success obtained in those divergent uses. Here the Z-car succeeds!

Let's face it, every production car is built by its manufacturer to a price. Even Datsun would probably have enjoyed lavishing Cost-Is-No-Object materials and workmanship on its 240Z, *if* it were to be sold in the Rolls-Royce price range!

I was more than willing to accept a less than absolutely perfect little sports-GT for the bargain-basement price of $3671 that bought my Z in 1970. To my jaded way of thinking, I got more value for my hard-earned dollars than a contemporary Ferrari buyer would have for $23,671. We both got automobiles that could never be truly perfect—true earthly perfection being unattainable, even from Maranello—but I paid 20 grand less for my imperfect machine!

But it is not in the province of *How to Restore Your Datsun Z-car* to go into custom or racing modifications, however attractive they might be to you or me personally. There are any

Decals, window slats and lots of other options were listed as original equipment. This 1977 280Z has all-too-scarce five-speed manual transmission as indicated by emblem on driver's side of hatch. Courtesy Nissan.

number of books, magazine articles and aftermarket suppliers catalogs that cater to the instincts we have to personalize our cars.

What applies to an original Z-car, be it suspension rebuilding, painting, headliner installation or any other process, also is basic to a customized version. Likewise, steps taken to install a windshield or steering box on an early 240Z are also relevant to a late 280Z 2+2.

As an aside, if you think you spot little non-original details on the principal subject Z-car of this book, please don't panic. I have made every effort to cover all points of originality in the text as well as differences in application. Like my Z-car, I am somewhat less than perfect!

Again, the niche Fisher Books and I determined to fill with this manual was that relating to the stock, original restoration. Even if you don't intend to show your Z in concours, the 240Z, 260Z and 280Z were very high-quality, fine performing automobiles just as they came off the boat. Most of us original purchasers were satisfied with only nominal personalizations. You may be, too!

I predict with great confidence that as the Z-car achieves true vintage-car status, the most valuable examples will be closest to original. If you're not convinced, check out prices for Corvettes, Mustangs or whatever "oldie" you prefer at the next collector-car auction!

"Frame-Up" Versus "Staged" Restoration

Well, obviously in unitized construction, you can't very well do a *frame-up* restoration because there's no *separate* frame. But this is the term usually given to any total, all-encompassing restoration done in one concerted effort. When all areas of concentration—drive train, suspension, interior, body and accessories—are underway at one time and the car is totally out of service, consider for our purposes this to be a frame-up restoration.

Frame-Up Restoration—Advantages
1. Thoroughness: When a car is totally disassembled, problem areas can be adequately appraised, then dealt with. Especially if your car has the dreaded "tin worm" (rust), repair work can be simplified and damage completely eradicated. Extensive floor/subframe rust is potentially dangerous. Eliminating the affected areas and replacing the unsound metal is messy and involved.
2. Cost effectiveness: The work can be done once and done right. This is efficient in labor costs as well as materials.
3. Total-use time lost can be less: Usually a restoration in one concerted effort will get your finished project back in service in less total time. This assumes your budget and planning are adequate.
4. Redundant and remedial work is minimized: Removing and replacing major components, such as drive-train assemblies or instrument panel, can be held to one time around. This helps preclude the inevitable damage that results from working around a previously restored area or from repeated disassembly-assembly.
5. Constructive use of shop time is maximized: When a lot of components are being restored at once, they may be worked on in turn. You can avoid time lost while waiting for some vital part that's at the plater or perhaps a seal that is backordered.

Staged Restoration—Advantages
1. You can retain the use of your car: Working on one specific area of the job at a time may let you keep you car in service during times you aren't working on it.
2. Storage space required is usually less: When the whole car is not disassembled and only the parts immediately under restoration are off, much less storage is required.
3. Costs come in smaller bites: You can wait until money is available to restore one specific area before committing to the outlay.
4. The car remains fairly portable: Transporting a completely disassembled project car can be a major expense. This could occur in the event of a job transfer that requires a move.

I admit to a prejudice. I doubt if a truly thorough restoration can be accomplished using the staged method. If so, the job would require a great deal of redundant time and labor—cleaning, prepping, refinishing . . . The wear and tear of assembling and disassembling inevitably would obviate a lot of painstaking work.

But the frame-up approach is a *luxury*. Although total costs are lower with a frame-up restoration, they will be higher over a shorter period of time. During the course of the job you may need other transportation. The various components will need to be stored out of harm's way. Some kind of efficient cataloging system will be required to keep all parts organized for the time that you need them.

Caution: Many times a completely disassembled car that was ostensibly undergoing a frame-up restoration suddenly becomes a parts car. The reasons for this phenomenon are many and varied. They usually involve problems with the restorer much more than with the car.

A career move or family upheaval can torpedo a restoration project. And discovering that commitments both in time and money will be much more than anticipated can stop a project. Even a hurried, ill-planned disassembly can create a basket case from a restorable automobile. Don't let this happen to your Z-car project!

Planning—This is the secret of a successful restoration. Plan subsequent steps your project will take and make allowances for problems *when* they occur. Anticipate what you will need in terms of time, tools, materials, services and so forth.

Moneywise, try to determine what your costs will be in advance and establish a realistic budget. Building contractors always add at least 10% for unexpected costs, price increases, over-optimistic estimates and so forth. You should, too, especially if this is your first restoration!

Use this book and your own good judgment to map out the particulars of your restoration project. A little research into the Z you have is time well spent.

Get out your Service Manual and familiarize yourself with shop procedures and component names as it gives them. Make an objective appraisal of your car, notebook in hand. Check each area systematically, looking for things you must deal with to bring it back to its original condition.

Using the Parts and Services index, page 204, order the latest editions of restoration-suppliers catalogs. Make a thorough study of what parts and supplies are available and at what prices.

Frame-up restoration lets me paint car in pieces, which is easier to do and allows better coverage. Fenders are *color-sanded* and ready for a clear coat. Note fresh-air respirator, lung insurance against catalyzed paints.

Whatever method you use, allow for both extra expenses and for extra time. Better to be overcautious than frustrated!

Used Parts for Your Z-car

When it comes to "pre-owned" parts, there are no hard-and-fast rules. But always try to get the best bargain possible. Rest assured that the junkie—recycled-parts person—will try to get as much of your restoration budget as he can.

Logically, it behooves you to:
1. Make sure the part in question is *exactly* what your car needs.
2. Pay as *little* as you absolutely must for the part.

Expanding on the first point, besides knowing exactly what you need, it is vital that you buy only a part that will serve well where it is needed. If a part or assembly needs restoration, it should be complete and rebuildable. At this juncture, take into consideration what it will cost in time and money to do whatever mechanical or cosmetic work is required. Don't end up paying twice for it!

Despite reassurances that most reputable dismantlers will exchange another used part for one that isn't serviceable, there is no guarantee that a replacement will be any better. You may have considerable investment in repainting or replating by the time a problem is discovered. So test for serviceability before actually installing the part. Tearing down a project to correct a defective part can be a trial.

Recycled parts are often perfectly acceptable on a concours-quality restoration. Sometimes they are the *only* correct part available for older cars. More so, an original factory item, even though it's used, will be of better quality and fitness than the best O.E.M. substitute or reproduction on the market. Keep in mind that this depends largely on the quality of the restoration work done on the used part.

Bits & Pieces—No recycler likes to *part-out* subassemblies. For example, he won't feel kindly toward selling a piece of trim for a door panel, even if that's all you need, if that drastically reduces the value of his used door panel. If he does sell you such a part, expect to pay the same as you would for the complete assembly. It doesn't matter to him that you've just reupholstered your panel. So you may find yourself owning another complete assembly—door panel in this example—just to get the bit you need.

Rarely can you get a real "deal" from a dismantler. More often than not, be prepared to *pay* for what you want. The cost of parts—from whatever source—is a major reason why seemingly nice-appearing Z-cars wind up being converted into parts cars. Problems they may have result in their being worth much more broken down into component parts than they were in their assembled state.

Too, the fact that a Z is a specialty car is not lost on those who price used parts. Even though a substantial number of first-series Zs were imported and there is a fairly appreciable amount of parts interchangeability between years and models, many parts are hard to find. Scarcity makes prices non-negotiable—the law of supply and demand rules.

Attrition of Z-cars was fairly high, whether from accidents, racing, rust or abuse. Paradoxically, those being parted out are not unusually plentiful. Zs that aren't already scrapyard-bound are like your project—either under loving restoration or already beautifully rebuilt. Several kit-car conversions are based on Z bodies. And the demand for good body/suspension combinations is growing.

Supply and demand leads to a scarcity of *good* used parts, thus premium prices for what remains available. A boneyard Z is usually picked-over in a few days. Hard-to-find parts seem to evaporate; what is in less demand deteriorates in the weather until the inevitable trip to the crusher. Unfortunately, a lot of good original brackets, clips, trim and pounds of fasteners are lost to the restorer this way! But unless you go the parts-car route, the law of diminishing returns to the junkie will tend to continue this cycle.

Large metropolitan areas often have salvage yards that specialize in Japanese cars, Datsuns . . . even just Z-cars. The latter are often an excellent source of information on availability and interchange. Bear in mind they are in business to sell parts. Such operations often have miscellaneous *new* stock on hand. It may pay to inquire.

Sound used parts are OK for a restoration. When thoroughly cleaned, rebuilt with such things like new bearings, seals and gaskets, then correctly refinished, they are as good as original parts.

What About a "Parts Car"?

Keeping an extra car to "mine" for parts is as old as the restoration hobby. Usually, a more-valuable body style is restored using parts from a less-valuable example. In days gone by, for instance, a collector might rebuild a used-and-abused Duesenberg roadster with drivetrain, fenders, instrument panel and so forth from a relatively pampered Duesenberg sedan. Though unthinkable now, quite a few vintage cars were sacrificed so their more rare and desirable brethren could live.

With the Z-car, substantial production volumes and relative commonality of bodies will preclude this unfortunate situation for some time. However, for a fortunate minority of restorers, the parts-car route can prove to be beneficial. Let's look at the pros and cons.

Parts-Car Advantages
1. Lower Cost of Parts: Probably the most common reason for taking on a derelict Z-car is to save money on parts. This assumes, of course, that you got a favorable buy on the specimen.
2. Availability of Parts: Some authentic parts or accessories may be obtainable only from another Z.
3. Reference Source: Don't discount the value of having an original Z as reference regardless of its condition to supplement the Datsun Service Manual, this book, your notes, photos, memory or whatever for reassembly time.
4. Trading Material: What you don't need may be barterable to another Z restorer for what you may need. Seldom will a restorer use every salvageable component from a parts car . . . and trading is a time-honored practice among car restorers and modifiers.
5. Selling Parts—Even the Complete Car: Obviously, you can dispose of surplus assemblies to other restorers for hard cash. Also, you wouldn't be the first to buy a fairly decent car for the parts you need, swap desirable for less-desirable and resell the car relatively complete with the substituted parts.
6. Scrap: Even the hulk of a "hangar queen" has scrap value. After you've cannibalized it for everything of value, it is environmentally responsible as well as remunerative in a modest way to cash in the Z-carcass at a metal recycler.

Parts-Car Disadvantages
1. Storage: This is the principal bugaboo in keeping a car to dismantle. The lack of appropriate storage precludes most restorers from enjoying the above advantages. Storage availability, especially in urban areas, comes at a premium. Outdoor storage invites complaints from neighbors and may violate zoning or other restrictions. Indoor storage for a parts car is truly in the luxury category for most restorers.
2. Disposal of Remains: Even though there's value in a scrap carcass, it may not be worth the hassle of hauling it off to sell it. If you removed the suspension, which you should because of its value, you may have to load and haul the hulk on a trailer or flatbed truck. At best, the salvage value may not pay for having the junkie remove it with his tow truck.
3. Cost-effectiveness: Depending on your situation, acquiring or keeping a parts car simply may not pay for itself in the end. This effectively negates our "'Vantage number one," as Winnie the Pooh said.

I've tried to find a parts car for all of my major restoration projects. The advantages for my situation far outnumber the disadvantages. If I can't find a parts car, I look for another restorer who may have one from whom I buy or trade for parts I need. A commercial dismantler is my distinct second choice.

Acquisition—The right parts car, like gold, is where you find it. Probably your best bet to find such a car is the classified section of a large-circulation newspaper. Equally good might be local swap'n sell classifieds. These are popular in rural as well as urban areas.
Note: Look for the best deals in the "Nissan/Datsun" classifications. What you find in the "Sports and Imports" or "Classic and Collectable" columns usually have higher price tags.

Word of mouth among restorers or racers is effective if you have such contacts. A classified want ad or even a 3x5 card tacked up near parts count-

Datsunisms? Nissyntax?

I'll say it again: You as a Z-car restorer should acquire and make constant reference to an authorized Datsun Service Manual. Japanese technical manuals, however, established a rather unique cachet for both distinctive and individualistic language usages as well as inimical vocabulary interpretations. See Parts Illustrations, pages 205—238, as an example.

The former obviously originates within the influence of the writers' native syntactic patterns—natural enough considering that those usages seem most clear and precise to the writers themselves. Undeniably, the result is hardly more obscure to the North American reader than the typical British manual!

I suspect that the latter stems from a deep nationalistic pride in being self-sufficient in every respect as a modern industrial and technological entity. The 240-260-280Z Manuals are a quantum leap forward from the first technical publications that arrived with the original wave of Japanese imports to the U.S. An early '60s Yamaha shop manual reads like a contemporary Pat Suzuki comedy monologue!

Following are other examples:

"Although the cleaner element looks dirty, do not intend to clean."

"It may be needless to say, however, to maintain optimum engine performance always, periodical adjustment (engine tune-up) is necessary."

"In this case, following trouble cause may exist, but in many cases, ignition system or fuel system may be in trouble."

And how about "Improper correct piston-ring clearance," or even the problem of a "Sticked valve guide"?

A small insight into the translator's frame of reference might be gained from the permutation of a brake-adjusting "spur" into a brake adjusting "claw." A certain poultry imagery seems to have crept into the interpreter's nomenclature.

Just so that no reader will take these observations to mean that your author has elitist notions, let me reiterate my admiration for both the Datsun Z-car and its designers, engineers and corporate people. The only Japanese I know is "sayonara," "arigato" and "banzai!" And which is more charming: our *phantom* view of a transmission or a *"clairvoyant"* view?

---

ers usually brings prompt results, but be aware that your taking the initiative may result in the seller assuming you will pay more than otherwise.

Know what you will need; refer to your continuing inventory to determine upcoming needs. What your project requires to be completed to your satisfaction will determine the kind of parts car to look for.

Accident-Damaged Cars—If your Z's drive train is shot, look for a wrecked car that is in relatively good mechanical condition. Therefore, a wrecked or rolled Z—as depressing as that sounds—would be your best choice. A car that was travelling fast enough to be totalled might be expected to have been a good runner.

Of course, if the accident was severe, the mechanicals may have been rendered useless, too. So look for a car that's suffered little damage to the engine-compartment area.

You should be able to appraise what your chances are of getting your money's worth while viewing a wrecked Z. Because this type of car is also in demand by dismantlers, if you can find a friendly junkie or body-shop owner to bid on a given wreck for you at an insurance company's auction, it could be advantageous.

On the other hand, if your project car is fairly complete and mechanically sound, you may be simply looking for body and interior parts—and possibly desirable options—with which to restore what you have. In that case, look for a parts car that has a major mechanical component blown-up or missing or one that has simply been driven to death. Sometimes a fairly presentable Z-car will be sold without title for legal reasons, or a recovered stolen Z may be sold by its insurer. Aborted race-car projects often yield a good parts car, if you don't mind sorting out a basket case. As far as that goes, a Z-car that was stripped to race often results in boxes of surplus street-usable parts.

A Z of any year with either of the above component areas intact usually doesn't come cheaply. There are exceptions. I recently found a 1971 240Z that went for $200 cash at the curb. Though unwrecked, it was definitely a parts car because a would-be restorer had almost completely dismantled its drive train and interior before giving up the attempt. After piling all the parts into the interior—the proverbial basket case—he sold out cheap just to get rid of the embarrassing evidence. From his perspective, someone made a good deal on his misfortune.

Actually, such tales are not uncommon, often involving much better examples than I've cited. Another 260Z showed up in a local wrecking yard sans its roof. No other damage or missing parts at all, but some backyard butcher had attempted to build a roadster. The dismantler loved it. My last parts Z was a 280Z—a rollover, less wheels and transmission. I got it for $250!

Kit Cars—The trend toward basing replica kits on the trusty Z-car body and chassis foundation has given street-weary but mechanically sound Zs a new lease on life. The Daytona Cobra and Alpha-1 Ferrari GTO conversions require a fairly competent and titled Z to build upon. This may increase the demand for rebuildable and parts-quality examples. Many kit builders install big V8s with their transmissions, so L24-26-28 engines and their transmissions may *not* be hard to acquire—if the trend follows old-time engine-swapping practice. Other than seats and front-end sheet metal, kit builders will be collecting and rebuilding the same suspension and interior parts as the dedicated Datsun restorer.

Any action on the Z-car hobby

front is good for all of us, causing more new and reproduction parts to appear on the market and at competitive prices.

In Conclusion—I'd like to hark back to the first advantage of what I mean by a "favorable buy" on a parts car. By this I mean you must get a bargain—and acquire just what you need for an truly low price. You can't use a bunch of junk that deserves only to be melted down.

Three Rules are applicable:
1. Don't invest more cash in a parts car than you think you'll get from it.
2. Be sure it has the *exact* pieces you need. Don't guess.
3. Be as sure as you can that the parts you want are in good enough condition to use.

Whether or not a parts-Z will fit into your restoration project depends on your needs according to the above rules. By now you should know!

2 Engine & Transmission Removal

Let's get started! The first step in a frame-up restoration is to clean the car thoroughly. I assume you've removed your keys and any personal items from the interior. Registration and insurance papers are safely filed away. That leaves the messy but very necessary job of cleaning the mechanical parts of your Z-car.

Cleanliness—I make it an absolute rule that any car I restore be as clean as I can make it before turning a wrench. This prerequisite has never failed me as a saver of time, trouble and money.

Depending on how much grime and crud has accumulated on your Z over its life, look forward to a more or less messy experience. I'm sure my wife thinks at least half the grease and soil that comes off my projects winds up on my clothes! For that reason I don't wear my best clothes while working on a car, as you can see from the photos.

As it came from Yokahama, your Z was very clean and tight. Professional auto detailers usually admit that Japanese cars are among the easiest to spit-shine under the hood because of the very high quality-control standards exercised. Even the most modest Japanese econo-box is relatively free of leaks, which are signs of shoddy workmanship, and rust or corrosion.

Compression Check—Because this may be the last time your engine will be in commission for the duration of the restoration, do a compression check and read the plugs. Even if it hasn't given any hints of weakness, now's the time to determine if any problems exist. It's much easier to make engine repairs with it on a stand rather than back in your newly

Use a steamcleaner or high-pressure washer to get major accumulations of grease and dirt off before you start under-hood work. Air cleaner was removed to improve access. Carburetor openings and master-cylinder caps are taped closed.

restored engine compartment. After warming the engine, I followed the steps outlined in *How to Rebuild Your Datsun/Nissan OHC Engine*.

Before beginning, list the cylinders from **1** to **6** in your project notebook. Remove and make note of the appearance of each sparkplug. Check out the plugs. Use a troubleshooting chart, such as that on page 10 of the above book, to analyze conditions inside each combustion chamber. With the cylinders listed front to rear, record your notes on each.

Pull the distributor-to-coil lead or, if your Z has electronic ignition, the distributor-to-amplifier lead. The plugs should be out. If not, remove them. Using a remote starter switch, connect one clip to the positive (+) terminal of the starter solenoid. Replace the ignition lead with the other clip. Crank the engine with a compression gauge in cylinder 1 and record the reading. Check the remaining cylinders and record your readings.

If all six cylinders are within 10 psi (pounds per square inch) of one another and the plugs are consistently tan or gray in color with moderate electrode wear, your engine is giving you good news. Bear in mind these

Mobile-wash unit was brought to my shop. This made it easier to put car on stands and gain access to underbody through wheel wells.

are not the only indications of engine condition—others are fuel consumption, manifold vacuum, oil pressure and consumption and operating temperature. Carbureted Zs often show signs of carbon-fouling. This is an excessively rich air/fuel mixture, inexpensively remedied by carburetor adjustment or perhaps rebuilding. You may have noticed some black, sooty emissions from the tailpipe as well.

The L24 in my car at approximately 100,000 miles had this condition. It responded to rebuilt carburetors. I also discovered a leaking head gasket on cylinder 6. Because this symptom required pulling the cylinder head, I had the head bead-blasted, pressure-tested and a valve job performed. While the head was off, I installed new rings and a cam chain. Ready for another 100,000!

The Datsun/Nissan L-series is truly a fine piece of engineering. Simple, durable, powerful and economical—I would never consider replacing it with a V8!

Automatic Transmission—If you suspect any problems with your automatic transmission, check it now. Troubleshooting an automatic for problems such as slippage or faulty shifting must be done in the car—it depends on oil pressure generated by engine rotation.

Leaks—Oil, grease or whatever type fluid are the primary cause of a filthy drive train. Oozing oil and grease are great dirt collectors. When engine heat is added, the result is a baked-on accumulation of layer upon layer of hard, sticky crud. Although oil seepage is symptomatic of high mileage, due care taken in reassembly will help to prevent such recontamination.

Other contributors are road oil, paint overspray, plain old mud, rust inhibitors and even insects plastered over the engine compartment and undercarriage of a car. The task of removing such debris is your first priority.

Methods to Use—For the extra-thick, farm-equipment-type accumulations, direct physical force is the first weapon. A putty knife, flat-blade screwdriver or gasket scraper is effective in breaking loose those big encrustations. The limitation to this is accessibility; you probably won't be able to reach all recesses and cracks with complete effectiveness. But loosening the deposits or decreasing their thickness is helpful to the finer techniques you will employ next.

Where practical, remove parts to increase accessibility. With the car on a flat, hard surface, jack it up and support it with sturdy jack stands. If you're working on asphalt, place the jack stands on squares of plywood to distribute the load. Otherwise the jack-stands will sink into the pavement. Take off the wheels to allow easy access under the fenders. The air cleaner can be set aside. Be sure to tape over carburetor openings or stuff them with clean rags. Take out the battery and its tray and retainer. Now you have a relatively clear shot at your goal.

After scraping with a sharp instrument, I often utilize a wire brush to loosen buildup in hard-to-get-at areas. These methods are done *dry*—without solvent or cleaning chemicals. At this stage, it is still purely a physical, mechanical effort. Take care not to damage any surfaces—painted, plated or cast.

Solvent or Detergent-Type Cleansers—Next, begin applying these. Many degreasing products are available at auto-parts or even discount-drug stores. They work fairly well on thinly layered deposits, but also may attack paint or other finishes you should preserve.

Most cleaners are alkali-based and are recommended for use on a warm surface, such as an engine that has just been run. I don't recommend any particular type, but you may want to ask around or experiment with different products in a safe area before going to work.

Be careful: Most cleaners are hazardous to eyes and lungs, especially the aerosol kind. Wear protective goggles, gloves and long sleeves.

Old-time mechanics will often attack with petroleum solvent and a stiff parts-cleaning brush at this stage. The solvent, whether it be mineral spirits, kerosene or diesel oil, softens and dilutes caked-on oil or grease that bonds dirt together.

Caution: Never use solvent on a hot engine! It will burn if it gets hot enough.

Some soil and stains will evade your efforts, so the final laundering should be done with heat, detergent and high pressure. Although steam-cleaning is the traditional method of choice, I prefer a high-pressure water washer. These can be rented in many locales, or you can hire the whole job done by a professional.

Communication—If someone else is going to handle the sprayer, talk with him. Let the operator know the car is

Engine & Transmission Removal

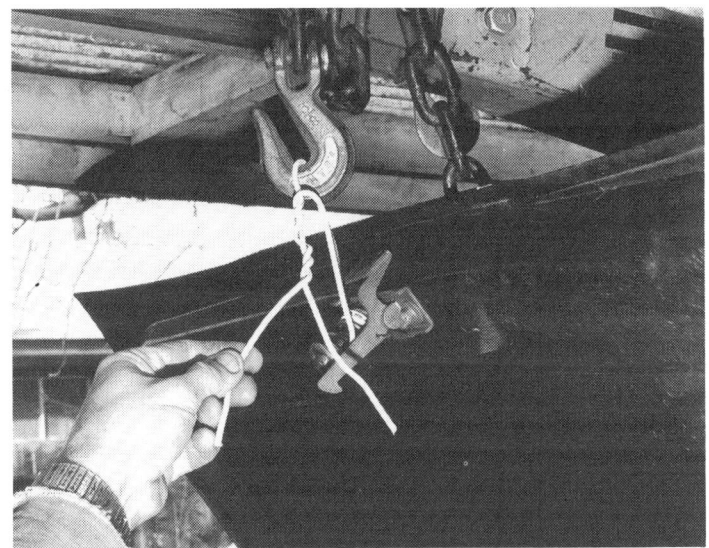

Cherry picker is used to help with hood removal. Electrical wire is used to support latch end of hood while hinged end is unbolted.

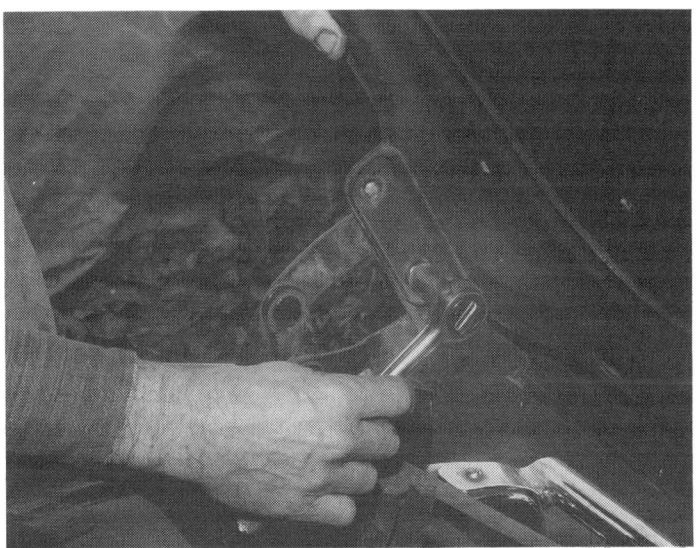

One bolt was left barely threaded in other hinge while I removed bolts from this one. Punch through bolt hole in hood and hinge will support this side while bolt is removed from other hinge. Z-car hood is not too heavy or bulky for one person to handle.

to be restored. Even though it should be *very* clean from bottom to top, be careful not to remove any decals or paint. Then make sure the pressure is strong, water solution hot and, if the unit uses a detergent, it is applied liberally.

Before using high-pressure cleaning on your engine compartment, seal off openings such as the carburetor(s), fuel and vacuum lines. Protect the ignition wiring if you plan on driving your Z home. Tape the caps on your clutch and brake master-cylinder reservoirs to prevent contamination of the brake fluid. I even mask decals or stickers I want to preserve, taking precautions the tape doesn't damage what it is supposed to protect!

In many locales, pressure-wash outfits will come to you, eliminating the need to start and move or haul your Z. Then again, you may want to put your car up on a lift so you'll have complete access to the undercarriage. This will save you a lot of aggravation and filth if your Z has heavy buildups of road accumulations. This didn't apply to my 240Z even though it led an active although fairly well-maintained life. We gave it a "two-bit car wash" top and bottom every few months for 15 years!

Even at that, after disassembly I spent days with my parts washer and brush, scrubbing steering arms, brake springs and the like. Dirt and grease contamination must be completely removed if you're to do a complete restoration. I have the cracked skin to show for it!

After your project is thoroughly clean and dry, you can get started with disassembly.

Fender Protectors—Cover your fenders if they are in top condition. But if yours are like mine were, don't bother. I knew a lot of work was in store for my good fender; the other was to be replaced. Just don't lean on them too hard; dimpling will result.

Battery—If the battery and attendant parts are still in place, remove them now. Don't store the battery on a concrete floor. Store it in a warm, dry place, away from children or pets. Clean the cable ends in bicarbonate of soda solution if you plan on reusing them.

Hood Removal—Before you loosen them, trace around the hood hinges to aid in remounting the hood so it'll have the same margins (gaps). If your car has been damaged or will be as thoroughly restored as my project car, it may not be helpful. If you choose to use this assist, make a neat line with a sharp-pointed scribe. Don't let it meander all around the bracket.

It best to have someone help you remove the hood and engine. But you can remove even a restored hood with the help of your engine hoist, or *cherry picker*. First, jack the arm of the hoist up above the raised height of the hood lip. (You can do this with a chain fall, too.) Then secure the hook to the hood with rope or wire. I use a length of household electrical wire or Romex. It is strong and its plastic insulation protects the hood lip.

After raising the hoist sufficiently to support the hood, remove the screws that mount the hood to the hinges. Be careful not to let the forward end of the hood get away from you and dent or scratch the fenders! Now, simply lift and swing the hood around on the suspending wires and lower it to a safe storage place.

Storage—As I noted in the previous chapter, I use zip-lock bags for storing many parts. Make notes on slips of paper and include them with the parts or stick a label on the outside of each bag. Don't use masking tape for labeling. Zip-lock bags can be tied to a part with twist-ties or "filed" separately.

Disconnect Radiator—Put a pan under the radiator-drain spigot and open it. Loosen the the radiator cap to speed draining. Use some penetrant on the hose clamps and loosen them sufficiently to remove hoses. The hoses may seem to have grown to the neck, so some wrenching may be necessary to break them loose. Or slit the

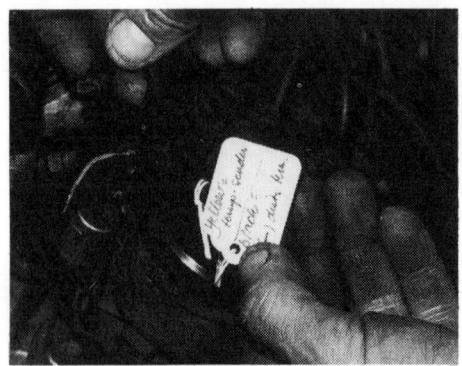

Disconnect electrical harness. Identify connectors with tags such as these before you disconnect them. Don't leave hose and wiring connections to your memory.

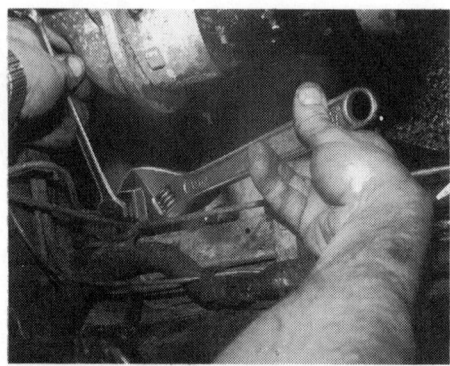

Don't forget any hoses, cables or wires. This is the clutch slave-cylinder hose. Don't plan on saving the fluid. All liquids should be replaced.

hoses lengthways and peel them off the necks. Leave the hoses on the radiator for the time being.

If your car has an automatic transmission, disconnect the cooler lines and hoses at the radiator. Have a pan ready to catch the automatic-transmission fluid (ATF) that leaks out.

Air-conditioning condensers are mounted in front of the radiator. The system must be bled before disconnecting the lines and removing the condenser. To do this simply "crack"— break loose—the large tubing fittings and allow the system to depressurize. Wrap each fitting with a shop towel or rag so you don't get frostbite from the escaping gas. The air-conditioning system will have to be evacuated and recharged with freon after reassembly.

Fan—Late Z-cars have fan shrouds that must be removed before you can remove the radiator. Partially unbolt the upper half of the shroud to get better access to the fan. Then loosen the nuts or bolts that hold the fan assembly to the water-pump shaft and work it out. The bottom half of the shroud can now be removed. I chose to leave the fan in place on my 240Z because it can be a real "knuckle-buster" to get at the nuts at the front of the flange.

Viscous-Fan Storage—All Zs came with viscous-drive fans. This is true with both the original steel model and the one-piece plastic fan introduced in 1972. The latter unit is a functional improvement—but must use its own fan drive. Store the front face down— water-pump-mounting surface up. This keeps the silicone fluid from leaking out, ruining an expensive part.

Unfasten the four screws that hold the radiator mounts to the bulkhead. For the time being, I run them back in the original holes to prevent loss or mixup. Store the radiator so its core can't get damaged. It's a good idea to tape corrugated cardboard onto the front and back of the radiator to protect it.

Wiring—"Flag" and disconnect electrical connections at the water-temperature sender, oil-pressure sender, starter solenoid and alternator. Remove wiring-harness clamps. As disconnections are made, use inexpensive pasteboard tags to keep track of wires and connections. If in doubt, make a note in your Service Manual or notebook. Do this *before* you disconnect anything. *Don't trust your memory!*

Fuel Tank—I drain the fuel tank before tearing down a car. Do this outdoors. Gasoline vapors collect near the floor and can be ignited by the smallest spark or a water-heater pilot. It helps if you haven't topped off the tank recently—the less to drain the better. Rather than storing this fuel, make sure it is clean and moisture-free, then dump it into the family car.

Fuel Lines—Loosen clamps and twist fuel and vapor-return lines to free them. Have a catch can and rag handy for fuel spills. A wood dowel or bolt can be forced into a rubber line to block flow if gas drains out. Compressed air set at low pressure will evacuate lines back to tank if you are draining it. Don't use high pressure and create a cloud of gas spray—it will be explosive!

Vacuum Line—Loosen clamp at intake manifold, twist and remove vacuum hose at MasterVac brake booster. Wire it and any other loose hoses up and out of your way.

Heater Hoses—Unscrew clamps and twist heater hoses to break loose. Pull off and be prepared for some coolant to spill!

A/C Hoses & Lines—Break loose the remaining connections and remove this plumbing. Store it so nothing can blow or crawl inside and contaminate the system. Neat plastic caps or plugs are available at plumbing-supply stores that fit these connectors.

Clutch Slave Cylinder—Use a 10mm tubing wrench to unscrew the flex line to the clutch slave cylinder. Give the clutch pedal a few pumps to purge lines of fluid before it leaks out by gravity.

Exhaust-Header Pipes—These disconnect at the manifold. Lots of penetrant on the three nuts, such as WD-40, can be helpful. Let it soak overnight before you try to remove the nuts.

Air-Cleaner Assembly—Early Zs: Disconnect hoses, remove cover, element and base. Late Zs: Remove air-cleaner snorkel and cleaner by removing the fasteners, both the obvious ones and those underneath. Remove the airflow-meter hose, disconnect the meter and store it carefully away. If your car is so equipped, remove the coolant-recovery bottle.

Accelerator & Choke Linkage—Z-car throttle-linkage rods rotate from a pivot at the firewall. For the time being, take the complete assembly loose from the firewall and secure it to the engine with twist-ties or soft wire. On carbureted cars, loosen choke-cable clamps with a screwdriver and withdraw the cables.

Air Conditioning—There were several A/C applications for Z-cars. Because of this and the fact that only a portion were so equipped, I don't cover A/C, either the approved aftermarket type or original Datsun. Use your Service Manual if your car has a factory A/C system.

It's easy to pull a Z engine with the air-conditioning compressor in place. Make all disconnections and label wire ends.

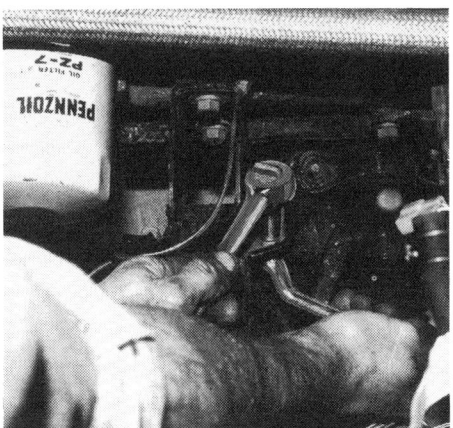

Hoses removed and tagged, I'm unbolting engine mounts. Note oil-pressure-gauge line immediately above engine mount. L-series engines weren't known for their accurate oil-pressure senders.

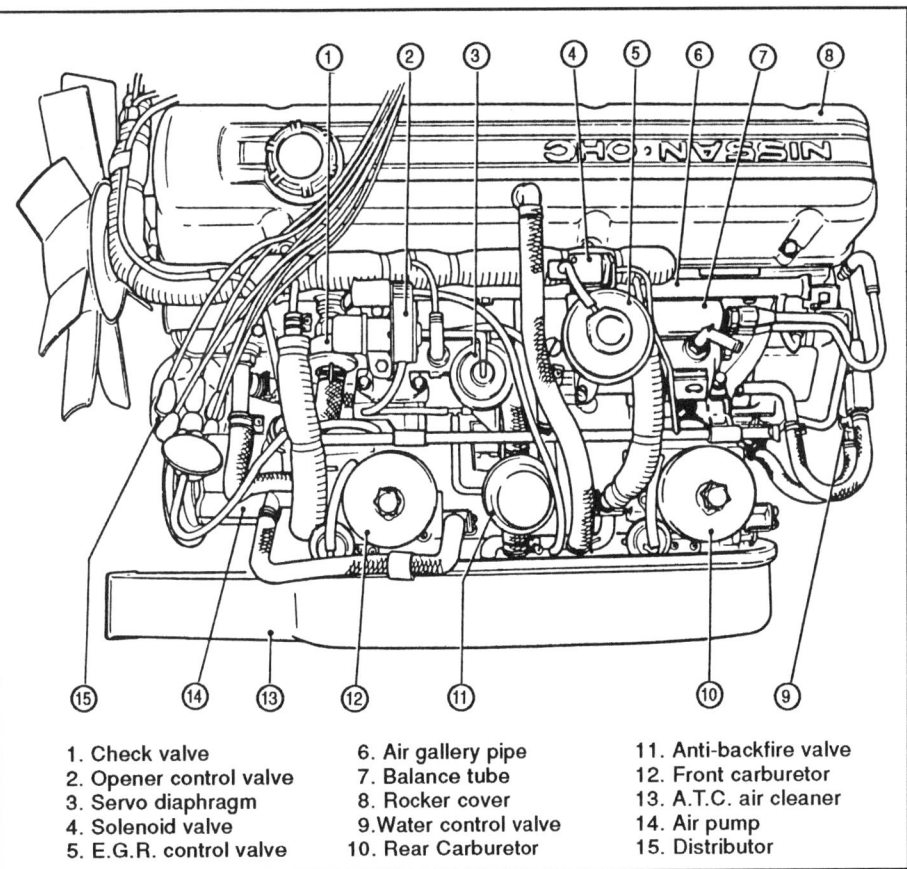

1. Check valve
2. Opener control valve
3. Servo diaphragm
4. Solenoid valve
5. E.G.R. control valve
6. Air gallery pipe
7. Balance tube
8. Rocker cover
9. Water control valve
10. Rear Carburetor
11. Anti-backfire valve
12. Front carburetor
13. A.T.C. air cleaner
14. Air pump
15. Distributor

1973 240Z engine, SU-equipped L24 is a snakepit of hoses and wires. Label all disconnects. Courtesy Nissan.

Engine-Mount Brackets—These come loose next. The engine isn't going anywhere because of the cradle effect of the mount system, but don't loosen them at the engine yet.

Under Car—Jack up the front of the car as high as necessary and support it with sturdy jack stands. Set the parking brake and/or chock the rear wheels.

Caution: Everybody knows of a horror story where the incautious shade-tree mechanic gets pinned under his car and expires before anyone notices. With such incidents in mind, I leave my jack under the car even though it is firmly supported by the stands, unless the jack absolutely gets in the way. I call it my "Second Chance."

Use the number-two crossmember—*front axle* as the old Datsun Manuals so quaintly call it—as your jacking point. Place the stands underneath the crossmember right at the lower-control-arm pivot points. Give the car a good jostle before sliding

under. You may find yourself giving a healthy pull on a wrench, so now is the time to find out whether it will topple the supports—not later! Don't trust jack stands on dirt, gravel or asphalt—set them on a square of plywood or metal plate. Don't even think about using concrete blocks for stands. They will give you a quick trip to the cemetery!

Speedometer Cable & Backup-Light-Switch Wires—Disconnect these from the passenger's side of the transmission. Also, get up under the dash and disconnect the speedo cable to get it completely out of the way.

Drive Shaft—Place transmission in neutral. Disconnect the drive shaft from the differential companion flange.

Transmission—If you want the transmission to come out with the engine, remove the shift lever. If the console is still in place, this job can be accomplished under the car. This leaves the lever in the console until you are ready to dismantle the interior.

Remove the inner shift-lever boot. Removing the shift lever is easiest on early manual-transmission Z-cars, requiring only two open-end wrenches to remove the nut. There's a corresponding flat on the shaft. Pull the lever up. Be sure to put the nut and washer back on the shaft. Later stick-shift Zs should be in neutral. Pull up the boot and remove the retaining clip and pin. Pull up the lever and replace the pin and clip on the transmission.

For automatic transmissions, disconnect the selector-range lever from the shaft. Disconnect wire connections from the inhibitor switch, vacuum tube from the vacuum diaphragm and downshift-wire connector from the solenoid.

Drain oil or fluid from the transmission now so it won't drool out of the tail-shaft housing when the transmission is tilted up by the engine hoist. Tag the transmission as **DRAINED** so you'll have a warning not to take that first triumphal shakedown drive with a dry gearbox!

26 How to Restore Your Datsun Z-Car

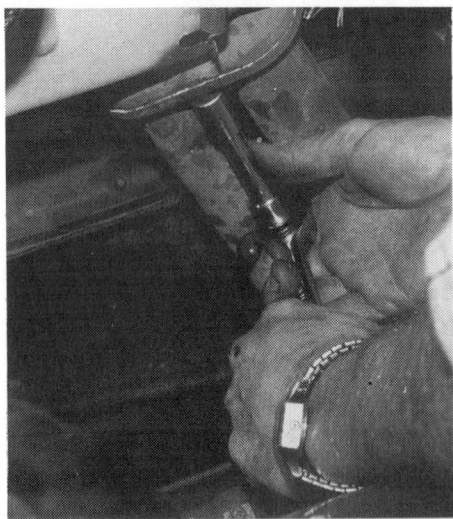

Exhaust-header pipe is accessible with air cleaner out of way. Even when lots of penetrant is used, studs still twist off . . . and one did!

Not the original exhaust system, most Z owners replaced original "whistler" mufflers early on. Remove remainder of exhaust system.

Transmission Mount—Loosen and remove the nuts holding the rear engine-mount insulator to the crossmember. Knock the captive-type bolts out of the transmission tail-shaft housing flange. The crossmember will support the weight until you are ready to remove the engine and transmission.

Exhaust System—Datsun used various mounting and connecting systems to attach and seal the exhaust pipes, catalytic converters, resonators and mufflers. And then there are the many non-stock systems hung on by owners and muffler shops over the years. If yours is of the latter variety, the question is, can you remove yours via something like the original hardware or will you have to resort to a hacksaw and torch? Either way, it helps to get the exhaust system out of the way at this point.

Remove Engine—Once all necessary connections are separated, you can proceed with pulling the engine and transmission. If you rented your engine hoist, you should have gotten a chain sling, nylon strap or cable.

Lower the car, but put the wheels back on if you removed them. Position the hoist hook so it's centered over the engine. Attach the ends of the sling to the engine-lifting lugs—one at the front of the block; another at the rear. Check that it is short enough so the bottom of the engine/transmission unit clears the radiator bulkhead. It should be long enough so you can set the engine down and unhook the sling. Position the sling pickup point so the transmission doesn't drag the back of the unit down too far. Before you commit yourself, experiment. Lift the weight off the mounts to check for good balance. If the pickup point is biased too much front or rear, adjust to suit.

Note also that as you lift the engine/transmission off of the mounts, the car will rise. Take this into account when deciding how long or short to make your connection. Don't forget that you'll have to set the engine/transmission down, too. Once the unit is free of the mounts, a combination of upward and forward motions are needed to get it clear of the engine compartment. This is where an extra pair of strong hands is helpful. It may be easier to roll the car out from under the engine, particularly if the hoist is on an uneven floor or soft ground, or you are using a stationary hoist.

If the unit hangs up even slightly, stop. Look for the cause before you proceed. An unconnected hose or cable will break itself or something else if you go on without checking. Watch out for the little nylon breather on top of manual transmissions. It can snag on the bracket on the firewall/transmission tunnel opening. Some "English" may have to be applied to snake everthing out, but it will come.

Be careful not to let the unit swing around and damage something—such as the windshield! Roll the hoist forward—or car back—and lower the engine/transmission. If you plan to store the engine, position it on a stout dolly or skid. Block it up solidly and remove the sling from the lifting lugs.

Up and out. Don't let bellhousing catch on fuel/vapor-line brackets on firewall. Fan could have been taken off, but it didn't inhibit removal of engine.

Engine & Transmission Removal

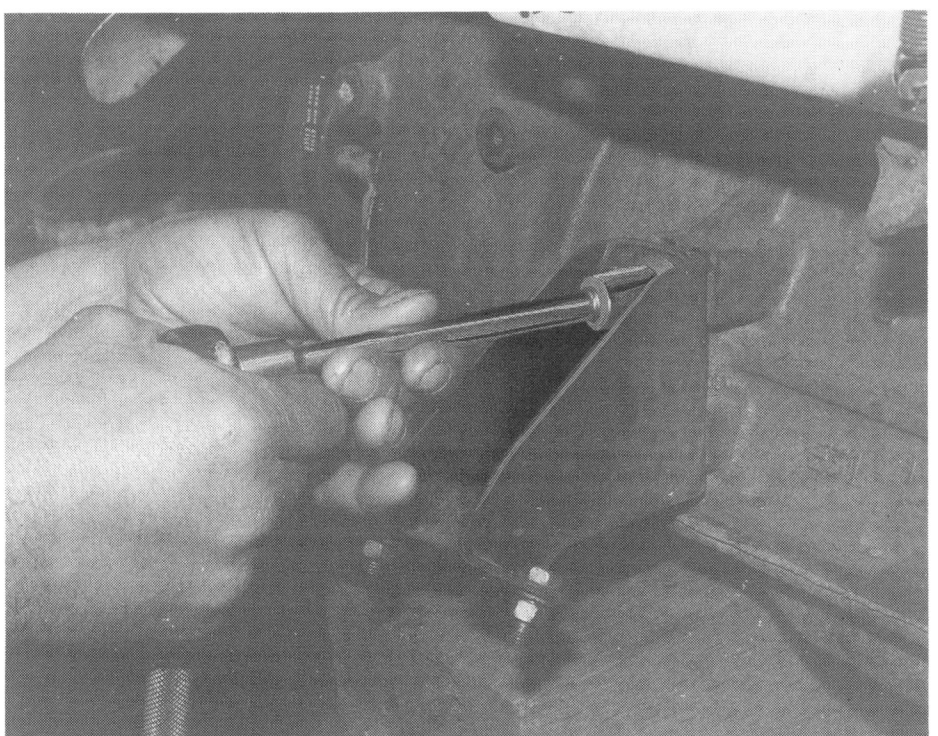

Once engine is out, remove bits and pieces such as engine mounts. Air pump is already off.

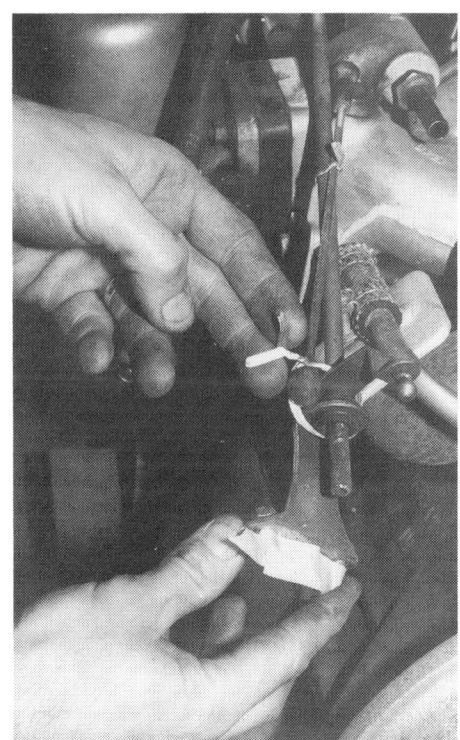

Until I get around to doing my engine work, items such as throttle-linkage parts are kept together with twist-ties and masking tape. Never leave tape on surfaces that are easily damaged.

If engine work is planned, mount the engine on a strong, roller-mounted engine stand. But first you'll have to remove the transmission, then the clutch and flywheel or flexplate.

Standard-Transmission Zs—While the engine and transmission are out, it is time well invested to separate the two and inspect the clutch and related components. Also check the pilot bushing in the back of the crankshaft, rear engine seal and front transmission seal. Now is an opportune time to replace anything that should be now or will need replacing in the near future.

Forethought—My stepdad H.P., a trucker of 50-years-plus tenure, maintains that only a greenhorn doesn't at least replace the throw-out bearing when an easy opportunity presents itself. His theory: An item as inexpensive as a clutch throw-out bearing is predestined to fail at the earliest opportunity after it is neglected.

Starter Motor—This must come off to remove a manual transmission. It can stay in place with an automatic. Remove the bottom mounting bolt and, while you support the starter, take out the top bolt.

Bellhousing—Remove the two engine-plate-to-bellhousing bolts and nuts. Remove the bellhousing bolt from under where the starter was. It goes in from the bellhousing side and threads into the back of the engine.

Give the clutch-disc friction surfaces careful scrutiny. Replace the disc if there's significant wear—more than half gone. Also, especially if the disc is worn thin, check the flywheel for grooving, hot-spots or, worse yet, cracking. An inexpensive trip through the resurfacer at your favorite machine shop will tell whether it is salvageable. Replacement of any of these items will be of negligible cost in time and money at this point. Replacement costs increase dramatically after your car is back together.

Automatic-Transmission Zs—If you detected any slippage, sluggish shifting or fluid leakage, now's the time to remedy the problem.

Some automatic-transmission maintenance can be done in the restoration shop—fluid changing, a filter screen that can be cleaned and gasket replacement are examples. Beyond these, you should have real automatic-transmission-service credentials to make repairs. The Datsun-supplied three-speed automatic box is efficient and serviceable just like the rest of the car. If you're in doubt as to your abilities compared to what your transmission requires, take it to your Nissan dealer or a reputable rebuilding shop for fixing.

If you want to put in a certifiably sound replacement for your automatic, consider trading it for a *guaranteed* rebuild. Don't, however, make the exchange until you are about ready to get your car back on the road. Transmission shops can be testy about honoring time-mileage warranties that show zero-miles but a year's elapsed time.

I can't improve on *How to Rebuild Your Nissan/Datsun OHC Engine's* directions on disconnecting the engine from an automatic, so I'll quote directly. Note, however, this describes the work done with the engine and transmission in the car. The work goes as follows:

"With an automatic transmission, you'll have to remove the flexplate-to-

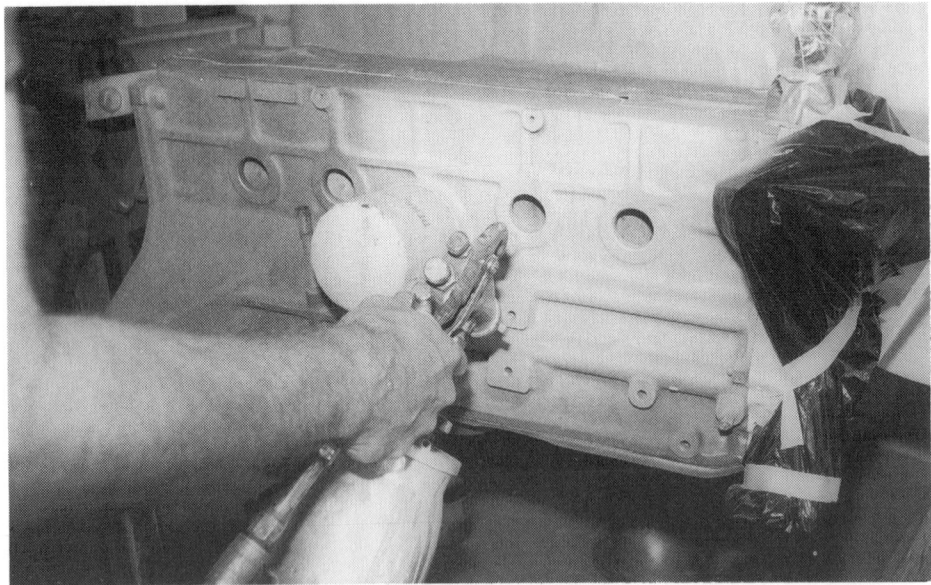

More than most restorers would bother with, I sandblasted my L24 block, then masked and cleaned it. I'm applying a light coat of primer filler. Although not installed here as in the factory, Datsun painted the core plugs blue and didn't bother with masking the aluminum parts. Consequently, they got overspray on the cam and front covers. Note early engine I.D. numbers—they don't correspond with body number.

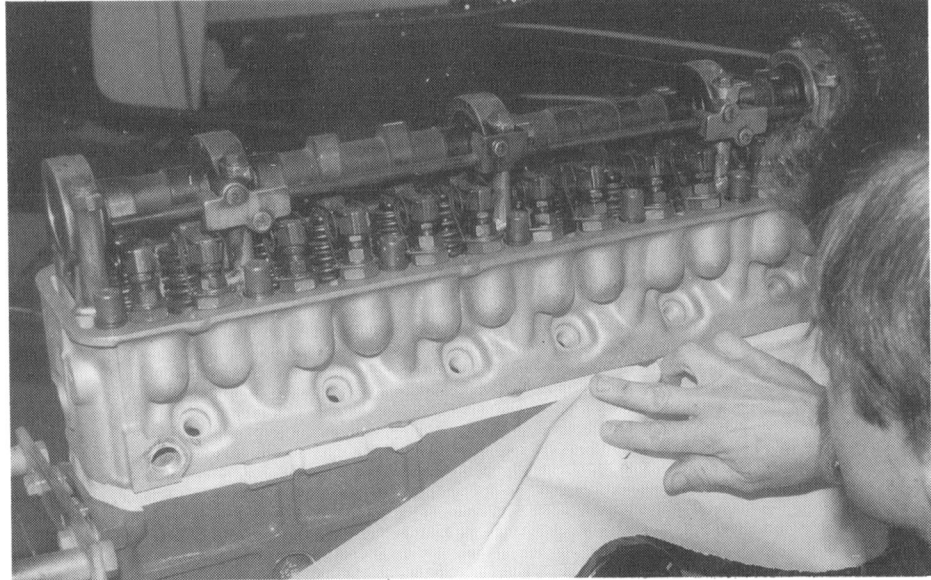

Yes, I'm over-restoring the engine. I'm masking the block in preparation for clear-coating the glass-beaded cylinder head. Only enough clear is applied to seal the metal. A thick coat is more likely to chip.

converter bolts. Start by removing the bellhousing cover plate—it's directly in front of the flywheel. *Before* removing any of the torque-converter bolts, use light-colored paint, chalk or grease pencil to put index marks on the flexplate and converter. The flexplate and converter holes must line up perfectly before the bolts can be installed, so here's one variable you'll eliminate at installation time.

"To expose each bolt, turn the crank with a socket and breaker bar on the crank-pulley bolt. This job is considerably easier with the sparkplugs out. Or, reconnect the battery and bump the engine over with the starter motor (if you haven't removed it) to expose each flexplate-to-converter bolt. If you use this method, make sure your helper at the ignition switch understands that he is to operate the starter only when you say so. Otherwise, you could be injured. After the first bolt is out, turn the crank to expose the next bolt and so on. If you use the starter to bump the engine over, disconnect the battery and remove the starter now."

Engine Mounts—Remove the engine mounts now. Store the bolts carefully or thread them back into the block bosses.

Exhaust Pipe & Muffler—Take a look at your exhaust system. Note the condition of the hangers, muffler and resonator, and the pipes. Don't economize on rusted-out exhaust plumbing. It's taking a chance with your life later on!

Now your Z is a "glider." A little trick I use with a body/chassis that moves only on muscle power is to *overinflate* the tires. Fifty psi won't hurt, and the combination of a reduced contact-patch and rock-hardness makes the car a breeze to push around the shop.

Engine Work—Major rebuilding necessitates engine removal, but even a quick valve job or simple detailing is much easier now that it is out. Mount the engine on a sturdy roll-around stand if you are going to do any work on it. If you don't have a stand of your own, buy one. But if you don't expect you'll need an engine stand for long, rent one. This approach will be fairly inexpensive providing you don't keep it for a year!

If you don't have an engine stand, use a skid or dolly. It will make handling any engine much easier—and safer. An inline six has a high center of gravity, so support or mount it so it can't tip over. Engine parts can be bent and broken; so can people.

Something to Remember—As with an automatic transmission, if you farm out engine work, wait until it's almost time for your car to go back into service. Most commercial shops only warrant their work for a mileage and/or time limit.

3 Body Exterior Teardown

Engine-mount cushions should be replaced, even if they don't look like they need to be. Save all original fasteners until you have the exact replacements.

Hood-to-cowl weatherstrip peels up easily. Note early Z-car identification plate in background. It's still on right strut tower. Z-cars from 1973 and up had it on driver's side firewall.

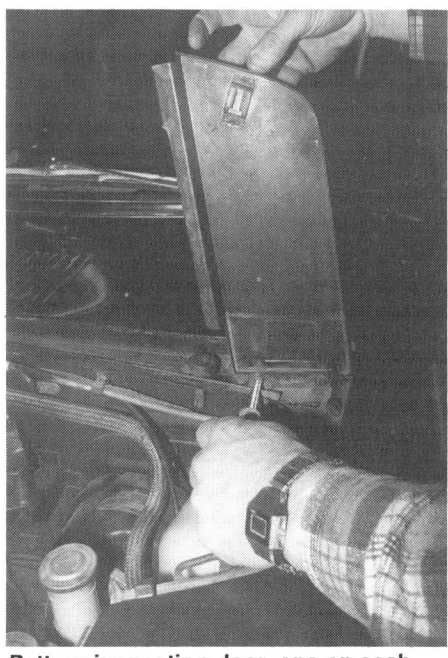
Battery-inspection door, one on each side: Early covers typically ended up with broken latch clips. Remove bolts and make note of shims, if any.

After the engine and transmission are out of the way, the remaining engine-compartment components are easier to remove. First some other parts should come off.

Hood Weatherstrip—This seals the rear of the hood to the cowl panel. A spatula or some kind of bladed tool helps get in behind the seal. Use a heat gun or hairdryer to heat the rubber and cement to help loosen the rubber. Be careful. It's easily broken!

Battery-Inspection Doors—Nissan calls *both* of them this because left-hand-drive models use the right side for the battery box and vice versa. These come off next.

Battery-inspection doors may have shims behind their hinges. Don't lose them. Note how many shims are used on each side. Write it down in your notebook.

Early-style plastic latch tangs usually broke, which is why Datsun switched to metal latches on later Zs. Check yours. If they are plastic, replace them with the metal type regardless of whether they are broken.

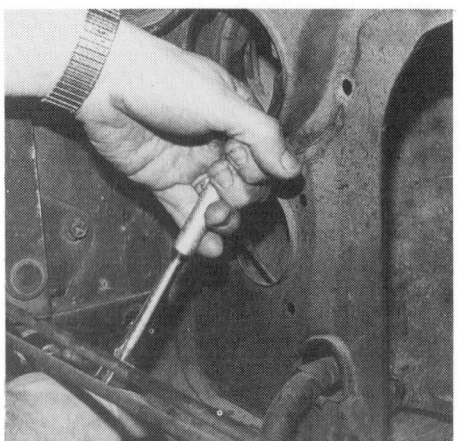
Unbolting hood hinges. And we thought we'd cleaned under the hood—ugh!

Torsion rods can be rotated out after they are unhooked from the hinge link. Note damage to early fiberglass headlight bezel, or fender extension, caused by contact with bumper guard.

Electrical connectors should be preserved if you expect to prevent problems on reassembly. To keep from pulling the wire out, grip male connector with needle-nose pliers to disconnect trouble-light lead.

Hood Bumpers—Datsun used a length of neoprene tubing to protect their threads, a nice touch. Remove both sides. Check to see if the rubber bumpers need replacing.

Grille—All Z-car grilles are fragile, regardless of the material. But the slats can be restored if they are not too far out of shape.

Remove the grille. Late Zs have a double bar below the bumper. They must have the turn-park lights removed to take the grille out—two screws hold the cover, two more the light unit. Put the grille in safe storage before it gets bent or worse. Make sure it can't get damaged in storage! Hang it high on the wall or above the rafters to keep it out of the way.

Front Bumper—Early Zs use a light, cosmetic bumper. It simply bolts to the front body/frame. Late 1973 240Zs used a much heavier, federally mandated, extended bumper. When removing this one, either support the bumper by blocking underneath it or get some help. These are mounted with energy-absorbing units. The heavy rubber end caps actually bolt to the sheet metal. There were two separate types.

1973 and early '74 bumpers are shock mounted; '74-1/2 and later Zs use the federally mandated 5-mph energy-absorbing type. None of the three types of bumpers interchange because of mounting differences at the body. There's no problem with mistaking one type for another.

Hood Hinges—Remove the hood hinges. The 1970 Service Manual omits this procedure, perhaps because it's so obvious . . . but it's also necessary. First, loosen the bolts holding the hinge to the body. Use the hinge to unload the torsion-rod counterbalance springs. These are lightly loaded enough to not require tools. Pull the anchor end out of the hole and remove the hinge assembly. Repeat for the other side.

Hood-Support Rod—Unbolt this now. Be careful on early 240Zs. If the metal support-rod clips are still sound—not cracked or otherwise broken—don't break them now! My ounce of prevention is to place a metal spray-can lid over the clip. After car is painted, I use a plastic tie-wrap instead of tape to prevent damaging the finish. Later cars used a replaceable plastic clip that attaches to the radiator support.

Grille Wiring Harness—It unplugs from the distinctively shaped connectors. This is one area where modern automotive practices are a boon to the restorer—it's very hard to mix up what connects where . . . but not impossible!

Trouble Light—Lenses on these break easily, so be careful not to drop yours. They often vibrated out of their bezel and ended up on the road. A nice touch, nonetheless. On all wiring, be sure not to pull the wire loose from the connector. If you do, stop to fix it then and there. Otherwise you'll forget it.

Coil—Remove the coil and ignition components. If there is any doubt when disassembling electrical hookups, record it in your notebook. Although a rarity, color coding in a wiring harness may not be consistent from connector to connector *or* may not jibe with the diagram. Don't take chances.

Plastic Guide Air Intake—As Datsun calls it, the *guide air intake* comes off by removing two screws. The vents should just pop out of the plenum, but be careful. Old plastic can be very brittle, especially when it's cold.

Feed the chassis wiring harness back through holes in the radiator bulkhead and unclip it from the frame clips. The plastic-covered clips are very weak and easy to break, so be gentle!

Engine Mounts—These can be removed from the number-2 crossmember if they're still there. Buy new insulators. Don't practice false economy—they are inexpensive!

Vacuum Line & Check Valve—Remove the rubber hose connecting the MasterVac unit to the intake manifold. Don't toss it, though. Use it to ensure you get the correct replacement. Old hoses should always be replaced.

Windshield-Washer Hoses—Back to the cowl area, remove the hoses

Body Exterior Teardown 31

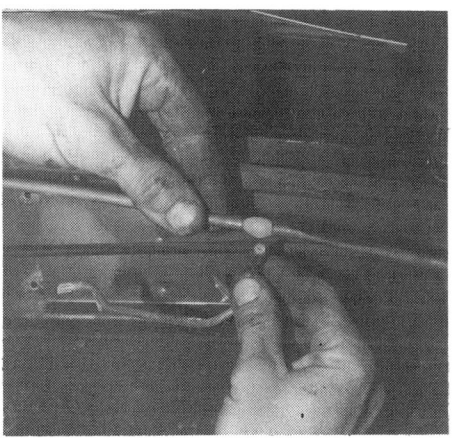
Old plastic becomes as brittle as a fresh soda cracker. Windshield-washer tee broke at a touch.

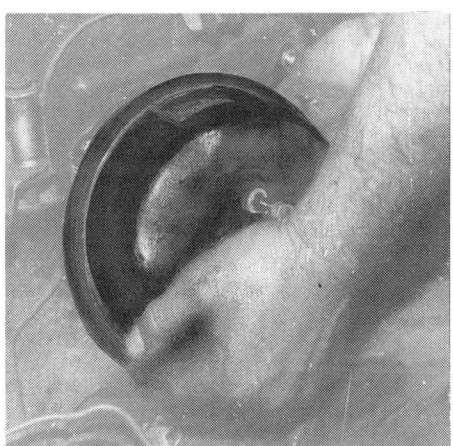
MasterVac brake-booster studs go through firewall, nuts come off from passenger-side of firewall. Studs and nuts also support pedal bracket at firewall. With nuts off, pull booster free of firewall.

Hood-latch-cable end is crimped into latch, so sides must be spread to release it. Inspect cable and replace if its action is stiff or cable is frayed.

and fittings attached to the firewall. Be very careful not to break the male fitting at the bottom of the windshield-washer reservoir/pump. Old plastic, like the tee, breaks like a soda cracker.

Brake Lines—Remove the brake piping from the proportioning valve. If you need to save the paint around the brake or clutch master cylinders, cover the area with shop rags. Bleed out as much fluid as possible before disassembly.

Conventional brake fluid is an efficient paint stripper if it's not wiped off immediately. Even if brake fluid doesn't take off the paint, it can discolor or craze it. Consider using silicone-based brake fluid when you reassemble the system. It costs more, but has the benefit of not harming finishes. Nor does it absorb moisture like conventional DOT 3 fluid—perfect for a car that'll only be driven on special occasions. On the other hand, it does have limitations when used in high-performance applications. So investigate before making a final decision.

All Z brake-component flare nuts are 10mm. Use a tubing wrench to loosen them even if you are going to replace the lines and hoses. Use a conventional open-end wrench and you're sure to round off the flare-nut corners. It's cheaper to invest in a tubing wrench.

Master Cylinders—Both clutch and brake master cylinders may be removed. The clutch-cylinder clevis pin must come out before it is free. You'll find this on the pedal arm under the instrument panel. Brake-cylinder removal is similar.

MasterVac—Remove nuts from the firewall side. Don't forget the clevis; put the pin and clip back on to avoid losing either.

Hood Latch—Take latch loose from the bracket now. Remove the pull cable by unscrewing the pinch bolt. These have a habit of breaking. Check yours for noticeable weakness or damage before reusing it. Usually brought on by cold weather, this phenomenon is frustrating to remedy!

Fuel Tank

If you've drained it, the fuel tank can be removed. Place the car on suitable supports and remove the right rear wheel. Remove the small metal splash shield that protects the vapor-return hose and filler tube.

This area is vulnerable to all kinds of road debris and water tossed up by the rear tire. You may have to drill out the screws or grind off the heads. If you took the splash shield off before you pressure-washed, it was at least partially cleaned. It is hard to remove all the buildup the first try, so a good

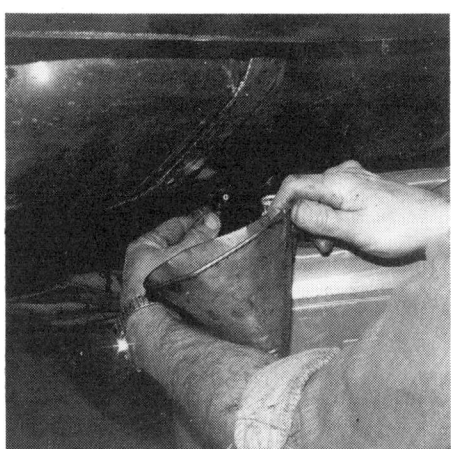
Drain fuel tank. It helps if it's not full—the less to drain, the better. First, make sure the area is well ventilated and there are no open flames or pilot lights. Keep an A-B-C rated extinguisher within reach.

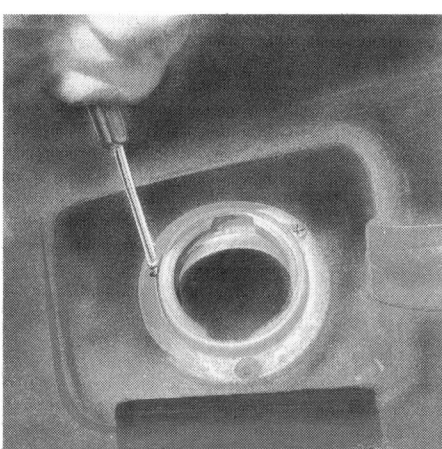
Early and late fuel fillers differ in several details—later version was a definite improvement. They remove similarly. Start by removing screws from flange.

Remove fuel-filler door. Note rust bubbles at the lower rear corner of opening. We'll tackle this later.

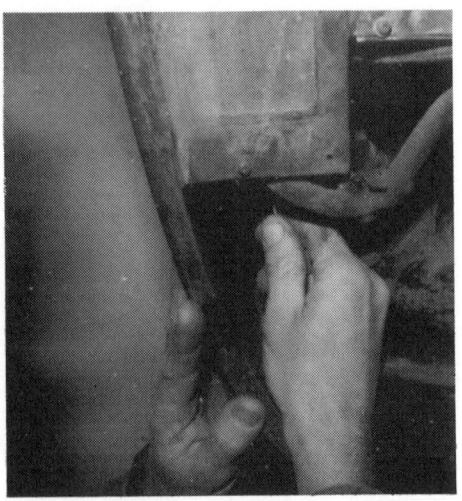

With tire off and splash deflector out of the way, loosen clamp on filler neck. This area accumulates lots of road crud—and rust!

flushing may be needed before you can effectively work in this area.

Disconnect the lower end of the fuel-filler tube. There's a hose-type clamp on the bottom of the filler. Three Phillips-head screws hold the flange to the floorpan. The latter may be corroded tight or rusted into oblivion. Do your best to get the flange plate off intact. You will have to move the vapor lines to gain access here. If the plastic-covered fingers holding the hoses are intact, gently bend them away and *maybe* they won't break off.

Fuel-Filler Top Flange—Remove the three machine screws from the flange and the fuel-filler neck can be removed. Early Z-car plastic filler necks are prone to crack. This lets fuel leak when the tank is topped-up—not safe. They may also leak from the upper vapor-return-hose joint. Late Zs had a two-piece filler with only the lower section made of plastic. The filler itself is retained similarly to the early style, but the flange seats against the body. It is considerably easier to remove. Check all joints for damage or potential leaks. Replace the plastic-tube section if it is not in good condition.

Fuel-Filler Door—This comes off after removing two screws that hold its hinge to the body. Early Zs—to July 1973—have a latch for the door held in place by a spring clip. After the door is off the car, remove the latch by withdrawing the spring clip with pliers. Later cars have only a finger indentation.

Fuel Lines & Fuel-Gauge Sender—Wiring should be removed now. Be sure to identify ends for future reference by tagging so there'll be no doubt as to which terminal each goes back onto.

Electric Fuel Pump—On Zs so equipped, disconnect the fuel hoses, wiring and remove the pump and bracket as a unit. Be prepared to catch residual fuel.

Fuel Tank—Loosen the strap nuts if you need to reach the vapor-hose connections before lowering the tank. Large vapor-collector hoses often rot at or near the tank nipples. Mine had new hose grafted on because the cracked ends allowed fuel seepage at about 50,000 miles!

Strap nuts can now be removed and the tank dropped. Use something to cushion the tank if you can't recruit a helper. Now's the time to finish draining *all* remaining fuel from the tank. Don't forget that vaporized fuel can explode, so take precautions before you store the tank.

I direct compressed air regulated to low-pressure air into the filler mouth, purging the tank of all vapors. Then I seal all openings with duct tape to prevent remaining vapors from escaping and debris from getting in.

Body Dissassembly

Rear Finisher—Remove the license plate, then the license-plate-light assembly. Remove the Phillips-head screws and disconnect the wire lead. Repaint or replace these parts.

Datsun uses reusable plastic rivets that resemble Pop Rivets to attach the finisher along the top ledge of the back panel. Before installation, these rivets have a small stem that extends up from the head. To install, insert the rivet into the hole and push the stem down flush with the rivet head to lock it in place.

To remove each rivet without destroying it, push out the stem with a small—no larger than 1/16-in.—Allen wrench, drill bit or even a nail. It will drop out the back side of the rivet. The top part of the rivet can then be pried up gently and pulled out. What could be simpler? These rivets can be reused, providing you retrieve the little plastic stems. Remove them all and find the stems.

If you experience ill luck with indispensable small parts such as this rivet,

Body Exterior Teardown 33

Early bumpers are featherweights. So is their protection against body damage. Wire exiting license-plate area was for CB antenna—definitely not Datsun.

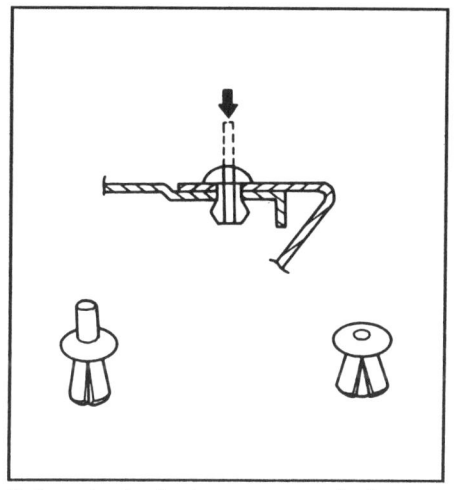

Datsun body rivets use same design as those for retaining interior trim panels. Courtesy Nissan.

you will be glad to know that supply has met the demand. Specialized Z-car suppliers such as Motorsports Auto, as well as Nissan, offer new replacements just for that reason.

Once the finisher rivets are safely together and stashed, remove the Phillips-head screws that secure the finisher under the license-plate area. Lift off the finisher. Store the parts where they won't get lost or damaged.

Stop-&-Turn-Light Units—Taillights to us, these have their own wiring harnesses. Unplug each so it can be removed with its light assembly. Also unscrew the individual light sockets now if you prefer. Remove the bulbs so they won't get broken.

Early units are secured with Phillips-head screws that thread into captive acorn-type nuts. These corrode, so apply some penetrant and let them soak. Take these out, then the lights. If a nut turns with its screw, gently squeeze it with pliers inside its plastic boss. They may have to be drilled out.

280Z-style lights come off with the

Rear finisher is removed by pushing rivet stems through, then pulling rivet. If you plan on reusing rivets, retrieve rivet stems from inside body. Bottom of early metal finisher is retained with clips welded to body lip.

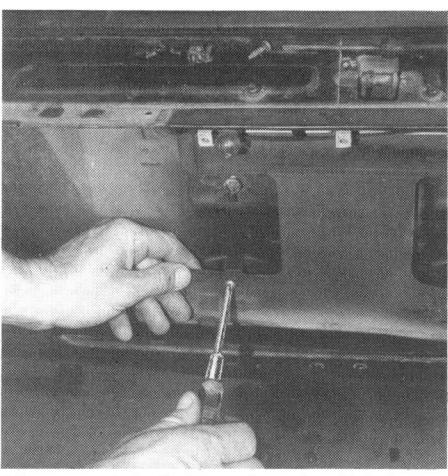

License-plate light and center finisher are retained with Phillips-head screws. Remove them, then the finisher.

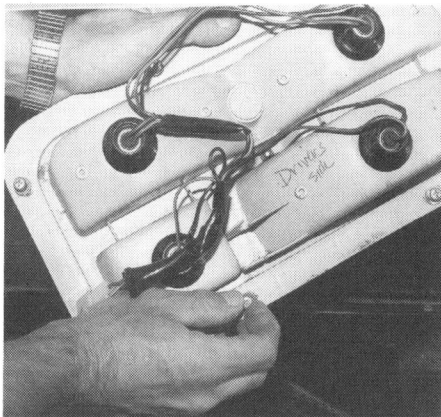

Remove stop-and-turn-light assemblies. Each lamp socket has its own place. Indicate side each assembly installs on as shown.

34 How to Restore Your Datsun Z-Car

Because I can't suggest a method of repairing a broken metal hood-support-rod clip, protect it like this—tape an old spray-can lid over it.

With screws out, lift cowl finisher and pull forward to disengage tabs at rear of finisher from grommets at base of windshield.

finisher side panels. They are held by nuts inside the passenger compartment. Light and panel are secured by Phillips-head screws.

Carefully pry light assembly away from the body opening. Sealer is used between the rubber seal and plastic housing, so seal should come away with the light assembly. Carefully peel the rubber away from the plastic. Try to salvage it. You will need to reseal the lights when reinstalling them. I use silicone for sealing because it effectively fills small gaps, such as those from a torn seal.

Early Z-car gaskets are protected from weather and sight by the metal finisher. Later Zs use a foam gasket. Both seals are relatively inexpensive.

Hood Bumpers—Two types of hood bumpers are used. The type used around the battery-inspection doors are cemented on. The others are attached with Phillips-head screws, which also help secure the fender inner lip. Remove them so you can do a quality refinishing job.

Cowl Finisher—Weatherstrip at the rear of the hood should be off. If not, remove it. Now remove the Phillips-head screws that retain the front edge of the cowl finisher. Pop it up and forward to withdraw tabs at rear edge of finisher from holes in the cowl.

Rubber inserts in the slots hold the tabs snugly and prevent squeaks and rust from metal-to-metal contact. Remove these, too.

Wiper Pivots—Each is secured with three screws. Remove them. Notice that cowl structure will accommodate right- or left-hand-drive wipers.

Wiper Motor—Remove four screws to free the wiper-motor assembly. Once free, it is relatively easy to work firewall grommet loose to remove the motor wiring. Lift the unit up and out.

First, move the motor and linkage rods up and out toward the passenger side. Next, slide the whole ungainly assembly back toward the driver side and lift it out.

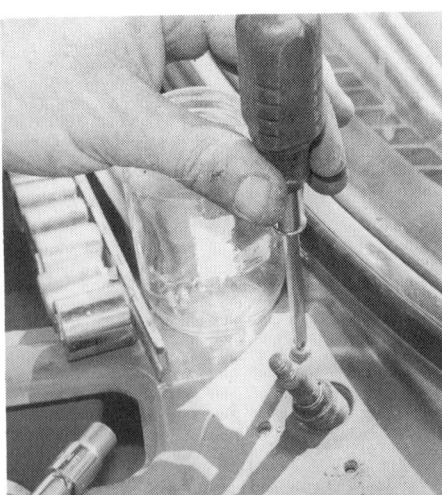

Three screws hold wiper pivots. They are tighter than my dainty grip on the screwdriver indicates.

Wiper motor-and-linkage assembly comes out through opening in cowl plenum chamber. Electrical pigtail and grommet—not seen—must be pushed through firewall. Wiper-motor insulator is missing from mounting bracket.

Body Exterior Teardown 35

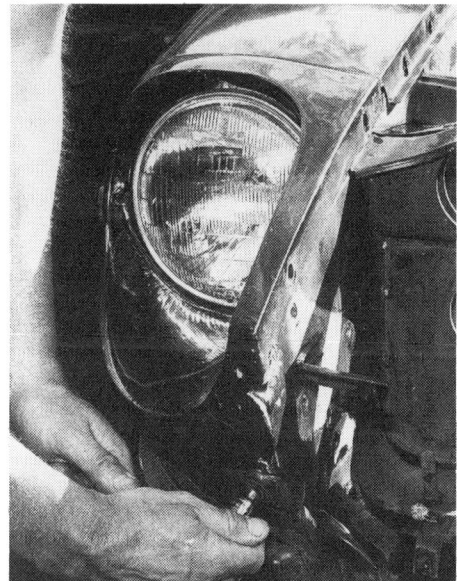

Front-fender lower extensions and apron may have nuts solidly rusted to bolts. Spray them with penetrating oil and let soak for awhile before breaking loose. Note holes in radiator bulkhead with plastic edge covers to protect wiring routed through them.

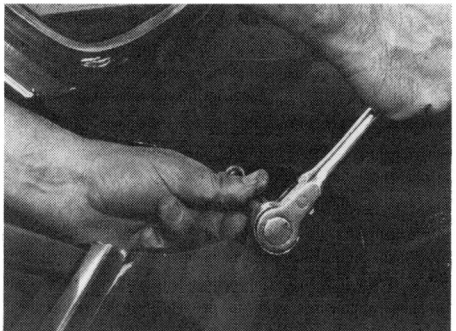

Remove all fender bolts except one in cowl area. Phillips-type impact driver is often needed to loosen these. This bolt hides in front of door.

Once *all* bolts are removed, fender and headlight bezel lift off as an assembly. Even though there's a seal to keep it out, note accumulated trash under fender. This is a rust-prone area, too.

Fender—Disconnect wiring for the headlights and marker lights if not already done. The rearmost Phillips-head screw can only be reached after taking off the cowl finisher. The rest follow the top of the inner fender. Leave the end bolts for last while you remove the rest. This keeps the fender from falling off unexpectedly. Work your way down to the bolts in the radiator-support area. Check them for reusability and store together.

There's a bolt in the rocker-panel area on each side. Because these were exposed to road contamination, they may be stuck and their hex corners rusted round. Be careful. Give them a shot of penetrating oil and let them soak. Try not to break or strip bolts down here.

In the upper door-jamb area, there is another bolt at the rear of each fender. Remove each.

Now the fender can be removed. The other side is identical. Remember to store it carefully. There is no sense in adding to your bodywork chores by having a fender fall over due to your carelessness. Hang them high on a wall or in the rafters.

Fender Upper Seal—This seal was originally held on with clips, though it will probably be stuck to the body.

Use a flat-blade screwdriver to loosen it along its length and remove. This is another area that is exposed to a lot of road slush, so be prepared to deal with rust. Like many body cavities, it was designed to flush and drain itself. As usual, though, this "drainage system" only functions for a short while. Remember that all Z inner front sheet metal has structural value. Be prepared to eliminate all the decay. Make a sound, *permanent* repair. Complete any welding and sealing *before* you paint.

Remove the front apron now. Early Z-cars have the shallow version to match their shorter bumper. There is very little complication up front, and precious little protection. The federalized 5-mph bumper, while adding weight and complexity, did a lot to limit damage to the Z's fragile snoot. The later Z's deeper front apron admitted more cooling air. More was needed with the advent of the 260Z.

Fender splash protectors come off next. They are only attached to the inner fender. Various models of the Z-car have different types of splash protectors. Only one type is shown here. All were designed to protect the unitized body/frame. But after the kind of use many Zs were subjected to, many

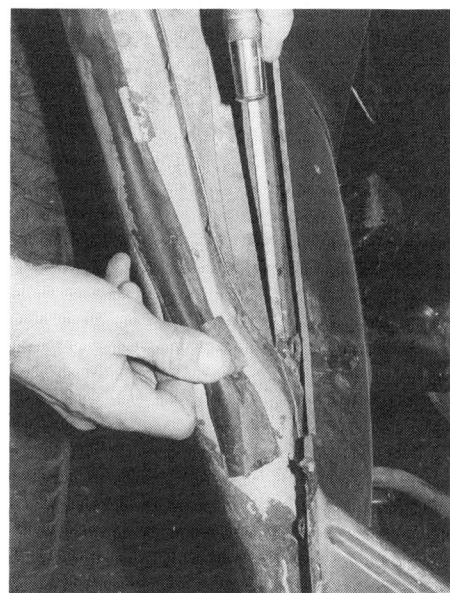

Removing fender seal. With fender-inner seal removed from weld flange, screwdriver point shows where a lot of road splash ends up.

ended up trapping road debris they were supposed to protect against. If so, they've been holding unwelcome moisture against the structure they were designed to protect. Don't be

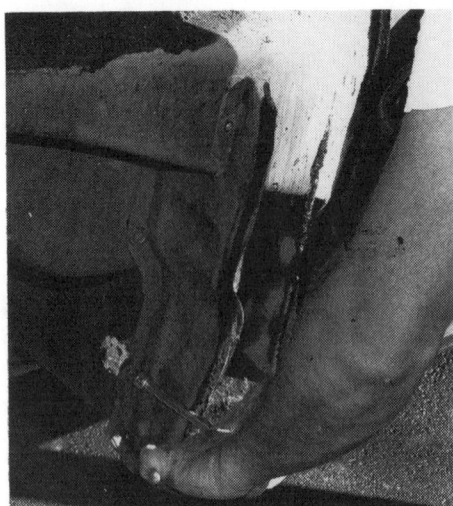

Unbolt splash shield from inner fender. Early splash shields provide less protection than later versions.

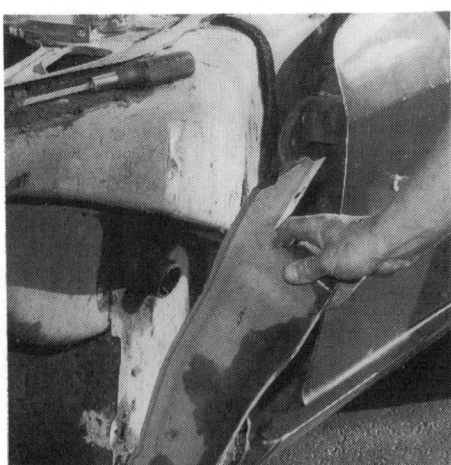

Look at all that accumulated debris! Luckily this Z isn't from the Salt Belt. Foam tape such as that in front of door hinges retains moisture and holds it against metal and rust eats away.

View from underside of fender: Headlight bezel and bucket are off, but gasket is still in place. Four skimpy studs that hold bezel to fender break off with regularity.

shocked if you find serious rust deterioration in this area.

Headlight & Bezel—With the fender off, the headlight is accessible. Before trying to remove it, scrub the fastener heads to get better screwdriver engagement. Remove the large Phillips-head screws from the backside of the headlight bucket to free it from the fender cap. It may be stuck to the cap by sealers or deterioration of the old rubber gasket. Store the unit so the headlight won't be broken.

The fender extension that holds the headlight assembly is attached to the fender with nuts on studs or bolts. Early cars have plastic extensions with studs imbedded in them. Take care not to break the studs if you have the early style. Metal extensions were standardized on all later Z-cars.

Park-&-Turn-Signal Assembly— Early type is easily removed as a unit. Don't try to disassemble them until you have them off the fenders and thoroughly cleaned. Late cars have these incorporated into the grille and are easier dealt with before removing the grille.

Marker Lights—These are retained with caged nuts and Phillips-head screws. Remove the screws to free the lights. If they are worth saving. If you want to keep the nuts, thread them back onto the screws or store them in a marked bag or can.

4　Body Repair & Paint

You've gotten this far, so you must have decided your Z is worth restoring. However, there are areas you can't see without doing major diassembly, so read this chapter and do what you think you must do before making a final go/no-go decision. For example, catastrophic rustouts can occur in such dark places as the upper cowl and floorpan areas. Major damage in either of these areas is very expensive. So look before you commit any more time and money.

Engine-Compartment Preparation

Minor Rust Repair—Not every Z will have major rustout, but even a garage-kept beauty may have the beginnings of body cancer somewhere. Let's look at what can be done to halt the corrosive process.

I choose to abrasive blast most of my body-rust problems. Sandblasters come in all sizes and specifications. All should be matched to the pressure and, more importantly, capacity—cubic feet per minute (cfm)—of the air compressor.

Bigger is better only up to a point when sandblasting bodywork. Too much pressure or blasting will seriously damage sheet metal. Using too strong a stream of abrasive or using the nozzle too close to the work will stretch the metal. This can have the same effect as playing a torch flame on light-gauge sheet—metal expands locally, causing distortion.

There are too many variables related to sandblasting, such as type of equipment, air pressure and such for me to make suggestions. I do, however, recommend that you use 30-mesh or #1 amber sand, nothing heavier. Wear eye and breathing protection. Don't forget gloves and wear a long-sleeved shirt.

Even if no rippling is evident, the peening effect of the bits of hard abrasive *work hardens* the metal. This makes it brittle, not receptive to further working, and susceptible to cracking. This often occurs where there is a deep-seated rust spot that takes prolonged blasting to eradicate—now the sound metal is very thin in places and even more rust prone! So be careful if you're going to sandblast.

Where Is The Z Prone To Rust?—Only parts that aren't plastic or rubber are potential rust victims. Seriously. Refer to the illustration, page 12, for areas most susceptible to severe rustout problems.

Outward sign of serious fender rust: You can bet rust damage is worse on the inside because it worked its way out from the inside. The only solution is to cut away all rusted metal from the wheel house and fender lip.

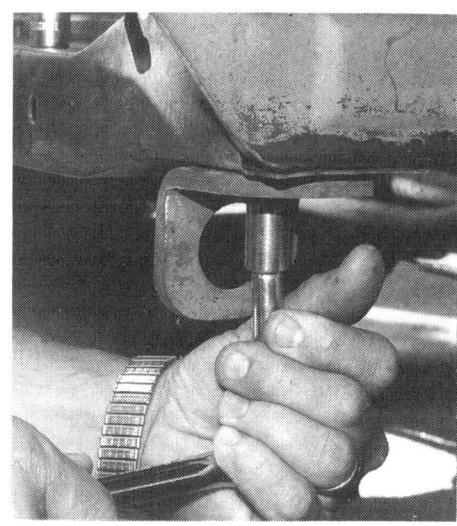

View under left front corner: Bolt in tie-down eye broke off just after photo was taken—much rust hides inside structural members, freezing threads. To repair, I drilled out broken bolt and retapped threads.

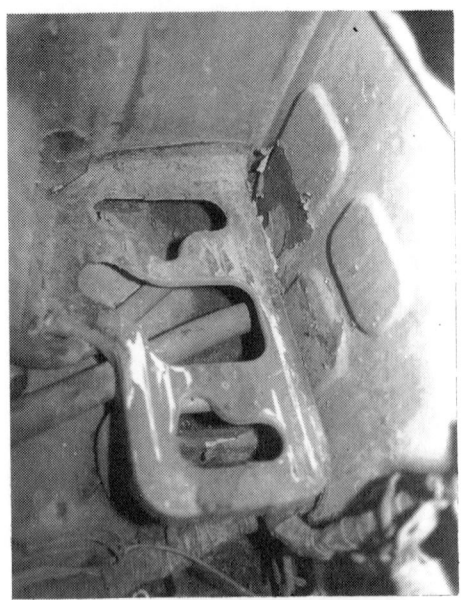

Battery tray didn't last long enough to prevent acid-stripping of paint and rust that followed around and under mount.

Sandblasted battery tray and cowl metal. Fortunately, corrosion and rust weren't major—now they're history. Don't leave metal bare any longer than necessary.

Engine-Compartment Refinishing—With the mechanical components out of the way, the firewall, inner fenders and front sub-frame can be returned to factory freshness.

This area contains many mechanical assemblies vital to the car's operation, all of which contribute to the accumulation of grime on painted finishes. Even after the best steam-cleaning job, baked-on grease hidden behind components that are now removed invites another cleaning. I'm talking about preparing the surface for quality repainting—not just getting it clean enough not to turn your stomach. You should have done that before disassembling your car!

Solvent and a good stiff brush are the old standby. The 3M Scotchbrite pad is a reliable cleaner if it doesn't have to deal with too much pure grease. There are a number of good non-petroleum degreasers on the market as well. Lots of vigorous physical scrubbing and thorough rinsing are vital.

Engine compartments inevitably harbor grease in a maddeningly hard-to-clean labyrinth of seams, welds and holes. Unitized construction such as the Z has created the worst environment to deal with in this respect. Persistence and exertion are the only remedies. After most grime finally seems to be off—and on your clothes, skin and floor—a trip to a coin-operated car wash might be a good bet for both! That's when you'll be thankful you have a car trailer.

When engine-compartment surfaces seem completely clean and dry, methodically wipe down everything with wax-and-grease remover such as Ditzler 330. Use plenty of clean rags saturated with it—not dripping—to wipe down each surface. Refold the rag to expose a new wiping surface when it begins to load up with residue. Continue wiping until all engine-compartment surfaces seem to come up clean, but make sure you get every cranny possible. Do this *before* you do any sanding.

Not only does petroleum residue cause problems with paint, so do errant deposits of silicone, such as Armor All. Even under primer-surfacer, silicone causes the dreaded *fish-eye* effect. Who needs it?

Besides these, there are other contaminants that normally lurk in an engine compartment. Brake fluid is one of these—DOT 3 brake fluid is a very effective, although gradual, paint remover. Both the brake and clutch master cylinders may have leaked onto the painted surfaces around them . . . or you may have spilled fluid while filling one of their reservoirs and didn't wipe it up. Although silicone-base brake fluid won't harm paint, it will cause fish-eyes. If your car has this problem, you may have extensive sanding to do on the inner-fender panel or firewall to bring it back to restorable condition.

Another nightmare: Most of us have experienced a leaking battery. The expense of replacing the battery can be just the beginning. Acid seeping down into the recesses of a unitized body can cause much more than paint damage. Datsun's original equipment battery tray was designed to catch battery seepage. But after 10 or 15 years of service, it may be cracked or the drain tube blocked. Not a pretty prospect!

Like rust, battery-acid corrosion must be thoroughly eradicated. Fresh damage, the furry-white deposits often first noticed, are fairly easy to correct. With good access this can usually be eradicated with a baking-soda solution and stiff brush. Wire brush or sand the cleaned metal immediately and apply an anti-rust primer to prevent the onset of rust.

If battery-acid damage is old or extensive, neutralize with soda and sandblast the affected area. Get it all and primer the entire area immediately.

Paint Preparation—Not much of the engine compartment can be machine-sanded, but where a D-A or jitterbug sander can reach, use it. Use 220-grit or finer *dry* sandpaper. Follow up by hand-sanding using the same grit in *wet-or-dry* paper.

When using wet-or-dry sandpaper,

Prepping New Body Parts

You just paid hard cash for a brand-new body part. It is well wrapped and finished with smooth-looking primer. You should be able to slap it right on the car, right?

"No" is the usual answer. Okay, you have been working hard to restore all that *old* damage in the original body and you deserve a break. But in real life, no experienced bodyman expects—or usually finds—a new body panel to be perfect as delivered.

A new replacement fender may not originate from the same country as did your car. Ironically, most original-equipment manufacturers don't have much interest in churning out replacement body parts for their products, especially those produced a generation or so ago. Most of the replacement-panel industry is supported by specialty companies that may or may not have supplied the manufacturer when the car was built. But, luckily for the restorer, at least they want the replacement business.

Quality varies greatly with aftermarket suppliers. Occasionally the biggest advantage of a replacement panel is the newness of its metal. Otherwise, it may need considerable trimming, drilling, straightening and massaging into shape before it qualifies as a replacement for the original panel. Original parts often begin to look good by comparison. Usually, the more major the part—fender, hood, etc.—the better it will be and the closer it will be to a bolt-on part. Replacement panels often live a hard life before they reach the user, surviving bumps and scratches on the jobber's shelves, in the freight truck and in the delivery truck. The old saw that they are just leftover, second-quality, original manufacturer's parts is unlikely. It's the rough treatment they get between the manufacturing plant and user that makes them look like they have already survived the torture chamber.

Preparation—First inspect the part for damage. Wipe the part with wax-and-grease remover on a clean rag. This not only removes unknown contaminants, you can feel for dings or waves in the metal while doing it.

Next, use 120-150 grit open-coat paper on a block to sand off the factory primer. It is there to prevent the part from rusting while in storage, *not* to provide a base for your expensive paint job. Don't trust what primer it might be—to me it always smells suspiciously like the inside of a cheap file cabinet! If a little is left, don't worry. You should use primer-surfacer and perhaps a sealer before your final paint job. Smaller sheet-metal parts such as patch panels usually aren't primered. Clean such parts with an acid-type cleaner right away and follow up with a coat of primer.

Do any hammer-and-dolly work now that might be required, but don't count on perfection until after you do a trial fitting. In case of weld-in patch panels, do the cutting and fitting.

Follow up with filler or spot putty anywhere needed and apply primer coats as needed. Watch out for razor-sharp edges on new sheet-metal parts. Knock off burrs and jagged edges with a file. Smooth with sandpaper.

Sandpaper might seem expensive, but as with most things, money spent wisely on good materials pays dividends in both the short and long run. This is especially true with using sandpaper to true a sheet-metal surface because sandpaper wears out just like anything else. Just because a sheet still cuts *somewhat* doesn't mean it is really effective.

The principle of block-sanding assumes that the block is flat and level and the abrasive is cutting consistently. Here's what usually happens: As the sandpaper-grit particles wear off or dull, we inadvertently compensate by using more pressure on the block. This depresses the metal surface—especially on critical low-crowned areas—and negates the leveling effect of block sanding. The result is either we underestimate the extent of the unevenness, missing small highs and lows, or we convert them into ripples and waves. Neither contributes to a smooth panel, thus wasting our efforts in the bargain!

Fresh, sharp sandpaper of the smallest grit—largest number—is sufficient to work on high spots *first*. It takes less pressure and considerably less work. This is true whether you are using dry strips on an air board or wet half sheets on a rubber block.

So don't skimp on materials in crucial stages. We budget-minded restorers can find lots of uses for semi-worn sandpaper after block-sanding is successfully completed.

Finish prepping the new panel just as you would any other part of the body. Save the final primer/sealer coat until the panel is mounted and adjusted on the body. Don't be surprised if a chip or scratch occurs during installing or aligning.

Resident Porsche-lover perfects his sanding technique on new Datsun fender. He'll remember this when he asks to use the 240Z for the Junior Prom!

40 How to Restore Your Datsun Z-Car

After all mechanical components are out, engine-compartment restoration can begin in earnest. Block-sanding can't be done in every area, but do it where possible. Fill areas where finish is bad, just as on exterior body.

Cowl-finisher louvers were sandblasted to save sanding time. Balance of work will be done with jitterbug sander after cleaning with wax-and-grease remover.

use a bucket of water and detergent rather than a garden hose for your water source, especially with preliminary sanding. Household powdered detergent is great for loosening and floating away remaining grease or contaminants. Change the water occasionally so you don't re-pollute the surface. Now you can use your garden hose. Use lots of fresh water in a strong stream to flush the sanded surfaces.

I spend at least one workday on just the engine compartment. All those brackets, holes and little plastic-covered wiring holders demand your attention. Little nooks and crannies respond only to lots of meticulous handwork. It will pay off in the finished product!

Primer—After the preparation work is done, blow out the whole area with compressed air. Then follow the *reducing* recommendations on the label of the primer/surfacer of choice. Apply it in thin, even coats. I like a *high-build* primer/surfacer such as Ditzler Kondar DZ3/7. It covers well, sands easily and will take even catalyzed-acrylic-urethane topcoats. Many restorers like a catalyzed primer such as Ditzler Epoxy Chromate Primer DP40/401 or Fiber Glass Evercoat Feather Fill.

Filler—Either the ubiquitous "Bondo" type polyester filler or a spot putty can be used to fill small imperfections. Pay more attention to areas that will be easily seen when the car is reassembled. There are a few spots that will strike the observer's eye immediately, so a sloppy job now will scream its presence in these areas when painted!

Painting—There is so much complication in the engine compartment/firewall area that I paint it separately. This requires masking the engine compartment when the rest of the car is shot, but this can be accomplished with a cheap plastic dropcloth and some masking tape.

When painting the engine compartment, use exactly the same materials and techniques as if you were spraying the body. Although not necessary, most painters use a smaller spray gun because of the close quarters and relatively small panels. Be extra careful of getting runs and sags in tight crannies and around brackets and so forth. And don't back into your work while spraying the opposite side!

Cowl—Like most manufacturers, Datsun uses an upper cowl cavity as an intake for the Z's ventilation system. It also contains the windshield-wiper motor and linkage. Because it's open at the top, the box-like cowl

Cowl cavity presents a real clean-out problem. Rust potential is high and access is not good. Cup brush turned with power tool helps.

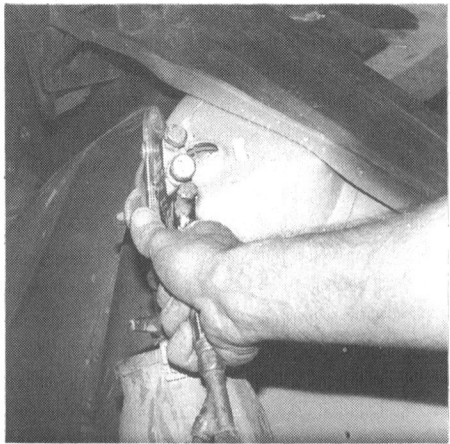

Primer applied to engine compartment will be wet-sanded with 320- or 400-grit paper.

Loose paint, sealer and corrosion are loosened and rooted out. Compressed air and vacuum help with cleanup.

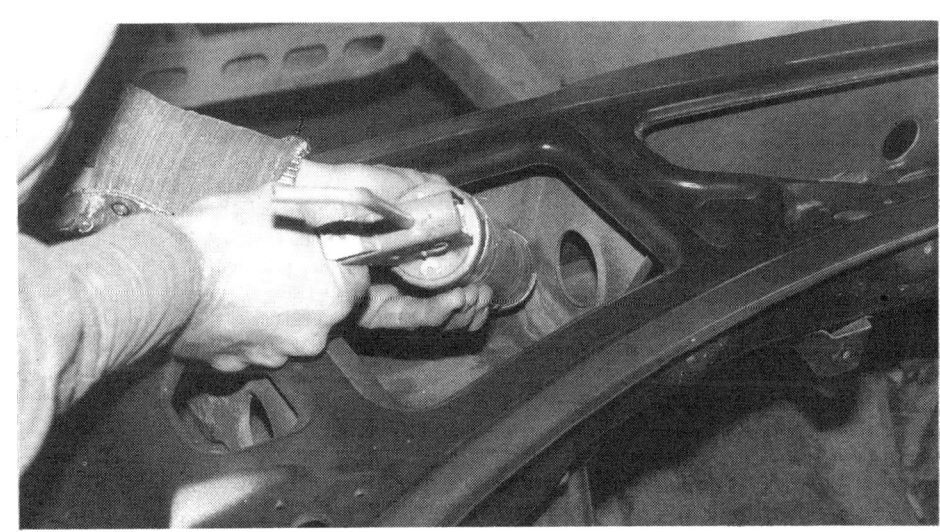

3M Joint & Seam Sealer is reapplied to all seams. It cures quickly.

collects its share of moisture from weather and washing. It also accumulates dirt and organic material.

The cowl has drains, but over time the drains get plugged. Unless the area was cleaned out regularly—something no one ever thinks to do—prolonged moisture exposure raises havoc with the steel in this area.

It is conceivable that a Z-car could be rendered unsuitable for restoration by rust damage in the cowl area. This is primarily because repairs in this complex structure might be too expensive to be justified by the value of the car—a virtual "total." But with time, more extensive repairs become practical as the Z's value increases.

If your car doesn't have major rust in this area, be diligent in cleaning and inspecting the bottom of the cowl and recesses where damage is most likely to occur. Apply sealant and caulking generously and be sure to check for free drainage afterwards. Datsun didn't use standard body finish in the inner cowl, but that doesn't mean you can't.

Underpan—Most Z-cars suffer from damage in the floor area. Rust, of course, is the number-one bugaboo. Fortunately, most cars can be saved even if rustout is major. You'll have to decide if it's worth the cost. A realistic assessment of the extent of the problem should answer this.

Once past that, decide whether you can accept the looks of the kind of repairs your car will need. Consider that a badly rust-damaged Z will require major reconstructive surgery to be functionally restored. Will the cutting, fabrication and rewelding required substantially alter the value of the car as a restoration?

As you can see in the illustrations from Auto Rust Doctors, pages 44 and 45, repairs of this magnitude leave more scars than those left by Dr. Frankenstein. Even if they can't be detected at first glance, will the unoriginality of the subframe, underpan and so forth hurt the car's value as an original? It certainly would at a concours event if the car were entered as a stock Datsun. As a daily driver, probably not. To make such repairs unnoticeable, either a portion of another car must be grafted on or panels scavenged from another Z must be used.

Another problem you may encounter is damage incurred by rocks, parking-lot dings and similar road hazards. Despite the Z-car's rather generous ground clearance, any veteran Z has its share of dings, dents and scrapes. Some are negligible; others may intrude into the footwells. Serious impacts to the front subframe or its attachment area can alter the car's suspension alignment. If you suspect problems in these areas, consult a competent frame shop while your car is still a roller. If welding or major mechanical realignment is required, have it done before you do any subframe and underpan refurbishing.

Pay attention to underpan areas that were exposed to wheel splash. The toe board, for example, tends to get sandblasted by road debris and gravel. Grind and prep these areas. Or really sandblast and refinish them as you would any other area of the body.

When major repairs are done—or only minor freshening-up is required—restoration of the firewall, underpan and fender wells is much like that for the exterior panels. Careful sealing, a good primer and an adequate thickness of the same paint as applied to the exterior is appropriate. Most of us will settle for a bit less high finish under the car.

Clean All Surfaces—These areas must be thoroughly cleaned for new paint to adhere adequately. This is never a fun job even if your steam cleaning was very thorough. After the mechanical components are removed, a whole new batch of grease, corrosion and crud seems to present itself. Use the same treatment that removed the severe soil to finish the job.

Old Undercoating—Asphalt-based coating from the factory was devised to reduce interior noise, not to prevent rust. Aftermarket undercoaters stress rust prevention. In my experience, a thorough undercoating can contribute to the preservation of an underbody *if* that car hasn't been seriously threatened with rust *before* the coating was applied. On a car that has weathered 10 or more winters in the Salt Belt, it can be less of a benefit. An undercoating can end up trapping

42 How to Restore Your Datsun Z-Car

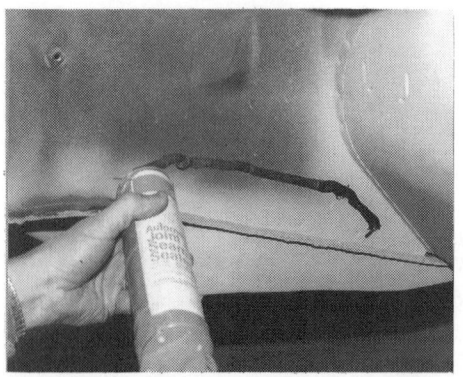

Inner fender looks pretty good. Be generous with sealer, particularly around sheet-metal joints in rust-prone areas. Body sealer takes paint well.

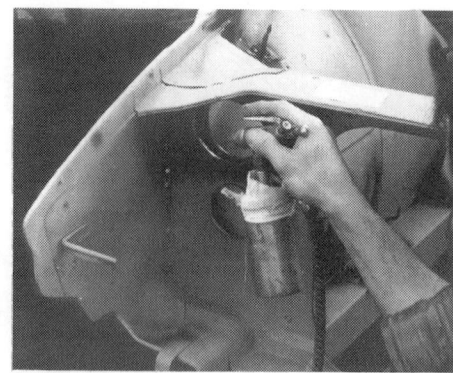

There are tight places that call for a smaller gun.

water between itself and the metal, causing problems much faster than it would otherwise.

When you strip off old undercoating, you may find it harbored lots of metal-eating moisture. In such cases the undercoating is easily removed—with some metal. If it helped to retard rusting and is still stuck to the painted steel, solvent and a scraper must be used to remove it. In this case, you may not have to remove it. Once you're sure the metal is sound, clean the surface thoroughly and apply another coat of undercoat over the old.

Note: It isn't good practice to slop undercoating on suspension components. It should be confined to sheet-metal surfaces. Undercoating can also be used for purposes other than rust prevention and sound insulation. A moderately thick layer of undercoat can be used to conceal carefully finished structural repairs.

Caulking & Sealing—Anywhere major structural repairs have been done may require resealing to prevent new rust damage. Body-supply shops carry a variety of quality products for such needs. Sealers and other compounds can be applied from a tube with an inexpensive household caulking gun. Non-hardening caulking, often called *dumdum,* is readily available, even from non-automotive sources.

Most of these products accept primer and paint. Just don't apply a body compound too thick. Let the sealer set up. They should at least *skin over* before primer or paint is applied.

Priming—Once everything you intend to refinish is structurally correct and the surfaces roughened, wipe it down with wax-and-grease remover. Then apply primer.

Make very sure every nook and cranny is given two coats. Some parts may have to be shot in two or more positions to get an all-around coat. Remember what they are because the same procedure will be required to paint them body color. If objectionable spots show themselves, take the time to bring them up to standard and spot reprime.

Painting—Before the color goes on, take time to blow out all cracks and pockets that might collect filler dust, bugs or water. A powerful shop vacuum is a big help.

Once everything is clean to your satisfaction, mix the color and spray.

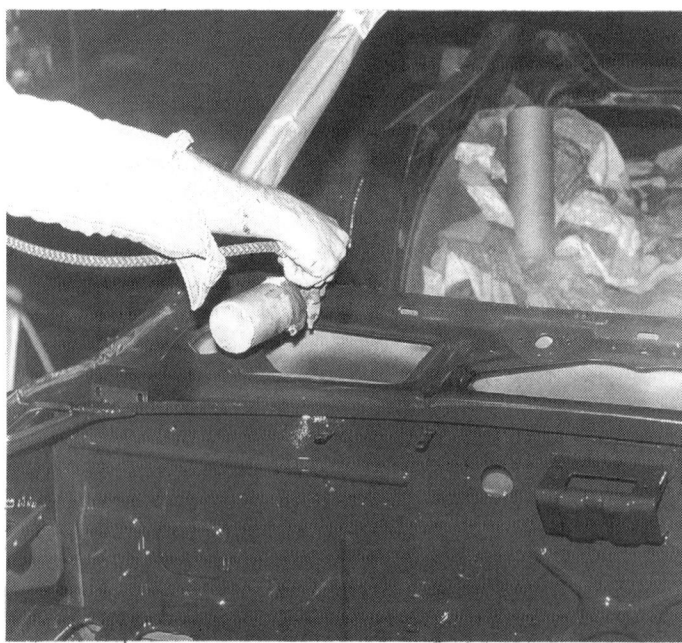

DeVilbiss EGA finger gun is ideal for spraying hard-to-reach areas such as this corner. I masked paint-code decal, then painted hard-to-reach parts first . . .

. . . then used a Binks 69 gun to get good coverage and gloss on broad areas. Don't let hose get against that fresh Deltron! Watch out for overapplication. Runs and sags aren't appealing, even in the engine compartment.

Body Repair & Paint 43

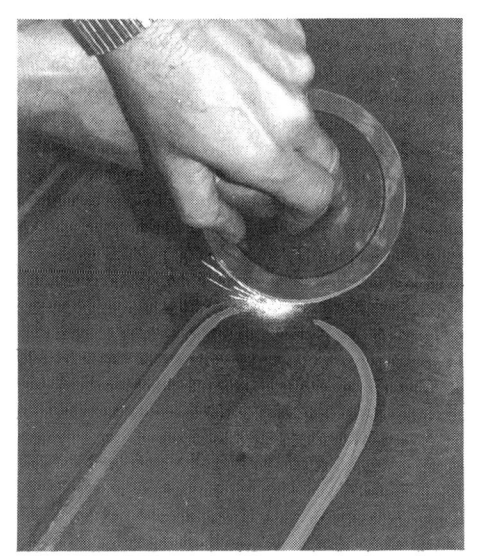

Pinhole rust can occur in floor and spare-tire well. This rust was caused by moisture that leaked in through door jamb, not the floor plug as might be expected.

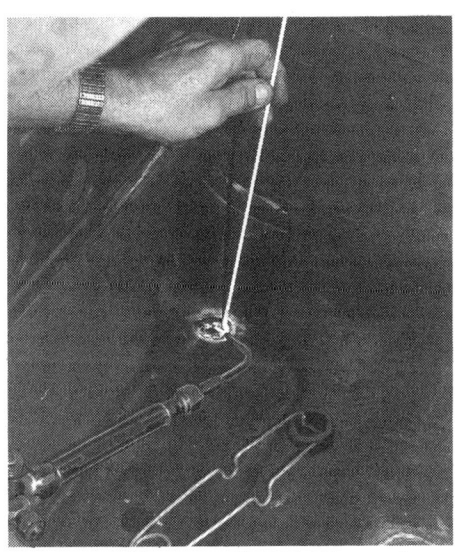

I removed floor mat that hid the rust. After removing rust by grinding, I flowed brass into the perforations. Brazing requires less heat than welding, thus there's less chance of warping sheet metal.

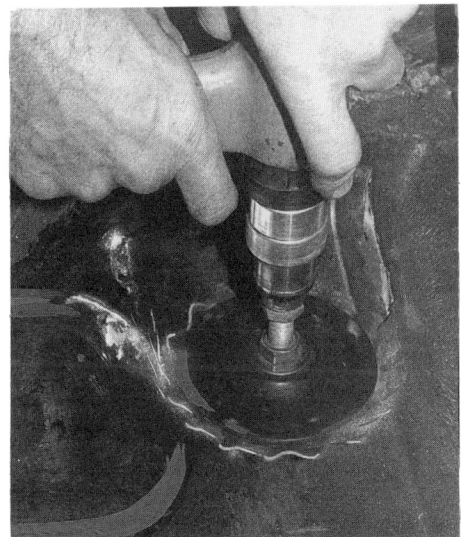

Braze is smoothed on this side and ground flush with underside of floorpan. More is left on upper side where it won't show. Serrated edge on 60-grit disc got all the flux and burned-paint residue. Then area was primed and painted.

Be forewarned that engine compartments, underpans, fender wells and the like take much more paint than similar looking outer body panels.

This is an opportunity to do a *better* job than the factory in ways that really make a difference. First, expend considerably more time and effort in handwork: sanding, filling, finishing and so forth. Secondly, use materials such as sealant, primer and paint much more lavishly. Third, upgrade the quality of the materials—substituting acrylic urethane for old-fashioned alkyd enamel, for instance. The latter would not be considered authentic by a purist, however. Datsun could hardly be accused of scrimping on the Z-car, but many improvements can be made without resorting to blatant over-restoration.

The bottom line on a fine restoration is often the detailing that is put into areas that aren't obvious. An example is the engine compartment. Quality of workmanship and attention to detail in this area usually draws the praise of knowledgeable judges.

Structural Rust Damage—Z-cars, especially the first three or four years' production, had a bad reputation for rusting out. Yet, they are in sufficient demand—or at least certain cars gained enough of a place in their owner's hearts—to warrant extensive repairs to keep them on the road. Again, geographic location determines how badly a Z-car will deteriorate from rust. The irony is there are Zs lingering away in Sun Belt dismantling yards that have nearly perfect subframes, floorpans and rear quarters. At the same time their less-fortunate, but better-loved brethren in the Salt Belt are getting four-figure repair jobs to keep them roadworthy.

How far can rust-cancer go in devouring a Z's sheet metal? Better yet, how much can be done to correct its ravages? In an effort to answer that question, I consulted Bob Hess of Auto Rust Doctors, deep in the heart of rust country. His shop specializes in repairing body rot on Z-cars, classic Mustangs and other cars that are valued enough to merit such radical remedies. This New Jersey firm supplies floorpan and "frame-rail" repair kits in 16-gauge steel that can be welded in by any restorer who has access to an oxyacetylene welder. As in the photos, MIG or wire-fed welding is the method of preference, but gas-welding or even brazing will suffice. Good shop practice and methods should be followed in either case. See *Welder's Handbook*, an HPBook by Tom Monroe and Richard Finch, for complete information on welding equipment and techniques.

The following description follows the same process as is used by Auto Rust Doctors, so you'll notice some inconsistencies relative to where you are in your restoration.

Start by removing all components that might burn or be damaged by heat—carpets, pads, floor mats, firewall insulators, rubber parts, upholstery—anything that can catch fire from direct or radiated heat. Also, if they aren't already out, remove the battery, radiator or anything that could impede the cutting or welding process. Be sure that any fuel, brake or transmission lines are moved well away from the danger area. Also move the wiring harness out of the away. Don't forget a fire extinguisher. A charged ABC-rated extinguisher within easy reach is more effective than the best fire insurance!

Jack up the car under the jacking point on the number-2 crossmember. Remove the front wheels and splash pan if so equipped. The bumper and brackets/shocks may be removed if necessary for access. Remove the stabilizer-bracket bolts and take off the bar or let it hang down. Then remove the four bolts/nuts that secure the crossmember to the sub-frame.

Jack up the car a little more, allowing the crossmember to drop away from the frame rails about 1 in.

Early Z-car doesn't have much floorpan left. Salt corrosion did the deed. Driver and passengers were fortunate not to have ended up on the pavement. Photo sequence courtesy Auto Rust Doctors.

One side with bad floorpan material cut away, the other repaired with Auto Rust Doctors' kit. This was done in their shop. The two beams are the hoist, not floor reinforcements! Note how seat mounts were saved.

Another view of the rust damage: Is there any doubt structural members are biodegrading? Stabilizer-bar mount has broken loose. No wonder car didn't handle.

Rot was cut away with an oxyacetylene torch. Bob Hess says this was one of the worst rust-damaged Zs he'd ever seen.

Using a torch or chisel, separate the frame rails from the wheel-well area. If you're replacing the floors as well, cut out bad floorpan areas. Use the replacement metal to guide how much to remove. You can cut farther if the rust extends past this line, but you'll have to piece in more metal to compensate. Don't cut out the seat mounts. They will be rewelded to the new floor. On 280Zs the passenger's floorpan and transmission tunnel must be trimmed over the fuel/brake lines to match the floor panels. The latter can then be shaped to make up the difference. Some metal may need to be trimmed from the new panels as well.

Watch your cutting flame for indications of bad steel. Rust won't cut cleanly—it curls and throws sparks. Use only enough heat to do the job—don't incinerate the metal. Some warping is unavoidable, but you should have some recognizable planes and curves to tack-weld the new panels to. Continue removing parts the kit replaces and use a grinder to remove slag and true edges. You will lose the use of any weldnuts that were originally in the frame rail—plan on using sheet-metal screws or through bolts in their stead. Save any brackets that can be reused and welded back on.

On the 280Z subframe, cut about 2 inches back from the visible compression-rod bracket on the bottom of the strut brace. You must find the inside brace—the new rail of the floor kit must be welded to it along both sides.

Now is a good time to sandblast all remaining rust and crud out of the frame rails, rocker panels or wherever you want to scour it clean. Cover or wrap anything you don't want full of sand with plastic sheet, garbage bags or duct tape.

When everything is cleaned, edges trimmed and trued and straightened—pretty scary sight—test fit the kit parts. New floors install from the underside. Frame-rail replacements should butt against the firewall. If the parts don't fit correctly, find the problem and cor-

Body Repair & Paint 45

Structural member is completely replaced. It ties in with original metal where it's sound and tied in with new sheet metal where it's not. Rear inner fender is patched; front comes next. Stabilizer bar can be reattached.

Opposite side of same car—would you call this a total? Most of strut tower is gone, as is mounting area for the front-suspension crossmember.

rect it. When they look just right, use C-clamps and Vise-Grips to hold them in place.

Tack-weld the new panels in place. Give the frame parts a good eyeballing for alignment and squareness. Use a tape measure to check dimensions. Trim either the old floorpan or kit panels or both to get a good fit. Around the interior area, try to use a lap seam—one lip will help support the other. Butt-weld if necessary or if you want to hide the seams by grinding and filling later. The floors don't have to be welded solidly—a 1/2-in. bead every 1-in. or so will suffice if the welds are sound.

Remove clamps as they are no longer needed and move them where they will help. When you have a good solid job—much welding rod later—take them off. Reweld seat mounts to the floorpan.

Lower the crossmember onto the new frame rail. Line up the holes with those already in the kit rails, add the reinforcing plates and run the nuts/bolts down finger-tight. Using body tools, shape the inner fenders to the new rails and weld them solidly.

The radiator crossmember must now be welded to the new rails. Use the plates supplied with the kit. Also reattach all brackets.

Tighten the suspension-crossmember bolts. Tack the two reinforcing plates from the strut tower to the rails. Reposition both with a body hammer and complete the welding.

New structure is attached at rear, will be joined to radiator bulkhead next. Suspension was supported by tall jack stands while new attachment holes were positioned to conform exactly with original holes. Service Manuals provide dimensioned diagram for this purpose.

Strut tower and inner fender panels replaced, everything welded securely and components bolted back in place. Metal will be primered, painted and possibly undercoated. It won't pass for original, but Z-car has a new lease on life. Front suspension must be aligned.

46 How to Restore Your Datsun Z-Car

Worm's-eye view of area immediately above right taillight opening. Rust in rear finisher/hatch jamb area occurs from water entering it through capillary action. Damaged area was sandblasted and filled.

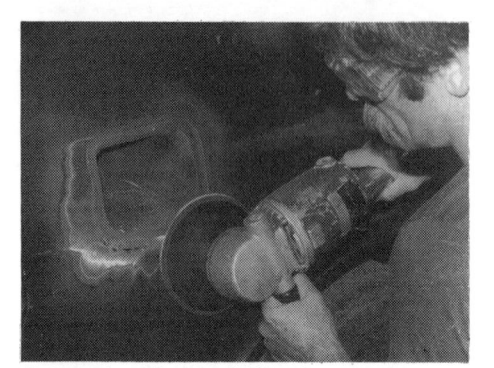

Datsun bonded fuel-filler box to the quarter panel. A fender-bender broke seal when car was nearly new, allowing rust to get a foothold. I wear eye-protection while feathering paint with a 150-grit disc.

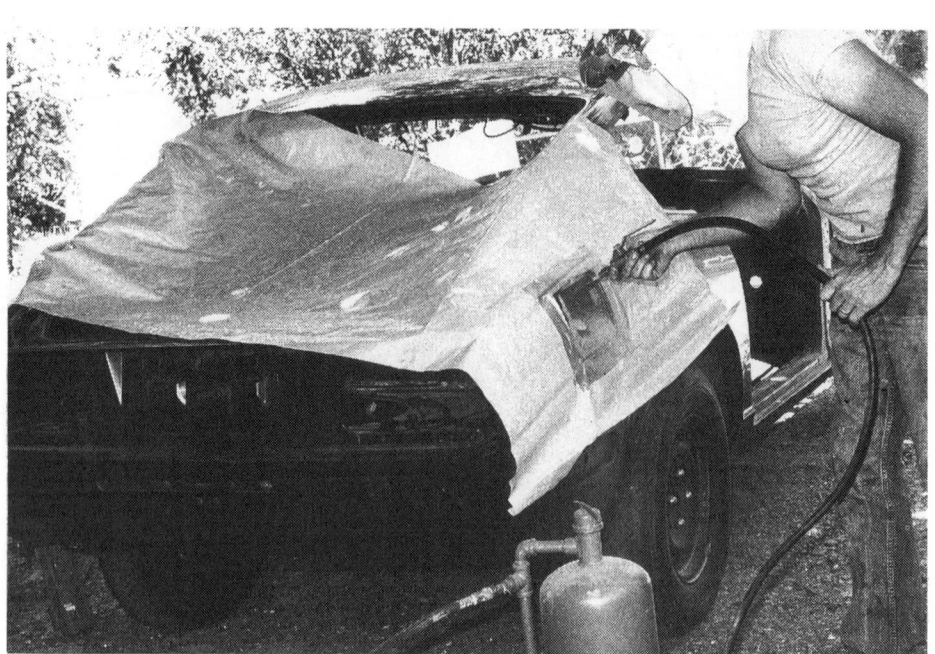

Rust blisters around fuel-filler box were caused by water seeping between fuel-filler box and inside of fender below the filler lip. Plastic and duct tape are used to mask area. Sandblasting eradicates problem.

Fender can be repaired with panels like these. Other areas such as the lower door, front and rear fenders and rocker panels are available in original-gauge metal. Courtesy TABCO, Inc.

Reinstall the stabilizer bar.

Clean all welds and inspect for cracks, voids and burn-throughs—quality must be tops. Another round with the sandblaster will remove slag, discoloration, old paint or anything else that could impede sealing and refinishing. Blow clean with compressed air.

Use a good non-sanding primer—Ditzler DPE1338 Satin Prime or DPE-1202 Ferrochrome Primer-Sealer—for additional rust protection. Then caulk all seams with something like 3M Body Caulk. I recommend using a spray-on undercoating such as 3M Body Shutz. Otherwise, regular enamel body finish should be shot on as soon as possible.

New floor-insulation pads are required for sound insulation. The resonance of bare metal creates too much noise.

Reinstall the components moved or removed. As soon as your Z-car is driveable, test it after you have the alignment checked at a good front-end shop. Continue to inspect joints and seams until you are satisfied that everything is correct.

A major project, to say the least. Not the kind of thing that will pass for a low-mileage Arizona creampuff—but it doesn't show from the outside.

The Z in the photographs is a true worst-case example. It shows how far a restorer can go to save an otherwise good Z-car. And you have to start somewhere.

Repair Panels—These go on the outside of the car, not underneath. Both metal and fiberglass panels are available for Zs. I'm biased. I like original metal. Too many poorly bonded fiberglass body parts come to mind—where the little hairline cracks start running around the edge of the filler just before the 'glass piece falls off onto the road! Even the best job eventually develops cracks because metal and plastic expand and shrink at different rates as they are heated or cooled. I leave fiberglass car parts for what they were intended—Corvettes and Avantis.

I prefer a method similar to that just described called *body sectioning*. HPBooks *Paint and Body Handbook* by Taylor and Hofer has a good chapter on the sectioning process—as well as rust removal. Tackling either can be done by a person with good skills using reasonable care and practice. Yes, it does require filler, but less filler on a more permanent base if done correctly. Tabco supplies a number of repair panels for the Z-car, some of which can be combined to replace a larger area. No doubt about it, there is an investment of hard work and hard cash, but *done correctly*, replacement panels can be as good as new ones.

Take precautions to make sure rust doesn't come back to infect your restored Z. Nothing is foolproof, but a good effort will be rewarded by good results—even in the Salt Belt!

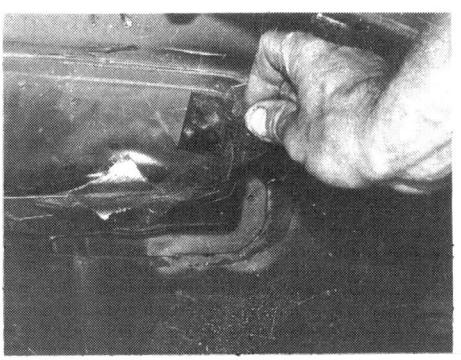

Taillight Assemblies

With the taillights out of the car, you can easily assess their serviceability.

New units are readily available. For the restorer who has badly deteriorated taillights *or* the concours-bound owner, installing a new set is the way to go. If yours are only showing normal wear—and you aren't trying for a 100-point show car—you can refurbish them.

This sequence focuses on the early style, but the techniques are the same for all styles.

Disassembly—Datsun never intended these units to come apart—but it can be done. I label the bulb sockets and corresponding holes in the lamp housing to save time at reassembly. Carefully remove the little pushnuts from the "chrome" plastic studs on the back of the unit. Then gently use two screwdrivers or similar tools to pry the lens away from the plastic housing. A thick gummy compound which serves both as sealant and adhesive for the two halves must be overcome. Use a small blade to get out most of the compound. Do the final cleanup with naptha.

With the halves separated, you will see more little pushnuts that secure the bright plastic trim. Don't try to pull these free. Crush them with pliers to remove them because the plastic studs are weak and brittle. Replace the crushed pushnuts with new ones. They are cheap and available at most hardware stores. Now press off the trim pieces and store them where they won't be damaged.

Wash taillight parts with dishwashing detergent and warm water. An old toothbrush will get into the cracks and grooves inside the lens. Don't use powdered cleanser, steel wool or Scotchbrite pad on the plastic. They're all abrasive and will scratch. Dry with compressed air. Using DX 330 or similar cleaner, remove as much old wax and waterspots as possible. The rear shell should come out as good as new.

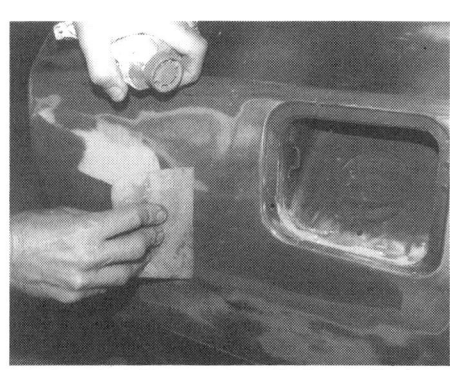

Because torch shouldn't be used in this area, I cut an L-shape piece of aluminum screening to fit where perforations occurred and used polyester filler inside to make repair.

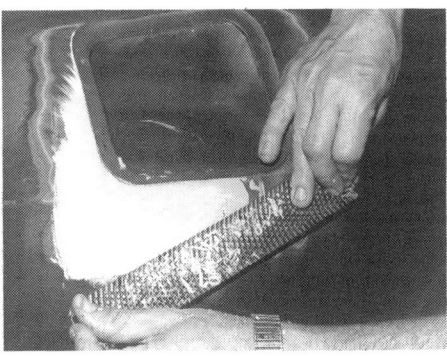

On the outside, Bondo is used to finish repair job. While still curing, it is shaped with a Surform file blade. Then most of the remaining filler was removed to achieve the original contour with 100-grit strip of sandpaper on a long board.

Some 150-grit sandpaper on a D-A sander removes errant scratches and old paint. Note light filler from earlier repair. A bit more filler was used to reseal the filler-box joint, then it was hand-sanded.

Ditzler Red-Cap spot putty is applied with a squeegee to suspected low areas and pin-holes. It was block-sanded dry. Never use wet paper on raw polyester because it absorbs water.

The lens will undoubtedly benefit from a good buffing. If you don't have the equipment to do buffing and polishing, commercial sign shops that work with plastic signs may be able to do the work for you. Buffing with a very fine compound—there are

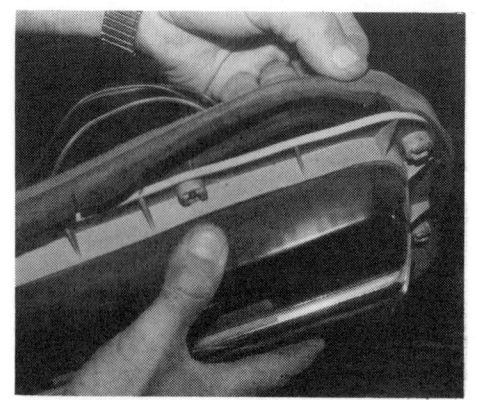

Early taillight assembly uses heavy weatherstrip/gasket fitted to its periphery. Replace gasket if it's in bad shape.

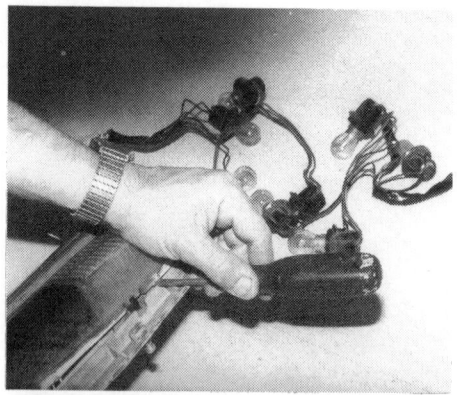

Taillight halves weren't meant to come apart. Thick sealant that joins halves is still pliable. Don't forget to indicate bulb-socket locations before you remove them. These are marked on tag at right.

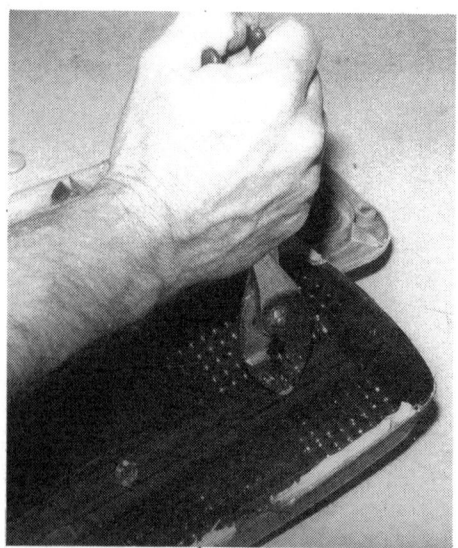

Vacuum-plated plastic trim is held on with pushnuts. There are vacuum-aluminizing services that can restore the original look. Matte-black inset appears to be hand brush painted!

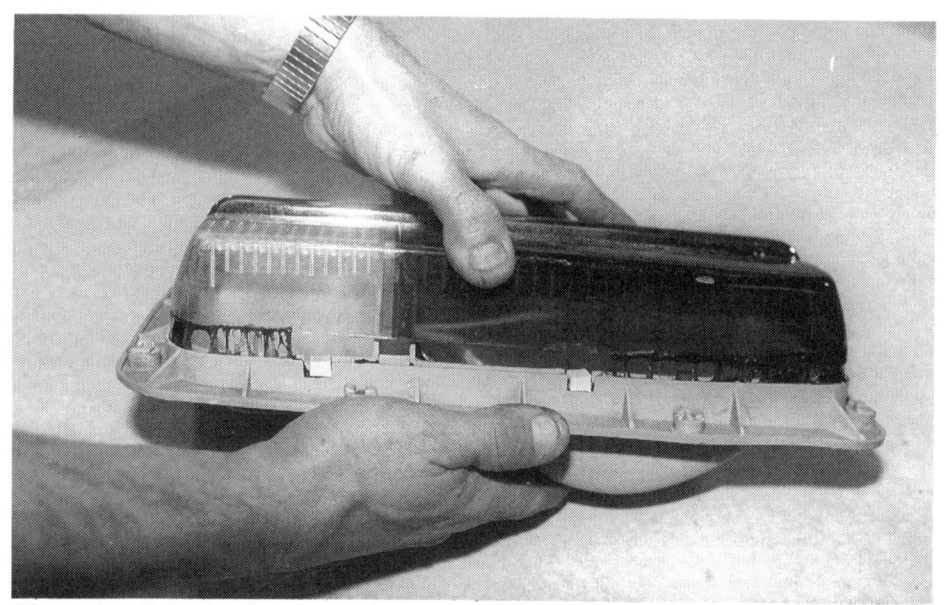

Cleaned, polished and reassembled, note urethane-foam cubes in the drain holes. 3M Weatherstrip Adhesive holds halves firmly.

grades of this abrasive just for plastics—will take out all but the worst scratches. A loose-sewn cotton buffing wheel will do the best job without burning the plastic. If you do your own, remember to buff with the wheel turning *away* from corners and edges—and always away from your person. Do a small area, recharge the buff with light compound and move on. You will be surprised at the results! Tight recesses will have to be done by hand.

The ersatz chrome trim can be redone by specialty companies—it is actually vaporized aluminum that is applied in a vacuum chamber. The process is not something that can be routinely done in the average shop.

When all parts are ready to reassemble, reattach the trim with new pushnuts. Consider using an adhesive on the mating surfaces for extra security. Then use a good commercial sealer/adhesive—available at auto paint shops—to join the shell and lens halves. Using weatherstrip cement, stick the taillight weatherstrip to the rear shell half. Reinstall the units and plug in the sockets to complete your taillight-restoration job.

Bumpers

This section applies mainly to early-style bumpers—240Zs through first-run 260Zs.

You must decide whether to replate your Z's bumpers or merely refurbish them with the existing chrome. They may clean up acceptably for your needs. A garaged car that was cleaned and waxed regularly may require only cosmetic attention to bumper plating. At the other extreme, a Z from a coastal area or where salt is used on winter roads may need new bumpers. Of course, collision damage is a factor regardless of geographic location.

If your plan is to replate the bumpers, choose a plating shop with great care. The best guarantee of satisfaction is recommendations from other restorers—especially those who have fine cars. Some shops don't have the time or equipment to do more than base-line collision-damage work. Stay away from such platers. A plater with top-quality equipment and skilled personnel will cost more, you can count on it. But the resulting quality will be worth the cost in the long run. As the old saying goes, "Buy the best and cry once."

Before you decide to replace, check the price of new bumper bars before shopping for a replate job—the cost difference may be negligible. And if you buy a new bumper, you may be able to sell your old one. On the other hand, a premium chrome

Body Repair & Paint 49

Bumper disassembly: Nuts on front bumper came off fairly easy. Where exhaust fumes got on the rear, bolts tended to break. Goodbye vintage decals. Off to the platers next.

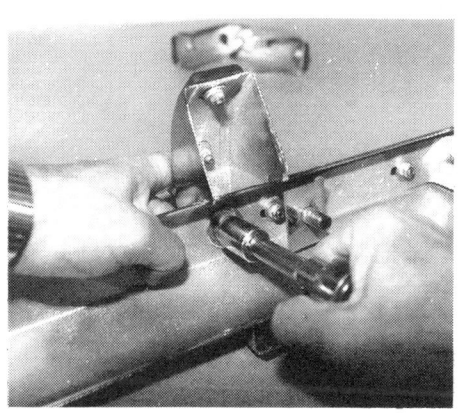

New chrome and rubber strips—what a difference! Note cleaned and painted back-side surfaces. This and generous lubricant on threads ensure a good appearance over a long life.

plater can put a smoothness and sparkle on a sound bumper that few new original parts will match.

There is more to a Z-car bumper than metal, however. These included the rubber guard strips and end caps, which are readily available. These parts can be used to refurbish even an old bar.

Disassembly—After cleaning the bumper assemblies with soap and water, strip them of their non-metallic parts. This uncovers more of the plating and may help you make the decision on whether to rechrome.

Soak all the fasteners with WD-40 or CRC penetrating oil before you start your disassembly. Remove the mounting brackets or shocks and label them if you think you'll confuse them at reassembly time. Remove the bumper guards.

Note: Different aftermarket guards were sold as original equipment for the 240Z.

Rubber Strips—You may be able to reuse rubbing strips from early Z bumpers. Usually a few studs will be so heavily rusted they will break before the nuts turn. Occasionally, the stud simply turns in its rubber mounting. Breaking off the nut with a chisel may be your only solution.

Brackets—Early Zs had what might be called *cosmetic bumpers*. Their mounting bracketry is very light. Later cars had Federally mandated bumpers that eventually incorporated 2-1/2- and 5-mph energy-absorbing shock mounts. While actually providing some collision protection, these were complicated and *heavy!* Either mounting system can be stripped or blasted clean and refinished with *low-gloss*—not flat—black.

Remove any loose plating or scale from the back of the bumpers with a wire brush.

Original Chrome—Clean and polish the chrome. Good chrome will tolerate cleaning with S.O.S. or Brillo pads, or finer steel wool. S.O.S. and Brillo pads are good because they are saturated with soap.

Give the plating a good scouring. Rinse, then redo questionable spots. If your bumpers clean up nicely, buff them with a light compound to give them the final *touch*. Plating shops have a grade they call *coloring* compound. Anything coarser will strip old chrome off the base metal.

Go over your bumper bars lightly with a loose-sewn buffing wheel and frequent recharges of compound until each surface reaches its best shine. Then give it a good coat of paste car wax. To protect the backsides, mask the chromed edges and retouch the back sides with silver enamel.

Rechromed—If your bumpers won't make it without replating, check the quality of plating work before writing that check.

Unwrap each piece, sight down it to check for straightness and examine the edges for roughness. Check the texture of the surface—it should be free of scratches, major ripples or peen-marks. Check the color of the plating and ask about any variations, lighter or darker. Check that you have every piece you brought in. Once you're satisfied, thank him and pay up! Show-quality plating will last the life of the automobile.

Back at The Shop—Clean the insides of the bars with solvent and coarse steel wool. The plating process often leaves a lot of scale on the backside of a bumper or guard. If you plan on showing your car, this can be a real negative. I've had to mask and glass bead areas on the back of a bumper or guard to eliminate *new* rust!

Then run a strip of masking tape along the edges to protect the chrome. Apply two coats of silver enamel to the back sides. Aluminum paint from a spray can will help, but I use a closed-surface acrylic enamel in a coarse metallic silver. This area is exposed to lots of moisture and never gets attention from the chamois or towel operator!

Wax the guards, bars and plated bolt-heads, too.

Rubber Strips—Reinstall new or

Trial Fit?

On a frame-up restoration, you may want to go to the trouble to reassemble your project for a trial fit. When using new body parts or when serious body damage was repaired, a trial assembly can save a surprising amount of new damage!

The handling and wrenching involved in putting together an auto can undo a lot of careful refinish work if your aren't careful in the extreme! If a degree of wear and tear doesn't bother you, this may not be a big factor. But if your goal is a better-than-new Z-car, this tactic can pay off in the elimination of redoing chips and scratches.

Before assembling those lovingly painted and upholstered parts, use reasonable precautions in handling and storage. I use furniture pads and old blankets to wrap or cover hoods, fenders and other large parts even though they are still in primer. Be sure the paint has thoroughly cured before laying any ostensibly protective surface against it!

Also be careful to keep any pad or cloth that comes into contact with high-gloss surfaces very clean, free of oils, debris or anything that could harm the finish. Lacquer finishes are the most susceptible to abrasives, but even hardened enamels can receive scratches that are frustrating to remove.

Small parts can be stored in crushed newspaper, styrofoam "p-nuts" or even wrapped in old towels—as long as the material protects more than it damages.

When it is time to put everything back together, fewer frustrations will result. What could be worse than saving a weekend to assemble your Z-car only to find that your kid's bicycle fell over and onto that unprotected hood or fender you parked against the garage wall?

It may seem like unnessary tedium, bolting a bunch of primered parts onto your Z-car's bare body, but most top restorers wouldn't consider waiting until everything was painted to find out that a bracket was misdrilled or an edge distorted. This means the parts must be completely adjusted and fasteners tightened—and if shims are needed, the location and number must be duly noted for final assembly.

Some builders run their cars through a frame shop to have all body/frame dimensions verified as per factory specs before attaching the body sheet metal. On unitized car bodies—especially those that have undergone rust repair—this is a sound and cost-effective practice.

When everything is snugged down and the doors, hood and so forth swing through their arcs without conflicting with or misaligning at the margins, you know they will also fit and function painlessly after painting.

Be certain all grease and soil that accumulated from handling sanded and primered parts is removed before shooting the final finish. Hands as well as tools can leave enough contamination on porous paint to cause trouble with the topcoats. Rectify any chips or scratches that result from the trial assembly and make a mental note of how they occurred. Write it down for later reference.

so don't tighten the nuts until you check height, straightness and clearances. Stand back to do this.

It often helps to run a strip of masking tape along the edges of the metal where it might accidentally contact the body. Not only does this protect the painted surface you will have worked so hard to achieve, a little scratch or nick might require that you remove the bumper to correct the damage!

Filler Panels—1973 to 1974-1/2 Zs have their own filler panels. They should be refurbished and reinstalled later.

Late-260Z & 280Z Bumpers—Only the heavy face bars are plated. The foregoing comments regarding plating and so forth apply to the later cars as well. Rather than rubber face strips, the Federalized-style have large rubber end caps and guards. Naturally, if these are in acceptable condition, they can be thoroughly cleaned and treated with silicone to restore their appearance. New rubber parts are a great improvement in appearance, but can be very expensive if they are all replaced.

Shock covers, brackets and so forth respond to similar refinishing treatment. Reassembly is covered in the installation section.

BODY & PAINT

No matter whom you consult on auto refinishing, you'll be admonished that a paint job is only as good as the preparation. This is contrary to what most laymen presume about hot paint jobs—they believe that a gorgeous surface is more the result of some combination of forbidden paint magic and someone's unfathomable skill with a spray gun. This is not so. You can do top-flight refinishing on your Z-car pride and joy. You just use good materials and practices, time, effort and a bit of well-earned experience.

Earlier in the process, I talked about identifying existing body damage and cataloging same for later reference. Assuming that through a process of dollying, shrinking, pulling and filling you have what seems to be a collection of pretty straight parts, let's proceed to the finishing step. The "Perfect Panel."

Anyone can do a *less-than-perfect* restoration, but you didn't buy my

well-laundered originals with new washers and nuts. Some grease or antiseize compound on the threads will ensure easy removal if the need ever occurs. The strips respond well to commercial whitewall cleaner and a stiff brush. Armor All or silicone brake fluid on a rag will give them a new look.

Reassemble the bars and guards and install the mounting brackets on early types. Use new nuts and washers and lube the threads lightly. Later shock-mounted bumpers should be assembled, but not with the shocks. It bolts to the body first. When it comes time to install the bumpers, you'll need assistance to prevent nicking the paint—and help hold the weight—while you get some washers on and nuts started. There is a little alignment latitude available with all Z bumpers,

Original Z-car fender—at least three repairs in 20 years! Fender was taken down with 180-grit open-coat paper on a long board except in the tight radius areas. Can you spot where problem areas will show up?

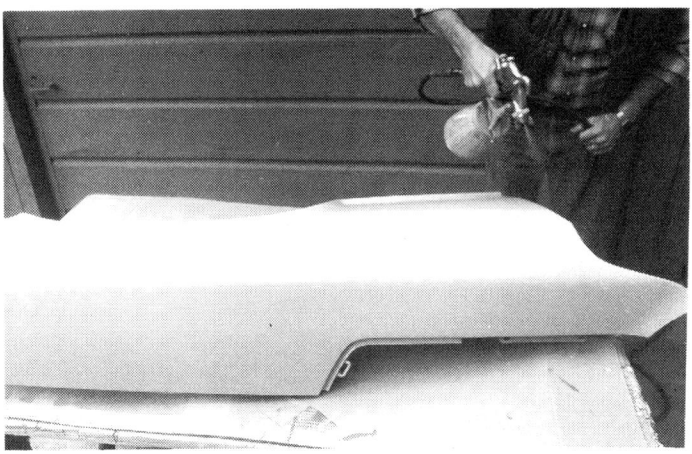

Light gray primer-surfacer is applied in a cross-pattern. It's OK to build up areas you suspect are a bit low, but be sure each coat flashes off completely.

book to learn how to stop short of superior results. Hotrodders have an old saw: "Speed costs money, how fast you wanna' go?" An accomplished body-person might paraphrase: "A perfect body panel takes time, how much you wanna' spend?" There is no substitute for thorough, painstaking and correctly done handwork in preparing that fender, hood or door for the spray gun. Thus, the quest for the "Perfect Panel."

Guide-Coating—The key to excellence is simple and self-correcting, even a novice can accomplish with a little practice—it is called *guide-coating*. A perfect complement to our identifying and cataloging process, pre-disassembly, a guide coat is nothing more than a light, even layer of contrasting color over your next-to-last primer-surfacer coat.

Many bodywork books allow aerosol spray-can work for the guide—it's cheap, fast and eliminates cleanup of the spray gun. I much prefer a *bona fide* refinishing product. It's not too much trouble in my shop to have a contrasting color primer available: dark gray, light gray and red oxide are available in almost all professional product lines. I will compromise with flat black or gray aerosol primer if it is lacquer; enamels dry too slowly and clog sandpaper, and you have little control over material quality.

Primer, primer/surfacer, polyester surfacer—what are their characteristics? Primer is comparatively low on paint *solids*—material that adheres to the surface after the solvent (vehicle) evaporates. Because of this, many coats of primer are necessary to build up mils of thickness to fill the typical run of pits, scratches and ripples. More useful is primer/surfacer, which has a higher proportion of solids to vehicle. It effectively fills surface divots in a reasonable number of applications. Both coatings harden by evaporation and can be readily sanded. They are basically lacquer products and will shrink as they dry.

Polyester surfacers harden by a chemical reaction—they must be catalyzed with an agent mixed in before spraying—and shrink very little. They go by such titles as *Feather-Fill, DZ40* and *Eliminator*, and might be characterized as sprayable Bondo. They provide a multi-mil-thick coat in as few as two applications, offering an appreciable timesaving as well as a tough, flexible surface. They are considerably more expensive, however. And you must use all that you mix and clean the equipment thoroughly immediately after use. Additionally, they can be sprayed on raw metal—such as a sandblasted area—and polyester filler can be applied OVER them, something that should not be done with conventional primer/surfacers. Some paint-company reps recommend them to help bond polyester filler to the base metal.

I use polyester surfacers but don't find them as sandable as lacquer-type products.

Putties come in all brands and colors. They are very helpful when used as intended. That is to say, not as you would use polyester filler. Glazing putty, which is lower in solids, can be spread with a rubber squeegee over fairly large areas. Use it for sand scratches—to about 80 grit—and small pits. Spot putty is thicker and is intended for voids and deep scratches (40- and 36-grit). It dries quicker, but resists spreading. Neither can be massaged around the area for much time—they skin over and start to roll up and adhere to the squeegee before long. Both shrink and may crack if force-dried with a heat gun or lamp.

Your Panel—Let's assume you have your panel as good as the eye and hand can make it, you can't actually see any imperfections. You've used your long board down to about 120- to 150-grit sandpaper and have eliminated pinholes and feathered the paint and filler edges and there are no significant 36-grit scratches or file marks. Now wipe down the whole area with wax-and-grease remover—Ditzo, Klix or similar product. Apply two to four coats of a high-build primer/surfacer. I use Kondar DZ-3. Correctly applied, it hides a multitude of small sins, and shrinkage is reasonable. Other makers offer similar products.

A heavy-bodied primer/surfacer must be applied in a fairly heavy coat, then allowed to dry sufficiently before recoating—don't rush the process! Again, in lacquer-type undercoats, the vehicle must evaporate out of the

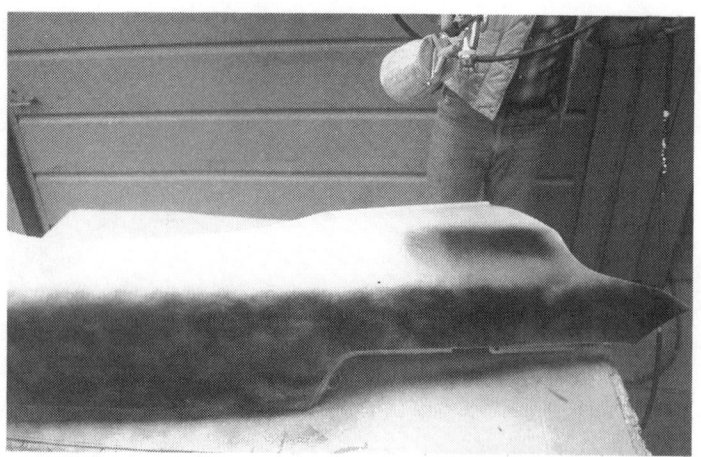

Darker, contrasting guide coat goes on fairly wet, with high pressure. It shouldn't be opaque, but close to full coverage.

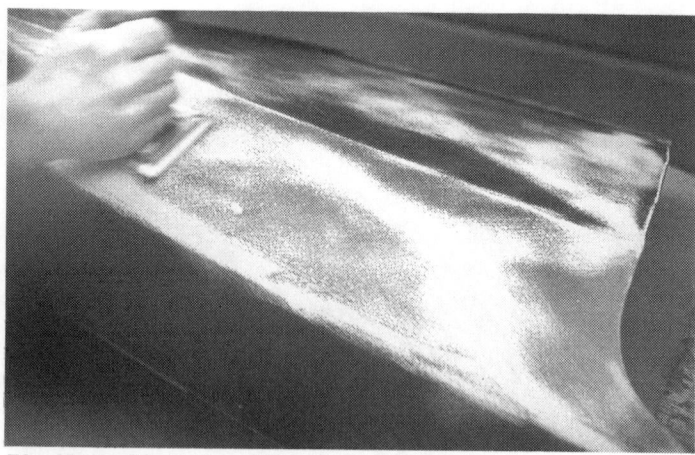

Blocking with 150- or 180-grit on long board—keep strokes across crown of panel, at diagonals. Note: dark lozenge shape at fender ridge, center; it's low. Bare metal in light gray area nearer dog-leg is high. Also, deep scratches from 80-grit paper show up.

solids. This first occurs from the top surface as it *flashes off,* often giving a false impression of dryness. Press a fingernail into an unobtrusive area if you need to experiment. Be aware that, though many use an economy "utility" thinner for undercoat work, there are thinners of specific *richness* to allow for correct drying times in hot, average and cool temperatures—you may find that they are worth the extra cost.

Spraying undercoats too thin will result in wasted pigment—it dries before striking the surface and blows away. Or there'll be excessive shrinkage of the undercoat as the excess vehicle evaporates. Too thick an undercoat creates an unnecessary *orange peel* or grainy surface effect. You should be able to wipe the surface with a cotton rag without it picking fibers from the cloth. I can sometimes eyeball surface ripples and other imperfections while the primer/surfacer coat still has its transitory wet-look surface.

Apply undercoats evenly, alternating direction of strokes each coat if possible. Then, when the surface has dried sufficiently, apply your contrasting-color guide coat smoothly and evenly over the whole surface. Guide-coat material should be relatively thin, but wet enough to give a consistent film. Remember, you're not trying to fill this time.

Tip: If you can afford an extra spray cup, you can save time by keeping the two color materials mixed and handy to spray.

To reveal what you need to know, put *new* 150- or 180-grit paper on your long board. Some authorities will urge you to wrap paper around a paint stir-stick, but this is much less reliable and a lot slower. Rubber blocks don't work—they are principally for finish work and color-sanding.

Pick an edge or body ridge and begin sanding in a direction that is approximately 45 degrees to the board with moderate pressure. Don't try to achieve a particular contour or flatness. You will do that later. What you are looking for is the pattern your abrasive is making on the surface in question.

Next, repeat the process. Stroke at approximately a 90-degree angle to the previous effort, taking care to key your board movements to an edge or body feature you know to be correct. As the contrasting color disappears, notice how the low spots show up. The flat abrasive will remove these surfaces last as primer/surfacer is removed. Also note the minor surface irregularities—heavy-grit scratches, pin holes, even patches of dry-spray undercoat and so forth—as they appear.

Continue the process over the entire panel in this manner, using the longest sanding board you can practically fit on the particular contour. Switch to a short board only on very restricted surfaces—this time you don't have to worry about overall smoothness. Instead, locate and delineate metal displacement.

Remember to use clean, sharp sandpaper. Blow the sand dust out of the grit with compressed air regularly. Change the sheet if you notice any loss of grit. It won't necessarily go to waste—much can be used on smaller blocks later.

As the process continues, you may notice holes appearing in your primer/surfacer, eventually some old paint areas or even bare metal. This is not a cheering possibility because it usually means that metal is still displaced upward. This will necessitate more dollying, shrinking and grinding, alas. You can't fill a bulge!

Low areas you identified, on the other hand, can now be remedied with further filling. Correct gross displacement using the above methods if low areas are really serious. Follow with polyester filler, glazing putty and/or more primer/surfacer applied where needed. As your proficiency increases, the latter two materials will be sufficient. Repeated applications may be required, however. And you thought tennis would give you a bum elbow!

Before considered ready for paint, the perfection of your panel must be confirmed by a repeat of the guide-coating procedure. You may be able to get away with lighter grades of sandpaper by now, however. Small radiuses, fender lips, panel edges and so forth can by trued with scraps of

Body Repair & Paint 53

My fender, completely blocked out. Circular areas are definitely low. Major filling will be necessary at ridge area! Lines and arrows are high, indicating that this fender suffered damage at some time and was inadequately repaired.

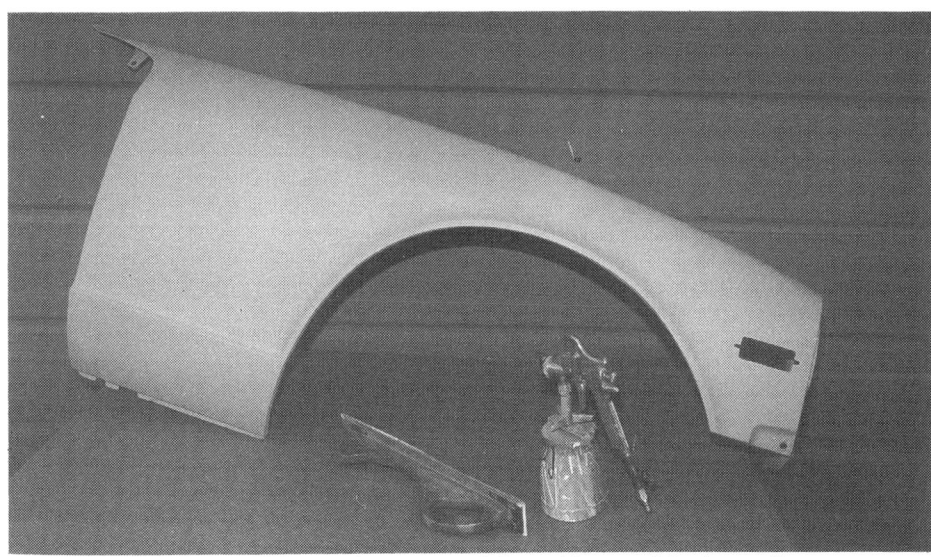

With further dollying, filling and a repeat of the guide-coat/block-sanding process a like-new appearance is achieved. Final sanding with 320-grit on trusty long board removes all residual pits and sand scratches. It's ready to paint!

sandpaper on the ubiquitous paint sticks, wrapped around a length of stiff rubber hose, or even just in a folded pad. Using two thicknesses of clean cotton rag, stroke your palm and fingers over the small or tight surfaces to find ripples—using this method will usually tell you if something is not right. Touch is a lot more reliable than the eye at this point.

Most finishing systems require no more than 320-grit depth abrading on the final surface to provide sufficient tooth for good adhesion. Cleanliness remains a factor, so use compressed air to blow—clean, dry air only, please! Wax and grease remover on clean rags will eliminate loose dust, sandpaper grit and grease from tools and skin.

Select A Paint System

It may seem to you that car paint is car paint, but not so. You have a choice of several different paint *systems* to use on your restoration—and by this I don't mean spray can or brush!

Which one you choose will depend on your needs and resources. Also, whether you intend to do the work yourself or not. For the sake of those who have not had experience with painting a car and think that they want the learning and satisfaction of doing their pet Z themselves, I identify and discuss the various systems that are available.

These are available from every major finish manufacturer. Although they are often very similar in composition and effect, they are not necessarily compatible. I never take a chance on mixing Ditzler and DuPont acrylic-enamel-system materials, for instance. They might work together fine, but on the other hand, why take a chance? Especially on jobs I want to be flawless!

Lacquer—The oldest spray-on automotive-paint system is lacquer. The first horseless carriages were painted with enamels, but these were laboriously brushed on—coats and coats, sanded, brushed and rubbed. In the late 1920's, DuPont developed Duco, a spray-on organic nitrocellulose-lacquer system, for General Motors. It was later supplanted by *acrylic lacquer*, a non-organic based system that is still very much with us today. Collision shops use it mostly for spot repair—but their needs are considerably different from the restorer, namely fast drying and ease of blending in.

It is attractive to the shade-tree restorer for that former aspect—rapid drying is ideal for use in garages and driveways, places where dust and bugs may not be as effectively excluded as in a professional's paint booth. This cannot be said of any other system, despite what the salesman tells you. Also, it requires about 20—30 psi less air pressure than enamels to apply, which is a boon if you have a low-capacity—low cubic feet per minute—air compressor. Generally, these have a 3- to 4-horsepower or less motor.

The other big "plus" for acrylic lacquer is it develops a fabulous inner luster when it is color-sanded and rubbed out with polishing compound like no other system. The very big "minus" with acrylic lacquer is it has almost no gloss of its own—fast drying doesn't let the paint *flow out*, thereby leaving a noticeable *orange peel*. This *must* be smoothed by *color-sanding* with a rubber block and ultra-fine sandpaper (600-, 1000- or 1200-grit), then buffed to a high gloss with rubbing/finishing compound, another abrasive product. Lots of elbow grease is required, even with a power buffer! Lacquer also requires a bit more attention to the final sanding process. Because of its inability to flow into and fill large sanding

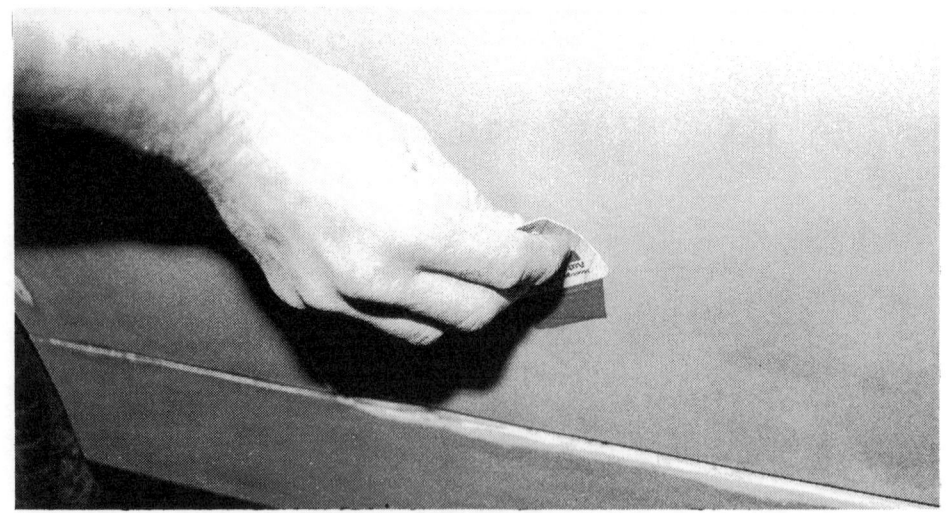

Spot putty is used to fill minor imperfections: deep sand scratches, pinholes, sanded-out chips, poorly feathered edges and so forth. (Please excuse: Car used for prep and paint sequence is an Austin-Healey Sprite. My Z-car photos were lost!)

scratches, using 400-grit is a good for that last smoothing of all surfaces before the paint goes on.

I have to admit I have a sentimental attachment to acrylic lacquer simply because it is what I learned to use as a restorer. It gives a *great* finish, and you certainly feel like a craftsman when your neighbor—or even a show judge—lavishes compliments on the result. However, there are two other factors you should consider:
1.) acrylic lacquer is not original for a Z-car and 2.) it tends to be more susceptible to deterioration when left out in the weather than other systems. So, if absolute loyalty to materials is not a problem and you will garage or cover your Z most of the time, you might be very happy with acrylic lacquer. Just be sure to use a good sealant coat before applying lacquer over any surface other than lacquer or certified compatible undercoats. It can cause lifting of material under sand scratches, bleeding of old color coats or even cracking of long-forgotten enamel layers! Again, it's your choice.

Enamel—Another older-style spray-on finish is generically typed *synthetic enamel*. This came along not long after nitrocellulose lacquer. It was used by Ford and Chrysler beginning in the '30s. Whereas lacquers harden by evaporation of the solvents in their vehicle, enamels harden by evaporation of the top layer only; after the surface skins over, enamel must oxydize to harden enough to be practical. Heat accelerates this process.

The *alkyd enamel* Datsun put on my 240Z is a synthetic enamel. As such, it requires a high-temperature oven for drying after it's applied. This is no big deal to a manufacturer or a well-equipped body shop with bake ovens for force-drying. Its high natural gloss results from a very slow drying time, rather the opposite of lacquer. After using synthetic enamel, you must bake your car for several hours or leave it in a dust-free environment for at least 24 hours. It is relative inexpensive, but not as durable as other enamel-type finishes. Synthetic enamel is getting harder to find because it's becoming obsolete as a system. It's not my favorite.

A huge improvement is provided by *acrylic-enamel* systems. This is much more durable than lacquer or synthetic enamel, and it dries quickly compared to synthetic enamel. It is less prone to chalking as it ages. It is superior in flexibility and resistance to chipping. Applied correctly, synthetic enamel has good flow-out properties for immediate gloss. Consequently, it hides surface imperfections that would make lacquer look terrible.

Acrylic enamel may also be catalyzed. By mixing in a hardening agent, both durability and gloss are easily enhanced and at reasonable cost. This option also allows this system to be color-sanded and rubbed out, much like acrylic lacquers. It can be force-dried, as well. I use acrylic enamel for many applications, and often rub it out. I let it cure for a few weeks despite what the directions say.

Urethane—The last system types are the urethanes and acrylic urethanes—often called *epoxy*. DuPont came out with their Imron first. Ditzler, R-M, Acme, Nason and others followed soon after. These systems are very "trick" and cost considerably more—they *must* be catalyzed before they'll harden. Most are mixed 50/50 with their hardening agent, as opposed to a 90/10 blend with acrylic enamels. They are super durable—although not as bulletproof as some advertising blurbs would have you believe. They resist scratching, chipping and chemical contamination from substances like brake fluid, gas, soy sauce, Dom Perignon—much better than other finishes.

Urethanes may be color-sanded and buffed, although their inherent

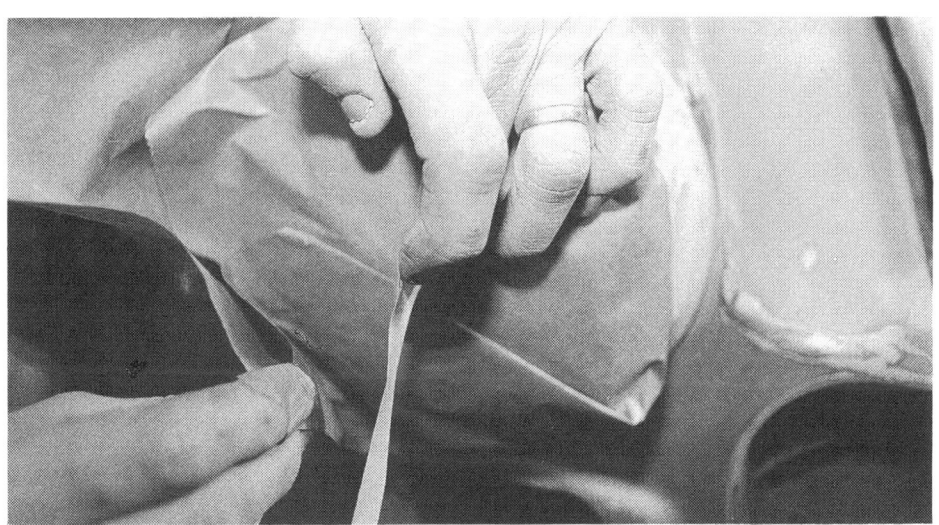

Masking should be done carefully. Use good-quality, fresh tape. Don't overlap any areas to be painted. Tape over all folds and creases in paper that can harbor sanding dust or dry paint. Never use newspaper for masking large areas. It harbors lots of tiny paper fragments which end up as dust in your paint job.

wet look is a much desired feature. They are fairly tolerant of undercoats, and obviously flow-out in superior fashion. They are undeniably non-original on any Z-car and those "in the know" can spot them!

Paint stores like to move customers upscale to *two-part systems,* especially if they know it is a restoration. I like them for their ease of application and the second-chance opportunity if a bug does a kamikaze into the hood.

Caution: You can't put leftover catalyzed paint back into the can. It will contaminate the whole lot. Likewise, you can't leave it in the gun beyond the *pot life* specified by the maker. Many good spray guns have been trashed by catalyzed material turning rockhard in their passages. They must be flushed out promptly. Estimating how much paint/hardener/reducer to mix is a skill that comes with experience. If you're not experienced with using catalyzed paint, brew a lesser amount than what you think you need—you can always mix more. I find that leftover mix will last much longer if stored in a cold place—not below 32F—but my Señora always takes a dim view of bottled Deltron in the refrigerator!

The counterman will also want you to use a clear-coat over the color so you'll achieve a more lacquer-like depth and higher gloss. This is up to you. I've used high-quality clears over acrylic lacquer, acrylic enamel and acrylic urethane with good results. But it's another expense and can really complicate spotting-in a damaged area later on, but many people think it is worth it. My project car is painted with Deltron with a DelGlo clear top coat. If you're not going to rub out your paint, add a bit of clear to the last coat of paint to improve its flow-out characteristics.

WARNING: Fumes from any paint system are not good for your health! Two-part systems, acrylic urethanes and acrylic enamels with hardener are particularly bad.

Always follow the instructions on the product label explicitly.

The primary concern is protection from breathing fumes and dust from sprayed paints. Wear a good-quality, tight-fitting approved respirator when spraying or working in a spray-vapor-filled environment. If the manufacturer of a paint system is concerned about your welfare while using their products, you should be no less concerned. Fisher Books and I are. We want you to be around to buy our next book! These paints contain petroleum solvents, particulate pollutants and various poisonous chemicals. They can cause respiratory disease, possibly cancer, and can even poison you with cyanide compounds. *Don't take chances!*

You must work in a well-ventilated area. And never spray anywhere near an open flame. Evaporating solvents and particulate matter are extremely flammable—to the point of being explosive. Don't paint near pilot lights such as those in a water heater or gas clothes dryer. Don't use a space heater with an open flame when spraying or even mixing paints. Don't let anyone weld—gas or arc—anywhere near your paint operation. In addition to keeping the work area well ventilated, it's a good idea to use a simple dust mask even when shooting primer or sanding.

Next to my great family, I am most proud of my showy body and paint work, but I compromise it rather than take chances on my health—I don't like the odds! End of sermon.

PAINTING

If you have chosen to farm out your paint work, use this section along with the expertise of your chosen painter to decide on a paint system. Do as much of the body and prep work as you feel comfortable with, and arrange for him/her to be responsible for the rest. Tell the person what kind of a job you expect, and

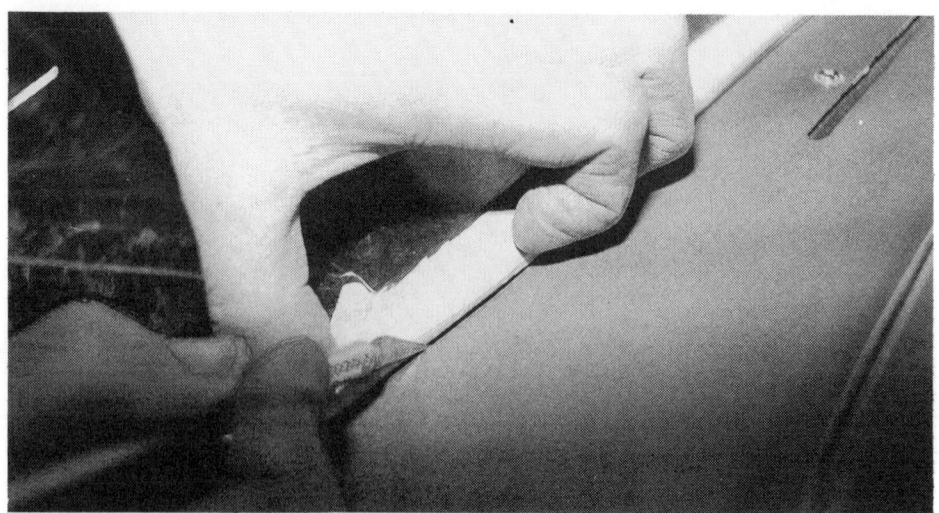

Just before spraying, carefully rub down edges of tape with blade, blow everything clean with compressed air and tack surfaces from top down.

that you won't accept less. You may save a few dollars by letting the shop use your car as fill-in work between their bread-and-butter collision work, but don't expect much relief. Check references. Don't take delivery if you didn't get your money's worth.

If you're going to do the shooting yourself, let's go! To paint the Z as Datsun did, you must spray the body *in white*—disassembled and stripped of soft parts, undercarriage, glass and so forth. The advantages of this approach are covered earlier. If you must paint the assembled car, you'll have to decide how to approach the body-color firewall and inner fenders, along with the door and hatch jambs, and so forth. *Remove* as much small trim, door handles, bumpers, finishers and similar obstacles as you can. You won't regret it!

Masking—This is easy and fun, at least for me. It usually takes longer than I estimate, however. You may find the same to be true. Buy your tape and masking paper where you got your paint supplies. Use only brand-name tape, the kind made specifically for masking.

A masking machine—one of those things that unrolls paper and tape together and has a serrated blade to cut them cleanly is a boon. However, I use skinny (1/2- or 3/8-inch-wide) tape by itself to do many edges, then follow up with paper/tape for the large areas. Important! Remember that some overspray on a nonpaint surface is easier to remedy than a lack of coverage on an area that should be painted! So, when masking, try to avoid the need to touch up strips of bare primer after the tape comes off.

You can expect overspray to contaminate every little bit that isn't masked adequately, so don't skimp. Mask it all. Lacquer may give you a break, but enamels and urethanes stay wet enough to stick for many seconds after they leave the nozzle. Conversely, you can't count on overspray to cover areas that should have a good multi-mil layer. You must consciously remember to shoot every coat on every surface.

Before shooting, blow all surfaces free of dust and wipe them clean of grease, water and other foreign substances—including oil from your hands. Use wax-and-grease remover generously, changing rags regularly. *Never* use those commercial red or blue shop rags. They are contaminated with residual grease and dirt, and solvent used in laundering them. Old cotton clothing is ideal, if clean. Remove buttons and zippers first!

Tape methodically, keeping the sides of the tape roll clean and without a dusty, furry fringe from the surroundings. I store my good masking tape in a plastic zip-lock bag. You can clean the edges of a roll somewhat with lacquer thinner. Keep an X-acto knife handy to make cuts where needed, tuck ends under weatherstrips and so forth. Keep folds and pleats out of big expanses of masking paper—they trap dust that will blow out on a freshly painted surface. Fold them flat, and tape down securely.

Visqueen or trash-bag plastic can be used to mask openings such as doors or to cover engines and components. Just be sure the masking tape will stick to the material—and won't let go when the paint spray hits it! I prefer to remove door panels or anything that will keep paint from where it should go. Door jambs are often a painter's nightmare—hinges and latches full of grease-adhered grime, old paint, stickers, decals, manufacturer's data plates and the like—hard to clean, hard to sand, hard to mask. Persevere and don't cut corners. Be sure your masking won't stick to wet paint when you shut the door after shooting the jambs—forethought is required.

Some parts—Datsun accessory door mirrors, battery-inspection doors, parts that should be body color from other areas—should be prepped

Good primer-surfacer is sprayed fairly wet. I use a separate cup for primer. Several medium coats are better than one heavy coat. Block-sand until the surface is acceptable, blow off and tack.

and set up on clean paper or hung from clean wires to be shot while the body flashes up. This is especially if you are using catalyzed paint, whatever you mix will have to be used in 8 to 24 hours.

Use commercial wheel covers or trash bags taped securely to the tires if they are still on the car. Sweep out your paint area, then use compressed air to blow away the residual dust. Don't fail to go over the car again. Even lacquer will make small bumps if sprayed over dust and debris. I wet down my floor if shooting anything other than lacquer. Be careful not to get any water droplets on the car. Start your exhaust fan a few minutes before you start spraying.

Mix Paint—Add hardener according to the directions on the can before reducing. Be sure the paint is well agitated—especially with metallics—before you do any mixing. Paint stores will often reshake an unopened can if you bought it previously from them. Avoid putting a stir stick in your spray-gun cup because of the potential for contamination.

All enamels are "thinned" with enamel *reducer,* lacquers use thinner. Bear in mind that these are also specific to the brand and product, don't mix types.

A good thermometer in the paint area—not in the stream of the exhaust fan or air filters—will tell you what *speed* of reducer or thinner to use. Most come in three grades: fast, to prevent runs and sags in cold weather; medium, a compromise evaporation rate for warm weather; and slow, for good flow-out in hot weather. Lacquer topcoats can be further slowed by adding retarder. Use clean buckets for mixing—paint stores sell nice one-time-use "dixie-cup" buckets if you don't have lots of clean 3-pound coffee cans or the like.

Strainers, like stir sticks, should be *gratis*—free—from your paint supplier. You've already discovered the cost of automotive-refinishing supplies—and virtually everybody pays list price! Strain your material into the paint cup just before you're ready to shoot. A couple of marbles in the bottom will agitate while you spray—especially important if you use metallics.

Tacking Off—You'll need a new, good-quality tack cloth to pick up any errant debris that has clung to the car. These are cheesecloth squares impregnated with a sticky resin. Ask you counterman's advice on which brand to buy. They know which are *stickies* and so forth. Don't approach tacking like you are waxing the car. Just lightly sweep the pad over each panel, starting at the roof and working downwards, turning the surface of the pad to expose clean areas. You'll be surprised how much crud is still on the surface, especially primer dust.

Sealer—For insurance against unpleasant surprises, spray on a good coat of non-sanding sealer. Let it have a few minutes to flash while you give your paint a final stirring and collect your thoughts. This will give you a chance to see if the hoses will reach without snagging or twisting, to check air pressure and to adjust your mask.

Most paint systems have their own specific instructions on catalyzing, reducing, air pressure (at the gun, not the compressor—check this with a gauge where your gun would be), distance to the surface, speed of gun movement, awkward areas to spray and possibly other variables.

The Moment of Truth—Test your paint on a neutral surface. I usually tape a piece of butcher paper to the shop wall and test the gun's spray pattern on it. A little wasted material can be worth a lot here, especially if your gun isn't as clean as you thought and something dislodges from the inner passageways—better on the wall than the hood! Optimize fluid feed and air pressure to achieve the fullest spray pattern. You can always reduce the spray pattern for nooks and crannies. Check the distance at which your

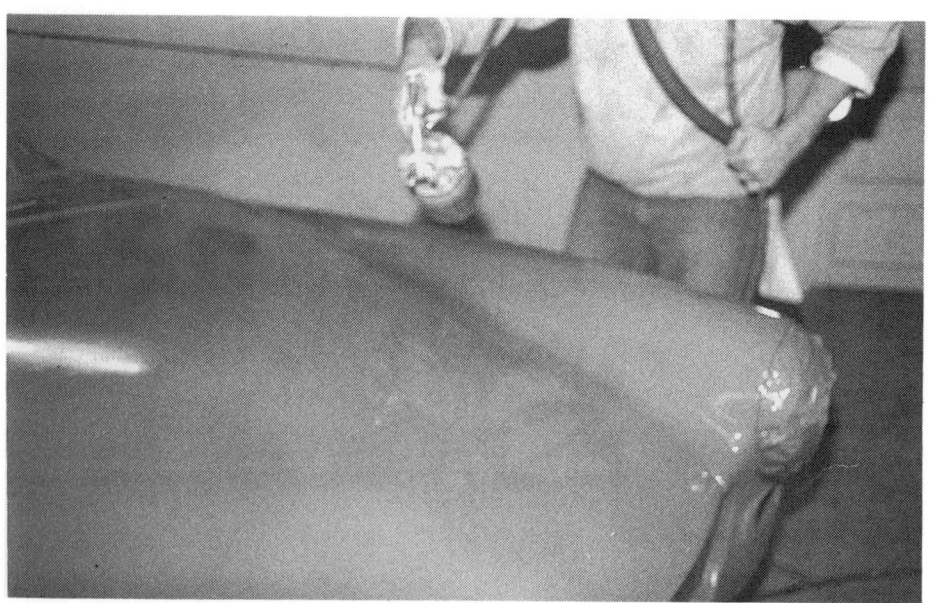

Apply color coats according to manufacturer's directions. Always wear respirator. I prefer the air-supply type even though it means dragging around another hose.

material is making the best wet but complete coverage. Paint mixed a little heavy can always be thinned, but not vice versa! Many of my thinner cans have test patterns on them as well—to confirm how much paint it takes to get a run at that particular pressure/thinness/temperature/distance. Now you're ready to paint!

Paint an assembled Z using the following sequence: roof and hatch to right quarter, right door, right fender to hood and cowl. Then grille/headlight/pan area, left side hood, left fender, door to left quarter and rear pan area. Also, remember the next pass around the car to sweep your strokes the opposite direction as the previous time. This will optimize coverage and prevent overpainting areas. While you're being the "perfect" shooter, don't lay on too much paint in areas on which you applied an "insurance" coat. Nor should you overload areas like the C-pillars and headlight buckets—runs and sags are easy to create on small areas—and hard to eliminate.

Start low and apply a coat to every underside surface—rockers, doors, wheel openings, etc. Then methodically do the door jambs, hood and hatch jambs, grille area, underside of the hood—anyplace that struck you as hard to get good coverage. Don't try to paint anything in one coat—it can't be done. The first coat is called the *tack coat*. It should be light, but cover completely. This gives the next full coat something to adhere to and lets you arrive at the particular sequence which you will use to progress around the body. You can give those rockers and hard-to-access areas their second coat after the tack coat is on.

After a suitable interval—check your label or refer to the counterperson—refill your cup and follow up with a *color coat*. Apply this coat more heavily. It will both hide the undercoat and impart a gloss of some degree to the surface.

I hope you didn't get any runs or sags. With many high-tech two-part finishes, these can be carefully wiped away with a clean, reducer-moistened rag. Be careful! Then spot in the wiped area immediately and get ready to shoot the next coat.

The *gloss coat* comes last. It is laid on almost exactly as the previous coat. Some systems call for *double wet coats* for proper coverage. This simply means that your spray patterns are put on to overlap the previous pass by about 50% of its width, similar to shingles on a roof. This keeps a consistent depth of paint without—it is hoped—overloading the surface and having it slide toward mother earth.

You can put as many coats of paint on as you want, but three is enough to get the depth in mils specified by the manufacturer. Classical balance is needed here—too much is as bad as too little. With lacquer, on the other hand, more doesn't hurt, especially if you want bragging rights on X number of coats of hand-rubbed lacquer. Old timers would shoot 6—9 coats—they go on pretty thin—and then wet block-sand, dry and tack down and repeat the process. At some point you get into the law of diminishing returns. A significant amount is removed when color-sanding. Add a bit of flex additive to prevent cracking.

Preview of the finished restoration, buffed out, fully assembled and ready to roll.

With enamels, remember that your goal should be to keep the pattern as wet as possible without runs *or* dry spots that detract from the effect. Otherwise you may end up color-sanding and buffing against your wishes! Establish a painting sequence that will maximize coverage for the amount of drying time that elapses as you move around the car.

Finishing Up
Unmasking—While the paint flashes off, dump your excess paint and flush out the gun with thinner/reducer. You may clean it later if you leave everything full and drop the air tip into the cup. Start unmasking before the paint is fully dry. This will be sooner for lacquer than for enamels. Too wet and it makes strings that may fall back into the good paint; too dry and paint film will tend to tear off with the tape!

Remove large areas of masking paper and plastic, if used. Roll them into a ball as you go so nothing drags on the new surface. Follow up by lifting off the tape where it makes edges with unmasked areas. Pull it up and back—and simultaneously at a bit of an angle from the masked line. In this way you will minimize the chance of pulling up a piece of good paint. If you should, though, stop immediately and cut the paint film away from the tape with a sharp X-acto knife. With a small paint brush, wet the film with thinner/reducer and try to re-adhere it to the undercoat. This often works. If it doesn't, the remedy is to reshoot that spot.

Let the car cure for as long as you can without moving it. This should be at least 24 hours with enamels and 3—4 hours with lacquer. You can theoretically begin block-sanding lacquer that soon, but I try not to rush it.

Color-Sanding—This is done with very light sandpaper on a rubber block or foam pad. I keep a bucket of water with a little detergent to wet the area, turning the paper regularly. Don't use the abrasive until you can't tell the front side from the back! With a bucket of water and sponge, flush the surface periodically to check your progress and remove debris.

Change water in the bucket at intervals and don't allow any sandpaper of *heavier*—coarser—grit near the project. I say this from experience. A friend who was sanding primer dropped a sheet of 220-grit sandpaper into a bucket I was using with 600-grit on a color-sand job. Before I realized that I had picked up his sandpaper, I had taken three or four swipes across the hood of a powder-blue show '51 Mercury. The air was a little blue around the car for a while, also!

Buffing—Use a cutting compound to bring up the gloss on a good-quality professional pad—Schlegel #5 is my old reliable. Steer clear of edges, peaks, corners—or cover with masking tape. Remember the direction of rotation of your buffer and how it will try to catch those areas and burn off the finish. A low-speed buffer motor is best—1750 rpm is about standard. Use the finest-grade compound you can get away with—those spec'd for lacquer are fine.

Do the really tight spots first such as inside radius corners and so forth by hand. Then follow up with a swirl-mark eliminator on a pad such as the

Schlegel Round-Up. Some have wax, some do not. Then buff with a soft cotton cloth, stand back and bask in the radiance!

Z-Car Exterior Colors

Datsun number and color, followed by dates used—if recorded—then name and Ditzler number. (# denotes clear-coat). Other refinish suppliers used different code numbers. Original alkyd enamels may not be available in these colors and may be matched by color chip. Beginning of production was 10-69, end was 2-78—"from" and "to" reflect these dates. This information isn't available for all colors.

901 Light Metallic Gray — (Lt. Gray Poly: 32910)
903 Blue to 8-71 (Blue Poly: 14239)
904 White to 7-75 (Ivory: 8879)
905 Red to 8-71 (Cherry Red: 71899)
907 Green to 8-71 (Green: 44403)
918 Orange — (Mexican Orange: 60636F)
919 Yellow to 8-71 (Yellow: 81908)
920 Gold — (Gold: 23576)
110 Red from 9-71 (Persimmon: 72000)
112 Yellow from 9-71 (Lime: 82040)
113 Green Metallic from 9-71 (Avocado Poly: 44681)
114 Brown Metallic — (Bronze Poly: 23750)
115 Blue Metallic from 9-71 (Blue Poly: 14467)
215 White from 8-75
214 Dark Brown from 8-73 to 7-76 (Cocoa Poly: 24062#)
240 Green Metallic from 8-75 (Racing Gr. Poly: 45208#)
301 Brown Metallic from 8-73 (Lt. Poly: 24062#)
302 Leaf Green Metallic from 8-73 (Leaf Poly: 44967#)
303 Green Metallic from 8-73 to 7-75 (Emerald Green: 44968#)
304 Gold Metallic from 8-73 to 7-76 (Deep Poly: 24097#)
305 Light Blue Metallic from 8-73 (Lt. Poly: 14748#)
306 Silver Metallic from 8-73 (Sterling Poly: 33143#)
307 Blue Metallic from 8-73 (Pacific Poly: 14749#)
362 Dark Purple Metallic from 8-75
517 Beige Metallic from 8-76 (Lt. Gold Poly: 24459#)
611 Wine Red Metallic from 8-76 (Burgundy Poly: 51013#)
901 Silver Metallic

Z-Car Interior Colors

1970-73 model years:
Black
Red
Tan
White
Blue (not available 1973)

1974 only:
Tan

1974-76:
Black
Dark Brown
Off White

1977-78
Black
Dark Brown
Off White

5 Interior Trim & Component Removal

Whether you're going to do your own work or have it done, Fisher Books *Trim Handbook,* by Don Taylor, should be on your reading list. I show specifics related to Z-car trim, but Don Taylor shares in-depth techniques and "secrets" related to his chosen profession.

Seats—Z-car seats are secured to the floorpan mounts with four studs and nuts. Each corner originally came with two black-plastic spacers shaped like nuts. These install between the seat tracks and floorpan to allow seat-height adjustment.

To prevent damage to the mounting-stud threads, place the spacers back on the studs and run the nuts on a few turns—not so far that the threads project from the nuts. Doing this also helps to protect surfaces the seat is placed on.

On 2+2 models, remove the rear-seat cushions. Also remove the seat-back hinges, latches and strikers.

A word to the wise: When putting seats into storage, clean the material first. Vacuum and sponge them thoroughly, particularly recesses that are hard to reach with the seats in the car. *Reason:* Mold or mildew loves to grow on organic material such as crumbs, spilled soda, even old deposits from carsickness—yuk! It can rot and ruin otherwise good upholstery and give off an intolerable odor.

Store these and other upholstered parts in clean, dry areas. Wrap them in plastic garbage bags to help keep out moisture, dirt and vermin.

If you're having your seats reupholstered commercially, get estimates from reputable shops. Have them order extra material if you plan on covering other interior parts to match.

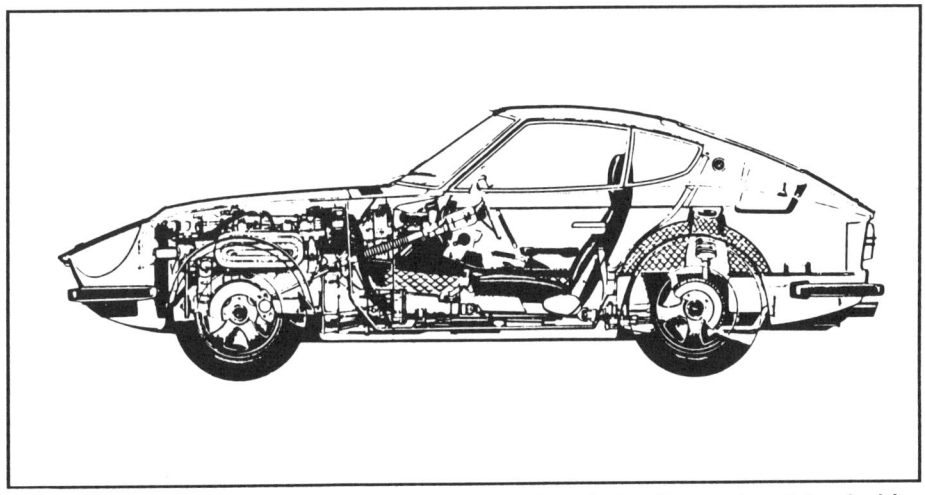

Interior trim such as that for the headliner, tunnel and wheelhouse is retained with adhesive–it's glued on. Courtesy Nissan.

If your plan is to install an interior-trim kit rather than having your interior work done commercially, check kit availability and prices. Some use more authentic materials, design and sewing details than others . . . and prices vary, too.

Seat Belts—Now it's easy to get a socket on the seat-belt-anchor bolts. Remove the lap belts, front and rear. Check carefully for wear. If the belts are original, chances are they should be replaced. Nothing lasts forever. Even lightly used seatbelts lose strength over time. Beyond that, inspect them for loose stitching, frayed or broken fibers and malfunctioning buckles. Check the retractors and their housings for serviceability.

Seat belts and luggage tie-down straps can be cleaned in a clothes washer—use warm water and moderate detergent. Clean any grease off the mounting plate and tie the loose ends together with a piece of household copper wire, the plastic-insulated kind. Connect the buckles and put them in with a load of blue jeans or towels. Use Grease Relief or similar stain remover on the badly soiled spots just before you pop them into the tub. A dash of 20 Mule Team Borax in the water will sweeten them.

If you don't want to remove the belts from the retractors, stretch each out on a piece of lumber and loosely nail down the ends. Scrub the webbing with mild soap. Lay each belt out flat full length to dry in the sun. Be sure they are thoroughly dry before storing or reinstalling. Luggage straps may be cleaned similarly.

Later series cars don't have webbing belts on the buckle ends. The carpet on the transmission tunnel will have to be lifted to reach the bolts.

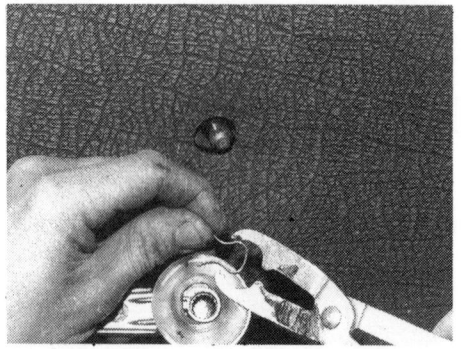

Window-regulator handle is retained with clip and has a plastic washer that does a good job of protecting vinyl trim. Tool shown is as adequate as any for removing clip.

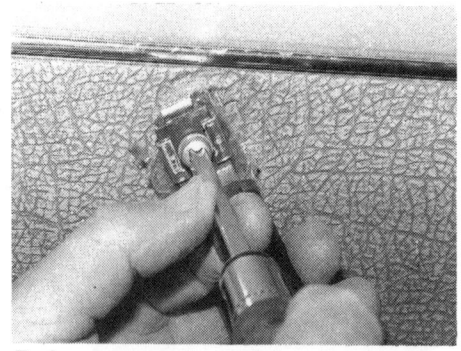

Early passenger's grab handle: Screws are accessible after plated-plastic covers are popped off their retaining tabs.

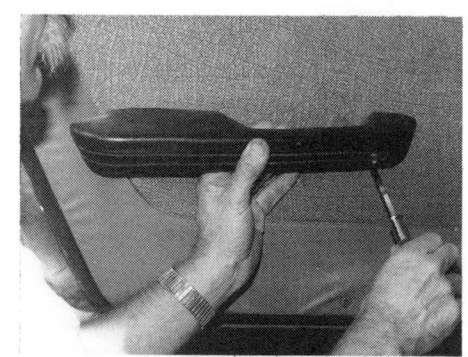

Door arm rest takes a beating, particularly on the driver's side. Early style has two screws, long late style uses three.

Remove them. Clean these bolts with a good cleanser and air dry thoroughly.

As an aside, the ill-fated seatbelt interlock was used on mid-run Z-cars. Many belts have wiring for this circuit incorporated in them, as do seats on Zs so equipped. They are no longer required to be operational.

Carpets & Padding—Remove the carpets and under-padding now. Some Zs require removing the deck trim and luggage tie-down straps to get the deck carpet out. You should take out these in any case.

The spare-tire cover and other deck parts can be removed as well.

Rear Deck—On later Zs, the jack, chocks and tools are contained under hatches in the rear deck. This utilized the space under the floor-pan kick up that was wasted in earlier Zs. Remove the rear-deck carpeting and jute mat in either case, page 68.

First unscrew the luggage straps and get them out of the way. These can be washed with the seat belts. Then remove the screws that hold the deck-edge protector and, on very early models, free the front edge of the carpet. After these are removed, take out the spare-tire cover and spare if they're still in place. On late 280Zs, remove the decking and hinged lid—the jack, tools and spare-inflation bottle lurk here.

Interior Disassembly

Door Panels—Datsun made it relatively easy to remove the upholstered door-finish (trim) panels. The first things that come off are the arm rests. The driver's side usually has a lot of wear and tear—it may be too loose to reuse. Then unscrew the door-lock stems from the lock-rod linkage.

Window-regulator handles are next. They are retained by the familiar spring wire clip shaped like the Greek letter Ω (Omega). Several tools are commercially available to remove this retainer. All work equally well . . . or poorly!

The inside door-latch screw hides behind the plastic trim. Using a screwdriver at the front or back edge, carefully pry off the trim. Try not to break the retaining tabs. Even the best plastic gets brittle with age.

A countersunk Phillips-head screw holds the chrome plate. A small rubber bumper was installed in the small hole at the front edge to meet the latch handle. These are often long gone from well-used Z-cars.

Grab Handle—Early cars have one on the passenger's door that is secured at each end with Phillips-head screws hidden by plastic trim. These must be pried up from the edge toward the *center* of the handle, not the more obvious outer end. Doing it the wrong way will damage the chrome-plastic trims. Late cars incorporate it with the arm rest.

The door-trim panel is made of a heavy hardboard. This is much preferable to the upholstery board many cars use. It is durable and relatively resistant to water damage. A number of spring clips along the front and rear edges snap into holes in the inner door panel. Early Zs have metal clips;

Inside door handles have a plastic cover that must be pried away from chrome finisher. Phillips-head screw retains finisher.

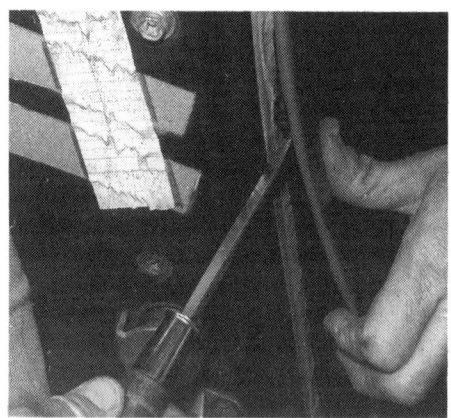

Don't yank the door panel off. Use a screwdriver to locate and lever out each attaching clip. This is good practice on both early metal clips and later plastic clip-and-socket retainers. Old hardboard panels tear easily and clips destruct. Be careful!

Interior Trim & Component Removal

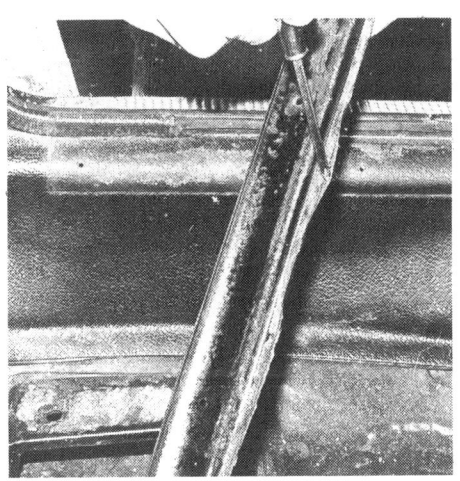

Water under weatherstrip destroyed this steel sill finisher.

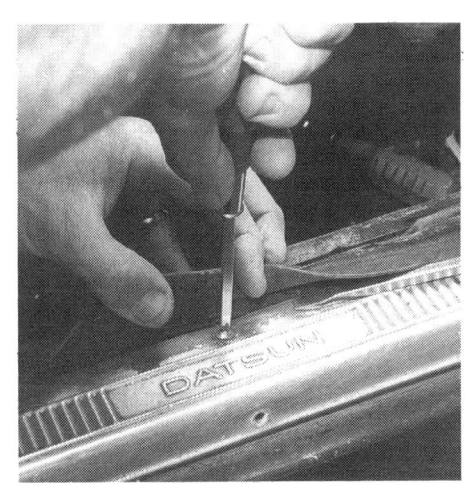

Don't forget to remove screws when trying to remove aluminum sill plate. They hide under the weatherstrip.

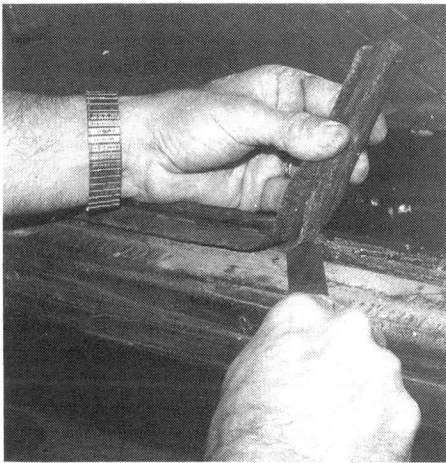

Ubiquitous spatula-type knife is useful for peeling old rubber and adhesive from weld flange. Then there's less to scrape off or remove with thinner later.

later ones use plastic bayonet clips and like sockets in the holes. *Very* carefully pry these out with a suitable tool while applying gentle outward pressure on the trim panel.

If you intend to reuse the panel, be careful not to rip the clip loose from its mounting hole in the hardboard. Without a clip, you may have difficulty getting a good, smooth fit upon reassembly. The edge in the area of a missing clip may not lie against the door edge. This gives an appearance that literally shouts "tacky."

The panel hooks over the upper edge of the inner door panel, so lift the trim panel *up* before you pull it off.

If a clip tears loose regardless of your efforts, you may be able to reorient it in its opening. Failing this, all is not lost if the panel itself is in good shape. The fix, however, requires detaching the glued-down edge of the vinyl-upholstery material.

Using a sharp utility knife or other cutting tool, simply relocate the clip-attachment hole adjacent to the torn hole and reinstall the clip. Then position the panel on the door and indicate where the clip will interface with the door inner panel. Use a marker to denote this position. With the panel out of the way, drill a hole of equal size in the metal door inner. Then reattach the panel in the customary manner. If need be, you might bracket the old clip position with *two* new clips done in this manner. This helps to ensure a tight, even mating of the panel to the door.

Door-Sill Plate—The door-sill plate is held on with Phillips-head screws that self-tap into the rocker sheet metal. Don't be surprised if you break off a few. This area is subjected not only to a lot of wear, but rust contamination, too. The metal is covered with black vinyl that can be replaced to hide deterioration. Replacements are inexpensive.

Step Plate—The aluminum step plate is also a candidate for stuck screws, so be careful not to gouge the aluminum with the screwdriver point. The best insurance against this is a snug-fitting screwdriver point that's not rounded off.

Three screws in the side of the plate are exposed; three on top are hidden under the flap on the door-sill weatherstrip.

Caution: Don't forget to remove all six screws before you pry up the plate. The soft aluminum will bend if you try to remove the plate with a screw still in place.

The rubber strip can harbor a lot of metal corrosion as well. Steel and aluminum don't agree with one another in the presence of water, so be alert.

Vinyl Door-Sill Trimmer—This part, which is retained with contact cement, can usually be peeled up. The area should be no less than room temperature for best success. To ease removal, warm the vinyl covering with a heat lamp, heat gun or hair dryer set on high.

Weatherstrip—It may respond to the same treatment. You'll also need a putty knife or round-edge spatula to free the weatherstrip from the body. Work from the joint at the bottom around the perimeter of the door jamb.

Eventually you should remove the cement residue from the door jamb. I have had good results with naptha. It will cut through the old cement, but is fairly gentle on vinyl. Be prepared. Removing all vestiges of the cement takes lots of clean rags and diligence!

Molded Door-Jamb Finisher—Found on early Zs, its metal core crimps onto the weld flange, thus is easily removed by working it off from around the door opening. Nissan replacement weatherstrip for the 280Z includes this feature—the 240Z style is no longer stocked, but the 280Z weatherstrip will work and is considered an upgrade interchange.

Door-Latch Striker—There isn't any point in scribing around the striker plates if you are removing the doors to refinish the body; they must be realigned at assembly time anyway. Remove the strikers and shim plate under each. Examine the contact surfaces for excess wear due to severe door sag or misalignment—replace them *and* the latch if the metal is chewed up.

Data Plate—This is your Z's pedigree, so ever so carefully use a 1/8-inch drill to drill out the rivets. Store

64 How to Restore Your Datsun Z-car

Vehicle-identification plate is riveted to door jamb. Very carefully drill off the rivet heads with a 1/8-inch bit. Store plate where it won't get damaged or lost.

Kick panel, or side-cowl trim panel, is retained with plastic bayonet-type fasteners and screws that hold electrical components to it. Thank heavens I didn't install these old-time speakers in the door-trim panels!

Early doors aren't nearly as heavy as the later Federal Side Impact Standard type. Hinge fasteners are susceptible to rust, making them hard to break loose and easy to break off.

the data plate in a safe place. I don't have any elaborate restoration suggestions for this part—just clean it carefully. Toothpaste will put most of the shine back on without removing the lettering. Perhaps a little patina of age might be considered a distinguishing feature on a restored Z-car.

Kick Panel—Just to the outboard sides of the foot area are the kick panels. Pop them off like you did the door trim panels, using the same care. This will expose the door-hinge bolts. Turn to page 67 for more details before removing them.

Door Removal—Here's another job where it is handy to have a helper! This is especially true of later Zs, where the hand of the Federal Government can be felt. Side-guard beams in the door structure add a lot of weight to late cars—especially 2+2s. This weight comes off with each door, and doors are awkward to handle, particularly if you're doing it *solo*.

If you must do it without the help of another human being, you'll still need some help. But this help can be an overhead rafter or something similar from which to suspend the door. It must be able to support the weight. A jack or block under the door is less useful because the door can topple over and get damaged. Simply roll down the window and attach a rope or similar material to the window

Wire or rope will support door when hinge bolts finally break loose and are out. Note my supply of electrical wiring hanging from door.

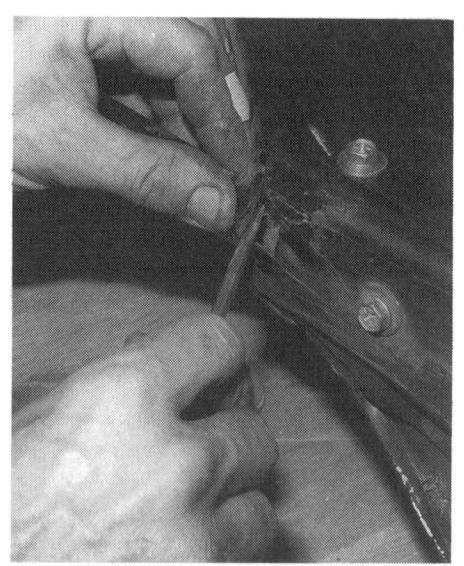

Remove sealing rubbers from door. They are retained with plastic push-in rivets and adhesive.

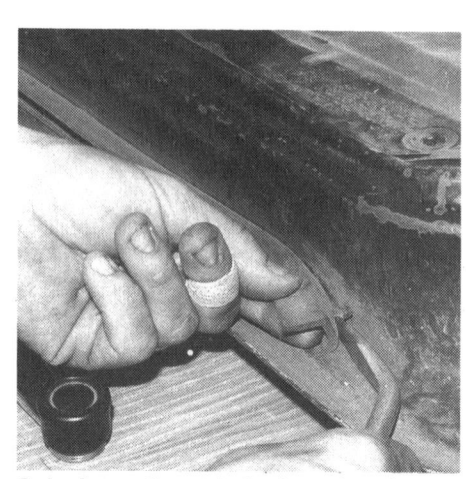

Splash weatherstrip is riveted and cemented to door. Brake-adjusting spoon makes a good lever for popping rivets loose.

Interior Trim & Component Removal 65

Remove hinges. Datsun marked them RH and LH. Glassbeading or carburetor cleaner will strip paint and old lubricant. Note front sealing rubber has been removed.

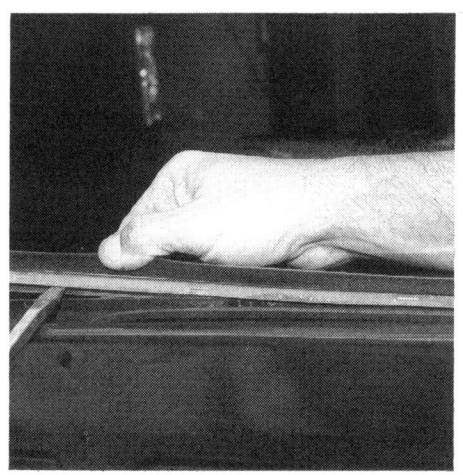

Stainless-steel trim and rubber whisker strip is gently pried off starting at one end. Screwdriver provides leverage.

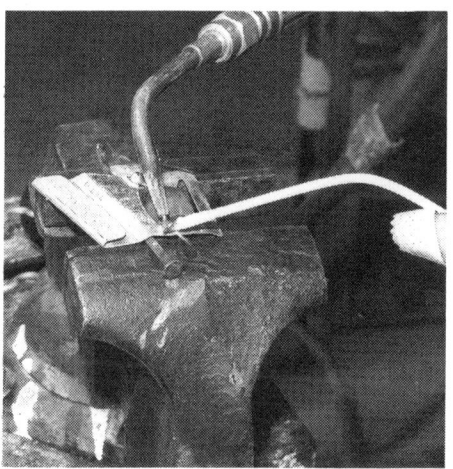

Window-stabilizing roller in my project car had broken. Pre-fluxed brazing rod and a low flame provided a quick repair.

frame, then to the support that's directly overhead. Be sure the rope is strong enough.

Here again, I keep some old-fashioned single-strand electrical wire on hand for jobs like this. Unlike bare wire, the plastic insulation protects painted and plated surfaces, but is easy to attach. Rope or webbing works just as well, though.

With a socket wrench, loosen the bolts that hold the hinges to the door pillar. You can reach them through an access hole in the cowl-side inner panel.

Once you have the door supported adequately—by a friend or overhead support—remove the bolts. Be ready to catch any shims that go between the hinges and body. These factory-installed spacers align the door in its body opening. If door alignment is satisfactory, be sure to note on which hinge you found shims and how many—write it on the shim(s) with a Sharpie. **L/T** for *left, top* shim, **R/B** for *right, bottom,* . . . Rethread bolts into the hinges for safekeeping.

Door Weatherstrip—Remove the splash weatherstrip from the bottom of the door. First, loosen the adhesive with a putty knife. Then pop out the plastic rivets using pressure on both sides. I do this with an upholsterer's tack puller or two screwdrivers.

Small rubber sealing tabs are contact-cemented where the window frame enters the door sheet metal. New ones are available, but you may be able to salvage these tabs if you remove them carefully.

The clear-plastic moisture barrier is often ruined or missing on vintage Z-cars. It is there for a specific purpose—to protect the backside of the trim panel against moisture. If missing, it should be replaced.

Door Hinges—If you're not sure whether your door hinges have succumbed due to inadequate lubrication, give them the once-over as you remove them from the door. These bolts tend to rust, so take care not to break off any in the door. If you do, it may mean the stub will have to be drilled out and removed with a bolt extractor. Failing this, the threads may have to be re-tapped.

Bad hinge action usually means one of the hinge pins is worn excessively. Nissan doesn't list replacement pins. Although a bit of machining might adapt a generic pin, it is more cost-effective to replace the entire hinge assembly with a better one. If the spring/detent assembly is broken or worn-out, the same remedy applies.

Door-Window Whisker Strip & Trim—In the US, this is called a *Schlegle strip* or *cat's whisker*. It installs in the slot in the top of the door through which the glass moves up and down.

With the window rolled down, gently pry this strip from front to rear away from the sheet metal with a flat screwdriver. A window-stabilizing roller is attached to the trim. The Service Manual quaintly refers to this as a *bamper*.

With the window rolled back up, take out the two bolts near the forward bottom corner.

Slide the window forward as far as possible, or until it drops off the regulator. Tilt the front corner down and lift the window up and outside the window frame. This takes patience and some "English" to accomplish, so don't get in a rush. Be careful!

Window Regulator—The regulator is secured with Phillips-head screws which are usually in tight. An offset-

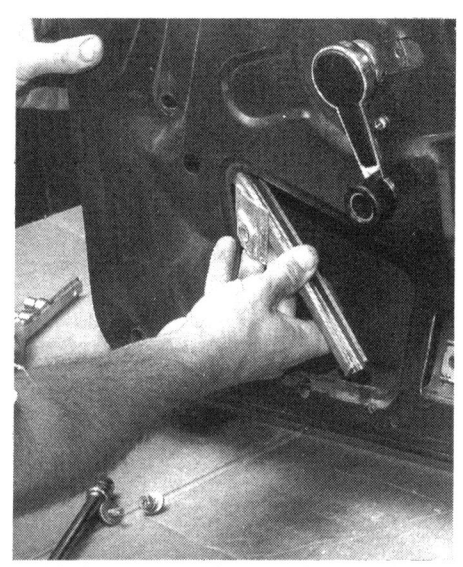

Guide is removed from early-type door. It should drop off window-support shoe.

66 How to Restore Your Datsun Z-car

Window-regulator handle was temporarily installed to maneuver glass. Even though fasteners are out, it still takes some strategy to work glass out.

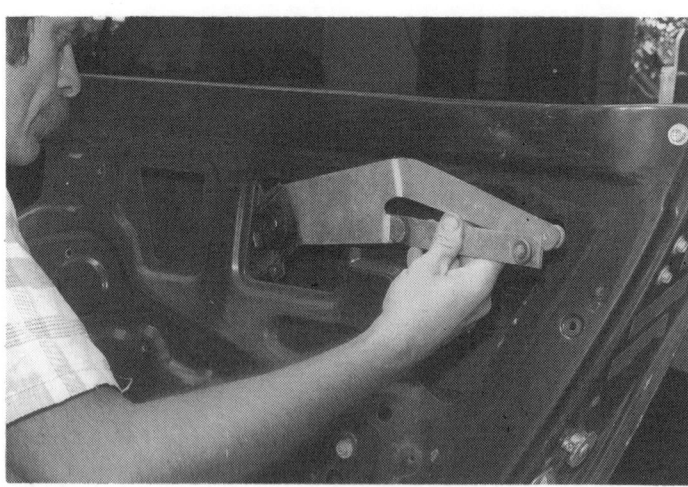

Window regulator slips out upper hole in door-inner panel. Don't wind it off sector or it may pinch your hand.

handle screwdriver helps a lot here—or put a 1/4-inch wrench on the shank of a Phillips bit. Push the regulator into the door cavity and work it out the window slot, then out the large access hole in the door inner.

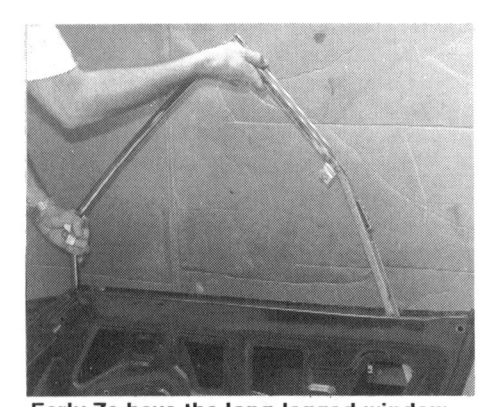

Early Zs have the long-legged window frame. Don't forget to remove bolts below door latch.

Two more bolts hold what the manual calls the *guide panel*. The door sash—I call it a *window frame*—is held in with eight bolts. Tilt the front end down and rotate the rear upward and out of the door. The mounting brackets may get hung up, so be patient and don't bend the stainless.

Inside Door Latch—Remove the Phillips-head screws that hold the latch assembly to the door-inner sheet metal. Next remove the big Phillips-head screws that hold the door-latch mechanism to the door. Also remove the striker dovetail, if so equipped.

The inside handle tips up to release it from the linkage eye.

Door-Lock Cylinder—Push the spring clip off with a screwdriver to release the lock. *Carefully* pry the linkage-rod tip out of its socket and remove the lock cylinder. A little penetrating oil helps.

Outside Door Latch—The easiest way to get handle off is to remove the two retaining bolts, then rotate the assembly up from the outside. Pop off the linkage so the rod comes out with the handle—it inserts into the lock assembly from above.

Inside the lower rear corner of the door is a bellcrank that connects the inside door handle to the lock mechanism. This pivots on a nut and bolt, so you'll need a wrench inside the door shell to remove it. Once the nut is off, pull the whole assembly out, inspect it for obvious deficiencies and reassemble as much as you need so you'll know how it goes together. 2+2 models have an additional inside handle.

Lock mechanisms have their share of linkage rods and levers. Take care not to break any of the nylon sockets

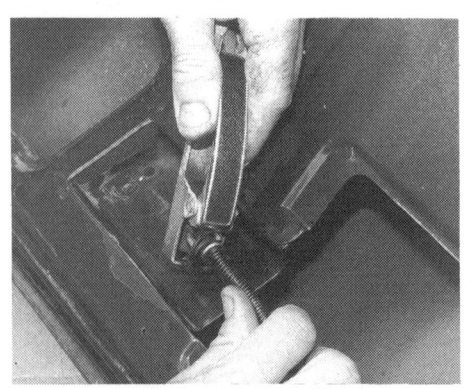

To release inside door handle, tip it up and off linkage-rod eye. Note how spring was loaded against handle bracket. It must be reassembled the same way.

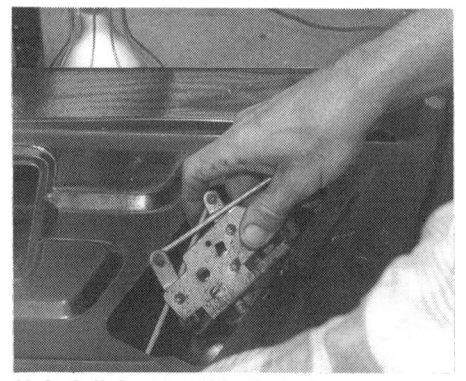

Unbolt linkage-rod bellcrank from door inner frame. With bolts removed, door latch and linkage rods can be removed.

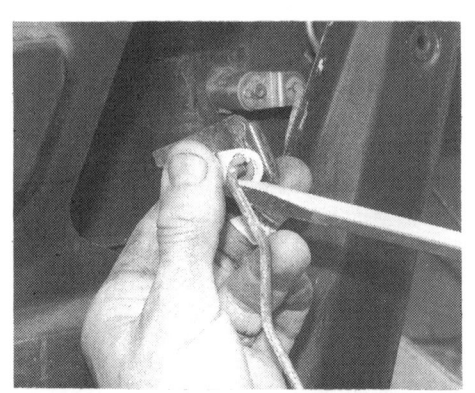

Linkage rods come apart at socket. Soak with penetrant, then pry apart gently with a screwdriver. Spring clip holds door-lock cylinder.

Interior Trim & Component Removal

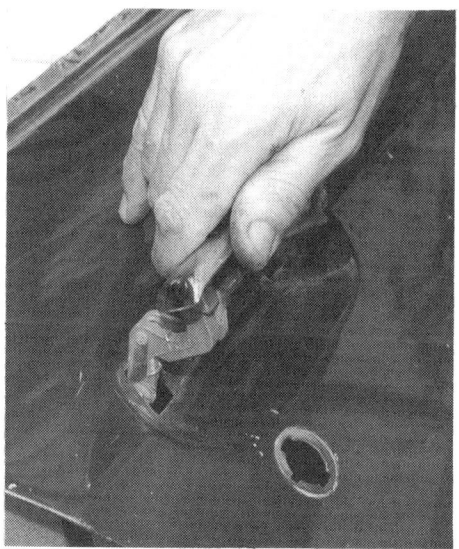

Remove nuts from inside door and simply lift off outside door handle. Scour off all built-up wax and debris before sanding the finish.

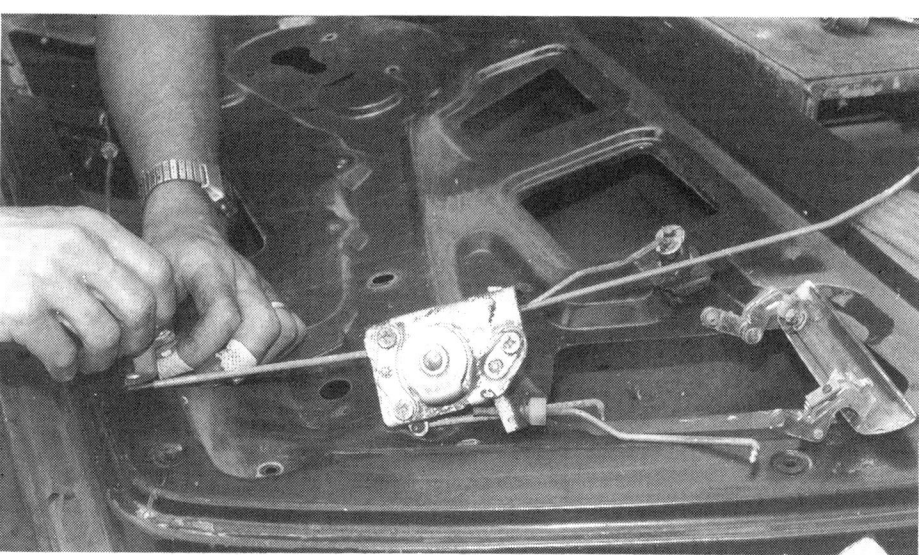

Reassemble bellcrank to keep parts together and organized until it's time to clean and reinstall them.

when disconnecting the linkages. So resist the urge to use striking forces or pliers to disassemble these.

As an aside, my project car had a broken window-stabilizer roller, which let the pane misalign with the channel and frame when rolled up. This may have happened when the window fell off the channel and into the bottom of the car when there was less than 1000 miles on the car. In an uncharacteristic lapse of Datsun quality control—perhaps because of the car's early production status—none of the screws holding the window to its guide/mounting plate were tightened!

The sheet-metal bracket holding the roller cracked, allowing the roller to drop to the bottom of the door. I brazed the pieces back together because of the lower heat needed for a mend. Only a drop flowed to both sides of the steel bracket should hold. Not even the rubber was damaged.

Kick Panels—These are encumbered with various electrical components on both sides. Flashers, relays, hood-latch release and so forth should come off before you remove the kick panels.

To remove, ease out the barbed, plastic bayonet retainers. Like the door-panel clips, these respond to gentle persuasion. A forked tool, one that applies force on both sides of the retainer, is easiest on the panel. A tack-puller, such as those used in upholstery work, is a good tool for doing this.

Caution: Interior-trim panels overlap at the edges, so plan the sequence of removal to avoid breakage. As old as these parts are, they won't stand much vigorous flexing.

Plastic Interior Finishers—These finishers are the semi-flexible plastic pieces used to cover the quarter-window frames, *B-pillar* header, rear-deck quarters and taillight area. The B-pillar is the post extending up from each door-lock jamb to the roof.

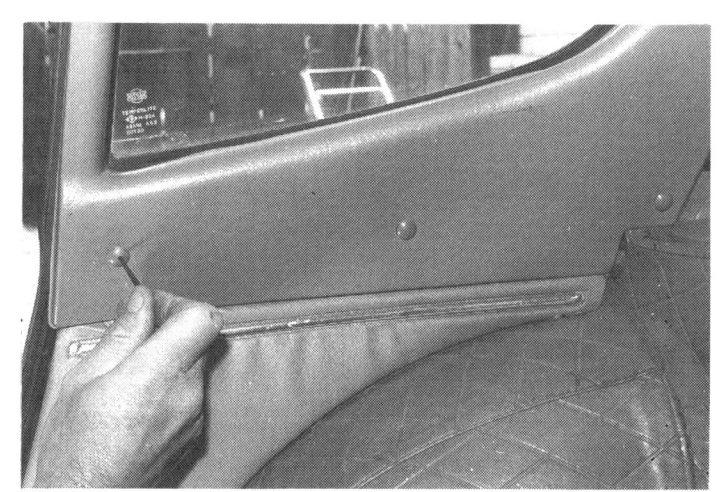

Interior plastic-trim pieces are retained by those plastic expansion rivets. A small Allen wrench works well to push stems through. Recovering them from inside body is another matter!

Early Z-car plastic trim was as thin as a kid's wading pool—and gets increasingly fragile with age. Later model's is more durable and makes a fair replacement if originality isn't a concern.

68 How to Restore Your Datsun Z-car

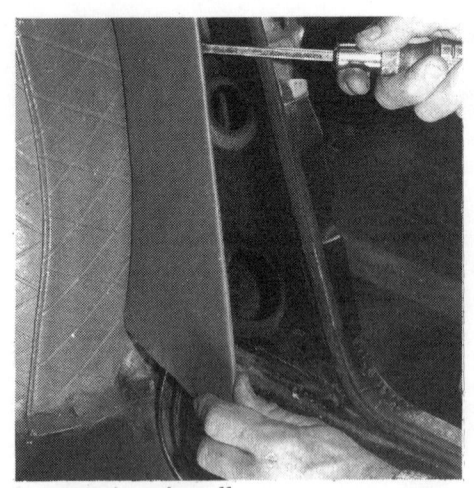

Dog-leg trim pries off just like door-trim panel.

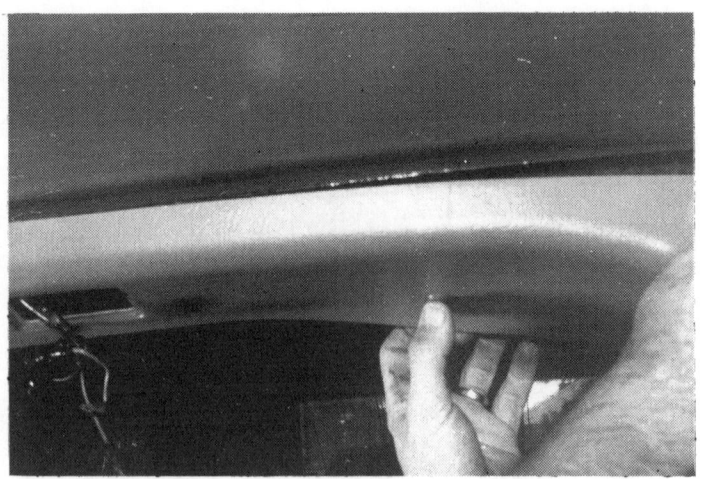

Rear-header finisher is held by rivets. Drill them out. Dome light and side trims must come off first.

Remove the dome light by gently prying down around the edge of the assembly and disconnect the wires. The clothes-hanger buttons should also come off.

Except for a few Phillips-head screws, these are retained by color-keyed plastic rivets. Though larger than those you removed from the rear trim panels, they are the same. Remove them similarly by pushing out the rivets from their centers. If you want to reuse them, you must search the "bilges" of the fender panels to find all of the rivet stems.

Make sure you store these interior panels in mild temperature—not too hot or cold. Don't handle them if they are very cold, otherwise they'll break. Ideally, they should be stored flat, not on end or with anything heavy resting on them.

Quarter-Trim Panels—These upholstered "dog-leg" trimmers are made of hardboard. They use wire-type spring clips like those used to retain door-trim panels. Again, don't force the clips.

Store trim panels with wire clips facing away from the other's vinyl if you hope to reuse them as is.

Vinyl Fabric—Zs, especially early models, utilize quite a bit of "quilted" vinyl material to cover the inner fenders, strut housings and transmission/drive-shaft tunnel. This was sewn into form-fitting units and hand-cemented to the painted metal or, in the case of the tunnel, to the jute padding.

Only if you're restoring to factory-original condition should you be concerned with the condition of this fabric. If your car is typical though, this material was subjected to some pretty rough usage. Removal is relatively easy. The older the car, the less sticky the adhesive. Just be careful peeling it back where there are tears, cuts or a series of perforations—along the rectangular edge of the strut-housing stiffeners is a good example.

The front panel of the rear deck area is a good place to start. Start at the edge and work across the panel evenly. Try not to cause a tear by overstressing any isolated point.

If you haven't already done so, remove the plastic caps that cover the strut fasteners. The segment covering the inner wheel housing went on last,

Very early 240Zs had stowage compartments behind seats, later models had stowage under deck. Carpet patterns are quite different due to these variations.

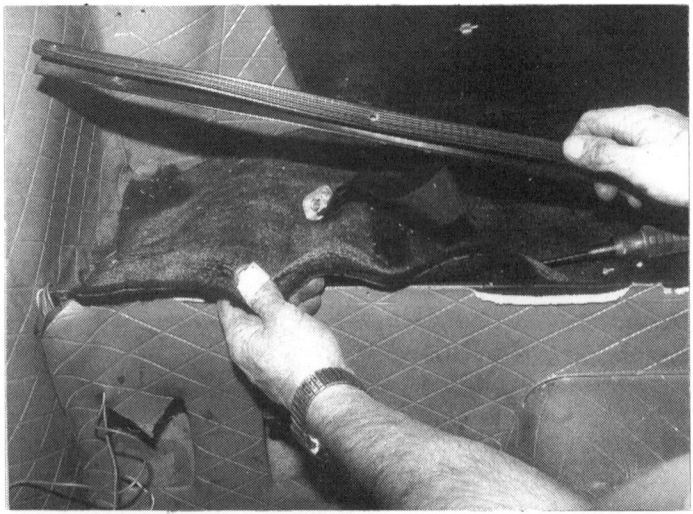

Deck molding retains front edge of carpet. Cargo-strap brackets screw down through material. Holes in deck-front trim and wires hanging out aren't original.

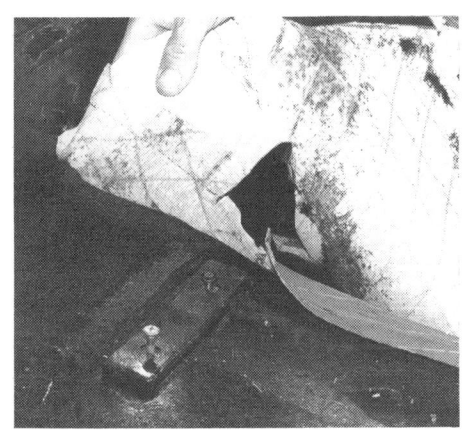

Interior Trim & Component Removal

Datsun's choice of material and pattern for early Zs was derided by car magazines, although it was durable.

Old cement doesn't maintain a strong hold on cloth or vinyl, but sticks like crazy to metal. The result is a big clean-up job.

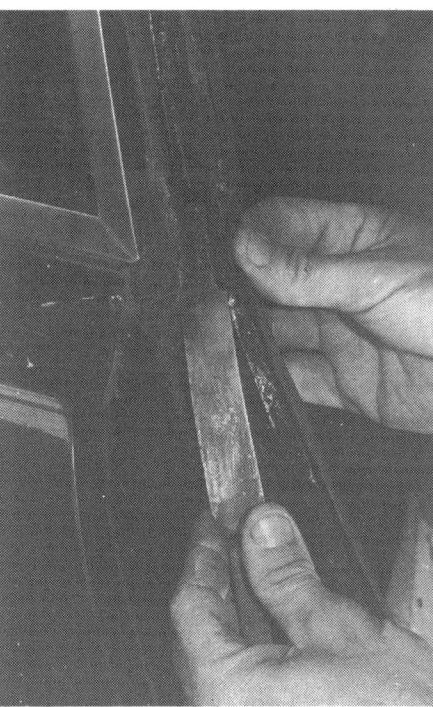

Early quarter windows have little sealing tabs cemented top and bottom. Later cars use a vertical finisher—they aren't interchangeable.

Quarter window comes out when machine screws are removed. Be ready to catch window.

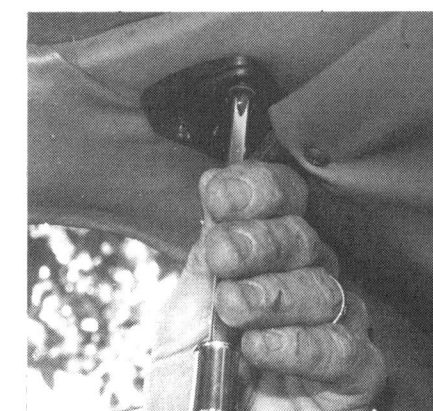

Two-piece mounting is used to support sun visors on early cars; one piece is used on later style. They look similar, however.

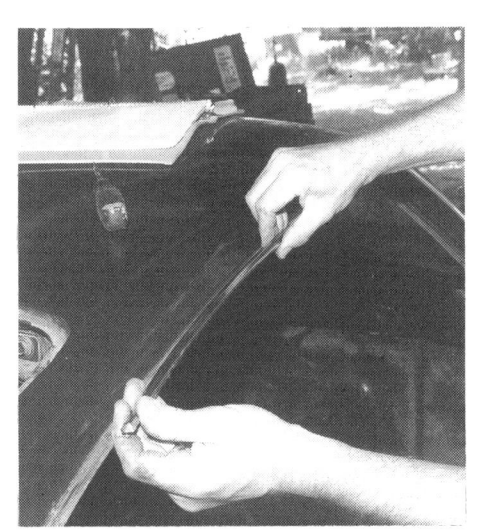

Start loosening drip trim with screwdriver. Roll trim up and away from metal lip on roof, but don't bend it. Be careful!

Gradually work trim forward, then roll off A-pillar. It makes one wonder how it stayed on so well.

so take it off first. Then remove the complex piece that covers the strut housing and stiffener.

On the transmission tunnel, loosen the toe-board insulation to get access to the tunnel covering. Peel the material back, rolling it so the cemented surfaces don't stick together. Several pieces are sewn together, making it hard to manage.

If you must make rust repairs to the floorpan or tunnel, you'll have to remove sections of jute padding that underlay the material. Also remove sections that are not in good condition and replace it with new padding. Jute padding is cemented in place the same as the quilted-vinyl trim, but is harder to remove because it has much less *integrity,* or tearing strength.

Soaking the padding with naptha and scraping it loose from the edges works, but is hard, messy and hazardous. Fumes from the naptha are dangerous to breathe and create a fire hazard. So open windows and doors. Set up a fan to circulate fresh air through the car and out of your work area.

Sunvisors & Rearview Mirror— These are secured to the windshield header with Phillips-head screws. Take them out them so you can remove the overhead trim. The sunvisor-mounting bracket also holds down the edge of the vinyl fabric, locating the fold on the finished edge.

The mirror assembly is designed to break away in an accident, so some pressure toward the front and an

70 How to Restore Your Datsun Z-car

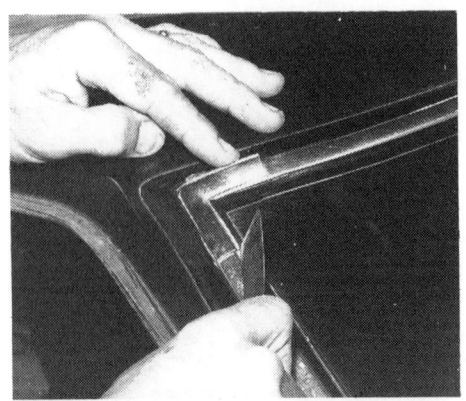

Garnish trim must be removed before taking out windshield. Trim is held under lips on weatherstrip. Proceed deliberately or you will kink the stainless. Corners and center trim pieces come off first.

Long trim strips come off next. I store them fastened together with garbage-bag ties and out of harm's way.

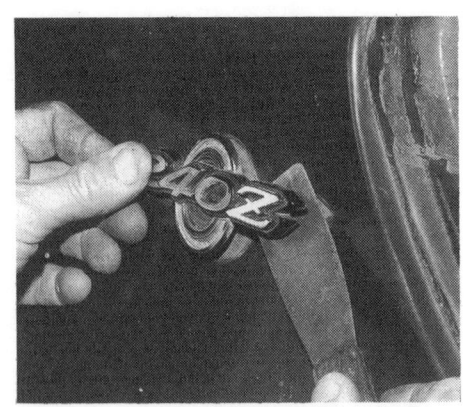

On later models, this is where interior air is vented, but on early 240Zs, it is purely decorative. Be careful not to bend.

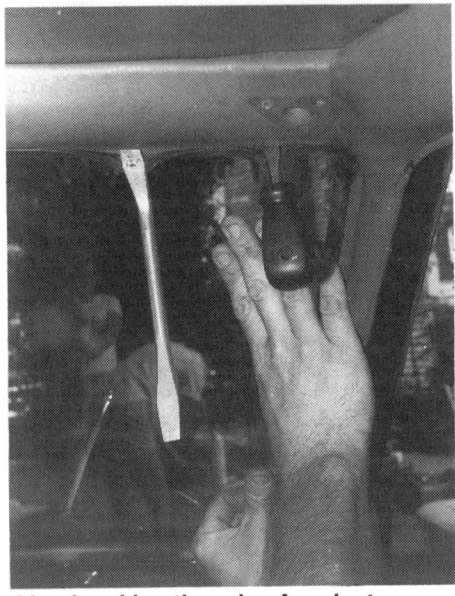

After breaking the grip of sealant on weld flange, gently wedge weatherstrip out of opening—have someone ready to catch glass. Don't get in a hurry.

assist from the rear with a screwdriver blade will release it. Once the mirror is out of the way, remove its mounting plate.

Headliner & Trim—You may not have noticed, but the Z-car's windshield was installed *after* the headliner and *A-pillars* (windshield posts) were upholstered. This means, logically enough, the windshield and its associated rubber setting strip (seal) must be taken out to remove and install the trim in this area.

A-Pillar- & Header-Trim Removal—All of this trim is cemented in place with a sprayed-on adhesive.

Starting at the top of the A-pillar, ease the vinyl away from the metal with a smooth, blunt-edge blade—like your venerable putty knife. This material is light-duty at best, and probably embrittled by sun and ozone damage, so be careful. I keep heat gun or heat lamp handy to soften vinyl and contact cement.

Problem: Under the vinyl is a 1/8-inch-thick layer of urethane foam, which is usually cemented to *both* the metal and vinyl. Whichever layer of adhesive is sticking the best will hold on . . . and sometimes it alternates! This makes salvaging the foam an iffy proposition. However, it is inexpensive and available at most upholstery shops. Keep peeling the material away until the A-pillars are bare. If damaged, save the vinyl for a pattern.

Along the inner roof rail, the top edge of the material seems to roll over and disappear behind the inner rail. Actually, a U-section flexible-plastic molding holds this side of the trim to the header. It can be dislodged from

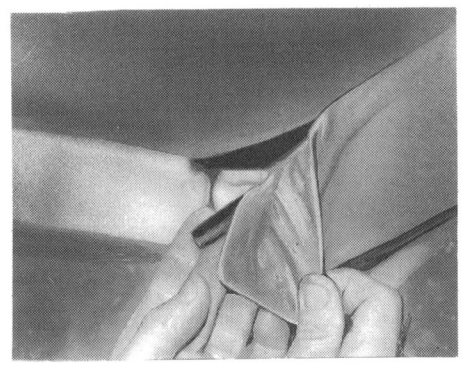

Header trim is held with a horseshoe-shape, metal-core plastic molding. This pinches the vinyl over the raw edge of the roof side-rail metal. Roll trim back from the end, noting how it attaches.

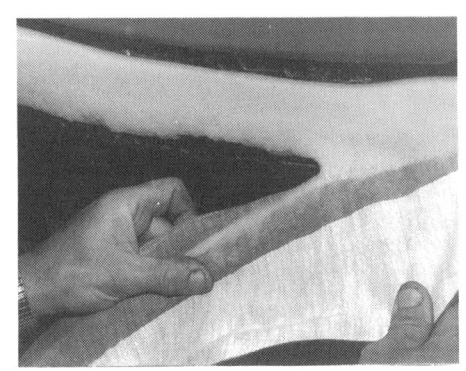

Vinyl material was cemented at the weld-flange edge, but not to foam.

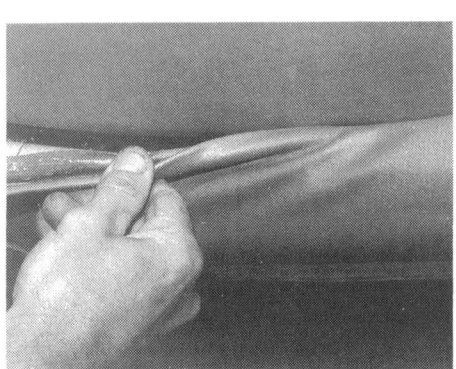

Roof side rails are next. Material is cemented around door-jamb weld flange. Trimmed edge was hidden by weatherstrip.

Interior Trim & Component Removal

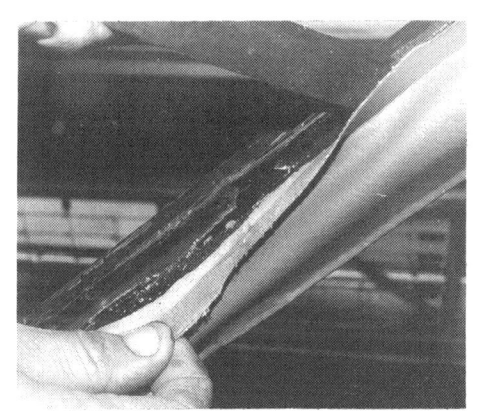

Blade eases material away from A-pillar weld flange. It can be saved if you carefully peel back trim.

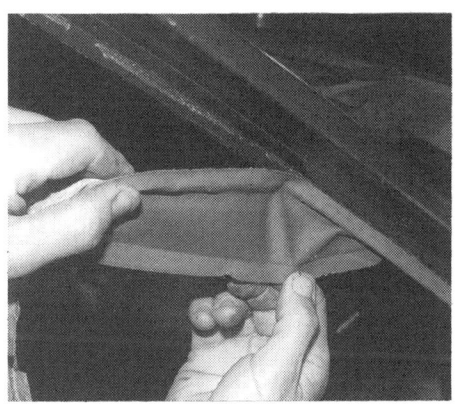

The factory wrapped vinyl around weld flange, then trimmed off excess where weatherstrip hid edge.

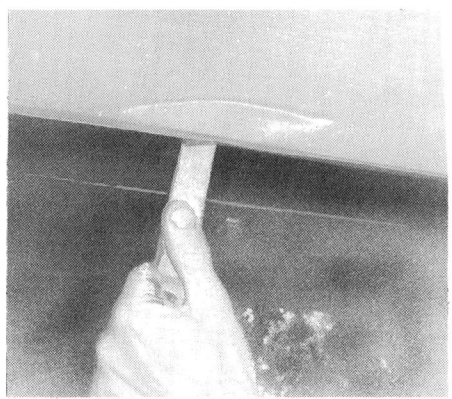

Find a place to begin separating from roof and use knife blade to start peeling foam/vinyl lamination free.

the extreme end by *carefully* inserting a small screwdriver under the lip. Once it begins to come loose, continue to roll the top edge and molding off the rail. Take the molding free from the material. Repeat this process at the other side.

It gets harder. Even if you don't care about saving the vinyl or foam, get at least one complete side off intact. Now ease the cemented-down side away from the edge of the metal. This side was covered up by the black molding you removed earlier.

Caution: This edge has several slits where it bends, perfect places for a rip to start. Find these slits along the edge and use your blade to loosen them before pulling away the material.

The last long strip to remove is at the windshield header because it went on first at the factory. Note how the roof-rail trim is finished at the juncture of the roof under the sun-visor mounts. Make the folds the same way when installing the new material.

Headliner Pad & Covering—A rectangular lamination of 1/4-inch-thick foam and a layer of vinyl is all you have to deal with here. A good starting place is right in the middle of a side. Work the blade back behind the header far enough to catch the edge of the sandwich and begin pulling it loose. Work toward the corners with your fingers. Don't hurry—do it right.

When all sides are loose and out from under the header, choose a side where the foam padding pulls free most evenly and begin working across the roof. Work the padding back and forth—use the blade to loosen the foam. Some headliners come out smoothly, like the one in the photographs. Others where the padding alternately clung to the vinyl and then the metal are more difficult to work with. These make it hard to salvage the original foam padding! If you are lucky, you'll only have a few little tufts of foam stuck to the metal "ceiling" when you're done.

I immediately use naptha and a clean rag to remove all residual contact cement, both from the car body and vinyl. Storing this gluey material, even for future use as a pattern for new material, can be a mess if it all sticks together!

Hatch Removal

This is listed under **TAIL GATE** in your Datsun manual. Doesn't sound like a sports GT car, does it?

The hatch can be removed whenever it is convenient, but you'll need

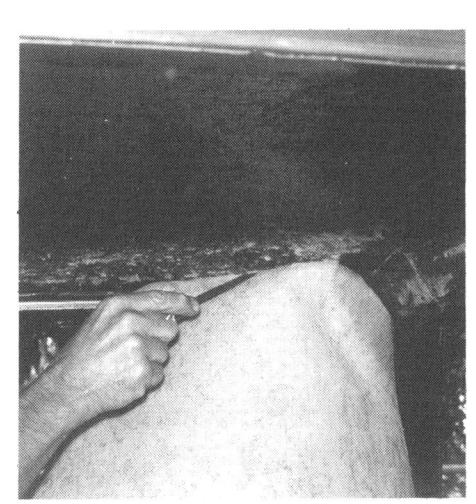

You may have to scrape every square inch free if adhesive was really tacky when applied. The less foam left sticking to the roof, the better the new headliner pad will adhere when recemented.

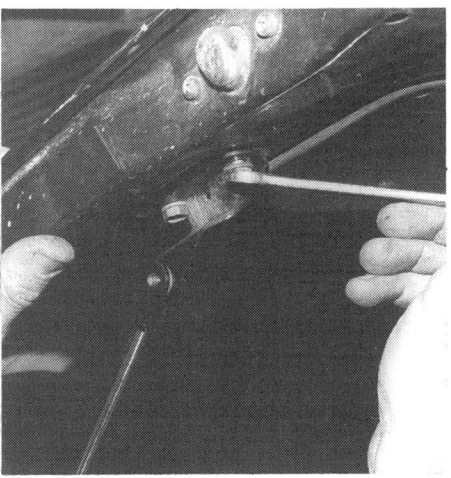

Support strut(s)—one is used on early models—should be detached either at the hatch or jamb. Other end can be removed next.

Hatch removal requires something or someone to support hatch. Countersunk Phillips-head screws at hatch hinges are easy to reach.

72 How to Restore Your Datsun Z-car

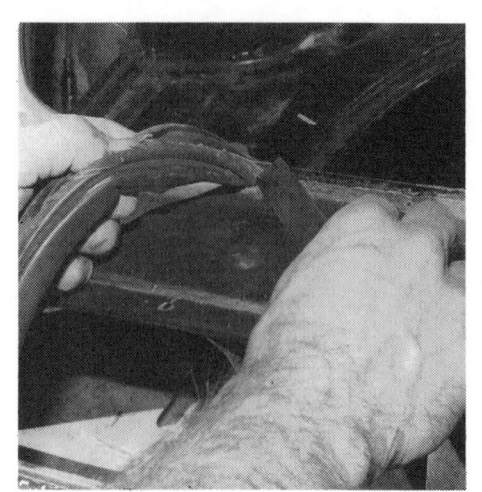

Hatch weatherstrips, both inner and outer, should be removed.

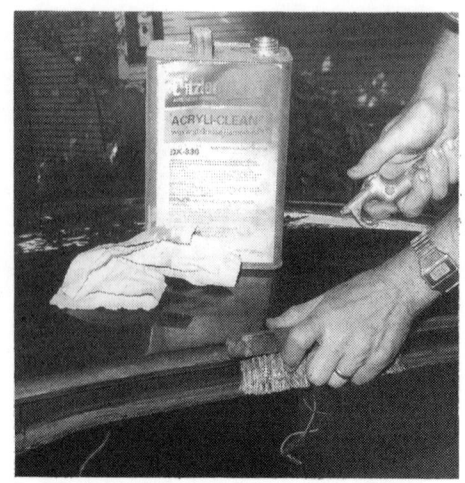

Lots of drudgery with scraper, wire-brush and compressed air are used to remove cement. Use Ditzler DX-330 Wax and Grease Remover or naptha and clean rags to remove adhesive, wax and silicone residue.

someone to help do it.

Start hatch removal by disconnecting the rear-window-defroster leads. Be very careful not to pull the male contacts off the glass. Hold the tang with a fingertip and gently work the connector downward. Use needle-nose pliers or a screwdriver tip if it's stuck.

Loosen—don't remove—the large countersunk Phillips-head screws that hold the hatch to the hinges. Unbolt the gas-charged strut(s) at the hatch, but hold up the end of the hatch. This can be done with a broom handle, 2x4 or whatever, but the hatch must be fully open. You now need an extra set of hands to support the hatch and window—it's heavy. Once safely supported, the hatch-hinge screws can be backed all the way out.

Set the hatch on edge in a place where it can't be damaged. This should be a side edge rather than the top or bottom.

Remove the strut bracket(s). Remove the bolts that secure the hinges to the roof header. Watch for shims between the body and hinges. Make a note of their location and number.

Hatch Weatherstrip—Peel the weatherstripping from the hatch-opening lip. Be careful that you don't tear it. Remove the hatch-latch assembly, too. If you need to work on the hatch hinges, remove them. Scribe around the hinge perimeters to assist in realigning them.

Vapor-Return Hoses—These connect the fuel tank with the vapor canister in the passenger-side quarter panel. To make sure you get the hoses connected to the correct nipples on the tank, put a strip of masking tape around each, indicating the corresponding tank inlet.

Early Zs used a plastic vapor-recovery canister. It was insulated from the sheet metal with a batt of fiberglass. Later Zs use a steel canister. One hose returns through the fender valance to the vapor-return lines in the transmission tunnel. Early canisters tended to crack or break at this nipple.

Both types of tanks are mounted to the B-pillar structure under the trim panels with Phillips-head screws. Loosen the clamps, pull off the hoses and remove the tanks. Check the hoses for deterioration. Replace them if their condition is at all doubtful.

Door Weatherstrip—Peel all rubber weatherstrip away from the door weld flange. Early Zs had a molded trim piece that was separate from the weatherstrip. Don't bother saving it if you're going to install a new Nissan weatherstrip. Remove adhesive and sealant residue with naptha on a clean shop towel.

Hatch-Glass Removal—With the hatch off the car, carefully remove the stainless trim in the glass-setting weatherstrip. Don't pull trim up to remove it. This will bend it. Instead, peel the rubber lips away from the trim and let the trim pop out.

Loosen the weatherstrip all around. Do a thorough job. With the hatch upside down on a padded surface, use several flat-blade screwdrivers and ease the strip away from the weld flange. Take your time. Free any sticky spots instead of forcing the glass. Some soapy water might help. Eventually the glass will fall out with the weatherstrip. Simply lift the hatch away from the glass. Leave the weath-

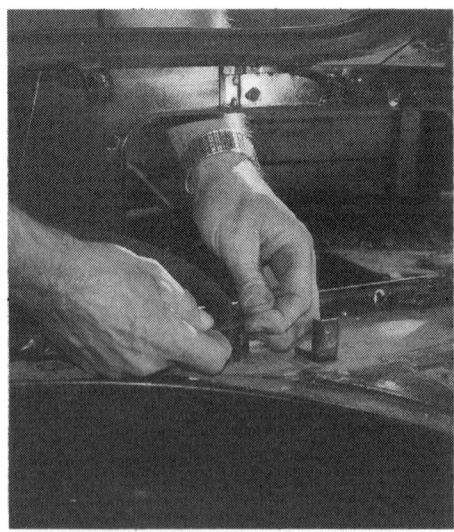

Fuel-tank vapor-return hoses have rubber nipples to seal them to the tubes. Save nipples if possible.

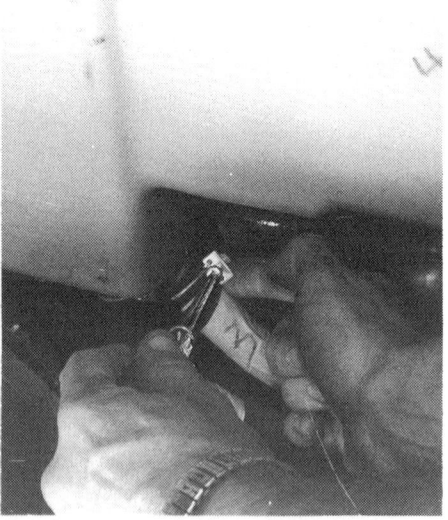

Number reservoir-tank nipples and hoses before you remove them. Later cars used a metal version. Plastic reservoir had tank-to-engine hose nipple snap off when almost new. It almost gassed the author (me) before I found the problem.

Interior Trim & Component Removal

Hatch finisher has a gasket that may still be cemented down. Early plastic finisher is fragile, so I'm being careful.

Technique for removing glass is exactly the same as windshield—just easier. Garnish, weatherstrip and sealer must be dealt with. Don't drop glass.

erstrip on the glass to protect its edges for moving and storing.

Remove all traces of rubber and cement from the weld flange with a razor blade and naptha. Remove old wax, dirt and so forth from nooks and crannies.

Early Hatch—Before flow-through-ventilation exits were moved to the B-pillars, Z hatches had these in their lower lip. Check for rust in this area, particularly if yours uses exterior grilles on the vents. I have never found primer on the interior of a Z-car hatch, so any moisture that gets in causes rust, especially around the lower lip.

Remove Finisher—It is retained with rivets and Phillips-head screws. The old gasket may be sticky, so a *little* prying with a flat-blade screwdriver may be in order. Don't pull on this panel. You'll bend it. Side dovetails, latch unit and lock cylinder can also be removed.

Vent collectors each have an outlet hose and plastic plenum sealed to the underside of the hatch behind grilles. Work hoses off the plenum neck and out through holes in the underside of the hatch lip. From the inside, ease collector plenums away from the metal without bending it. Slip plenums out of the hatch.

Hatch Trim—All chrome is held on by barrel clips that fit tightly into holes in the metal. If you can, push them out from the inside. If not, use a flat-blade tool and very carefully pry underneath them up from topside. Vent grilles are attached similarly. These vacuum-plated plastic trim pieces are easily broken. Take care when removing them.

Hatch-Jamb Hardware—Remove the striker, rubber bumper and rubber plug in each.

Rubber Plugs—Remove any rubber body plugs you encounter and note their number and location. Replace any that aren't in good condition.

Lock cylinder is retained by big spring clip. Little bolt and locknut adjust stroke to accommodate latch lever.

Brake spoon or other flat tool can be shoehorned under rear plenum to loosen barrel-clips and gasket. Place paint paddle or something to support spoon to prevent damage to back panel. Trims are tough to remove if they've never been off.

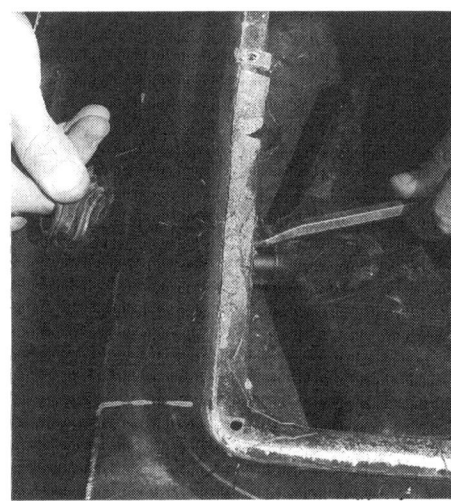

Early hatch has vent collector (plenum and tube) to remove. Don't lose clips that are on gasket.

74 How to Restore Your Datsun Z-car

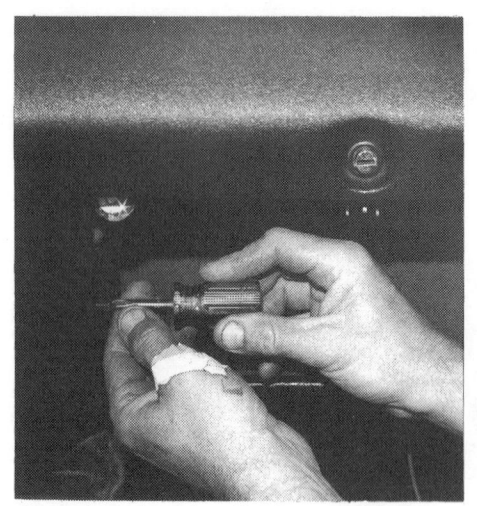

Glove-box door is off. Liner and light come out next.

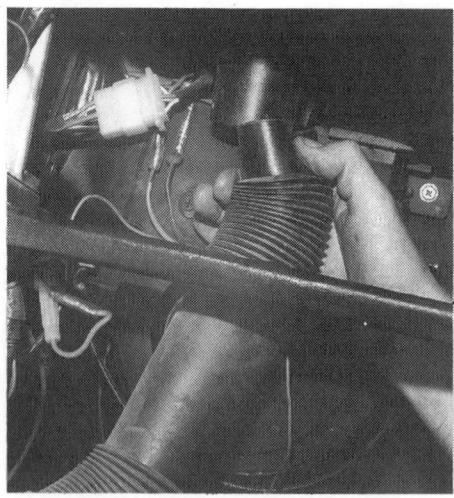

Z-cars have a variety of underdash ducts. Don't forget to remove securing screws at heater plenum.

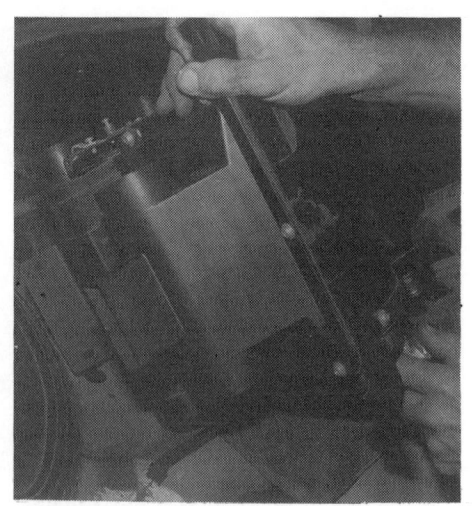

Once you have heater assembly out of car, blow it out thoroughly while rotating it to remove all leaves, bugs, dust and any other debris.

They are inexpensive and provide a barrier against moisture entering the body cavities. Bear in mind there are several that seal sub-frame cavities, so there will be a matching plug on the opposite side in those locations.

Instrument-Panel Area
Glove Box—On an early Z, the first thing to attack in the instrument-panel area is the glove box.

Plastic glove-box doors are often in miserable condition. Even examples that have been well cared for are usually warped—they tend to bow inward in the area of the latch and outward at the upper corners. And the thin hinge area eventually cracks.

Removing the glove-box door is simple. Start by taking out the metal travel limiter. Rotate it up and out of the slot. Then remove the self-tapping screws that hold the hinge to the panel.

Liners are held in with screws. If yours is cardboard-box like, compress it to get it out of the instrument panel. This and the lid are often candidates for the trash bin. Luckily, replacements are available and relatively inexpensive. If your liner doesn't need replacing, remove the heater unit first. If you're wondering why the order of photos doesn't agree with what I'm telling you, accessibility for photo taking in the instrument-panel area dictated the sequence. So, follow what I say, *not* the order shown in the photos.

Unsnap the vinyl cover on the wiring-harness trunk. With this out of the way, remove the duct to the passenger-side defroster. Then remove the vent-flap-cable mounting and lever clamps.

Heater Unit—Disconnect all control cables from their levers and brackets. Disconnect the gang plug for heater wiring, too. Pull off the flexible heater/defroster ducts.

Air Conditioner—Disconnect remaining A/C lines, heater hoses and cables and label them. Store these components together so they don't get mixed up with others or damaged.

Underpanel Wiring—You shouldn't encounter problems in the future with reassembly if you carefully pull apart wiring-harness connectors now. Datsun's color coding is usually consistent, but *not* infallible. So don't start disconnecting things until you're ready to label or code all of them. Better safe than sorry!

Be sure you have a firm grip on the connectors and not the wires before you start to pull off a connector.

Steering-column jacket is a two-piece affair. Early style is secured by three different types of Phillips-head screws!

Interior Trim & Component Removal 75

Occasionally a wire that isn't tightly crimped into its connector will pull free. Besides, you never know what abuse previous owners or mechanics may have inflicted on your car and its circuitry!

Once you have the main harness free from the engine-compartment harness, push the firewall grommet loose and work the latter through the hole.

Early Zs are blessedly uncomplicated in comparison to fuel-injected 280Zs—the same procedures apply, but the later series have many more electrical components to deal with. Remove all plastic covers and systematically detach the relays, fuse block and other "black-box" components.

Steering Column—You may want to leave the steering column in place to help when moving the rolling chassis. You could pull the steering wheel to allow more working room and set it back in place only when needed for steering. Turn to page 77 for a description of how to remove the wheel. But if you're ready to remove the steering column, let's proceed.

The plastic cover that conceals the upper section of the steering column has two halves. They are screwed to one another and to the column. Don't break the plastic trying to wrestle the bottom half free. Check to make sure you've removed all screws!

Move pull controls for the vents out of the way. You may find several connections for the vent cables under the dash. Only two are screwed onto the outlets. The rest are bayonet-style push-ons, which disconnect when you apply the right motion. The hood-latch remote control is removed by dismantling its handle and pulling the cable through the grommet it shares with the speedometer cable and bracket.

Now is a good time to disconnect the speedometer cable from the back of the speedometer. Work the grommet free from the firewall, bend over the metal support tab and pull the cable through. Make sure it isn't globbed with grease and dirt, or you will create another cleaning job for yourself.

Instrument-Panel Removal

The Z-car instrument panel assembly has a welded sheet-metal support with a molded-foam cushion and

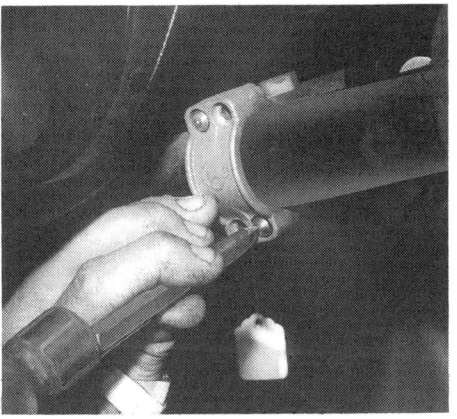

Two screws that held ignition-switch-mount cap on had duplex-style heads that break away for theft protection. They must be center-punched before drilling. Combination switch is already removed.

Here drill bit has just cut through screw head. Shafts can easily be backed out with pliers after cap is out of the way.

Front steering-shaft U-joint is splined to rack-and-pinion input shaft. Someone applied too much torque to this bolt. Although it hadn't caused any trouble, I cleaned up threads with a tap and replaced bolt.

To remove intermediate steering shaft, steering coupler or upper spline can be disconnected.

vinyl covering bonded to it. The various year and model changes notwithstanding, the basic instrument panel and its removal and replacement are virtually the same.

On the underside of the panel and on the transmission tunnel are Phillips-head screws that must come out. Another row of screws holds the top of the instrument-panel assembly to the upper cowl. These are usually the hex/Phillips style. I prefer a socket wrench, but the screwdriver option is a versatile alternative. Remove the bolts from the radio mount.

Steering-Column Combination Switch—This is retained with two Phillips-head machine screws. Remove it before you tackle the steering lock.

The steering lock came from Datsun assembled with four screws, two of which had breakaway-type heads. This was to foil would-be car thieves by making it difficult to change ignition locks.

Breakaway screws are not generally available. If your Z needed a new ignition-switch assembly at sometime during its existence, it may not still have them. Or . . . your Z-car could be "hot" in a way you may not have expected! If your Z is among the majority and the breakaway screws are still there, you have to go through the hassle that was meant to deter perpetrators of Grand Theft, Auto.

Very carefully centerpunch the stubs of the breakaway screws. Use a sharp punch and get it as near center

76 How to Restore Your Datsun Z-car

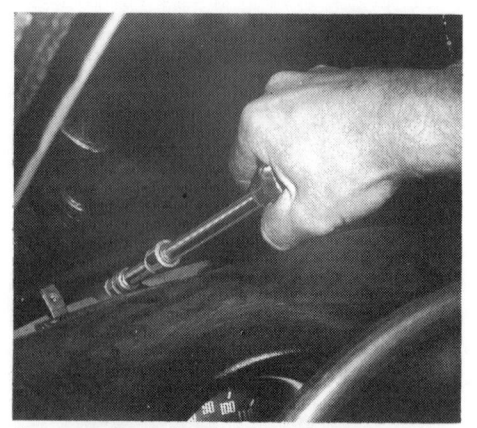

Screws along front edge of crash pad are accessible after garnish trim is removed. More mounting brackets are under each end and on the transmission tunnel.

After removing fasteners at steering column-and-pedal-support bracket, instrument-panel assembly is lifted up and out.

as possible. Once punched, start a pilot hole with a small drill bit in both screws. Drill in no more than the depth of the blank head. Then follow up with a bit equal to the diameter of the screw shaft. About 3/16 inch is adequate. If your punch mark was accurate, the head should be cut off cleanly. If not, stop the bit before it wanders into the metal of the lock itself.

Use a small, sharp chisel to knock off the screw head without marking the lock assembly. Remove the other two screws and take off the lock halves. You should now be able to grasp the stubs of the breakaway-head screws with pliers and unscrew them.

Steering-Column-Tube Clamp—This clamp secures the steering column below the instrument panel. On early cars—up to July 1973—it is held on with four bolts that thread into weldnuts in the steering-column-and-pedal-support bracket. In Zs with the later steering column—260 and 280—these are replaced with two bolts with insulators. The clamp is held to the column with four bolts.

Caution: Once the support is disconnected, the column is vulnerable to damage that might require its replacement. Due to the energy-absorbing requirements Datsun built into the steering column, the mast jacket can be bent very easily. Every precaution should be taken not to apply pressure to the column while it is still bolted at the firewall.

Steering Coupler—On the engine-compartment side of the firewall, remove the bolts/nuts that hold the steering-column coupler assembly together. This will free the upper section of the steering column from the lower.

Then remove the four bolts from the steering-column-mounting flange on the passenger-compartment side of the firewall. Now withdraw the column into the passenger-compartment area. Again, be very careful not to put undue stress on the collapsible-mast jacket, especially the corrugated type.

To remove the lower steering shaft, remove the clamping bolt from the lower half of the U-joint at the steering gear. Pull the U-joint free of the splined pinion shaft. This may require *gentle* persuasion with a screwdriver between the U-joint and steering-gear housing. Replace bolt in U-joint for safe keeping.

Heater—The coolant control-valve cable on the passenger side of the heater unit comes off with two screws. Be sure to label or otherwise identify the cables to simplify their reinstallation.

Carefully disconnect the gang plugs connecting the main instrument panel-to-fuse block harness, checking for mismatched or duplicate color codes. On early Zs, remove the fuse block and its harness. On 240Zs, watch for melting where the large red and white wires enter. Replace the fuse block and affected connector if damaged from overheating. The heater and vent cables on the driver's side must also come off the engine side of the firewall. A/C controls are similar, but more numerous. Refer to the illustrations in your Service Manual to get their correct names.

Ease the heater hose through the firewall. There will be some coolant in the hose or heater core, so take precautions against spilling it in the passenger compartment. The core plenum may be full of leaves and debris as well. Blow it out with compressed air and inspect for heater-core leakage.

The vent intake-duct assemblies are attached with Phillips-head sheet-metal screws. Check for debris, rust and free movement of the valve flap.

For 240Zs, Nissan published a supplement that covers heater repair and instrument-panel, console, instruments and revised electrical details.

Instrument-Panel Removal—It isn't essential to have a helper to muscle out the instrument-panel assembly, but it helps. If everything is loose, a few good tugs on each side and it should lift up and out. If your instrument panel appears reusable, be careful. Don't set it on the crash pad. The

Interior Trim & Component Removal 77

Steering wheel is secured to steering-shaft splines by a large nut. Don't strike steering shaft for any reason. Use a steering-wheel puller to free wheel. Threaded holes in steering-wheel hub used for pulling wheel are ISO type; SAE bolts won't work.

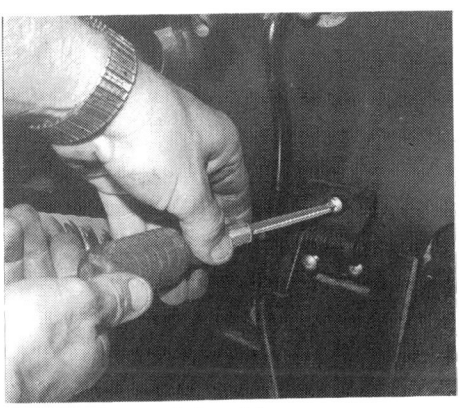

Accelerator pedal and lever are retained by pivot which bolts to bracket on firewall.

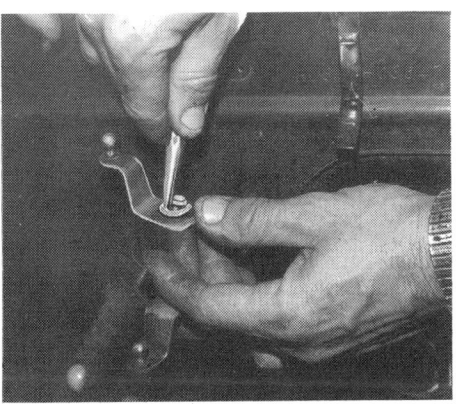

With accelerator-rod-socket ends popped off balls, bellcrank can be removed. Retaining ring comes off with needle-nose pliers. Don't lose ring or two bushings that go on bellcrank shaft.

old vinyl may choose that moment to crack. Also, don't drop it on the back sides of the tachometer/speedometer units.

Steering-Wheel Removal—Early style: The cushioned Datsun horn button simply pops off with a good tug. Late style: Turn it counterclockwise while pushing down.

You will probably need the leverage of a breaker-bar or some sort of "cheater" to remove the 23mm nut (7/8-inch socket will work) that holds the wheel to the steering shaft.

Before you pull off the wheel, use a sharp punch to matchmark the relative position of the wheel hub to the shaft. Don't deform either part, just make a prick mark on the top next to the splines and a corresponding one where the washer rested on the wheel hub.

Remove the horn-attachment rings and spring. You may not need a puller to pull off the wheel. A light rap or two from behind the wheel hub is often sufficient. If yours is tight, attach a screw-type steering-wheel puller to the hub and tighten until the wheel breaks free. Don't use a jaw-type gear puller or you'll mar the hub.

Pedal Assembly—Besides the clutch and brake master-cylinder studs, the entire unit is held in place with four bolts, two on the upper side and two below. When these are out, the assembly can be worked free, even if you left the steering column in place. Most need only a little judicious lubrication to be restored to good service. Under-instrument-panel parts are usually the best preserved parts of any "old" car!

If you experienced sloppy action and noise in the pedals, the culprit will probably be the fulcrum pin and bushing. These can be replaced—as a set preferably. Remove the return spring, then unscrew the pin. Lubricate with light grease and reassemble.

Accelerator & Linkage—The ball-and-socket joints in the linkage should be popped apart. Take care not to break the plastic socket. A shot of WD-40 or equivalent helps if they are dry and sticky. Remove the screws that retain the accelerator and its pivot and pop out the rubber firewall boot.

Note: The various boots and grommets in the firewall should be replaced. All are cemented in. Make a note of which ones you will need, but don't discard the old ones until you have *all* replacements in hand. These are readily available from Nissan or suppliers listed in the directory beginning on page 204. Spend what little they cost. You'll never get a better opportunity to renew them.

On the engine side of the firewall, remove the circlip from the accelerator bellcrank. Unscrew the inside ball and socket and the wing nut, then pull the rod through. Remove the bellcrank bracket from the firewall and loosely reassemble. Take off the kickdown switch if so equipped.

Firewall Insulators—These usually take quite a beating. The three pieces are held in place with bent-over metal tabs that can be straightened. However, the insulation was also cemented in place. So, if you intend to save yours for reinstallation, be careful when you pull it free.

Any spatula-like tool can be used to separate fibers from the cement. Expect some to remain on the firewall.

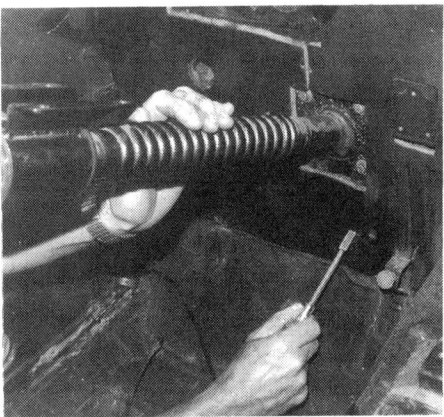

Firewall insulator is made up of three pieces. They are held in place by metal tabs (like the one I'm straightening) and spray-on adhesive. Late-style steering columns have a flange that covers raw edge of insulator around column.

78 How to Restore Your Datsun Z-car

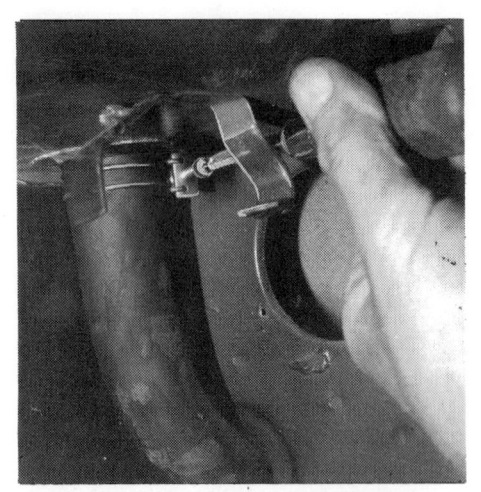

Cowl-drain hoses are clamped at top, run through rubber grommets to vent into fender area. Expect to see lots of debris—leaves, filler dust, rust flakes—when this comes free.

Accelerator-pedal stop threads out of bracket—it has a jam-nut for adjustment. Note steering-column mounting-flange gasket hanging loose and lots of adhesive residue.

Wiring for courtesy light and hatch-window defroster is fed through holes in rear roof header. Don't pull any connectors loose without tagging them first.

Try not to tear the insulation. New ones were not available as of this writing. Store yours in a safe place until they can be restored.

Interior-Light Switches—Installed in the door jambs, these may take some persuasion with a screwdriver. Pop them loose and thread their wiring out through the hole. These switches deteriorate, so check their operation and replace if necessary.

Body-Wiring Harness—With instrument-panel and engine-compartment wiring out of the way, turn your attention to the main-body wiring harness. You may not see the need to remove this harness, nor should you if it isn't necessary. It is the best protected, residing away from the elements and from wear and tear. Also, it is the most difficult to get out and, likewise, the most difficult wiring assembly to reinstall. You be the judge.

If there were no shorting problems or obvious damage to your Z's electrical circuitry, simply check all wiring-harness connectors and obvious wear points—such as in the floorpan area. Make any needed repairs with the harness in place. If you can't get *continuity*, page 116, through all circuits or someone has obviously butchered the harness, you should remove it. Here's how:

First, straighten all the plastic-covered retaining tabs that hold the exposed harness. Then work the rear harness through the rubber-grommeted hole in the rear-fender inner structure. Carefully pull the rear-window-defroster and dome-light wires through the rear header—it's immediately ahead of the rear hatch.

The main harness has to come through to the lower passenger-side door-sill area. The large hole here provides access for the harness trunk. Work the bundle of wires out carefully. Don't jerk on it if it hangs up. You could pull off some connectors.

Wiring harness is sealed to firewall with a rubber grommet. These grommets often suffer from acid damage due to battery leakage—hole is under battery.

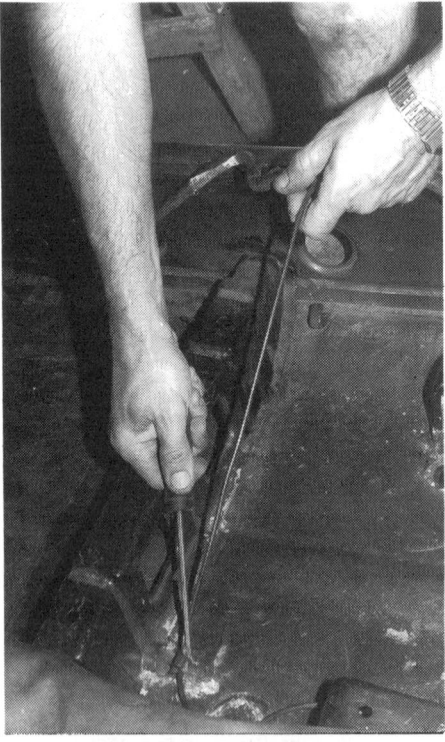

Clips hold parking-brake wiring to floorpan—also seat-belt interlock wiring and other harnesses.

Remove the parking-brake warning-light circuit. Then work the header wires out to the rear until the gang plug and connectors are accessible. Disconnect them and label the ends for future reference.

Keep fishing the body harness out through the fender-panel hole. If the rubber grommets are reusable, leave them on the harness. Then unclip wires from the driver's side rocker area and remove. The antenna lead pulls through the large lower hole in the fender panel on that side.

When all wiring is out, roughly reassemble the *complete* harness on your garage floor so you can make a visual inventory of its general condition. A little naptha on a rag to clean the various taped and colored branches is helpful. Check the connectors and adjacent wires. Look especially for frayed or burned insulation.

Engine heat can melt or embrittle neoprene insulation, but so can a short or an overloaded circuit. Either way, that strand will need attention. Sometimes electrician's tape or heat-shrink tubing can be used to make an acceptable repair. If the damage is severe, only a new length of the correct-gauge wire or a new connector will do the job.

The engine compartment and under-instrument-panel wiring are often turned into a restorer's nightmare by an amateur electricians' cutting and splicing. The addition of sound systems, driving lights, burglar alarms or musical horns that play *La Cucaracha* are often done by inexpert installers. Replacement wiring harnesses are expensive . . . if you can find them. I have renovated poor examples using wiring and connectors from another salvage harness, commercial crimping joints and lots of checking with a continuity meter. Consult the wiring diagram in your Datsun Technical Manual, label the ends you removed and good luck!

For detailed information on your Z's electrical system, including wiring-harness troubleshooting and restoration, read Chapter 8.

Console Removal—Z-cars use basically similar consoles, but there are differences. Removal is simple and fast.

Early Z: Before starting, disconnect the two choke cables from the carburetor linkage. If your car has the seldom-seen hand throttle, detach the end from the accelerator linkage and bracket. Choke cables must be threaded back through their boot as you remove the console. These early models incorporated the fuse block as well as console-mounting screws under the ash-tray panel.

Unscrew the gearshift knob from standard-shift cars; remove the setscrews in the handle of automatics and remove handle. Remove the lighter, lift this out and remove the machine screws. Remove the arm rest if your car has one.

At the rear of the console, remove the screws that secure it there, including the one in the coin box. Are you sure you have all of the screws out? OK, then ease the console up from the rear, letting it pivot out from under where the instrument panel was. Slip the boot up over the shift lever to free the console.

Carbureted Zs have two different choke-lever locations—the first style combined the choke/throttle/rear defroster switch in a panel, as above.

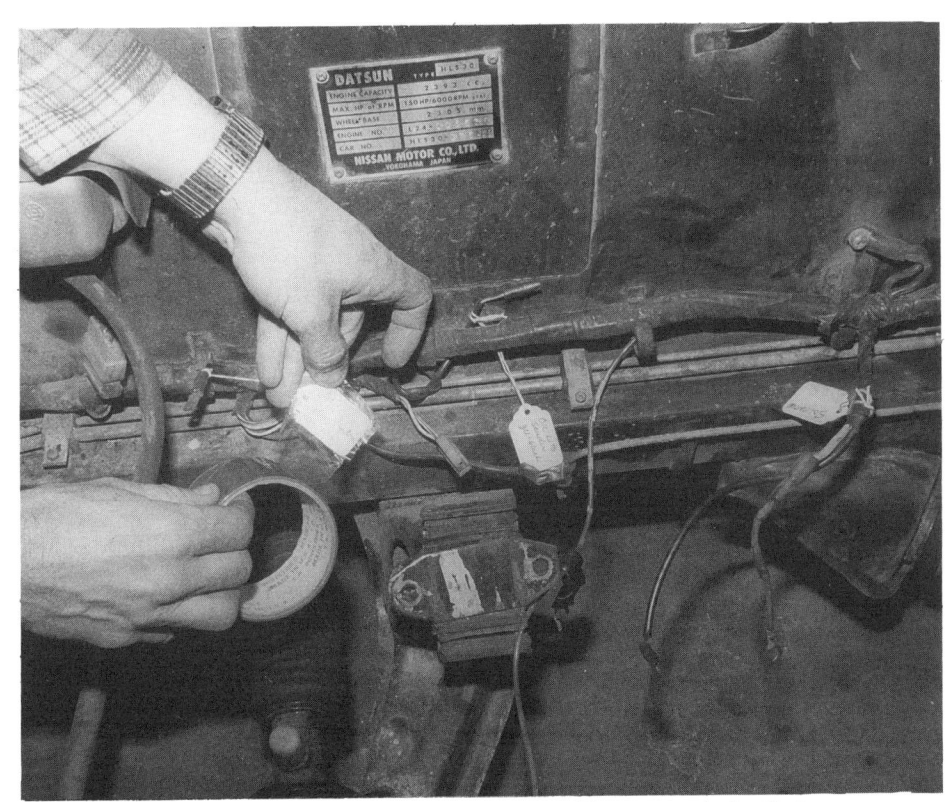

Note tags on engine-compartment wiring harness. Transparent plastic tape protects paper tags so they can even survive steamcleaning.

Using a very small flat-blade screwdriver, remove the choke lever and hand throttle if so equipped. The second style moved the choke forward even with the shifter. Remove these controls now.

Late Z: Consoles still have the three screws to the top rear, but are attached by two at the sides of the forward part. Remove the shifter knob, as explained above, as well as connections to the electrical harness. Depending on the year or equipment, there are radio connections, hazard flasher, choke-on and overheat warnings, automatic-transmission lights and lockouts, and rear-window-defroster switch. After the console is out, remove the radio.

On early 240Zs, there are two storage areas behind the seats. The passenger-side storage holds the wheel chocks, jack and handle; the driver-side storage hides the tool-kit pouch. Both have black-plastic covers. The hinge on former unscrews from the outside; that of the latter from within. The securing knobs unthread from their retainers with some persuasion.

Parking-brake lever mounted to right side of tunnel removes from inside car. It isn't likely you will confuse the warning-light lead with any other.

Parking Brake—Now is a good time to get the parking-brake-handle assembly out of your way. Its boot unsnaps from the transmission tunnel. Remove the brake-warning-light wire and take out the two bolts that hold the unit to the tunnel.

Parking-Brake Linkage—Underneath the car, remove the cotter key and pin that hold the linkage together at the rear. Then the brake linkage comes off the tunnel with two bolts. Back inside the passenger compartment, withdraw the complete assembly from the hole.

6 FRONT SUSPENSION, STEERING & BRAKES

Raise the front of the car and place jack stands under the front subframe. Remember, don't take any chances here. The car should be on a hard surface and supported with top-quality jack stands. Double-check that the jack stands will safely support the the car and that the stands don't restrict access to the front-suspension area.

Remove the lug nuts and front wheels. Soak all suspension-fastener threads with a good penetrant. More than one application may be required due to rust or filth accumulated over years of use.

Some fasteners may need extra effort to remove. Use discretion when applying oomph with a "cheater" so that you don't break bolts unnecessarily. An oxyaceytlene torch can be used to heat nuts to help loosen them

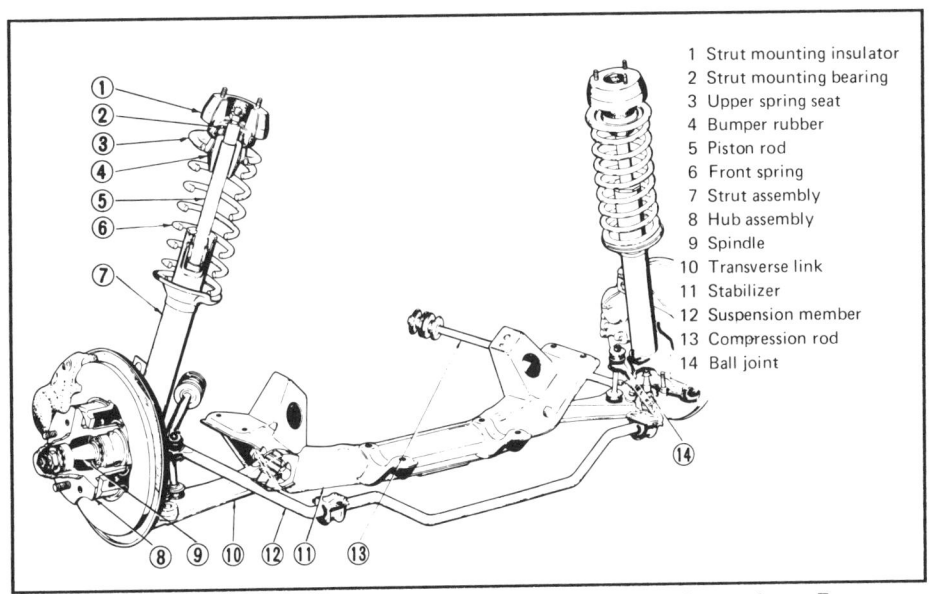

1 Strut mounting insulator
2 Strut mounting bearing
3 Upper spring seat
4 Bumper rubber
5 Piston rod
6 Front spring
7 Strut assembly
8 Hub assembly
9 Spindle
10 Transverse link
11 Stabilizer
12 Suspension member
13 Compression rod
14 Ball joint

Z-car front suspension: It shares some pieces with home-market sedans. Because it served all nine seasons of the S30 series, suspension must have been a sound design. Courtesy Nissan.

Flare-nut wrench is a must when loosening or tightening brake-line connections. Here caliper line is being disconnected at hose.

Stabilizer bar can stay with front suspension, but is easier to take it off before removing front-suspension assembly. Strut rod has already been removed from control arm.

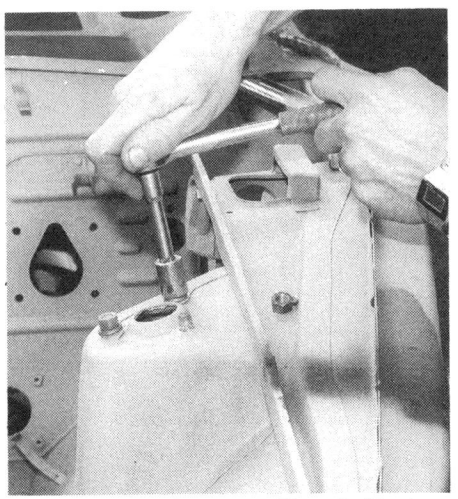

Strut-mount nuts come off next. Strut assemblies were secured to body with wire so they wouldn't fall when pulled free of spring tower, possibly damaging something—or someone.

81

Front-suspension crossmember is bolted through flange to underside of unit body. Brake hose has been removed—note standoff bracket. Floor jack is under jacking point in center of front-suspension crossmember; body is securely on jack stands.

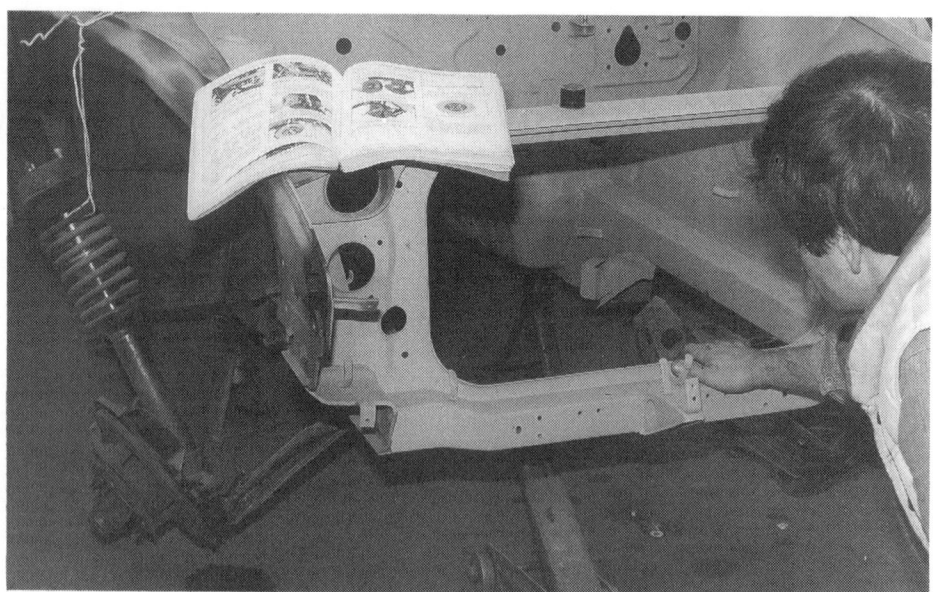

With everything unfastened, lower front suspension to the ground. Note Datsun Service Manual. Keep yours nearby.

if they aren't near rubber, paint, floor insulation or a fuel line. If they are still stubborn, use a chisel, nut-buster or hacksaw to split the nut. In extreme cases, drilling out the bolt will get the part loose at the expense of trashing both the nut and bolt. Be aware that you may inadvertently damage the component you are trying to remove if you're not careful. Above all, work safely.

Brake Lines—Before you can remove the front suspension, disconnect each front disc-brake hose at the bracket on the strut. Use a 10mm flare-nut wrench on the line side and have a rag underneath to catch old brake fluid. Pull the retaining clip after the flare nut is loose.

Tension/Compression Rods—Remove the nut and big washer from the rear of each rod. Then unbolt the forward ends from the lower control arm. Pull the rod forward and collect all the washers and bushings from the subframe-bracket end. If the bushings aren't in good condition, order new factory replacements or the ABS plastic/aluminum kits intended to improve handling.

Stabilizer Bar—Stabilizer bar, or *anti-sway bar* as it's sometimes called, has a link assembly at each end that attach the bar to the front-suspension control arms.

These stabilizer-bar links are typically in bad shape. If a wrench at each end of the link doesn't free it, clamp Vise-Grip pliers on the middle part of the shaft. Don't be surprised if the bolt breaks. Replace the link assemblies if they're if not in good condition.

Remove the frame side mounts for the stabilizer bar. Check the bushings on the bar.

MacPherson-Strut Assemblies—Remove all three nuts from the top of each strut housing. Don't worry about the coil spring, it will still be secured by the top of the strut assembly.

Suspension Crossmember—The crossmember must be supported by a

Stabilizer-bar link is dirty and corroded. Lots of penetrant should be used when disassembling under-car components.

Steering assembly is removed from crossmember. Locknuts on wire are saved so they can be reused.

Front Suspension & Brake 83

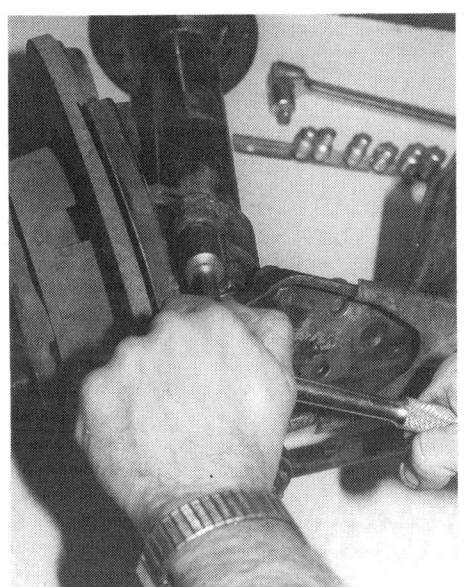

Struts are held to each steering arm with two bolts. Don't lose O-ring that seals bottom of strut to steering arm.

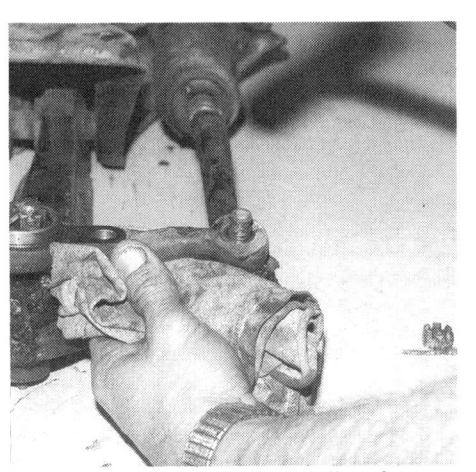

Remove cotter pin and castellated nut. Then support back side of steering arm and knock tie-rod ball-joint stud out of steering arm with a soft-faced hammer. If this doesn't work, you'll have to break it loose with a pickle fork. Note grease oozing from ball joint. Boot is long gone!

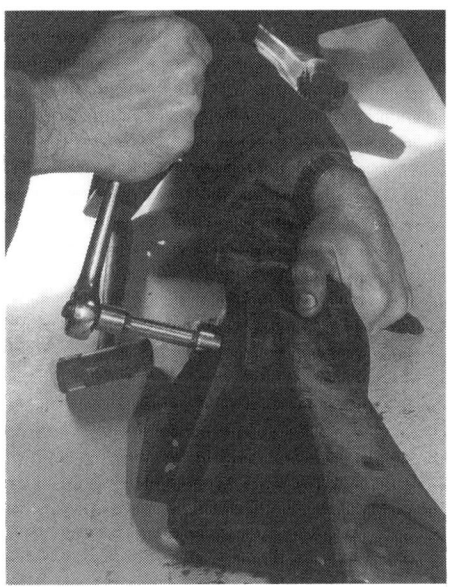

Remove nut from control-arm-pivot bolt and drive out bolt to free control arm. Note that control arm installs with long side of bushing to the rear.

jack before it is loosened from the subframe. Place a floor jack under the center of the crossmember.

If you are working alone, tether the tops of the strut assemblies to the body with wire. This will help keep the struts from falling to the sides and causing the steering knuckles to reach too great of an angle as the strut drops down. It will also keep you from getting a rap on the head.

Now remove the bolts and nuts in the wheel well where the crossmember attaches to the body structure. There is a stiffener plate on the underside of the subframe flange above the washer and nut.

When the assembly is free, lower it with the jack. Remove the wires and roll the crossmember-and-suspension assembly out from under the car. How is that for a simple, but effective front suspension? It is light enough for one person to set up on a bench for better access.

Struts—At the bottom of the *knuckle arm* (steering arm) are the *fixing bolts*, as the Service Manual so charmingly calls them. Remove these to free the strut assembly. They can be difficult to break loose, as you may have discovered. There is an O-ring at the bottom of both strut cylinders, apparently to keep water from collecting around the ball-joint stud. Set the struts aside.

Steering Gear—All Zs have rack-and-pinion steering. To remove the steering gear, take the cotter pins out of the tie-rod ball-joint studs and remove the nuts. Solidly support the back side of the steering knuckle (steering arm), then give the end of the ball-joint stud a good rap with a soft-faced hammer or mallet. If it doesn't yield to the hammer, don't beat it to death. Use a suitable puller such as a *pickle fork* and separate the two.

Z-car tie rods are mirror-images of one another. The driver side is marked **L** on the round end; the passenger side is marked **R**.

Note: The driver-side tie rod has left-hand threads! Count the number of threads showing on each side. Record this so you can return the tie rods to these positions to achieve the same basic toe-in.

The steering-gear assembly is mounted to the suspension crossmember with two rubber-insulated compression clamps. A locknut is used on top of each of the four captive nuts to lock the clamp bolts. Don't try to remove the weldnuts. Remove the locknuts before you attempt to unscrew the bolts. Access to the bolts is gained through two access holes in bottom of the crossmember. Remove the bolts, then the gear.

Rack-Stopper Assembly—This is not found on all Z-cars. Apparently it was an interim fix to remedy or prevent some steering-gear problem.

A rack-stopper doesn't appear in the 1970 240Z Service Manual. Also, the illustration in the parts book is upside down. If yours has this part, make sure you reposition it correctly.

Steering Arm—Remove the cotter pin from the control-arm ball-joint stud, then remove the castellated nut. It may require some leverage, especially if water got in and the nut and stud rusted.

Control Arms—These are retained at the inner pivot on each side with a large bolt and Nylon locknut. They are often frozen in place. Extra leverage on the wrenches may be required to break them loose, followed by a hammer and punch to knock out the bolt.

The large, bonded-rubber bushing inner pivot must be pressed out. A press becomes a necessity here. Datsun special tools aren't necessary for doing this job. A deepwell socket acting as the punch, a pipe collar for backup and a spacer to keep the control arm from being collapsed work just as well.

If you don't have an arbor press, hydraulic press or very large bench

After you unbolt ball joints from control arm, push out bushings. Dave uses hydraulic press to push out control-arm bushings.

Separate rotor from hub. A few taps on chisel frees it once bolts are out. Lots of meat is left on rotor—it's never been turned.

vise and an extra set of hands, get this job done at a local shop. For now push out the bushings. Just make sure you push on the small end. Replace them with new ones after you've refurbished the control arms using the same method, but in reverse.

Ball Joint—Remove the four bolts that hold the ball joint to the control arm. Support the steering arm on something solid and strike the ball-joint stud with a solid blow. This should dislodge it from the tapered bore in the steering-arm forging. If you're going to reuse the ball joint, place a brass punch against the end of the stud and strike it with the hammer. This will keep the threads from being damaged.

Ball joints are not expensive, so replace them unless yours are practically new.

Note: Only 280Z ball joints are available as of this writing. Earlier models must use the late steering arm or have their ball-joint-stud holes enlarged by reaming.

Spindle—Pop off the grease cup, then pull out the cotter key and unscrew the spindle nut. The hub and rotor should pull right off, bringing the large washer and outside wheel-bearing roller assembly and inner race. Remove the inside bearing similarly. Mark the hub-and-rotor assembly so you'll know which side it came off.

With the hub's lug side facing down, use a large punch and hammer to drive out the outboard outer bearing race. Make sure the punch is solidly against the back side of the bearing race. There are two reliefs in the bearing-seating flange that allow the punch to seat against it. If the bearing race doesn't feel like it's budging, make sure the punch is against the bearing and not the hub flange. Work the bearing race out by alternating from side to side. Once the outer bearing race is out, turn over the wheel hub and drive out the inboard outer race using the same process. Remove the inside inner race from the spindle.

The inboard grease seal will come out with the bearing race. Clean the old bearings and inspect for abnormal wear or lack of lubrication. Replace anything that looks questionable—these bearings are not expensive. If yours are good enough to reuse, keep each individual bearing cage together with its own races. *Never* mix bearing components. Replace the seal. Now is a good time to clean the old grease out of the hub cavity and the cover.

Brake Rotor—Take out the four bolts holding each rotor to its hub. With the rotor clamped in a vise—please use soft jaws to avoid scarring the friction surface—separate the hub and rotor with a large chisel.

Work around the hub/rotor, wedging them apart at the wheel studs. Once separated, mark each hub and rotor so they can be rejoined and installed on the same "corner." These should be matched with spindles, but rotors and calipers can be mixed.

Coil Springs—Back to the suspension-strut assemblies and the curse of Mr. MacPherson. Even though the MacPherson strut does a great job of suspending an automobile, maintenance procedures such as changing shock absorbers require that you remove the coil springs. Z-cars run around on long-worn-out shocks just because of the hassle and expense of working with MacPherson struts. Compared to conventional shocks, struts are a lot of work and constitute a hazard because of stored energy in the compressed spring. However, they aren't impossible. As with any job you must use the right tools and a fair amount of common sense.

The tool you'll need for disassembling the spring and shock/strut is a screw-type spring compressor. The compressor illustrated in the Datsun Service Manual is a special tool.

Unless you can promote something like it from a dealer, you'll have to settle for the universal type. Although one can be purchased, it makes more sense to rent a spring compressor for a one-time application. These are sized to work with the largest automotive-style coil springs, so they'll be larger than necessary for compressing your relatively light Z-car springs. Look for two features: The smaller the end hooks are, the easier it will be to use. And because rented tools tend to get abused, make sure the threads are in good shape!

With the strut on the bench, position both compressor hooks to include as many coils as possible. This may require disassembling the clamps to work the end hooks into place.

Hot Tip: I use Vise-Grip pliers on the spring wire just *down-coil* from each compressor hook. This prevents the hook from sliding down the spiral of the coils, letting the clamp assemblies slide together—and the coil from springing out like a "Slinky" on the now-unclamped side. Scary!

Once you have the hooks and clamps positioned to your satisfaction, alternately tighten the clamp nuts until the coil no longer is putting pressure on the spring seats.

If you're satisfied everything is stable and secure, remove the 19mm locknut on the top of the strut shaft. Put short lengths of rubber vacuum hoses over the studs on the upper spring seat to protect the threads. Then, using a big screwdriver as a lever spanning two of the studs and a socket on the nut, break the nut loose and thread it off. Now the spring seat assembly—consisting of the metal seat, a bearing and bushing, and a jounce bumper on early Zs—can be removed.

Unless you are going to put the spring right back on, unload the spring using the same gradual technique as when compressing it. It will extend to its unloaded length, so more unscrewing will be necessary. When both springs are off, place them on a level surface and visually check for uniform height. A coil that is a little shorter indicates it should be replaced. If so, replace them both. Springs should be replaced as a pair.

Shock Absorbers—I would show how to rebuild the stock strut, but it has been a long time since the factory

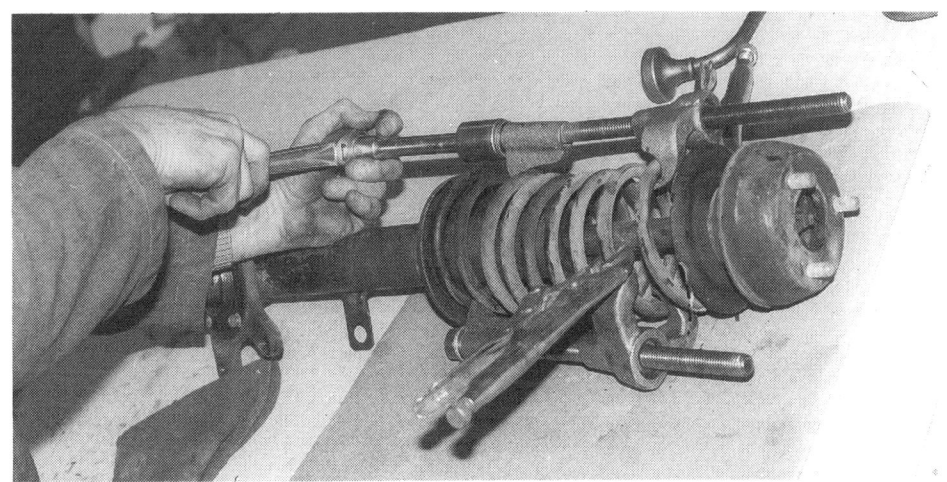

Coil-spring compressors slide "down hill" on spring helix. This can be prevented by clamping Vise-Grips onto "down-hill" side of spring coil. Slit short sections of rubber hose, then put one between each Vise-Grip jaw and coil to protect spring.

has stocked all of the parts necessary to renew the original strut. Any such parts you might find would be from obsolete dealer inventory (New Old Stock, or NOS), so if you are fortunate enough to find all of the necessary parts, you'll have to rely on the Technical Manual's instructions.

Nissan recommends using aftermarket-replacement strut cartridges—a highly economical alternative, considering the wide variety of types and manufacturers competing for your business. As a bonus, you have the option of choosing firmer, high-performance units.

If your car still has the original shocks, they will undoubtedly be worn out. To remove, place two pin punches or equivalent into the two holes in the gland packing. Then, with the strut held firmly, place two big screwdrivers between the strut and drifts and unscrew the gland packing from the strut tube. Pull the rod and shock cylinder out of the strut and empty the shock fluid into an appropriate container.

If you have a tired aftermarket cartridge, use a large wrench—a pipe wrench is fine if the cartridge is to be trashed—and unscrew it.

280Zs should have an accordion-style neoprene dust cover mounted to the upper spring seat. Sometimes damaged covers are not replaced when strut cartridges are installed. Do your Z a favor and renew the dust covers now—they are a good idea. Automobile manufacturers aren't in the habit of spending money for unnecessary items. And these were installed later in the Z-car's life, so that should tell us something, too. Installing 280Z dust covers on a 240Z or 260Z will require 280Z upper spring seats.

Repeat this process with the other spring-and-strut assembly. Inspect all suspension parts closely before you declare them roadworthy. If you suspect a crucial part such as a steering arm or spindle, take it to a machine shop and have it checked for cracks by Magnafluxing or dye testing.

Fast-ratio steering arms are available—these Nissan Competition approved parts use 280Z ball joints. If you plan on substituting these on your early Z, be ready for a substantial increase in steering effort. Without power steering, you may find that it is unacceptable for around-town driving.

Front Brakes
Calipers

While you're rebuilding the front calipers, take this opportunity to detail them for eye appeal. The latter isn't necessary, but requires little effort compared to the improvement in looks. It also makes sense to rebuild the rear calipers at the same time because the same tools, materials and processes will be the same.

Disassembly—Remove the steel brake lines. Use your 10mm flare-nut wrench to do this and to loosen the bleeder tap. While holding the bleeder over a catch can, flush out the old fluid by applying low-pressure air

86 How to Restore Your Datsun Z-Car

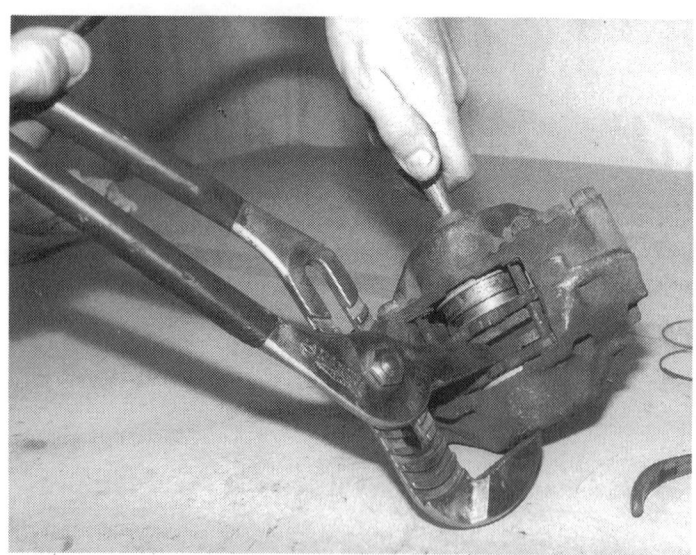

Hold in opposite brake pad with Channellock pliers while forcing out each piston with compressed air. Boots and retaining rings are off and pads, pins and anti-squeals are quickly removed.

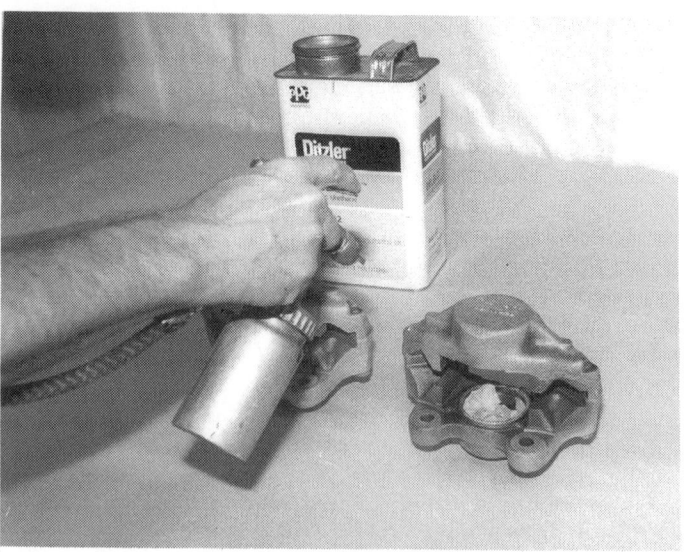

After calipers are completely cleaned and glass-beaded, give them a light coat of catalyzed clear with flattening-agent added. This helps retain the new cast look.

to the line fitting. When it's all out, retighten the fitting.

The piston retaining rings come off before the pads. To get the old pistons and seals out, use compressed air again.

Caution: Don't hook your thumb over the edge of an unrestrained piston like the man shown in the 240Z Service Manual. When a piston comes free, it is with surprising force. To get an idea of what would happen picture yourself slamming two bricks together with your thumbs in between!

With the pads still in place, apply air pressure until one breaks free. Clamp it, then force out the second piston. Now pull the spring clips out and free the caliper pins, anti-squeal springs and pads. The pistons should be free now. Be careful not to scar the chromed-piston surface if more persuasion is needed to remove one. Clean the pistons thoroughly and inspect for corrosion or pitting.

Look inside the piston bores in the caliper. Using a toothpick or some other non-metallic tool, remove the piston sealing ring. Likewise inspect the bore walls for rust.

Clean Up—Any parts that will be replaced by those in the rebuild kit may be disposed of now. I clean the remaining caliper parts by soaking them in fresh carburetor cleaner. It is not necessary to separate the caliper halves. In fact it's best not to break the internal fluid-passage seal between the two halves.

If any parts are beyond repair, get a new or rebuilt caliper assembly.

Detailing—A nice touch you can make at this stage is to bead-blast the caliper forgings. Before you do, though, all orifices must be positively

Silicone-base brake fluid won't harm paint, including clearcoat. Clean hands here: Lubricate cylinder and seals with fluid before installing pistons. Seal appears to be way too large, but of course, isn't.

Piston goes in next, then dust cover and retaining ring. Repeat with opposite piston and replace bleeder and cover.

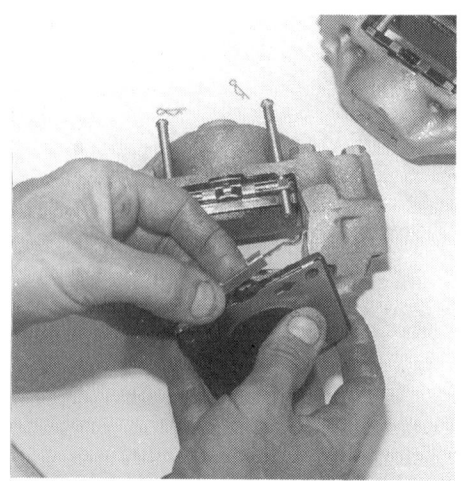

Reassemble pads and attendant hardware. I buy new steel parts or replate original ones.

plugged and the cylinder area should be completely masked to form a positive barrier to prevent abrasive from entering the interior passages.

After the caliper is spotless, lightly but thoroughly coat it to prevent corrosion and contamination. I use several thin coats of DAU 82 DelGlo clear, a tough acrylic-urethane top coat that requires a catalyst. Unless you want a wet-look finish, add a bit of DX 685 Flattening Agent. This will give a low-gloss finish like new metal. An alternative, especially if you don't wish to glassbead the calipers, is to use Eastwood Hi-Temp Stainless Steel Coating. Just be sure the caliper is totally clean and free of grease and fluid.

I send out the rest of the brake parts that aren't replaced with new ones to be replated. New parts are often no more expensive. Check prices and make your decision. It helps to have everything—kit, pads, lines and so forth—on hand and ready to reassemble.

Polish the caliper bore with 600-grit sandpaper or 000 steel wool and blow out with compressed air. If you find pitting in the surface the piston seal rides against, *stop*. Don't take chances on losing your brakes. Get another caliper.

If the calipers are clean and in good condition, reassemble them. Start by wiping a bit of brake fluid inside the bore. Then carefully position the rubber seal in its groove. It may seem too big, but it will fit just right.

Piston—Coat the side of each piston with some clean brake fluid or grease supplied with the brake kit. Insert it, cup side out, gently into the cylinder bore and push it past the seal. Don't force it. Do all four at this time. Follow by installing the dust covers and retaining rings.

Anti-Squeal Shims & Springs—Assemble these onto the new pads and insert into the caliper. Strive to keep the pad face free of grease and fluid from your hands. Put just a drop of oil on the retaining pins and push through the pad assembly. Secure pin with clips.

Bleeder Taps—New ones look and work better . . . and they are cheap. Run them in finger-tight, then install the dust caps. This completes caliper reconditioning. Wrap each in a plastic bag and store them until you're ready to install your "new" calipers.

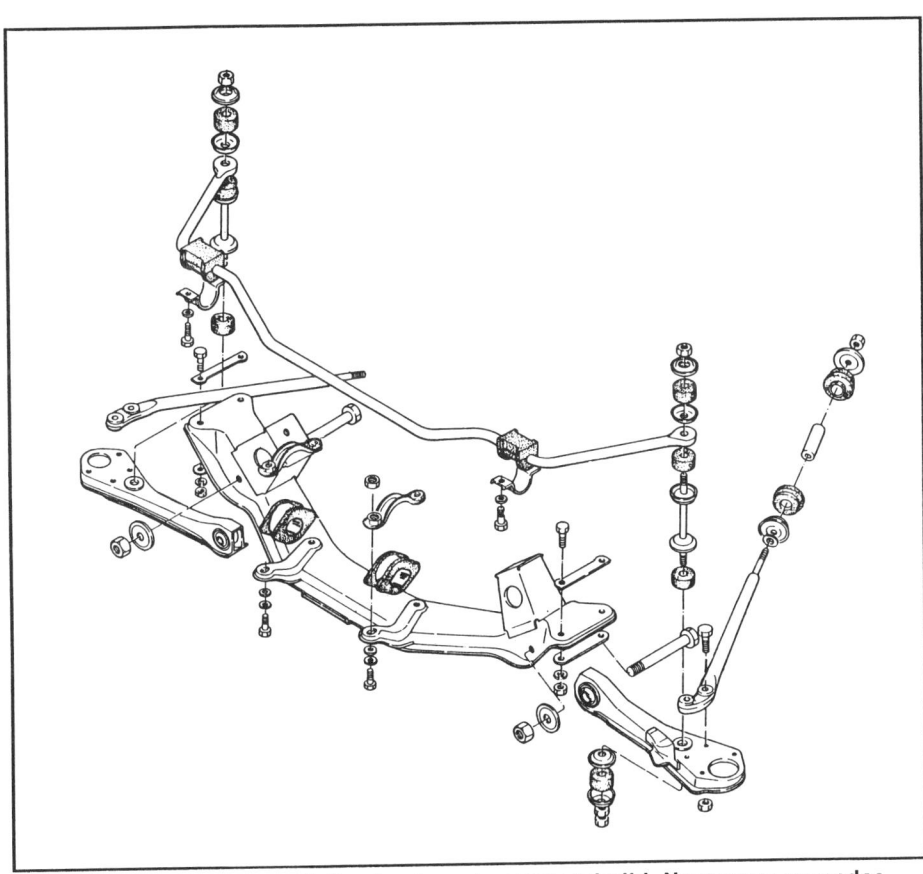

Front suspension is beautifully simple and easy to rebuild. Numerous upgrades are available for better feel, handling.

Front-Suspension

Suspension Refinishing—Refurbish all suspension parts as I describe in the rear-suspension section, page 106. Parts that normally wear should be evaluated and refurbished or replaced as needed.

Lower Control Arms—New inner-pivot bushings should be installed. Although these can be driven in, it's better to press in the bushings using process described for removing the old ones, page 84.

The bushings are necked down slightly. The shorter, small-diameter end installs forward relative to its in-car position. With the left control arm positioned right-side up and the ball-joint end to the left, the bushing's small end goes in the back side of the control arm. The right control arm is the same, except the ball-joint end is to the right.

To make the bushing installation easier, lightly coat the outer shell of the bushing with oil or grease, then press in the bushing. Install both, then wipe any grease or oil off of the control arms.

Attach control arms to the sub-member, small end of the bushing forward. Coat the attaching bolts with lubricant and insert it from the rear. Install the Nylon locknut—it doesn't need a washer—and torque to spec.

Ball Joints—Fasten these to the control arms using bolts that have **9** on the head. They are crucial to the operation of your Z's suspension and steering, so torque carefully to specification.

Datsun went to a slightly larger stud for the 280Z ball joint. So why should this concern you if you have a 240Z or 260Z? Well, only 280Z ball joints are available. The later part is heavier but constitutes only a *conditional interchange* for the early steering arm. This means either the early steering-arm ball-joint taper must be reamed larger to accommodate the larger ball joint or 280Z arms must be used. Paying a machine shop generally costs less than buying new arms. Sound used arms may represent a saving over either, however. Just in case you were wondering, simple drilling *is not* a substitute! A taper reamer

88 How to Restore Your Datsun Z-Car

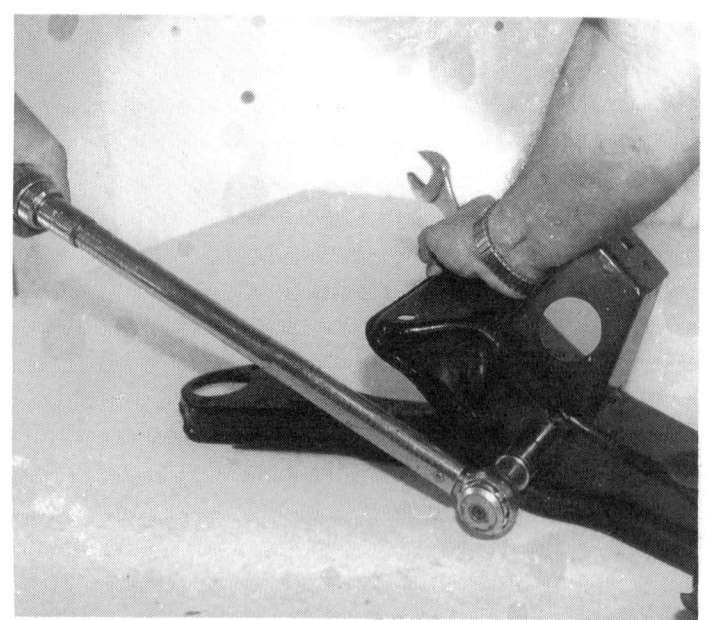

Front-suspension installation begins with bolting control arms to suspension crossmember.

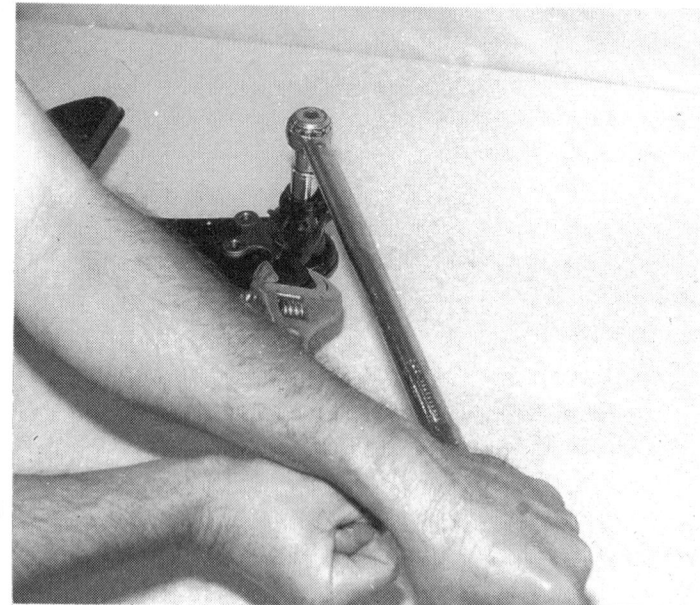

New ball-joint is bolted on control arm. Then steering arm is installed and nut is torqued to spec. Lock castellated nut with cotter pin.

must be used. The smaller ball-joint stud uses a 17mm castellated nut; the larger uses a 19mm nut.

Place the arm on the ball-joint stud and tighten the castellated nut. Keep the steering arm from turning while you torque the nut 40—54 ft-lb.

If you had your 240Z or 260Z arms reamed and you can't get the cotter key in because the cotter-key hole is below the castellations, remove the ball joint and have the machinist check it again. Take both arms and joints with you.

Steering-Gear Housing—The Z-car rack-and-pinion steering doesn't wear much as long as lubricant is maintained and is not contaminated in some way. Early and late boxes are similar, but don't share components and are not interchangeable. One reason is the rubber bushings used to insulate the housing from the suspension crossmember are different. Many drivers complained the 240Z's bushings allowed too much lateral steering-box movement, especially as the rubber aged. This was corrected by shimming and stiffer replacement bushings.

Left- and right-side bushings are different. The one with the oval inner cross section installs over the alloy boss on the driver's side; the thicker one with the circular hole goes to the

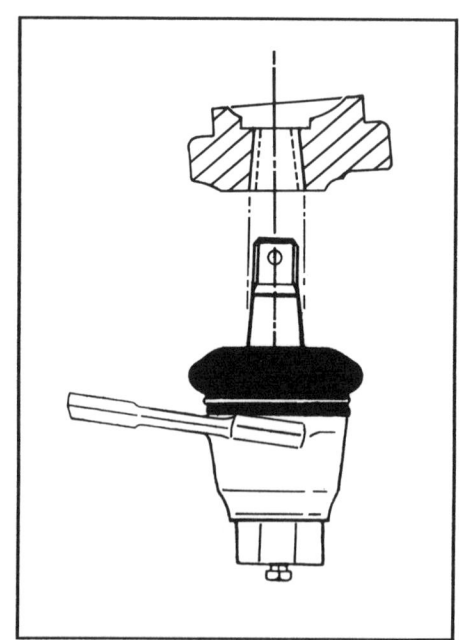

Relative size difference between early and late steering-arm bores. Either ream out early arm—bore indicated by dashed lines—or substitute 280Z arms. Replacement ball-joints are no longer available for the small-bore early arms.

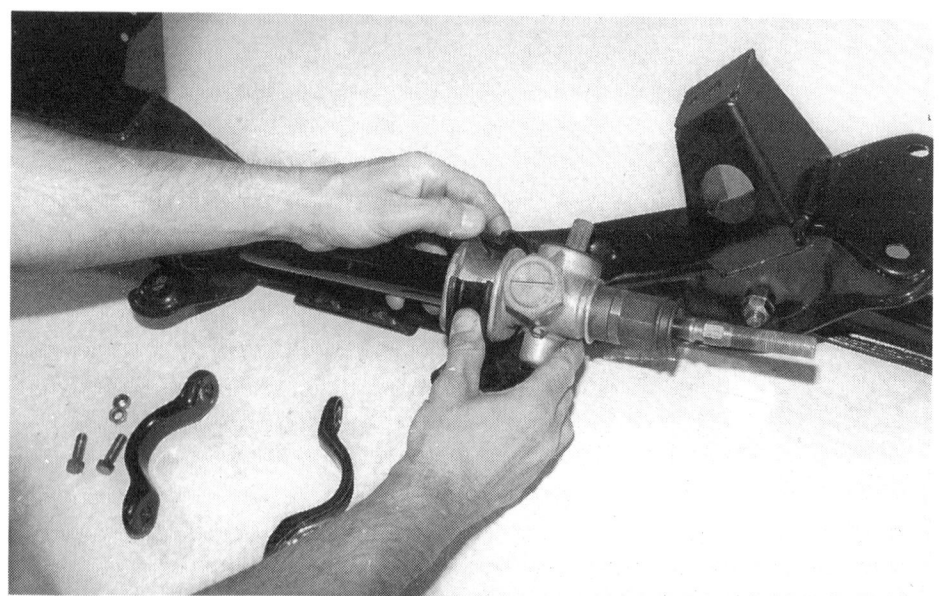

Steering-gear bushings spread open, fit between mounting-boss flanges. Although not visually identifiable, replacement bushings have a firmer-than-stock compound, giving more-positive steering action.

Front Suspension & Brake

Push boots over flanges at ends of steering-gear housing. Use clamps to retain them in place. Install jam nuts, then thread on tie rods so they are in approximately the same position as they were before teardown. This will have to do until front end can be aligned.

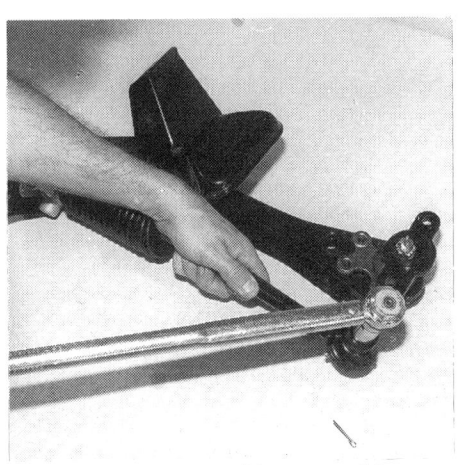

Tie-rod ball-joint stud is torqued to steering arm, then locked with cotter pin.

Rack stopper can be positioned and clamped to steering-gear housing. Don't collapse the tube while tightening it.

passenger's side. Open up each bushing and wrap around the correct boss. Early bushings are split at the center, late ones are off-center. Lay the steering gear in its saddles and install the caps with bolts from the bottom side.

Eyeball the housing for alignment before you tighten the bolts—make sure it's not cocked or twisted. Once torqued to spec, snug the locknuts against the nuts. I coat these with clear lacquer or grease to prevent rusting—the concave locknuts hold water.

Lube Reservoir—On early Zs, there is a fragile plastic thimble that threads into the housing, ostensibly to supply lubricant to the steering gears. Replace this now or wait until after the engine is installed to preclude accidentally snapping it off.

Boots—Install the accordion boots that go over the ends of the housing. Slip the big end of the boot over the lip on the end of the housing. The small end just clears the 13mm flats on the ends. Moisten the end with brake fluid to lubricate it for ease of assembly.

Some very early Zs had no boot retainers. Spring-type clamps at each end and one that corresponds with the groove in the inner socket were used. One later type is similar, but uses a hose-clamp-type band that tightens with a screw on the large inner end. This can be slipped on before the boot is installed or opened up and installed afterwards. Finally,

Datsun went to a rubber O-ring style that has two pull-rings.

Tierods—These are either marked **L** for the driver's side or **R** for the passenger's side. If you don't remember, you'll find out while installing them that the driver's-side tie rod has left-hand threads.

Lightly coat the threads on the steering-gear stubs with oil or grease.

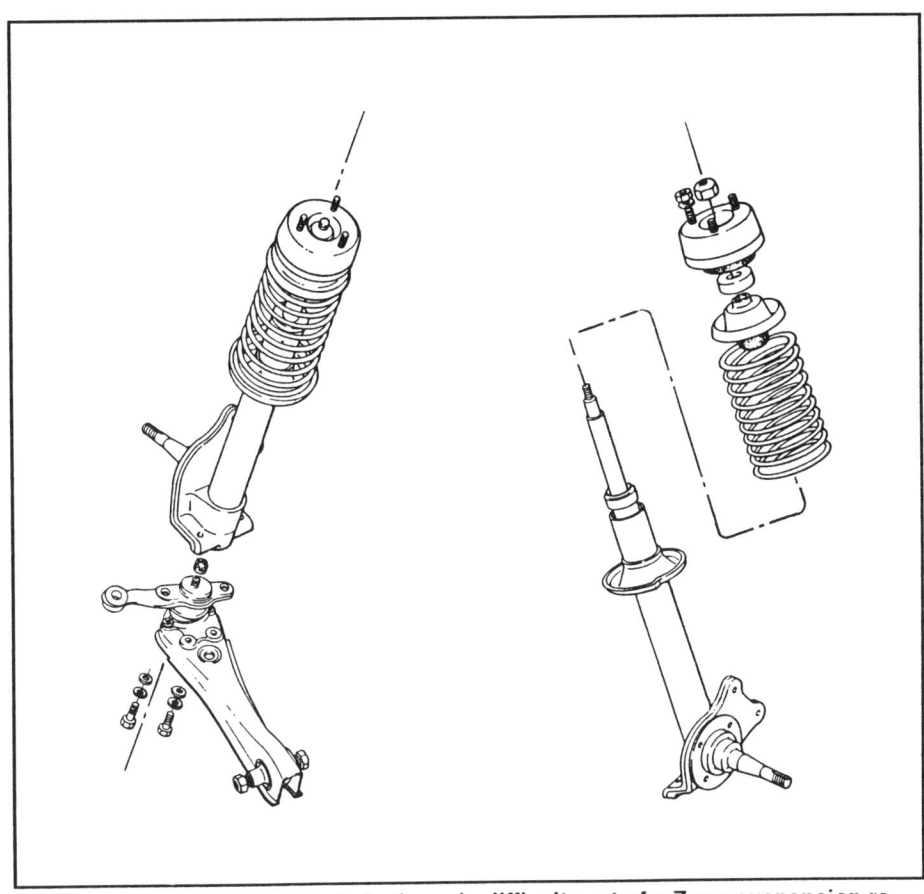

Assembling MacPherson struts is the only difficult part of a Z-car suspension rebuild. You'll need a spring compressor again and O-rings for base of struts.

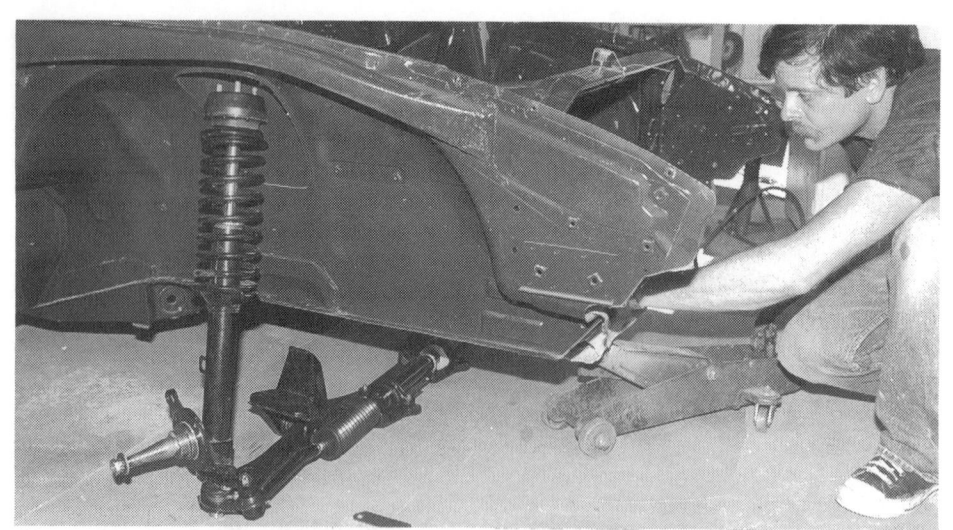

After under-fender metal is repainted, suspension-and-crossmember assembly can be raised back into place. It will hang from the struts until crossmember can be bolted to body structure. Be sure reinforcing plates are in correct positions. Check drawing, page 211, for reinforcing-plate positioning.

Orient "hockey-stick" end of strut rods to control arms and secure with bolts.

Spin the tie-rod locknuts on, then thread on the tie rods. Don't tighten the locknuts yet. If you noted the number of threads showing when you removed the tie rods, use that as a rough setting until you can have the car aligned by a front-end specialist. As a rule of thumb, between 8 and 10 threads is typical.

Now that the inner ends are on the rack, attach the outer ends to the steering arms. Insert the ball-joint studs into the bottom of the steering arms, install the castellated nuts, torque to spec and secure each with a new cotter key. Bend long leg of the cotter key over the top of the ball-joint stud and the other down over the nut.

Rack Stopper—Install the little stabilizer that fastened to the steering-gear housing. Load the rubber bumper firmly against the surface of the suspension crossmember. Tighten the Nylon locknuts. Reference the punch marks you made to align it to the gear.

Front Struts—Bolt the MacPherson strut assemblies to the control arms. Don't forget the rubber O-ring that seals the bottom chamfer of the strut tube to the ball joint. The parts are self-aligning and need only to be bolted together.

Springs & Shocks: The installation of these is virtually identical to that of the rear struts with one important exception.

Strut-mounting bearing: Where the rear struts have a spacer ring under the mounting insulator, the fronts require a bearing here to allow the struts to rotate when the front wheels are steered. Pack the recess created by the inner bearing race and shock rod with grease before installing the mounting insulator.

Install Front Suspension—Now that the needed steering and suspension components are hung on the crossmember, move the assembly under the front of the car.

Getting the strut-and-crossmember unit in place can be done two ways: raising the crossmember to the car or lowering the car onto the crossmember. Don't use the second method if your engine and transmission is in the car. Datsun didn't mean for the front crossmember to support the load. Let's look first at the method I illustrate.

Using a floor jack, raise the assembly until it meets all mounting points at the frame rails and towers. As you should always do before working underneath, check that the body is firmly supported.

You'll need someone to operate the jack or keep the assembly from tipping over. Or tie the strut tops to the body with wire as I suggested on disassembly. Guide the spring-seat studs into the three holes at each side and thread on the nuts.

Attach the crossmember to the frame-rail brackets and secure with two bolts per side inserted down through, the scalloped plate on top with its straight edge outboard, the other plate underneath, and a flat washer, lock washer and nut on each bolt.

As an alternative, position the suspension directly under its mounting points. Then using a floor jack under the front crossmember, lower the body to meet the suspension. Replace the jack stands as soon as the unit is in place.

Guide the spring-seat studs up through the holes in the strut tower and thread on the nuts. Shim the suspension up from the floor—I use a few scraps of lumber—until the mounting holes line up with the pad on one of the frame rails. Put the scalloped reinforcing plate—straight edge out—in place and start the bolts in from above. Position the straight-sided reinforcing plate below, along with the large flat washer and lock washer, and start the nuts.

Repeat with the other side. Then torque the suspension crossmember bolts. Torque the six strut nuts.

Strut Rods—In order, place the flat washer, cupped washer, rubber cushion and tubular collar onto the rod and seat on the machined shoulder. Insert the threaded end into its cupped hole beneath the frame and position the forward end over the control arm so the holes match.

The curved end should bend toward the front of the car. With a bolt

Front Suspension & Brake 91

You'll need some help here. With Jerry helping push strut rod into its socket, rubber biscuits and washers are reinstalled. I'm using my big Channellock pliers to compress rubber biscuits enough to get nut started on threaded end.

New stabilizer-bar links are inexpensive. Tighten link nuts until rubber starts to bulge so they assume shape of a barrel. Then install jam nuts.

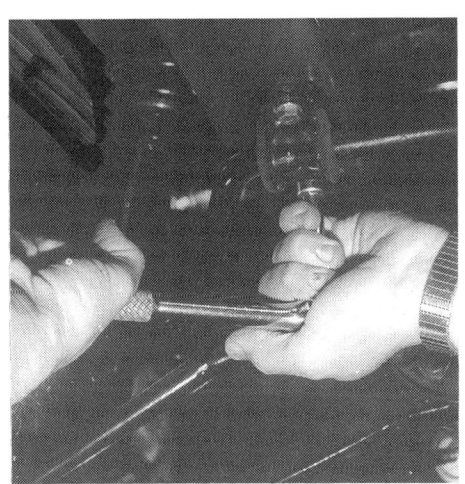

Using clamps, bolt stabilizer bar to underside of front body members. Rubber bushings can be replaced with stiffer, higher-performance items at nominal cost.

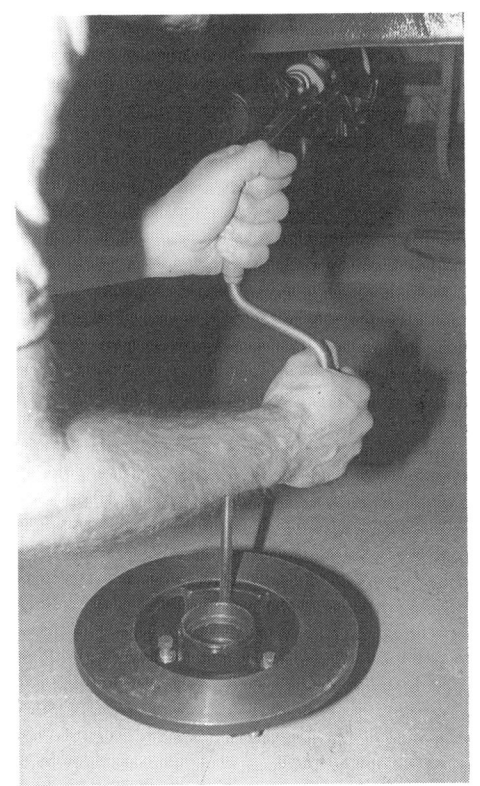

Freshly machined rotor bolted to hub. Early and late rotors interchange, but early-style hat is slotted. Later one is solid.

Installing new wheel bearings may not be imperative, but is inexpensive insurance. Use high-temperature grease regardless of whether you install new bearings. Just make sure your hands are clean when repacking bearings.

in hand, push the control arm forward until you can drop in the bolt. The inner-pivot bushing will resist, so make sure the car won't move forward and fall on you! Drop in the other bolt, run on the nuts and torque them.

Back at the rear of the compression rod, slip another rubber cushion and cupped washer on and compress them enough so you can start the Nylon locknut. The cushions, of necessity, provide firm resistance, so you may need to clamp the cushion assembly to expose enough threads so you can get the nut started. Run the nut down until it bottoms on the sleeve. This automatically preloads the cushions. Torque the nut.

Stabilizer Bar—Wrap the split rubber bushings around the bar where they will mount to the frame rails. With the flat reinforcing plates in place, fit the brackets over the bushings and bolt them in place.

Assemble the inner cupped washers and rubber grommets onto each stabilizer-bar link. Fit this assembly between the hole in the control arm and the eye on the bar. Add a washer, grommet, another washer and locknut to the upper end. Repeat sequence at the other end of the link below the control arm, but thread on two conventional nuts. The second is to lock the first nut. Tighten the link until the rubber grommets bulge slightly—don't try to bottom the thread. When you estimate the links are tight enough, jam the nuts together. Then tighten the locknut—you may have to hold the link with Vise-Grip pliers. Try not to scar it.

Rotor & Hub Installation—Turn your attention to the rotors. I abrasive-blast and paint the rotors before having them refaced, but the reverse will suffice.

Have your rotors checked, particularly for runout and thickness. You can see if they're grooved. If there's a problem, have them refaced to make their surfaces smooth and parallel. Early and late rotors aren't identical,

92 How to Restore Your Datsun Z-Car

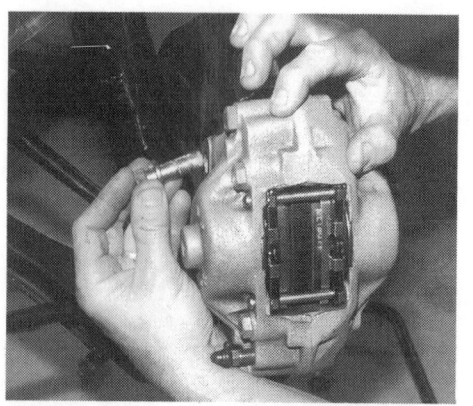

Slip good-as-new caliper over rotor and bolt it to suspension upright.

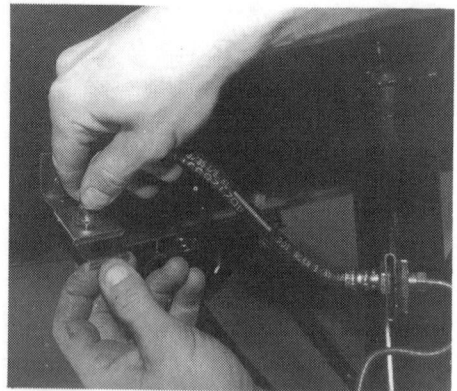

Brake line and hose going back on. Clips secure hose ends to mounting brackets. Use flare-nut wrenches to tighten line-to-hose connections.

but do interchange if yours end up being too thin to be safe.

Assemble rotor to the wheel hub with the four bolts. If you want to reuse your old bearings, thoroughly clean them in solvent. Be careful not to mix up a bearing cage with another's bearing races. When they come clean, wipe off and dry with air.

Don't let the bearing spin as you blow it off. This will damage the bearing. Check the individual rollers and races on which they run. Any discernable irregularities such as pitting means you must replace them. They are so inexpensive it would be false economy not to do so. New seals are a must in either case.

With the new or cleaned bearings in hand, pack the bearing cages with a good high-temperature wheel-bearing grease. Work with one bearing at a time to prevent mixing components. New bearings are factory-lubed, but I see if they will take a bit more. But don't make the common mistake of overpacking the bearings. This can also cause bearing damage. A palm full of grease is the typical amount a front-wheel bearing should take.

After you have one set of bearings lubed, put a bit of grease in the inboard side of the hub. Drive the outer bearing race into position with the large inside diameter (ID) facing out. I use a large socket and a big washer in lieu of the factory's special driver. Turn over the hub and repeat with the outboard outer race. Using a spatula, pack the inner recesses of the hub with grease. Install the packed inboard bearing and its inner race into the inboard side. Pack the lip of the grease seal with grease and drive it into place.

Cover the newly assembled hub to keep out dirt and dust while you assemble the other one.

Brake Baffle—If they aren't already on, install these sheet-metal parts onto the spindles.

Thoroughly coat the spindle from its base to the threads with grease. Take care that your greasy hands don't transfer dirt or grit to the bearing surfaces. Frequently wipe off your hands on a clean rag.

Collect the parts necessary for installing the hub and rotor assemblies: outer bearing and inner race, inner wheel bearing, washer and castellated nut. With the big bearing in place, carefully slip the hub assembly onto the spindle. Install the outer bearing, washer and castellated nut in sequence and tighten the nut to seat the bearings. Rotate the hub as you tighten, loosen and retighten the nut.

Back the nut off until the rotor spins freely. Then retorque the nut to 18—22 ft-lb. Back off the nut again about 1/8 of a turn or slightly more until a castellation in the nut aligns with the hole in the spindle. Install the cotter key and bend over the legs to lock it in place. Check for severe drag. New bearings will take a bit of rolling to get settled, old ones usually less.

Put a gob of grease into the bearing

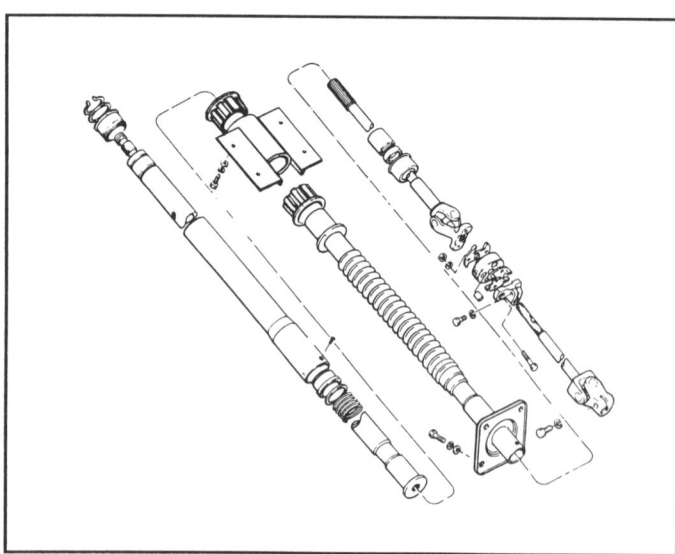

Early-style steering column exploded view: Mounting to dash is unique with rubber collars.

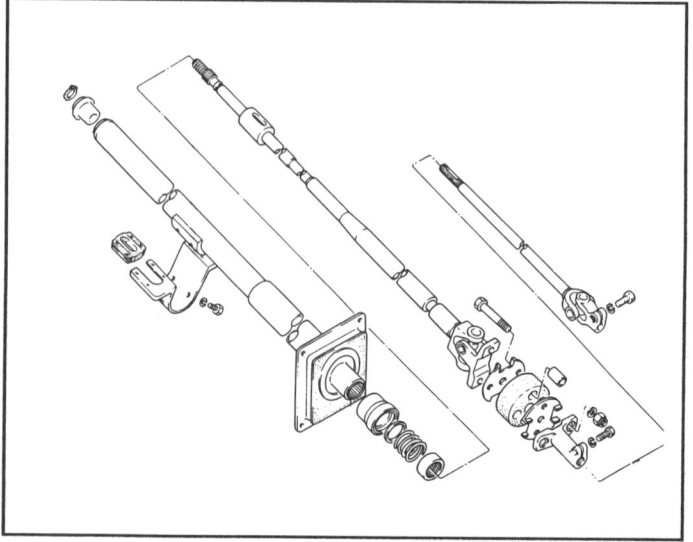

Later column is similar, but note firewall flange, smooth upper tube, dash mounting with insulators (one shown).

Front Suspension & Brake 93

Remove steering column from firewall. All Z-car steering systems are basically the same, differing only in some details and appearance.

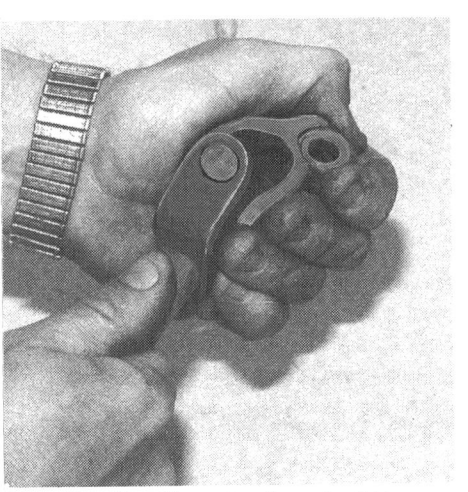

Here I'm checking steering-shaft U-joint for side play. They can be disassembled for inspection and repacking with grease.

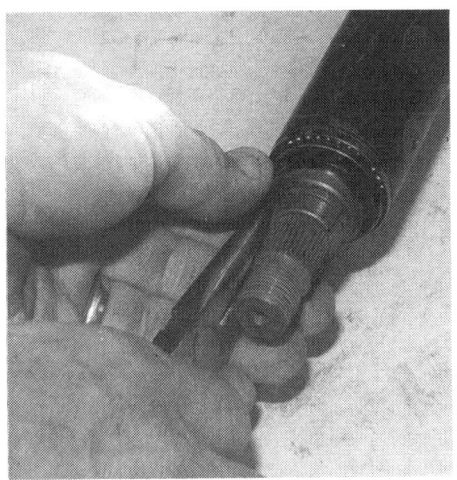

Retaining ring comes off steering-wheel end of shaft.

cup and tap it into place. Wipe any excess grease from the brake and hub. Be sure the disc friction surfaces are spotless.

Brake Caliper—Replace the calipers by bolting them to the ears on their respective spindles. Do yourself a favor and lightly coat the bolt threads with grease or anti-seize compound in case you have to unbolt them someday. Any suspension or brake component that is exposed to road splash and spray will benefit from the rust proofing, especially components like brakes that tend to get hot.

The brake line should be reattached using a flare-nut wrench. Steel lines only fit one side. Put the plated sleeve over the bracket on the MacPherson strut tube. Be sure the 12-point hole faces inboard so it will match the hex on the hose. Insert the line into the caliper and run the other end into the bracket. Then tighten the fitting.

Steering Column

If you haven't done so already, dismantle the steering coupler—this connects the steering-column shaft to the intermediate shaft. Remove the pinch-bolt and remove the splined end of the shaft from the clamp.

There is a miniature universal joint on the column and at the steering-gear end of the shaft. Check these for excess play. Hold one side of the yoke in one hand and work the other yoke back and forth while rotating the U-joint cross on both axes. It should move smoothly and freely, but not exhibit any play in the needle bearings. There is no provision to relubricate these U-joint bearings without tearing them down, probably because they don't take much abuse—nothing like those in the drive train.

To lubricate, dismantle steering U-joints by driving the cups out using two sockets. Use one smaller than the cup as a driver, a larger one as the receiver. Cups and bearings should be kept together and returned to the same arm journal, so keep track of where they go. Contamination by moisture and loss of lubricant are the enemies of steering-shaft U-joint bearings. They are easily inspected and relubricated while dismantled. Don't forget to check the neoprene seals. If you find any broken or missing bearings or galled journals, replace the joint. If all is OK lube the bearings and reassemble the U-joints. Use the same grease you used for packing the wheel bearings.

Column Removal—Unbolt the column flange from the firewall. Also detach it from the pedal-bracket assembly if this is still in the car. Pull the column from the car.

On the workbench, carefully remove the tapered collar and spring ring from the upper end if it's so equipped. Don't lose these parts! Remove the retaining-ring from the upper shaft. The spacer ring may have to be pried off. It's a tight fit.

On the early-style steering, remove the screws and pull apart the upper and lower column sections. Then pull the upper shaft from its tube. Using a soft-faced hammer, knock the column bracket off the rubber bushings. On later cars, simply remove the four bolts holding the bracket to the tube.

Slip the lower shaft out of its tube the collapsible, corrugated tube. The later smooth-looking tube uses a one-piece design. They work similarly in practice, though. Notice the sequence of the spring and ring disassembly.

The lower column retainer is installed a little like a bottle-cap.

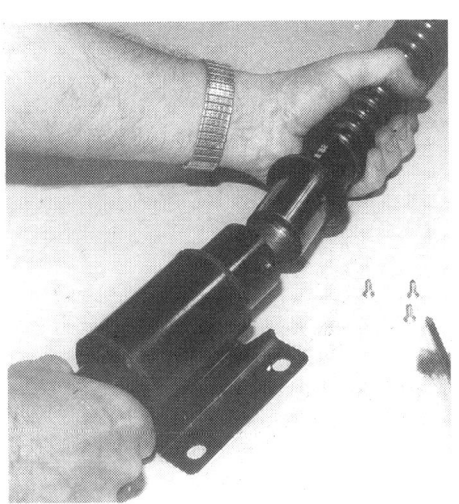

Early column is held together by three Phillips-head screws. Pull upper and lower assemblies apart and take out upper shaft.

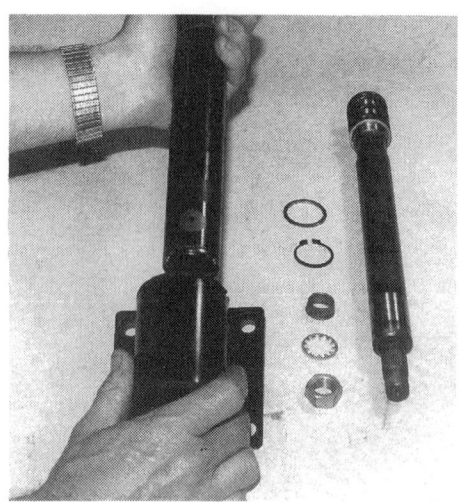

94 How to Restore Your Datsun Z-Car

Column bracket slips off upper column. It has two rubber insulators inside bracket. Late style doesn't use this setup. Its bracket is bolted solidly to the column; rubber insulators go between it and the dash/pedal bracket.

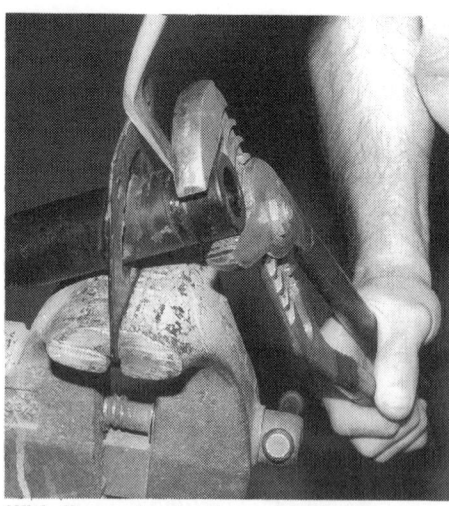

With flange in vise jaws, rotate lower retainer to disengage locking tangs and pry it off gradually.

You'll need something like this homemade tool to drive lower bearing and seal out of tube. It directs impact to circumference of bearing housing. Keep in mind you're working with sheet metal, so don't overdo heavy blows.

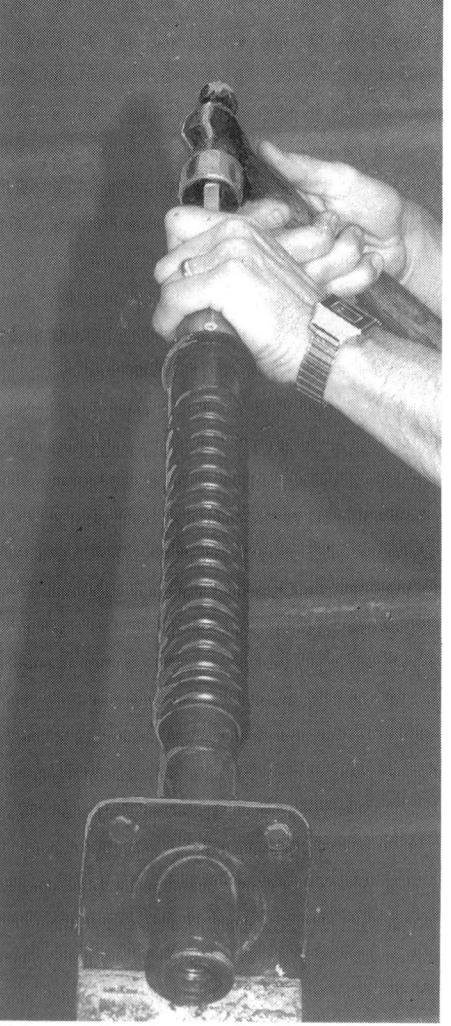

Drive out bearing evenly. Move driver around bearing about 90 degrees or so after each blow. A bit of penetrating oil to start with may help.

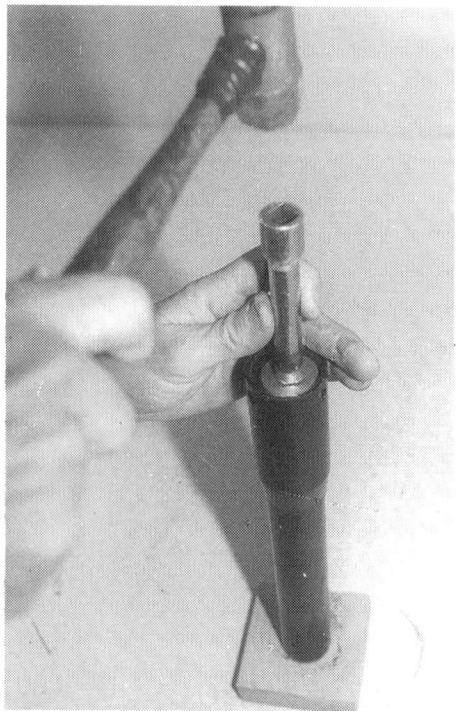

After you've repainted the steering column, drive new or reconditioned bearings back in. A socket and extension make a suitable drift. Use a soft-faced hammer to apply the impact.

Remove it very gently so it can be reused. Do it by twisting it carefully back and forth while prying the lip against the column-to-firewall flange. Retainer should work off. If not, use penetrating oil and let it soak before trying again.

The bearing and seal were pressed into the column tube, so it must be pulled or driven out. A specialized puller may work, but even the Service Manual doesn't indicate how to do the job. So let me suggest using "Wick's special tool." Devise a drift similar to what I show in the photograph. This, with some judicious hammer work, can be used to drive out the bearing and seal while the tube is held in a vise.

Direct the impacts around the inner race of the bearing as evenly as possible—alternate from side to side after two or three blows. Don't lean on the collapsible section of the mast.

The early-style upper mast has two similar bearings. Both can be removed using the same method. There is also a white plastic sleeve that matches the steering-lock hole. Don't remove it unless it is damaged.

Later columns are considerably

Front Suspension & Brake 95

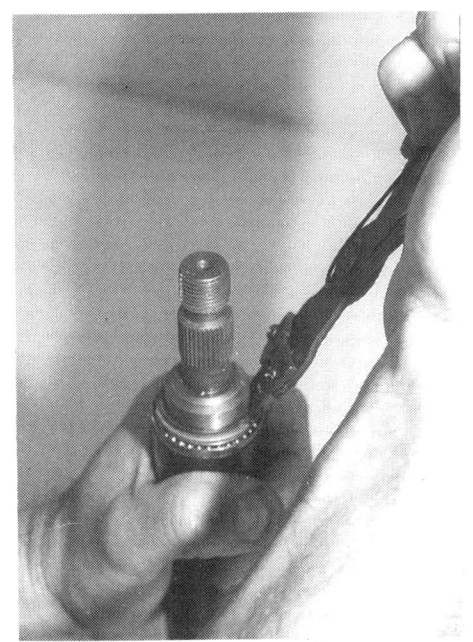

With everything together, slip upper shaft into housing. Set lower end on a deep socket and push down on housing until groove in shaft shoulder is exposed so retaining ring can be installed.

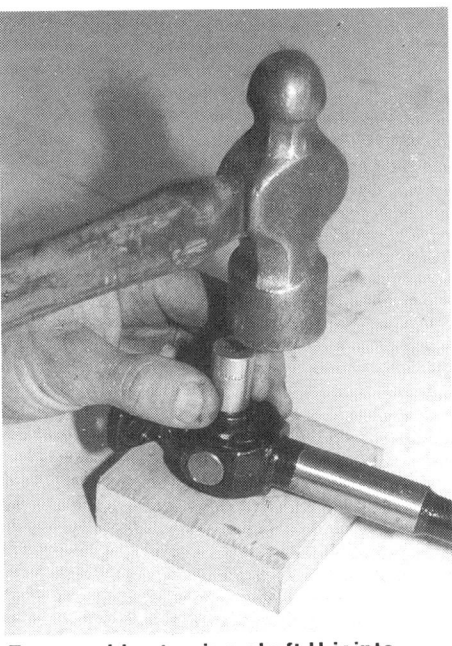

Reassemble steering-shaft U-joints. Bearing cups don't have any form of retaining clip or ring—retention is by interference fit.

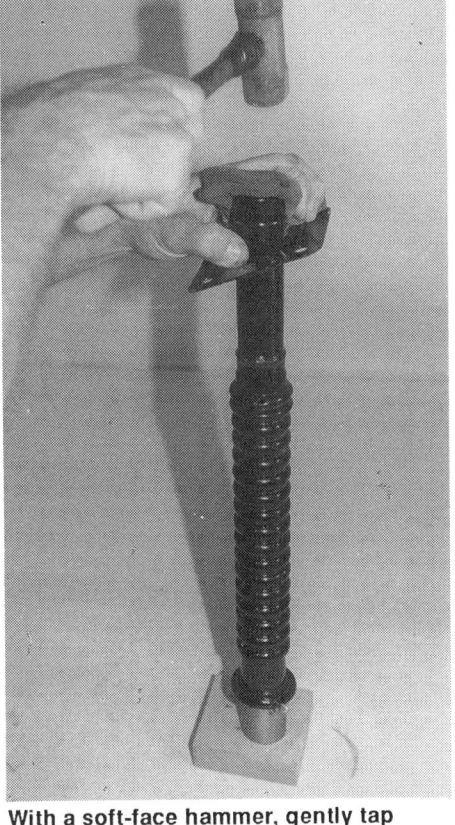

With a soft-face hammer, gently tap new bearing and seal into lower housing. Follow with the retaining cap. A light coat of grease on housing ID will ease installation. Note rag on top of bearing to protect paint from chipping.

easier to service. See the Datsun exploded drawings, page 92. Inspect all bearings and seals for wear, missing balls, out of round and so forth. Replace any that seem defective. These parts live a fairly easy life, but even Nissan products wear out. Refinish all column parts before you begin reassembly.

Column Reassembly—Lubricate the lower column bearing and carefully tap it back in about 1/4 inch below the end of the tube. This will allow the seal to seat flush with the tube end. Put a dab of grease on the seal ID and install it. Follow with the cap/retainer. Check that the retaining tabs line up with the rectangular holes in the tube.

Upper Column—Lube the upper bearings and drive one—they're identical—into the upper end of the tube until it seats on its shoulder. Invert the tube and repeat with the other bearing until it seats in the neck, about 3 inches down the tube.

Upper Steering Shaft—Place the ring and spring back onto the shaft and slide it back into the tube. I place the bottom end of the shaft on a big socket, so when I push down on the tube, the big spring compresses enough to force both rings into place. Lubricate all moving surfaces with light grease or a coating of engine oil. Replace the upper spacer ring and reinstall the retaining ring.

On an early-style column, cement the rubber insulators back into the bracket. Then slip the tube into the bracket. Slide the lower tube end inside the upper neck. The steering-lock hole should be oriented toward the passenger's side. Align the screw holes and reinstall the Phillips-head screws.

(Text continued on page 98)

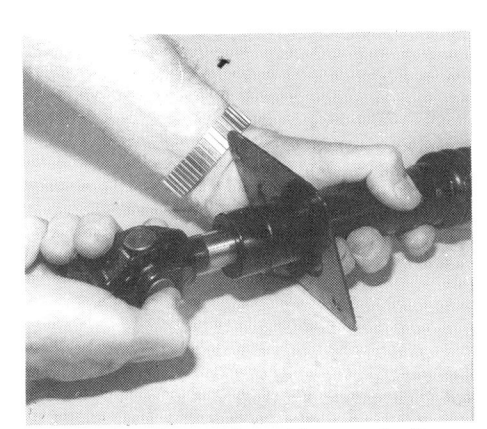

Oil bearing ID and insert lower shaft into column. Upper column with bracket can now be reassembled to it. Lube splines lightly first. Make sure hole for ignition lock is oriented toward passenger's side of car when before securing with three Phillips-head screws.

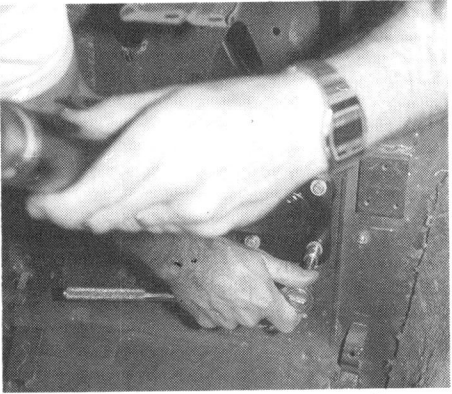

Reinstall steering column soon after the front suspension is back on. It will be easier to wheel your project car around the shop—you'll be able to push and steer at the same time.

FASTENERS

What do I mean by *fasteners?* Anything that holds individual parts together, excluding adhesives: Nuts, bolts, capscrews, cotter keys, rivets, pins, self-tapping screws, clips and anything else used to hold a Z-car and its individual assemblies together. An individual fastener doesn't seem like much, but a major industry does nothing but supply our society with such fasteners. The various fasteners on your Z may vary in condition from perfectly reusable to unusable after you wrench, chisel or burn them off of the car.

Japanese cars have always used metric measurements, thus all original fasteners are specified in millimeters (mm). Since about 1969, their auto industry standardized on the ISO (International Standardization Organization) thread pattern. To make any sense at all, you must conform to this standard. Although working in metrics is intimidating to some, it isn't difficult.

The Z-car has some unique fasteners. Some bolts and screws especially are specific to the model. Then again, some are shared with other Datsun cars due to rather broad parts interchangeability. This aspect is a real advantage to the restorer.

Some parts and assemblies from such diverse models as the 1600 and 2000 roadster, the PL510, 610, 620, 710, 720, 810 series sedans and trucks and the 200SX sedans are related. There are far too many to enumerate here, but you shouldn't have a problem identifying the specific parts if you encounter them.

Warning: Don't take for granted that because your local dismantler's interchange book says a part fits your Z that it is up to the performance of your car. When in doubt, check with your dealer's service people or a specialist who should know!

I cover storing fasteners and other parts starting on page 12. But now let's look at what you may face in dealing with them in the restoration proper.

When people talk about the essentials of a project, they often refer to the "nuts and bolts" of it. Threaded fasteners are the most common on any machine. They offer strength, versatility and, best of all for the manufacturer, ease of assembly. What happens to the threads, the actual working surfaces of the capscrew, nut, bolt or self-tapping screw after it leaves the factory is another matter. This is where the restorer gets vitally involved with fasteners. The thrust surfaces—faces of a hex-head fastener or slot or recessed area of a screw—are vulnerable to wear and misuse.

Using Existing Fasteners—The principal determining factor in whether or not to reuse a fastener or group of fasteners is the condition in which you find them. A number of contributing factors come into play here. Where the fastener was used is a major one—if a bolt has spent its life in a particularly exposed area where it receives more than its share of scraping on rocks, soaking in road salts or frequent applications of a wrench, it may be due for retirement. At the other extreme, if it is in a dry, secluded area and has a light coat of oil on its exposed surfaces, it probably will continue to serve faithfully for another lifetime.

A good clue to the probability of remedial action needed is how difficult a fastener was to remove. Once it and its siblings are removed, inspect them. Badly corroded threads go hand in hand with hard removal and may indicate the fastener's useful life is over. Not only does rust reduce the strength of a fastener, it also affects accurate retorquing. Sometimes threads can be restored, but if they are crucial to an assembly related to the safe operation of the vehicle, replace it!

Threads—What can you do with questionable threads? After giving them a thorough cleaning in solvent or degreaser, a rotary wire brush can be used to remove most surface scale on *external* threads. Capscrews, bolts and sheet-metal screws are examples of externally threaded fasteners.

Caution: When cleaning plated parts, use a petroleum solvent (not gasoline) if at all possible. Phosphate cleaners attack the finishes of plated parts if they are left immersed for any length of time. Discoloring or etching of the protective surface will occur.

Be sure you wear eye protection when using a wire wheel. And keep hair and loose clothing well away from the wheel, motor, shaft or any belts.

If the head, unthreaded length and threads look sound, a trip to the derusting bucket may be in order. On large threaded fasteners, a bead-blaster may be the answer. Either way, reevaluate threads after all crud has been removed. Make sure the threads will have sufficient engagement to be fully functional.

Hex Heads—If your wrench slipped off the bolt head or screwdriver bit jumped out of the screw slot or recess, suspect that the thrust faces are deficient. Do not reuse a rounded-off hex-head fastener. The same goes for slotted, Phillips or Allen head screws. They are so inexpensive in relation to the frustration you may encounter while trying to remove them in the future, don't practice false economy here. File defective fasteners under "scrap metal" and replace them with new ones. You'll thank yourself later.

How about the fastener's finish? The manufacturer plated every metal fastener on your car. On the Z-car, it is predominantly what platers call *yellow zinc*, that multi-tinted golden finish used on most bolts and nuts exposed to the elements. Plain natural-colored zinc is also used on some parts.

Not only does plating guard against rust, it looks good. For the most part, paint similar to that used on the sheet metal can be used to protect the refurbished fastener if it has complete coverage. However, *single-step* plating gives superior durability because the coating is electronically bonded to the surface. Plated fasteners are also more original. Unlike chrome plating, which requires three successive *strikes* (copper, nickel and chromium), as well as an expensive labor-intensive polishing step, single-step plating is less expensive.

Plating shops in most urban areas can do yellow zinc, though they require a large order. Otherwise, you may find in the case of fasteners, small brackets and similar parts that buying brand-new ones is no more expensive than replating. Of course, this assumes that a specific part is available. Don't discard anything until you have the exact replacement in hand!

Some hazards with replating parts: A large order will require that you scramble all your carefully sorted screws, nuts and bolts. To make matters worse, it is common that parts *will* come up missing after the shop is done with your batch, even in the best-run operation. This is much more common in the case of loose fasteners than readily identifiable small parts. It seems the process just "eats" a few assorted bits and pieces at random.

An advantage of having parts plated is the ones you deliver for plating need only be visually clean of grease, dirt and debris. The plating process includes an acid bath to remove corrosion, exposing clean base metal for the plating to adhere to.

What about replacing fasteners that are unusable or simply get lost? There are several approaches, depending on what authenticity you require. Your friendly Nissan dealer should oblige your needs for fasteners, just as he would for other parts. Be aware, however, you will quickly become a pest at his parts counter if you go to him for every little lock washer or Phillips-head screw you may be short. Think benevolently about his profit margin on a ten-cent bolt, to say nothing of the counterman's patience. I go to the dealer mainly for those vital but esoteric bits that only can be obtained from Nissan.

Don't overlook aftermarket suppliers when fastener shopping. Chose one that is involved with just the type of car you are restoring. Such suppliers take pains to stock a lot of often-needed small parts you're likely to be looking for. They simply charge enough to make the practice worth their while.

More and more aftermarket suppliers offer prepackaged fastener sets for collector cars, often at appreciable bulk-lot savings. Although you shouldn't need to replace all of the fasteners, having a complete new set of bolts, nuts, screws and the like on hand could save you a considerable amount of time and trouble.

Check the list of suppliers, page 204, for where to get fasteners. It doesn't hurt to ask.

Of course, for some pieces any dealer of Japanese autos may suffice—there's a high degree of standardization between manufacturers from "Japan, Inc." Along this line, fasteners pirated from your own parts-car *or* any Nissan-Datsun derelict *or* any Toyota, Mazda, Honda or Subaru may get the job done. Like many other things, suitable fasteners are where you find 'em.

Cotter Pins, Clips, Roll Pins & Retaining Rings—Fasteners without threads are found in several areas. Many such fasteners can be reused safely, although I recommend that you use new cotter pins. The bending that is done to fasten them causes a cotter pin to become unreliable after a few uses. Domestic sizes are suitable. Don't bother looking for metric cotter pins or keys.

Retaining Rings—Sometimes known as *snap rings, Circlips, C-clips* or *E-clips,* depending on specific type—should be replaced like-for-like. Usages are usually specific and some set a certain clearance. Others such as spring clips for mounting hardboard interior panels are generic.

Non-Metallic Fasteners—What are they? Plastic rivets, for the most part on Z-cars. Most hold plastic trim panels in unupholstered areas of the passenger compartment. These plastic, color-matched rivets are reusable. Just don't lose the plastic center stem that fixes them in place. If you need new trim rivets, suppliers such as Motorsport Auto carry a complete selection. Nissan/Datsun dealers may have a supply as well. They aren't free, but just be glad new ones are available. Even at the listed price, damaged ones aren't worth your time to restore.

There are some bayonet-type fasteners, door-panel sockets and miscellaneous plastic holders to deal with. If they are not serviceable, restoration suppliers and dealers usually carry a supply of new ones.

ISO—It stands for *International Standardization Organization.*

ISO Bolt Grades—Don't make the mistake of interpreting the number you may find on your car's bolt heads. It is not the same as the SAE grading system most North Americans are used to. The "points" or geometric-figure markings seen on SAE-rated fasteners are codes that indicate the strength of a bolt regardless of size. For example, three lines arranged in a star pattern or "three-points" on the bolt head indicates the bolt is SAE Grade 5.

On ISO fasteners, the grade is indicated by its number—4, 5, 9 and so forth—on the bolt head. But this doesn't mean a bolt marked 5 is equivalent to SAE Grade 5. Unfortunately, the ISO number indicates a torque capacity lower than the SAE number—a negative safety margin if you mix them up. For instance, the ISO Grade 7 is equal to approximately an SAE Grade 5—for a 14mm bolt, Nissan's torque spec on this bolt is 56—76 ft-lb.

ISO Grade 9, the highest number I've found on any Z-car bolt is torqued 80—108 ft-lb if it's a 14mm bolt. At the other end of the spectrum, anything ISO Grade 4—as are many of the 10mm/Phillips-head bolts found on the Z—is comparable to unmarked "hardware-store" grade bolts. This means they could conceivably be snapped off with only an overenthusiastic twist on a Phillips screwdriver if Murphy's Law applies to you. Remember to use the right bolt for the job. And use the torque values your Service Manual specifies for each fastener. And on unmarked bolts, take it easy!

Turn to page 158 for some typical bolt-torque specifications.

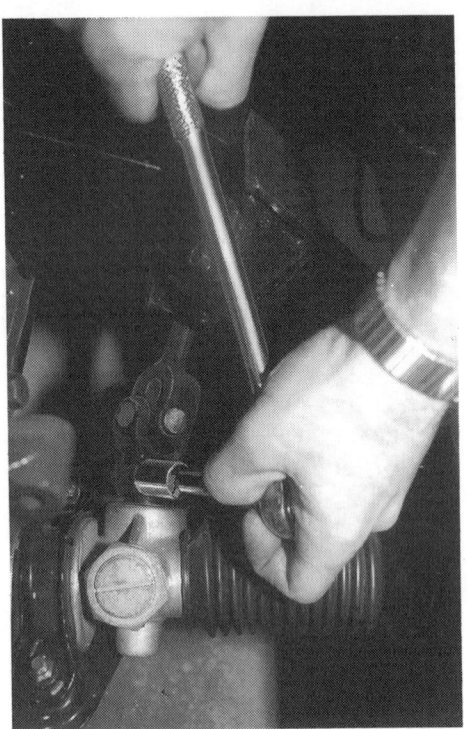

Lower Steering Shaft—With the U-joint assembly reinstalled and the shaft splines and journal lubricated, slip this into the lower column through the seal and seat the splines into the upper shaft. It probably won't seat flush against the retainer.

Reinstall the split-collar and spring ring. The column is now ready for reinstallation. Late-style columns can wait until now to have their brackets and insulators replaced.

Steering Coupler—With the column bolted to the firewall and pedal-bracket assembly, reinstall the upper coupler flange on the splined end of the lower shaft. Be sure the split is centered over the machined relief for the pinch bolt. With the bolts in the upper-column U-joint yoke, assemble the plate-coupler-plate sandwich. Then secure it with nuts to the lower flange. If the steering box is in place, slip the U-joint yoke into engagement with the steering-gear-pinion spline. Align the bolt hole in the yoke hub with the relief in the pinion shaft, then install the pinch bolt. Check your Service Manual for more illustrations and front-end-alignment details.

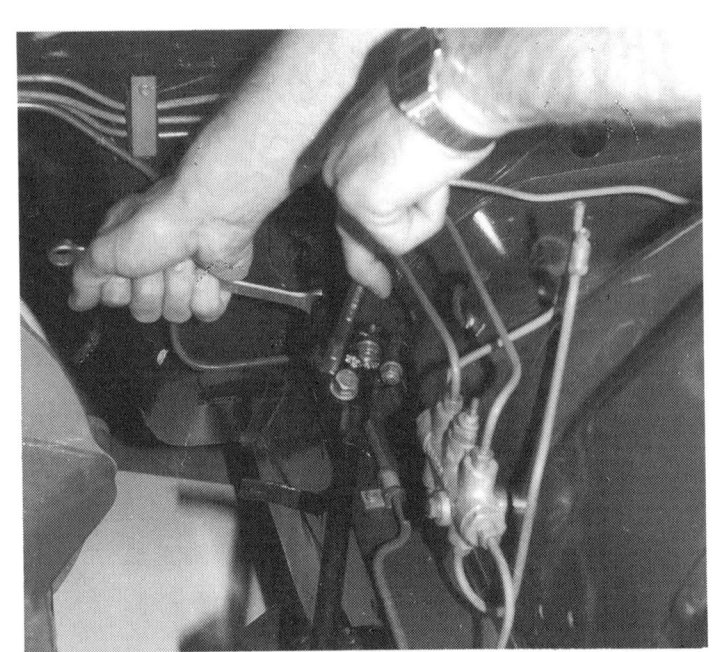

Align lower U-joint-yoke bolt hole with relief in steering-gear-pinion spline. Insert bolt and tighten.

Attach lower shaft to steering coupler. This was taken late in the restoration process, so pretend you don't see brake lines and warning-light switch.

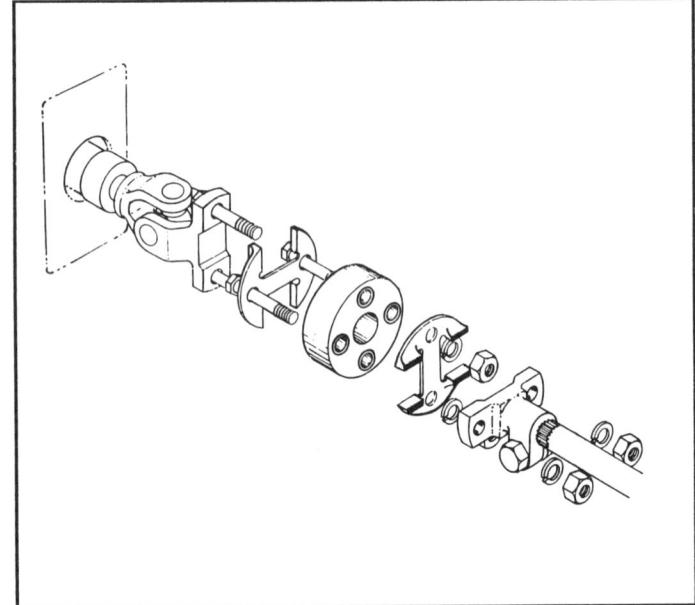

Assemble Z-car steering coupler using drawing as a guide to position parts. If performance is your game, replace original rubber/metal coupler with solid plastic for better steering "feel." Be prepared, though, for increased harshness. Courtesy g-Machine.

7 Rear Suspension, Differential & Brakes

Jack the car up until the rear tires are 3 to 4 inches off the ground and place jack stands under the jacking points. I've said this before: It'll be your body under that automobile and the supports are no safer than you make them, so take all the precautions you feel necessary. I do.

Removing the rear suspension requires that the brake hose and parking-brake cable be disconnected and exhaust system and drive shaft removed. It can be done with the fuel tank in place if need be.

At this point, a transmission jack is nearly essential. I rent one when I'm almost ready to pull the assembly. This way I can usually get by on a two-hour minimum-rental rate. If a transmission jack is not available, prop up the assembly under its center of mass with wood blocks or something similar so it doesn't fall to the floor or on you. Have at least one *strong* helper on hand.

Place a support—a jack is shown in photos—under the center of the differential/suspension assembly and adjust it to match. Although it will get in the way occasionally, the added safety factor is worth the hassle.

Rear Stabilizer Bar—Remove the nuts from the stabilizer-bar links. Take the stabilizer-bar mounts free from the rear subframe and remove the entire assembly. Check the rubber-link and mount grommets for wear and deterioration. Make a list of rubber parts you'll need so you can have them on hand for reassembly.

Control Arms—Loosen the bolts at the front and rear of both control arms. These large, fine-thread fasteners may take considerable leverage to budge. Breaking them loose is easier while the assembly is still fastened to the car, but make doubly sure the car is firmly supported and you don't rock it off of the jack stands!

Front Differential-Mounting Member—Remove the four bolts holding this crossmember to the body.

Link-Mount Brace—That's what the Service Manual calls the two supports that mount the rear ends of the control arms. Remove the four bolts that hold them to the body subframe.

Differential-Mounting Rear Member—This steel leaf spring-and-rubber insulator assembly is secured with two studs to the backside of the differential. Outboard insulators are bolted to the rear floorpan. The bolt heads are accessible through holes in the rear compartment under the shock-tower braces. You may be able to unscrew the nuts without a wrench on the bolt heads. If not, a helper with a wrench on the bolts will be handy.

Caution: These are the last parts to loosen from under the car. The assembly will drop as they are removed, so have your jack or supports close underneath.

Strut Mounts—The three nuts at the top of each strut can now be removed. This will free the complete rear suspension-and-rear drive assembly from the body.

With the aid of a helper, lower the assembly and work it out from under

Z-car rear suspension and differential. Courtesy Nissan.

99

Transmission jack is barely visible under all that machinery. Suspension can be removed without disturbing the differential, but jack makes operation relatively easy.

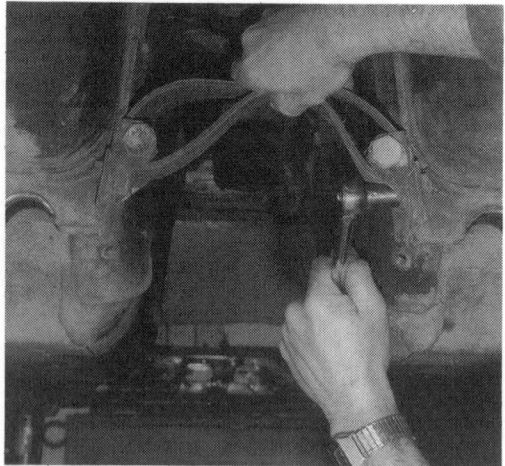

Torque-arrester belt must come off to refinish underpan. Check its condition.

With the body stripped down and supported by jack-stands, clean and repaint underbody. Balaclava and mask are protection against spray mist during this tedious operation.

the body. If you haven't raised the car high enough, it will take considerable effort to move the whole unit out.

If the exposed assembly needs more cleaning, now is the time to do it. While it's still on the jack, move the suspension-and-differential assembly away from the car. Raise it to make the cleaning job a bit easier. Be sure to clean up the jack and your garage floor or driveway afterwards. Move the suspension-and-differential assembly to your work area.

Back underneath the car, the two large bolts that mount the differential-mounting rear member are threaded into the rear floorpan. Before backing these out, remove the big rubberized insulator washer from each side. Put a socket on the bolt head and back it out. Access is gained to these through the rear deck under the strut-tower brace.

Differential Torque Arrester—The heavy rubber/fabric strap that loops over the differential nose is held by a bushing bolted at either end. Remove these, then the brackets can be unbolted from the subframe.

The strap can often be reused, but replace it if its condition is at all questionable. Check it for deterioration and other damage.

Underpan & Subframe—Now's the time to assess any underneath rear-area damage or rust. You'll never have a better chance to remedy problems in this area.

Undoubtedly there will be road debris and contamination to clean off. Look carefully at the rear body sill, around the exhaust-pipe opening and in the strut towers. Go over the fender-well flanges with care and check crevices for trouble. When you are satisfied with the condition of the rear-body underside, seal cracks and seams, apply a thorough coat of primer and paint with your choice of finishes.

I use a finger-gun until all tight areas are covered, then finish up with a standard spray gun. It pays to mask threads, especially internal ones, to prevent paint clogging. *Be careful*—spray mist can get very thick in confined areas—wear your respirator!

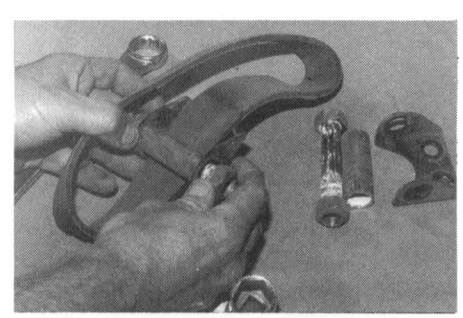

Torque-arrester strap, brackets and mounts. Black vinyl dye will give an old but sound rubber part a new look.

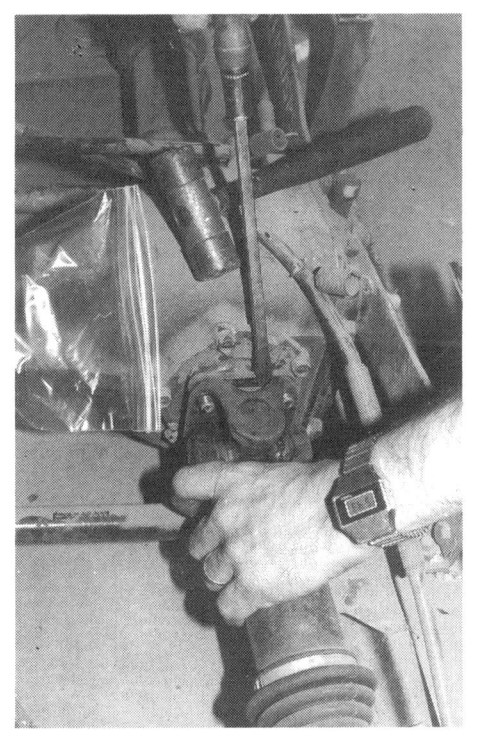

Rear Suspension, Differential & Brakes

Of all U-joints on the Z, those on the halfshafts work hardest. Early models don't have grease fittings, but most aftermarket joints do.

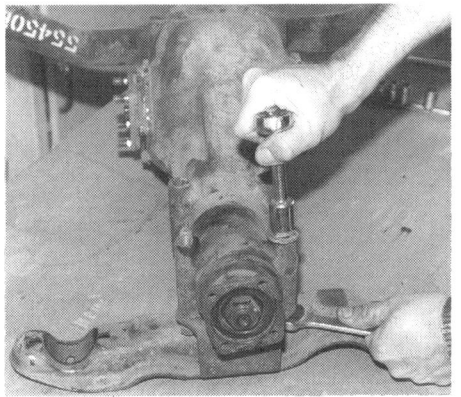

Halfshafts unbolt from wheel end on all Zs. A little leverage from pry bar will free U-joint from drive-flange studs. Side-flange type is fastened similarly at differential end; side-yoke-type uses one center bolt holding inboard U-joint yoke to splined stub shaft.

Front differential mount has its own insulator. It bolts to the two forward bosses. Stenciled number on rear differential mount is Datsun parts number. Number can be restenciled after part is refinished to restore authenticity.

Rear member fits over studs in the differential rear cover and is secured with Nylon locknuts. Stud at left chose to back out of cover; nut came off other stud.

Axle Halfshafts

These are called *drive shafts* by Datsun.

Two different differentials—and, consequently, halfshafts—were fitted to Z-cars. Automatic-transmission-equipped cars used the R180 differential, which has its own drive-shaft design called the *side-yoke type*. The other was the R200, fitted to cars with manual 4- or 5-speed transmissions. These used *side-flange-type* shafts. Because I don't cover differentials in this book, only the removal of drive shafts will be addressed. Other than this difference, procedures are basically identical between the two types.

R200 Type—Prop up the differential mounting at the extreme end with a 2x4 block to make two nuts angle upwards for easy access and then rotate the shafts to remore the other two nuts. Pull the halfshaft U-joints from the differential drive flange. You may need to use a soft-faced hammer or chisel to separate the U-joint flange from the drive flange.

The outboard halfshaft U-joints are retained with bolts rather than studs and nuts. Once the bolts are out, use a similar technique to remove the outer flanges from the stub-axle companion flanges. We'll deal with the halfshafts' ball-splines later.

R180 Type—Reverse the sequence for the automatic-transmission car—take the outboard ends loose first. Then, looking behind the universal-joint cross, find the single side-yoke bolt. Remove these bolts and pull the side-yoke splines free from the differential shaft.

Handle the halfshafts with care, they damage easily if dropped on a hard surface.

Differential-Mounting Members—Remove the two bolts that hold this member to the bosses at the forward end of the differential casting. The front mounting insulator comes off with a stud and nut accessed through hole in bottom of crossmember.

The rear mount should be removed now. Two nuts on studs hold it and sometimes a dynamic damper and bracket to the rear of the unit.

The damper is basically a metal weight Datsun dealers were supposed to install when owners of 240Zs with automatic transmissions complained of vibrations. According to the Technical Bulletin, it would "... reduce the vibration levels arising from the differential mounting and the power-train torsional motions to an acceptable level."

Also, at the outboard mounting points, additional rubber spacers were installed to bolster the existing castellated spacers. These were split for

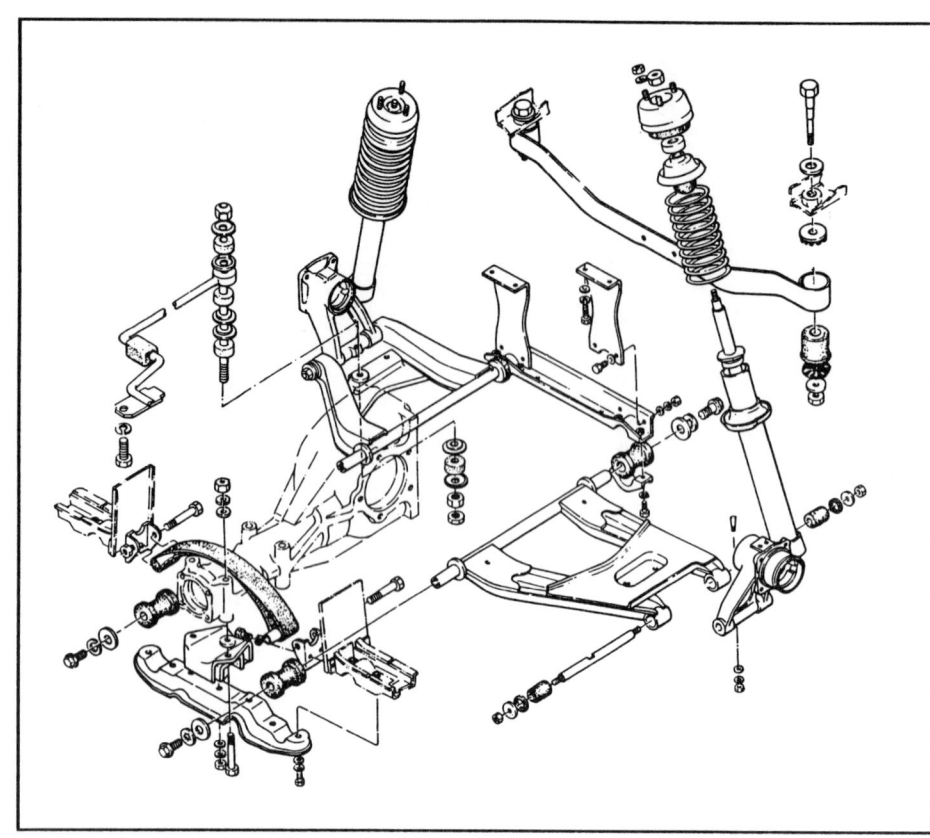

Fairly early rear suspension-and-differential assembly can be identified by its straight control-arm-mounting member and differential-mounting member.

Control arms mount to hub carrier on a spindle shaft and rubber bushings. Shaft is retained by a tapered lock bolt—flat on bolt corresponds to notch in spindle shaft. Flat goes toward the front, or on side opposite strut mount.

easier installation. Z-cars often suffered from apparent vibration-related noises, and Datsun used several "fixes" to rectify complaints.

The rubber-bushed insulator can be driven out with a length of 1-1/2-inch pipe and a big hammer. You shouldn't need Special Tool 33260000! Original bushings should be replaced.

Control-Arm Spindle

The rear-hub carriers are supported by a shaft and bushings that pivot it at the outboard ends of each control arm. Remove the self-locking nuts, washers and rubber washers that secure both ends of the spindle shaft.

Spindle Lock Bolt—At the bottom of the hub carrier is a spindle that serves as the lower control-arm outer pivot. At the bottom center is a nut and washer that must be removed. These secure a tapered lock bolt against a flat machined in the spindle to prevent it from turning in the hub-carrier bore.

Use a soft-faced hammer to dislodge the lock bolt, driving it up and

Note offset of notches in spindle shafts, lots of rust and mushroomed threads at one end of each—result of driving out rusted shafts.

With a big pipe collar supporting the hub, work back and forth across the brake-drum flange with hammer against something such as this brass bar to spread force of blows. If drum doesn't budge, heat it around hub pilot and try again before it cools.

out of the carrier. You may have to drive it out with a punch or drift, as it and the spindle are likely rusted tight! Both will benefit from an overnight soaking with penetrating oil before you attempt to remove them.

On a brand-new Z, the spindle might come out with a one-handed pull, but that's not likely with an older Z. Chances are you'll have to drive or press it out.

Don't mushroom the threaded ends of the spindle when you're attempting to dislodge it from the control arm and carrier. Again, a punch or 5/8-inch drift may be necessary to move one that's rusted to the hub. If it's really ornery, you may have to take the hub-and-control arm assemblies to a machine shop and have the spindles pushed out with a press!

Control Arm

Remove the big bolts from the inner control-arm pivots. Give the two rubber bushings on each control arm a critical look.

The control-arm inner rear saddles come off as well. Finish removing the link-mount braces if you haven't already done so. Note that the links are actually the same part: The passenger's side fits with the *hat section* right-side up; the driver's side is reversed for idiot-proofing!

Rear Brakes

If the drums on your Z-car haven't been removed recently, you may be in for a struggle. Each drum must have an exact and *close* fit where it pilots over a register at the stub axle. This is so the drum rotates wobble-free against the brake shoes.

The combination of dissimilar metals—aluminum drum and steel axle hub—results in a process called *electrolysis* when exposed to moisture. This causes corrosion at the drum/hub interface that effectively bonds the two metals together in their tight proximity. Before you curse those finned aluminum drums, be aware that steel-to-steel drums and hubs *rust* together, too. Either way they must come off, and there are ways of doing this. But first you must retract the brake shoes.

Retract the shoes by rotating the brake adjusters. These spur-like wheels at the end of the hydraulic cylinder inside the brake assembly expand or retract the brake shoes. With a brake-adjusting tool or flat-blade screwdriver, access the brake adjuster through a hole in the bottom of each brake backing plate. Rotate the wheel one way or another. Check to see if you went the right direction by rotating the drum. If it's locked up or difficult to turn, rotate the wheel in the other direction and check again. You don't have to back off the shoes very far. Just make sure there's more than normal running clearance between the shoes and drum.

Now soak the pilot between the drum and stub-axle hub with penetrating oil. This will help break loose the bond between the two and you may—although unlikely—be able to pop the drum off into your hands. A well-equipped brake shop should have pullers that can remove a stuck drum, but other methods you can use are effective and safe. One method that won't work—without destroying the brakes—is a big hammer on the drum flange, especially on an aluminum drum. Relatively little pounding on the fins of a drum will render it useless for further use. *Don't do it!* And don't use a pry bar between the drum and backing plate. The Datsun Service Manual calls the backing plate a *brake disc,* but because this can be confused with the *rotor* of a disc brake, I use the Americanized name.

If the drum doesn't show signs of loosening with a few blows of a soft-faced hammer, stop. Other steps must be taken to free it.

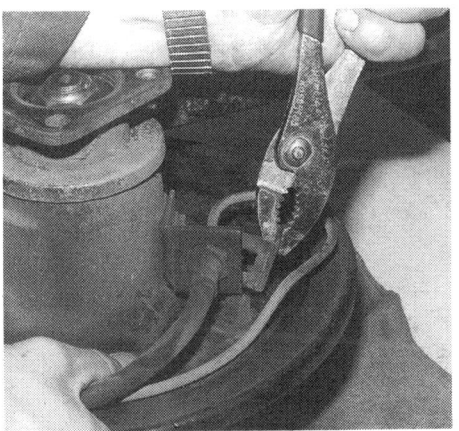

Off comes the rear brake hose and line. Break connection loose—remember to use flare-nut wrench—before removing clip.

Brakes disassemble next—shoes don't look bad. Caution: Don't clean brakes with compressed air. You fill the air with brake dust . . . and it's very dangerous to breathe.

If a few applications of penetrant haven't had sufficient effect, apply heat to the area of the drum immediately around the stub-axle-hub pilot. Don't heat the hub! Using a torch flame about 1 inch or so from the surface, heat the drum between the lug holes and center evenly all around. The heat should expand the drum enough to break the bond with the hub.

Before the drum cools and assumes the same temperature as the hub, place the wheel lug-side down with the hub seated against a big socket or piece of pipe. Repeat the blows to the outer edge. I used a brass bar to spread the force around as much of the rim as possible and constantly moved around the drum circle. Once the hub-flange area has broken loose, carefully pry with a screwdriver in that area to finish removing the drum. Again, don't pry against the backing plate.

Honing Brake Drums—Your Z drum has a cast-iron friction band cast into its inside perimeter. Have this surface honed at a shop that does such work. They can also check it for thickness. If it has been machined several times previously, it may not have enough material to be reused safely. A drum brake must not be so thin in this area that it is unable to absorb and dissipate heat effectively.

The brake-shop man will not turn a dangerously worn drum—he can't by law. And so be prepared to buy a replacement drum on his say-so. After

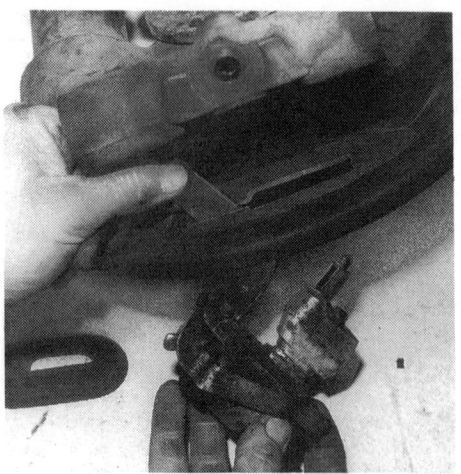

Early-style brake from the back—single-piston wheel cylinder moves in slot on backing plate to actuate both shoes; later two-piston type is fixed.

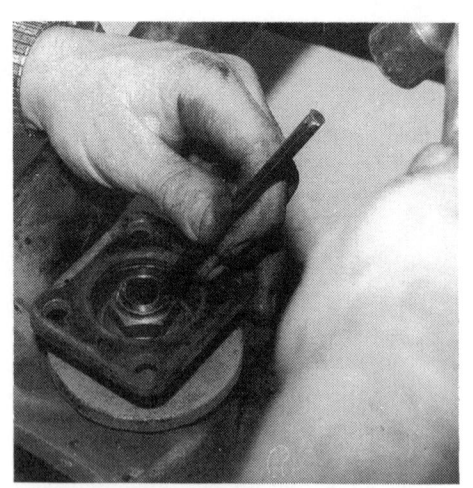

Big nut is staked to flats on threaded end of stub axle. Use a chisel to bend nut away from flat. Nut is relatively inexpensive to replace, but avoid damaging stub axle.

With backing plate supported by 2x4s, knock or push stub axle out of its bearings. Pry out seal.

all, it's for your safety.

Caution: At this point, you are exposed to another, more immediate danger—asbestos dust. *Do not* blow out the brakes with compressed air. Asbestos was used in most brake linings, and we now know that the material not only can cause asbestosis, it is also linked to cancer. There are a number of brake-cleaning solvents available in aerosol cans.

If the hub assembly is off the car, you can use a garden hose to spray off the dust. The trick is to get rid of the dust without breathing it, so use common sense here. Wash up after the job and dispose of dirty rags and so forth properly.

Brake Line & Hose—Use a 10mm flare-nut wrench to loosen the brake-line flare nut at the backing plate. Free the brake hose and line at the bracket by pulling the metal C-clip, then disconnect the metal line from the wheel cylinder.

Check the rubber hose for any cracks or chafes. Unless it looks as good as new, replace the hose now. These parts are important but inexpensive relative to the safety of you or your family. Also inspect the metal line for signs of rust, crimping or other damage. If the flare-nut shoulders are rounded off from someone using a conventional open-end wrench, replace it, too.

Brake-Hose Bracket—The bracket you just removed the brake hose/line from can be removed. It's bolted to the top of the hub carrier.

Brake Shoes—The brake-adjuster wheel should be backed off completely now. Hold the self-adjusting pawl off the wheel with a screwdriver and turn the toothed wheel inwards.

Push the shoe retaining pin up from the back side and turn the retainer plate 90 degrees while pushing down against the spring. This releases the brake shoe from the backing plate and it will pop up.

The brake-shoe retracting springs come off now, green is on top, black on the bottom. Using needle-nose pliers or the brake tool that unhooks and spreads the springs at the same time, twist the hooked ends back to free them from the shoes. This should free the shoes so you can take them off. Inspect the shoes for wear, cracks or greasy contamination. Brakes shoes are inexpensive, so replace them with a good-quality rebuilt or new set. Most parts suppliers give credit for the old shoes as cores.

Note: Datsun front and rear drum-brake shoes are not the same. The *primary,* or front shoe, has the lining positioned low, and the secondary or rear shoe has the lining positioned high. Don't assume any labels are correct, even on Datsun replacements. Also the rear shoe must be installed so the rectangular hole is at the bottom. Be sure yours follow this scheme on reassembly.

Wheel Cylinders
These are different depending on the model, but operate similarly.

240Z & 260Z: With the hub inverted, pry up the rubber dust seal to expose the wheel cylinder. There are two retainers, though Datsun calls them *shims* or *locking and retaining plates.* These allow the early Z wheel cylinder/adjuster to float back and forth with the shoes, a necessity because the wheel cylinder has one piston rather than two.

Unlock the inner retainer from the outer and remove. Use a screwdriver to release the indentations while you pull the upper retainer free. Hold the wheel cylinder from moving and withdraw the lower one. Then take out the wheel cylinder and parking-brake lever from the bottom.

280Z: With the hub inverted, remove the dust cover and the two retaining bolts. Now remove the cylinder and parking-brake lever/adjuster.

The late Z wheel cylinder has two pistons, thus the adjuster doesn't need to move in the backing plate. Obviously, these are not interchangeable without replacing the entire assembly.

Anchor Block: Two bolts hold this part on the early Zs, but on the late Zs it is permanently attached.

Rear Hub

The stub axle is held to its flange by a large nut that is staked to flats on the stub axle. The flats are parallel, 180 degrees apart on the threaded stub-axle shaft. Use a small, sharp chisel to move the deformed sections of the nut away from the flats, but be careful not to damage the threads on the axle in the process. The nuts should be replaced, so don't worry about saving them.

You'll need a socket wrench to remove the nut because of the way it's recessed in the center of the stub-axle companion flange. And it may be frozen tight. If it is, an oxyaceytlene torch can be used to unstick it, but again don't damage the threads on the axle. Heat the nut cherry red by concentrating the flame around the nut.

There are several ways to keep the stub axle from turning while you remove or replace the nut. The simplest is simply to drop the hub studs back through a wheel and tire that's face down on the floor while you apply the breaker bar. If you have a solidly mounted vise with jaws that open wide enough to grip the square shoulders of the stub-axle flange, that works very well. I found that a short section of 2x4 clamped into a smaller vise mounted on my floor jack will lock the hub studs without damaging the threads or bending the studs.

The stub-axle companion flange is splined to the axle. It may need a bit of penetrating oil and a few blows from a soft-faced hammer to dislodge it. Place the hub carrier face down on two 2x4s. The backing plate will have to support the weight of the assembly and the impact of the hammer. The stub axle can be broken loose by striking downward on its threaded end. Protect the threaded end from mushrooming by using a soft punch or plate between the stub axle and hammer.

There is a *distance piece* (spacer) on the axle that should be kept with that side. It is marked with a letter to denote what clearance the assembly requires. As long as yours have the same letter—**B** for instance—they are interchangeable. If yours don't have any, just keep them separated side-for-side. Check the ends of the distance piece for deformation that would change the clearance.

Brake Backing Plate—Four bolts hold this to the carrier. Remove them. The backing plate fits tightly over the carrier flange, so a few taps with a wood hammer handle may be necessary to dislodge it.

Bearing & Seal—The inner bearing can be driven out by placing a drift

Remove bolts holding backing plate to hub carrier and knock backing plate loose. Note that coil spring has been removed—procedure is exactly like that for the front strut.

If you don't have a hydraulic press or arbor press, take the stub axles to your local auto machine shop. Take along new outer bearings, too. Outer bearings must be pressed off stub axles. Once off, press on new bearings.

against the bearing-race lip. Two slots in the inner carrier flange give access to the bearing. You may have to clean out some of the packing grease to see them. The seal will probably come out with it.

You'll need a hydraulic press to remove the outer bearing. Don't attempt to hammer it free. You'll destroy the threads long before the bearing budges.

Wash all the brake and hub parts in solvent. Again, because you've gone to the trouble of dismantling the hub, reinstall new bearings and seals. Take all suspension parts and a can of grease remover to your local car wash. Give the nastiest areas a good soaking with the grease remover, let them soak according to the directions on the can, then spray them off.

I bead-blast every piece that was not plated, then repaint them. I recommend that you do the same. After bead-blasting or stripping, check for obvious scars that were the result of use. Don't be concerned with machine marks and nonstructural flaws left by the factory, but smooth them over. You may want to go further in smoothing cast or forged components. Be aware that excessive grinding and plating may weaken mechanical parts.

After you've removed all dirt, grease and paint, and inspected the suspension parts, give them a coat of primer-surfacer. Never leave bare metal uncoated. A lot of work can be done while the parts are in primer, but don't get them greasy!

Use a good two-part black for painted parts. The best paint from a spray can doesn't compare. Your paint-store counterman can supply you with a catalyzed-acrylic enamel and will mix flattening additive to kill its high gloss when required.

Hang the parts on soft wire and give them a minimum full-coverage double coat of paint. Be sure the paint is hard before handling them. Take precautions against breathing the spray mist/fumes.

Plated parts that still have an acceptable appearance after a thorough cleaning—solvent or carburetor cleaner and a very fine wire brush—

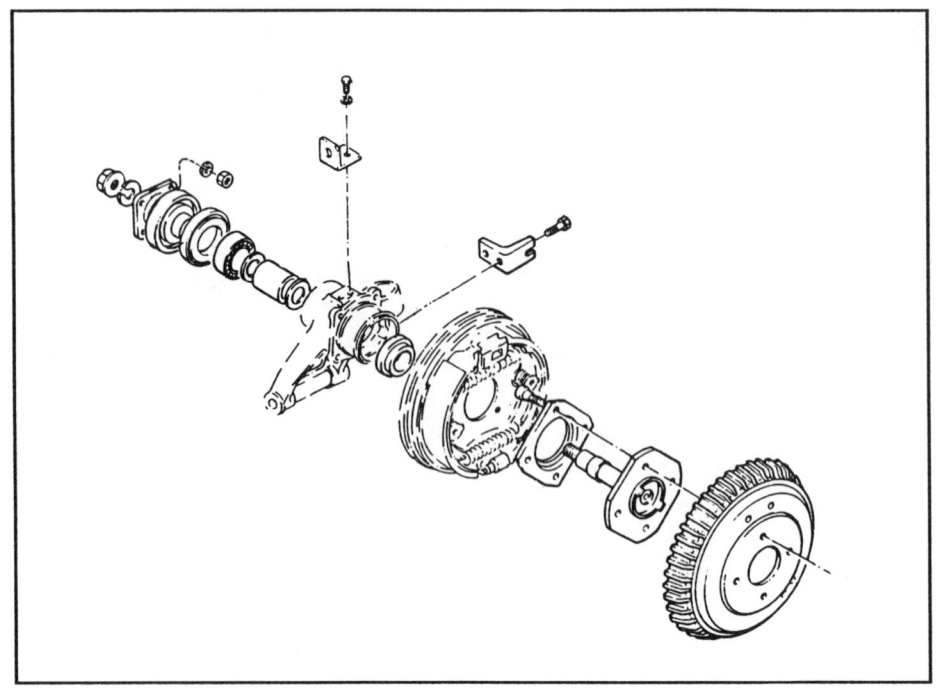

Stub shaft, bearings, brake parts and brackets that mount to rear-suspension hub carrier. Courtesy Nissan.

can be protected with clear lacquer. Otherwise, find and get to know a quality plater.

Suspension Refinishing

While the suspension is completely dismantled, all separate components should be inspected and either replaced or reconditioned. This includes the principal components, such as the struts and control arms. It also includes the bearings, bushings and U-joints. I replaced virtually all the latter with new parts on my project car. The remainder were inspected for straightness, soundness and serviceability. Although they were steam-cleaned before disassembly, I recleaned each part with solvent and a stiff brush and air dried them. This and the inspection process go hand in hand.

After cleaning and inspecting, mask the parts with duct tape in areas sensitive to abrasive, such as bearing surfaces, exposed threads and threaded holes. Sandblasting is a messy project at best, but it provides an excellent surface for refinishing—clean of rust, paint and all lubricants and chemicals. It is the method I recommend.

I use a small pressure-fed blaster and a 5-hp air compressor, which is adequate. A blast cabinet is the best as long as the part fits completely inside so you can shut the door. Bead-blasting gives a finer finish, but takes longer and generally will cost more. Wire brushing, sanding or strippers aren't adequate. The effort is high and results are less satisfactory. Whatever method you use, keep in mind that you should protect yourself against injury. Always wear eye and skin protection when using abrasive blasters or chemicals.

Use an enamel-type paint, never lacquer, to paint suspension components. A small spray gun—called a *finger gun, spotting gun* or *touch-up gun*—is ideal for painting small parts and tight areas. Again, spray cans have their place, but for restoration purposes neither the applicator nor paint they contain is adequate. Datsun, of course, used a *utility* black enamel on undercar parts. Neither high nor low-gloss, it was applied directly to bare metal.

I use a thin coat of a good-quality all-purpose primer-surfacer on freshly sandblasted metal. This helps fill pits and scratches, and restores the original smooth surface if it was prepared correctly. Where there was damage that detracts from the appearance but doesn't threaten the safety or serviceability of a suspension component, some filler and primer-surfacer will suffice. Never leave stripped parts for long without covering with some kind of paint. Rust begins immediately. I use red-oxide primer to protect bare metal.

High-build surfacers—usually two-part spray-on *filler* types—are favored by some show-car builders. They like the smoothness spray-on fillers impart to mechanical parts—even rough castings. Most parts require a light sanding to have maximum effect. The problem is that parts covered with a spray-on filler are less attractive when the inevitable chipping occurs.

When in doubt buy a new part—or at least a better used one. Control arms, front and rear, suffer the most from road hazards, so check yours carefully for damage. They hang 'way down, move and are sheet-steel stampings.

Some restorers paint mechanical parts after assembling them. This is based on the notion that, if painted first, they will be chipped and scratched during reassembly. This is more or less true, depending on the care taken during reassembly. But if you paint them afterwards, elaborate masking is required, which is sometimes only partially effective. And too many parts have the potential for getting overspray—some that should get none and others that need a good, unbroken finish coat! I prefer to take precautions against damaging the paint, then use a fine brush to touch up mistakes.

Don't overload parts with paint. Several thin coats are always superior to one or two thick ones, especially from a durability aspect. Drippy, thickly applied paint dries poorly and often comes off in large chips when nicked by road hazards such as gravel. And there's the handling involved in installing universal joints, springs and so forth. Mars and scratches are inevitable, and overly thick layers of paint are harder to touch up.

If your heart's desire is a slick "wet-look" finish, try this: After refinished parts are assembled to the their new as-manufactured condition, hang each assembly with wire and give it an overall coat or two of a good acrylic-enamel clear topcoat. This will not only gloss everything evenly, assuming you've gotten good coverage, par-

After you have all rear-suspension components replaced or reconditioned, reassemble the hubs. Pack outboard bearing with grease, install stub shaft in hub and pack inboard bearing and install. I'm packing seal before tapping it into place. What have I forgotten?

Align companion flange to stub axle and drive it into place. Now I remember to put the brake backing plate back on. Ouch!

After I removed the stub axle, installed the backing plate and reinstalled the stub axle, we're back on course. It's time to secure stub axle. New locknut requires a lot of torque; 189—231 ft-lb. Great! But how do you hold the shaft when applying this torque? Easy. Lay a wheel with tire mounted face down on your shop floor and set the upright-and-brake assembly into engagement with it. Loosely install a couple of lug nuts. This will counteract the torque reaction. After you have the nut torqued, check axle's turning resistance. If it rotates smoothly, stake nut to flats on the stub axle.

ticularly in tight spots, it will also protect plated parts and metal edges from road splash. Catalyzed Ditzler Del Glo or Del Clear are great for this effect.

Suspension Reassembly

New Parts—This applies to both front and rear suspensions. Have *all* new and refurbished parts accounted for and close at hand. If possible, check bushings, U-joints, bearings and so forth for fit and application. Nothing is more frustrating than to be stopped halfway into a complicated job to run down a missing part.

With a car as old as the Z, most parts will be "over the hill," if they're not already. As I've said all along, it's best to replace all of the bushings, bearings, fasteners and similar hardware now. And the availability situation, as well as cost of parts and ease of replacement, won't be any better in the future. Finally, it's nice to know everything is new between you and the road. And new metal and rubber surfaces look great, too!

Reassembly Sequence—Don't be afraid to deviate from my recommended sequence of assembly if, for instance, you have parts on hand for a certain area and not for another. I show what I consider to be a logical progression for clarity's sake, but some sub-assembly steps can be done in whatever sequence is most convenient for your restoration. Use common sense however, or you may be doing some disassembly to get access to an area. Much of the following can be done under the car. For clarity though, I show as much as possible on the bench . . . and it was easier to photograph.

Brake Backing Plate—These must go onto the rear hub carriers before the stub axles are installed. Make sure you have the correct side and attach each with four bolts. Clean and repaint them first.

Rear Stub Axle—The next step is to install the outer stub-axle bearing—the one that faces the outside of the car.

To avoid thread damage, don't support the stub axle with the wheel studs. Grease the stub axle lightly. With the flange side positioned toward the outside, drive the bearing onto the stub axle until it seats firmly. Drive or press against the inner race, not the outer, to prevent damaging the bearing. You shouldn't need a press for this, but it would work nicely. I use a 6-inch-long, 1-1/2-inch water pipe and a big hammer.

Once you have the outboard bearing on, thoroughly grease the stub axle. Pack the recesses of the bearing and shaft, then insert the axle into the hub carrier. Now pack the recesses of the carrier with grease and inboard bearing. This bearing doesn't have a wide inner flange as does the outer bearing, but it has the same diameter.

Slide the tubular spacer onto the stub axle. With the axle and hub carrier centered and safely supported, drive in the inner bearing until it seats against the spacer.

Grease Seal—Fill the seal recess with grease and tap it into position in the carrier. Put grease on the exposed side, where it will face the companion flange.

Companion Flange—Drive the companion flange onto the splined end of the stub axle. Use a short section of pipe or a large socket to hammer against. Replace the lock washer and thread on the special locknut. Use a new nut, too. This must be torqued tight: 189—231 ft-lb is a lot. Hold the stud side of the stub axle and tighten. I use a 2x4 block of hardwood clamped in a vise with the studs

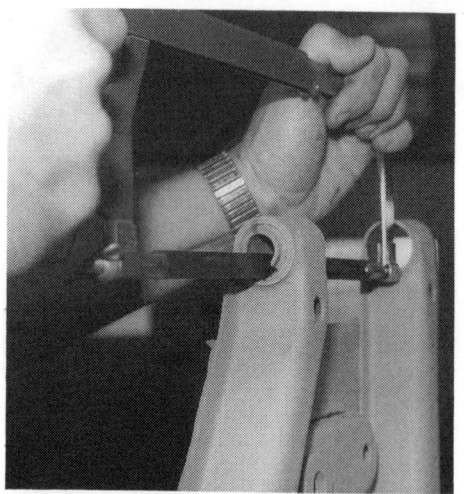

Spindle bushings are pressed into control arm, making them difficult to remove. And, because of the control arms' awkward size and shape, they don't fit well in a press. So, you'll have to cut them out. Remove hacksaw blade, insert it through bushing and reassemble saw. Cut notch out of bushing, being careful not to cut into control arm,

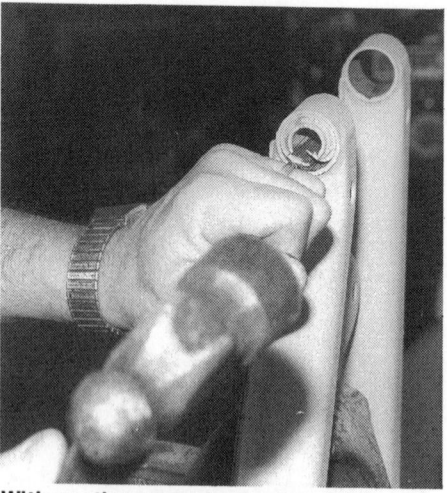

With section sawed out of bushing, it will relax in bore—chisel curls up cut ends to complete loosening process.

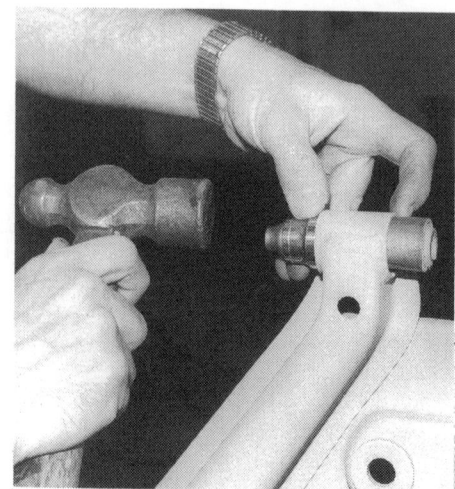

I use socket with old extension to drive out old bushing.

straddling it because the wood won't damage the threads. You can also use a wheel and tire on the floor with a couple of lug nuts threaded on to do the holding.

Check that the stub axle turns freely. You will feel some resistance, especially at first, but it should turn easily with moderate pressure on the studs. If it is locked or turns grudgingly, disassemble and make sure you have everything in the correct sequence and turned the right direction.
Note: Datsun's Service Manual makes much over mixing spacers. This may have resulted if you assembled stub-axle or hub parts from another car, or simply got yours mixed up. Otherwise, it is doubtful this is the problem. A number of spacers—as well as hub carriers—I have seen are not even marked **A**, **B** or **C** as referred to in the Service Manual. If the spacer is too short, the axle will stick or bind when rotated. Conversely, if it's too long, there will be noticable end play. Satisfy yourself that each side is OK after torquing the nut.

If you are satisfied with your job, carefully use a flat-nosed punch to stake the flange of the special nut to the flats on the stub axle. Don't booger up the threads just in case you or someone else has to dismantle the hub again some day. Daub a bit of clear lacquer on the nut and exposed shaft to inhibit rust.

Rear-Suspension Control Arm

Remove Bushings—There are four bushings in each rear-suspension control arm, two at the inboard pivot and two at the outer. These are press-fit at the factory and, with the addition of rust, become very tight. Due to the shape of the rear-suspension control arm, using a hydraulic press without special tool ST38800000 as a receiver isn't possible. Fortunately, the shade-tree approach works just as well.

Clamp the control arm firmly in a vise so the bushing axis is near horizontal. Assemble a hack saw so the blade runs through the center hole in the bushing and saw all the way through the metal inner sleeve in two places about 1/4-inch apart. Dislodge the narrow strip of metal with a cape chisel and pull it out.

Use the saw blade to chew out enough of the rubber so it doesn't bind the saw. Then carefully make a clean cut through the outer metal shell without rocking the saw from end to end. Avoid cutting into the control-arm bore.

Drive a long punch down the saw kerf, curling the metal inward to relieve the pressure on the shell. This will loosen the shell so a suitable drift can easily drive it out. As shown, I used a 7/8-inch socket with a broken extension to hammer on. Remove the rest of the bushings.

New bushings may be pushed in now or after the control arm is painted. To prepare the control arms for new bushings use a sanding drum on a drill motor. Clean and deburr each bushing bore.
Outer Control-Arm Bushings—To ease assembly, smear grease or oil

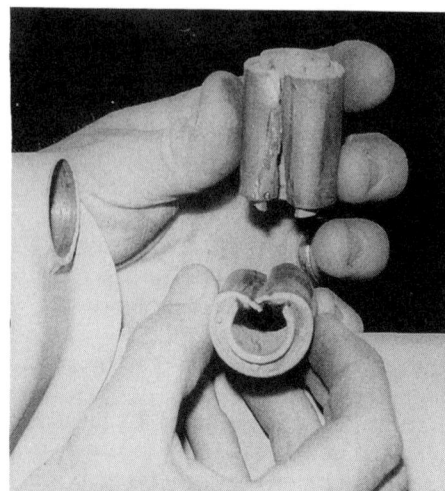

Both bushings are out. New bushings can now be reinstalled.

Rear Suspension, Differential & Brakes

New bushings drive in easily with socket. Both inside and outside are well lubricated.

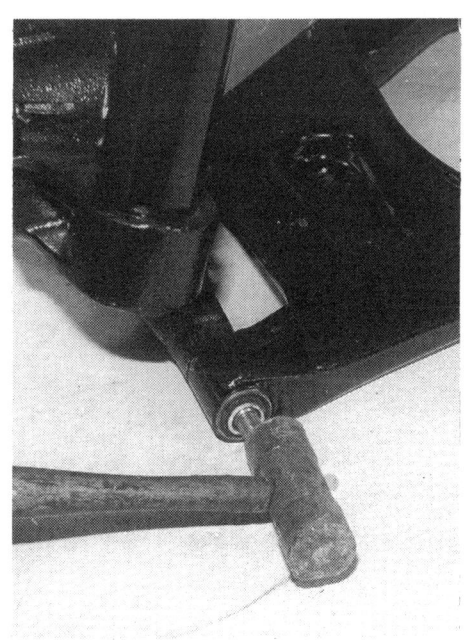

Position control arm and upright so bushings align with bore in upright. Lube control-arm spindle and drive it in. Remember, notch goes to front of hub, or side opposite strut. Try to align notch with lock-bolt hole on your first try.

With notch aligned and equal amounts of thread showing at each end of spindle, fit lock bolt and nut, and tighten it. Now install washers and Nylon locknuts on spindles.

either on the bushing shell or in its bore. With the control arm well supported, drive the bushing into its bore. Install the other three.

Use a socket or piece of pipe with a hammer to drive them in or, if you have a press, press them in. The outer shell of the bushing should be flush with the shoulders of the bore in the control arm. With all four bushings in place, reinstall the rear-suspension components and differential.

Inner Control-Arm Bushings—There are two sets of these, the rear bushing is somewhat shorter than the front one. Although they look similar, don't be fooled and mix them up. Compare them to be sure.

Start by lightly lubricating the inner tube and threads. Install all finger-tight with the big bolt and washer. Don't grease the rubber outer area. Coat them with a bit of silicone brake fluid, if anything.

Control-Arm-Mount Braces—Reinstall these two uprights to the control-arm mounting member with their nuts and bolts. The upper flange should point to the front of the car.

Link-Mount Caps—Position the control arms with the rear bushings under the mounting member and install retaining caps. Make sure bushings are centered, then tighten the cap bolts.

Control-Arm Spindles—Position a hub-carrier assembly to its control arm so the spindle and bushing bores align. Grease the spindle thoroughly to prevent corrosion. There is no way to do this once the spindle is installed. The flat on the side of the spindle should be toward the front when the spindle is installed—it isn't exactly centered from end to end. Also, the spindle should be oriented so the flat corresponds with the lock-bolt hole in the hub carrier.

To accomplish this, start the spindle with the notch oriented toward the forward end of the assembly and rotated so it will align with the lock-bolt hole once it's in place. The notch needs to wind up matching the hole and not lost somewhere inside its bore. The spindle can be rotated to match the hole once it is driven in. But get it as close as you can on the first try. The job will be much easier.

Put a nut on what will be the rear end of the spindle. With the hub carrier and control arms positioned correctly, drive in the spindle using a soft-faced hammer. Keep driving until the shoulder gets about even with the front end of the forward bushing. A bit of adjusting of the two assemblies may be helpful. This is another place where a helper facilitates the process.

Spindle Lock Bolt—Use new lock bolts and nuts. Used ones usually aren't worth reusing. Note that these bolts have a tapered flat on one side. This flat should match the notch in the spindle when installed.

Check spindle position by looking through the lock-bolt hole. If the notch isn't aligned or doesn't show, double nut one end of the spindle and rotate it until it does. If it doesn't show regardless of how much you rotate the spindle, maybe it is in backwards or has been driven past the hole. If it is just a bit off, don't worry—the lock bolt will make itself fit as you drive it in from the top. Install the nut when the threads appear at the bottom—I have seen these with either lock washers or Nylock-type nuts. Install and tighten the locknut.

Spindle Nuts—These are the Nylon locking variety. A large rubber washer and plain metal washer go on in that order under each nut. Tighten them.

Struts/Shock Absorbers

Before you install the new shock-absorber cartridges, put a little oil or even enamel paint into the strut tube and swish it around. This will inhibit

110 How to Restore Your Datsun Z-Car

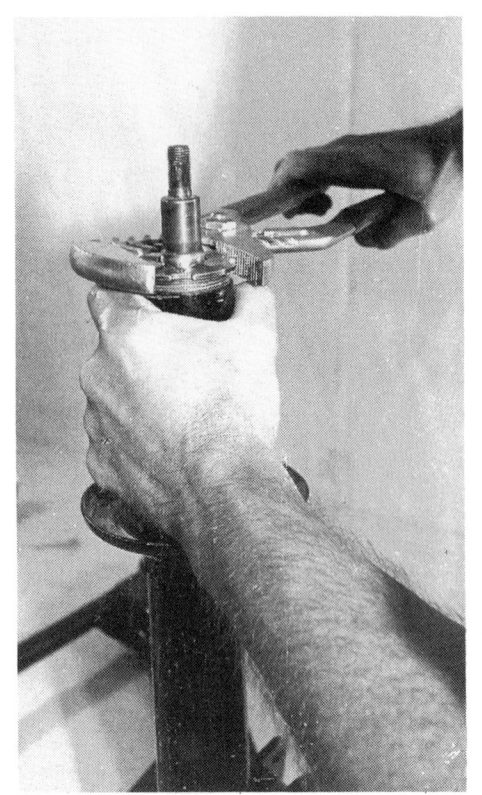

New shock cartridges just drop in tube and thread to original shock nut threads. From standard to full-race, almost any type shock is available. All are improvements over originals.

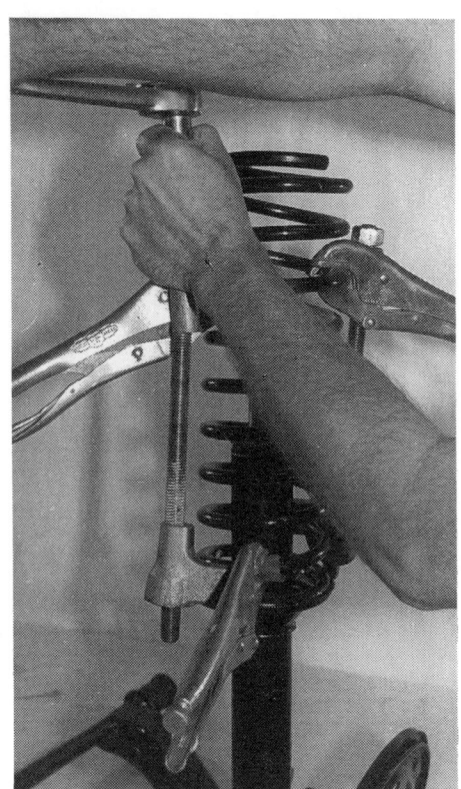

Run spring compressors down in steps, alternating side to side. Grease on compressor threads eases turning. Again, Vise-Grips are on spring to keep compressor clamps from "walking" sideways.

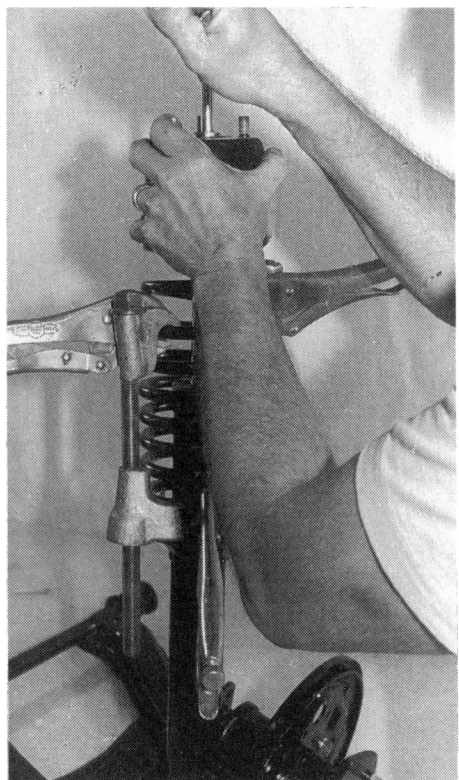

While spring is compressed, install spring seat. Secure seat with a single nut. Back off on spring compressor and remove it to complete this part of the rear-suspension assembly. Note that rented spring compressor is well worn.

rust in the bottom if water seeps in over time. Insert a new cartridge into the tube and secure it with the retaining nut supplied with the cartridge. The longer cartridges are for the rear suspension.

Spring-and-seat reassembly is basically a reverse of the disassembly routine. It's straightforward, but if you encounter a problem, refer back to that section. If you remember, you need a spring compressor.

There are a few things to consider when installing springs. When seating the spring, make sure the end of the bottom coil fits the pocket of the lower spring-seat cup. And remember to use the Vise-Grip-plier trick to prevent the spring-compressor hooks from sliding on the coils.

On 280Zs, reinstall the dust boot and its retaining rings.

Fully extend the shock rod and place the spring in position on its seat. If you don't have three hands and your shock rod keeps sliding down into the shock, here is another Lone Wrencher trick: Before the spring goes on, drop an appropriately sized worm-drive hose clamp over the rod. Pull the rod to its top and tighten the hose clamp on the rod so it's against the top of the shock cartridge. Be careful that it doesn't scar the rod—and don't use pliers on the rod. To protect the piston rod, wrap it with several layers of masking tape before you install the hose clamp.

Put on the strut upper seat, bushing and insulator, then secure with the Nylon locknut. Back off the spring compressors *gradually*—be careful. When the compressors are fully relaxed, remove them and take off the Vise-Grips. Don't forget to remove the hose clamp if you used one.

Rear Suspension, Differential & Brakes Installation

Although it was easier to remove the differential and suspension as a unit, I reinstall the cleaned and refinished parts separately. You may choose to assemble the suspension and differential as far as possible first. Either way is OK. Take gravity into consideration, though!

Differential

If the performance of your differential was flawless and you've refinished it to your satisfaction, reinstall it. If you are replacing the plastic breather, position it so the arrow on top points toward the front of the car.

Rear Mount—Reattach this to differential cover with the nuts and large washers. Orient eyes at ends to the rear on 1970-71 cars; to the front on later Zs. Be sure to torque all suspension pieces "by the book," especially when they thread into aluminum parts.

Using two pieces of pipe, one as driver and another as receiver, install the rear mount insulators from the bottom. Lube the insulator or mount loop and use a big hammer. Incidentally, the later mount can be adapted to early Zs, but the benefits are nebulous.

Front Cushion—Rubber mount goes on the forward bosses of the differential nose.

Rear Suspension, Differential & Brakes

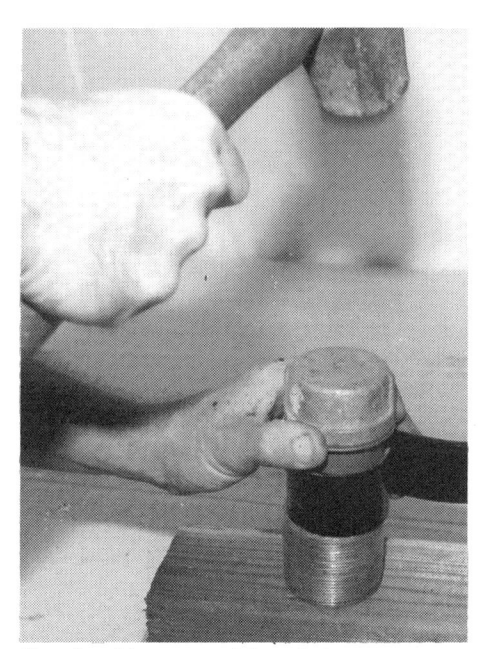

New bushings are driven into rear mount—big hammer and pipe fittings don't have a Datsun part number, but work just as well. If you're having a problem holding it steady, rear mount can be reinstalled.

Differential-limiter brackets go back on before rear suspension is mounted. Install strap after differential is in place. It loops over differential hose.

Supported on transmission jack, suspension-and-differential assembly is easy to position under car. Install rear-mount bolts first, then install front control-arm bushings and mounts.

Differential-Limiter Strap—Brackets for this part attach to the floorpan reinforcement forward of the differential area. Attach one side of the strap with its bushing, but don't fasten the other end until you've positioned the differential on its front mount.

Rear-Mount Insulator Bolts—Install the large bolts through the holes in the rear deck area under the strut-tower braces. Push them through and tighten the nut to let the bolts act as studs.

Front Mount—With this mount placed correctly—larger kick-up on the driver's side—thread the bolts in about two turns.

Using a floor jack or transmission jack, position the differential cushion over the front mounting member. Allow the stud at the bottom of the cushion to drop through the hole in the mount. Start the nut.

Raise the differential and align the rear-mount-cushion holes with the bolts extending down from the floorpan. Put the rubber-metal serrated washers on the bolts and work the cushions into place on them. Put the lower serrated washers in place and tighten the Nylon locknuts.

Install Rear Suspension

Use shop towels to pad the underside of the suspension components against scuffing or chipping. As you should remember, this assembly is heavy and very cumbersome, so a transmission jack will help. If you have one, raise the control arm/hub and strut assembly and move it into position under the differential. If you don't have a jack, set the assembly on a piece of heavy cardboard or a tarp and slide it underneath. Be careful that the top of the strut doesn't strike your fenders and damage the body or paint.

Struts—Guide strut studs up into position and loosely secure with nuts. This takes much of the weight off the control arms and rear mounts. A helper will facilitate this operation greatly, but you can do it alone.

Link Mount & Brackets—Raise the mounting member and move it forward. Aim for the gap in the front mount that you left partially tightened with the two front control-arm bushings. You may have to withdraw the

Using a jack, raise suspension and guide strut into engagement with upper mount. Get a nut on from inside and remove jack. Note early and late serrated washers on rear mount bolt. Datsun recommended using the fat late version on all Z refits, but I wasn't able to get two more until after this sequence was photographed.

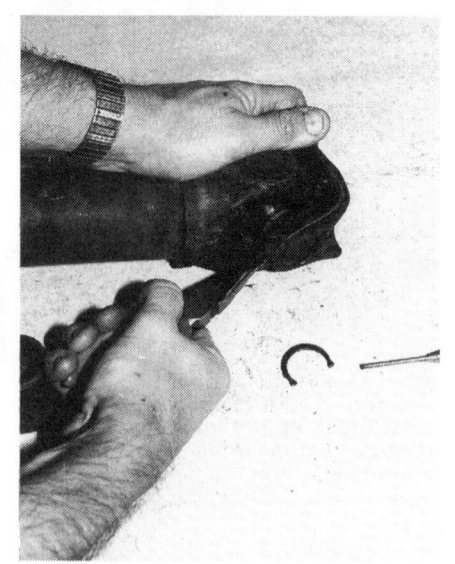

Halfshaft U-joint clips are removed with pin punch and pliers. These can fly off with some force, so wear eye protection.

Use a short section of pipe or socket with an ID large enough to allow clearance for the U-joint bearing cup as support and a driver on the other side. Knock out the cups and remove the cross shaft. New U-joints are cheap insurance against future problems.

Halfshaft, or "Drive Shaft" to Datsun

These transmit engine torque from the solidly mounted differential to the suspended hubs. Because they have to flex, both are provided with two universal joints as well as an enclosed ball-spline.

Universal Joints—With the shaft firmly supported, locate the locking clips on the four caps of the joint. Wearing eye protection, use a pin punch to dislodge the clips and remove with pliers. *Be Careful!* These spring-steel clips are capable of flying 25 feet—they can easily injure an eye or at the very least get permanently lost! I prefer to merely drive them partially off the cap and remove with needle-nose pliers.

Then using a hydraulic press or hammer, force one bearing cap out of the bore. Either method requires a couple of sockets or pieces of pipe—one smaller than the diameter of the cap as a drift to push it out and the other larger to act as the receiver. After one cap is removed, reverse direction and drive the cross—the center unit—back out with another appropriately sized drift.

Repeat with the other pair of caps and then work the cross out of the yoke. It helps to have the assembly very clean. I use penetrating oil liberally. All four are done the same way. The companion flanges—outer side of the joint—are identical. If your joints are worth saving for reuse, keep the bearing cap with the arm of the cross it came from. Also check all caps for lost or damaged needles, lack of lubricant or damaged plastic ring seals. *Recommendation:* Replace them as a set. They are available at very reasonable cost. Most replacements come with a grease fitting for easy maintenance, and they don't need cleaning!

Propeller Shaft—Universal Joints on 240 and 260Zs are removed in the same manner as the drive shafts. Because the yoke flanges are parallel on these two parts, the process is even easier. If these had proper maintenance—were lubricated at regular intervals—they may not need replacing. With its rigidly mounted differential, the IRS Z-car doesn't give the prop shaft U-joints much work to do.

On 280Zs, the U-joints are not replaceable—barring machine-shop modifications—and the shaft must be replaced as an assembly if problems occur. If you are hunting for one of these items, be sure to specify what transmission your car has.

Propeller shafts are factory-balanced. If reassembled differently from original—or damaged—they may contribute to vibration, noise and premature failure if not rebalanced.

---

large bolts and washers to squeeze the bushings into place. If you do, replace them immediately. The bushings have molded flanges on opposite ends. Orient these horizontally for better alignment with the front mounting.

Getting everything aligned takes patience. Raise the front of the differential slightly to clear the cushion. There is enough flex in the rear bushings to do this by hand. As the front goes in, position the link-mount uprights on their mounting pads and bolt in place.

Up front, tighten the front-mount bolts and cushion nut. Reinstall the inner-pivot control-arm bolts and torque all fasteners to specification. Finally, finish installing the differential-limiting strap.

Install Halfshafts

Begin reinstallation of halfshafts now by bolting the outboard universals to companion flanges on stub axles.

On R200 differential-equipped cars, fit the inboard U-joints over the side-flange studs and secure with nuts. On R180-equipped cars, reinstall the large bolt and torque to spec. To hold the halfshaft so it won't turn as you torque the bolt, slip the plastic-coated handle of large slip-joint pliers into the joint yoke. The plastic coating will protect the paint.

Stabilizer Bar; 260Zs & 280Zs—Reinstall the stabilizer bushings and clamps on the bar. Assemble the washer and bushing "sandwich" for both links and install.

Recondition Rear Brakes

The first step in rebuilding the rear brakes is to thoroughly clean all of the components. As I mentioned, take precautions not to breathe or

Rear Suspension, Differential & Brakes 113

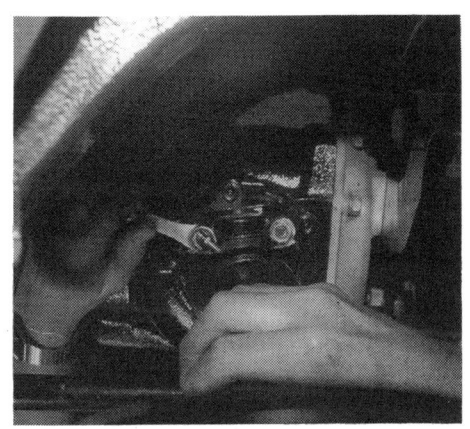

Axle halfshaft goes onto differential. Aluminum differential cover was originally painted black, but looks prettier clear-coated after bead-blasting. If your replacement U-joints have Zerk fittings, lubricate while you're under the car.

Now that the rear suspension and differential are back in place, turn your attention to the brakes. First, clean the wheel cylinders and install new seal kits. Lubricate the rubber parts with brake fluid.

Brake Fluid—Should you use silicone?

If you are considering using DOT 5 silicone-base brake fluid, here are some points to consider. The first you should know before you use silicone-base fluid. It is *not* compatible with conventional brake fluid. If you're restoring your brake system from top-to-bottom however, it should be free of any contamination. That makes it a good time to switch to silicone.

There are some definite advantages to silicone for non-racing applications—long a favorite of show-car owners. As I mentioned in the text, traditional brake fluid will damage a car's finish if left standing for long. Silicone, on the other hand, will not discolor or loosen even a fragile finish like lacquer.

Another feature over conventional brake fluid is it won't absorb water. This helps prevent rust pitting and corrosion so often found in hydraulic systems during brake overhauls.

There are a number of parts, especially underbody rubber parts, where silicone fluid can be used as if it were a thick Armor All to shine and preserve.

Beware: Like any silicone, it can contaminate body finishes. Especially before you use a primer-surfacer, be super-thorough in cleaning up to prevent later paint lifting and "fish-eye."

One last disadvantage is that silicone fluid is about twice as expensive as DOT 3 fluid. If you decide it is worth the expense, completely purge your brake system and clutch system of non-silicone fluid. This includes all cylinders and lines.

---

overly expose yourself to the asbestos dust. If you choose to have any zinc plating redone, get the parts to the plater.

Brake Drums—All Z-cars have aluminum-alloy drums with a cast-in friction liner. Unless you are satisfied this is smooth and of adequate thickness for reuse, take the drums to a reliable shop to have them turned. This will ensure a smooth, concentric surface with which the shoes can efficiently make contact. As mentioned earlier in this chapter, the machinist will measure the remaining thickness to ensure they have sufficient "meat" to be legal.

Aluminum alloy takes glass-bead-blasting very well, but don't bead-blast the iron liners. Give the outside a light coat of low-gloss clear—a thick coat will impede heat dissipation.

Wheel Cylinders—Dismantle each wheel cylinder and inspect the bore before rebuilding unless you've decided to pop for new ones. If the bore is pitted, replace the cylinder. There are two distinctly different types. Be sure you get the correct kits or replacement cylinders.

The 240 and 260Z early series had only one piston, the cylinder being free to slide to the reaction of the piston. Pop the dust cover off and pull the piston out of the cylinder. Look down inside the cylinder and inspect for pits and scuffing. If there appears to be a problem, thoroughly clean the unit and check the suspected irregularities with a sharp tool. If they aren't severe and are behind the stroke of the piston, the cylinder can probably be reused. If there are irregularities in the swept area—where the piston and cup ride—try refinishing it with a bit of #400-grit sandpaper. If it still looks bad, replace it. Aluminum cylinder walls can't be honed like iron ones.

Remove the conical spring by unwinding it from the top and pry off the old rubber cup. Clean the piston thoroughly with a wire brush. If it shows advanced rust or wear, replace the wheel cylinder. If all is OK, clean the cylinder and install a rebuild kit.

Rebuild Kit—This contains a new sealing cup. Lubricate the cup with some brake fluid and install it on the piston. Install the spring and carefully work the seal back into the cylinder. Wipe some fluid on the dust-cover lip and spread the cover over the end of the cylinder. Put spring clip on cover.

Fit the parking-brake lever/adjuster on its pivot at the rear of the cylinder. Clean and lightly grease the adjuster wheel and screw. Run the screw into its retracted position and insert in the back end of the cylinder. Also lube the shoe-contact slot on the back side.

Cylinder Installation—Put a daub of light lubricant on both sides of the cylinder slot in the bottom of the backing plate where the unit slides. Insert the assembly through the slot and rubber dust cover. Secure with the two horseshoe-shape clips. The curved one with dimples is nearest the plate, the flat one with holes fits on top. Check the assembly for free movement. If it slides with light effort, push the outer dust cover snugly in place. If it's loose or too tight, remedy the problem. Then install the bleeder tap finger-tight and slip its dust-cap retainer over the neck.

Brake shoes reassembled on backing plates. Pay attention to which way they go on. One's the leading shoe, the other the trailing. Adjust shoes so drum will fit over them.

Once drum is on, readjust shoes so there's a slight drag against drum. Check by rotating drum as you make adjustments. Drum is glassbeaded and has a thin coating of clear. More could inhibit cooling and would discolor if it got hot. I smeared some heavy grease on the drum pilot and center hole of the drum.

Parking-brake cable is reinstalled— clevis to lever, clip to cable bracket.

Later series brakes (280Zs) use a more conventional double-piston cylinder that is fixed to the backing plate. Follow the steps above, except do both pistons. No significant irregularities can be tolerated in the bore of this cylinder as the pistons slide at both ends. Once assembled, bolt each cylinder to its backing plate. Make sure the adjuster is fully retracted so the drum will fit over the shoes.

These brake cylinders were supplied by Tokico or Nabco. Although the cylinders are interchangeable as an assembly, their parts are not. In other words, you can't use a kit meant for one to rebuild the other. Similarly, 280Z brakes interchange as complete assemblies—that is, brake line, backing plate, cylinder and all.

Anchor Block—On early types, reattach this part to the top of the backing plate and lubricate the slots where the shoes ride. It is riveted in place on late backing plates.

Brake Shoes—With the cylinder in place, install the shoes. These are so inexpensive that unless you find negligible wear on the existing linings, replace them. There are many excellent brands available. Most offer more efficient semi-metallic linings for improved performance.

Before you install the shoes, lubricate the six raised rubbing surfaces around the plate's circumference. Any high-temperature grease will do. Also lubricate the adjusting screws where they contact the shoe.

Z brakes require two different shoes for each side, a leading shoe—it installs to the front—and a trailing shoe. The leading shoe's lining is mounted low—it seems to have slipped down on the shoe. The trailing shoe conversely shows some bare shoe at the bottom. On early-type brakes, the shoe with the rectangular slot is always trailing because the parking-brake-lever tang fits into the slot.

Insert the nail-like retaining pin through its hole in the backing plate, slip the appropriate shoe in place and install the short coil spring and retainer button over the pin. Hold the pin from the back, position the slot in the retainer so it aligns with the flat on the end of the pin and push the retainer against the spring and over the pin. Turn the retainer or pin 90 degrees to lock the shoe in place. Be prepared. The little spring can shoot the retainer off with some considerable force if it slips off the pin! I have a humorous photo of falling brake parts that happened just before I took the one used to illustrate this section.

Repeat the process with the other shoe. Put a daub of grease on the two return springs and reinstall them into the appropriate holes. On early types, the top spring is usually black, the bottom green. Look for the green spring first; black is harder to see on older springs. On later brakes, the bottom spring has a straight center wire section and can't be interchanged mistakenly.

Reinstall Drums—Put a skim of grease or anti-seize compound on the inside chamfer of the center hole of the drum to help prevent sticking the next time you need to remove it.

Slip the drum over the shoes until it fits tightly onto the hub. All drums have a hole in the face for adjusting. It is closed with a rubber plug.

Parking-Brake Cable

Reinstall the cable bracket on the hub carrier. Run the cable ends down to each bracket, slip the cable through the slot, position the housing end in the bracket and clip in place. Fit the clevis end to the lever, put in the pin and secure with a cotter key.

Brake Line—Bolt the bracket atop the hub carrier. Fit the steel brake line around the backing plate on the forward side. It will only go one way, so if you have it on the wrong side or the line is upside down, you'll figure it out. Using a flare-nut wrench, reattach the fitting to the wheel cylinder and tighten it. Then secure the line to the bracket.

8 Electrical Components & Wiring

Final metamorphosis—luxury, beef and about triple the sticker price. Just what a couple of hundred-thousand folks wanted! The electrical system of a fully-equipped 280Z is much more complex than an early 240Zs. Courtesy Nissan.

Modern automobiles have literally miles of electrical circuitry to accomplish the myriad tasks we buyers opt to have done by electrical power. This is to say nothing of the lights, buzzers and whistles that are required. Z-cars have their share, especially the electronic fuel-injected 280Zs. I don't attempt to tackle the minute specifics of the many circuits, connectors, switches and attendant electronic marvels Datsun built in. That I leave to the various Service Manuals and your test light!

Electrical malfunctions can be a real problem in a restoration. Fortunately, we are dealing with a modern, well-engineered automobile. And this extends to the electrical system. There were problems with some of the switches in early Zs, but overall electrical circuitry is easily serviced.

Let's take a look at a few pertinent aspects you may encounter with your car's electrical system. First, no matter what quality is built into a product, there isn't anything some hack can't foul up. I find the formidable job of replacing an entire wiring harness preferable to trying to make sense of a butchered original. Unless electrical work is your specialty, replacement rather than wiring repair may be your best bet.

Top-quality wiring harnesses are not cheap. They cost what they are worth and may require a substantial backorder wait. As Zs get older, there will be a growing demand for brand-new harnesses for specific models. On most collectable cars, this results in a period of scarcity, eventually followed by the relief that reproduction of parts engenders. If the parent company—Nissan in this case—senses that the demand for such parts is solid and ongoing, they may keep any part, including wiring harnesses, in the dealer inventory. Otherwise, buy any wiring harness you *think* you may need without hesitation. If you do get a new or repro harness, confirm that you got the right one by laying it on top of your original harness and comparing lengths and connectors.

If you aren't successful in finding a replacement harness, specialized

115

116 How to Restore Your Datsun Z-Car

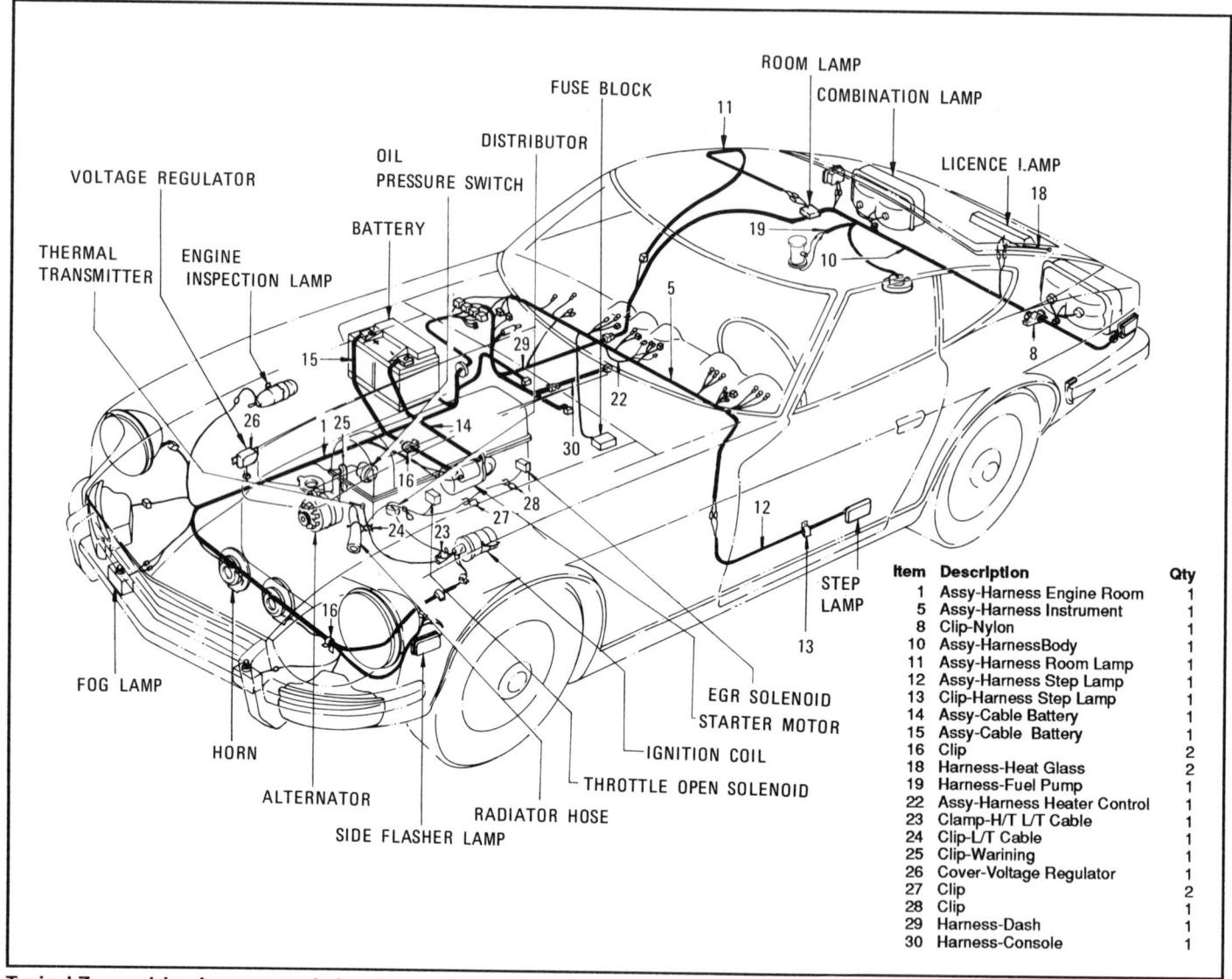

Item	Description	Qty
1	Assy-Harness Engine Room	1
5	Assy-Harness Instrument	1
8	Clip-Nylon	1
10	Assy-HarnessBody	1
11	Assy-Harness Room Lamp	1
12	Assy-Harness Step Lamp	1
13	Clip-Harness Step Lamp	1
14	Assy-Cable Battery	1
15	Assy-Cable Battery	1
16	Clip	2
18	Harness-Heat Glass	2
19	Harness-Fuel Pump	1
22	Assy-Harness Heater Control	1
23	Clamp-H/T L/T Cable	1
24	Clip-L/T Cable	1
25	Clip-Warining	1
26	Cover-Voltage Regulator	1
27	Clip	2
28	Clip	1
29	Harness-Dash	1
30	Harness-Console	1

Typical Z-car wiring harness and electrical components. Courtesy Nissan.

automotive-electrical shops can functionally rewire just about any car if your budget can handle it. Repaired wiring correctly done will meet or exceed the original specifications, but it won't look original and it will cost a lot.

If your harness performed well and looks good, keep it. A thorough cleaning should be the next move. I use naptha and clean shop towels, cleaning a foot or two at a time. Be careful you don't lose track of the tags at the terminal ends you placed there at disassembly time.

Inevitably, there will be grease, lint, paint overspray and other less readily identifiable substances on the loom tape, even on wiring from the interior. Solvent will remove most if not all of the crud that gums up a bundle of wires. Keep the cleaned *end* portion out of the dirt and work from the middle out to the ends. This will help you identify and mentally inventory any broken leads or lost connectors.

Troubleshooting
If your project Z has been victimized by an amateur or has evidence of fire damage, be prepared to do a considerable amount of troubleshooting. An inexpensive tool you should not be without is the electrical *multitester*. These can be acquired at auto-parts stores or hobby outlets such as Radio Shack. With very little experience, you can pinpoint some shorts and broken circuits in a Z wiring harness that would otherwise be impossible to find.

Using the wiring diagram in your Technical Manual and continuity function of the tester—scale that reads *resistance* in ohms—you can probably verify the integrity of most circuits. If the circuit is installed and energized with 12 volts, the voltmeter function—set to read 12 volts—can be equally handy. An inexpensive test light will perform the tracing job equally well and is very convenient to use, though most benefit from a longer jumper wire.

Let's look at some specific problems.

Color Coding—Generally a restorer can trust wiring diagrams found in factory manuals. However, a Nissan Service Manual Supplement disclaims:

Electrical Components & Wiring

"Individual wire color tracers do not always terminate as they are begun and may at times vary in color within the harness manufactured for a given model series." This means you can't take anything for granted when it comes to the color of wires. Note that while not all Z harness *tracers* are consistent, most are. And usually the variation is detectable by the process of elimination. Only one tracer color will be inconsistent; others will conform throughout the system. I don't think it will constitute a major stumbling block to a successful rewire.

A graphic illustration of the increasing complexity of the Z-car through its evolution from sports coupe to luxury GT can be seen by comparing the respective wiring diagrams for the 240Z and 280Z. No one could be blamed for getting a migraine from the latter's five-page spread. The 280Z Service Manuals take pity on us by including separate circuit diagrams for the major circuits.

A trick I like to employ is the use of colored pencils or flo-tip pens to highlight circuits I'm trying to trace. Just be sure you use a straightedge and highlight the right lines to start with! A clear photocopy or Xerox of the diagram is a big help with this technique—and it saves your original from getting messed up. Tape it to a piece of cardboard or tack it up on the shop wall.

Restore Wiring Harness

If you are refurbishing your present wiring harness, the most common problem you are likely to encounter is mangled or missing connectors or taped splices in place of such. If originality is of particular concern to you, an ideal source of parts can be found on old wiring harnesses from wrecked Z-cars.

Correct terminals and color-coded wires can be reused in their original location, providing the wires are carefully spliced. I find some length can be added to a harness, which sometimes comes in handy. Commercial butt-type splicing joints can be hidden inside the taped part of a harness. Resourcefulness is necessary to repair wiring correctly!

A negative factor may arise if you need to replace a worn or damaged component. The same component tends to receive the same wear or damage on other Zs. You may be able to find wires or plugs that interchange from other Nissan products, providing you have the time and patience to investigate at your local dismantlers. Otherwise, commercial aftermarket splices and connectors will have to suffice.

Keep in mind when purchasing wiring components and materials that black magic has nothing to do with malfunctions in a car's circuitry, but there may be a times you'd swear your Z has a hex on it. Although you can *see* the physical presence of a wire, electricity—or absence of—cannot be detected by sight. What looks like a perfectly good wire may have a hidden break. Connectors and gang plugs, of which there are plenty in any automobile, are the perfect hiding place for shorts or opens. Worst of all, electrical malfunctions always seem to be secreted in some inaccessible spot, such as in a body panel or up under the dark recesses of the instrument panel.

The solution? Use the best materials you can and carefully and methodically ensure your connections are correct and sound. Attention to such detail will go a long way toward eliminating puzzling electrical problems. Remember: A professional auto-wiring technician may be able to correct your botched wiring, but only after he's exhausted a generous portion of your restoration budget.

If the connector or plug is sound, but the plastic insulation on the wire has suffered from chafing, heat or contaminants, heat-shrink-tubing insulation is a viable repair. Granted, it won't be the correct color, but it is inexpensive and readily available at electronics hobby stores. Simply by sliding the appropriate size tube over an exposed wire and applying heat, you can make a functional repair.

Note that a wire with heat-shrink tubing on it lacks flexibility. And the tubing shrinks in length as well as breadth. Bear these points in mind when determining how much heat-shrink tubing to use and where. For really heavy-duty applications, I have often added a second, larger diameter section to a repair, making it doubly thick.

Similar to electrician's tape, but without the adhesive, is a product made especially for wrapping harnesses. It is called *loom tape*. It is offered by OEM suppliers such as Essex. Their loom tape is part number BT-079. The problem is finding it. Because you probably can't find it at your local auto-parts store, inquire at electrical supply houses that specialize in automotive or aircraft applications, or contact one of the following suppliers:

BWD Corporation
11045 Gage Ave.
Franklin Park, IL 60131

California Terminal Products
(Cal Term)
1990 Friendship Drive
El Cajon, CA 92020

Del City Wire Co. Inc.
2524 S.E. 15th St.
Oklahoma City, OK 73129

East Penn Mfg. Co.
Deka Rd.
Lyon Station, PA 19536

JT & T Products Corp.
206 Commercial St.
San Jose, CA 95112

Mize & Company
300 Industrial Ave.
Kingman, KS 67068

Murphy Industries Inc.
Whitco One-Stop Electrical Centers
2801 Rockcreek Parkway
N. Kansas City, MO 64117

Narragansett Reproduction
Ed & Miki Pease
Woodville Rd., P.O. Box 51
Wood River Junction, RI 02894

Ron Francis' Wire Works
167 Keystone Rd.
Chester, PA 19013

Standard Motor Products
37-18 Northern Blvd.
Long Island City, NY 11101

Taylor Cable Products Inc.
301 Highgrove Rd.
Grandview, MO 64030

Terminal Supply Co.
1800 Thunderbird
Troy, MI 48084

Wiring harness is restored, ready to reinstall. I'm attaching rear harness to a "fish" wire and taping it so harness won't hang up in B-pillar. Grommet will be cemented to hole.

Same harness being fished through quarter panel. If you don't have a helper feeding in the other end as you pull, feed some in, then pull it out, repeating this back-and-forth process until you have the harness installed. Use metal fingers to secure harness in rear fender/finisher areas.

If the harness is salvageable, but the tape is loose, peel it off and rewrap it in manageable sections. Duplicate the "factory" look when retaping a bundle of wires by starting from the extreme branch end by the terminal and taping toward the thicker bundle. By using a *blind-end technique*—taking a wrap or two toward the terminal end and then overlapping back toward the trunk of the bundle—a very slick appearance can be obtained. This also helps prevent the bundle from unwrapping later when age and heat have taken their toll.

Fusible Links—Datsun used these in several places—starter and alternator connections are common locations. Serving a function similar to a regular fuse, they "self-destruct" when their circuit is overloaded, protecting the expensive component they service. A blown fusible link can be identified by its insulation being crisp or blistered from the resultant heat.

When replacing a fuse or fusible link, find out what caused its failure. Don't replace a fuse or fusible link with tinfoil or ordinary wire. This is asking for big trouble. Fuses and fusible links are readily available from Nissan dealers or auto-parts outlets.

Replacing Electrical Components

Repair or rebuild of electrical assemblies such as alternators, starters and F.I. "black boxes," are better left to the specialist. The amount of specialization of equipment and knowledge required makes these parts inappropriate for the restorer to tackle. There are several areas of concern to be aware of, however.

If you purchase a rebuilt component on an exchange basis, be very sure what you get is like-for-like. A number of alternators used by Datsun were similar and often are listed as direct interchanges by rebuilders. Differences usually involve the specific output rating the manufacturer listed—some alternators spec'd for the 510 series fit Zs, but don't have the needed amperage output. If authenticity is a must, be sure the rebuilt part not only looks like the original, but has the same part number, rating and so forth.

Otherwise, take your original to a shop that will recondition and return the *same* unit to you. Often, they will be glad to bead-blast or otherwise treat the housing so it looks like an off-the-shelf factory part. Telling the technician what you're doing makes good sense. This will prevent such disasters as getting your alternator back with the tag blasted off or painted flat black! It would look much better with a coat of clear enamel over the freshly beaded casing before it gets greasy.

Small electrical components such as relays, regulators and so forth are inexpensive. New components are clean and brightly plated! Be prepared to accept functional interchanges that don't look like the original on occasion. Remember—electrical parts are seldom returnable, so take your old one in to match it against the parts store's replacement.

Beware—Counterfeits!

Responsible auto-parts retailers are reporting increasing numbers of bogus "name-brand" replacement parts turning up as returns. Not that your trusted counterman sold the part. The typical scenario is it failed in service and the unlucky buyer tried to get some satisfaction from him because it carried his recognized brand name.

With depressing regularity, investigation of such a part reveals it was not manufactured by that company at all, but was cleverly faked . . . and usually sold at a radically discounted price by a "gyppo" retailer! I won't characterize this miscreant further. But the victim should count himself lucky if it was only that part he needs to replace with a quality part. All too often, a blown engine or a serious traffic accident is the result of counterfeit parts "polluting" a repaired car.

With this information in mind, be aware that everything bearing a recognized trademark—even Genuine Nissan Parts—may not be genuine. Expect to pay a fair price for quality goods. And know your supplier. Parts of imported origin are probably easier to fake than domestics with their plethora of brand names and cryptic—to the English-speaking public—labeling. Caveat Emptor—"Let the buyer beware"—and good luck!

Install Wiring Harness

The body wiring harness that came out easily won't necessarily go back in the same way, but it doesn't have to be an ordeal, either. The only challenging installation is routing the main body harness from the passenger floorpan area to the inner rear fender.

Question: How do you get that limp bundle of wires through the hole in the inner fender just behind the door jamb and up through the B-pillar?

Answer: Take a page from the construction electrician's book and use a *fish wire,* or *tape,* to pull the extreme end wires of the bundle up and out the desired path.

For your purposes, a 5-foot piece of soft wire will do. Any type that is rigid enough to push from the accessible area in the C-pillar—up where the fuel-vapor canister is normally mounted—forward and down to the hole in the B-pillar where the wiring should enter.

When the end of the fish appears at the hole, grasp and pull out a few inches. Bend a loophook into the end and push the extreme end connectors of the harness through. These will probably be the speaker and antenna power leads. Bend them over and tape them tightly to themselves so they won't hang up as you pull them through the double wall of the body. The taillight connectors should be secured close to the harness also, but *not* the branch to the dome light and rear-window defroster.

Now pull the fish back through the C-pillar, alternately tensioning the harness and guiding it through the access hole, until you can reach the end of the harness. Remove the fish and continue drawing the harness into position in the same manner. The twists in the wiring as well as the protruding connectors will hang up occasionally, so be patient as you snake it through.

Put all protective grommets back into their holes in the sheet metal. Route the harness through the rear inner fender hole, across the taillight panel and through the driver-side hole. Secure it by bending over the rubber-covered fingers. Remove your identifier tags as you make final connections, but not before!

Dome-Light & Hatch-Window-Defroster Wires—Fish back through the rear roof header and pull these wires back to their positions. The hardest part of this maneuver is capturing the wires from the main harness. Hook them up later.

Secure the trunk of the main body harness to the floor/sill areas all the way up to the firewall. Run the parking-brake, speaker, fuel-pump and seat-belt-interlock leads to their locations. Tape to the body any wires, such as for the electric fuel-pump, that were originally so secured.

Engine-Compartment Harness

This harness is the easiest to install.

Switch such as this can be installed so it will shut off the entire electrical system. Knob removes for security. Another advantage is it can be removed to return car to complete originality. Courtesy Bathurst, Inc.

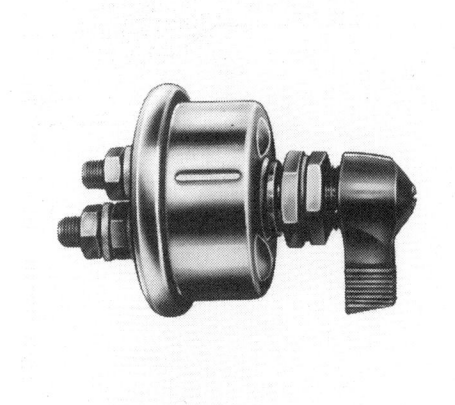

Battery shut-off switch needs to be heavy duty. It can be mounted inside passenger compartment, but longer cables will be required. Key-operated switch is another security variation. Only end of lock cylinder needs to show from outside car. Courtesy Bathurst, Inc.

The main connection between the two trunks of all Z-car electrical systems is made under the instrument panel on the passenger's side. The engine-compartment harness must be threaded back through a hole in the firewall under the battery box.

The type of grommet used varied somewhat from model to model. It is in a vulnerable position right under the battery. Engine wiring takes a beating in general. Being exposed to the dribbling of hydrochloric acid from an ailing battery is even more destructive. If the original grommet is in good condition, count yourself fortunate.

You may be able to find a new grommet that will serve as an identical replacement, but I have yet to find one that is comparable. Nissan supplies the firewall grommet on a complete new harness, but the part is not available separately. So for now replace it with something similar—until some sharp aftermarket supplier discovers the need and reproduces a substitute. Of course, if you opted for a new replacement harness, you will avoid this and other drawbacks of old wiring. It is a joy to work with factory-fresh wires and connectors!

If you're using the original wiring harness, but must replace the grommet, you'll have to do some detective work. I made a substitute grommet

Battery-switch knob can be removed, rendering switch inoperative. Cap replaces knob, protecting switch from the elements. Courtesy Flaming River.

using one from another harness, but there is no practical way to stretch even a relatively new original one or a grommet of the correct size over the main connectors. So split the grommet and put it over the wiring bundle, then rejoin the cut ends with a quick-setting glue. When the grommet is in the hole, it should present a neat, original appearance.

In any case, a ring of sealer should be made on the engine side of the firewall hole to leakproof it. If you are stuck with using the old grommet, be liberal with the sealer. A wrap or two of black *dumdum* or an overall coating of body sealant will conceal the effect *and* appearance of a cracked or loose grommet. At least the battery support partially hides this part from view!

Route Wiring

Using illustrations from this book and the Service Manual, return the harness to its original routing. Datsun provided abundant retainers in the form of those plastic-coated metal fingers. Follow the routing forward with the main trunk, securing it as you go. Pass the front branch through the radiator bulkhead and route it across the front. I don't crimp the retaining fingers down tight until I have all the twists and kinks out of the trunk and the connectors at their destinations. There is a certain amount of slack in the harness until you secure it tightly—be patient and methodical because if it fit originally, it will fit again.

Route the other branches toward their ultimate reaches similarly. Remember that many components have their own sub-harnesses or short pigtails that also provide length and accommodation. The Service Manuals provide fairly detailed information on each specific year/model which can be referred to as you rewire.

Caution: Use your powers of observation and common sense as you proceed, both in the harnesses and dash wiring. Especially in the area of wire color coding, no manufacturer is above committing discrepancies or providing isolated misinformation. Check for similarly sized wires—not 12 gauge connecting to 18 gauge, for instance—compatible connectors and logical destinations.

A complete rewiring in a restored car that is electrically crippled because of careless or hurried work is disheartening. Remember the old saw: If you don't have time to do a job right, how are you going to find time to do it *again?*

Just in case, have your amp-and-continuity meter or test light handy for when the circuits are energized. Don't be "shocked" if you have to run down a few glitches, even if you've done a conscientious job.

Battery Shut-Off Switch

No, this isn't something you'll find in a Nissan parts catalog. On any valuable automobile, I recommend the installation of an accessory switch to kill the car's electrical current. These are available from several suppliers for a reasonable price, considering what they can save you—your restored car. Installed between the battery and circuitry, they provide a positive shut-off for all current. This has saved more than one collector car when an unsuspected short threatened to burn up the wiring. An added bonus is it provides a measure of anti-theft deterrent. Disadvantages are a degree of non-originality though, like seat belts on old classics, this is often overlooked in deference to its safety value. Also it stops the electric clock. Many longtime Z-car owners have lived with a purely ornamental clock.

My project 240Z and virtually every car I restore are routinely equipped with an electrical shut-off. Yes, I know the "Prince of Darkness" jokes, but the Lucas switch in my car has been in service since 1970. This model has a hot contact to run the clock. I'm not sure it is still marketed in this country, but it has been reliable. *Don't* use the open knife-type switch often found on RV's.

Electrical shut-off switches are available from many sources. For example, Bathurst, Inc. supplies a battery-post-mounted underhood model similar to the unit on my project car. This type can be temporarily removed for original appearance such as concours. They and the venerable J.C. Whitney & Co. carry both a keyed and non-locking version. Another is available from Flaming River. It has a removable handle and a cap that seals the switch from the elements.

On a Z-car the most practical mounting point is on the engine-compartment firewall adjacent to the battery. Either utilize two short cables—battery post to switch terminal and switch terminal to starter—or cut the original cable and install two 3/8-inch terminal ends. A battery shop can do this for you. The switch can even be mounted so it is accessible from the interior, but this may require longer cables.

If you aren't using a shut-off, leave off one battery clamp after rewiring your Z-car until you've checked for short circuits.

9 Interior Restoration & Assembly

The most complex assembly on the interior of your Z-car is the instrument panel. It's also the largest. Consequently, it's the most difficult to restore and install. However, if you break the instrument panel down into its separate components, the job is not so difficult.

Restore Instrument Panel
Instruments & Controls—With the instrument panel (I/P), or dash to some, out of the car, the gauges, switches and controls can easily be refurbished or replaced. As with many other assemblies on a car of recent manufacture, it makes sense to buy new ones rather than repair them. As long as new or good used items are available, the expense of tinkering with the likes of a tachometer or clock mechanism is not cost-effective.

Glove Box & Door—If these weren't removed to get the instrument panel out of the car, they should come out now. Check the box for serviceability, especially if it's cardboard.

Remove the various knobs and store them carefully. Don't lose the little setscrews that hold them in place. These have either Phillips or conventional heads.

Remove all face plates from the heater-control panel—courtesy light, radio/stereo and so forth. Disconnect the wiring and make sure the heater or A/C-control cables are free. Take the panel off and put it safely out of the work area. It's plastic and easily damaged.

Radio/Stereo Tape—Remove the unit and any related connections now. Not only did Datsun equip the various Zs with differing sound systems, but yours may have an aftermarket unit—

"The car that started it all"—as they say. Factory photos can often be used to verify originality, vintage of features on collector cars. Courtesy Nissan.

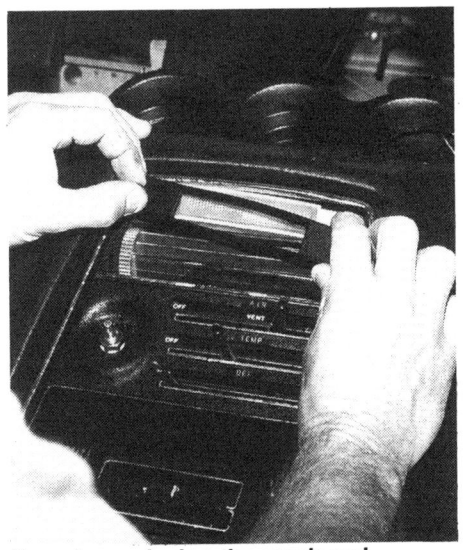

If you're replacing the crash pad, which is the basic instrument panel, everything from old panel must be transferred to new—and work! Radio knobs, bezels and so forth come off. I use ziplock bags to keep parts organized.

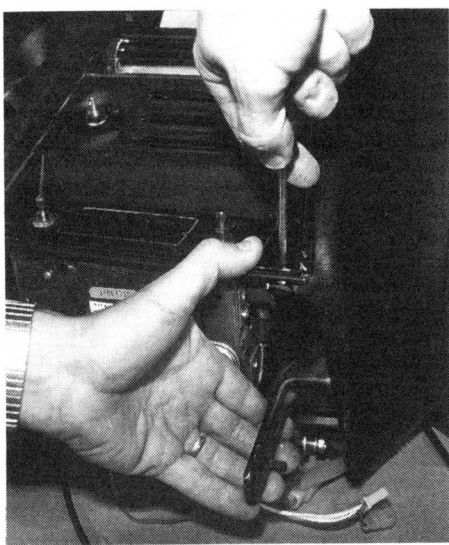

Disassembly must be methodical. Does the radio need work? Did the heater controls work smoothly? Don't lose those identifying tags on wiring.

122 How to Restore Your Datsun Z-Car

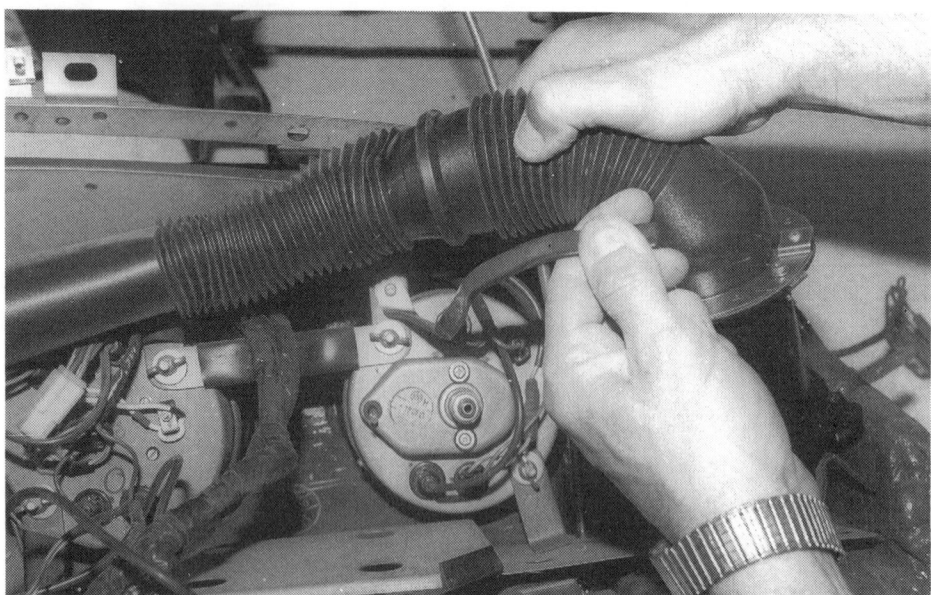

Wiring harness and ducts are held in place by plastic-covered fingers. Some are tack-welded to I/P frame and can't be moved, others transfer to the new crash pad.

Trip-odometer reset cable has setscrew on speedometer housing, but sleeve won't fit through cable housing. This must be carefully released from speedometer-like cable.

Speedometer and tachometer remove from front of panel on early style, from rear on late. New crash pad is a major investment, but often necessary on well-used Z-cars.

or you may be upgrading your car's sound system. All that is beyond the scope of this book. I show the original 1970 AM radio only. At least these are mounted similarly.

Tag all electrical connectors just to simplify reinstallation. Then remove the fasteners holding the sound system and store it away from heat and moisture.

Flasher & Cigarette Lighter—Remove these now. Store everything with care in labeled bags or other small containers. Don't forget where they are stashed!

Instrument Panel-End Vent Outlets—The *eyeball* vent outlets come out from the backside of the panel. First remove the Phillips-head screws, then the vents. Next are the flexible hoses. Remove them by moving the plastic-covered metal retainers aside.

If the plated-plastic deflector is damaged or worn, you will be money ahead to replace the whole assembly. But it comes apart if you find a deflector in better condition.

Defroster Vents—On early Zs, the vents are attached with screws to the I/P flange. They are marked **LH** and **RH**. On late Zs, they attach to the body cowl.

Instrument Cluster—With the vents/hoses and defrosters out of the way, the gauges are accessible.

Trip-Odometer Reset Knob/Cable—This is a chore that was easy at the factory, but will take you considerable time and effort. The sleeve that connects the cable to the odometer shaft is held by a setscrew. Removing this effectively disconnects the gauge for removal. However, if you're going to replace the whole cluster as on my project car, the cable must be removed as well.

Remove the retaining clip with needle-nose pliers. Unfortunately, the sleeve is too large to fit through the cable housing on the lower panel frame. Datsun crimped the sleeve to the speedometer-like cable *after* it was through the housing tube. Eight little crimps on the sides of the sleeve must be carefully drilled out with a 1/16-inch drill bit. When this metal is removed, the pressure that holds the cable in the sleeve is gradually released. At some point you should be able to pull the cable free. Slip the cable and its wire sheath out of the panel proper. Then use a 1/8-inch bit to clean out the bore of the sleeve for reuse.

Panel-Light Rheostat—Tag the wires, pull off the knob with a steady pull, then remove the Phillips-head screws that hold the switch. Put the knob back on the switch until time to reinstall it.

Tachometer & Speedometer—Mark the color codes of the terminals and bulb holes with a Sharpie pen before removing the wiring and bulb sockets. The harness connectors should be unique, thus self-identifying.

240Z Versions—Remove any nuts that secure the two large gauges to the panel frame and their braces. Panels in 260 and 280Zs retain these with screws in the top of the bezel and a flange at the rear to the frame. Gently push the tach and speedo rearward until they are free of the instrument

Interior Restoration & Assembly 123

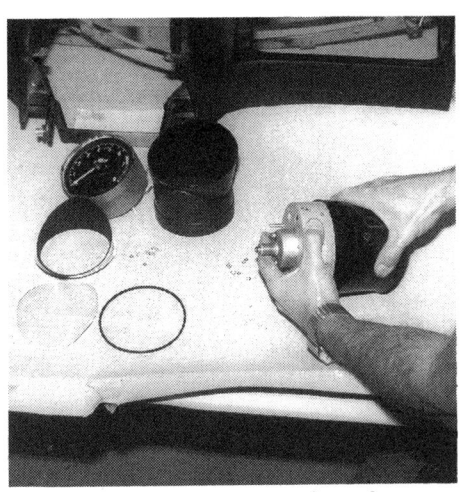

Tach and speedometer can be refurbished to look much nicer. They disassemble similarly. Try not to scratch or get fingerprints on lens or face of either.

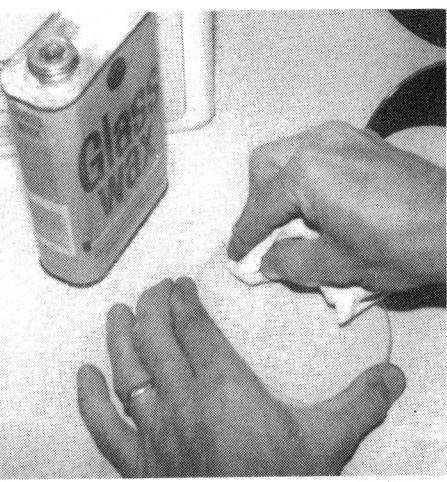

Plastic faces may not be restorable if they are deeply scratched or burned. Buffing wheel and super-fine compound will eliminate hair-line scratches, though. Preliminary cleaning with DX-330 and a clean soft rag or thorough polishing with Glass Wax may tell you if it is salvageable.

Camera-lens cleaning tissue is good for final cleaning on inner face of lenses. Compressed air and camera brush or artist's paint brush will dust out bezel and face.

panel. If either hangs up on padding, don't force it from the lens side. The lens could break or pop out of place in the unit. Pull on the metal housing instead.

Refurbishing Gauges

Now's the perfect time to remove crud and insect parts from your gauges. First clean the outside of each gauge and take out the small Phillips-head screws. Using a twist/pull motion, separate the bezel from the head assembly.

Lenses: These may be scratched or otherwise occluded, so push them rearward gently to separate from the inner parts.

Clean the faces first. A cotton rag and a few drops of DX330 or naptha work well to remove greasy deposits. Use solvent *sparingly* on plastic, especially a clear lens! Follow up with dishwashing detergent and warm water. Now examine the lens in the light. Be careful to protect the back side from damage while it's exposed.

Very bad scratches may be irreparable. The same goes for cracks and crazing. They mean you'll have to hunt for a better lens. Minor damage—shallow penetration of the material—can be polished out with a buffing wheel.

Use a loose-sewn wheel with the lightest possible compound—rouge or coloring grade—and very light pressure. If you only have access to a finish buffer, such as is used to polish paint, do this: Clamp the buffer securely in a vise or suitable fixture, put a bit of very light compound on the lens, lock the machine's trigger down and hold the lens to the edge of the wheel. Use a new bonnet with plenty of pile and take care not to lose your grip on the plastic lens. And don't forget the eye protection, which you should use with any kind of polishing machine . . . right?

If your gauge lenses look pretty good to start with, just give them a once over with a good plastic polish—available in most paint departments—or a cleaner-wax such as Glass Wax. Wash your hands afterwards and don't get any on the matte-black bezel! Using a soft cotton cloth, buff the lens until it looks clean in direct sunlight, especially on the side you can't get at when reinstalled.

Use compressed air at low pressure to remove any dust or bugs from the meter assembly. Clean out the recesses of the plastic bezels, too. A badly damaged face may be beyond repair, but some Testors 'Namel®, somewhat thinned on a #1 sable brush can be used to touch up either the numbers or the face. It is available at model counters in either flat black or white. Don't expect it to cover in one coat. Use a matte lacquer, such as Ditzler Low Gloss Black 19, to restore bezel finish.

Drop the lens back into the bezel from the rear. Be extremely careful not to get fingerprints on the back side of the lens or face of the gauge. There's no wiping off fingerprints from the interior surfaces of a gauge once it's back together.

Spacer with the gasket pops in next—check where the little tangs go at top and bottom. Tangs fit into slots in the lens and spacer. Check for dust or threads on the lens or gauge face

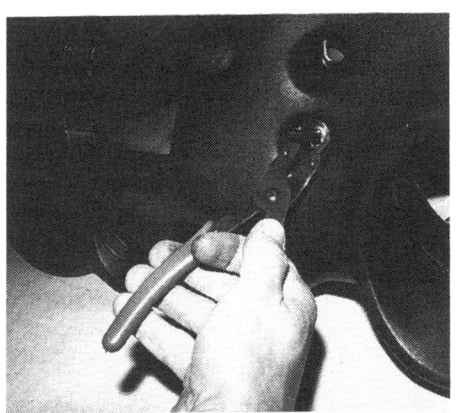

Retaining-ring pliers being used to remove hazard-flasher-switch nut. This was moved to accommodate switch for fog-light circuit, which is already wired into early Z harness.

124 How to Restore Your Datsun Z-Car

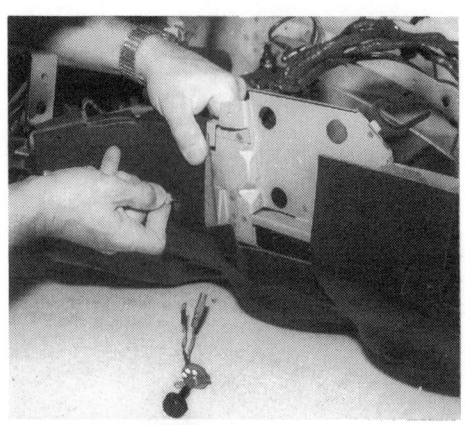

Wiring is in. Dash-light-rheostat and trip-odometer-reset-knob holes must be cut into dash padding. Refer to old dash for locating holes.

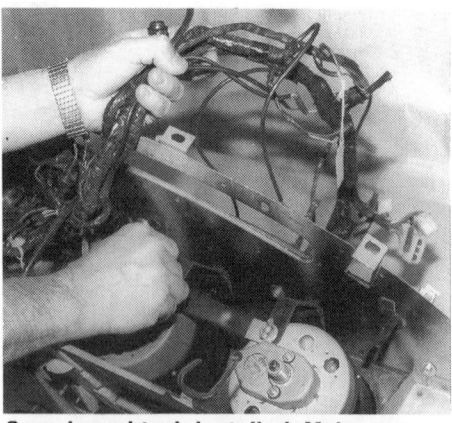

Speedo and tach installed. Make sure they are aligned, then tighten wing nuts. Brace installed between units is necessary to limit vibrations.

Reattach gauges and align their faces for uniform appearance, then tighten fasteners. Hook up wiring as you go to get it out of way.

and reassemble the unit with the Phillips-head screws. Repeat process with the other gauge and store the tach and speedo where they won't be contaminated with dirt or paint overspray.

Hazard-Flasher Switch—This has a circular trim nut on the face side. Loosen it with a pair of retaining-ring pliers. Don't chew it up with needle-nose pliers. Remove the switch and run the nut back on for safekeeping. On early panels there's a support that screws to the instrument-panel frame. This must be removed and transferred to the new panel.

Combination Gauges & Electric Clock—Remove screws that hold these gauges, the clock and their brackets to the instrument panel frame. You may notice these are designed to provide fore-and-aft adjustment to position the gauges in their sockets. Z-car panels have those plastic-covered fingers to secure the major wiring-harness bundles. Straighten these and lift the harnesses free. The gauges should now be easy to remove. If you're going to transfer the gauges to a new I/P right away, leave the plugs and bulb sockets in place.

Vehicle Identification Number (VIN) Tag—Now is the time to transfer the VIN tag to the new I/P. Don't wait until later. Access to the VIN tag requires removal of either the instrument panel or windshield! The special rivets must be drilled out, but *be careful* not to allow the bit to "walk" across the plate. The rivets are a bit smaller than the common 1/8-inch Pop-type rivet.

Use a 1/8-inch bit to remove the rivet heads. Once they're drilled off, use the same bit to enlarge the holes in the new instrument panel so they'll accept 1/8-inch rivets. Then simply position the plate so it reads from the windshield side and reinstall with 1/8-inch Pop Rivets.

Do a neat job of this operation. You won't want to unnecessarily excite the curiosity of law-enforcement personnel with a scarred or bent up VIN plate should you ever need to register your Z in another state.

New Dash Pad—Don't work on an expensive replacement panel in the cold—under 60F. The crash pad should be stabilized at no less than room temperature—about 70F—before attempting to stretch or stress the covering. Open the holes for the hazard flasher, panel-light rheostat and odometer-reset cable with a sharp tool. Proceed cautiously and don't cut away too much material.

Wiring Harness—Place the harness as in the original panel, running it inside the braces from the center outward, but don't secure it yet with the plastic-covered fingers until the five gauges are in place.

Tachometer & Speedometer—These should insert into their respective openings easily from the front of the panel. Tach is right, speedo left, remember? Secure with nuts from the rear with brace reinstalled. Or reinstall Phillips-head screws if so equipped. Hook up the wiring if it won't interfere with other installations.

Combination gauges have various brackets, depending on year of manufacture. All accommodate full range of adjustments to fit dash.

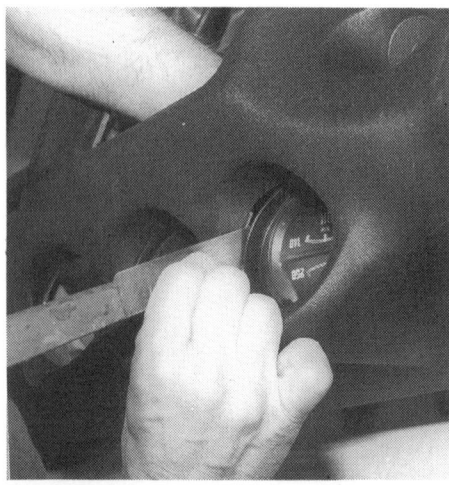

Combination gauges may need a bit of shoehorning with thin blade. Use a dull blade so it won't cut vinyl as you work in gauges.

Interior Restoration & Assembly 125

Gauges—Insert the gauges from the rear of the panel in contrast to the others. For this reason, you may need to use a flexible blade to "shoehorn" the bezel past the raw edge of the foam and covering. Use the adjustment feature now to align the three units with the instrument panel and one another. Secure as much wiring as is convenient—some may be easier to do after other parts are in place. Utilize as many of the plastic-covered fingers as are helpful to you now, do the remainder after you've finished the assembly.

Hazard Flasher—Transfer the support to the new instrument-panel frame now and install the switch from the rear. Install the nut and tighten with retaining-ring pliers. If your car has the rare fog-light switch, reinstall it now. Reinstall the cigarette lighter if so equipped. This applies to later models only.

Panel-Light Rheostat—Reinstall this switch, making sure the knob turns freely. Reattach the connectors.

Odometer-Reset Knob—Thread the cable through the hole you carefully cut until the circlip can be snapped on. Cut approximately 1/2 inch from the spring cover to allow for the cable lost in removing the attaching sleeve.

Resolder the sleeve. You'll need at least a 75-watt soldering iron and some good rosin-core solder. Clamp the sleeve so your hands will be free to hold the solder and cable, as well as the iron. Heat the cable and *tin* it with a coat of solder. Then insert it into the bore of the sleeve and flow solder into the holes left from drilling out the crimps. Allow the solder to penetrate to secure the cable. To check your job, tug and twist the cable after it has cooled. Don't close the setscrew hole with solder!

Clean up the job, put a drop of light oil on the sleeve and replace the screw. Now it can be reattached to the odometer-reset stem and tested.

Vent & Air-Conditioning Ducts—Whatever combination of ducts your panel utilizes, they may be reinstalled now. Use a bottle-brush and compressed air to remove any dust and spiders that may have taken up residence in them.

Defroster Ducts—Note which is **LH**

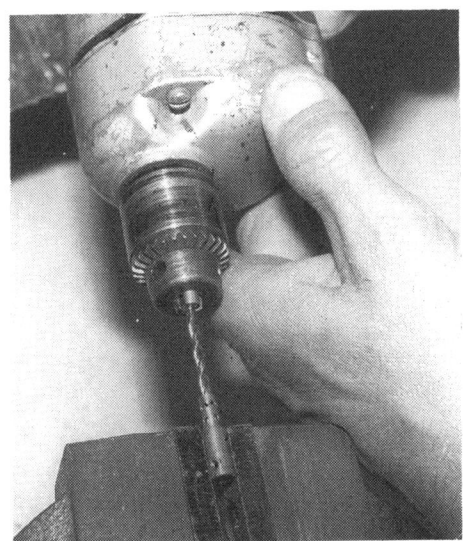

I used trim nut as a guide for cutting new hazard-flasher-switch hole. Dash is a bit later than originally installed in my car. Note depression in pad for flasher on/off label. Metal strip between lower dash brackets is only for shipping. Remove before installing center-mounted components.

Panel-light rheostat and wiring harness can be transferred directly to new instrument panel.

Reaming trip-odometer reset-cable sleeve prior to reinstalling on cable. Note small holes. These make soldering easier and improve solder retention.

Be sure you have cable through dash with its sheath installed before you resolder sleeve. Retaining clip holds knob in place.

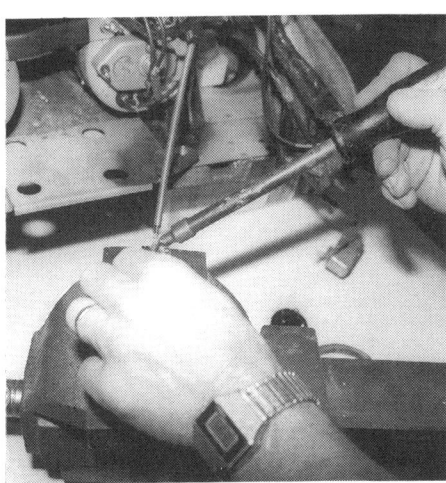

With sleeve firmly clamped, flow solder through small holes and into cable. Clean and put a shot of WD-40 on cable, especially if you used a flux, then reattach to odometer shaft.

126 How to Restore Your Datsun Z-Car

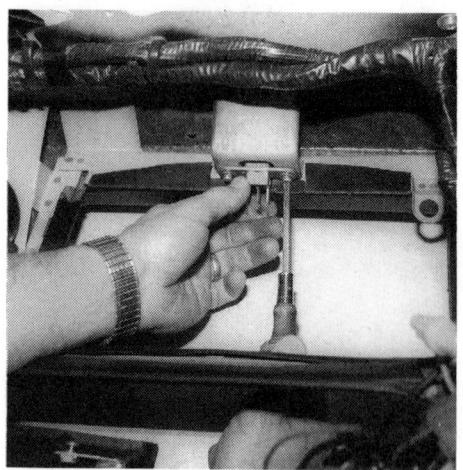

Eyeball registers and glove-box latch can be installed.

Ducts can be replaced now. Defroster diffuser fastens to I/P frame on early unit, to cowl on later type. Plastic glove-box liner must be installed now; cardboard can be done later.

and **RH** and install accordingly.

Glove-Box Striker—Don't forget this from the old panel. I wait until after the instrument panel is in the car before reinstalling the glove-box liner and door.

Heater Controls—This part of the panel varies in configuration—even between the different years of early or late series. However, Z-car panels remain similar in attachment and are very simple and straightforward to remove and replace. The early example I show was replaced because of wear and tear even though it was still functionally serviceable.

Instrument-Panel Finisher (Bezel)—Early Zs have a deep bezel that fronts the heater controls, courtesy light and radio. Late Zs have the radio in the console, use a shorter bezel to house warning lights and surround the heater/A/C controls. Levers and knobs are attached directly to the system control. Both have center air-duct outlets.

These finishers take a lot of abuse and, as a result, should be replaced. On early cars, after finisher is on, install heater-control switch and knob. Early 240Zs have **OFF** to the far left. This was changed later. If you need to refinish the levers on either system, mask and paint them matte black.

On early cars, reattach the heater-control unit. Then fasten the finisher to the panel with Phillips-head screws. Using a small straight-blade screwdriver, put on the control-lever knobs. Install the radio controls and panel-top courtesy light. On later cars, reattach the warning lights and fasten as above.

Be careful not to bend the levers or cables before or while you're installing the panel.

Interior Restoration

Painting Exposed Metal—After Z-car production began, Datsun evidently discovered the tacky appearance of contrasting body colors in the gaps left between interior panels. Imagine red paint showing around white interior panels! To correct the problem, some assembly-line worker wielded a paintbrush with matte-black enamel to kill the effect—a far cry from today's robotics, cheaper in 1970 Japan!

These areas should be repainted before you begin interior upholstery work. Included are the inside lip of the door jamb from the quarter window around to the windshield pillar, encompassing the interior body sill to the firewall, the seat mounts and, on early 240Zs, the little tabs that hold the knobs for the tool compartments.

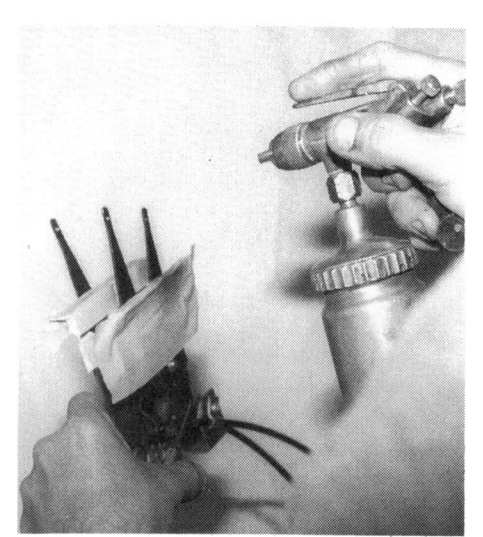

Heater-control arms get a new coat of matte black. It isn't necessary to disassemble control for painting. This one has cables cut from old Z choke cable—much stronger than early originals.

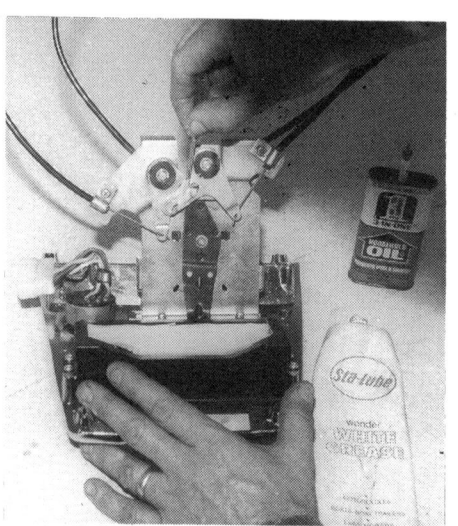

Assembled control head gets a thorough lubrication, including cables. White grease and light machine oil stay in place well.

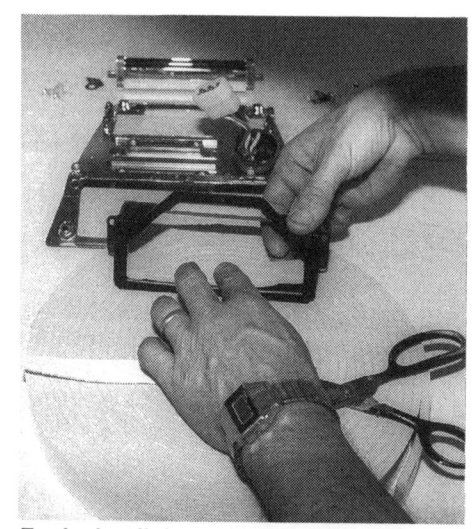

Replacing lining on heater-duct opening with foam tape that's been cut to shape. New console bezel has blower switch installed.

Interior Restoration & Assembly 127

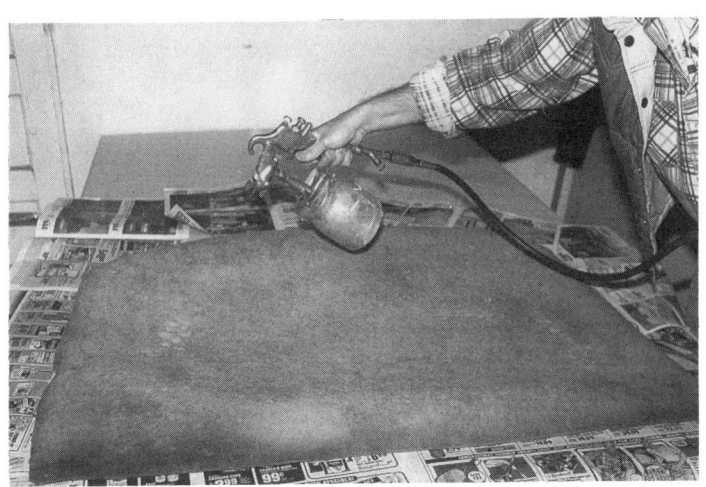

In preparation for installing headliner, contact cement is sprayed in an even pattern on the foam backing. Newspapers catch overspray. Replace them afterwards because they'll stick to anything and everything.

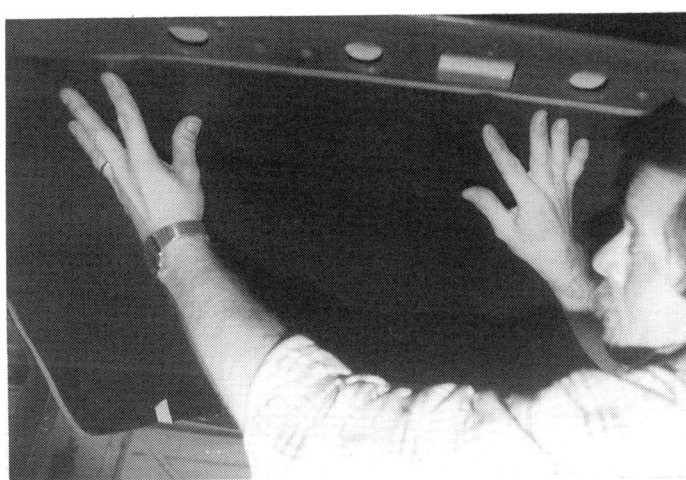

Roof was sprayed next. Tack time is short, so be ready to install the headliner. Line up V notch with center of mirror-attaching holes and hang forward edge of headliner from windshield weld flange with strips of masking tape. Headliner must be "spot on" the first time it touches underside of roof. As you work back and out from the center, rub headliner firmly against roof.

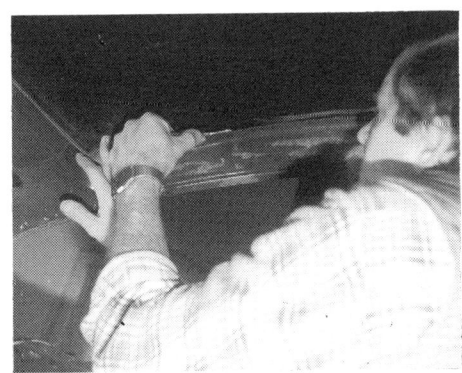

Tuck headliner under header and side-rail lips. I'm using a headlining tool to push edge under, but a new Bondo squeegee would work just as well.

Reinstall Headliner

The Z-car headliner is a foam-pad-backed rectangle of vinyl material rather than the traditional cut-and-sew fabric and bows. By cementing headliner directly to the roof sheet metal, headroom was gained and insulation and finish value were retained.

New headliner material can be glued directly to the old without removing it from the car. Start by cutting out the replacement material about 1-inch larger all around than the headliner dimensions. Adhere and trim it using the general technique I describe as follows. Be aware, however, that original headliner material is not yet available, so this approach only applies to a custom installation.

To reinstall a good usable Z-car headliner, use a good grade of contact cement and follow the instructions. As with any contact cement, apply it to both surfaces and let it tack. Then the two must be mated exactly and compressed long enough to assure a permanent bond.

The trick is to position the headliner exactly so it doesn't need adjusting afterwards. A cement strong enough to hold the pad securely will not allow any movement to get a good fit without possibly tearing the bonded foam.

Adhesive—On large areas such as for the headliner, use spray-on contact cement. Bear in mind though, the cement won't make a pretty spray pattern as you would need for paint. Actually the squiggles and droplets that squirt out allow the cement to build up as needed. And most cements can be lightly thinned to spray with low air pressure. Check the container label to see what solvent is recommended for the cement you have.

Spraying has the advantage of fast coverage of large areas, the disadvantage of requiring masking to prevent gross overspray onto adjacent surfaces. Carefully done, it tends to be less expensive as well.

Caution: Protect yourself. Using adhesives that have evaporating solvents can constitute a health hazard. Work in a well-ventilated area and wear a mask or respirator. Don't use near open flame or other high heat source. Protect your hair from airborne adhesive, too. Rubber gloves will protect your hands from solvents and make cleanup easier.

Place the headliner foam-side up on newspapers or some other disposable surface and give it a good overall coat of contact cement. Don't reuse the surface as it can contaminate other parts with cement overspray.

Now spray the inner roof panel with adhesive. Don't worry about overspray on the roof header sections as they will be covered in their turn.

Most, if not all, headliners have a triangular notch at the center of the forward edge. This notch should be positioned so it's at the center of the rearview mirror-mounting holes. If you are alone, simply attach several strips of masking tape from the forward weld flange so 4 or 5 inches of each strip hangs down. Then position the headliner on them so when you swing it up, the center notch and edges will align correctly. This operation is sort of like breeding porcupines—a sticky business if not done carefully! Either way, take the time to get good alignment because there isn't much leeway—maybe 1/2 inch.

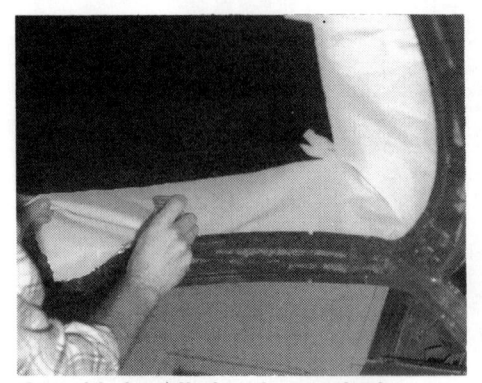

Once it's installed and smoothed down, mask headliner in preparation for spraying adhesive on headers and roof rails. Push paper under the lips to hold it at outer edges; use masking tape to hold up inner edges.

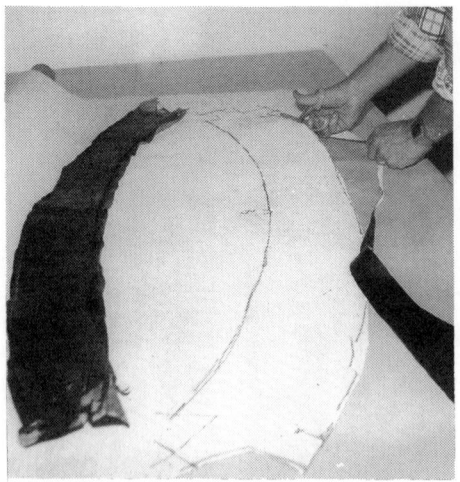

Old header covering is intact enough to use as a pattern. Cut new material slightly larger and remember that slits and irregular edge of old piece resulted from trimming in place.

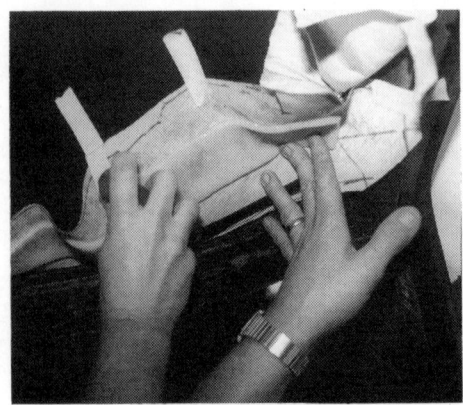

Windshield header was sprayed with adhesive as was new material. Padding foam could be adhered directly to header, then adhesive reapplied. Masking tape holds material away from header until I am satisfied with its position.

Stick the pad to the roof only on the center line and cautiously lift each edge out to the side—don't touch it to the roof—to make sure it won't come up short and leave the roof showing. If the position is good, begin adhering the headliner from the center outward by rubbing it with a section of towel. If it's too far out of position, gently tug the bond apart and try again. Don't take too much time as the cement will begin to lose its tack. Avoid wrinkles. If one develops, stop and work it out before going on. Heat from an infrared lamp or heat gun can now be used to relax slight imperfections, but it won't cure a ripple.

At the edges, use a smooth, flat tool to tuck edges up behind the metal header section. The last 1/2 inch of headliner must be well bonded even though it's hidden behind the header lip. Smooth the material firmly all over and check for cement slop. Remove with the recommended solvent. Acetone used sparingly seems to work best on many contact cements.

Header Trim—The windshield header and two door side rails must be recovered with foam and vinyl. The two side pieces also include the A-pillars. This operation can only be done with the windshield removed because the windshield weatherstrip covers the raw edges of the material. (You may want to use a professional glazier to help with windshield installation, page 130.)

Salvaging the original foam and vinyl is hard enough, but repositioning it is nearly impossible, so use the old pieces as patterns for cutting out the new trim pieces. Use new vinyl that closely approximates the original texture and colors.

Before going further, mask off the perimeter of the headliner to protect it when you spray or brush on cement for the windshield header and side rails. Using a strip of masking paper, simply push one edge between the headliner and the metal header and side rails and tape it up to the vinyl at intervals. The masking paper for each side should have enough width—6 inches is about right—to prevent the adhesive from spattering on the headliner. If you spray the adhesive, mask around the roof side of the weld flange, too, to keep it off the paint. This seems tedious, but it's necessary!

The windshield-header trim must be applied first because the side portions form the joint between the two. Remember where the folded edges were secured by the sun-visor brackets?

Place the new header material face down on a clean work surface. Arrange the old material as a pattern, taping it fabric side up to the new vinyl to assure it will provide an accurate shape. It helps if your old material is warm, so it will lie as flat as possible. When you are satisfied with the alignment, trace around the pattern as accurately as possible—don't worry about your new piece being slightly large, but don't overdo it. Don't make it too small, though.

Note that there is another V-notch at the forward edge of the original material. Transfer this to your piece as you'll use it to center the material. A number of slits were put in the edge of the original trim, too. Mark the location of these, but don't cut them yet. Wait until you're putting the new vinyl into place. The depth you need to make each slit will vary as to the stretch and positioning of the individual piece. These and the irregular edges on the original pieces result from trimming after installation.

As an aside, I refer to the material as *vinyl* because that's what Datsun used. If you are installing a custom interior, you may have opted for a woven upholstery, which is your choice.

Be aware that at the windshield weatherstrip there is a danger of moisture wicking through the cloth. This could cause staining and even mildew damage. With this in mind, use a liberal amount of sealing compound when installing the weatherstrip to ensure complete water-tightness. Datsun installed a fairly light grade of vinyl in areas that would be considered non-wearing, which makes it that much easier to stretch and work wrinkles out of as well.

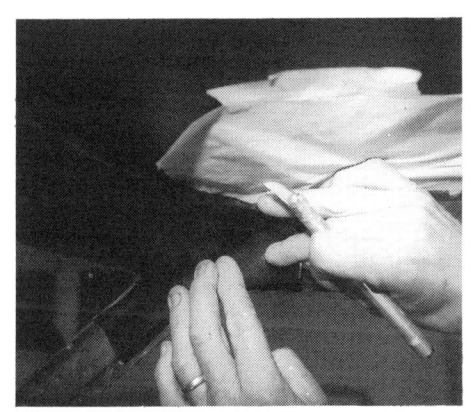

With pinch molding holding upper edge in place on header, vinyl is stretched over windshield weld flange. Here I'm getting ready to trim and position end. Masking paper for side rail is still in place.

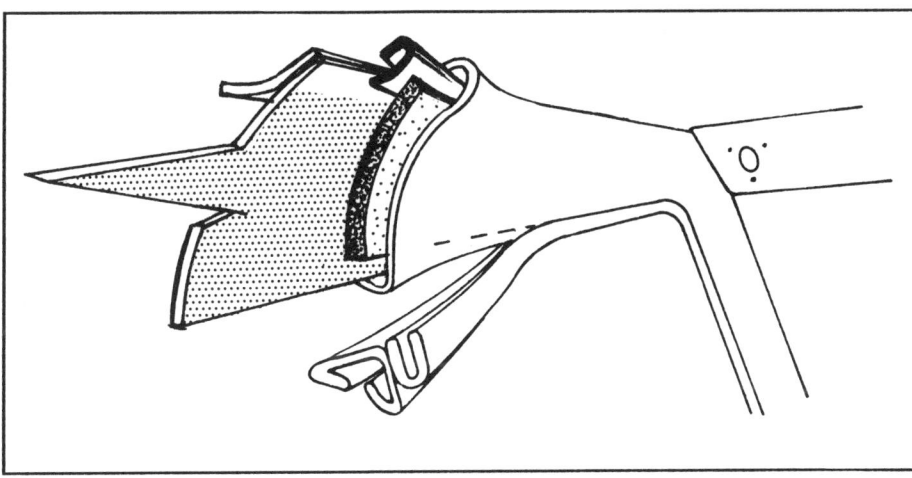

Here is how side rail is covered; front header is similar. Remember how material folded under pinch molding? Weatherstrip hides lower weld flange very handily. Shaded area is where adhesive is applied.

Urethane foam should be cut using the old pieces as patterns if possible. Keep edges smooth and even. Sloppy work may show through vinyl covering.

Spray contact cement onto masked roof header as well as the upholstery backing and foam strip. Apply the foam to the header. Don't put it too far forward or it will interfere with the weatherstrip later. The exposed side must be coated with adhesive also. Remove masking tape and paper as you no longer need it.

The plastic pinch molding holds the rear edge of the header—the one you see. It should have a small white dot of paint at its center. The vinyl makes a wrap around the molding so it is crimped to the rear edge of the metal header.

Start the new vinyl onto the header at the rear center. Use masking tape to hold it up against the headliner if you're working solo. Make sure there's sufficient material to wrap forward edge and up over the roof weld flange. Then using the white dot to line up between the mirror-mounting holes, push the pinch molding on for a few inches to both sides of center. The material will go a little slack as you press it forward into position. From here on, work vinyl across the header, alternately stretching and pressing molding onto the metal edges. If the plastic molding came out off-center after all, you may be able to slip it to the side. Failing that, pull it off and reposition it. Keep wiping off excess cement as you go.

When you are satisfied with the rear edge, stretch the material forward toward the weld flange and work out from the center. Don't get discouraged if you don't achieve perfection at first. Proceed carefully and deliberately. Speed is not of primary importance. You shouldn't let the cement dry out, but it can be renewed with adhesive on a small brush if the tack *dies back.*

Keep pulling the forward edge of the material up and stick it to the adhesive at the weld-flange edge of the roof as you go. If everything looks good, press it down for a permanent bond. Continue in this fashion until the header is covered and all edges are well adhered. Wrap forward edge up over the weld flange, make sure it is sticking down flat. Use a blade to trim the excess. Notice that some material will extend down the A-pillar. Also, some should be wrapped over the metal edge where the weld-flange molding no longer extends. This will be covered by the vinyl on the side-rail weld-flange moldings.

Side-Rail Trim—With header trim satisfactorily in place, mask it off at approximately the outermost visor-bracket hole and apply adhesive to length of the header. Cut both the foam padding—two pieces per side—and hockey-stick-shape vinyl pieces just as you did those for the front header. Stick the foam in place—windshield pillar first—then side-rail strip, which overlaps somewhat. Check the trim and recoat with adhesive.

Do the section over the door first, fastening the upper edge with the plastic pinch molding. Start this strip just where the metal edge becomes straight and work front to rear. Check hang of the A-pillar strip before pressing the molding tight.

There is that crucial fold that must be made in the vinyl where it joins the windshield header. This occurs just inside where the sun-visor-bracket corner falls. The corner of the triangular bracket—or on early Zs, its plastic mounting plate—captures the folded edge and secures it to the header. It may be necessary to trim the cut edge of the material to prevent too much bulk in the fold if you wind up with an excess at that point. Put a daub of cement into the backing at the fold to hold it until you install the visors. It isn't necessary to cement it up to the underlying material. This is a nice touch and looks great when done correctly.

You will probably need to make several *small* slits in the vinyl where it meets the curve of the A-pillar where it joins roof. Again the windshield weatherstrip covers the material where it meets the A-pillar weld flange. A plastic pinch molding that attaches to the door weatherstrip will neatly finish the edge that ends at the door-jamb weld flange. Be sure to trim any excess right on the edge of the weld flange.

Check the bottom of the A-pillar vinyl for a neat edge. It can be seen by someone looking at details. The rearmost edge is covered by the plastic quarter-window finisher. Again,

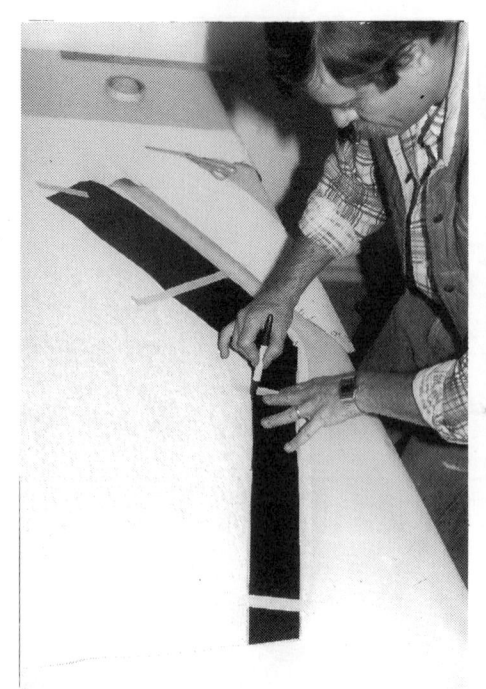

Side-rail covering that was cut out is used as a pattern for opposite side. Don't forget they are *mirror-images*—place them back to back when laying out pattern. Otherwise you'll end up cutting out two for the same side!

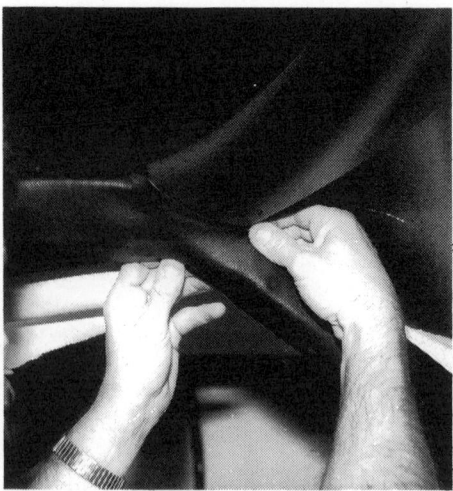

Same procedure is used to cover side rail as for windshield header. I'm making crucial folded joint at A-pillar junction—sun-visor mount holds fold in place as long as there's enough material to reach visor.

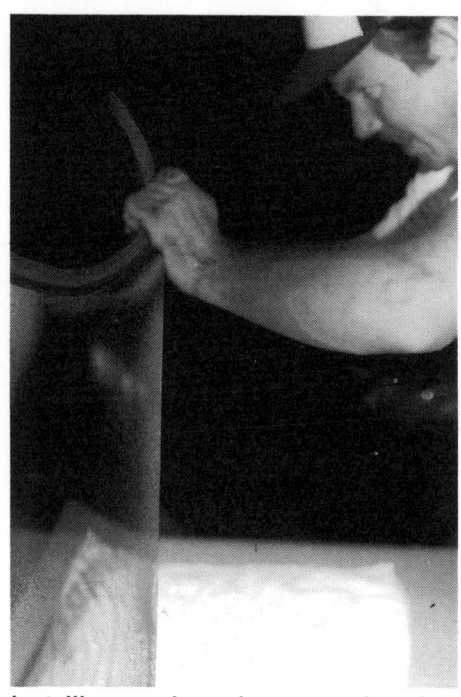

Installing weatherstrip on top edge of windshield.

heat from an infrared lamp or heat gun can be used to smooth out slight imperfections.

Check painted areas for excess contact cement and clean with solvent before it starts collecting lint and dust.

Install Windshield

Do-It-Yourself or hire pro? Because I replaced the windshield, I took advantage of my glass man's vast experience for this sequence of pictures. It is nerve wracking enough to handle a couple of hundred dollars of new tinted windshield without having to juggle a Nikon as well!

You shouldn't have much trouble deciding whether to tackle setting the windshield glass yourself. You may find putting the hatch glass in first is easier and good practice for the windshield job. Read this section carefully. And although it helps to have a partner, installing the windshield isn't all that hard or risky.

Whether you have a new windshield or are reusing your old glass, the procedure is the same. With previously used glass, clean both sides thoroughly. Pay particular attention to mineral deposits or "water spots."

I recommend that you use a new weatherstrip, but an old strip can be used if it isn't hard or cracked. Check for splits or cracks at the corners in particular. Check the full circumference and pay attention to the channel used to hold the stainless-steel garnish trim. Really "tired" rubber won't hold the edges of the stainless securely, especially where the corner and bottom center transition pieces must fit over the strips.

Clean and polish the stainless before reinstalling it. If you are looking for that "high-tech" look and aren't concerned about originality, you could trim off the lips and eliminate the bright trim altogether.

Install the weatherstrip on the glass. Start by spreading out a clean furniture pad or blanket of some kind to rest the glass face down. Start the weatherstrip on at a top corner. Work the setting channel over the edge of the glass across the top and to the opposite corner.

If you have a helper, balance the glass on its bottom edge and pull the rubber down both sides. It will get more taut, but the farther you go, the easier it will be to slip it over the long lower curved edge. When you have the seal on all the way around, lay the windshield flat again.

Pull String—Next operation is to set a piece of cord or screen-door spline into the channel that grips the windshield-opening weld flanges. Start somewhere at the bottom edge, leaving 6 inches or so extending out of the channel. Tape the free end to the inside of the glass with masking tape and run the cord all the way around in the channel until you come back to the starting point. Overlap this end with the other and fasten it to the inside of the glass with the same strip of tape.

Sealant—Run a bead of windshield-setting compound around into the channel with the cord. Get this in cartridge form at a glass shop or auto-parts store. Don't leave any gaps to leak. Check the windshield weld-flange area. Be sure your upholstery material is trimmed back so it's at least flush with the weld-flange edge. Remove any errant globs of weld slag or old rubber/sealant.

Easy Does It!—Carry the windshield to the car and set it in place against the weld flange. Don't push it into

Interior Restoration & Assembly 131

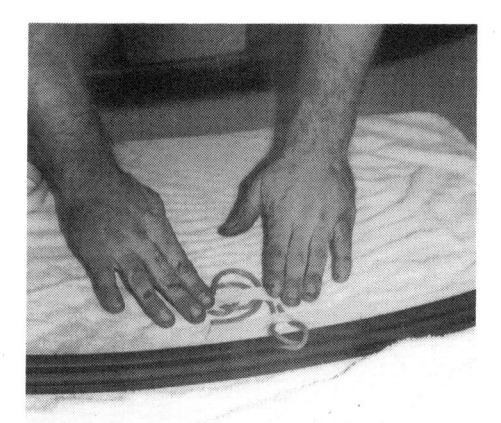

Pull cord is wrapped in and around weld-flange channel, then taped to glass until needed. This is plastic screen-door spline.

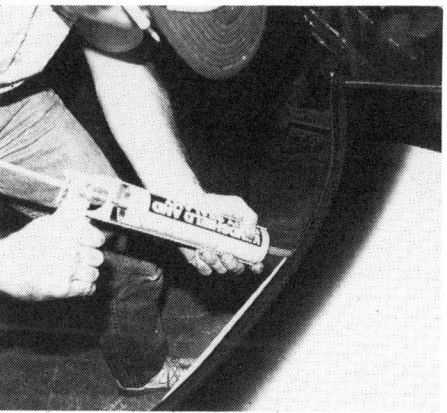

Sealant gun is used to apply sealer to windshield-weatherstrip setting channel. Modern sealing compounds stay flexible and weathertight forever . . . almost.

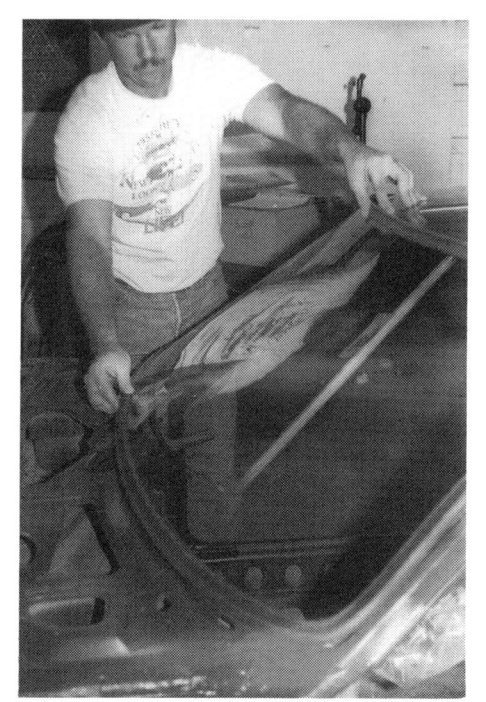

Cameron had help positioning the glass—it's heavy and expensive.

place yet. Just make sure it nests into the opening. Now climb inside and check the position. If everything looks good, untape the ends of the cord and begin pulling the cord over the weld flange. This "peels" the weatherstrip lip over the weld flange. If you have a helper, have him follow the action of the cord, pressing firmly down against the opening to assure a positive fit. Don't get carried away—brute force won't help.

Pull the cord evenly so each end is at about the same point on either side and watch the weatherstrip lip. Use a plastic or wood flat-blade tool with rounded corners to encourage the lip into place if need be. Make sure it doesn't have a cutting edge because the weatherstrip lip shows rather prominently and gashes or nicks won't add to the professional look you want to exhibit. If you have problems, remove the windshield and start over with a better placement. Keep a rag handy with some solvent on it to clean up any mess caused by the sealant-soaked cord.

When weatherstrip seems to be in place, work around the outside edge with your fist, thumping the joint lightly—use your good judgment—to work lip and sealant into comfortable accommodation with the weld flange. Wipe excess sealant off the paint or upholstery material.

More Sealant—Squeeze the tip of sealant applicator under an exterior lip of the weatherstrip and pump a bead of sealant into it. Give both the weld-flange channel and glass channel the same treatment. Be generous with the sealant. Better to waste some than to have to chase down a leak the first time you wash the car!

Rub your cleaning rag back and forth over the lips to force the goo into all recesses and corners. Finish by wiping up excess sealant that oozes out.

Stainless Windshield Trim—This fits into the shallow channel on the exposed face of the weatherstrip. Slip one leg of the trim into the *outboard* weatherstrip lip—the one farthest from the glass—and work it on as far as seems practical. Then, using your dull, flat-blade tool, carefully work the inboard lip over the strip. Continue this until the entire length of the strip is secure. Do the same with the other stainless strips.

Don't get in a hurry! The inboard lip is *very* fragile, especially on an old weatherstrip. It tears and nicks easily.

When the long strips are in place, put a few daubs of weatherstrip

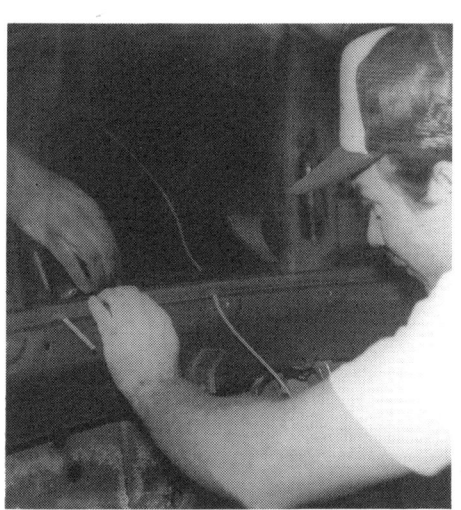

With everything set in place and you inside car, begin pulling one end of cord back, watching how lip rolls over weld flange. It should do this all the way around. If not, remove windshield and start over.

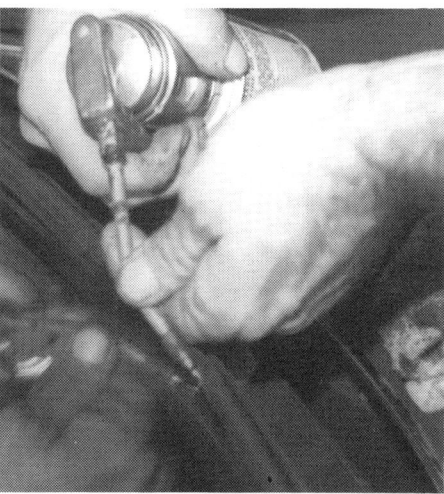

Hand-pump gun flows sealant into setting channel after weatherstrip is solidly in place. Lots of solvent and towels are used up to remove excess.

132 How to Restore Your Datsun Z-Car

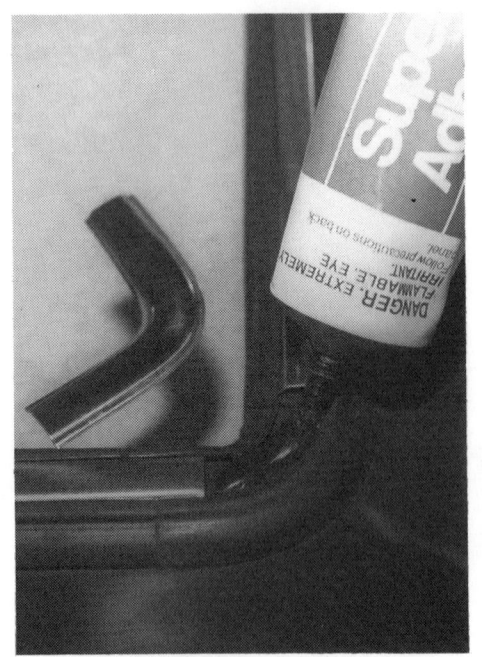

Hatch glass is installed the same way. I've snapped stainless trim under rubber lips, but corner trim needs additional retention provided by weatherstrip adhesive.

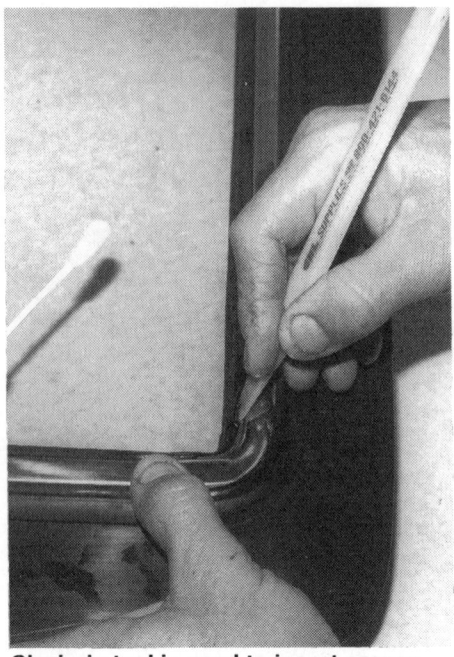

Glazier's tool is used to insert corner trim. Note center-gap filler trim on glass. Excess adhesive must be cleaned up quickly. Q-tip swab is moistened with silicone brake fluid, a good lubricant for installing trim. Just don't get it on surfaces where you want paint or adhesive to stick.

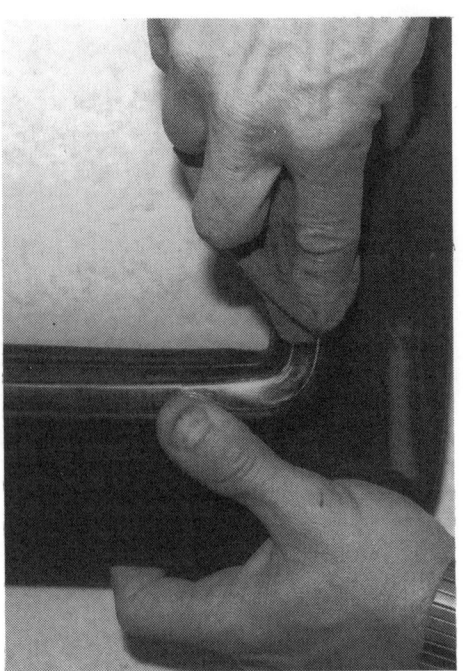

I press down while wiping off adhesive to make sure stainless is seated. Windshield trim installs the same.

adhesive into the channel and position the short center and corner pieces. These must overlap the long strips and hold down their ends, so the small rubber lips have a lot to do—take time and care. The shorter pieces will fit, although tightly. A tiny bit of silicone brake fluid, applied with a cotton swab, can provide enough lubricant to ease a particularly tight fit. I find cement is good insurance to keep these short pieces in place. Wipe up excess cement immediately.

If your car is weathertight otherwise, test the seal with a hard stream of water from the garden hose soon. If not, keep the sealant can handy for fixing leaks found in later testing.

Sun Visors—Using an awl or sharp punch, locate the three tapped holes for the visor mounts. Although the triangular mounts look like they could be attached in any orientation, only one allows them to rotate correctly. The angle can be found most simply by test fitting the visor mounts—castings are marked **L** or **R** on their back sides. Make slits to accommodate the countersunk Phillips-head screws and attach both visors loosely.

Mirror & Visor Retainer—This plate mounts exactly at the center of the windshield header. Attach it the same way you did the visor mounts, but tighten it down. Put the visor-pivot ends into the retainer clips to be sure of alignment and tighten the visor screws.

Rearview Mirror—A spring clip on the mirror-retainer mount snaps into the back of the mirror bracket. Hold the bracket in place and give it a good thump with your fist. It should attach firmly. This clip is a safety breakaway feature. If it seems too stiff, put a tiny bit of Door Ease stick on the edges of the mount.

Hatch Glass

This goes in exactly like the windshield, except it can be done on the bench or floor. However, doing it on the car has its advantages: The weatherstrip and glass sit on the hatch weld flange courtesy of gravity while you pull the cord from the bottom side. The six pieces of stainless trim install the same as those on the windshield.

Be careful with the rear defroster-wire contacts at the edge of the glass—these are easily broken off, ending the usefulness of the defroster grid.

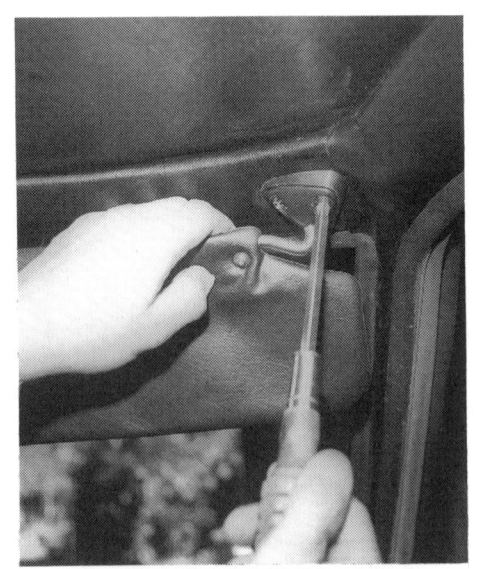

Attach sunvisors with Phillips-head screws. Note how corner of triangular mount pulls down against fold in header vinyl.

Interior Restoration & Assembly 133

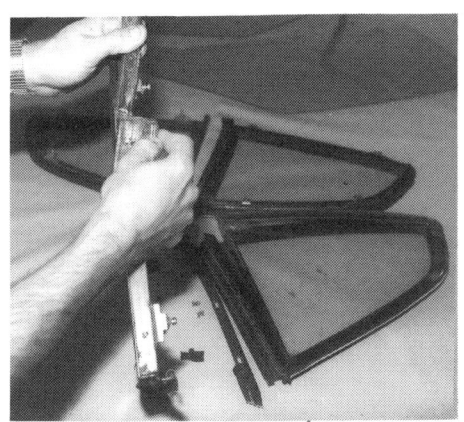

Remove old outer strip with a razor blade. Late-style quarter window at right shows different molding in place of sealing tabs.

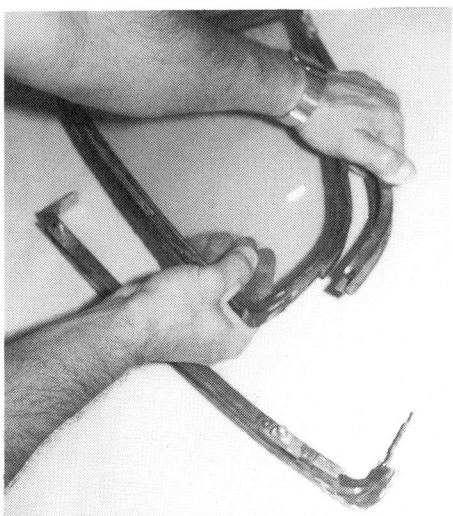

Screws removed, quarter-window frame comes apart to free glass and inner weatherstrip.

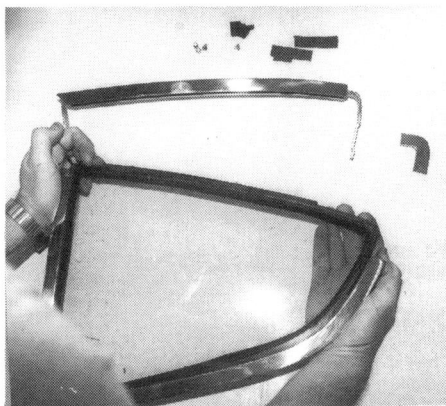

With stainless frame repolished, it can be reinstalled around weatherstrip. Window frame, corner trim, shim rubber strips are above.

Quarter Windows

With the windows out of the car, clean them thoroughly with soap and water and a stiff brush. Crud seems to accumulate on these, both inside and out.

There are two separate weatherstrips on Z-coupe quarter windows: One seals the frame to the body opening. It is made up of a flexible strip and either two small tabs (early) or one long molding (late) that interfaces with the door weatherstrip. The other one-piece weatherstrip mounts the glass to the window framework. Chances are you should replace the window-to-body weatherstrip. But the glass setting channel may not need replacement unless the pane is cracked and you have to remove it or the neoprene is in real bad shape.

Remove the outer weatherstrip first, removing cement from the stainless-steel frame as you go. Use a single-edge razor blade to remove stuck neoprene. Use naptha to remove adhesive.

On early Zs, if the upper and lower tabs are still on the frame, note how they are installed. Often as not, these stick to the door weatherstrip when it comes off. On later models, the metal-backed molding comes off by removing four screws. If you wish to take the glass out of the frame, take out all screws; top, bottom and at the rear upper joint.

Early cars are often heavily shimmed and caulked at the upper, rear corner joint. Note how much shim rubber is used as you remove it because this material should be replaced similarly for a tight seal. Carefully pry up the top frame molding until it is loose from the glass setting channel and pull the upper corner joint straight up and away. Carefully slip the L-shape trim piece off the corner. Now separate the lower frame from the channel, being careful not to bend the bottom joint!

The glass can now be removed from the channel. Use care around corners where neoprene will be most likely to crack.

Clean the glass with a new razor blade and lacquer thinner. Get all the dirt and mineral stains now, use Windex later. The setting channel can be cleaned like any rubber-neoprene product.

Clean the stainless carefully as you did the windshield molding. Don't use any abrasive that will scratch the finish. Of course now is the time to do any polishing if needed. Z-car stainless didn't have a high polish, but a satin sheen.

Reassemble the pane to the channel, using a sealing compound in the recess. Firmly compress the channel to the glass and wipe off any excess sealing compound immediately. Clean up with naptha. Late-style channels extend farther into the interior, fitting closely to the window trimmer—a nice detail improvement.

Squeeze the setting channel into the lower frame section. Repeat the process with the upper section, inserting the tips of the end brackets into the lower frame, *then* push the dogleg trim corner on to the top frame. Seat the top frame section so the "L" trim telescopes over the bottom frame end and seats tightly. Replace the countersunk screws at the rear and the two at the top with the early version.

For early cars, several layers of flat rubber shim material must be added over the top rear corner to make up for the way the corner reinforcement is designed. This part on later models is different—probably to eliminate the need for shims. The corner should be thoroughly caulked—black weatherstrip adhesive works well—and shims added to give the weatherstrip an even surface to stick to. Inner-tube rubber is good enough—cut it into strips with sharp scissors and clean it with naptha.

Apply black trim adhesive to the metal, press the shim into it and pull back to get it tacky, then adhere. Repeat the process with slightly longer shims until the surface is fairly level. Weatherstrip for the quarter window isn't molded to the shape of the frame, but comes cut from stock. New Nissan rubber should be long enough for some excess to stick out top and bottom.

This fits on with the longer lobe—looking at it from the end section—to the outside of the car. If you miss this distinction and cement it to the wrong

134 How to Restore Your Datsun Z-Car

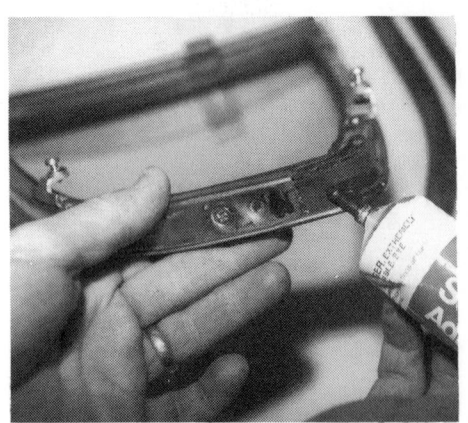

Early cars must have height deficit made up with shims. Each is longer than the previous; must be cemented on in turn.

Outer weatherstrip is cemented on. Masking tape temporarily holds it in place. Ends should be trimmed flush.

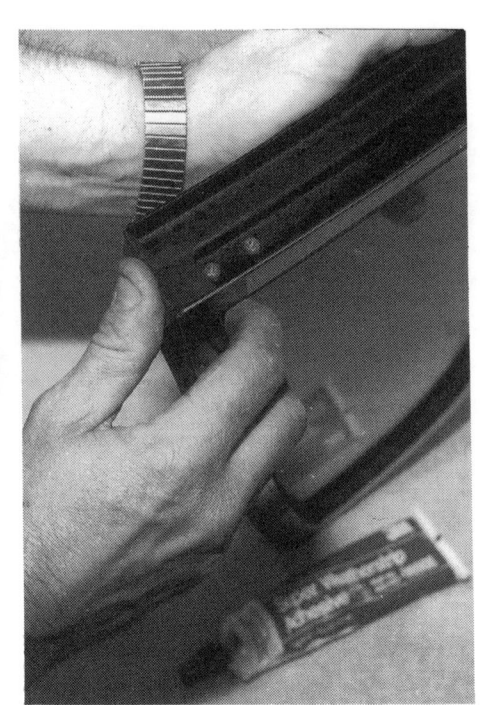

Upper sealing tab can be put on now. Other tab is put on after window is installed.

window, you'll discover your error when you try to remount it.

Wrap it around the frame to establish the rear corner point and begin cementing it from there to one end or the other. Hold what you have adhered with short strips of masking tape until it sets up completely.

On early models, check that your shimming was neither too little nor too much. Apply enough adhesive at the corner to build up the inside corner so it's smooth and flush level.

When both windows are weatherstripped, trim the extra material off flush with the forward edge of the frame. On the early models you will cement the little sealing tabs *after* you install the quarter-window assemblies. On later cars, attach the vertical molding loosely now or wait until the window is installed.

Installation on Body—When the weatherstrip cement has set up firmly so the strip won't move, carefully set the quarter window in place. Using an awl or punch, lever the frame rearward until the threaded tabs are within reach of the retaining screws. These are fairly short—I make judicious use of Vise-Grip pliers to fight

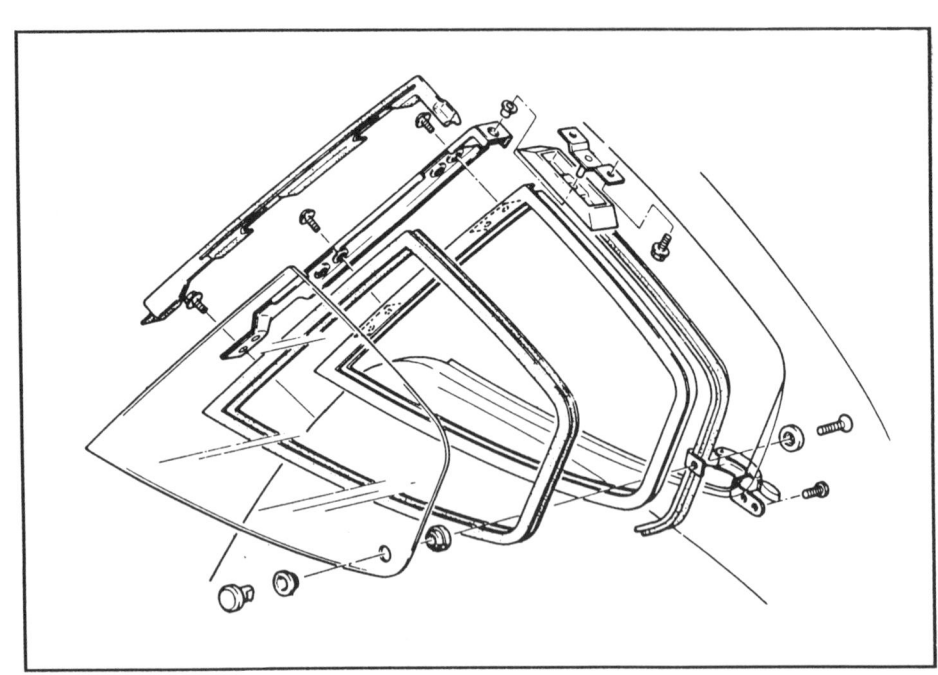

2+2 window is unique to that model, has its own weatherstrips.

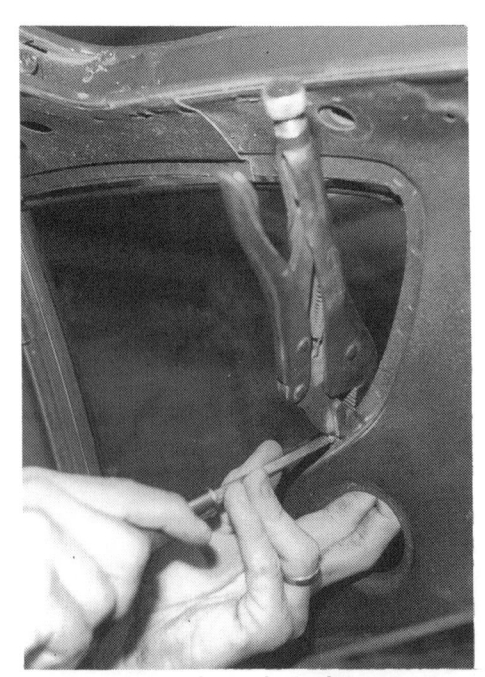

New outer weatherstrip resists compressing into window opening. Window must be forced both in and to the rear before screws will align with holes. Vise-Grips provide an assist.

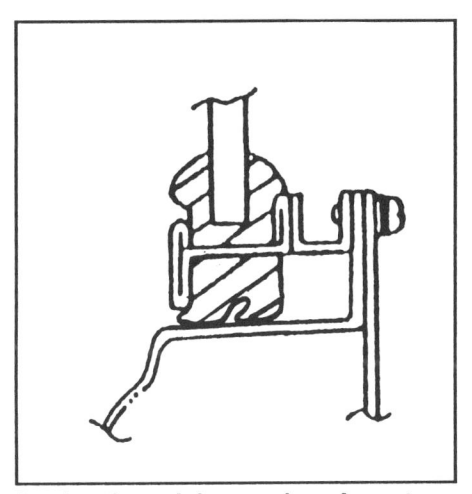

Section through lower edge of quarter glass and window frame: Outer weatherstrip looks like this when window is tightly in—the only way to get a positive weather seal.

Contact cement holds vinyl sill trim to inner sill. Be sure notches and seat-belt holes line up.

the springiness of the new weatherstrip until the screws get a grip.

Datsun used machine screws, but if yours are damaged or you have trouble getting them started, you could use self-tapping screws with good results. Another possibility: 280Zs used longer screws—possibly because the assembly-line workers had the same problem. These work on earlier cars.

Early Zs can now have the two little filler tabs cemented at the ends of the weatherstrip. Late Zs should have the vertical sealing molding screwed down tight. Add some sealer where gaps appear. The latter type can be used on early cars, but only if you change the complete window unit. Keep in mind that some of the forward frame will be covered by the door weatherstripping.

Sill Trimmer—The textured-vinyl strips that cover the inner door sills are cemented in place. Datsun didn't provide any padding or covers for the stamped holes in the sill panel under it. These strips often show a wear pattern that matches the holes. Check yours to be sure you will be satisfied with its appearance. If not, vinyl dye does a creditable job of renewing the surface.

Apply contact cement to both the sill surface and back of the vinyl. Mask any areas not to be coated if you're using spray-on adhesive. The trim should be securely adhered to the sill. Start by lining it up to the seat-belt hole, then align the upper edge of the material with the door-opening weld flange.

Press the vinyl down firmly along the top edge. Using a soft cloth, smooth it down the length of the sill. If your first try is too far out of alignment—misses the seat-mount member or seat-belt hole for instance—pull it up gently, reapply adhesive where missing and try again. Repeat with the other side. Remove excess adhesive.

Door-Jamb Weatherstrip—These not only provide a seal against wind and water, but also provide trim for the door-jamb weld flange and roof side-rail upholstery. If yours is an early Z, you'll find Nissan replacement weatherstrip is somewhat different. Instead of separate plastic weld-flange trims and glue-on segments of weatherstrip, the factory supplies the late 280Z style preassembled strip. This has the weld-flange trim and neoprene foam bonded together and all segments preattached except at the very bottom.

Also included is the window-frame strip that fits under the drip-molding jamb.

Obviously the more continuous a weatherstrip is, the less likely it will leak as compared to those on early models. It contains a non-hardening adhesive/sealant in the "U" of the weld-flange trim that was not previously specified. This precludes the hassle of applying yards of contact cement as the part goes on. The only areas needing weatherstrip adhesive are the aforementioned window-frame strip and joint in the bottom sill.

Take new weatherstrips—this applies to all of them—out of their plastic bags and arrange them in approximately the shape in which they will be installed on the body. The temperature should be warm to help them relax. To speed the process, lay them out in the sun if the weather is warm. Folding strips for packaging places unwanted bends into the material. Laying them out will make the installation job easier.

Door weatherstrip secures and finishes edge of trim at weld flange. Start installation at rear upper corner and, using butt of hand, bump U-section onto weld flange in stages. Weatherstrip has its own adhesive.

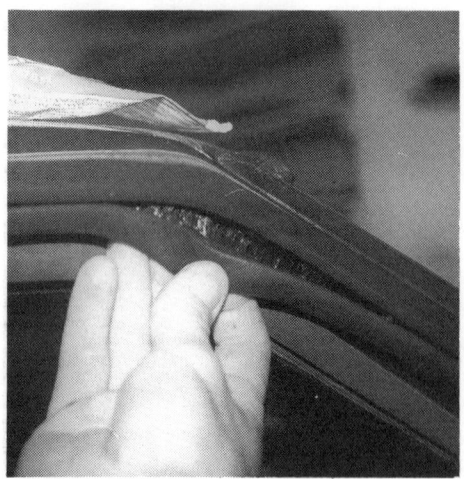

Strip that fits under drip-channel molding must be secured with weatherstrip adhesive. Press surfaces together, pull apart to let cement tack and press into place.

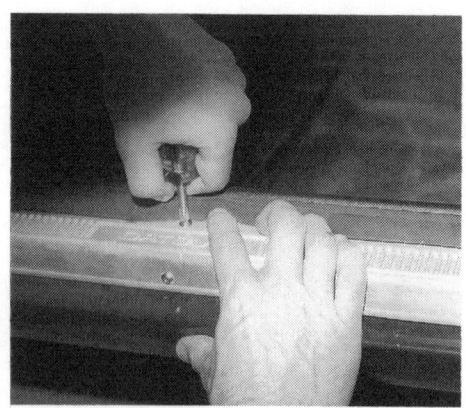

With strip ends butted together and cemented, put on the inner-sill trimmer. Then install door-sill plate.

weatherstrip adhesive and tape it in place until it is securely adhered.

Sill Trim
This steel molding has textured vinyl bonded to it. It is secured with black Phillips-head screws. New trims will undoubtedly be the late style, which has three screw holes spaced 14 inches apart. Early models have five holes, 7 inches apart. It is necessary to drill two extra holes to use these replacements on early cars. The trim neatly covers the weld-flange trim and edge of the vinyl sill trim.

Door-Sill Aluminum Plate—The sill plate is secured with six bright Phillips-head screws. If using your old ones, they can usually be cleaned with steel wool and cleanser, followed by an application of Duro Aluminum Jelly. Wear eye and hand protection when using this product. Afterwards, thoroughly rinse the acid jelly off the parts and your skin! A light coat of acrylic clear will forestall premature tarnishing.

If your sill plates are badly corroded or dented—slamming the seat-belt-buckle tang in the door will do this—replace them with a new set.

Reassembling Underdash Area
A number of variations exist in this area, depending on the model and

One person can do the weatherstrip-installation job, but that indispensable extra hand helps at the start. Be sure your upper and lower sealing tabs are in place on early Zs. Also check to be sure you haven't left excess vinyl-upholstery material overlapping the weld flange along the windshield post and roof.

Start weatherstrip installation at upper rear corner of door where the quarter window meets the roof header. I tackle upper-sill area along roof first to help manage the rather cumbersome strip better. But you may find the rear-jamb stretch easier.

Either way, tap the weld-flange trim tightly up into the corner from both directions. Then follow the weld flange around the door jamb until the end is reached and repeat with the other leg. On the forward jamb, be sure the pinch strip and neoprene don't take shortcuts across the inside curves of the windshield pillar and hinge-area jamb. Bump it into place with your fist or something similarly soft. Don't scar the plastic with a tool.

Where the two ends meet at the bottom, trim and cement them together. Cut the unneeded section off, but leave about 1/8 inch or so extra length. Put weatherstrip adhesive on one end, push both together, then separate until they tack. Then carefully align the neoprene-foam sections and let them mate for a nice-looking joint. This will be seen, only the weld-flange trim is hidden.

If you find the stretch at the top doesn't stay in place, gently squeeze the pinch molding's metal core to give it a better grip. It is a necessity with the newer-style weatherstrip to cement the window-frame strip to the upper jamb. Again apply adhesive, let it tack up and firmly readhere it. Don't attempt to shut the door on the weatherstrip until it is fully cured. If any section still won't stay put, add black

Pedal-support bracket on early cars installs like this. I had column and bracket in and out several times during restoration.

Interior Restoration & Assembly

Insulators

Until someone decides to replicate Z-car insulators, you must make do with used ones. It's nearly impossible to find new old stock (NOS) insulators.

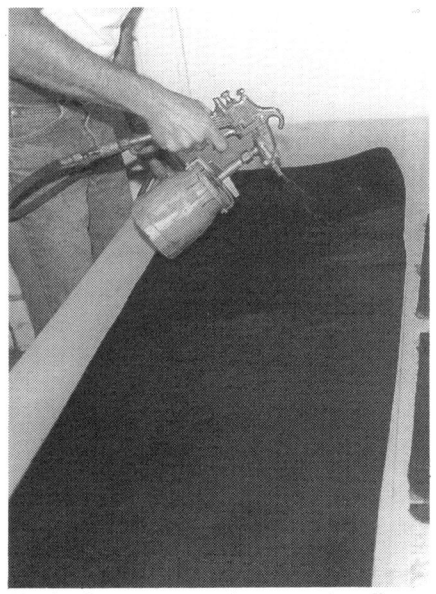

I'm in the process of recovering firewall insulator. Sections of insulator (jute padding) are at right. Contact cement is sprayed on reverse side of covering. Passenger-compartment side of padding is already coated.

Even in wrecking-yard cars, insulators are usually functional—they just look bad. The composition backing (fronting?) is not very durable in the first place and usually takes a lot of abuse. Golf shoes or loggers' boots can take a toll!

Unless yours has had water or fire abuse or someone has hacked it up for some reason, it may be restorable. I'll assume it was removed from the car with reasonable care so the jute padding is reusable and the composition board is only bent or cracked. Z insulators come in pieces for ease of handling and installation. But don't try to recover these while they are still in the car.

By and large, they only interchange model for exact model, but you may find restorable parts at the recyclers if yours is too far gone.

Upholstery shops and suppliers sell a black-vinyl convertible-top material that simulates the matte black of the insulator very well. It also has the desirable characteristic of being very durable and washable—probably more so than the composition board ever was!

Clean your insulator parts as well as is practicable—make sure they are thoroughly dry, too. Put down clean newspaper and put your new material face *down* on it. Arrange the insulator parts face *up* nearby. Make note of any holes or slits that should *not* be reopened—not all the ones provided are needed.

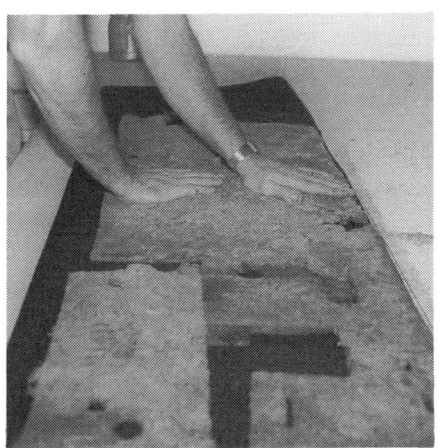

Lay padding on covering and press it down all over. Then cut sections apart, invert and smooth material again.

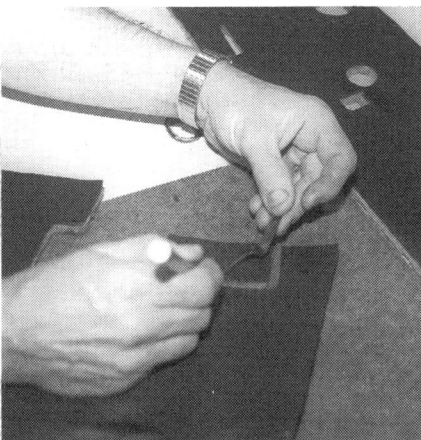

Contact Cement—Spray or brush an ample coat of good adhesive on both the backside of the vinyl and fronts of the insulator parts. Let the adhesive tack up briefly, then carefully set the cemented faces together. Press down all over the jute side to stick them securely, then cut the pieces apart. Leave 1/8 to 1/4 inch all around each piece to trim later. Flip them over—not in your cement overspray—and finish bonding the vinyl to the board.

Now very carefully use sharp scissors and an X-acto knife to trim edges, open holes and make necessary slits. Check for any spots, especially edges, that didn't adhere completely and re-cement. Wipe off any visible adhesive with naptha.

Attach the rug snaps if you are going to use the original snaps in rugs that came with many Zs.

This makes a world of difference in the appearance of a small but significant item—one that would attract a lot of attention only if you didn't do it!

I'm cutting out holes and slots with my trusty X-acto knife. Some holes and slots weren't used on my car, so I omitted cutting them out.

---

equipment involved. Injected 280Zs have a good deal more electronics to mount and connect than carbureted Zs. And air-conditioned cars have considerably more controls and plumbing than others. Numerous other small differences occur, but all Z-cars use basically the same body shell—thus the restoring of the under-panel equipment is similar. It boils down to "what came out must go back in."

The Datsun 280Z Service Manual devotes 73 pages to its heater and air-conditioner; the first 240Z manual makes *no* reference to air conditioning. I cover general concerns and procedures, but space does not permit detailed instructions of each variation and option. Refer to your factory manuals for specifics. More important are your notes and labels. Be patient and logical. Recheck each fitting and connector as you assemble them. Consider the alternative: Spending days troubleshooting leaks or tracing a short under the instrument panel

138 How to Restore Your Datsun Z-Car

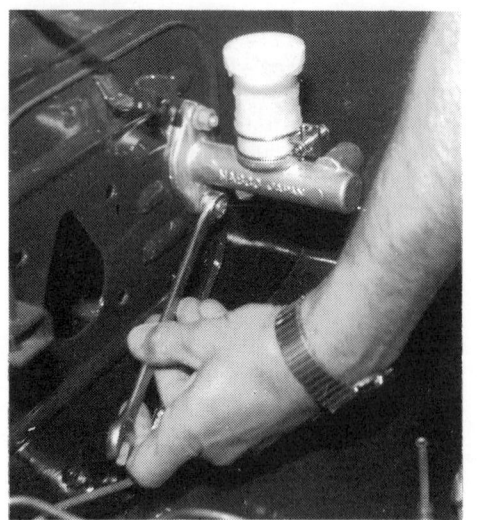

Clutch master cylinder is secured to firewall. Pushrod clevis must be connected to pedal arm. Lubricate pedal pivot and its connection at the clevis.

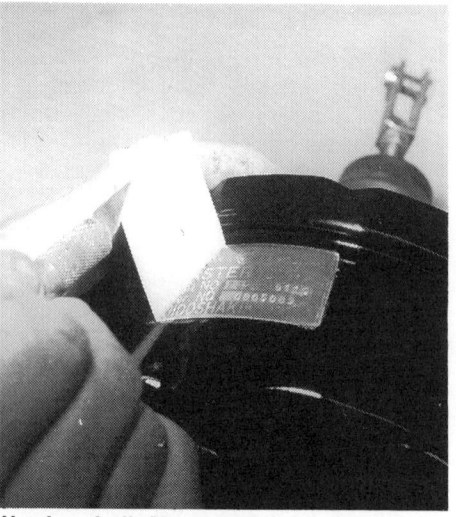

Newly rebuilt MasterVac brake booster: I managed to salvage original sticker with repeated maskings.

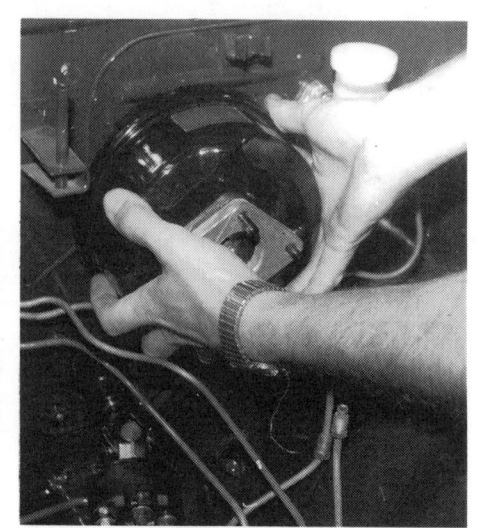

With adapter plate on, brake booster can be slipped in place. Nuts go on inside of firewall. Adapter plate is sealed to booster with silicone sealer.

instead of cruising your favorite winding road.

Cowl Drains

Reinstall the rubber grommets in the aft fender area. Attach drain tubes to the drains with hose clamps and route them through the grommets.

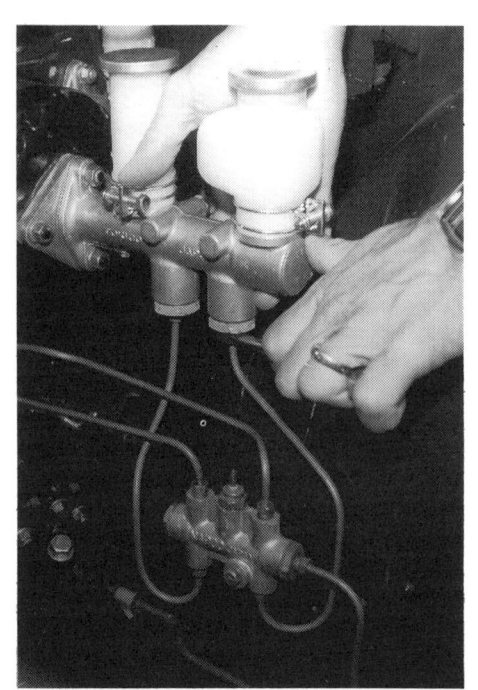

New brake master cylinder is later vintage. Lines are installed between master cylinder and brake-failure warning-light switch.

Pedal-Bracket Assembly

On cars with the first instrument-panel version, this is mounted with four bolts to the instrument-panel brackets and four more to the steering-column bracket/instrument-panel connection. On the later style, it mounts with five to the instrument-panel brackets and two on the column bracket. Don't tighten these until the MasterVac studs are in and loosely nutted—the holes might not line up.

Clutch Master Cylinder

On standard-transmission models, put a little bead of silicone sealer around the outside of the firewall holes and install the clutch master cylinder. Then tighten the pedal-bracket bolts. Remove the retaining clip and clevis pin, lube all pivot points and install the pushrod clevis to the pedal.

Brakes

MasterVac Power-Brake Booster— Install the power booster to the firewall. Run its nuts down on the inside of the firewall and tighten the pedal-bracket bolts. Repeat the process with the pushrod clevis and pedal arm. Lubricate the interface with stiff grease.

Brake Master Cylinder—This is secured to studs on MasterVac unit. Don't forget the diamond-shaped flange.

Install and connect the brake- and clutch-cylinder hydraulic lines. Use a flare-nut wrench and don't cross-thread the fittings.

Install the brake-failure warning-light switch on the inner fender and hook up the remaining brake lines. Bleeding and adjusting brakes is described on page 185.

Transmission-Tunnel Coverings— All Zs had a thick jute pad cemented to the transmission and drive-shaft tunnel. If you removed the jute pad, you'll need to find replacement material. If you have trouble finding jute, a one-inch-thick sheet of high-density urethane foam can be substituted with good results. Don't worry about heat from converter-equipped cars. If your floorpan gets hot enough to melt urethane, it would damage jute as well.

Another possibility is Fiber Glass Evercoat. Evercoat markets floor-insulation called *Q-PADS*. These self-adhering, waterproof insulators can be cut to shape with scissors. They are available at auto-paint stores as part number 117.

Once you have the insulation cut to fit and have checked it, apply contact cement to both the metal and material. Now install the material on the tunnel. Be sure you have holes, notches and so forth where Datsun had them originally.

Tunnel Upholstery—Zs used three vinyl patterns in their console and wheel-housing coverings, progressing from the notorious early bold dia-

Interior Restoration & Assembly

I was able to salvage transmission-tunnel jute pad for my project car. Duct tape holds top in shape and won't be visible after console is in place. Original vinyl is tricky to position, but cements down nicely.

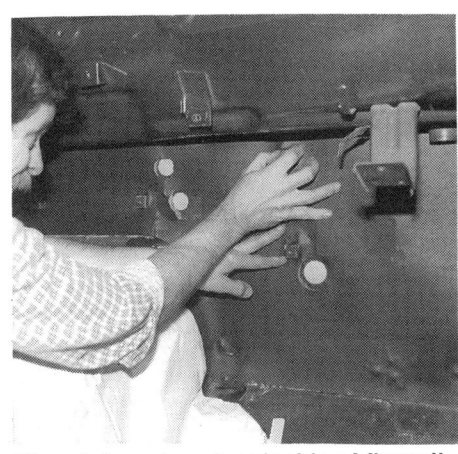

Place jute pad against inside of firewall after covering both surfaces with adhesive and secure with metal tabs. Seams can't be seen from the normal sitting position after instrument panel is in place. Snaps for early-style rugs are omitted.

mond pattern, through a more subtle diamond and ultimately to a plain pebble-pattern material. Although the former are restorable, only a restorer striving for originality will reinstall the factory material. Otherwise, new material, cut and sewn to fit—or carpet—finds its way into restored Z-cars.

Before you get into reinstalling the original material, thoroughly clean and inspect it. Use naptha to remove unwanted cement or overspray, a good detergent and brush to launder the pattern. Hang it to dry in the sun. Don't put it in a clothes dryer!

Most damage is sustained in the luggage area, especially around the strut towers. If you find any blatantly bad abrasions or holes, look for a parts car from which to procure sound material of the same color. Clean it and match the pattern in an area large enough to provide your needed section, plus hems.

Remove the seams on affected sections. Use the original material as a pattern, cut out a new piece and sew it into your upholstery. Professional upholsterers don't necessarily welcome this type of material to work with—especially if it's coated with a lot of old contact cement. But the services of a commercial sewing machine are vital when joining heavy upholstery materials. The job should be fairly small, but expect to pay enough to make it worth their while.

Installing Interior Vinyl—If you are spraying on contact cement, do some rough masking. Tape a 6- to 12-inch strip of masking paper to shield areas from adhesive. It takes a little time, but not nearly what it would take to remove drizzles of adhesive from new paint.

Start with the U-shape tunnel piece. Lay it face down on clean paper and coat with cement. Then, when areas you don't want contaminated with adhesive are well masked, coat the console padding. Let it tack up briefly. This depends on the adhesive, solvent and weather, so experiment if you aren't sure.

Then position the rear "saddle" of the material and drape it over the tunnel up one side. Keep aligning the top edge with where the edges of the console will fit. Repeat with the other side. Keep in mind that if you are using an original piece of material, there isn't much room for error. Misposition the material—it's easy to do—and you'll have to pull it up and repeat the process. With new material, you can cut the cover somewhat larger than original pattern and trim it back after it's down. Datsun also put a small rectangle of vinyl in the area under the ash tray on early models.

Straighten out any puckers or wrinkles. Pull the covering into place and rub it down with a clean towel, securing it as you go. A heat lamp or heat gun should help take out minor problems, but don't count on it for big ones. This job is easier if you have a helper.

Check edges and re-cement any that lift. Mask the tunnel to protect it from overspray.

Install Firewall Insulator

This is held on by both contact cement and metal tabs. Check that the tabs are straight and not bent over against the firewall. Mask off the steering column, pedals and tunnel covering at the forward edge. Mask all open holes in the firewall from the opposite side if you're spraying on the adhesive. Otherwise you may get some interesting adhesive designs on the engine or compartment surfaces! Coat the firewall and jute side of the insulator pieces with a generous coat of adhesive. Remove the masking materials so the messy jute doesn't hang up on it.

Start by positioning the center insulator piece accurately and press it firmly into the adhesive. Then repeat with the two outer pieces. You'll have to work around the steering column on the driver's side. On late cars with

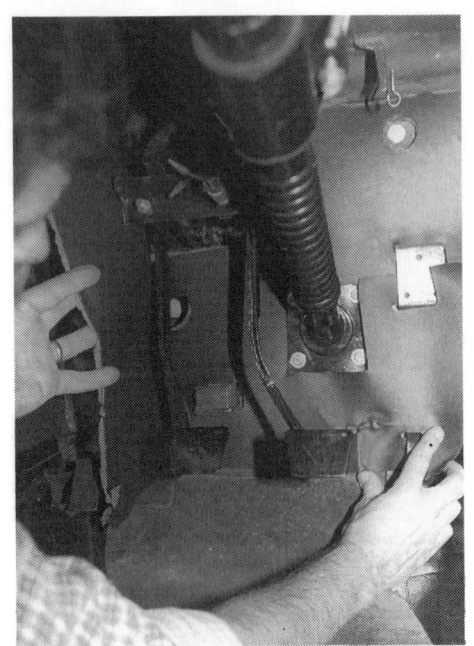

With tunnel vinyl taped against adhesive, I'm sticking lower section of insulator onto firewall. Metal tabs help position and hold it in place.

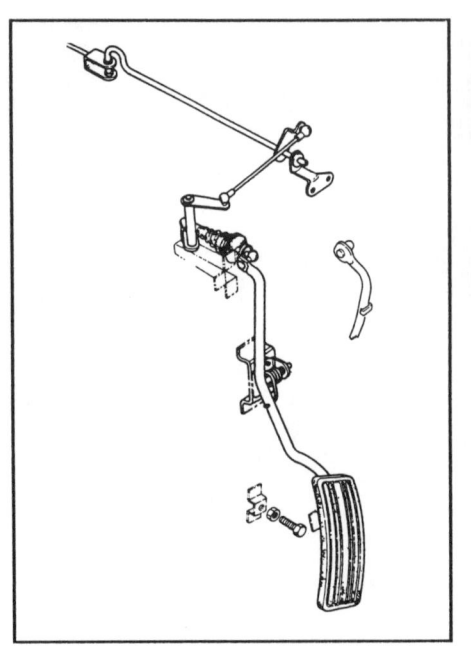

Accelerator linkage from pedal to throttle shaft. Inset is automatic-transmission lever end—pad contacts downshift switch.

Early throttle cable fastens to bracket. Cable has a plastic grommet that pops into accelerator lever, providing one-way action.

the revised steering, the factory provided a nice flange on the firewall plate to cover the raw edges of the insulator. However, this makes it a little more difficult to install because the insulator has to be stretched farther. In several places, insulator tabs must be inserted under or around existing brackets and bumpers.

Rub the insulator pieces down vigorously and bend the metal retaining tabs over. Check the edges and clean up adhesive before it dries completely. If your wiring was not removed, unobtrusive slits in insulators can be made to accommodate it.

Accelerator Linkage

I recommend installing a new rubber grommet/boot in the firewall hole when replacing this linkage. Mount the accelerator-pedal arm and pivot assembly to the inner firewall. Push the first joint rod—the short rod with sockets on each end—through the boot and thread on the wing nut and interior socket. Put a daub of light grease in the socket and snap it over the ball on the arm. Run the wingnut to the full-out position.

The bellcrank is mounted on the pivot post on the engine-compartment side of the firewall. Lube the post and drop the lower bushing over it. Place the bellcrank on the bushing, lube the top bushing and drop it on also. The balls on the bellcrank point upwards. Install the retaining clip in the groove on the pivot post. Snap the first joint rod socket to the bottom arm ball.

With the torsion-shaft bracket bolted to the firewall, fit the torsion shaft—lightly lubricated—into its bushing. Install the forward end to the carburetor-injector linkage with its washer and cotter key. Make sure it doesn't bind.

Lube both sockets on the engine-compartment rod and snap them over the balls on the pivot and torsion rod. There is some adjustment in both the first and second joint rods. Remove the threaded socket and rotate either on the threads to adjust length.

Install the bolt-like pedal stop and adjust it. The accelerator pedal should open the induction to full throttle, but no more, when it's against the stop. Set the locknut when you are satisfied with pedal travel. Check the joint-rod adjustments. Set the upswing limit with the wing nut if necessary.

Check the entire linkage for binds or return problems. Make sure the throttle-return spring(s) is correctly attached—especially if the return isn't positive! Get the throttle-return action working right before you go on to another task.

Heater/Air Conditioner

Heating and air-conditioning components occupy a large portion of the underdash space. Before you reinstall either, be sure all flapper valves are clean and lubricated. Check interior spaces and ducts for debris. Leaves and dust love to hide inside these units.

Install heater and connect all new hoses—there'll never be an easier time to do this.

Interior Restoration & Assembly 141

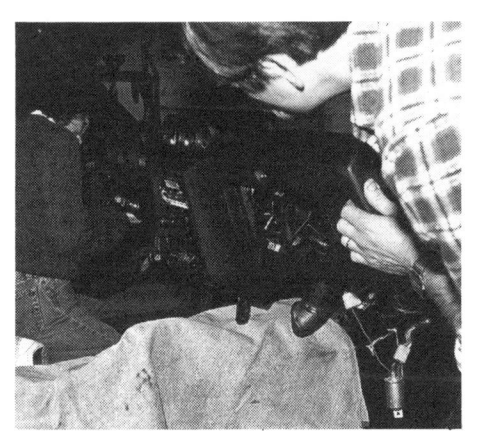

Lady who enjoys Z-car even more than I helps me lift new instrument-panel assembly in place.

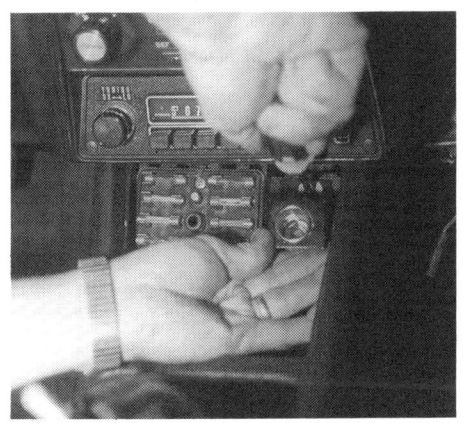

With console in place, fuse block and lighter can be installed on this 240Z. Later-style console accommodates sound system and many other components.

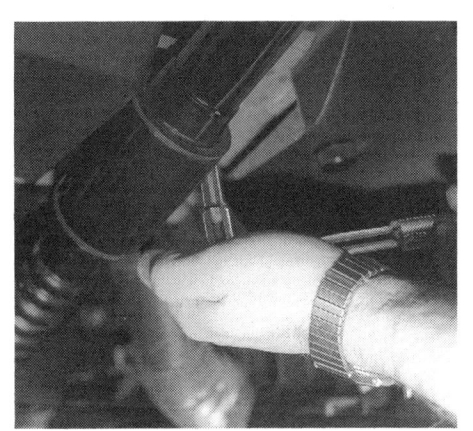

Early-style steering column is remounted to instrument panel and pedal-support bracket.

Use a soft bottle brush and compressed air to dislodge debris while holding the heater or air-conditioner case in several positions—upside down, on its front and so forth. Inspect all gaskets and valve pads for gaps or looseness. A bit of weatherstrip cement to renew their grip will save headaches later.

Take a critical look at all coolant/refrigerant fittings and valves. Be particularly aware of evidence of leaks. If you see suspicious discolorations, determine whether they are from old hose joints or from deteriorated or cracked tubing. Look at the heater radiator for similar evidence. Don't be afraid to dismantle the unit if you suspect impending leakage. Z-car heating/cooling equipment has a good reputation, but is not immune from the need for occasional repairs. A competent radiator shop can often clean and repair simple leaks for minimal cost. Don't tempt fate if you're in doubt.

Mount the heater or A/C case to the firewall and tunnel. Attach new coolant hoses and pass them through the firewall. Use new grommets to ensure a tight seal. Tighten the clamps securely. Align fittings to prevent cross-threading and tighten only enough to get a good seal. Don't fracture the tubing by over-tightening with a pipe wrench. Tighten only against another wrench or you could twist the tubing.

Next, add the blower unit. If the gasket to the cowl plenum is dubious, apply a bead of non-hardening sealer—silicone types are fine here. Blower motors are relatively inexpensive, so replace the original if you had any problems with it. Check to make sure it wasn't a switch or wiring problem, however.

Install Instrument Panel

This job is hard to do without a helper. But you won't need help for any longer than it takes to carry the instrument-panel assembly to the car, pass it over the tunnel and set it in place. Before moving the instrument panel, make sure all air ducts are in place.

Before you place the instrument panel in the car, consider some things first: The late-style Z-car instrument panel has its defroster ducts mounted to the cowl rather than the instrument panel as with the early style. So first install the defroster ducts to the cowl if you have the later style.

The glove-compartment liner on the early instrument panel is composition board and possible to install after the instrument panel is in place; the rigid-plastic version used on the later instrument panel must be in place *before* instrument-panel installation. Attach the latch striker.

Check to see if wiring connectors are accessible. If you put the steering column-to-pedal support bolts in place, remember to remove them temporarily. By now you should know *not* to let the instrument-panel assembly rest on the column.

Be sure the duct to the central

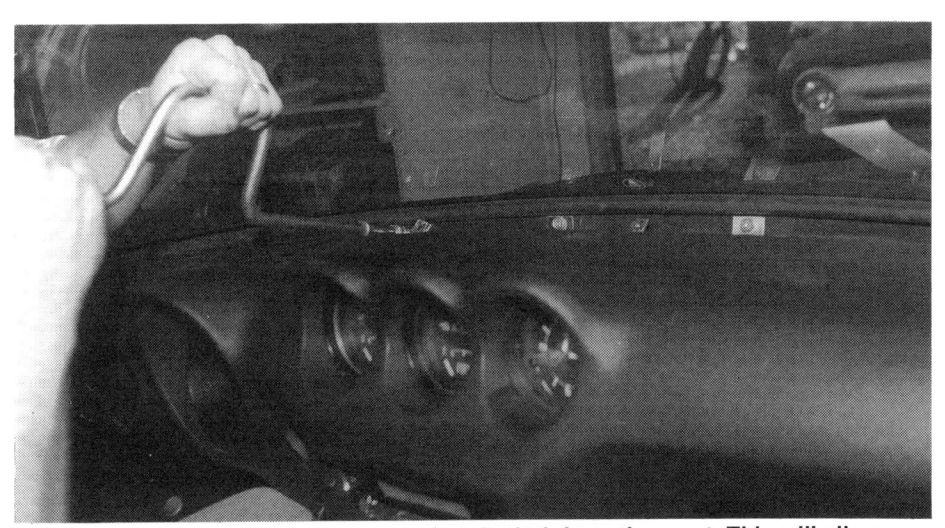

Install upper panel-mounting screws, but don't tighten them yet. This will allow you to shift panel slightly for installing the lower screws. Once lower screws are in finger-tight, tighten them all.

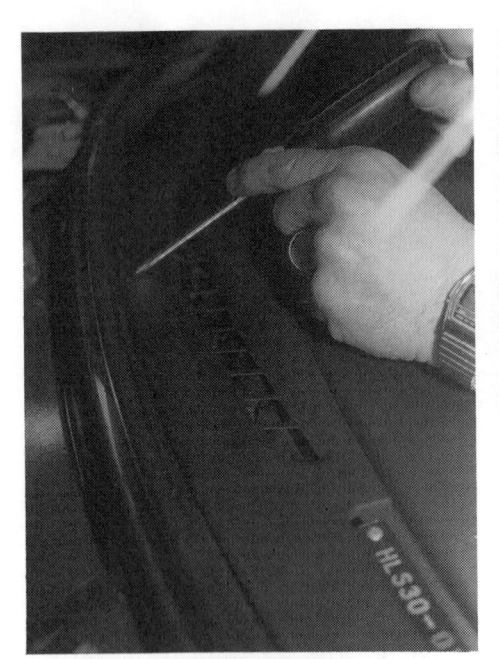

Instrument-panel-garnish trim installs next. Note VIN plate at right.

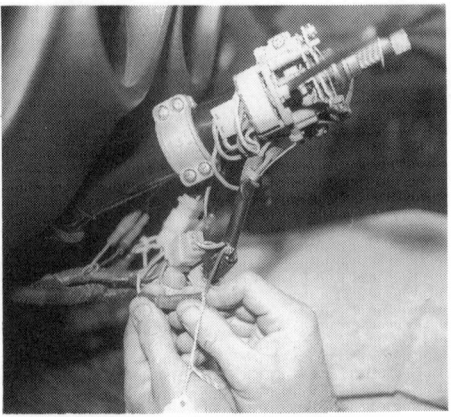

Install combination and ignition switches. This is where your tags, notes and patience are tested—any connections that aren't correct will come back to haunt you!

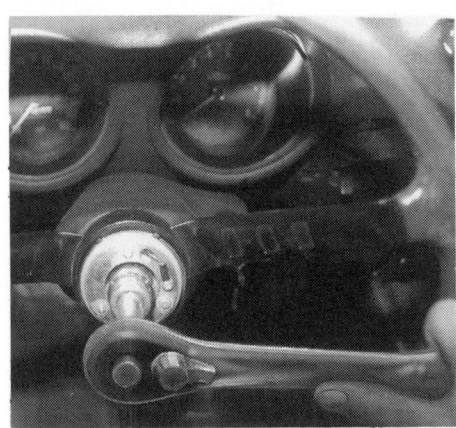

With column jacket on, steering wheel can be reinstalled. This photo doesn't flatter my restoration job on wheel.

heater/air-conditioner duct mates with the diffuser. The remainder of the ducts have enough flexibility to allow for later installation and routing.

If your instrument panel is new, the slotted bolt holes in the metal armature may not be in exact alignment with the mounting holes in the cowl. This is because the armature is somewhat flexible . . . which will permit enough movement for aligning.

Use a punch in a center hole to align an adjacent hole and get a screw started. Then work toward the ends of the instrument panel, starting the next screws. Don't tighten them yet. Go instead to the two brackets that support each end of the instrument panel from beneath. Again, the instrument panel will stand a certain amount of distortion for alignment. Insert the punch to hold it until you can start a screw in each side, then start the second ones.

Replace the steering-column mounting bolts, but only finger-tight. Early Zs have four, later ones six. The early instrument panel has two mounting ears at the bottom that mount to the tunnel, the later type has two braces that fasten to the tunnel and instrument-panel armature.

Tighten All Screws—When your instrument-panel alignment is good, start tightening the upper fasteners and work down. Don't miss any. A loose screw may result in a lot of noise when your car is in operation. Tighten the steering-column bolts and check the pedal-bracket bolts.

Instrument-Panel Trim—This is held with Phillips-head screws that thread into clip-nuts in the instrument panel. If these don't mate readily, adjust the nuts—or their tabs—slightly until they are satisfactory.

If your 280Z instrument panel had spacers under the longer trim-mounting screws, don't omit them. These were a remedy on some early 280Zs to prevent the forward edge of the instrument-panel padding from slipping out from under the trim. By letting the trim extend rearward, the unsightly edge was prevented from curling up.

Heater-/Air-Conditioner Control Cables—Route each cable and attach to its respective arm. Move the control through its travel, observing the arm action. If all is OK, tighten the bracket clamps. Be methodical and check that all cables have a smooth, positive action. Put a daub of light grease or machine oil on the moving parts—pivots, slides and so forth.

Wiring—Rely more on your ID tags and configuration of the connectors than on Service Manual schematics. These are often just accurate enough to be more confusing than helpful. Wiring diagrams are more accurate.

Begin making the more obvious connections, but try to correlate both the wiring size/color and labels you made. There are a few connectors that will mate, but result in an incorrect circuit. Remove tags when you are sure the connections are correct. Again, work carefully and methodically to minimize mistakes.

Some incorrect or shorted circuits can cause a fire in inaccessible areas. In the best case, you'll be cleaning fire-extinguisher chemicals out of your new interior and looking forward to an extensive/expensive repair job. In the worst case, you'll be hauling a burned-out hulk to the scrap yard, so be attentive.

Early Fuse Block—This can be connected now or after the console is in place. Do whichever is more convenient. The late fuse block as well as the junction block, EFI control box and so forth go in the kick-panel areas.

Steering Column

Ignition Switch—Reinstall the switch/steering lock on the column. Breakaway-head screws were unavailable at the time of this writing, so I used four Phillips-head screws. Check the lock action.

Combination Switch—Next reinstall the two halves of this switch above the ignition on the column. Lubricate the moving parts of the turn signal with light grease or oil. Be careful not

Interior Restoration & Assembly 143

Horn cushion presses into engagement with early wheel. Later models install with a partial turn. If horn circuit is energized, you'll make a lot of noise doing this.

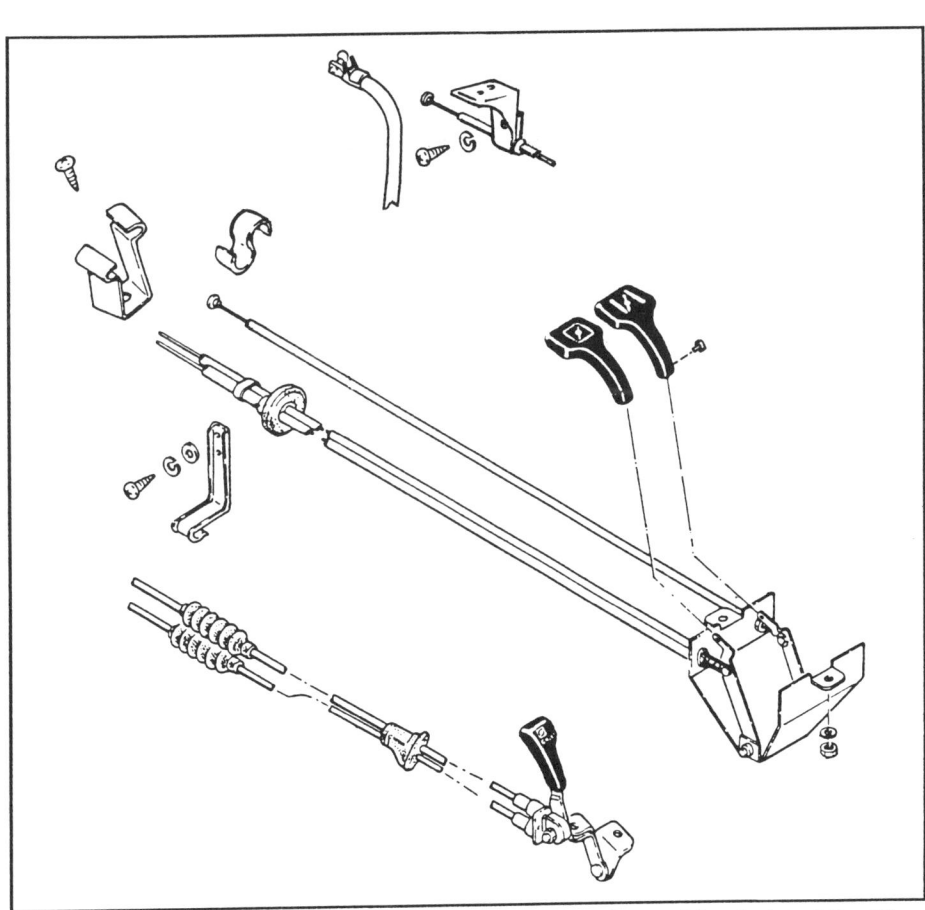

Choke and throttle mechanisms for carbureted Z-cars. Inset at top is hand throttle to accelerator-lever hookup. Most Zs only had the choke control. Bottom is later-series choke lever.

to bend the horn-contact arm.

Column Jacket—Reattach the two halves. Be sure to use the correct screw in each case—they are specific for the location.

Steering Wheel—Datsun used imitation wood grain rim on early Zs. Thoroughly clean the rim with lacquer thinner and recoat it with clear lacquer to give it a new look. The matte-black spokes may require sanding as well as cleaning. Mask rim and respray with matte-black lacquer or enamel.

Wheel has the horn-contact ring lead-and-spring assembly mounted with two countersunk machine screws on the top side. Late-type wheels have a cushioned vinyl rim. If this is deteriorated, the only alternative is to replace the wheel. This type also has three screws to retain both the horn-spring assembly and mounting blocks for the horn cushion.

Center the front wheels and orient steering wheel in the straight-ahead position. Install the center onto the splined shaft. If you marked these, realign them with the marks. Put on the lock washer and nut and torque to specification.

Horn Cushion—Early models: Orient the logo and push cushion down over the spring clip. Late models: Fit slots on the reverse side over the plastic mounting blocks so a clockwise turn of about 10 degrees will lock it in the correct orientation.

Back to the Instrument Panel

Speedometer Cable—Make sure this is routed correctly and reattach it to the speedometer. Support the cable with the plastic-covered metal fingers.

Dash Bezel—Early Zs have a deep bezel that fronts the heater controls, courtesy light and radio. Late Zs have the radio in the console proper and use shorter bezels to house warning lights and surround the heater/A/C controls. The levers and knobs are attached directly to the system control. Both have the center air-duct outlet.

These bezels take a lot of gaff and, as a result, usually need replacement. On early cars—after the bezel is replaced—the heater-control switch and knob go back on. Early 240Zs have the **OFF** position to the far left. Later, this was changed. If you need to refinish the levers on either system, they may be masked and painted matte black.

The urethane-foam lining of the duct deflector can be relined by using foam tape sold at recreation-vehicle outlets. Simply remove the deflector and scrape out the old foam. Then cut new pieces from the tape. Don't trust the adhesive, use contact cement on both sides. Reassemble the unit and attach it to the bezel.

On early cars, reattach the heater-control unit. Then fasten the bezel to the instrument panel with Phillips-head screws. Using a small straight-blade screwdriver, install the control-lever knobs. Put on the radio controls and instrument-panel-top courtesy light. On late-instrument-panel cars, reattach the warning lights and fasten as above.

Be careful not to bend the levers or cables before or while installing the instrument panel.

Recondition & Install Console

Z-cars used a variety of consoles

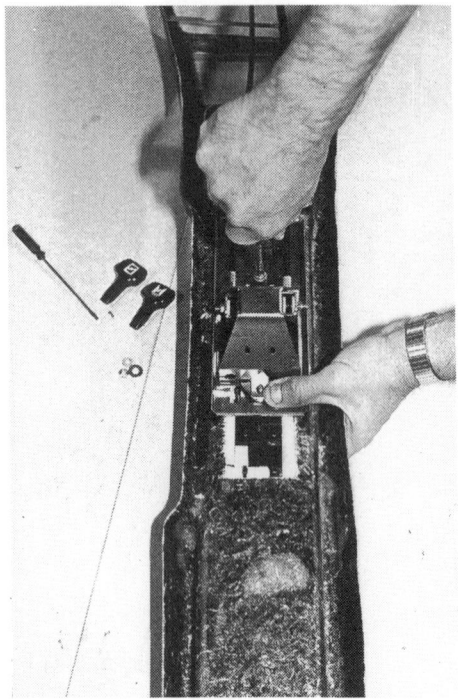

Early-style console from underneath; choke and hand-throttle assembly nuts onto captive studs. Handles go on levers after they fit through plate. Rear-window-defroster switch fits behind them. Other blank hole is for European parking-light switch, which was never used on North American models.

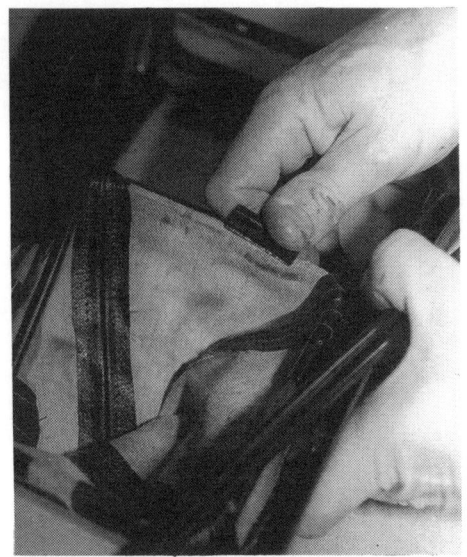

Cosmetic upper shift-lever boot clips to lip of console opening. Cables have retaining clips on sides of console.

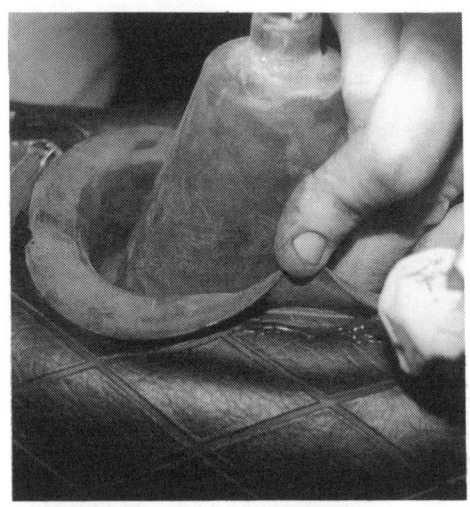

Lower boot must be cemented or sealed from both sides to provide weathertight joint at tunnel opening. Manual-transmission shift lever is in place.

over the years, but these were constructed and installed basically the same way. They do not interchange, however, even between standard- and automatic-transmission models.

Built of molded light-gauge fiber-reinforced plastic (FRP), they tend to deteriorate after years of exposure to burning tobacco, coffee spills, repeated drillings, heat from the sun or occasional use as a seat. As a result, a console structure usually needs to be replaced. Fortunately, these parts—the first of many, I predict—are being reproduced for the restorer.

Motorsport Auto, one of the first to reproduce Z-car parts (see Suppliers Directory, page 204), has new consoles available for all six varieties. They are authentic down to their design, finish and fixtures. If you tried to find a restorable console in wrecking yards, you know their scarcity. If you found a good one you know their cost.

If your Z's console is damaged beyond repair, don't hesitate to replace it with one of these excellent new replicas. On the other hand, if it only has a few cracks and blemishes, you can repair it. The material responds well to fiberglassing from the back side. Close up any cracks by truing the structure and clamping it in place with a piece of reinforcing material. Then apply the resin/hardener mixture and fiberglass cloth to the reinforcement. When it cures, cut or grind off any surplus. Vee-out any cracks with a knife or file and fill with polyester filler or glazing putty. Sand the filler smooth and repeat until you are satisfied with the appearance.

There is no satisfactory way to restore the pebble-grain effect molded into the original material, but Cal Custom's Wrinkle Black paint—applied correctly—gives a close approximation. Sprayed from an aerosol can in light coats, it will recreate a light texture and charcoal-black finish that is close to the original. Be sure the console is spotlessly clean and free of grease before painting—even in cracks and crevices. I use a heat lamp, hand-held, to get the light texture.

Consoles hold various controls and accessories: choke and throttle levers, fuse panels, ash trays, cigarette lighters, defroster switches, seat-belt and catalytic-converter-overheat warning lights and more, depending on year and equipment. The sound system is even housed in a 280Z's console.

These must all be replaced as they came out. Be sure to lubricate the levers on reinstallation. Check all bulbs and clean the plastic lenses with mild soap and a brush. Aftermarket armrests, such as the Amco, were offered as dealer-installed options by Datsun, so they may be considered original equipment.

Install the upper shifter boot—mainly decorative—to the console opening on standard transmission cars with its eight clips. These are available new or can be made by any competent upholsterer.

Standard-Transmission Shift Lever—This should be installed now if it isn't already in place. On early transmissions the lever is nutted to the shifter extension. On later transmissions, position the lever concentric with the holes in the guide and reinstall the pin and clip.

Lower Shift Boot—If you haven't installed this, do so now. It pays to use a new rubber boot due to the proximity of the exhaust pipe, rear transmission seal and a generally hostile underfloor environment. The factory-replacement boot is thick and pliable. It has a generous lip that seals to the tunnel-opening edges.

To seal the boot to the tunnel, apply a bead of weatherstrip cement or other sealant under the boot lip and let it set up before disturbing.

Automatic-Transmission Shift Mechanism—This bolts to the tunnel sheet metal and is linked to the selector lever. With the shifter in place—be sure you have a good seal—reconnect the rod to the lever. It is adjusted at the threaded end of the rod. Set it to

Interior Restoration & Assembly 145

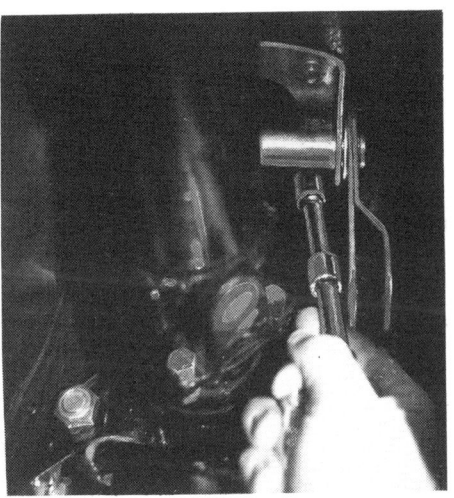

Back underneath, parking-brake-equalizer bracket and linkage installs in transmission tunnel. Notice that drive shaft is in the way. I did!

Grommet for hood-latch cable and speedometer cable must be slit before it'll fit over cables. This won't hurt seal. Cut only far enough to accommodate them.

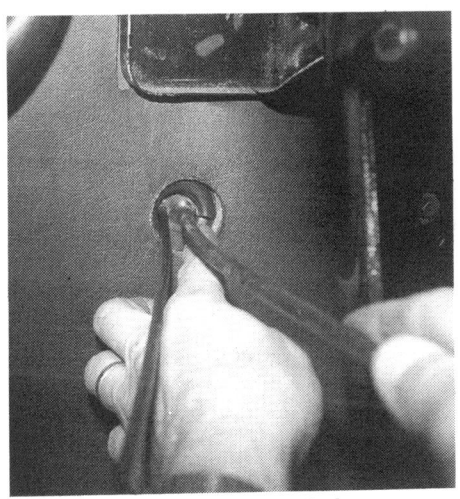

Grommet should be cemented or sealed to firewall.

engage **N** at the transmission, but confirm this by running the shifter through the gears before taking your car out on the road.

Parking Brake
Clean and lubricate the parking-brake-lever mechanism and linkage. If there's much damage to the wearing surfaces or ratchet, replace the mechanism. Install the lever by feeding the shaft and arm through hole in the tunnel. The nylon-bushed end of the shaft should seat in the pocket on the underside. Seal mounting plate to the opening with a strip of dumdum or sealer. Tighten the mounting bolts.

Under the car, mount equalizer and attach the cable yoke to its clevis with the pin. Hook up control rod(s) and adjust the clevis or turnbuckle with parking-brake lever in the released position. Take out slack, but don't tension the cables against the actuating levers on the brakes.

Note: The following can be done before or after the tunnel upholstery goes on. Slip a plastic bag over the lever to mask it from contact adhesive. The parking-brake warning-light lead should be hooked up to the switch pigtail after the material is in place.

Hood-Release- & Speedometer-Cable Grommet
This grommet accommodates both cables in the same firewall hole. If you're installing a new grommet, the hood cable will fit through its nipple in the grommet; the speedometer cable won't. Neither end of the cable housing will come off and the ends are too big to fit anyway.

Fit the hood-release cable through the grommet, then use a sharp blade to make a slit from the other nipple directly to the adjacent edge of the grommet. Slip the speedometer-cable housing into its nipple and cement the slit section together with weather-strip adhesive.

Push the cables through and seat the grommet in the firewall hole. Install the speedometer cable to the transmission if you haven't already done so. The other end feeds through the pedal-bracket assembly. This or any other grommet can be cemented in place. Wipe up excess with naptha on a rag.

Hood Latch—Caution! If you are using the old hood-latch cable, inspect it very carefully. Make sure cable action is smooth and free. It may need lubrication. Light oil will suffice to restore its performance. Inspect the small knob on the end for fraying, broken strands, bending and so forth. The latch should also be cleaned and well lubricated so it works without dragging.

The experience of having your hood-latch cable seize *or* the end knob break off with the hood shut is no fun. To open the hood requires reaching up past the engine from below the car to release the latch! Replacing a marginal cable or latch is cheap insurance against this.

Install the cable end into its retainer on the latch arm. Squeeze this shut with pliers. Install the hood-latch assembly to the bracket on the firewall. Don't tighten the bolts until you are ready to adjust the hood-sriker-to-latch interface.

Shock-Tower Trim
Recover these next. All models that don't have shoulder-harness reels should have a hardboard filler across the top cavity as well as wrapped around the angled braces between the tower and rear-deck floor. Don't forget to replace the rubber plugs in the differential-mounting-bolt access holes under the braces!

Some early cars didn't have hardboard fillers, but they are a good idea for improving upholstery durability. Either get some from a parts car or cut your own. If yours have begun to sag, simply reverse them side for side to restore the desired appearance.

Cement one side at a time. This process can be a bit time consuming. If the solvent evaporates out of the adhesive, more adhesive will have to be applied. Cement the hardboard fillers on first, then coat their exposed sides. Turn the strut-tower covers inside out and coat with cement. When it is the correct tackiness, position the material to the top of the tower by the

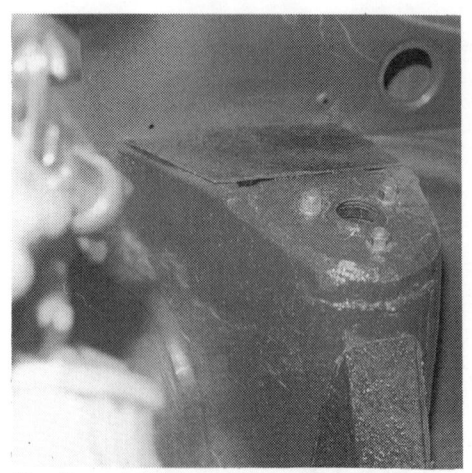

Hardboard fillers are cemented to strut tower, then sprayed with adhesive to take vinyl covering. Upholstery should be sprayed (or brushed) fully outside the car—do one side at a time.

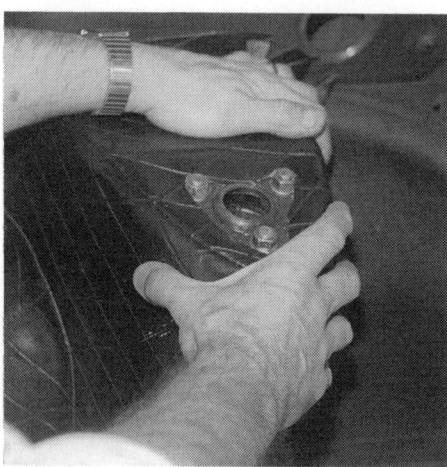

Installing strut-tower covers is a challenge. An extra hand or two helps keep everything from sticking to everything else. Start applying cover at the strut-mounting holes while trying to get good alignment. If the cover is not lined up, pull it free and start again until you get it right. Then progressively stretch and smooth the cover onto the adhesive until all edges are down tight.

strut nuts. Roll the cover down over the tower, stretching it carefully and rubbing to get a good bond. I do the back side first, then the front. Be sure the edges are well adhered even though they don't show. Then repeat with the other side.

Parking-Brake-Lever Boot—Snap this to the upholstery now or later.

Wheel-House Trim

Now you will have to determine where the edge of the adhesive should be on the forward edge of the strut-tower cover and mask it appropriately. Also mask the door jamb/sill area. Apply adhesive and remove masking, then coat the vinyl piece.

This piece of vinyl has to match the front lip of the deck. There should be a slit in the material at that point. Start it there, then work up and down away from it. Do clean, careful work for results you will be proud of later. If you left any crud or debris on either cemented surface, it will show up under the otherwise-smooth vinyl! Repeat by covering the other side.

Deck-Front Trim

Again mask off the vinyl of the tunnel and wheel house. Apply adhesive to the panel in front of the rear deck and to the vinyl. The crucial part is where it meets the tunnel—the bound edge must be very close to the original position or you will have a tacky-appearing transition to say nothing of coming up short at the edges. Oddly enough, Datsun left a raw edge where this strip meets the wheel houses! If you are reupholstering with all-new material, this will look better with a bound edge.

Work the material down over the tunnel junction, then stretch and rub it down for a good bond. Early 240Zs have slits for the tool and jack stowage lids which must match up. You don't have this extra hassle with later Zs. Check exposed edges for adequate cement so they don't curl up later on. Remove adhesive from exposed upholstery surfaces.

Install Choke Mechanism

This applies only to carbureted cars, of course. Clean and lubricate choke lever—and throttle lever if so equipped. With the handle(s) removed, install the assemblies in the console. Reinstall the handles and secure with their setscrews. Route cables through the metal retainers on

Because I am spraying on adhesive, masking is necessary to keep adhesive drools off cover material. Wheel house is next. It overlaps strut-tower vinyl at the edges.

Slit for front lip of deck is the key position here. Start applying cover from this point and work away from it. Try to get a good bond where the materials overlap. Other edges will be covered.

the inside of the console. Also install any other switches or lights.

Install Radio
Install the radio or sound-system unit into the forward console on 260Zs and 280Zs. Put on the face plate and knobs.

Install Console
Fit the forward end snugly under the instrument panel. Check routing of the choke and throttle cables—make sure they don't kink or bind. Make any necessary electrical connections. If you hooked up the fuse block on the early style, feed it between the forward mounting bracket and cross piece. Take off the cover and work it a bit—it will go.

Early: Two screws attach the forward mounting bracket. One also secures the fuse block, the other the cigarette-lighter element. Don't forget the ground wire. At the rear, put on the seat-belt minder if so equipped and the plastic change tray. Insert the three screws, recheck console alignment—test fit the ashtray and lighter—and tighten.

Late: Install the two screws that enter from the sides of the forward portion. Check alignment and install the three screws at the rear. Replace the arm rest—either Datsun or approved accessory—on cars so equipped.

Gearshift Knob—Thread knob back on the lever so the shift pattern is readable.

Transmission tunnel is masked, as are stowage-lid tabs.

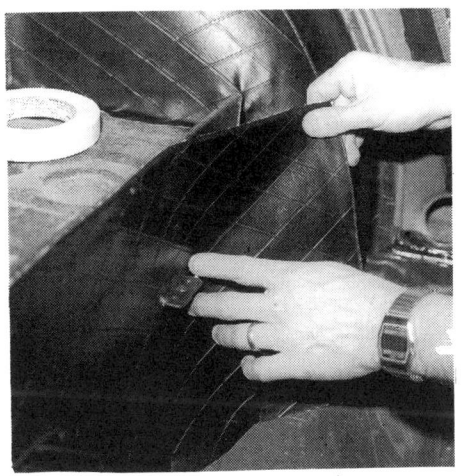

Vinyl should be positioned at tunnel with top edge matching lip and cut out centered on hump. On recycled material, you'll have to hit the stowage-lid tabs right "on the money."

Throttle Cable—Route the hand-throttle cable through its clamp. Snap the nylon bushing behind knob on the cable end into the little bracket on the accelerator-pedal arm. Then put cable through slot in the bracket and attach the crimped-on end fitting tightly. Tighten nut on the bolt to keep it in place. Check throttle travel and lubricate the cable end for free movement.

Choke Cables—Install choke-cable boot into the firewall. Route both cables in as direct a path as possible to and through the grommet boot. Connect cable sheath to the retainers on both carburetors and cables to the choke linkages. Follow adjusting procedures to be sure the chokes fully open and close.

Interior-Light Switches—Clean and check these for operation. Put a daub of grease or stick lubricant on these and push them back into their holes in the door jambs. Pull pigtails out of the jamb rear and connect to the harness.

Radio-Antenna Lead—This routes over pedal support and clips along the driver's toeboard and along the lower sill. Fish the female end up through the lowest hole in the right B-pillar and out behind wheelhouse. Plug the male end into the radio.

Restore Seats
Bucket Seats—When you removed the seats, I suggested you identify them side for side. The driver's seat has more fore-and-aft travel—for reasons unknown because there is adequate room for similar travel on the passenger side. The seats interchange and many well worn Z-cars have had the buckets switched to equalize wear. Adjusting handles go on the tunnel side. So do the rake-adjusting knobs on the early series. These were replaced with levers on the later cars.

Seat Disassembly—If you haven't done so already, clean both seat

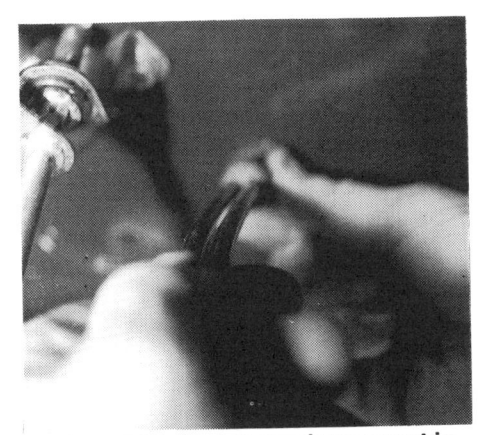

Choke cables feed through grommet in firewall and attach to carburetors. Grommet I used is later than what came on my '70 Z, but it was the only replacement available at the time.

Installing interior-light switches. I don't remember if these worked before they were removed. If not, new switches are now in order.

148 How to Restore Your Datsun Z-Car

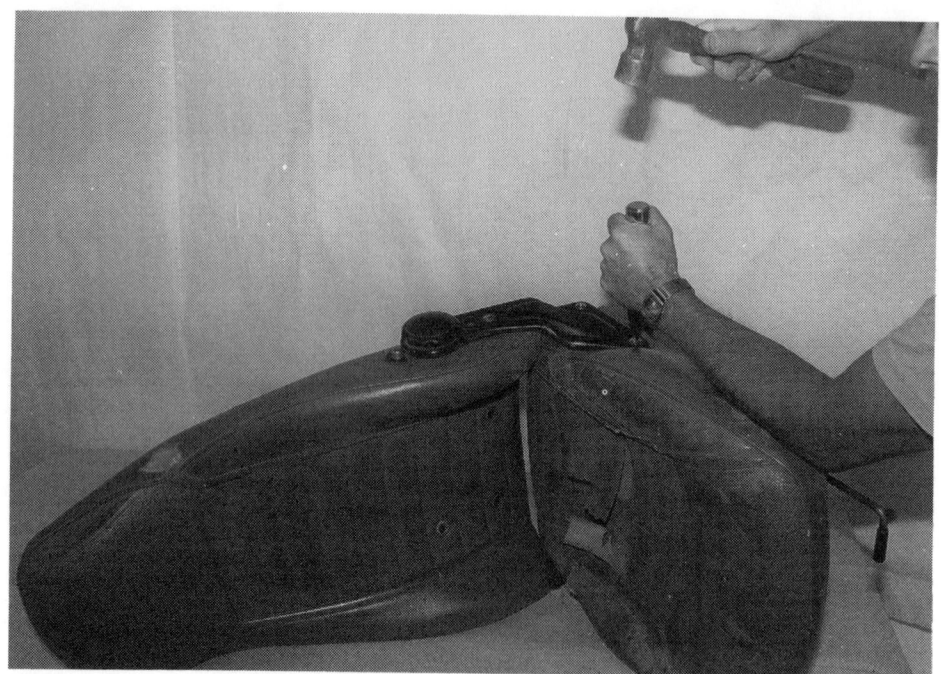

Impact driver is needed to loosen big oval-head Phillips-head screws on these early seats. Cover kit is a quantum leap from duct tape that was on seat cushions!

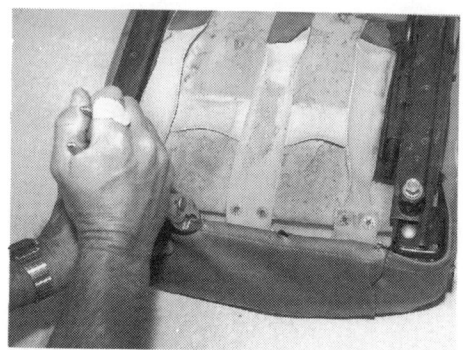

Points on seat frame must be bent back to release wire in hem. There wasn't much support left in them.

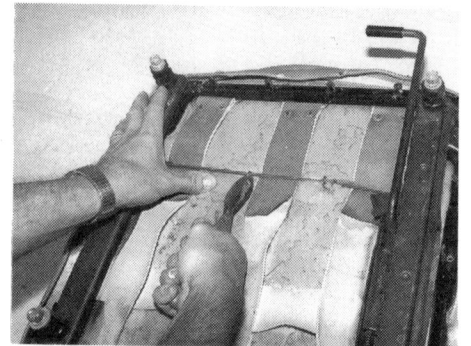

Cut hog rings that hold listing to wire. Cushion cover should now come off.

assemblies. Take them outside and blow out the peanut shells, McDonald's coffee stirrers, meter change, spiders and whatever. Get into the cracks and under the seat cushion as much as possible. This will reduce the crud that would otherwise get all over your work area.

Remove the seat-belt-minder hooks and plastic bolster guards. Then take out the Phillips-head screws and bolts that attach the back to the seat-to-back brackets. The early style uses a countersunk screw that may require an impact driver to break loose. You may have to rotate the seat backs to their full-back positions for access to the lower screws. With all fasteners out, separate the seat, back and brackets. Early cars had clear-vinyl scuff protectors under the brackets.

Refinishing Hardware—Metal brackets should be thoroughly cleaned and repainted now so they will be ready to go back on when the upholstery is completed. Use a low-gloss finish and be sure to get good coverage. Flex the parts between coats so you don't end up with unpainted "shadows." Plastic parts can be replaced, especially if warped, cracked or otherwise unserviceable. Vinyl dyes will cover, but in high-use areas, expect these to wear off quickly.

Seat Cushion

With the seat cushion inverted, padded side to the workbench, you should see that the bottom edges or pull-tabs are held in place by short, pointed metal tabs. These are welded to the seat's tubing frame. Release them simply by bending up with pliers. It may take a little prying with a screwdriver or similar tool to get access to the points. Start at the rear of the seat.

Peel off wire-reinforced edge of the vinyl covers. You'll need to reuse these soft-steel wires, so remove and store them where you can find them.

Listing—You probably noticed there is an indented area in the seat cover just where your posterior fits. If not, you should notice that the cover isn't free yet. The reason for both is there is a strip of listing—a loop of material hog-ringed to a wire on the bottom of the padding. Using side-cutter pliers, nip the wire hog rings to free the listing. Then pull the old cover off the seat frame and foam squabs.

Seat Frame—Straighten the triangular points that held the hem of the covers. Try not to break any off. If you encounter several broken-off points, your car may have had the covers changed previously. This means you'll have to weld or braze new ones back on. If the seat frame is rusty, now's the time to thoroughly abrasive blast and repaint it.

Cushion Repair—Seat-cushion, or squab foam is made of urethane. Now is a good time to evaluate the serviceability of your seat cushions. If the vinyl is long gone, there may be considerable erosion of the foam, where frequent contact with your jeans rubbed the surface away over time. Don't despair. Find some scrap polyfoam of approximately the same firmness.

Using a sharp bread knife, cut it to fit the voided area. Keep slicing

Interior Restoration & Assembly 149

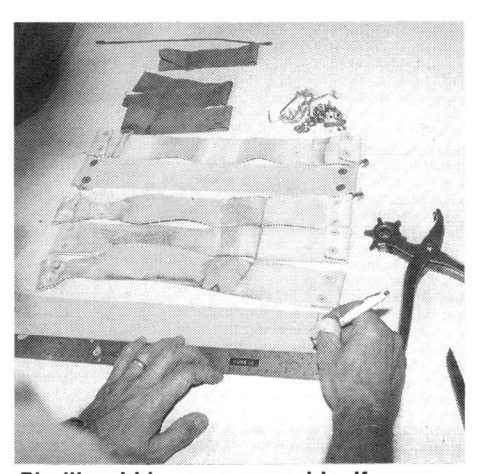

Pirelli webbing was unusable. If yours is in similar condition, new material is available in bulk; buy the number of feet you need. Wire hooks are easy to remove with foam cushion squabs out of the way. Measure each strip 16-1/2 inches long to give about 14-1/2 inches between hook wires.

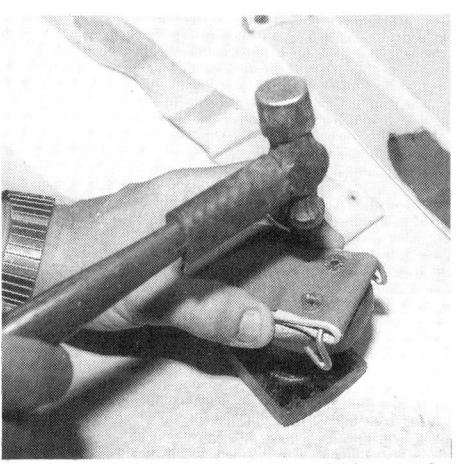

I salvaged rivets from old webbing and punched new holes with a leather punch. With reinforcement cloth cemented to webbing as was done originally, wrap webbing around hooks. Then reinstall rivets and washers. Peen ends down firmly.

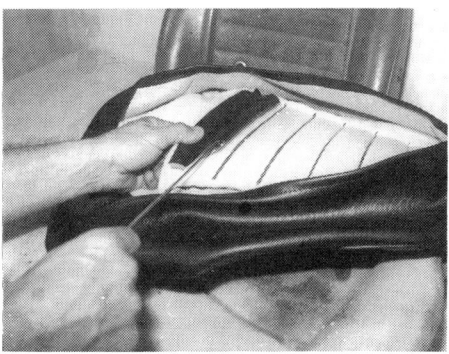

With webbing and foam back in place, reinstall cover. Listing wire is reinserted. This will be hog-ringed just as it was originally.

pieces from the bottom of the patch piece until it fits, but is a little on the plump side. You might need to laminate two pieces to build up the needed thickness, then sculpt it to fit. Coat both mating surfaces with a good grade of contact cement and carefully adhere them. Check feel and appearance of the cushion. Upholstery will hide some unevenness, but not much.

Seat-Belt Warning—If you have one of the Zs that was blessed with the automatic seat-belt interlock—and it is still in place—remove the sensor and wiring before going further.

New Cushions—At the time of this writing, new foam cushions are not available for Z seats. This may be rectified, though, given the upswing in popularity of the first-series Z-cars. Bear in mind that old foam doesn't become *more* resilient with age. If you can't find sound foam cushions for your Z-car seats, recreate the cushions from foam stock available at a good upholstery supplier. New foam comes in several firmnesses. Generally, the firmer the better for support and durability.

Because they're pros at it, have an upholstery shop shape the cushion(s) using your old ones as a guide. If you choose to do the job, rough the block into shape with an electric knife. Further trimming can be done with a common wire brush, if used judiciously. Gradually scrub away the foam in light passes over the surface. Laminate blocks of foam using a good spray contact cement to get shapes otherwise unattainable. I use a very thin layer of foam or cotton batting to add smoothness to a repaired or roughed-out replacement cushion.

Pirelli Webbing—On early seats such as those illustrated, the seat cushions are sprung by rubberized fabric straps called *Pirelli webbing*. The name comes from its Italian manufacturer. These probably have lost their effectiveness by now even if they don't look bad. If yours are due for replacement, slip the wire hooks out of their holes in the seat frames and remove.

You should be able to find new webbing at any good upholstery-supply store or local shop. Cut four replacement strips per seat 16-1/2 inches long. In their finished state, this will give 14-1/2 inches between the wire clips. You'll need three lengthwise strips and one lateral strip.

Original rivets can be reused if you remove them carefully. Pry up flared ends with a knife blade, slip off the washer plate and push out the rivet.

Use a punch—a cheap leather punch works fine—to make new rivet holes. When these are in the same position as the old ones and the distance between the looped ends is 14-1/2 inches, apply contact cement to the mating surfaces of the webbing and wrap it around the wire clip. Line up the rivet holes and reinstall the rivets. When the cement has had time to dry, stretch the webbing between the seat frame and snap the clips into their holes.

Later Zs use wire springs sometimes called *Never-Sags,* which denotes good durability. However, they sometimes fatigue and break, especially at the outside edges. Spring wire is available by the foot at Z-car parts suppliers. An alternative is to use a good spring from a derelict seat cushion. The trouble, as usual, is finding one.

Whatever you use, simply bend the ends of the spring wire into the attachment point and continue as follows.

Covers—I illustrate recovering seats using a commercially available kit. These are available from several manufacturers. They are offered at varying prices by many different retailers. Whether you use a kit or sew your own from scratch, the installation is the same.

Kits are similar in quality to the original covers and utilize almost the same if not identical colors and patterns. In some cases "seams" are heat-pressed instead of being top-stitched by machine. Because kits are

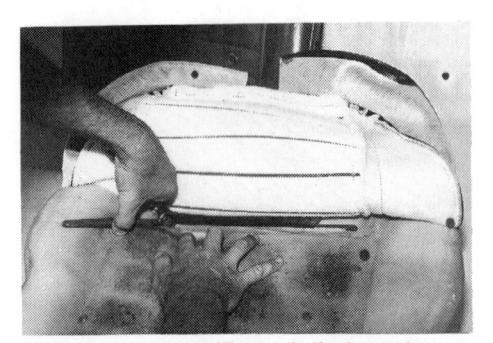

Hog-ring pliers will reach listing wire below webbing if foam is depressed. Upholsterers have strong, but tired hands.

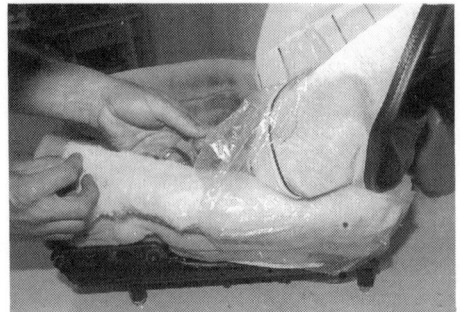

Extra cotton layer plumps up seat bolsters—light plastic sheet helps padding stay in place, prevents material from hanging up.

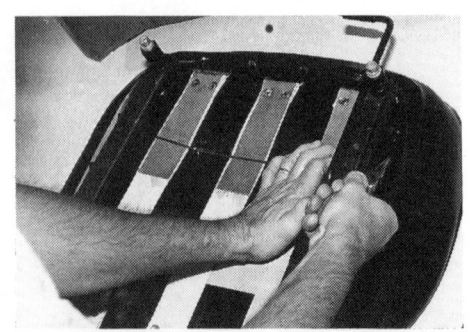

With wire-reinforced hem stretched into place, retaining points are pushed through and bent over. Plastic hammer with duct tape on face was used to bump them down.

relatively inexpensive, I recommend their use unless you want to substitute a different type of material.

If you must do your recovering in a cold shop, pre-warm the vinyl cover in direct sunlight or in front of a forced-air heater. It should go without saying: Don't burn it!

The kit shown has nylon cord in hemmed-edge of the covers. I prefer wires, so I bend a tight loop in one end and use the cord to fish original wire into its place. Don't forget short piece that goes into the center listing.

With your foam cushion positioned on the refurbished frame and webbing or spring assembly, stretch the cover over both. Then roll the rear section back over the front to expose the listing. Push the wire-reinforced listing through the slot in the cushion. Then, while holding the whole thing together, invert it on your work surface. Using three or four hog rings, clip the wire in the listing to the wire that runs beneath the webbing. This gives that deep, contoured look and feel to the finished seat. Now, turn the unit right-side up.

Check the seat-cushion bolsters for height and smoothness. You can add some cotton or polyester fiber batt to fill out the corners or edges. Careful trial and error is the only way to judge how much. Once the edges are fastened to the frame, it will be too late—unless you want to repeat the process. So make it look smooth now. Some light plastic such as that for dry-cleaning bags works well to facilitate fitting the cover. Cut a couple of strips and intersperse them between the cushion and cover. They won't survive much manipulation, but once may be enough to keep the foam where you want it.

Pull the cover over the foam and down around the frame. Work the stretched areas over the bolsters with your hands until the cover fits pretty smoothly and the cushion feels even underneath. Invert everything again and begin hooking the retaining points through the hemmed edge. The points should poke through between the hem seam and wire. Tired, old foam will allow more room in the cover, so build the height back up with a 1/2-inch layer of foam or more. Don't build up the foam to where the cover will be stretched too tightly.

Begin at the center of the front, get a few hooked and repeat at the back. Hook two at the middle of each side, then flip the seat over and check your progress. If it looks satisfactory, continue with the hooks until all are engaged and recheck.

If pronounced wrinkles are developing at the sides, move the edges one forward or rearward relative to the original hooking holes. If they are in the rear part of the embossed center section of the cover, these can be eliminated with the rear pull-tab—it doesn't have a sewn hem and will allow more adjustment. Just don't get it too tight and cause a pulled seam or tear in the tab.

Repaint and lubricate the seat tracks. Reattach the seat tracks now or when you reinstall the seats in the car.

Seat Back

The back cover is slipped over the back cushion and frame like a pillow case. It's secured with the metal points at the bottom. As you did with the cushion, carefully pry these back to release first the back, then the front. Slip the cover up until the listing strip is accessible, snip the hog rings that hold it down and remove. Take the wires out of the listing and hemmed edges. Straighten the metal points that secured the hems.

Foam Padding—Again, take remedial steps necessary to get a good base for the new cover. But back cushions usually take relatively less abuse

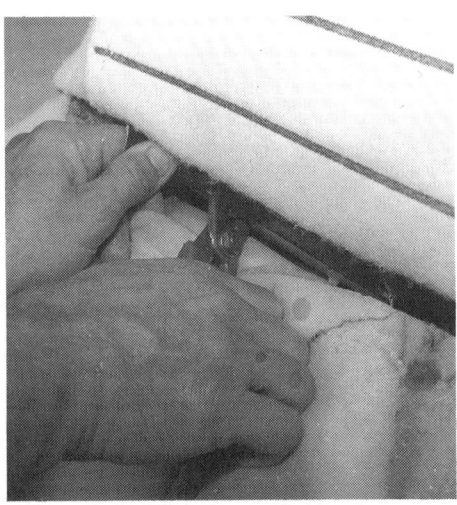

With seat-back cover rolled back over itself to listing tab, I pushed top over headrest. Listing must be hog-ringed before unrolling cover downwards. Plastic sheet is very helpful while installing cover.

Interior Restoration & Assembly 151

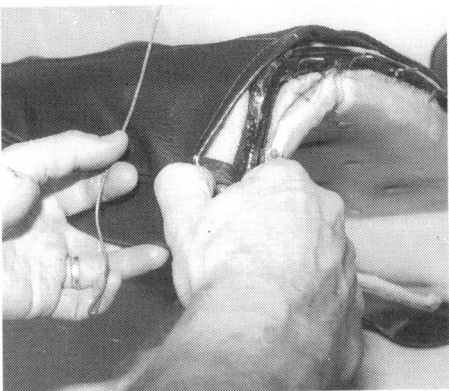

Wire reinforcements in hems are important for a good stretch. Kit didn't have wire reinforcements, but tiny slit—just above my right thumb—admits wire just like original.

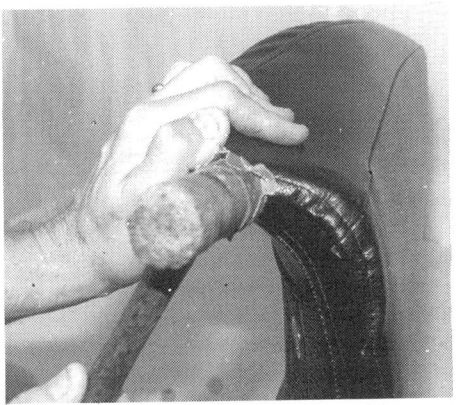

Considerable stretching and working the material down is required to install cover. Front hem is attached first, then the rear.

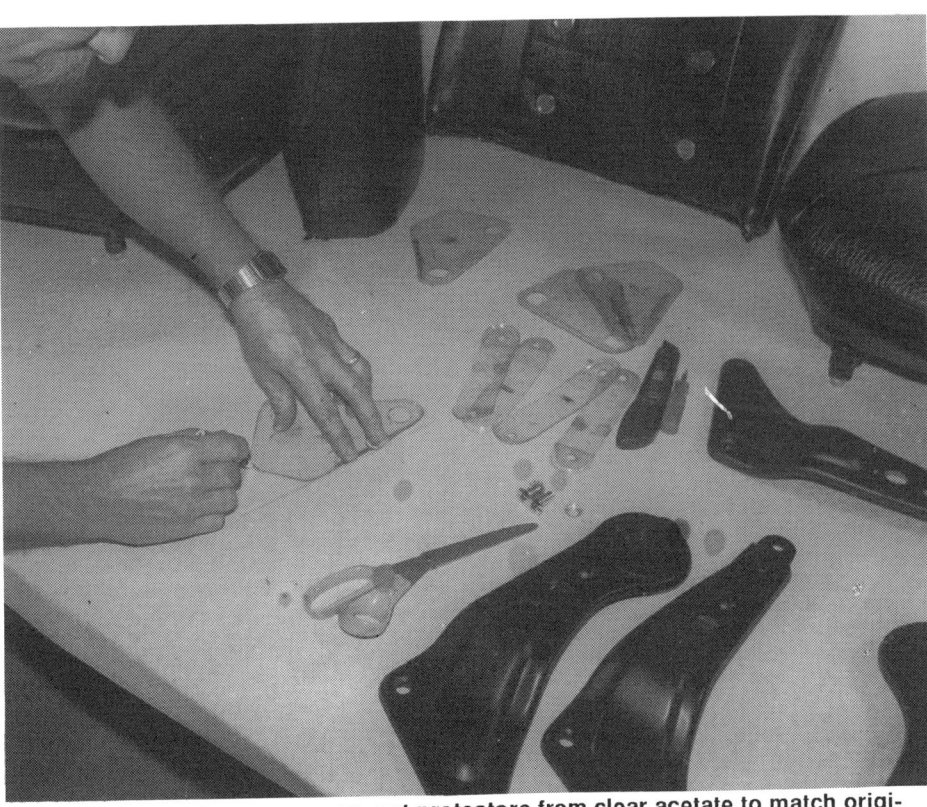

Once both sets of covers are on, cut protectors from clear acetate to match original ones. Brackets are refinished. There isn't much you can do with plastic parts except clean them thoroughly or replace with new ones.

than seats, so you should have less work to do here.

New Cover—Roll up the new seat-back cover like a sock. Start at the opening and roll it inside out until only the headrest portion shows. Put a bit of light plastic as used on the cushion over the headrest and shoulders of the back. The cover should be warm and flexible. Force it and you may tear a seam!

Put the wire into the new listing strip and gently ease it over the headrest until the listing reaches the anchor wire in the padding. Center cover before you get more than one hog ring in place. Check the listing and rings for secure attachment because you will have trouble getting back to them if they pull loose later!

Carefully roll cover down the back, working creases out with your hands as you go. Check for padding that doesn't look right and fix it now. With cover smoothed on, reinsert the wires in the hemmed tabs. You may have to make a tiny slit to feed wire through. There is a considerable amount of tension on the vinyl, so the wires are necessary both front and rear.

Because the seat-back front is the hardest to stretch—there isn't much to hang on to at either side—it is the first to be clipped under the metal points. An extra set of hands helps with this operation because you must stretch the material *and* secure it to two or three of the middle points simultaneously. Keep the material very warm, never cold. Avoid relaxing tension on the cover with only one point clipped as the point or vinyl may be overpowered and break or tear. Hang on until you're sure the cover is straight and taut, plus the hem is well secured. Keep an X-acto knife handy to start the points through the thick vinyl, especially toward the sides. When you're satisfied with the fit, bend over the points with a soft-face hammer.

With the front hem secured, repeat the process with the back hem. The same steps are necessary, but less strenuous. The extreme ends take extra care. This is where the edges will look ragged if the stretch isn't just right. Try for a clean, well-finished look, even though this end of the seat back doesn't show prominently.

Wrinkles & Stretch Marks—There will still be a few . . . and in new vinyl? Here is a trick, but you have to be careful—use a heat gun or, in a pinch, a heat lamp and play the heat on the general area where you have

152 How to Restore Your Datsun Z-Car

Once attaching points are cut through and protector is in place, brackets can be loosely installed. Don't tighten one side until all back screws are started.

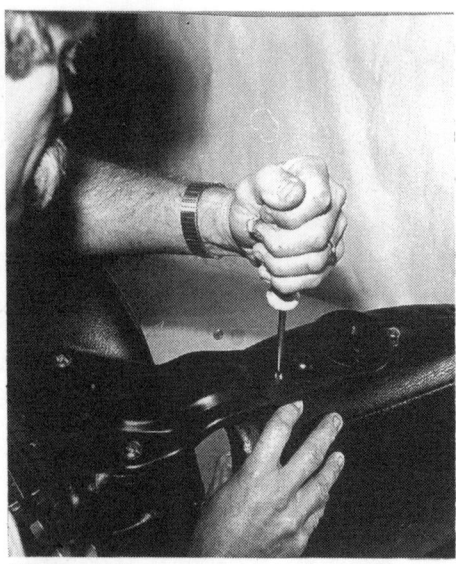

With seat back in place, tighten all bolts. Early adjuster knob goes on last, then finisher cap.

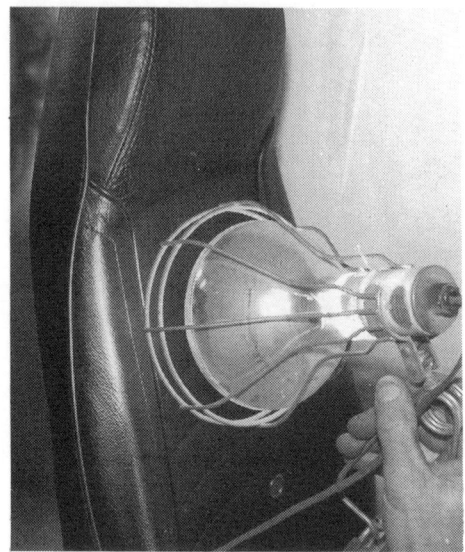

Looks good! Judicious application of heat from lamp or professional heat gun will allow stressed portions to relax. This lets wrinkles flatten out in a most gratifying way. *Don't overheat!*

stretch marks and wrinkles. *Don't* concentrate the heat on any one area. Keep it moving! You should see the tightly pulled areas between loose areas slowly relaxing as the vinyl gets hot. This will allow the highs and lows conform to the padding underneath and give your job the look you were hoping for in the first place. If you get carried away with the heat, however, you will get smoke and unsightly blisters. This will definitely not be what you spent all your time and money for. Take my word for it—don't learn by your experience. Learn by someone else's.

Assemble Seat

When both the seat and back are done, cut little X's where the bolts will go through the cover. The vinyl should be in its final position before you do this, so double-check before cutting.

Early cars used a clear plastic protector under the bracket to prevent chafing the vinyl. These can be duplicated from many kinds of transparent upholstery plastic or inexpensive acetate. Trace the old one with grease pencil and cut it out with an X-acto knife or sharp scissors. Slip it in between the adjuster and upholstery.

Seat brackets, or *devices* to Datsun, should be loosely screwed to the seat cushion. Then position the back, start its bolts, and with everything aligned satisfactorily, tighten. Replace the knobs and caps on the early style, the plastic covers on the later ones. Add seat-belt-minder hooks and interlock devices if you choose.

The later-style seat brackets are similar, though they have a different appearance. Restoration procedures are the same.

1970—74 Taillights

With the parts cleaned and polished, reattach the plated-plastic trim to the lens. Use a bead of weatherstrip adhesive as well as the original push nuts and washers.

Reflector—Run a bead of adhesive around the mating channel. There are little squares of plastic foam in the drain holes—keep these free of cement so condensation can escape. Fit the lens to the correct reflector. Let

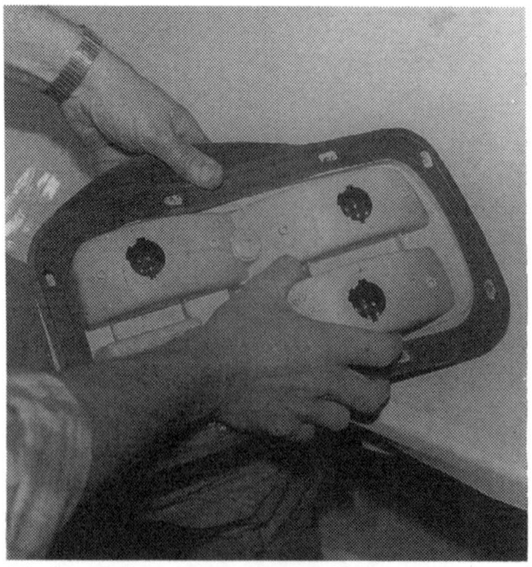

Early-style stop-and-turn light gets new gasket. Apply silicone sealer between ribs on rear face.

Attaching light from inside deck. Early light uses Phillips-head screws; late style uses nuts on studs to retain light/finisher assemblies. Note sealer on vapor hoses at lower left.

Interior Restoration & Assembly

Install vapor canister and connect lines. Secure canister to body structure. Plastic version is shown. Seal vapor hose to deck floor with dumdum or heavy bead of sealant.

Dog-leg panels behind doors just bump on, but check alignment of clips to holes first. Don't break hardboard.

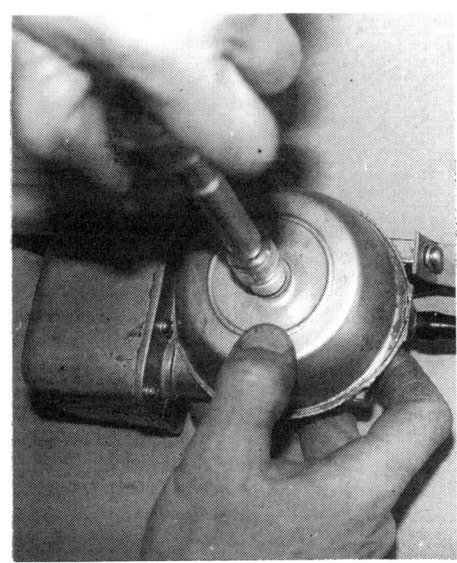

Remove radio-antenna-reel cover. Set each piece aside in order. Unit looks deceptively sound, but it was full of crud because of plugged drain hose.

the adhesive tack and squeeze them together to get a good bond. Set aside and repeat with the other unit.

Weatherstrip—Fit the neoprene to the taillight circumference. This must fit over the flange to make a seal, but doesn't need to be cemented. Taillight weatherstrips are marked **L** and **R**.

Installation—Put a good bead of sealant—silicone works well—on the face of the weatherstrip. Datsun even provides little dams to ensure correct positioning. Line up and press the unit into its place on the back panel. Have the eight Phillips-head screws handy, then secure each light by screwing these into the captive acorn nuts in the reflector. Repeat with the other side.

Sockets & Bulbs—Check all bulbs for burned-out filaments and replace. Top bulbs are dual-filament turn-and-stop bulbs; backup-light bulbs (clear lens) are single filament. Install these in the reflector holes. Don't forget the rubber plug for the unused smaller hole.

1974-1/2—78 Taillights—These appear similar to the early style, but are different in appearance and mounting. The lens and reflectors may be restored similarly to the earlier units. There is no exterior trim to worry about, and the reflector and lens need not be cemented together because studs and nuts are used. A small bead of silicone will suffice to seal out moisture. A foam gasket instead of a weatherstrip is used to seal taillights to the rear panel.

Installation—The later-style lights support the gray plastic rear finisher, so they should be mounted to them with Phillips-head screws. You may want to seal the side of the gasket to the back panel with silicone. Install the unit with locknuts on the long studs. Don't forget the plastic spacers on studs that originally had them. No washers are needed.

Sockets & Bulbs—Install essentially the same as described for early Z-cars. Fasten the connector to the reflector.

Antenna-Mast Repair

Nissan can supply a new antenna mast and plastic extender coil. Despite the fact the antenna could be retracted, many owners forgot to do so and had their masts broken by vandals. Also, the extender-coil material didn't have an unlimited life. Z owners needed a less-expensive alternative to replacing the complete antenna assembly, especially if it was otherwise serviceable.

The kit is still cost-effective if the motor and retractor are not too worn. Another problem was the little drain tube would plug. This eventually causes the retractor to rust and seize. If your antenna mast isn't performing—even if the mast is unbroken—consider installing a new unit if yours is the original part. Performance-wise the more costly alternative is probably the most cost-effective remedy.

Disassembly—Remove reel cover and pay attention to the removal sequence of all mast parts. The extender-tube spool has another cover held on with three screws—remove this. The cover has a hole that appears to be a drain. Mark the position so you can install it in the same position.

Clean all parts thoroughly, watching for evidence of water damage. Clear out drain passages and plastic tube. Run a wire through the drains or clean with a pipecleaner and compressed air. Inspect the worm and gear for adequate lubrication if you removed the spool reel. A few drops of machine oil will ease the load on the motor and prevent rust. There is an adjustment for the little worm gear at the bottom end. This has no moisture-drain passage, and any moisture makes it corrode tight. Remove the set-screw on the side and back out the adjuster to clean it.

Keep all removed pieces in sequence—clean and lube them before reassembly. Put only a light lubricant on the overrunning clutch behind the reel. Remove the antenna-mast tube by taking out the two screws. Discard the old mast and extender tube or

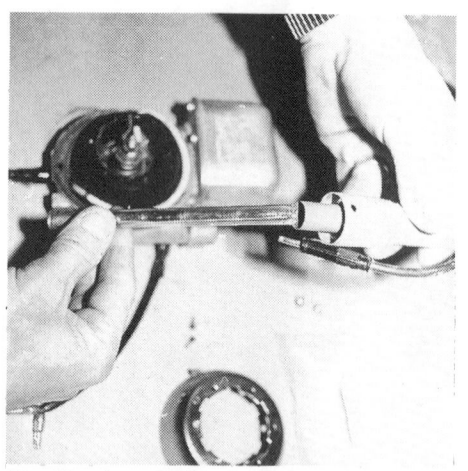

Mast broken off by vandal was beyond salvaging. Mast tube is held on with Phillips-head screws.

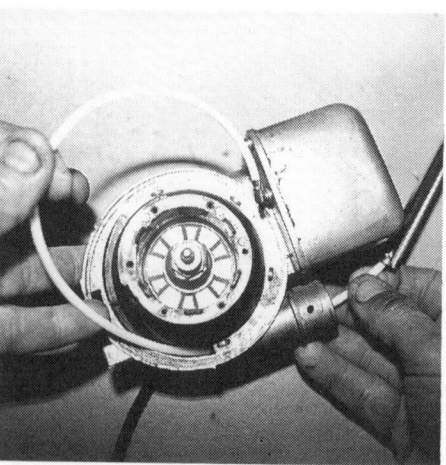

With gears cleaned and lubricated, I replaced spool cover, spring and nut. This is retained by ears crimped to flats. Now replacement mast extender tube is fed into reel. It is held with a cotter pin. After securing tube, coil must be wound around spool. Spool cover goes back on.

what is left of it.

Replace this with new mast from kit and install it. Extend mast fully to make the extender more manageable. Push metal tip of the coil tube through hole in spool.

Pin tip of the coil on the inside of the spool with a little cotter key. One is not supplied in kit. Put a skim of light lubricant—white grease is good—on the spool.

Wrap slack extender around the spool and replace cover. Attempt to get drain hole back into the 6-o'clock (bottom) position when it is fully retracted.

Newer models have a plastic extender guide that helps direct coil back into the reel. Replace it under the inlet passage and secure with Phillips-head screw. This can be added to an older unit.

Replace washers and reel cover. Reattach drain tube.

Note: The antenna won't retract manually. If your car's circuits are hot, connect unit before installation and use the switch to retract it. Or power from a 12V battery charger set to TRICKLE will usually work. Failing that, the unit *can* be put in while extended.

Install Antenna—With the inner mounting ball in place, route mast through the fender hole. Z antennas have a bracket that fastens to the bottom of the unit. The lower end fits onto a stud just under the edge of the deck lip. They used a wing nut, for what reason I don't know. Attach these parts and tighten.

Route drain tube through grommet behind the wheelhouse. Put sealer

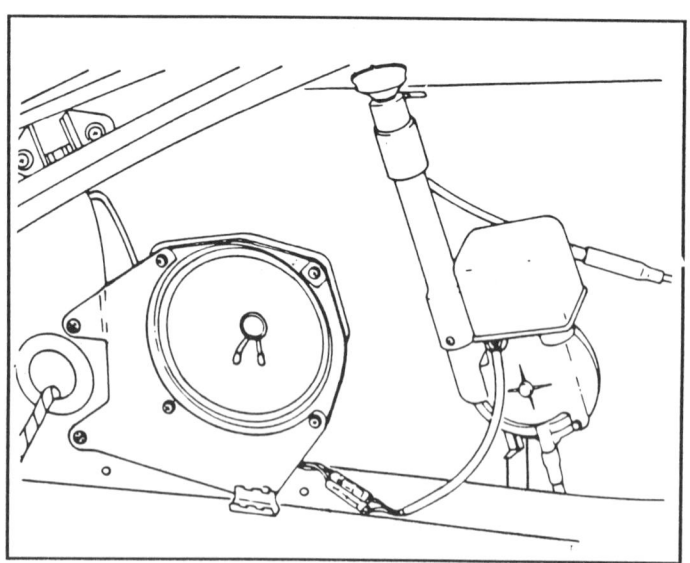

Speaker on early cars was mounted to rear of antenna. On late models they are mounted above strut towers. Courtesy Nissan.

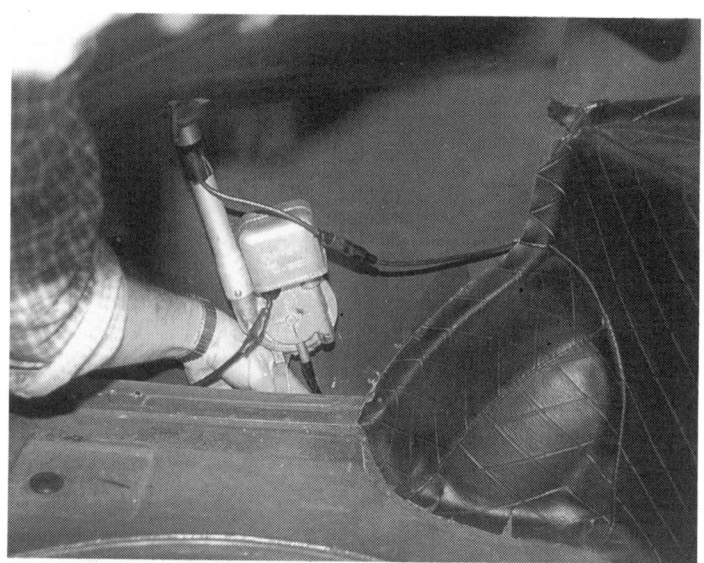

Install power-antenna unit. Feed mast through hole in quarter panel and attach bracket to stud below deck edge. Antenna lead and power harness are already connected.

Interior Restoration & Assembly 155

around these, even if new.

Attach the antenna-motor connectors and the antenna lead.

Outside Hardware—Orient the inner mounting-ball half so that outer half matches the contour and slope of the quarter panel. Put a bead of silicone sealer around the hole. Drop the rubber gasket, outer ball half, trim washer and nut down over the antenna mast. Align the ball and washer and tighten the nut carefully. Test the motor unit before replacing the inner finishers.

Vapor Canister—Attach all vapor hoses to the appropriate fittings, clamping them securely. Early Zs have a plastic reservoir; later models have a metal one. The number and size of the hose nipples are specific to each model which doesn't encourage interchange. Find the mounting holes on the inner body structure and remount the canister. Also mount the protector on cars so equipped.

Interior Panels

As with the door trim panels, the dogleg trims behind the doors are vinyl over hardboard. They are held in place with metal clips. Position clips to mate with the holes in the inner body panel and snap on by pushing or bumping with your fist.

Molded-Plastic Panels—To replace the remainder of the panels, an adequate supply of serviceable plastic rivets is a must. These are inexpensive and available in the original colors.

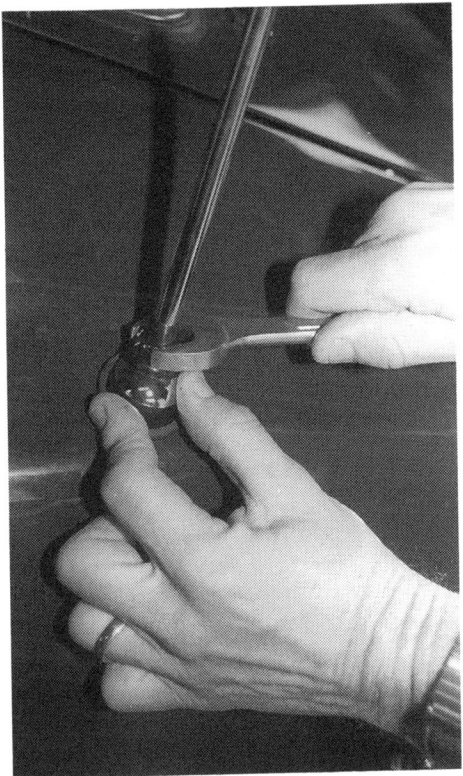

Antenna nut, washers and ball are reinstalled.

Hardware required to mount the radio antenna on the quarter panel. It holds antenna at the correct angle, seals its base and tightly secures it.

The originals can be reused if enough rivet heads and expander stems were saved after removal. Every Z-car in existence probably has a supply rattling around in inaccessible crevices—and plastic can't be retrieved with a magnet!

Assuming the speakers have been installed, begin with the rear quarter-trim panels. These are fragile and prone to crack when below 70F or so. The 280Z's plastic trim was much heavier than early trim and many will interchange with a little work, but there are a number of detail variations.

To install, carefully bend and fit the rearmost panel into position. Replace the plastic rivets. Push them through

Plastic rivets, caulked right and uncaulked left.

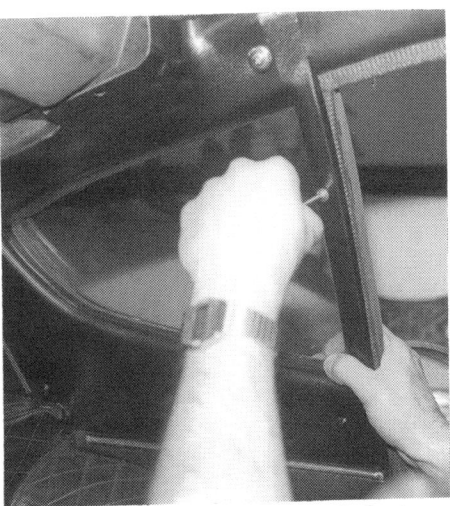

Rearmost panel and quarter-window trim is in place. Coat hook or knob helps secure trim at top; trim washer and screw hold it to B-pillar.

Rear roof header trim is next. Dome light helps secure plastic finisher.

156 How to Restore Your Datsun Z-Car

Rear trim panel is last. Spare tire is mounted in place.

Jute pads on rear floor are in place. I'm installing stowage boxes in my early 240Z.

the panel and hole in the body metal. Don't bump the stems in flush until alignment is good. Remember some go in after the next panel is on and overlap the previous edge.

Next to install are the quarter-window trim panels. These have a coat hook at top center and one screw and trim washer on the B-pillar. Early Zs use a chrome knob held by a screw, later models a plastic hook.

The roof-rail trim follows. It overlaps the quarter-window trim where they meet.

Dome Light—This has three leads, each with its own terminal. Check the bulb and push the unit into the hole. It helps to hold the trim snugly.

Carpets and cargo straps on deck: To make like new, straps and seat belts can be washed, then dyed with vinyl dye.

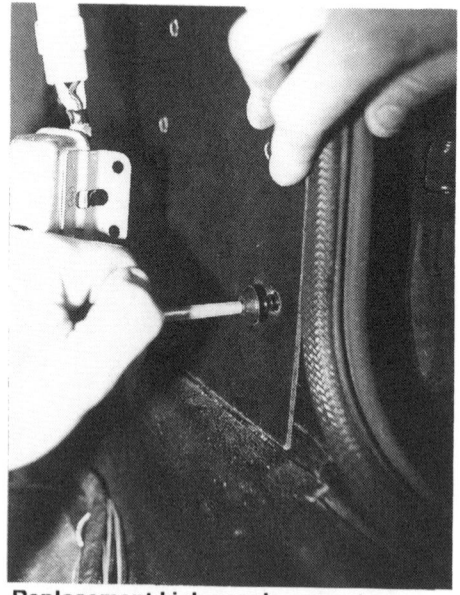

Replacement kick panels are not specific to any year/model Z-car, so chances are they won't look exactly like what came on your car. Regardless of the year, plastic rivets hold them in place. With the rivet in its hole, push in center pin so it's flush with the head to lock it in place.

Rear Interior Finisher—This often requires a bit of wrestling to get in place. Only early 240Zs don't have the screw-down panels that allow access to the light sockets, consequently requiring removal of the trim to change a bulb.

Rear-Window Defroster—Reattach the two leads to the metal connectors.

Spare-Tire-Well Lid—Most Zs came with the round hardboard lid. It was supposedly held down by postage-stamp-size bits of Velcro. Late models have a hinged lid. Install this now.

Jack- & Tool-Stowage Boxes—Replace the liners and lids in the deck.

Deck-Lip Molding—This straddles the rim of the deck and is held to it with chrome Phillips-head screws. On very early 240Zs, the deck carpet was retained at the front by this molding. All later cars had removable carpeting.

Early 240Z Jack-Stowage Lid—Again a unique part. The underseat carpet and pad installs first, then the plastic cover screws down. This also holds the chocks.

Tool-Stowage Lid—Similar to jack stowage, but this lid hinges on the inside. Both are retained by screw-down knobs.

Deck-Cargo Straps—Zs had straps running both with and across the deck. The anchors are secured by Phillips-head screws. Early 240Zs mount through the carpet at the forward end.

Strut-Tower Caps—These should be snapped into the shock-nut hole.

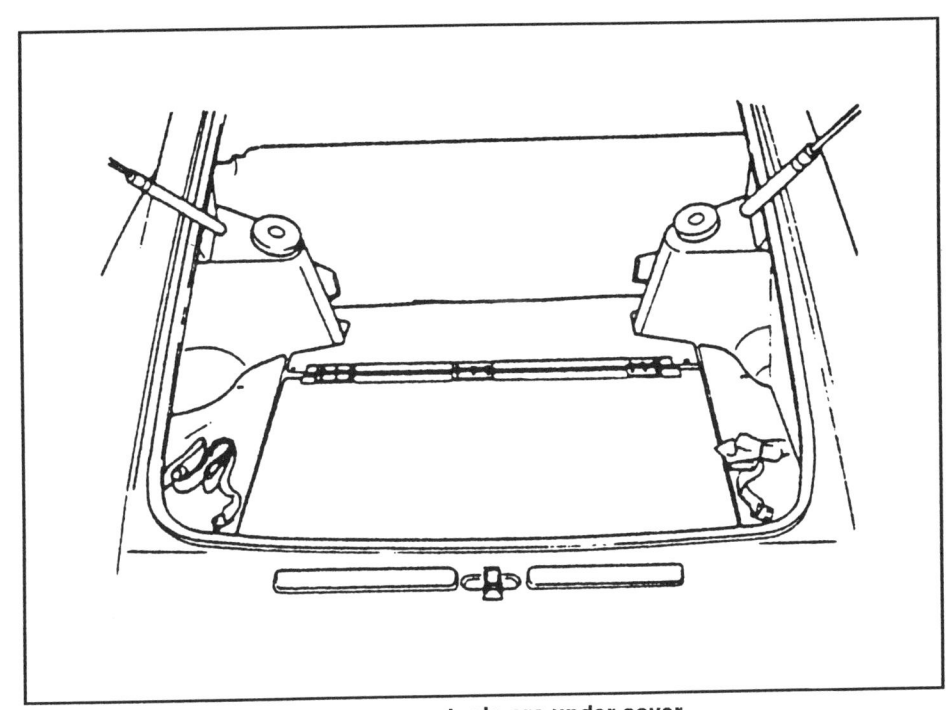

Late rear decking: Space-saver spare, tools are under cover.

Shoulder-Belt Retractors—On 280Zs these mount on the strut tower. Install them and their covers. On some 260 and early 280Zs, the retractors mount back on the roof rails as do early non-retractor shoulder-harness anchors.

Seat Belts—Retractor-type lap-belt mechanisms attach to the door sills below the quarter trims, approximately where the previous non-retractor belt bolts. The inboard belts bolt to the transmission tunnel. If you have an interlock-equipped Z, reconnect the wiring now even if you disabled the interlock itself. The warning is a safety factor.

Kick Panels—These are retained to the side-cowl panels, primarily with plastic bayonet-type fasteners. Before remounting, be sure the doors are aligned to your satisfaction and the hinge bolts are tight. Install these and

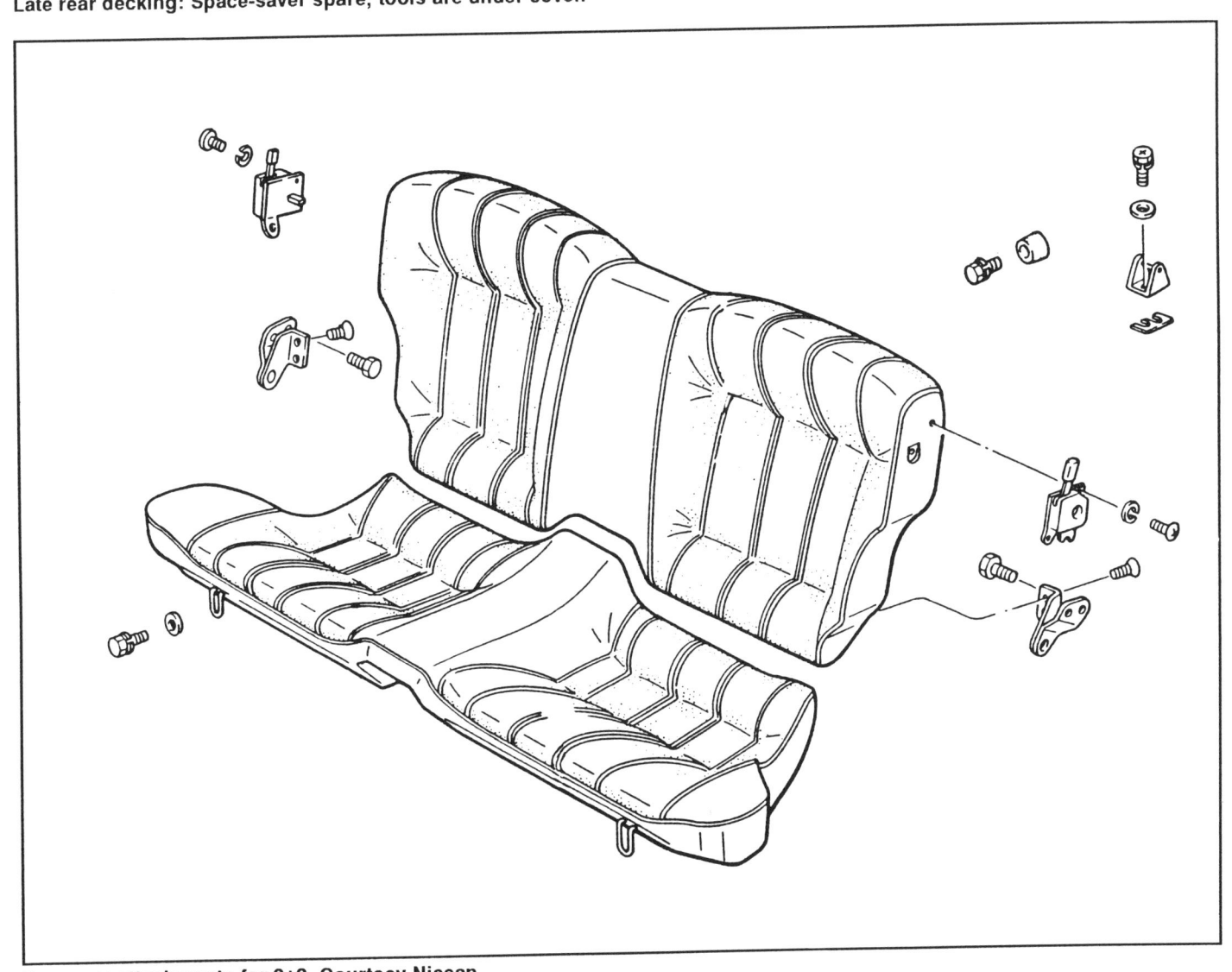

Rear-seat attachments for 2+2. Courtesy Nissan.

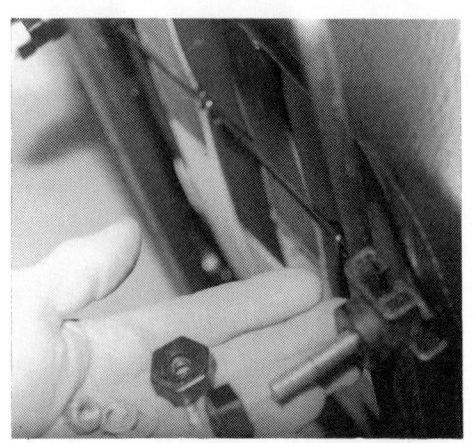

Seat spacers can be stacked to achieve desirable height and rake relative to seat-bottom cushion.

attach the various electrical components that mount to them. Route and clip down any loose wiring in the area.

Hood-Latch Handle—Remount the latch-cable bracket. Orient the graphic so it is logical. It's a shame Datsun didn't use a silhouette that looked like a Z rather than a PL510! Be sure the cable and shaft will seat fully so the latch seats fully.

Vent Controls—Reattach knobs and remount brackets under the instrument panel.

Carpets—Replace carpet padding and carpets. Early Zs had snaps at the front of the footwell and Velcro at the rear. Snaps usually pulled out of the firewall insulator, tearing it. Trash and dirt clogged the Velcro, causing it to lose its grip. The carpet could then bunch up forward, possibly hanging up the accelerator. A better, although not an original, solution is to install the old-fashioned "Dot" convertible-top snap-on fasteners.

Seats—Reinstall the seats now—rear cushions first on 2+2's.

Be sure to stack the plastic spacers for maximum comfort. Carefully—don't gouge anything—install the seats on their mounts and tighten the nuts.

STANDARD DATSUN BOLT-TORQUE SPECIFICATIONS

Bolt Diameter (mm)	ISO Grade*	Pitch	ft-lb	kg-m	N-m
6	4	1.0	2.2-2.9	0.3-0.4	3-4
8	4	1.0-1.25	5.8-8.0	0.8-1.1	8-11
10	4	1.25-1.5	12-16	1.6-2.2	16-22
12	4	1.25	22-30	3.1-4.1	30-40
12	4	1.75	20-27	2.7-3.7	26-36
14	4	1.5	34-46	4.7-6.3	46-62
6	7	1.0	4.3-5.1	0.6-0.7	6-7
8	7	1.0-1.25	10-13	1.4-1.8	14-18
10	7	1.25-1.5	19-27	2.6-3.7	25-36
12	7	1.25	37-50	5.1-6.9	50-68
12	7	1.75	33-45	4.6-6.2	45-61
14	7	1.5	56-76	7.7-10.5	76-103
6	9	1.0	5.8-8.0	0.8-1.1	8-11
8	9	1.0-1.25	14-19	1.9-2.6	19-26
10	9	1.25-1.5	27-38	3.7-5.2	36-51
12	9	1.25	53-72	7.3-9.9	72-97
12	9	1.75	48-65	6.6-9.0	65-88
14	9	1.5	80-108	11.1-15.0	109-147

*Bolt grade embossed on bolt head

10 Body Exterior & Drive Line Assembly

You've now reached the final stage of your restoration; bolting on the exterior parts, engine, transmission and underhood components. Let's start with the doors.

Door Restoration

Disassemble door glass from metal backing by removing the screws, washers and insulators. Thoroughly clean the glass. Use new single-edge razor blades to scrape off mineral deposits and crud, but be careful not to scratch the glass. Double-ought (00) grade steel wool works more slowly, but is safer. Don't use Scotchbrite pads because they will scratch the glass. Use lacquer thinner or acetone to remove all contamination. Follow up with a glass cleaner such as Glass Wax or Windex. You'll never have a better opportunity to get the glass totally clean.

Also clean the backing and mounting parts, including the rubber backing molding. Dry everything and lay the parts out on a clean work surface.

Assemble the backing molding and rubber insulating washers to the backing. Place the door glass in position and screw down the plastic and metal washers with the machine screws. Later Zs also had lock washers—a better idea!

To rehabilitate the frame, remove the old window *runs* (glass-channel weatherstrips)—undoubtedly bald—from the stainless-steel frame. I use an old screwdriver sharpened to loosen cement from the metal that holds the furry insulating runs. Then pull and hope they come out fairly intact so there won't be too much tedious scraping. Don't leave any chunks of runs or any big deposits of cement.

Factory-fresh 280Z is fitted with final Z-car hubcap design—plastic/aluminum composite with chrome acorn lug nuts. Courtesy Nissan.

Check the frames for general condition. Replace any that have cracks or bad distortions. Now is the time to clean and polish the frames.

Glass-Run Channels—Lay out new weatherstrips in their positions. Let them relax for a day or so. Put a bead of weatherstrip adhesive in the bottom of window-frame "U." The channel material has probably taken a set in the curved positions in which it was stored. Start with short rear upper section. You'll be able to spot this because of the notch for the upper corner. Insert this into the frame and seat it firmly into the cement. Push it rearward and up relative to how it fits on the car. Work fast because the cement is drying. Continue with the long run, following down the frame to the bracket.

Cement the short felt-like channel into the frame below, butting it against previously installed short run.

Tip: The best way to get the strips into the frame is to collapse one leg of the channel flat against the opposite side and push that side in first. Then, letting the run expand, push the other leg into place. Using both hands, follow the channel to the end, one hand inserting, the other snugging it in. The

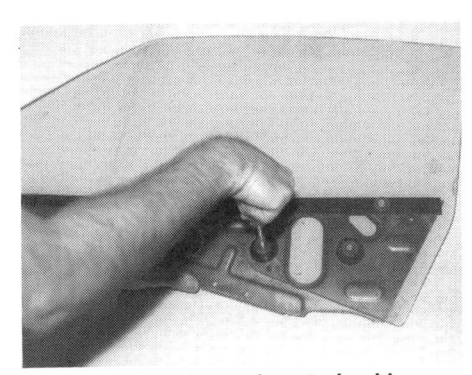

Reassembling door glass to backing: Rubber molding and washers are in place. Add lock washers to screws if your assembly didn't have them.

159

160 How to Restore Your Datsun Z-Car

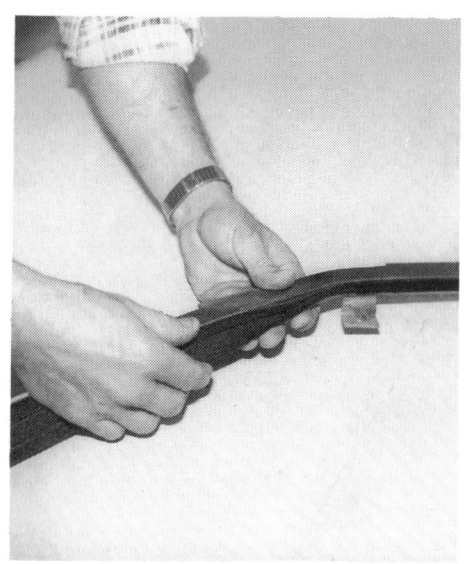

Channel is pinched together, then pushed into cement in window frame. Paint stirrer or other blunt tool can be used to smooth channel into place.

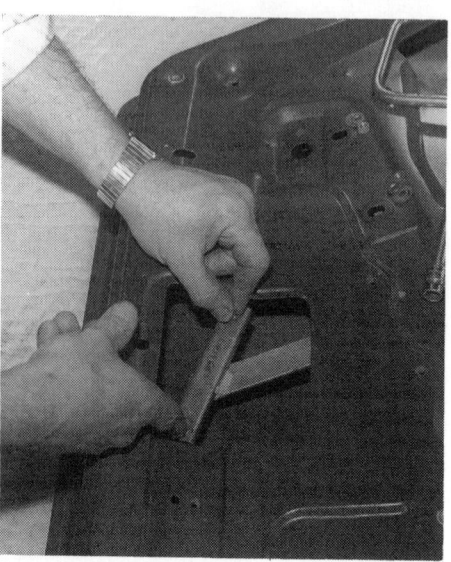

Install window regulator after liberally lubricating it and other related parts with white grease. Guide channel slips onto regulator arm. Note clean furniture pad door is laying on.

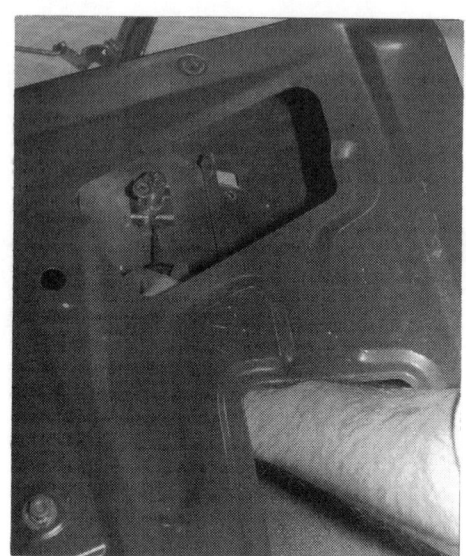

Lock cylinder and handle go back on before window and frame are installed.

edges wind up roughly flush with the frame. Try to scoot it back up from the ends toward the corner to ensure the notch closes up tightly. Use a blunt tool, something that won't damage the furry material, to force the runs into complete contact with the adhesive. Trim off any excess. Slide the window into place and set the assembly aside to cure.

Door Reassembly

While the window-frame channels are curing, place a door outer side down on a soft clean surface like a clean moving pad or old bed spread. Some of the following steps are more easily accomplished with the door laying down, others with it in its normal orientation leaning upright. Proceed carefully and don't damage the finish now!

Outside Mirror—For the driver's side only, fasteners for these mirrors install from the inside. Consequently, they are easier to attach before the window is in place.

Position the mirror and gasket over the holes and insert the bolts from inside the door. Check alignment using the door edge as a guide and tighten.

Window Regulator—Before reinstalling the regulator mechanism, put the handle on and crank it through its full range. Watch your fingers. It can pinch if run off the end of the sector!

Using medium-weight grease, lubricate the sector teats and the pivot and rollers. Make sure grease gets where it will do some good, then wipe off any excess. Slip regulator into the door and push the shaft through its hole. Install and tighten the screws.

Window-Guide Channel—This short roller guide fastens to the two holes toward the lower rear of the door. The early style has two studs on the back, later is retained with screws. Slip lower end of the regulator pivoted arm into the channel and install, but don't tighten it completely.

Lock Assembly—Check and clean lock assembly thoroughly before reinstalling it. Generally the passenger's door components will be in decent condition in comparison to the driver's side. If you had any problems with the door latching solidly or if there is visual evidence of damage on the contact parts of the latch, get a new latch.

Some poor latch performance may be due to latch and striker misalignment, but if left uncorrected, these parts will be damaged beyond serviceability. A new part is the best insurance. Dismantling a Z-car latch is not practical, so buying a new one is the easiest way to get new zinc plating!

Assemble the entire mechanism, including the bellcrank(s) and linkage rods. You will install the outside handle from the outside, so leave it separate. Lubricate the latch assembly with machine oil and work the mechanism to make sure it operates freely before installing. Pay special attention to the plastic snap-on bushings. If one of these is broken or worn out, you'll end up with a loose or sloppy linkage rod flopping around inside the door. Late Z-cars have these bushings built like a clevis for added security. This is a good modification for the early latch mechanism if you can get the replacement parts.

Lock Cylinder—Lock cylinders install from the outside of each door. If you are going to polish the stainless bezels, do them off the car. Again, check and lubricate the mechanism. Use your key to verify smooth action. This is one part that can be interchanged side-to-side. If the driver's side cylinder is showing its age, swap it with the opposite cylinder. You may have to file the hole slots to get the cylinders to fit. Slip cylinder in flush and secure it with the spring clip.

Door Handle—Slip door-handle lever and mounting studs through the rectangular hole. Be careful not to nick the paint. Early Zs are retained with nuts and no plate to back them up. Later cars have a backing plate for

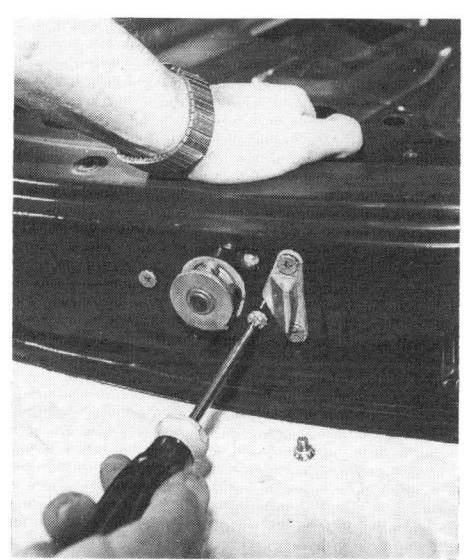

Dovetail guide and latch are installed next. Later-style door latch reversed striker and latch positions.

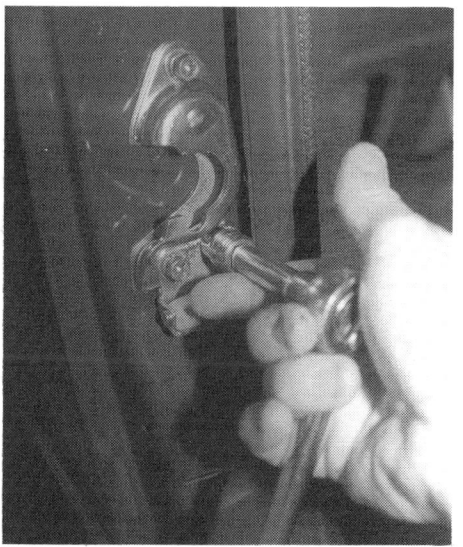

Early-style door striker is bolted on loosely. As you can see, new plating is worth its cost on often-seen parts such as this.

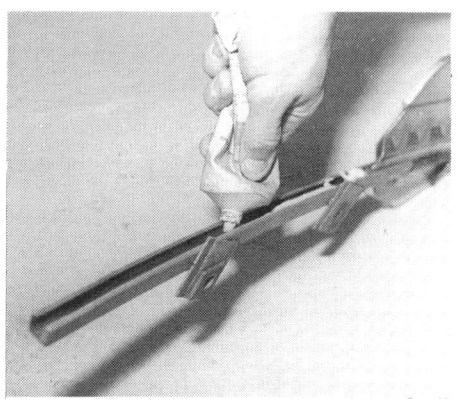

Front window sash gets plenty of lubricant where guide shoe will ride. This part can be loosely bolted to door first and window fitted to it. Or, it can be inserted with the window.

reinforcement. The rubber protectors on the hinges of the handle are not available as replacements. You can substitute used protectors from other handles, but they must be slit and reattached with contact cement. A stopgap at best.

Install Latch Assembly—Insert the latch and its attendant linkages through one of the holes in the inner door panel. Sort out the linkage rods as you go. The principal ones to hook up should be the rod to the lock-cylinder arm and pushrod from the door handle. Position the latch and install with three screws. There is an adjustment provision on the outside-handle pushrod. Run the nylon nut down if the latch fails to trip when the handle is fully up; run it up if there is insufficient free play in the handle itself. Some Zs have an additional metal nut below the door-latch lever.

Bellcranks—One on the inside door-handle connecting rod attaches to the lower rear corner on all Zs. Late 280Zs also have one on the door-lock-knob rod (Say that fast three times!). These should be installed so the bellcrank is right side up and there is no binding in its action. Rotate them after installation to make sure the bushings are concentric and work freely. 2+2 models have a somewhat different door, incorporating a rear inside lock lever with the lock bellcrank.

Tip: Zs are prone to noises developing from all those linkage rods vibrating around inside the doors. I've found that sliding a length of rubber vacuum hose over the offenders—especially the lock rod on models without the second bellcrank—greatly quiets the racket. Secure it at the center of the rod with electrician's tape or weatherstrip adhesive.

Inside Door-Latch Handle—The spring and washer on the linkage rod must be positioned behind the bracket flange. In other words, it isn't installed correctly unless it puts tension on the rod eye to hold the handle in the shut position.

To install, pull the washer back. Tip the bracket and slip the eye into the slot in the flange. Push the eye forward and work the hook of the lever into it. Let the lever shut as you restore the bracket to its normal orientation. Then attach to the door frame, but don't tighten.

Dovetail—Install this below the latch on cars so equipped.

Door Striker—This installs on the door jamb. There are two types, one like that in the photos. It's for 240 through early 280Zs and a post-type for late 280Zs. See illustrations, page 165. Both have an important adjustment function, so don't tighten yet.

Work the inside and outside door handles as well as the lock rod to be sure they function smoothly *before* you assemble the rest of the door.

Binding, catching or sticky movement is a sign of incorrect installation. Sloppiness may be due to a worn-out latch or linkage—especially on the driver's door—so don't be shy about replacing it. Even though it may not be dangerous, a faulty door latch can be a major frustration.

Window Frame—Datsun calls this the *sash*. Early, late and 2+2 models have somewhat different frames and attachments, but installation is basically similar.

Drop the frame into the door. Be careful not to damage the finish. Start all retaining bolts, but don't tighten.

Window Assembly—Before you install this, make sure guides are lubricated with some medium grease. Sta-Lube has a white grease that is just about ideal—it spreads easily and stays put.

Lay the door on a soft, non-abrasive, soft surface—moving pad or blanket—and at a comfortable work level. Keep unneeded tools and fasteners—anything that might damage the finish—off the work surface.

Early Z: Tilt the window down at the front and insert it through its slot. With a bit of juggling it will fit. I find that it even fits with the front sash installed—channel in which the front guide shoe of the window glass backing rides.

Crank window regulator to the midpoint of its travel. Work the window

With window frame loosely installed, I put door down on the floor—pad is underneath to protect new paint—then slip window and sash into place.

Now run glass up into frame and tighten fasteners. If after the door has been mounted and aligned but doesn't jibe with the door jamb, the frame and window positions can be shifted accordingly.

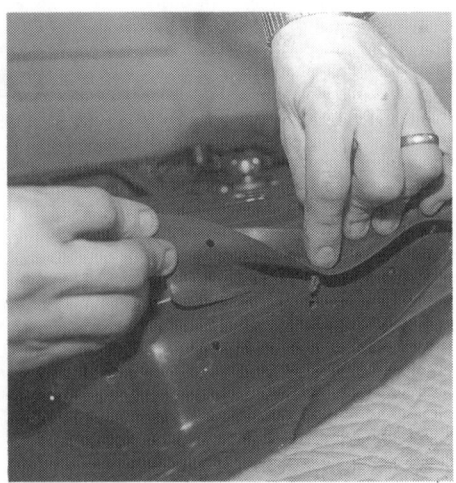

Front sealing rubber should be positioned by center rivet, then weatherstrip adhesive applied. Other rivet can be replaced as it cures—then top tabs cemented in turn.

assembly down and toward the forward end of the door. Now align channel on the window backing with the rollers off the regulator. These fit on in turn and take some maneuvering of regulator arms and window. Finally, get the lower roller onto the guide channel. Patience is a virtue here!

Now, position the front sash and start the two screws that hold it in place. Make sure the guide shoe is in place. Adjustments fore and aft can be made with the front sash screws.

Carefully establish the front and rear edges of the glass in the window-frame channels and roll the regulator up. Observe both sides and don't let the glass hit the edges of the channel and break the adhesive bond. The first fit is important to avoid problems with the expensive channel. Snug the screws on the front sash, guide channel and window frame, but not to their final tightness—just so these parts aren't wobbling around.

Roll the window to its full-down position and observe its travel. If it doesn't have both a smooth start and windup, play with the adjustment of the front sash until it has a "ball-park" fit. Roll the window to its full-up position and observe how it meets the top channel of the frame. The principal adjustment for this interface is in the guide channel. If the glass seems to be cocked to the front, move the studs down in their holes; if to the rear, move them up. It helps to stand the door up in its normal position at this point. Have a helper hold it up or lean it against something solid with a moving pad or old bedspread in between to protect the door's finish.

If the glass is topped out front and rear and doesn't seat in the top channel, it may be too far forward. Loosen the front sash and adjust it rearward. If the gap is too great to compensate for this way, check rollers and channels again. Something may have jumped out of engagement.

Further frame work is incidental to its adjustment to the door jamb in the windshield/roof/B-pillar. We'll get to this after the door is installed. Snug but don't tighten all window-frame screws.

Late 280Z: Notice differences in 280Z window-frame structure and how the window-glass guides function. Otherwise, procedures and window operation are fundamentally similar. Where earlier models have the short front-sash channel and the frame channels extending to the bottom of the window run, later 280Zs utilize two long parallel guide rails that mate with rollers on the window assembly to control the glass better. Correspondingly the window frame is abbreviated at the rear and mounts differently. It should be removed—much easier to accomplish on this model—before installing or removing the window assembly.

Guide Rails—Install these by pushing their studs through holes in the door inner and loosely installing their nuts. Fore-and-aft adjustment is made with these six mountings as well as alignment with the frame channel. Line up the rollers with the guide channels and insert the window assembly. Roll the regulator to the bottom of its travel and install the guide channel that attaches to the glass backing plate.

Window Frame—Late 280Zs have a rubber molding that fits into a groove in the top of the window frame. If the old one is cracked or simply "dead" and no longer serviceable, strip it out. Clean the groove completely and run a small bead of weatherstrip adhesive along the bottom. Make sure you have the correct side! Push one edge of the new rubber under its retaining lip for a foot or so, then repeat with the other edge. Pull on the molding to keep it from bunching up and continue until the entire length is adhered. Trim off any excess.

Remount the frame/channel assembly and adjust the fit via the guide channels. Snug the fasteners, but don't tighten them until after the door is mounted. Adjustment of the window assembly to the frame is similar to that already detailed.

Front Sealing Rubber—This is held on by weatherstrip adhesive and black-plastic rivets. New rivets are available . . . and they look much nicer. If yours is an early Z, note that

Body Exterior & Drive Line Assembly

1. Door-window-channel weatherstrip
2. Door weatherstrip
3. Quarter-window weatherstrip
5. Windshield weatherstrip
6. Door upper molding/chrome strip
7. Under door seal
8. Front door seal
9. Cowl-to-hood weatherstrip
10. Radiator support-to-hood weatherstrip
11. Hood bumper, side-rail
12. Hood-height-adjuster

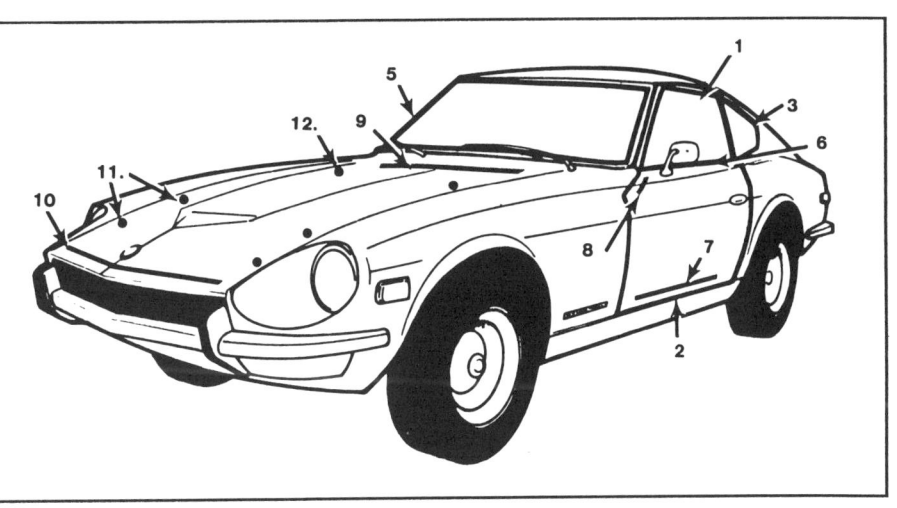

Door, window and hood sealing weatherstrips. Motorsport Auto.

the replacement rubbers are superior to the originals.

Install rubber with the center rivet to position it on the door. Apply a generous bead of black weatherstrip adhesive to the lower half of the rubber and press it down once you have it correctly aligned. Lift rubber and let adhesive tack. Then put in the lower rivets as you line up each hole. A bit of tension may be necessary on the end of the piece. Repeat with the upper section.

Note that the rubber is molded to conform to the contours of the door/window-frame transition. A small tab at the inside top should roll around the frame and into the channel. Apply adhesive sparingly in this area, but let it tack so rubber adheres well. Remove excess adhesive with naptha or thinner after it has cured.

Use solvent sparingly. If it gets into uncured adhesive, the solvent will prevent a good bond.

The rectangular tab at the outside face is not cemented now. It will go on the forward face of the stainless-steel trim.

Rear Sealing Rubber—This little seal is cemented on as well. It has one specific place it fits and no other. Note that the small outer tab wraps around and secures *under* the edge of the stainless trim, unlike the front. Make a trial fit of the rubber and note the adhesive must be applied to different sides of the part, where it interfaces with different parts of the door and frame. Take your time and get a neat, secure bond.

Window-Stabilizing Roller—Slip this over the upper door lip so it fits into its slot. This is easier than recombining it with the trim molding.

Stainless-Steel Outer Molding—This trim has a rubber sealing lip stapled to it. If the sealing lip requires replacing, either purchase a new molding or search for a substitute lip and bond or rivet it to the part. As of this writing, no replacement rubber lip is available. Install the trim molding starting from the aft end so it can fit over the aforementioned tab. This will hold it securely. Work along the length of the trim, bumping it down

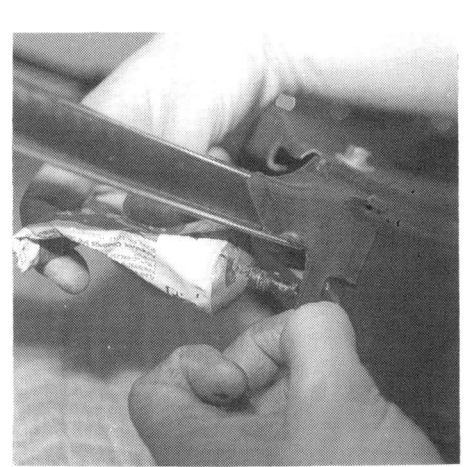

Rear sealing rubber must be cemented in steps. Little tab is further secured by window-trim strip.

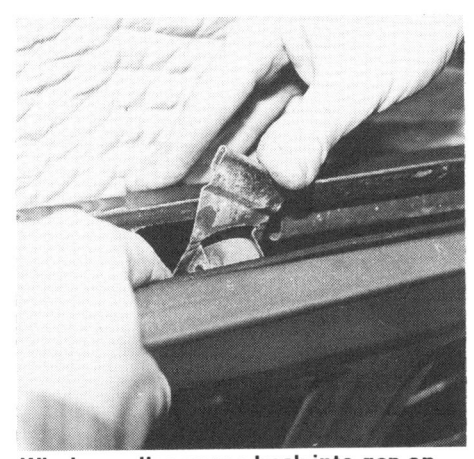

Window roller snaps back into gap on door lip, then stainless trim fits over it.

Drip-channel molding rolls onto channel at A-pillar, then snaps onto channel over door and quarter window. Installation is easy if trim and channel corners match. Caution: Don't use strong-arm tactics or you'll bend trim.

164 How to Restore Your Datsun Z-Car

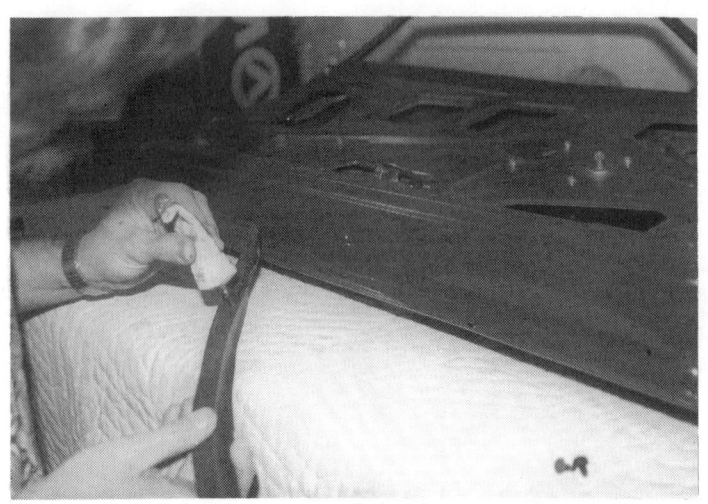

I want a neat job, even on weatherstrip across door bottom. So one rivet goes in, then cement, rivet, cement . . . .

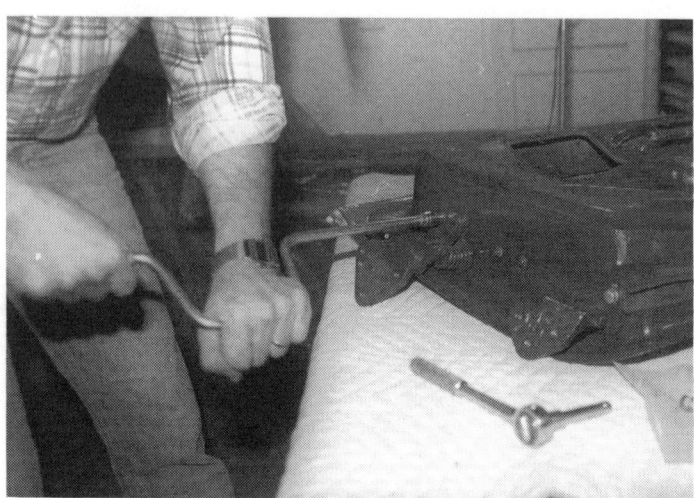

Install door hinges. Although they were in good condition, I painted and lubricated hinges before installing them.

with your fist, being careful not to get ahead of yourself and kink it!

When the outer molding is secured, trim the rectangular tab with scissors so it matches the shape and size of the forward end of the molding. Cement it in place.

Door Sealing

Door-Bottom Weatherstrip—This is riveted and cemented in place just as the door front rubber. Install it using the same process. Again be sure to oriented it correctly for a good seal.

Door Hinges—Install these on the correct door—they are marked **L** and **R** for driver's side and passenger's side, respectively. Screw them down tight as they don't adjust on the door.

Rehang Doors—You will definitely need assistance when doing this operation, especially if you had the doors off the car. It is all too easy to do damage that will waste hours of time and money to rectify.

I describe how to replace the original doors. If you're installing doors from another vehicle, test fit them before painting, page 50.

Bear in mind that new weatherstripping is fatter and fuller than what it's replacing. Also, on an older Z, replacement door seals are improved 280Z versions. This will tend to make the door harder to close and align. It'll be OK once it takes a compressed set in its new environs.

Put the big thimble-shaped door bumper in its hole in the jamb. Mount the striker-plate assembly *almost* tight. If you traced around it and you can see the line, you have a good approximation of the correction location.

Round up the screws that held the hinges to the jamb, place them and your socket wrench on the floorpan. Position the door hinges and, while your helper balances the door assembly, thread a screw into both hinges. Some weight can now be shifted to the body, but until the door is close to

Jerry wondered why I was taking so long. He was lucky this wasn't a late door with the internal side-guard beam. Adjusting door involves shutting, checking gap, changing hinge bolts and repeating process over and over. Jack has 2x4 padded with towel to protect door bottom—this one needed a bit of persuasion.

being correctly aligned, *don't* attempt to shut it.

I use a floor jack to support the door, though this only helps when the door is open and stationary. Protect the paint with several rags on the jack pad!

Turn all six screws until they begin to tighten. Carefully swing door toward the closed position, paying close attention to the gap at the rocker panel. Naturally, gravity will pull the door down, so it will chip the paint if you try to shut it. If your helper is not around, use a clean paint stick or two as a spacer to help establish the margin at the bottom. When you think door adjustment is close, see if the door will latch.

Check the margin and alignment at the rear of the door. Does it hang out beyond the body?; this depends on the position of the striker plate on the jamb. Attack the margin first, as it is adjusted at the hinges. This is done by juggling the position of the hinges and their shims. However, only two bolts—one at top hinge and one at bottom—need be tightened to hold alignment.

Be patient! Don't pry or jimmy the edges, hinges or latch. If the door fit before, you'll eventually get it to fit again. A similar process is used to adjust the striker plate. Once you get one side right, repeat the process at the other side. You now know how to do it, right?

Next point of adjustment is at rear of door—the striker. Loosen bolts and adjust it up or down and in or out so door is positioned correctly and closes smoothly. This may require going back to the hinges to get it right. More than one cycle of loosening, moving, tightening and retrying will be needed unless you're extremely lucky.

Same is true of late-style striker. These only adjust for degree of "shut" on door, not gap. Window frame and glass may need readjusting as weatherstrip compresses.

Put a few drops of light oil on hinge pins and limiter. A daub of Door Ease in the right place on striker plate will facilitate latching, and won't get on your clothes. Make a few test closings and adjust as necessary. Once you're satisfied with door fit and operation, move to the next item.

Moisture Barrier—Datsun put a plastic sheet, much like commercial Visqueen, on the inner door panels. This was to prevent moisture inside the door from permeating the door-trim-panel backing. Make sure you give your trim panels the same protection. Use any durable vinyl sheeting or the original material and cut it to fit.

Use the door trim panel as a pattern to trace around with a Sharpie pen. The moisture barrier should be at least 1/2 inch smaller, so cut the plastic 1/2 inch inside the mark all the way around. Double the sheet and cut both at one time.

Install Barrier—First, make sure you finished with all door adjustments and

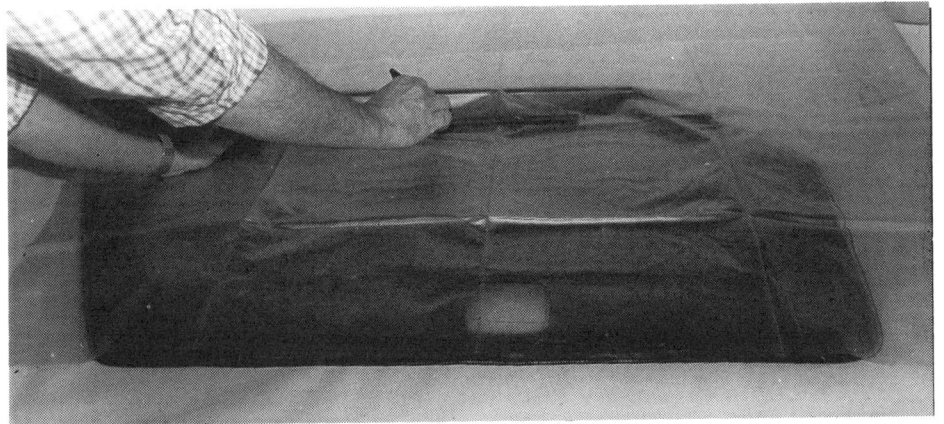

Using door-trim panel as a pattern, trace shape onto moisture-barrier plastic. This is the genuine Datsun article, but other plastics will suffice.

Trim plastic about 1/2 inch smaller than traced outline, then glue it to inner door panel. Tape holds it in place until cement sets up. If late-style plastic clips are used to retain door-trim panel, puncture barrier plastic over holes the clips will go in.

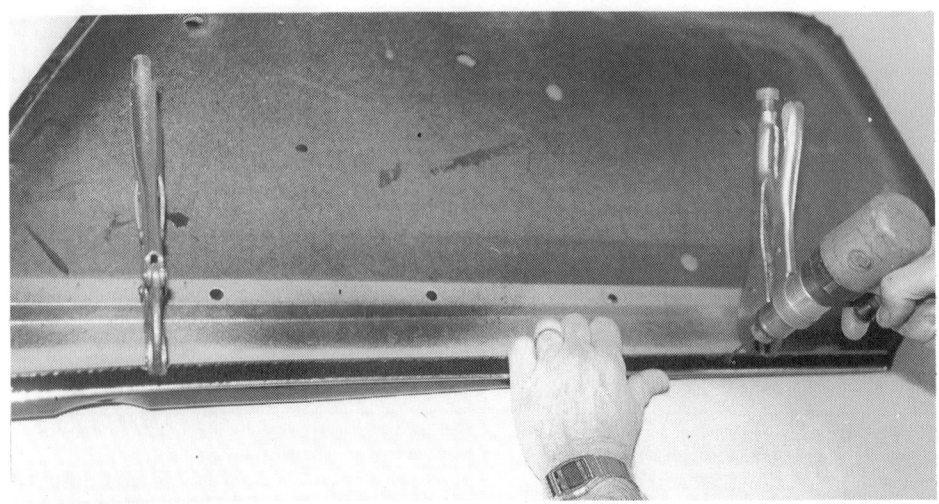

Door-finisher whisker strips are reattached with rivets. With the old strip removed, I positioned new one and clamped it in place with Vise-Grips. Then five or six evenly spaced 1/8-inch holes were drilled. Strip has a front and rear—don't reverse it.

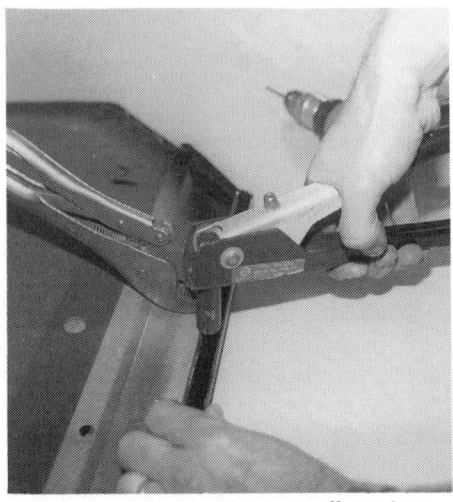

Check rivet heads for protruding stem nails. If you find any, correct the problem. Any metal that projects above whiskers will scratch glass.

all fasteners are tight. Hang the plastic from the upper door with a few strips of masking tape. When you are satisfied with the position and edges, run a bead of adhesive around the perimeter, approximately 1/2 inch inside. Do one section at a time and get a good bond.

Even a new door trim panel won't fit completely down on its clips, so unless you want to see the plastic and adhesive, keep it well back from the edge. Use tabs of masking tape to keep the plastic tight while it sets up. You don't need to put adhesive on the the top section.

Cut holes for the handles now, but no bigger than necessary. An X-cut will do for simple holes, but trim the inside door-handle cutout(s) rectangular. If your car had door-mounted aftermarket speakers that you are reinstalling, they should be moisture-proofed with sheeting so the purpose of the barrier will not be defeated.

Restore & Install Door-Trim Panels

Either replace your door-trim panels with new ones or recover the originals. There is no way to duplicate the original material because it is heat-embossed both in pattern and attachment. It can be repaired, although results vary with method and skill. Dye with commercial vinyl dyes. As long as new panels are available, you'll find them to be a good bargain, especially for maintaining your car's originality.

Door-Trim Whisker Strips—These are the toothbrush-bristle cushions (*Schlegle strips* or *cat's whiskers*) for the glass. Datsun used heavy staples to attach the strip to the lip of the door trim, but this attaching method isn't available to most restorers.

I drilled 1/16-inch holes to match the original staple holes and counterfeited the original look using stainless-steel wire. Doing this is tedious at best.

A serviceable alternative is to rivet the new strip in position. Position the correct strip—left or right side—to the panel and clamp it exactly in place with two Vise-Grip pliers. The bright stainless bead should just break over the top of the vinyl upholstery. Be careful not to bend or kink the trim.

Using a 1/8-inch drill bit, make five or six evenly spaced holes in both the strip and lip. Bias the holes below the centerline of the strip, down where the bristles will hide them.

Starting in the center and working outward toward the ends, use short aluminum rivets to fasten the strip to the trim panel. Important: Inspect the rivet heads for protruding stems. Also be sure the heads are pulled down and flush. Otherwise they may scratch the window glass. A daub of black silicone rubber on each head will complete the camouflaging if need be.

Put the lock-rod-plunger grommet in place if needed. Replace the retaining clips if necessary. No matter where the metal type is attached to their holes, the trim-panel-clip legs must be lined up to mate with the holes in the door panel.

Install Trim Panels—Hook the top lip of the trim over the upper edge of the door-inner panel. Be sure the door-lock rod is in position.

Check the trim for fore/aft alignment. Bring the inside door-latch handle through its rectangular hole. Pull the trim panel down to seat it and match the retaining clips with their holes in the inner panel.

Starting with the uppermost clips, either front or rear, press them into the holes. The less these are manipulated, the better for the hardboard backing and clips. Try to get them in

Door-trim panel hooks over upper door-inner panel. Check alignment of clips *first*, then press on.

Body Exterior & Drive Line Assembly 167

correctly the first time!

Early Zs have a chrome Phillips-head screw and clear-plastic trim washer to secure the lower corner at the rear.

Arm Rests—Another item that you will probably have to replace with new ones because they take a lot of abuse is the arm rests. Reinstall the arm rests with their screws. Early cars use two, later versions combined the door pull, so they require three. The early door pull was only for the passenger side and installs with two screws. Push the chrome-plastic trims over the ends and snap down. These help secure the trim.

Escutcheon—I am tempted to call the door-handle chrome a *finisher*, but Datsun uses *escutcheon*, so I defer to their terminology. Install the escutcheon in the rectangular hole and fasten with the countersunk Phillips-head screw.

Note: There should be a tiny rubber bumper at the forward edge of the escutcheon—where the handle hits when it's released. If yours has nothing but a hole there, use a fuel-filler-door bumper to replace it.

Check the handle for smoothness and actuation. Pop the plastic escutcheon cover into place. If yours is a 2+2, replace the rear door-handle assembly.

Window-Regulator Crank—Replace the omega-shaped E-clip on the crank. Put the plastic washer back on the shaft and mesh the crank splines with the regulator shafts. Push the handle on until the clip catches in the groove. Position the crank so the knob is at a certain position when the window is full up or down. I suggest a position away from your knees, pointing forward.

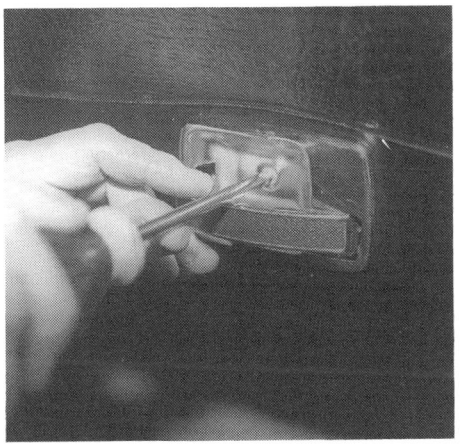

Test-Shut Door—Make sure the trim panel will not interfere with the door jamb.

Hatch

Weatherstrip—Zs have a three-piece weatherstrip on the hatch jamb. The tubular segment goes across the top run. Apply weatherstrip cement to the jamb lip and press the rubber strip into it carefully. Let it tack and adhere that segment thoroughly. Continue down one side similarly with the plain strip and repeat the process again on the other side. Trim off any excess strip at the bottom ends.

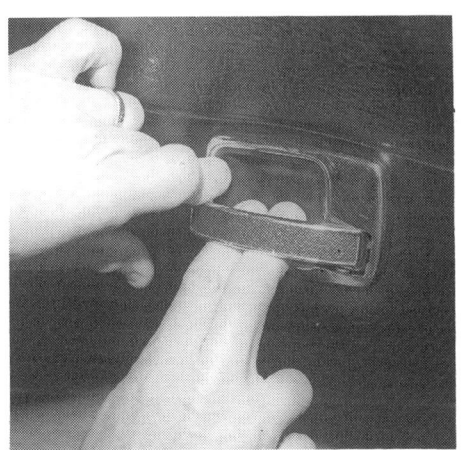

Inner Sealing Strip—The inner lip mounts the one-piece rectangular strip. This can be a handful to put on without getting adhesive where it isn't wanted. Keep a roll of masking tape and a clean naptha-wetted rag handy.

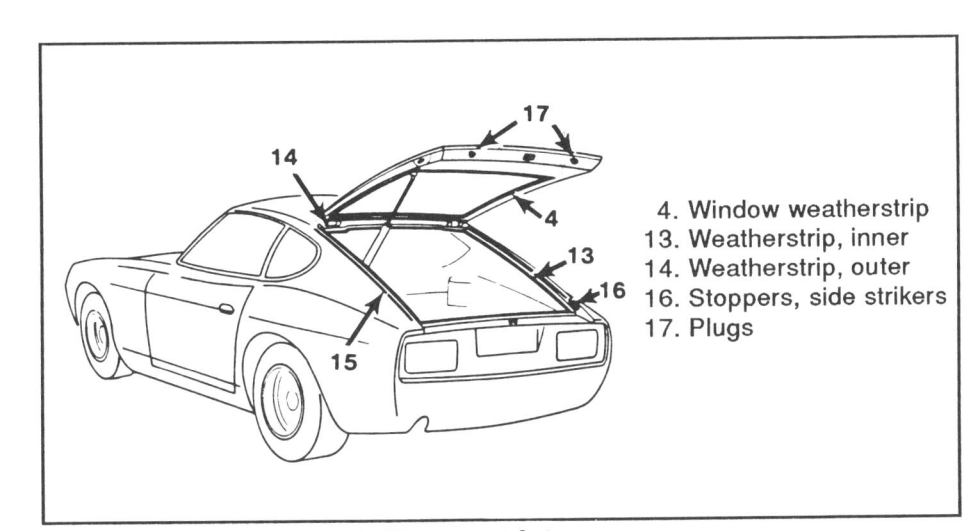

Door-handle escutcheon—or finisher—also helps hold door panel in place. Try handle. It shouldn't bind or make undue noise.

Plastic trim snaps into place. These won't fit tightly if retaining bumps are worn out. Rubber fuel-door bumpers can replace bumpers on escutcheon plate. New ones are available.

4. Window weatherstrip
13. Weatherstrip, inner
14. Weatherstrip, outer
16. Stoppers, side strikers
17. Plugs

Rubber components for hatch. Motorsport Auto.

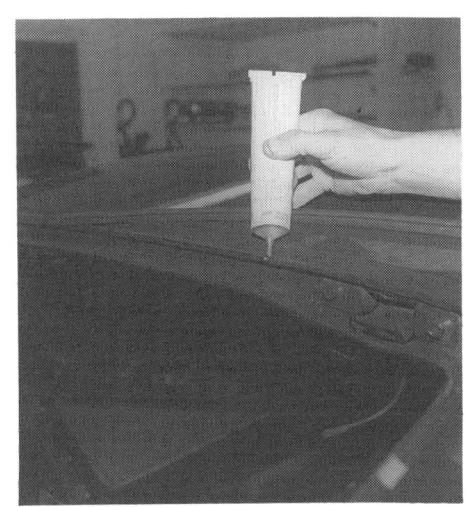

Hatch weatherstrip is made up of three pieces. Side pieces are in place, taped until solidly adhered. Outer strip is being cemented on and will be trimmed so ends will butt. Don't stretch weatherstrip as you install it.

168 How to Restore Your Datsun Z-Car

Large inner sealing strip has a spongy core. It can be a handful to get adhered correctly. I tape it in place at the 12-, 3-, 6- and 9-o'clock positions, then apply adhesive in sections.

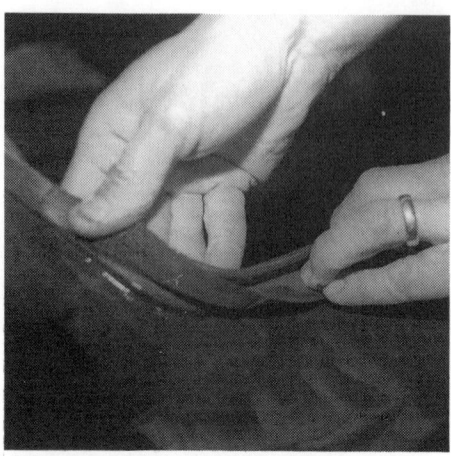

After pressing strip into adhesive, pull it back an inch or so to let it tack—then carefully press it into exact position and rub down. More tape will be needed to hold weatherstrip in place.

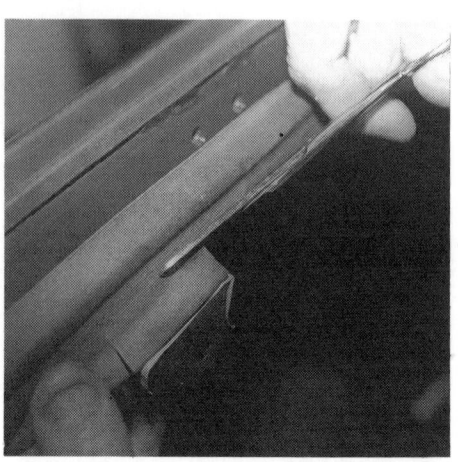

Where the lower lip crosses over hatch-strut mount(s), a section must be snipped away for clearance. Masking tape keeps mount bracket from being covered with cement.

Mask the top(s) of the hatch-support-strut brackets. Arrange the strip around the opening and tape each side approximately in the middle. It's a big help to lay this strip out flat to let any twists or kinks relax as a result of packaging or storing. Neoprene rubber is more pliable when warm, so it's best to do this in a warm shop.

Cement the top run in position and tape into position at the corners. Use as much tape as required to hold it firmly. Cut a notch out of the edge of the strip at each side where it meets the support brackets. Cement sides and tape them down. Repeat with the bottom run.

Check all cemented areas and remove the inevitable slop-over and stringers. Remove the tape when the cement has thoroughly set up.

With the glass installed, assemble the remainder of the hatch. The early 240Z is the most involved because of its air vents. All use the same latch and hardware.

Latch—With the hatch upside down on a soft, non-abrasive surface, install the lock push-button to match the slotted hole and secure it with the spring clip. Cock the latch mechanism and bolt it on finger-tight.

Dovetails—These insert from the inside. Install the Phillips-head screws and tighten.

Early Air Vents—Two outlet hoses install in holes at the lower, rear edge of the hatch. Put both of these in—one at each side. Later cars have a simple rubber plug in these holes.

The vent collectors are two-piece: the rectangular plenum that connects to the outlet hose and a foam-gasketed flange that mates to the rectangular slots in the hatch. First, attach the two with weatherstrip cement. When the pair are set up, put a bead of adhesive on the gasket face and slip them inside the hatch. Mate the hose and plenum, and wedge the unit against the hatch flange with a hunk of cardboard under the hatch-opening lip. Leave these until thoroughly dry.

Hatch Finisher—Reinstall the finisher to the underside of the hatch with screws and plastic rivets. Be sure

Lock cylinder and dovetails are installed from inside hatch cavity—as are vent-collector tubes and plenums.

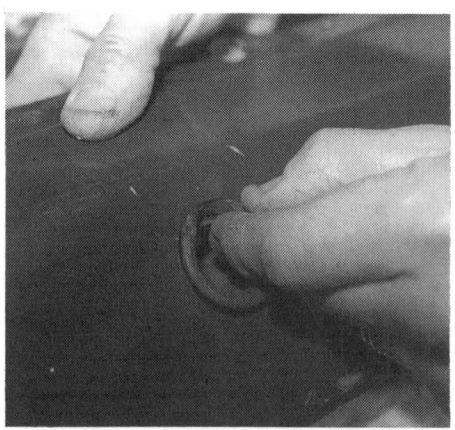

Early Z has tubes to fit in these holes; later cars use rubber plugs.

Early or late hatch finisher is retained with rivets and screws.

that the clip-nuts are in place where the screws go. Early 240Zs only have a hard-plastic finisher with vent slots. Check the rubber flapper on the reverse—it may be brittle and not doing its job. Later 240Zs and newer finishers are hardboard upholstered with plain vinyl over thin padding. If the material needs replacing, do it before installation. The fasteners will help hold the edges in place while the cement dries.

Jamb Hardware—On each hatch jamb, install a striker, rubber bumper and rubber plug. Install the latch striker to the body sill, but don't tighten it yet.

Hatch Strut(s)—Attach a strut to its mounting bracket, usually one on each side of the jamb. You could mount them on the hatch, but the hatch will be more difficult to handle. So I prefer mounting them on the jamb.

Zs with one strut can be modified to take the second one, but this requires welding a second mounting tab to the passenger's side. There is a pad on the hatch that corresponds with the strut-rod bracket, but the captive nuts are not installed—use self-tapping screws. One strut will suffice if it is in like-new condition.

Install Hatch—Replace the hinges and shims if any. All side-to-side and fore-aft adjustment is made between the hinge and jamb. The dovetail stoppers will move fore-aft, but only to conform to the dovetail. With a helper, carefully position the hatch

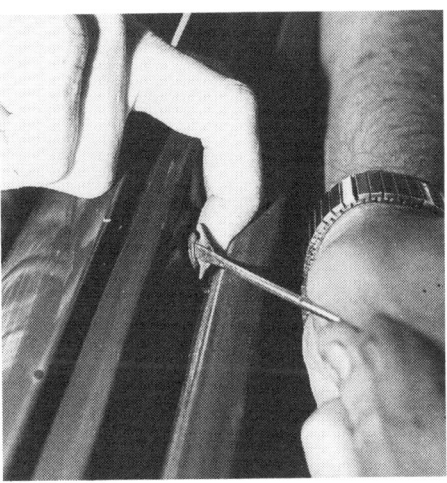

Reinstall rubber plugs in hatch-jamb area.

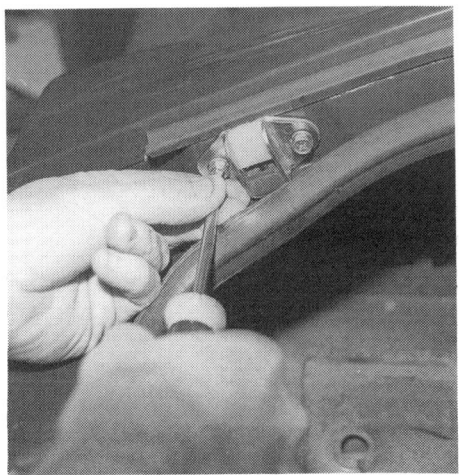

Install dovetail striker and hinges. Remove tape from weatherstrip if adhesive is thoroughly set up.

and start a screw in each hinge. Z-car hatches usually conform very nicely to the jamb, even from car to car.

Now, attach the strut rod(s). Install and tighten all hinge screws. Carefully shut the hatch and check margins at the roof and sides. Make adjustments by loosening the hinge-mounting screws and carefully shifting the hatch and/or adding or removing shims. Shut the hatch again and check margins again, especially at the roof edge. Readjust if necessary.

Look into the gap at the rear edge of the hatch and see if the latch jaw is meeting the striker. Tighten the latch screws so the jaw makes good contact with the striker.

Adjust the gap at the rear of the hatch with the striker. New weatherstrip will increase this gap. With the latch closed, press down on the trailing edge of the hatch to compress the weatherstrip and, when the hatch is aligned, tighten the striker bolts. If you can't get it down far enough, open the hatch and check the dovetail stoppers. They should be fully down.

Check latch and lock functions. A daub of Door Ease stick lubricant on the striker bar is helpful.

Vent Grilles—Their studs are secured by barrel clips. If the barrel clips are not new, put a daub of weatherstrip cement on each before pressing into holes.

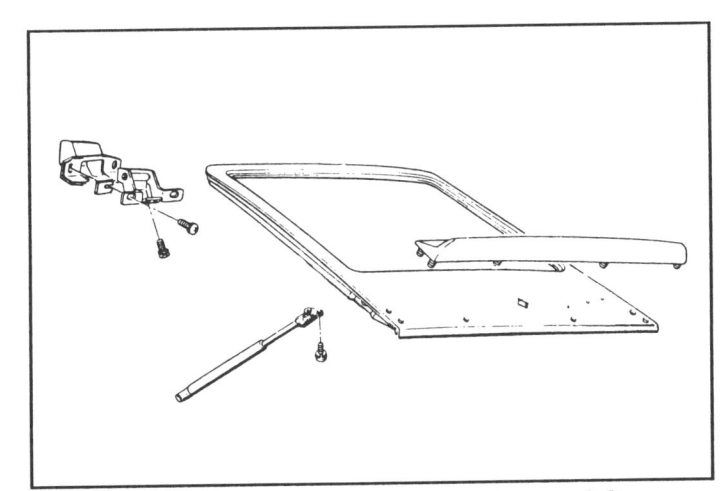

Hinge with shim and single strut rod are shown at left. Spoiler was standard equipment on European Zs and a bonafide dealer option in North America. Early and late versions were sold.

Install hatch-support strut(s) to jamb before installing hatch. Hatch is heavy enough to require a helper to prevent damaging finish. No leeway is available at these attachments, only at the hinge-to-body interface.

170 How to Restore Your Datsun Z-Car

Strut rod(s) are bolted to hatch. Second rod can be adapted to early models, but it requires some creativity to mount extra bracket.

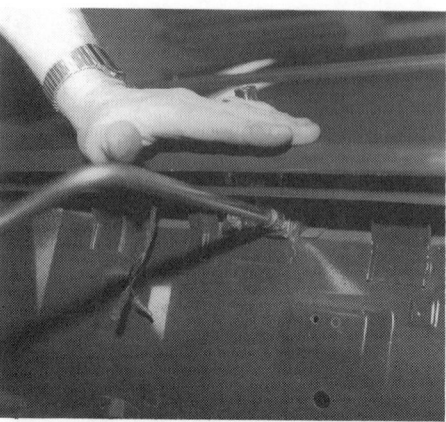

Bolt hatch striker finger-tight, then test shut hatch against new weatherstrip. While pushing down firmly on hatch lip, tighten striker bolts. Then check that it latches readily.

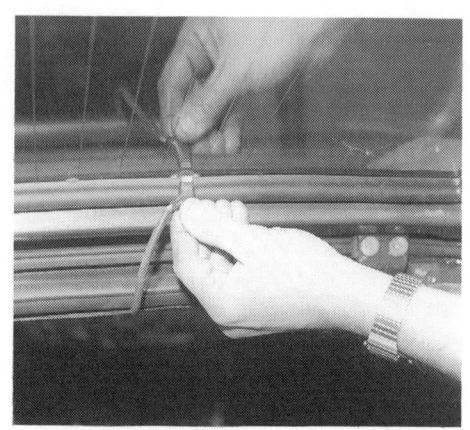

Connect hatch-window defroster-grid leads. These late-style connectors are lower profile and less prone to snag than early ones.

Engine & Transmission Installation

Engine Mounts—Engine-mount insulators can be interchanged from side to side, but should be oriented correctly. Pay attention to how they bolt to the suspension crossmember. Don't tighten these bolts yet or, for that matter, any engine- or transmission-mount bolts until all engine- and transmission-mount components are loosely bolted in place.

Engine-mount brackets also have their own side orientation. If you removed them, be sure they are attached to the correct side of the engine or chassis before you begin the engine drop.

Transmission Mount—Up to HLS30-46000: Install cushion to the transmission crossmember and install the assembly to the underbody member. Alternately attach the crossmember to the mounting pad on the transmission tailshaft.

After HLS30-46001: If the cushioned engine mount needs new insulators, install them now by pressing or driving in with a drift. Install the insulator to the spring engine mounting. Orient the forward side of the cushion toward the forward side of the rear engine-mount member. Install the assembly to the underbody member. Alternately attach the assembly to the mounting pad on the transmission tailshaft. Go back to the engine mounts and tighten their bolts.

Drive Shaft—You installed new U-joints on the drive shaft . . . didn't you? If not, do it now.

Check the splines on the transmission output shaft for bad scratches or rust. Clean up imperfections with fine emery cloth. Check for dirt or obstructions in the splines and correct any problems. If all is OK, squirt some oil on the splines and slip the spline onto the transmission flange and bolt it up. Give the U-joint zerk fittings a shot of grease until it barely begins to show around the seals.

While you're under there, check to be sure the access holes and tubes for the vapor hoses have a sound rubber nipple or are securely caulked with dumdum, flexible body sealer or other suitable caulking.

Fuel & Vapor Lines

Whether you chose to replace, replate or merely clean these steel lines, now's the time to reinstall them. Various Z models have different sizes and numbers of lines that vary somewhat in mounting. Check the rubber-insulator blocks for hole

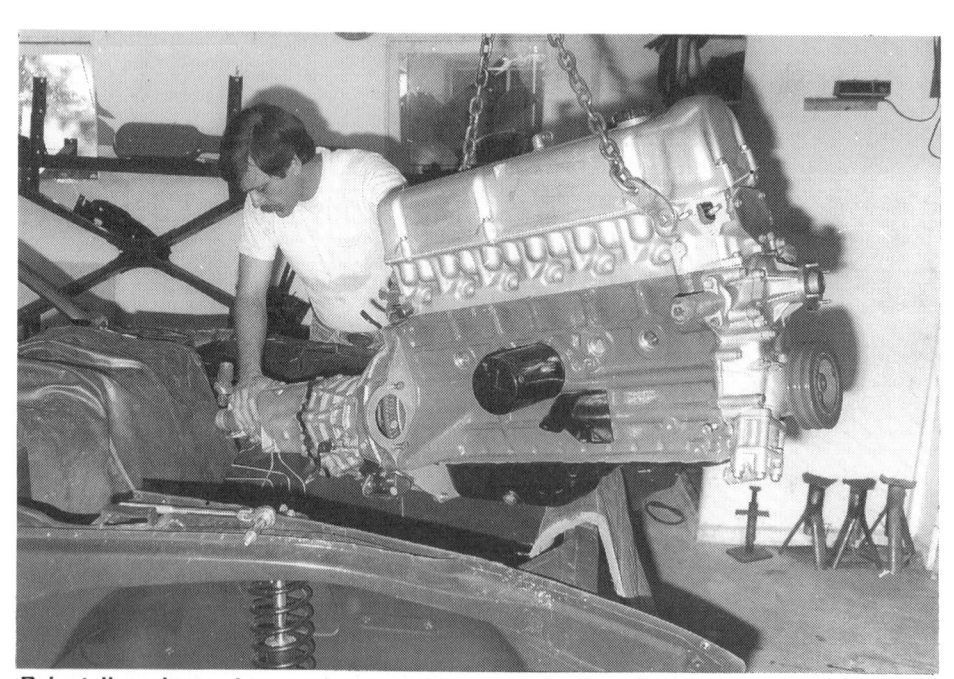

Reinstall engine and transmission. I think it should look *right* at least once. Block, crank pulley and engine plate are blue; brackets, engine mounts and oil pan are black; and aluminum components are clear-coated. Thick plastic protects firewall from damage—and don't stick transmission tailshaft through windshield if you're installing transmission with engine! Note evidence of other restoration in progress. Frame against wall is a 1935 Packard.

After tightening engine mounts, I wrap engine in plastic. How much time you put into maintaining cleanliness or finish is your option, but the extra care will show in the end.

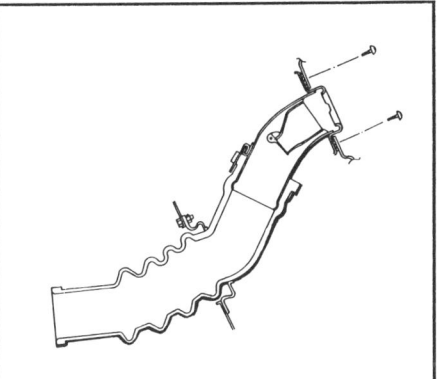

Cross section of late-style fuel filler shows restrictor for unleaded fuel nozzle. Lower clamp is not shown. Courtesy Nissan.

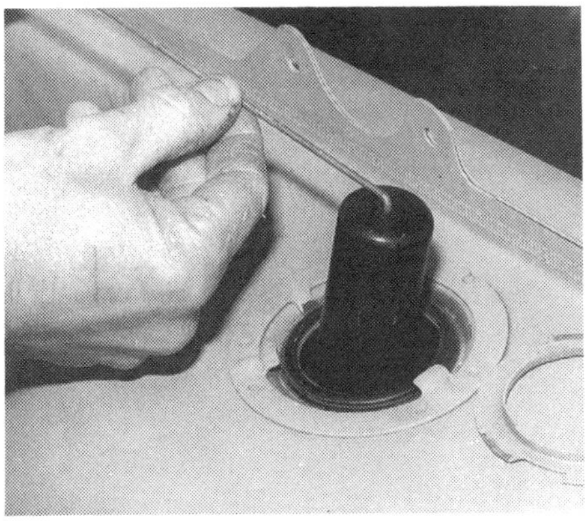

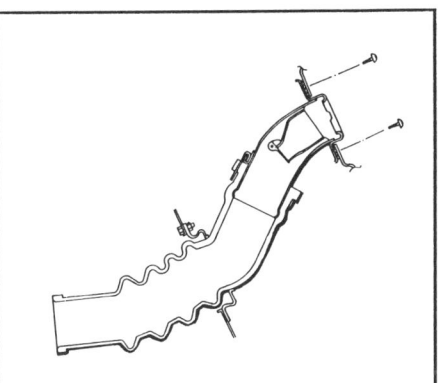

Fuel tank is in primer and ready to slush. I'm removing sending unit. Other openings are taped closed.

size. Organize the line arrangement to this. Putting them back is considerably more difficult than removing them. Unless they were twisted or bent while out of the car, their shape will indicate how they should lie.

Work methodically and don't be discouraged—they will all fall into place eventually! Be sure all clamps are tight and no lines contact the body or each other. Otherwise, rattling and chafing will result.

Fuel Filler

On early Zs, the fuel-filler neck must be returned to position by pushing it up through the hole in the inner fender, then the hole in the fuel-filler box. The only way I know to get the plastic flange through the holes is to heat the top of the filler until it collapses slightly and stuff it through the openings. Either a heat gun or heat lamp will work. Don't use an open flame. Heat it only enough to get the required flexibility. Repeated heating and cooling seems to cause some permanent shrinkage, something not desirable when it comes to mounting the top flange to the filler box on early cars!

The lower opening gets peppered with considerable road splash, so apply a ring of sealant to its circumference—dumdum, body sealer or silicone sealer will suffice. When the neck is through the bottom hole, reinstall the metal ring around the hole with its screws. The fuel-tank neck will mate with the filler, so slip the screw-type hose clamp around the plastic neck, but don't tighten it yet. The 280Zs use a metal filler neck in the filler box that must be installed from inside the rear compartment. It has a gasket on the top side of the flange.

Early Cars—The upper end of the filler neck must be fitted through the filler-box hole and secured with the metal filler flange and Phillips-head screws. I use an awl or punch to find and hold the screw holes in position while I wrestle the fasteners in. This end shouldn't need a sealer if the neck is in good shape and installed securely. After this operation, it won't be hard for you to understand at least one reason Datsun changed filler designs!

Don't forget to refit the rubber "bib" body protector.

Later Cars—Fit the plastic neck through the lower opening from the interior. The flange seats on the inside of the body metal, but the screws attach from outside. It should be sealed both on the tube and at the opening.

Fuel Tank

Restore—This procedure is easy to do and very beneficial, but must be done safely. First, you should have drained any gasoline from the fuel tank before the fuel system was disconnected. After it has been removed, all remaining fuel and fumes must be purged, page 32. Even at that, never assume a fuel tank is free of combustible fumes.

Fuel-Gauge Sender—Remove this to facilitate inspection of the tank interior. Remove the sender assembly by unscrewing the locking ring. Using a punch and hammer, rotate the ring counterclockwise by lightly tapping it. Inspect neoprene O-ring for cracks—don't hesitate to replace it for safety's sake.

Be careful with the float-and-arm assembly when removing or storing it. Check the float for leaks—if it has liquid inside, it definitely isn't doing its job. If you had problems with the gauge registering correctly and the sender appears to be the culprit, now is the time to replace the sender. Check it with an ohmmeter. The fault may be in the wiring or gauge itself.

On late 240Zs through 280Zs, there is an electric fuel pump and attendant plumbing to disconnect and remove. Be careful of electrical sparks where there might be gasoline fumes! Check for a clogged fuel filter. It's inside the electric pump on 1973 240Zs and '74 260Zs.

I sealed all openings with silver duct tape, but plastic caps can be used if you have them. I then sandblast the outside of the tank. Datsun tanks aren't plated on the outside, so don't worry about removing any rust protection. Consider using a boil-out service such as is often available at many radiator shops. This can be particularly valuable to determine

172 How to Restore Your Datsun Z-Car

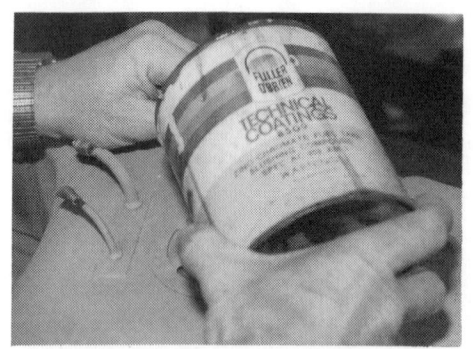

Gauge-sender hole is fine for pouring in Fuller-O'Brien Slushing Compound. One quart will do three tanks this size. The fumes are fierce.

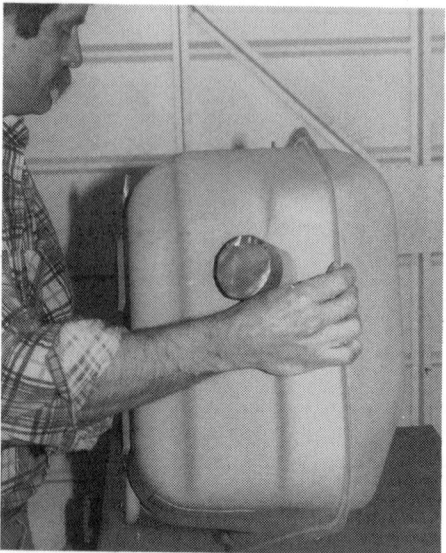

Turn and move tank so liquid "slush" covers every square inch of tank interior. Lots of methodical turning and moving is imperative.

Because water is heavier than gasoline, it will stay against bottom. Therefore, bottom of tank is most susceptible to rust. Let compound run out of drain hole to make sure heaviest coat is deposited on bottom. Slushing compound never hardens.

whether there is rust damage on the inside of the tank. Make sure the drain plug is tightly seated.

After blasting, carefully remove the tape from the holes and replace it with fresh to prevent abrasive from entering the tank. Thoroughly blow out crevices with a strong stream of compressed air before you remove the tape, though.

Slush Fuel Tank—A special coating is available to renew the usefulness of fuel and chemical tanks. It is known as *slushing compound.* I use Fuller-O'Brien 8509 Zinc Chromate Tank Slushing Compound, which I purchase at an aircraft-supply house. It is a heavy-bodied non-drying paint product that uses Methylethyl Ketone (MEK) as a solvent. Avoid breathing the fumes—they are fierce and volatile. So don't do this process indoors or around open flame. Similar products are available at paint stores or some of the suppliers in the list at the end of this book. For example, Eastwood offers both a gas-tank sealer and a gas-tank etching compound. They recommend using the gas-tank etch to prepare a rusty tank for the sealer.

Pour the entire can of slushing compound directly into the tank and seal the opening as tightly as possible. Rotate the tank 360 degrees on all three axes until you are satisfied every side, corner and seam is thoroughly coated with the compound. This is important, so take your time and repeat the process until you are convinced coverage is complete.

Because water is heavier than gasoline and sinks to the bottom of the tank, that's where rust will be the worst. Consequently, the bottom of the tank should be thoroughly sealed. Support the tank so it's level and place the can under the drain hole. Remove the plug and all tape. Check the small vent tubes for clogging—the liquid is thick enough to plug a fairly large hole!

You won't get all compound back, of course, but drain as much back as will flow. Leave it draining and set up in this position for several hours. This will ensure the bottom of the interior gets maximum coverage.

Remember, sloshing compound will never actually dry. It remains elastic for maximum sealing. It not only will hold residual rust and dirt in check, it also plugs pinholes in the tank. Gasoline will not dissolve the sloshing compound, so the tank may be filled soon after using it if necessary.

Replace the drain plug and give the tank exterior a good coat of black

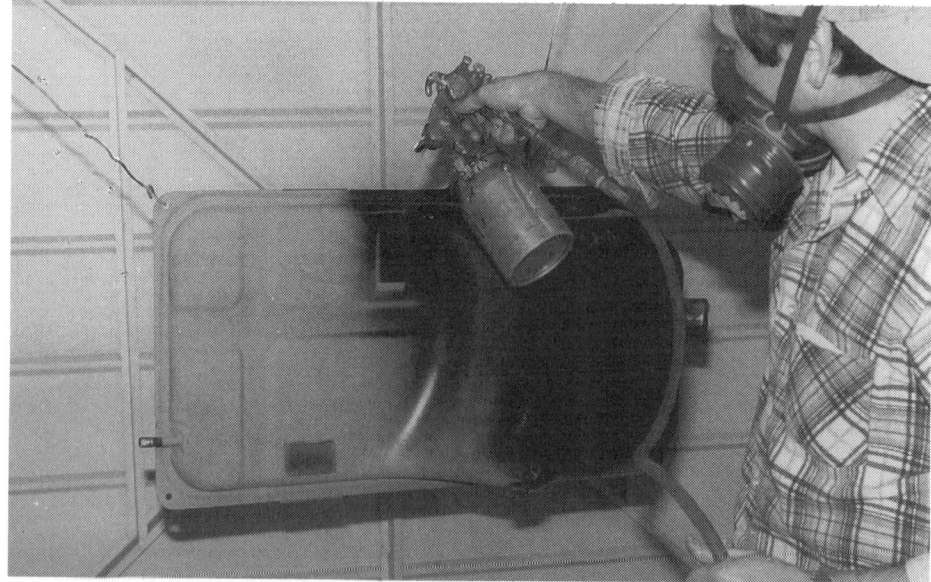

After sealing inside, I give tank a good coat of catalyzed black. Notice how I hang parts painted off car. The ceiling of my shop is studded with screw-hooks for wire hangers.

Body Exterior & Drive Line Assembly 173

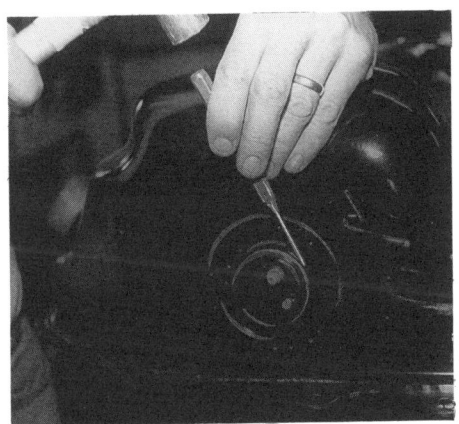

Tape is removed, paint is dry and fuel sender is reinstalled by tapping ring ears with hammer and punch.

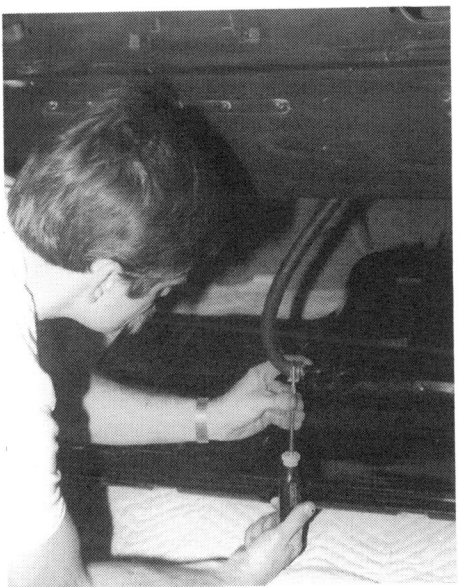

Fuel tank is protected by pad. Large sheet of cardboard also works. Replacement vapor-recovery hoses don't have distinctive braiding on outside.

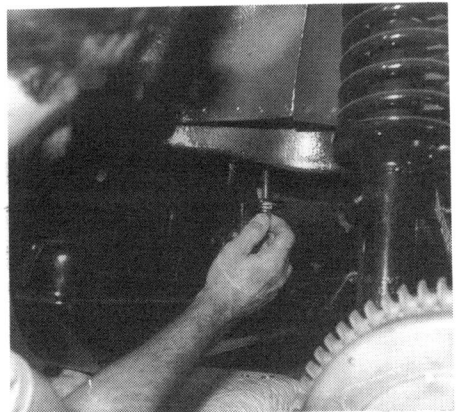

With fuel-filler tube in place, lift tank to meet its lower mouth. Don't forget to put clamp on first! Pull collector hoses up through holes in deck flooring. Adjust tank hanger-strap fasteners for long reach, then slip them into keyholes in brackets. Rack tank around to settle it before tightening fully.

enamel. It can now be reassembled. Double-check the neoprene O-ring and replace it if it's at all deteriorated. Install the fuel-gauge sender. Secure it with the locking ring by tapping it tightly into position.

Install Fuel Tank—Place fuel tank under the car, then the mounting straps and insulating strips in the grooves provided. An old furniture pad or sheet of cardboard under the tank will help protect it while you position it. I cement the insulating strips to the straps so they won't slip out of place while I manipulate the tank into position.

Run the vapor hoses down through the tubes provided for them in the deck floor. Be sure hoses you use are marked for fuel or vapor use. Don't court trouble with water hose or some other inadequate substitute. Clamp the hoses to the fittings on the tank.

Now, raise the tank and straps until you can hook the rear ends of the straps into their mountings. They have to be rotated 45 degrees to match the triangular holes, then twisted back to their final positions. Pull the vapor hoses up through the deck. Don't let them kink under the floorpan. Swing the forward end of one strap—whichever appears to be the easiest—up and slip the retaining-bolt head into the keyhole-shape slot. Then insert it into the bracket hole and slip on the washers and nut. Repeat with the other strap, then check alignment. Tighten straps when alignment is good.

Fuel-Filler Door

Two bolts attach the door to the filler box. Tighten these only enough so the door can be swung through its travel. Be careful that misalignment at the front edge doesn't knock a big chip of paint out of the fender lip! Make several trials before tightening the bolts. If necessary, add a washer or two under the hinge bracket, or *carefully* bend the hinge to gain some clearance. The lid and hinge are bonded together, so be careful not to break them apart! At the rear lip, install the two tiny rubber bumpers in the holes provided. Moisten the attaching stems and pull through from the inside. These will help establish the correct gap at the rear edge.

Early 240Zs have the little thumb latch that is retained by a spring clip on the inside of the hole. As an aside, these were often replaced by keylocks during the '70s fuel inflation. Later models had only a finger loop at the rear edge.

Rear Finisher

Restore—On early Zs with three metal finishers for the back panel, a big improvement in appearance can often be made by simply refinishing

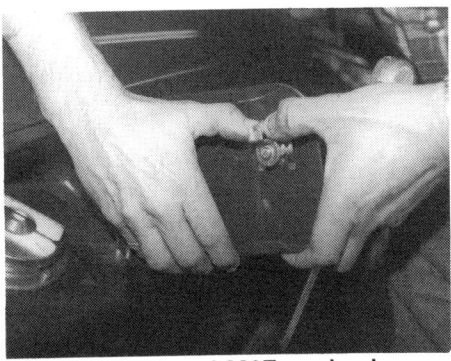

Filler neck, bib and 280Z cap in place: Early cars have latch to install. Under car, install electric fuel pump and connect fuel and vapor lines. Remember to replace splash deflector.

them. The original paint is a silver-gray "match scratcher" finish, which retains all sorts of contaminants, especially paste wax.

For this reason, it must be carefully stripped of the old enamel. This is complicated by the slim stainless-steel taillight-opening trim strips. These can't be removed without unacceptable damage occurring and are very hard to protect from abrasive, whether they be sanded or sandblasted. So you'll have to use chemical stripper, which won't harm the trim. Just make sure you remove all residual stripper that may have seeped under the trim itself. If you don't, it

174 How to Restore Your Datsun Z-Car

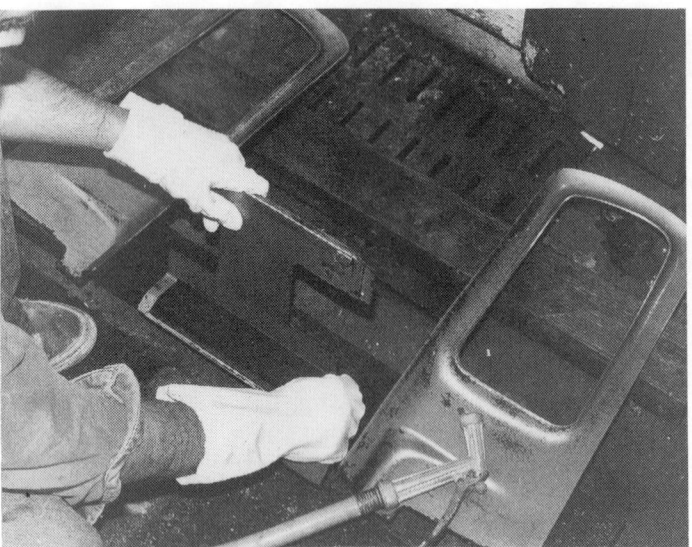

Metal rear finisher on early Zs can be refinished. Aircraft paint stripper won't harm thin stainless moldings and it rinses off with water. Rubber gloves protect my numerous Band-Aids while I use 3M Scotchbrite pad to urge last scraps of paint free. When doing your final rinse, make sure you get all paint remover out from under stainless trim. Moisture should be blown from behind trim with compressed air.

Because trim around taillight openings can't be removed without damaging it, I use 3M Fineline tape to mask them.

will sneak out and spoil the new paint.

Rinse the three metal panels carefully and blow all moisture out of the trim strip crimp with lots of compressed air. Don't use an acid metal-prep on these parts—it can hide under the trim. Shine the stainless with very fine steel wool *before* you paint. Carefully mask strips and primer the panels completely. Check for damage, pits and so forth. Use spot putty and block-sand, being careful not to scratch the stainless trim.

Restore License-Plate Light Housing

Disassemble the housing, but don't strip it. Instead, hand-sand it to prepare the plastic for paint. Prime it just as you do metal, though. Clean the clear plastic "lenses" and check the sockets and wiring.

A good match for the original paint is Ditzler Duracryl DDL 2862 Argent with quite a bit of *suede* additive. The formula is:

1 Pint DDL
200 units DX265
300 units DX264
Thin 100—150% and spray on fairly

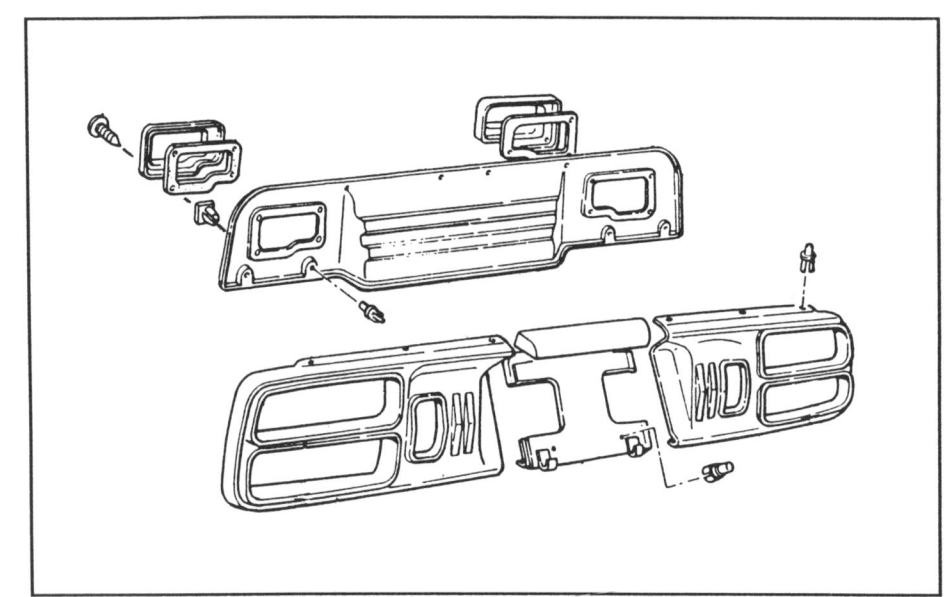

Late-style rear finisher and trim panel. Most Zs have access covers for taillight-bulb sockets. Early style is a pain to remove and replace.

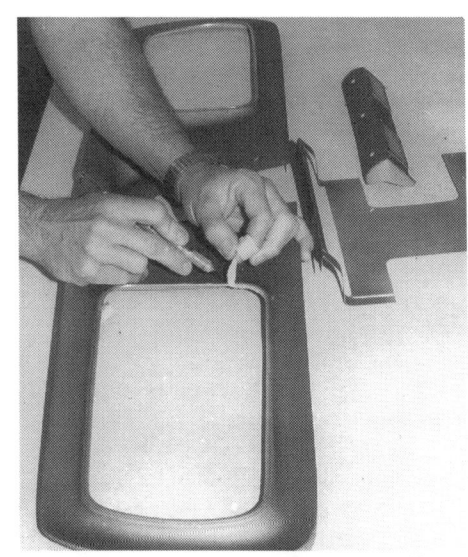

Gray lacquer with suede agent duplicates original-finish texture. License-plate light was sanded clean and painted simultaneously. I'm using X-acto knife to urge tape off. Never leave it on too long!

dry. Regulate air pressure to the high side. Swirl paint around in the cup constantly to help keep texture additives in suspension. Maintain spray-gun distance and overlap coverage on the final coat, or variations in surface texture may be unacceptable. This paint should have no gloss, so don't expect any!

Unmask trim as soon as paint has had a few minutes to flash up. You'll be surprised at the improvement this procedure will make on a nicely refinished Z-car—or perhaps I should say you'll be disappointed with how punk the effect will be if you don't!

Install Rear Finisher

Early Z: With the taillights installed, replace the three-piece finisher. Mount the center portion first—it is held with screws at the bottom. Side pieces help secure the upper section.

Snap a finisher end-section onto the retaining clips on the lower panel. Make sure the finisher lip fully enters the clip. Press the top edge forward until the rivet holes line up with those in the hatch-ledge lip. Hold the alignment if necessary with an awl or pointed tool and insert a rivet. If paint has built up on the edge of the hole, this may take a bit of effort. Set the rivet by pushing the stem down flush. Used rivets may need a drop of lubricant. Finish installing that side and repeat with the remaining finisher.

License-Plate Light—This is held together with three Phillips-head screws. Before reassembling, be sure the bulbs are good. Check the gasket to make sure it is seated. Cement it to the housing to make sure it doesn't "walk" out of position.

Connect the electrical leads to the harness. Position it on the center finisher—it retains the upper part—and reinstall to the hatch ledge with the two Phillips-head screws.

Late Z: These finishers install with the taillight, but utilize rivets along the hatch ledge and under the license-plate area. Attach each finisher to its light assembly with the two Phillips-head screws and remount them.

Install License-Plate-Light Housing—Check the bulbs, install in the sockets and insert them into the light unit. Pass the two electrical leads through their hole. Position the light assembly and reinstall it to the hatch ledge.

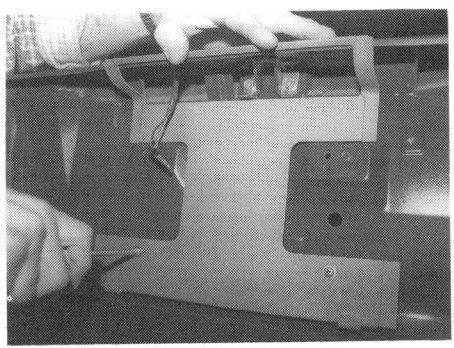

Early rear finisher center section attaches with Phillips-head screws.

Outboard rear finishers clip on at bottom and are retained at top with plastic rivets. New rivets are not a luxury. Considering the price, they are a necessity. Push in center pin so it's flush with top to lock rivet in place.

Front Fenders

Fender Inner Gasket—This is held to the big weld flange atop the front inner-fender structure by metal clips. The fat section of the strip goes to the bottom; the thin upper lip turns out. Check the clips to be sure they will hold tightly. Do this by squeezing them shut on the gasket with pliers.

From the rear of the gasket to the end, fold a strip of dumdum over the weld flange.

Before the fender can be installed, the splash protectors must be installed. In an effort to cure the unfortunate tendency of Zs to rust, Datsun improved splash protection over the years. At least three different protectors were used during the nine seasons of Z-car production. All attach to the side/cowl and inner-fender structures similarly. For positive sealing, sandwich a 1-inch-wide strip of dumdum between the splash-protector flange and car.

Rubber Flap—Don't forget these little deflectors that attach to the bottom of each rear splash protector. If yours are serviceable but look tired, just swap them side for side.

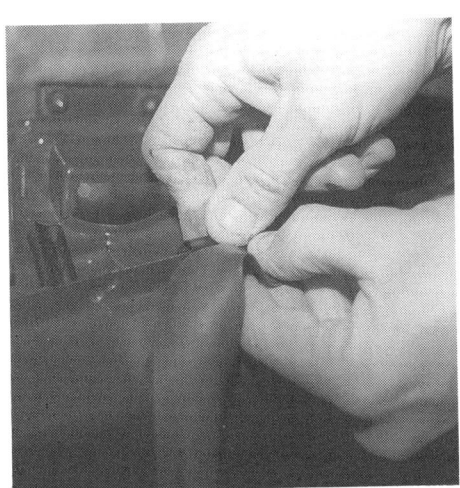

Install front-fender inner gasket. Believe it or not, gaskets and clips are original. Rubber lip should flare to outboard side of car.

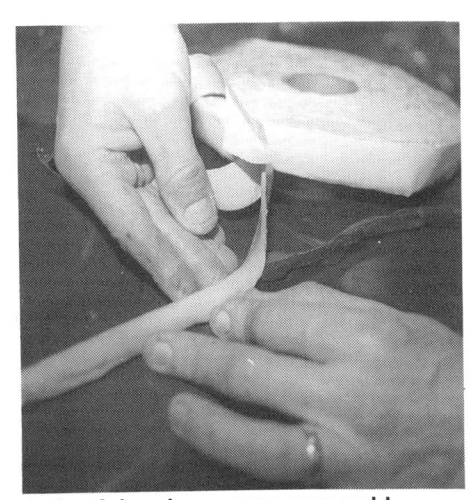

Strip of dumdum wraps over weld flange. This stuff can be procured at good paint shops, from folks who build metal buildings or at some RV supply stores.

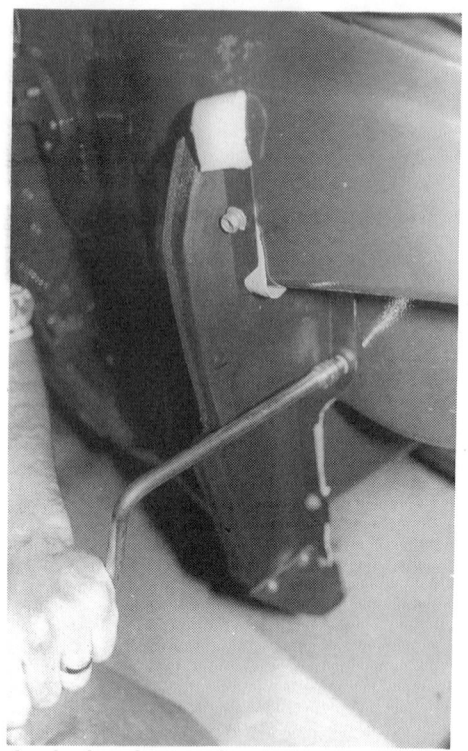

Apply dumdum under splash protectors, then tighten screws. Don't forget to install rubber flap at bottom. Later protectors surround splash area, attach to inner fender and each other.

Carefully position fender over the inner lip. Rear edge must not hit door or A-pillar. Note matte-black area at side of radiator opening.

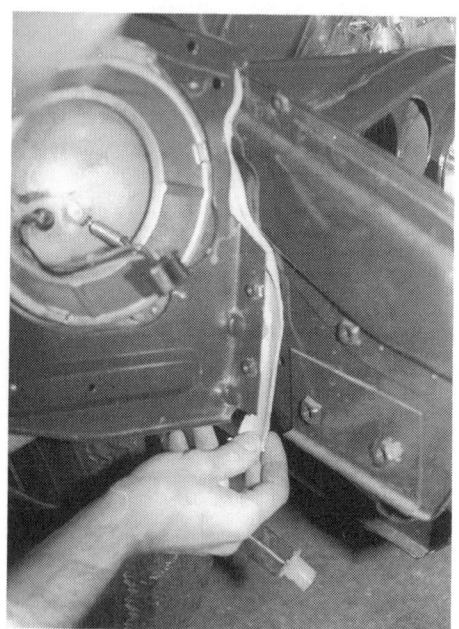

Before installing any fasteners, place strip of dumdum between fender and inner panel. Now start bolts and screws here and in cowl area.

Foam Gasket—You can get a good closed-cell urethane-foam weatherstrip at many recreation-vehicle-supply houses. Complete the sealing job by putting a strip of this across each inner fender and down the outer protector flange. The pressure-sensitive adhesive on these is usually pretty wimpy, so add weatherstrip cement to be sure. Also, you may need two layers of weatherstrip to fill the gap, depending on tape thickness and the distance between the fender and protector.

On the fenders, another strip of closed-cell-foam tape goes on the baffle filler—the big flange at the inner rear of the fender. Originally it was applied to the inner fender, but unless you know where the filler meets the fender, it's better to apply it to the edge of the baffle filler. This automatically positions the foam when the fender is installed.

Headlight Bucket—This can be installed now or after the fender is on. I installed mine first so photo taking would be easier. The sealed-beam unit should be in place. A bead of silicone seals the gasket to the rear of the fender. Four Phillips-head screws hold it.

Mount Fender—Very carefully hang the fender over the top of the inner-fender structure. Keep an eye on the rear edge of the fender. Don't let it hit the front edge of the door and chip the paint.

Run another strip of dumdum over the top of the inner-fender lip and down the body where it will contact the fender flange at the headlight. You may need to build up the thickness, especially the 6 inches over the wheel, to ensure a positive seal against road splash. Start the two screws that go into the weldnuts on the flange, but don't tighten them until alignment is good.

Start the two screws that hold the top of the fender to the cowl. Datsun used Phillips-/hex-head machine screws, but standard hex-head screws can be used. Because it is an area that gets a lot of trapped moisture, put some oil on the screws.

Don't forget the fastener in the door-jamb area. Run it in tight, then back off a turn so you can move the fender to align it.

Two more bolts hold the bottom of the fender to the front of the rocker panel—one in the fender lip and the other in its little well. I put the latter in first and tighten both when I'm satisfied with fit.

Install the bolts that secure the upper lip of the fender. Some are hex-heads with washers that only serve to secure the fender; two are pan-head Phillips head that also hold the hood bumpers. Leave them loose until the hood is aligned.

Check the gap between the front edge of the door and fender—if it's not even or one of the edges isn't parallel, adjust the fender. Also note the fit of the fender where it joins the A-pillar/cowl area. There isn't a lot of leeway, but it should be enough. I use a large, worn-out Phillips screwdriver whose tip I ground sharp. Inserted in one of the screw holes, it gives enough leverage to move the fender the needed distance. When I can see that the adjustment space in the fender hole is expended, I tighten the

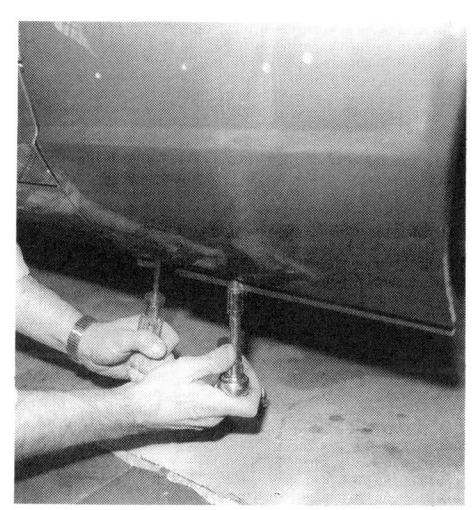

Two bolts secure fender at bottom. I hope the threads are sound—now's the wrong time to find out. Sharpened screwdriver is used in rear hole to pry so fender aligns with rocker panel.

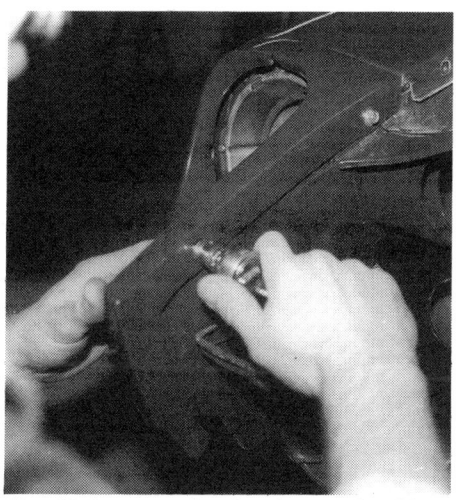

Headlight-mounting hardware should be installed before bezel is installed. Bezel attaches to inner-fender structure. It has four studs at rear that are secured with nuts. Tighten all fender fasteners.

Fender finishers at lower corners go on next. Tighten fasteners after apron is on.

Clear headlight cover isn't legal in all states. Shown on 280Z, it fits all models. Courtesy Motorsport Auto.

adjacent fastener and check my progress. Be careful not to ruin the threads if there is a weldnut in that hole. When fit is good, tighten all fender fasteners.

Headlight Bezel
This can go on next. Early 240Zs have molded-plastic bezels—called *fender extensions*—with studs that engage the fender. All later Zs used a die-cast metal bezel mounted with screws in the same positions. Also, these use a gasket between the fender and rear of the bezel. On the early type, run a bead of sealer around the perimeter, far enough in so it won't squeeze out so it's visible. Fasten bezel loosely to the fender and put in the screws that hold it to the inner fender. Check alignment of the two parts by sighting over the gap. They should match. Tighten all headlight-bezel fasteners if they do.

Run headlight wiring to the harness and connect. Repeat the process with the other fender.

Fender Lower Extensions
These sheet-metal panels fit below the headlight bezels. Install both, but don't tighten the fasteners yet.

Front Apron
Now install the apron—valence panel—and align it with the lower extensions. When you are satisfied with the alignment of the extensions and apron, tighten the screws, including those in the brackets.

Bumper Filler Panels
If your Z has the plastic bumper fillers that attach to the headlight bezel/fender extension joint, install them.

If it has the metal bumper filler and shock-absorber covers, they can be installed now or later.

Turn & Park Lights
1970—74
Again, bring parts up to par appearance-wise. Clean inside and out and buff plastic. See page 123.

Lens—Replace the little square of plastic sponge in the drain hole. I use a few drops of Super Glue—it holds well and is unnoticeable.

Reflector—Replace mounting studs if they were removed. Fit a new neoprene weatherstrip to the reflector circumference. This needs no adhesive or sealant. Fit lens to the face of the weatherstrip and replace the six screws. Be careful not to strip the threads out of the plastic! Repeat with the other side. Put good bulbs back in the sockets and lock them into the reflector.

Installation—With the front fender extensions and pan in place, push the studs through the holes and install the washers, locks and nuts. Route the wiring pigtails into the grille cavity.

1974-1/2—78
These are restored in much the same method as the earlier style. The lens and gasket are held to the reflector with two screws as is the bulb socket.

Installation—The later style mounts to the grille with two screws.

For early and later models, Datsun provided rubber protectors where the wiring runs over the sharp edge of the sheet metal. It is a good practice to duplicate these—inner-tube rubber can be substituted for the original, but new stock looks better. Check the plumbing-supply department of a good home-improvement store. They should have sheet-rubber gasket stock that can be substituted. Cut a rectangle that can wrap around the raw edge and bond with contact cement.

Battery-Inspection Doors
Be careful not to mar the finish on inspection doors or surrounding jambs while installing or aligning—this is

178 How to Restore Your Datsun Z-Car

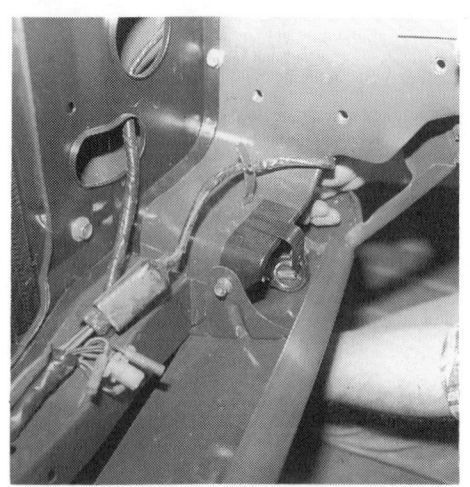

Apron fastens to brackets, has captive nuts where it joins fender finishers. Tighten all bolts when alignment looks right. Connect headlight wiring.

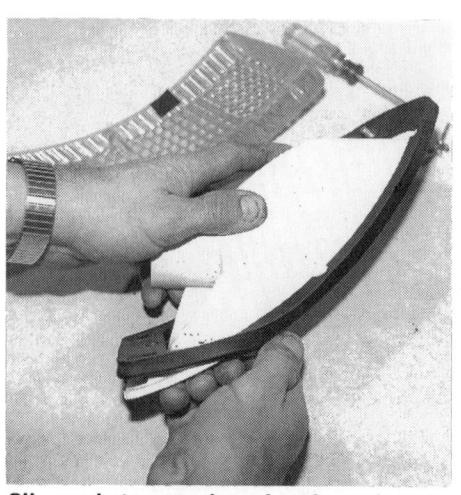

Slip gasket over edge of early park-and-turn signal housing. Gasket hides clip-nuts that secure housing. Lens goes on next.

Install park-and-turn signal in finisher. Route wires to main harness. Later signals mount in grille.

easy to do! A strip of masking tape applied lightly to interfacing edges can be a great headache remedy.

Fasten with bolts, there should be enough leeway to provide side-to-side and high-low door adjustments. Fore-and-aft adjustments are made with shims—flat washers also work. Check to be sure the hinge isn't bent or distorted if good alignment is not easily achieved.

Latch—Early Zs use a plastic fork that slips into the little bracket. Late Zs have the more-durable metal latch that attaches with screws. Put this on and set it to meet the wire loop that's welded to the fender lip. A daub of Door Ease lubricant applied with a little screwdriver will smooth the action.

Rubber Cushions—These cement to the fender-lip channel and must be in place before the inspection door can be aligned accurately.

While you're at it, cement the rubber strip back into the front corner of the door lip where it will interface with the hood lip. You can cut this piece from stock, but it must be the same thickness as the original.

Caution: The cowl finisher must fit so there's clearance between it and the rear edge of the battery-inspection doors. Check clearances there before you fully open either door or you may damage the paint.

Windshield-Wiper Drive Motor—Datsun equipped the Z with a sealed windshield-wiper motor and gearbox. If problems exist, replacement is the remedy. Be sure there are no problems in the switch gear or in the wiring or connectors before buying a new motor.

Early Z-car wiper mechanicals are covered by a black ABS plastic shell; later ones are snapped inside a plastic bag. Otherwise, they interchange.

Wiper Linkage—There isn't much to maintain on the linkage arms, but the pivot balls and felts can benefit from a drop or two of light machine oil. Take the old boots off the wiper-pivot shafts and thoroughly clean off any dirt or corrosion. These rust from moisture trapped under the rubber boot. If they did their job before you tore the assembly down, they will benefit from the lubrication. Push its cover back and oil the crank joint. Rotate the linkage to check for free movement.

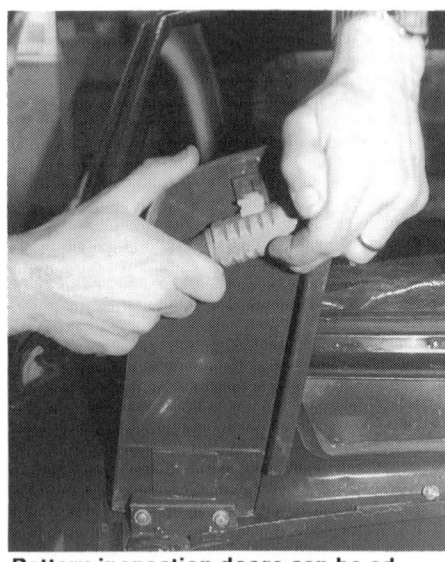

Battery-inspection doors can be adjusted at hinge brackets. Replace shims that were removed if there were any. I hope you noted where they went. Early latch is plastic. Slot on little bracket allows some adjustment to allow it to mate with loop on fender. Late cars have metal latch that adjusts with slotted screw holes.

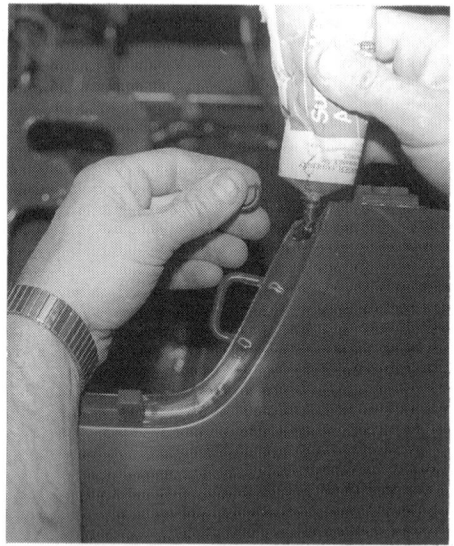

Rubber bumpers cement to lip of inspection-door opening. Piece of plastic hose pushed over threads near battery was a Datsun trick used to protect them from battery-acid fumes.

Body Exterior & Drive Line Assembly 179

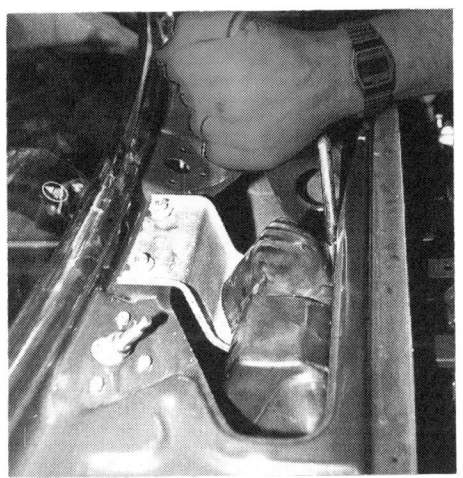

Route wiper-motor wiring through its hole in lower cowl and seat grommet. Guide linkage into place, then install and tighten all fasteners on pivots and motor.

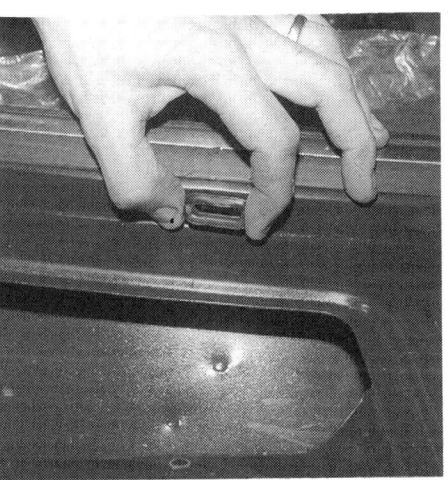

Don't forget to install plastic pockets for positioning cowl finisher. Otherwise finisher will vibrate and make noise. It will also rust in the local area as paint is chipped off metal edges.

Slip cowl-finisher tabs into pockets—without chipping the finish—and install screws in front flange.

Wiper linkages are relatively trouble-free, but if you find serious wear or a bent arm, replacement is the best remedy. Don't attempt cobbling used parts back together.

Cowl Finisher

Replace the plastic grommets at the base of the windshield that position the metal tabs on the rear of the finisher. These will show just a bit, so be sure they are presentable.

You should have some help with installing the cowl finisher to reduce the potential for paint damage. Insert the cowl-finisher tabs into the grommets in the cowl. Start wherever you prefer—at one end or the middle—and hold them in place as you go across. Keep an eye on adjacent edges and lips. Paint chips in this area are painfully obvious. Push an awl or punch into one of the center screw holes to hold alignment and install the screws.

Cowl-to-Hood Weatherstrip

Run a bead of weatherstrip adhesive inside the vee of the strip. Center it on the cowl lip and smooth across to the sides. It doesn't need to be trimmed.

Side-Marker Lights

All Zs have the same basic side-marker lights, so all installations are basically the same. Later models use a better splash boot, so these make a good replacement on early cars. Check bulbs before assembling the lights. Rear lenses are red, fronts amber.

Replace clip nuts at the two screw holes. The marker lens is held on by the stainless-steel bezel. The edge of the bezel snaps into the lip of the rubber molding. The Phillips-head screws that hold the unit together are also stainless steel—the bezel and screw heads polish up well. Don't polish zinc-plated screws.

I put a bead of silicone sealer around the hole and screw holes. Insert the light into the hole and thread the screws down until the rubber just begins to compress, but not so much that it bulges out. Route wiring to the harness and make the connections. Repeat with the other three lights.

Restoring Emblems

Most exterior trim is available new for Z-cars, but why spend the money if yours has good plating and attachment pins? This is especially true with early Zs. Their trim is heavily chrome-plated pot metal which is relatively easy to restore. Later cars often have vacuum-plated plastic trim—much more difficult to restore.

The first step is to scrub the parts with a non-scratching cleanser such as Bon-Ami and a fairly stiff brush. If the plating isn't pitting or flaking, they may be worth your effort. If, on the other hand, you see specks of plating coming off or little eruptions of the base metal on any parts, discard them and get replacements.

To remove the old finish, coat the entire front with a good paint stripper,

Wiper-pivot nipples slip on through cowl finisher. Wiper motor should be in "parked" position before installing wiper arms. If you're in doubt, hook up battery, turn on wiper motor, then turn it off. System will automatically go to the "parked" position.

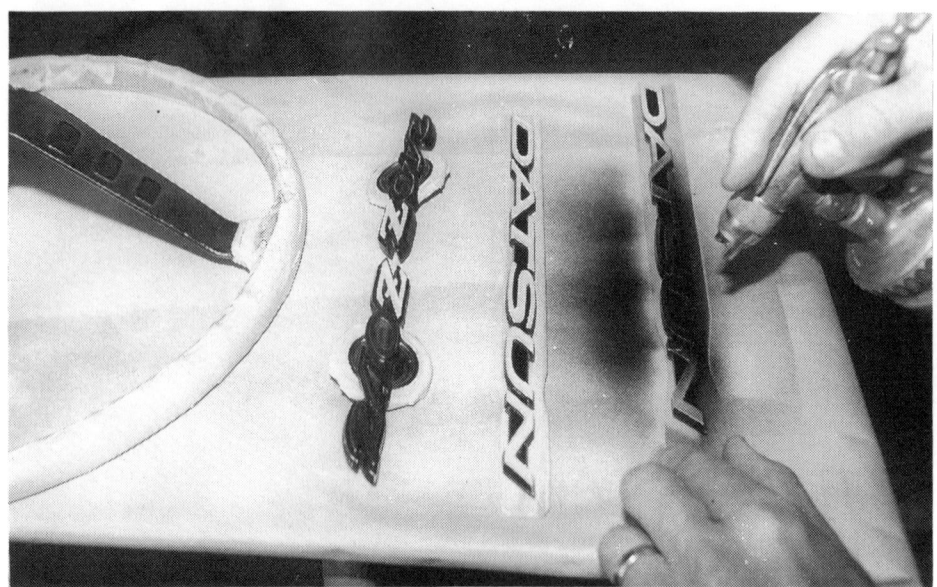

DATSUN logo has white letters as does the Z on 240Z trims and outer rings on circle background. To ease handling while painting, I mounted trim pieces to paint-stir sticks. Holes are drilled in sticks to match mounting pins. After spokes are painted matte black, early psuedo wood-grain steering-wheel rim is shot with clear lacquer.

Handling during assembly tends to put spider-web scratches on new paint, especially if it has already been buffed. I wait until just before it's time to install trim and emblems to rub-out surface with something like Liquid Ebony. Schlegel Round-up bonnet is less likely to burn or catch on edges. Splatter wipes up with a towel.

let it work and clean off with an old toothbrush. I particularly like using brass-bristle brushes like those sold at plumbing-supply stores—they won't damage the plating, but will remove any paint and wax that has accumulated in crevices. Plus, the bristles last much longer when used in chemicals. Rinse both sides of each piece with a stream of water. Use that stiff brush and detergent or cleanser to remove all stripper.

Wipe parts thoroughly and dry them with compressed air. Do they still look promising? Polish plating with very fine steel wool, using wooden matchsticks or toothpicks to get all those crannies and cracks.

Now, you must either mask and spray *or* hand brush the paint colors back on. Use 3M Fineline masking tape for places where 1/8- or 1/4-inch widths are useful. Otherwise the usual 3/4- or 1-1/2-inch-wide tape should be laid carefully over the entire emblem and the parts to be painted exposed by trimming the tape with a sharp X-acto knife. This is easier than it sounds because the edges of the chrome detail provide a guide for the tip of the knife blade. Plus, unless you are very careless, you won't damage the hard chrome plate. So use finesse and do a good job.

Matte Black is used on many Z trims. Ditzler Low-Gloss Black 19 DDL 9381 is good. Spray this on in several thin coats for good coverage and sticking power. Do white areas next—they are so small that white spray-can lacquer will suffice. Unmask and check for overspray. A bit of lacquer thinner on a piece of cotton T-shirt material stretched over a finger tip will remove most overspray. Use a Q-Tip swab or toothpick for really tight areas.

After you've let the parts dry overnight, apply a good paste wax for protection—unless it will present a problem for show judging on the low-gloss black or in inaccessible crannies. I use wax on street-driven cars because of the vulnerability to moisture and salt of scoured-up plating. Armor-All or some other protectant may do the job for you.

Your parts should now look new!
Hood Trim—Reinstall the **DATSUN** hood badge—on late 280Zs, the louver trims, also.

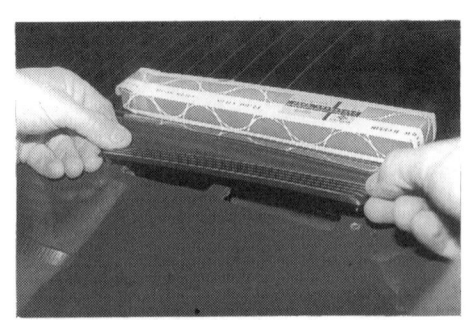

Early air-extractor grilles are plated plastic. New parts are fun to install! Note there should be no buffing-compound residue on trim or under edges.

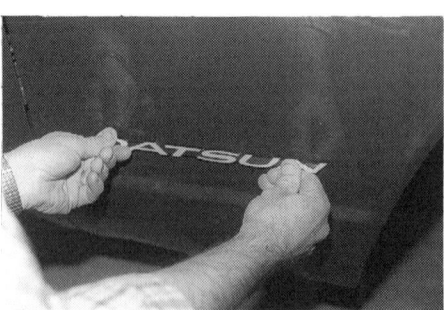

Most Z-car trims are held on with barrel clips pushed in holes in the body—these are available at most body and paint suppliers. They are worth the cost if your old attachments are the least bit doubtful.

Hatch Trim
Reinstall the chrome trim on the hatch deck with barrel clips. 240Zs and late 5-speeds have the most hatch trim.

Fender Trim
The 240Zs have **DATSUN** script in chromed-zinc trim; 260Zs and 280Zs use plated plastic. Replacement fenders are drilled for either type, but an extra hole is hidden. If yours has an unused hole, plug it with dumdum or weatherstrip cement to prevent road splash from running out from behind the emblems.

C-pillar Trim—Early 240Zs have their model designation here, but later cars have the vent-outlet trim. They install with barrel clips.

Tip: Trim for the early series, which is a nicely chromed-zinc piece, will interchange with the later plastic version. It looks spiffy.

Engine-Compartment Assembly & Detailing
MasterVac Hose
Run vacuum hose from vacuum tap on the intake manifold to the check valve, then from the valve to fitting on the MasterVac unit. Tighten clamps. Recheck in a few days because they'll relax after a while.

Radiator
Zs tended to overheat in hot weather, especially after accumulating some miles. The problem was compounded on early Zs equipped with aftermarket air conditioning. These retained the original two-core radiator—not a good way to ensure a cool-running engine.

Consider upgrading your car with a three-core late-type radiator if you are faced with an overheating problem or repairs are needed on the original two-core radiator. On the other hand, if you've had no problems before the teardown for this restoration, a good overhaul may be enough. Use only a shop with a good reputation for quality work. It pays in the long run.

Refinish radiator to match the original matte-black paint. Don't use too much paint. A radiator functions by rejecting heat to the air and excess paint buildup will inhibit heat conduction. Save those extra coats of enamel for the sheet metal. One good double coat is sufficient to cover all the bare metal, even on the tanks.

Use an industrial urethane enamel with a flattening agent.

Installation—Make sure the drain tap is in and tight. Carefully position the radiator and start the four screws. Take care not to smack the fan and bend radiator fins or scar any finish. When the radiator is square against its

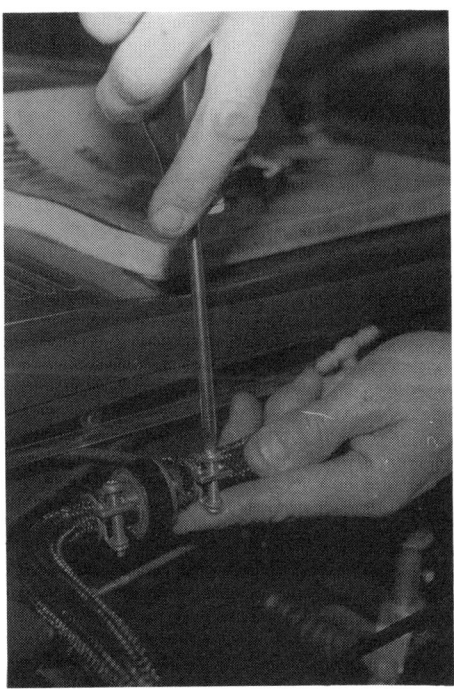

Installing original two-core radiator. Next, install fan shroud on cars so equipped.

Nylon aftermarket dress-up is reminiscent of original braiding on vacuum hoses. I scrounged nice wire-type clamps from my parts-car and Datsuns found in wrecking yards. Dipping in clear lacquer restores shine to clamps.

Fans: early metal at right and late plastic, left. Metal fan is more durable, but plastic one is lighter, thus easier on water-pump bearings. Their bolt patterns are common with viscous-drive hub, so all are interchangeable. Courtesy Motorsport Auto.

182 How to Restore Your Datsun Z-Car

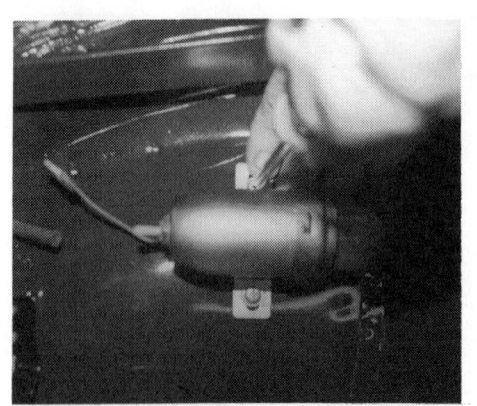

Trouble light, regulator and fuel-filter bracket are in place. Strut-tower hole caps go on next.

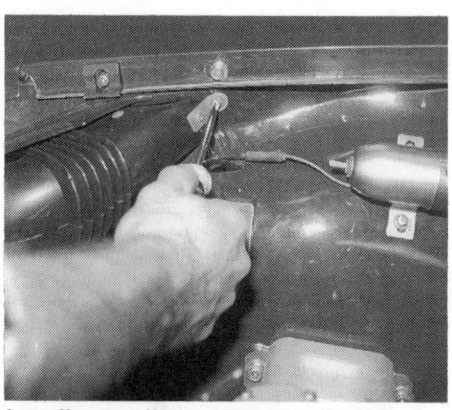

Install vent elbows. Some early fuel-injected cars had later-style snorkel routed to elbow opening and vent cable disabled by dealers.

Not everyone thought stock horns had a tone becoming a classy sports GT, but they're part of the car. Put them back on.

support, tighten bolts.

Put on the radiator hoses and tighten the clamps. Early Zs use braid-covered hose—new replacements are impossible to find, but the plain later style is a functional interchange. Slip-on braided-nylon covering will give a fair approximation of the original look. You can get this at automotive custom or performance shops.

Fan Shroud—On cars so equipped, reinstall the bottom and top halves and tighten all fasteners. This is another piece that is a functional addition to all Z-cars—it improves cooling.

Coolant—When all hoses are installed and tightly clamped, add at least a gallon of good-quality antifreeze. Top with clean water. Put the radiator cap on and start engine. After the thermostat opens, top the level again. Check all cooling-system joints for leaks, including heater core, valve and connections. Move the heater control to **HEAT** until the heater core and hoses are full of coolant. Feel both heater hoses. If they're warm, coolant is circulating through the core.

When bubbles cease to come up in the radiator tank, top it to about 1 inch below the neck—it needs some room to expand when hot. If so equipped, fill coolant-recovery bottle to the upper line. Put both caps on securely.

Don't scrimp on antifreeze coolant. This is a restoration, remember? Even in a moderate climate, a good commercial solution will prevent corrosion of the engine-cooling system materials and provide lubricant for the vulnerable Z water pump. It also increases the temperature at which the coolant will boil, so it improves the hot-weather performance of your engine's cooling system.

A/C Condenser
Remount this ahead of the radiator on its own brackets. Reconnect the refrigerant lines.

Vent Elbows
These simply push through their holes in the bulkhead and attach with one Phillips-head screw.

Horns
These can be disassembled and refinished or replated, but new horns are available. Reinstall them to the front crossmember and connect the wiring.

Hood-Support Rod
Remount bracket to the top of the bulkhead. If your car has the plastic retaining clip, reinstall it now. Snap rod into the clip.

Strut-Tower Caps
Snap one into each shock-absorber-nut access hole. They keep water out of the recess.

Windshield-reservoir assembly slips into bracket. Connect new plastic lines and electrical connections first.

Washer nozzles are next. Hook up plastic lines and elbow.

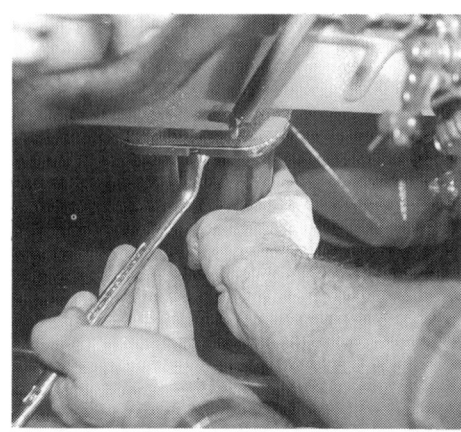

Fit exhaust-header pipes over studs at manifold. Everything should be new including studs, nuts and gasket.

Body Exterior & Drive Line Assembly 183

My Z's header pipe was fabricated at a muffler shop. It was custom fit, had no leaks and is guaranteed. Higher cost reflects labor cost. This is a good route to take because original systems are not available.

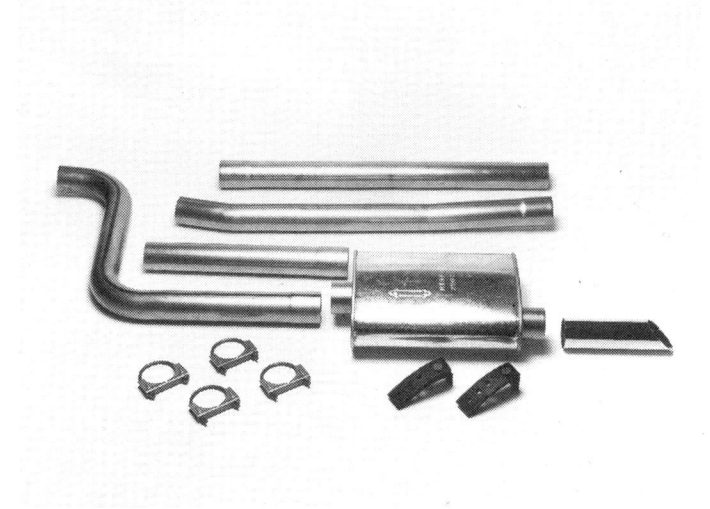

Mail-order tailpipe-and-muffler system: Pipe has large diameter and quality looks good. It has to be in this many pieces for shipping, requiring clamps for every joint. Original-style header pipe is also available to fit it. Courtesy Motorsport Auto.

Window Washer

Feed washer nozzles up through holes in the firewall and secure each with a Phillips-head screw. They should be positioned just below cowl finisher between the louvers. Adjust the spray pattern with needle-nose pliers after the washer nozzles are functional.

Measure and cut a new vinyl hose so it routes from the farther nozzle to the nearer. Attach to the tee and connect the tee to the near nozzle with a short section of hose. Then route another hose to where the washer motor will be when installed. Cut it to length and slip it over the motor tube.

Slip the windshield-washer tank-and-motor unit into the slot on the driver's side inner fender, but connect the motor electrical connections first. Fill and test the system.

Wiper Arms

With the cowl finisher in place, reinstall the windshield-wiper arms. If the rubber nipples that protect the shaft are cracked, replace them first. Then start the wiper motor and stop it so the shafts stop in the parked position.

If you put the arm onto the shaft splines in a chance relationship, you may find the wipers trying to remove paint from the cowl finisher the first time you turn them on. Position the arms carefully and mesh the splines.

Tighten the cap nuts. Replace the wipers, but check the rubber filler first for condition. Replace if necessary and secure to the wiper. Check the windshield-wipe pattern.

Exhaust System—Just about any kind of exhaust system is available for Z-cars—except perhaps one that is an authentic original. There are any number that sound better, flow better and perhaps look better, but it is unlikely even Nissan dealers stock exactly-as-produced pipes, mufflers, hangers or tips. The fact is the vast majority of Z-owners either accept or *prefer* a non-original system. Only if you will compete in concours d'elegance against another owner who somehow came up with a sound "stock" exhaust will your car suffer.

So what's my point? Simply this—choose and install the exhaust that suits your needs. A muffler shop can simulate stock resonators, catalytic convertors and mufflers with relative ease. Suppliers such as Motorsport Auto, Bob Sharp Racing, Z Accessory Products and Nissan Motorsports Department can supply complete systems in kit form that should fill any need. If you are in doubt as to which of these to run, consult *How to Modify Your Nissan/Datsun OHC Engine* by Frank Honsowetz.

Be sure the exhaust-manifold studs and nuts are serviceable. I use new parts whenever possible—they are murder to change after everything is assembled if a stud breaks or threads strip. Use a new gasket. Install the resonator, converter and hangers. Route the tailpipe aft and install the muffler.

Check all hangers and shake the system to be sure it doesn't strike any underbody or suspension components. Make sure you reinstall any heat shields originally used. Position end of the muffler extension almost even with the rear face of the bumper. This will help prevent the exhaust gasses from getting on the bumper and discoloring or corroding the plating.

Jim gets muffler (a non-original "turbo") just right, then finishes welding all joints. I jury-rigged old system just to get it from my shop to his.

184 How to Restore Your Datsun Z-Car

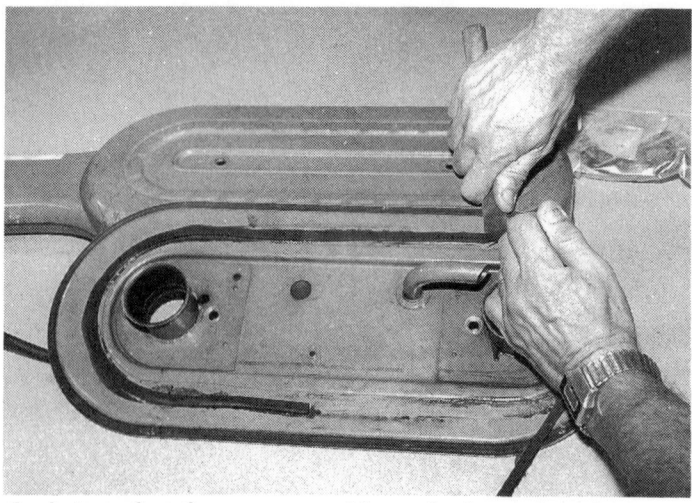

Gaskets and seals are removed from air-cleaner housing. New seals may have to be fabricated if old ones aren't serviceable.

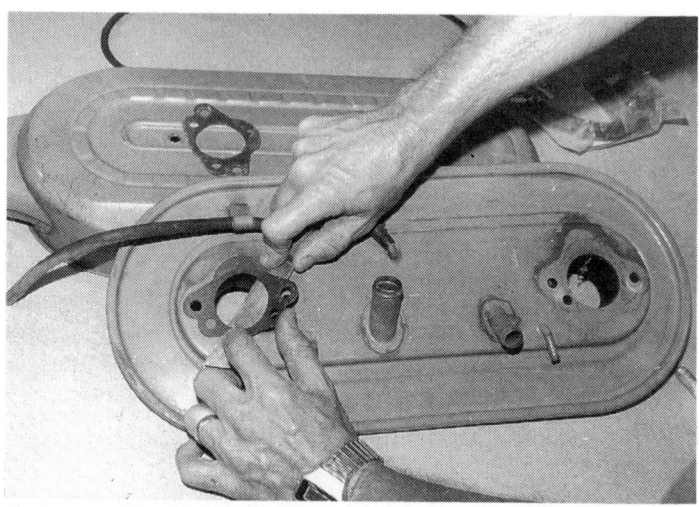

Stripper will take off old adhesive, sealer, paint and decals. Housing is primered before it can be painted just like any metal part.

Weatherstrip adhesive is ideal to secure seal strips. Tape ends until cement cures.

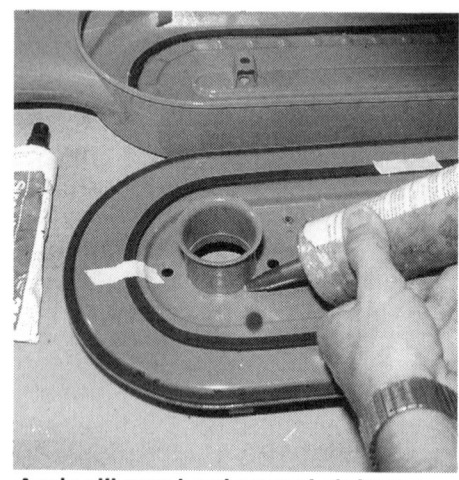

Apply silicone bead around air horn. Late carburetor air cleaners have more ducts, a flapper valve and related hardware. Air-cleaner housings for fuel-injection can be restored using the same procedures.

Battery Tray, Retainer & Cables
Reinstall these electrical parts and any other wiring you have. I hope all connectors are still labeled. Secure all loose cables and harnesses.

Battery
Clean terminals and charge the battery to capacity. I always use corrosion-preventive felt washers under the cables. Anti-corrosion spray also works well, but be careful not to get overspray where it's not wanted.

Air Cleaner
On carbureted Zs, install the air-cleaner base to the carb flanges. Don't overtighten any screws on the carburetors—their threads are easy to strip. Put a new filter element in the cover and install it with the wing bolts. Hook up all fuel, emissions and vacuum hoses.

On fuel-injected Zs, route hose from the airflow meter to the air cleaner. Bolt air cleaner to the radiator support. Install air-cleaner snorkel and tighten all clamps. Put a new filter element into the housing and latch it.

Differential & Standard Transmission
With the car level, check lubricant levels in both. Make sure the drain

Air-cleaner base attaches to carburetor flanges. Don't overtighten bolts! Note restored smog pump (lower left) and labyrinth of hoses and gadgets. Who would ever have thought emissions-controlled cars would be restored!

Body Exterior & Drive Line Assembly 185

Brake-shoe adjustment is done through hole in side of drum. When you're finished, replace plug.

Bleeding starts with at rear brake farthest from master cylinder. For a left-hand-drive Z, this means the right-rear brake. You'll need a helper, someone to pump brake pedal while you open and close bleeder. Immerse hose end in clear, clean jar containing clean fluid. This will keep air from being drawn back into lines. Check level in reservoir. Don't let it run dry and suck air. Finish the right, then move to the left wheel. Front is separate system, bleeds similarly. Note: If you're using it for the first time you may notice that silicone fluid is more difficult to bleed. This is because of its higher viscosity.

plugs are in and tight. If they were drained completely, recheck fluid levels after the first test drive.

Automatic Transmission
Engine has to be running to check the transmission-fluid level. Don't overfill it.

Bleed Hydraulic Systems
Brake Master Cylinder—You must fill and bleed the entire brake system, both front and rear before car is moved.

Start by shutting all bleeder taps, then open them very slightly. Fill both reservoirs, replace the lids and pump brake a few strokes. Top reservoirs with fluid and repeat the process until you get signs of fluid at a bleeder tap.

Start bleeding the wheel farthest from the master cylinders. With a left-hand-drive, this would be the right rear wheel. But first, tighten the other bleeders. Don't let the fluid level get too low in the reservoir or you'll just pump in more air.

Push a 12-inch piece of clear-vinyl hose over the bleeder and stick the other end in a clean, clear glass or plastic jar or bottle that has an inch or so of clean fluid in it. Position the hose end below the level of the fluid in the catch jar. This does two things: Lets you see when air ceases to flow from the system as the brake pedal is pushed down. And it prevents air from being drawn back into the system on the backstroke if you don't get the bleeder shut first.

When bubbles no longer appear, close the bleeder and repeat the process on the opposite wheel. Then repeat the process at the front.

When you finish bleeding the last wheel, push the brake pedal down hard and hold it. Do you have too much travel or a spongy pedal? If so, check rear-brake adjustment. If they are OK, you may have more bleeding to do. Once you have a "hard" pedal, make sure all bleeders are tight, inspect all flare connectors, junction blocks, the proportioning valve and hoses for leaks. Did you forget to replace or tighten any joints or plugs? Better to get fluid on the garage floor than on the road at the end of the block!

Try several hard stops in your drive before you road test the car. Proceed carefully until you are confident the system is sound.

Clutch Cylinder—Shut, then slightly reopen the bleeder tap on the clutch slave cylinder. Fill the master-cylinder reservoir and replace the lid. Pump the clutch pedal a few strokes until there is a sign of fluid at the bleeder. Put a hose on the bleeder and pump the air from the line and hose. Check fluid level in the reservoir and replenish if necessary. When no more air

Filling clutch master cylinder with silicone fluid. Slave cylinder is bled the same as wheel cylinders, but there's only one. After bleeding, adjust pushrod to get positive clutch release and free-play.

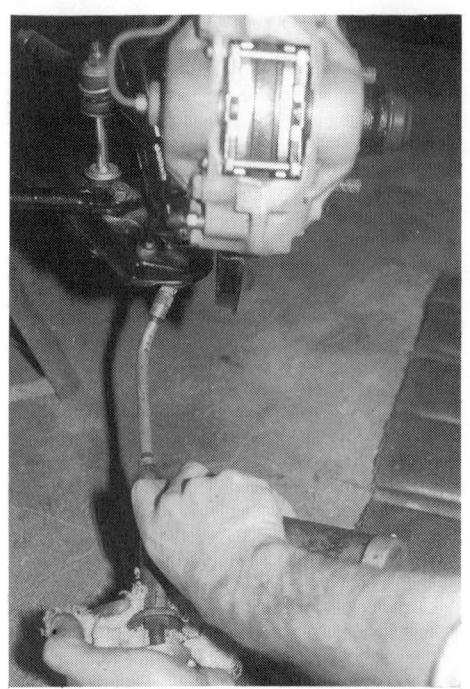

Restored Z needs to be greased before it turns a wheel. Give each zerk fitting a shot of grease and wipe up any excess that will collect dirt—again.

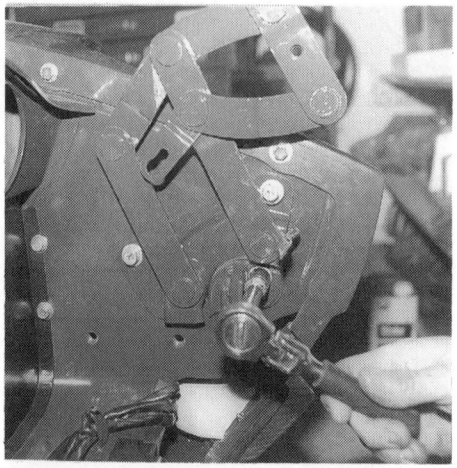

Remount hood hinges, but leave them loose so they'll move. I succumbed to the temptation of leaving fasteners bright. Datsun painted over both hinge- and fender-bolt heads.

First torsion rod slips into anchor. This rod loads right hinge.

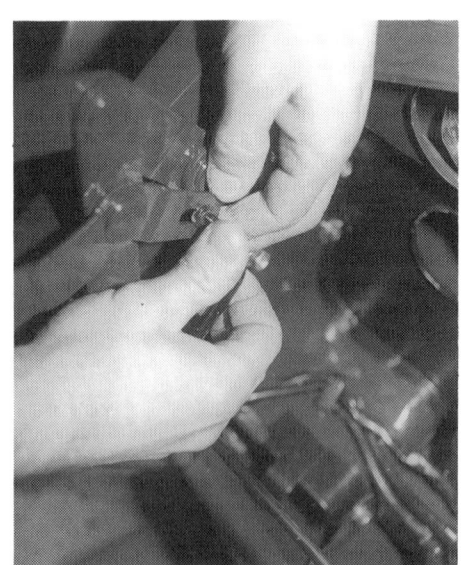

This end with nail-like head slips into keyhole-shape slot in short linkage. Install other torsion bar.

bubbles are evident at the bleeder, shut the tap.

Check slave-cylinder-pushrod travel—a full stroke should disengage the clutch fully. With the car running, put the transmission in gear and determine whether the clutch engages and disengages. Adjustment should be available on the pushrod. If lengthening doesn't rectify a dragging clutch, you may have to bleed the system again. A too-short adjustment may cause the clutch to slip under full power.

Grease Fittings

Remember to grease all zerk fittings before you use the car. Even factory new ball-joints, steering tie-rod ends and U-joints need to be "topped up" with lubricant. Don't overdo the grease. Wipe off excess grease before it collects dirt.

Install Hood

Hood Latch—Position latch where it originally fit. Run the bolts in finger-tight.

You have an advantage if you are remounting original body parts and scribed around the hinges, mountings and so forth. On my restoration, I installed a new fender and hatch from another car. Add to this a stripping and refinishing job so complete that virtually no original paint was left. So premarking these components would've been meaningless.

Hood Hinge—Remount both hinge mechanisms with the three bolts, but leave them very loose. Put the L-shape end of one torsion rod through the oval slot in the bottom of the hinge mount. The L fits up into the notch in the hat-section bracket.

The opposite end with a nail-head tip fits into the upper slot. This is the deeper of the two. Bend rod to the rear and mate the tip with large slotted hole in the short link. Release slack until the tip seats into the narrow slot. Install the other rod. The torsion bars should now load both hood-hinge mechanisms in the open positions. Run bolts down almost tight.

Hood Bumpers—These rubber-cushioned adjusters thread into the cowl area. Run them all the way down for now.

Hood—If you've ever needed a helper, now's the time. The second, alternative (which I don't recommend), is to suspend hood from above while you lift and position it. Place hood against the hinges and run the bolts down finger-tight. The hinges will now support the hood.

Shut hood gently while watching the edges for interference or gross misalignment. Let the two latch parts meet and determine if the tongue and striker will mate correctly. There is some adjustment in both.

Compensate for fore-aft and high-low hood adjustment at the front attachment. With grille still out of the way, you can use a socket to loosen or tighten these bolts to manipulate hood position. Sight across front corners of the headlight bezels to determine these adjustments. A bad job here will be obvious. When adjustment at the front is satisfactory, check rear edge. Because the cowl finisher can't be moved, a too-close relationship will have to be rectified at the hinges.

Determine how low the rear hood bumpers are and run them back up until they contact the hood at both corners. If the hood is too low, raise the bumper(s) on the low side(s) until the hood aligns with the cowl finisher and fenders. Tighten the bumper locknuts when you are satisfied with adjustment. If the rear of the hood is too high, use a screwdriver to thread the hood striker in to allow it to latch lower. While you are at it, make sure the hood-latch release works smoothly and positively.

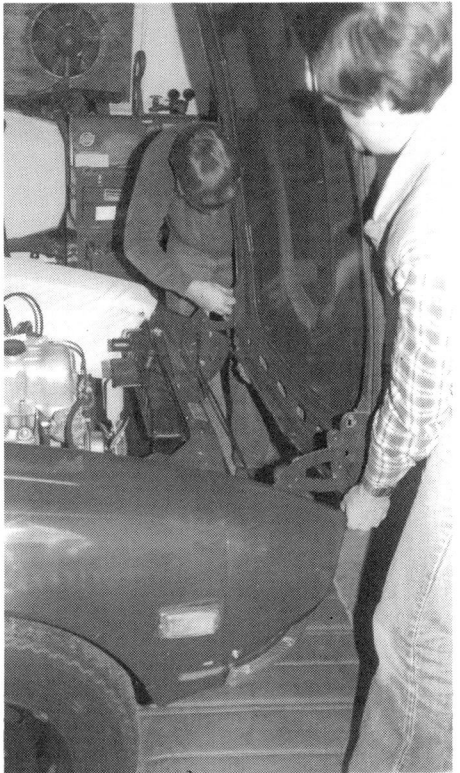

Grille

Restore—North American spec Zs had a very tasteful grille of steel slats assembled with long through-bolts and rivets. Although your grille may not require restoration, it is relatively easy if it's not too badly damaged.

The finish is enamel, the same as on the rear finisher on early Zs; matte gray-black on late versions. This first step is to remove the finish, either by stripping chemically or sandblasting. Be sure you get all paint off. And if there's rust, remove it down to sound metal.

You may want to dismantle the grille into its separate parts before or after stripping. Remove the fasteners that hold the slats, uprights and brackets together. Check each part for residual paint, stripper, rust or damage. If any slats are bent, they can often be straightened with some hammer-and-dolly work.

Primer each part, spot fill any pits and block-sand them. Then reassemble the grille bars and uprights using 3/16-inch rivets in place of the originals. Have a 3/16-inch drill bit and motor handy in case you have to enlarge the rivet holes. Double-check alignment and tighten everything. On the 280Z, you will have both upper and lower grilles to deal with.

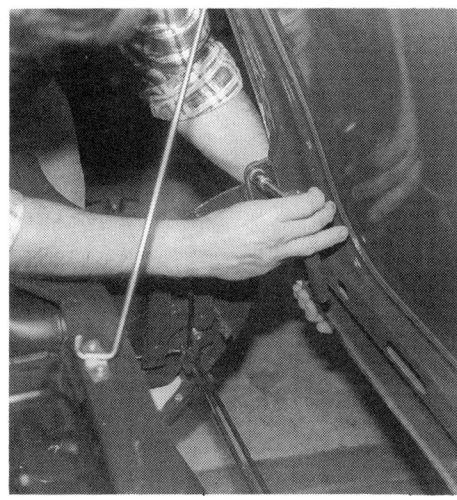

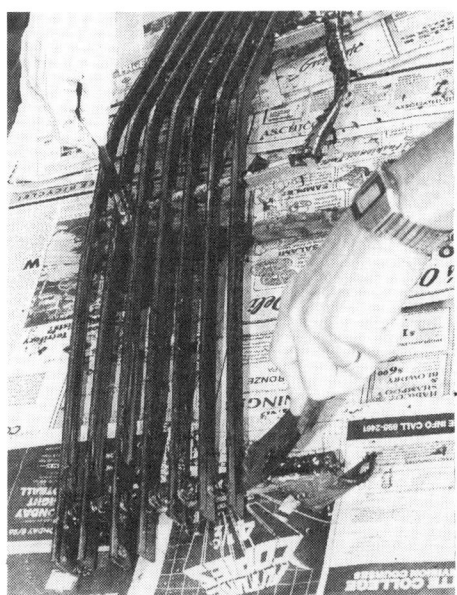

With all bolts started and hood support helping, align hood. Adjusting hood alignment is strictly a trial-and-error job. Don't forget that bumpers in cowl area and along fender lip provide adjustment, too.

Easy does it with installing the refinished hood. Use a helper to install this awkward-to-handle piece of sheet metal.

Stripper should be liberally applied. Grille has lots of crannies to clean out, disassembled or not.

Grille bar was bent, stretched slightly. Clamped against strip of bar stock in vise, it is heated and lightly hammered to shrink stretch area. Filler won't improve appearance of bent bar.

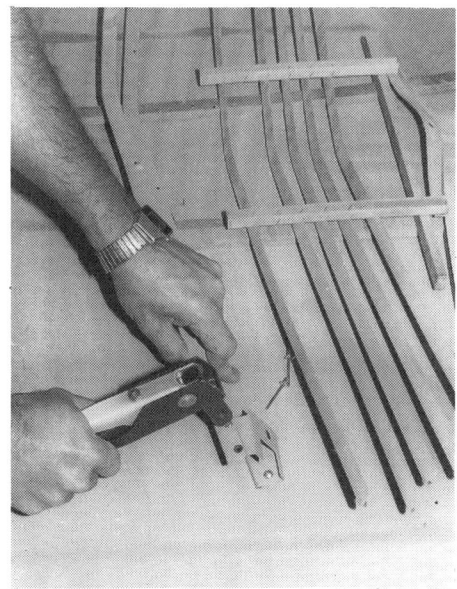

Primered grille parts must be carefully reassembled before painting. Rivets are easy to replace.

Trued-up and long screws tightened, grille assembly can be painted. Rear was done first from all angles to get those tight-in spots. Then front gets a good pattern of same paint as used on rear finisher. Late grilles take matte black.

Grille for early car is one piece. Late style has lights and bezels in upper section; smaller grille goes in apron.

Repaint grille, spraying it from all angles to ensure full paint coverage. By waiting until it is reassembled, you will avoid damaging the paint while fitting slats into the uprights and so forth.

Install Grille

Early Zs: With the hood open, position grille over its mounting points and thread in two screws. Shut hood and start the other screws. There is quite a bit of adjustment at the mounting points, and the supports can be bent to improve access to the screws or align the grille. Shut hood and recheck grille alignment. Loosen it and readjust as needed.

Late Zs: Mount lower grille section loosely. Remount large upper section, but don't tighten until it is aligned.

Install park-turn lights and their housings in the grille. Tighten the screws, first on the upper grille, then with a good eyeball alignment, the lower grille.

Bumpers

Early Bumpers—240Z and early 260Z—is simple compared to the later style. Although these are uncomplicated, light and attractive, they don't provide much protection. The later bumpers and mountings—late 260Z and 280Z—are heavier, but do a better job of protecting the bodywork.

General procedures for handling, positioning and protecting the body finish are applicable to all Z bumpers for the most part. Use common sense and care.

Front-Bumper Installation—There are several places where the bumper can damage body paint. To protect against chips and scratches, pad rear edges of the bar with masking tape or shop towels. And a helper will be very useful when installing them.

With the two bumper mounts loosely nutted to the bar assembly and rubber end-bracket protectors on, carefully ease the bumper into the grille cavity. Start in bolts that hold mounts to the front body.

Back off and check fit and align-

Early bumper is light enough for one person to handle. Check clearance between hood and bumper guards. North American Zs are the only ones with bumper guards.

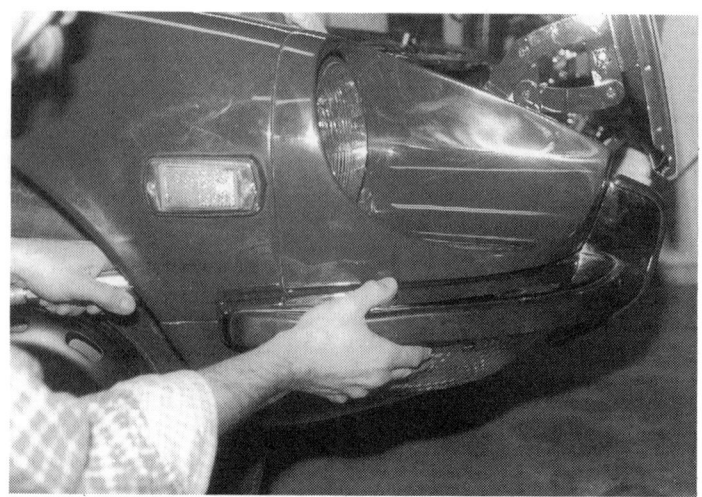

Air ratchet is a big help when only one hand is free.

Body Exterior & Drive Line Assembly

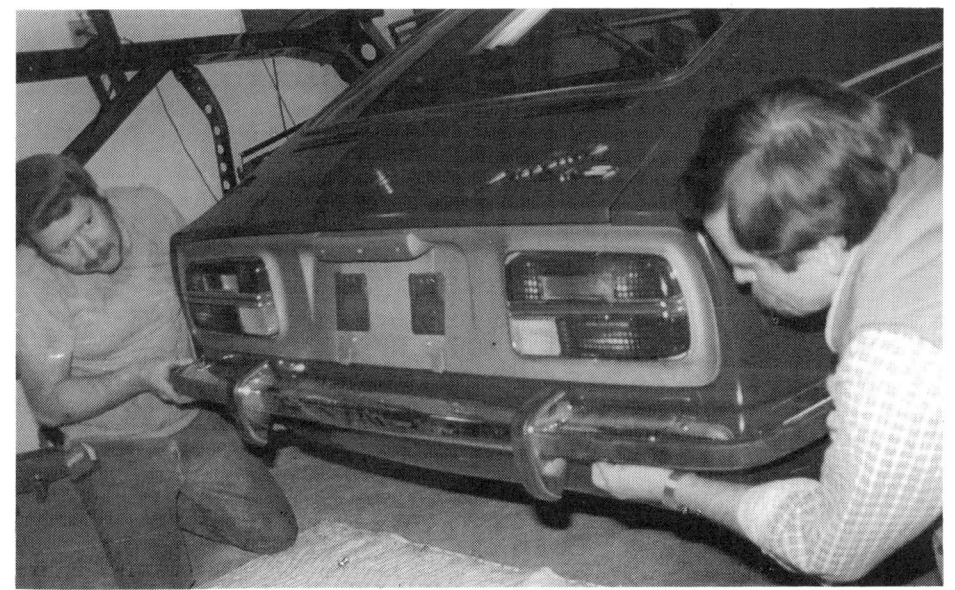

Rear bumper is more cumbersome—enlist help. Only one tow-hook came on this car. It mounted to bumper bolt on passenger's side.

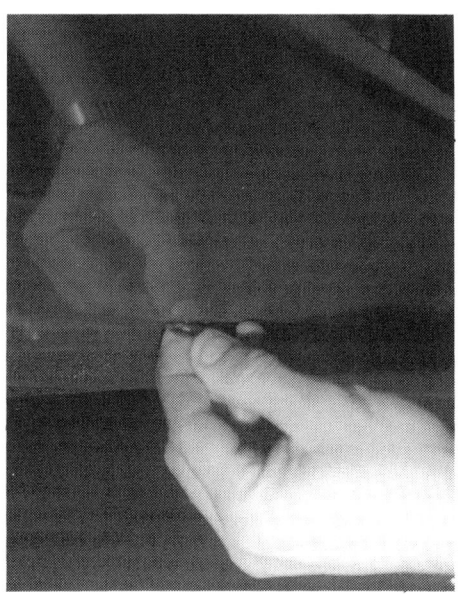

Small rubber plugs go into bottom of rocker panels. Make a visual check of entire underbody to be sure no holes have been left open.

ment. Not much adjustment is available, but now's the time to be sure there's as much clearance between the bumper/guards and body proper as possible. With this established, thread in the bolts to the end attachments. When you have the ends horizontal to the body lines, tighten bolts at the mounts and finally at the end brackets.

Carefully open hood, watching its relationship to the bumper-guard tops. If clearance seems adequate, rock hood forward against the hinge stops while looking to make sure the hood won't clip the guards.

Rear Installation—With the mounting brackets nutted loosely to the bumper bar and the end-bracket protectors on, carefully position bumper against the mounting pads on the rear pan. Start two bolts while holding the ends away from the finish. Start the two bolts that hold the end brackets.

Add towing hooks to the other rear bolts and start these in also—all bolts may be finger-tight. Then step back and check alignment, especially at the ends. If satisfactory, tighten all bolts.

Install Late Bumpers—Install energy-absorbing units (shocks) to the body structure, but don't tighten the bolts yet. Position bumper brackets on the shocks and start the nuts. Align both end mountings and start the bolts. Check the bumper for alignment and tighten the fasteners, working from the body out.

"Standard heights" quoted in the Service Manual are mainly for the Fed's bumper standards. They also reflect car ride height.

Install Rear Bumper—Replace the rear shock absorbers to the body by reinstalling the acorn nuts and bolts in the deck floorpan. Install the end brackets. Reinstall the filler panel to the rear body. Position bumper brackets on the shocks, but don't tighten the nuts. Also start the end-bracket bolts. Check for alignment and tighten the fasteners from the body out.

Early Shock-Mounted—These are characterized primarily by their metal end sections.

Late Shock-Mounted Bumpers—These are characterized primarily by their heavy rubber ends.

Front Installation—Reinstall the metal filler and shock covers. Install the shocks, then the bumper bar. Shims fit between the shocks and bar. Install the rubber ends to the bar and fender. Align and tighten all fasteners. Replace the rubber plugs in the ends.

Rear-Bumper Installation—Replace the shock absorbers as above. Reinstall the filler panel. Position and attach the bumper bar—don't forget shims. Replace the tie-down hooks. Install the rubber ends to the bar and body. Align and tighten all fasteners. Replace the rubber plugs.

As described in Chapter 3, two types of bumpers evolved after the Federal impact standards went into effect. Both were shock-mounted and required plastic filler panels due to the extra distance between the bumpers and body. Restoration procedures are essentially the same as with the early style. The metal should be straightened and replated. Replace the rubber parts if worn.

The Service Manual has performance specifications for the shock absorbers—replacement is the only fix for sub-par shocks. Brackets and hardware can be repainted, of course. Filler panels that are body color should be refinished with the body, however you must add a flex agent to paint shot onto these. Flex agent prevents cracking and peeling.

The additional weight of these bumpers requires either a helper or a tire-shop-type bumper jack to position them. Again take precautions against damaging body finish.

Rubber Plugs

Z-cars have a lot of various-size plugs in the floor area. Reinstall these before you install the carpet. I use new plugs and lighty coat the

190 How to Restore Your Datsun Z-Car

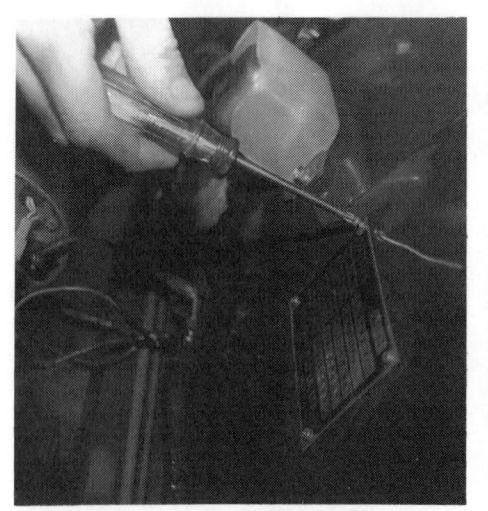

Data plate is the finishing touch to a detailed engine compartment. After 1972, it was mounted on the driver's side hood-ledge panel.

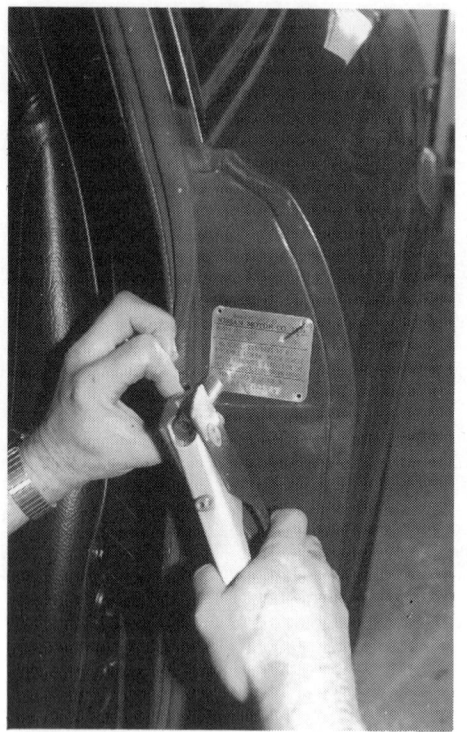

Carefully rivet vehicle identification number (VIN) plate to driver's door jamb. Unpulled rivet holds plate in position while other one is "popped." Without the loose rivet in place, plate will "walk" toward pulled rivet, moving remaining three holes out of alignment.

Stock Z-car steel wheels with tires mounted so whitewalls are on inside. Earliest rim started out silver, then was oversprayed matte black on outer side.

flange with clear-silicone sealer. This makes the plug slip into the hole more easily and provides a secure seal. Excess sealer should be wiped off with a clean cloth.

Don't forget the two drain holes in the bottom of each rocker panel, just outside the weld flange. These need plugs.

Plates

Data Plate—Reinstall the data plate with its Phillips-head screws. Early cars had this on the passenger's side front-strut tower. On later cars, this plate is on the driver's side of the engine compartment.

Vehicle Identification Number (VIN) Plate—This goes on the driver's door jamb. Mount it with 1/8-inch Pop Rivets. You may have to ream the holes with a drill bit because Japanese metric rivets are slightly smaller than 1/8 inch. Also, paint on the lip of the hole makes it tighter. Hold one corner with a loose rivet to prevent plate from "walking" away from the other holes while you *pull* one in the diagonally opposite corner.

Decals

If you weren't able to save your original decals and stickers, the only source of supply at this writing is the musty back shelves of your local dealer. When demand becomes sufficient for someone to reproduce them, they'll become available. There were quite a number of these under the Z-car's hood, air filter, radiator, inner fenders and assorted supplier's components. None were particularly adrenalin-pumping—like those found under the hood of a Shelby or other supercar—but they would be considered the finishing touch for a restored Z.

Steel Wheels

Two sizes of stamped-steel wheels were originally installed on Z-cars. Early cars have 4-1/2J-14 wheels, later ones got the 5J-14—a 1/2-inch increase in width. All have four lug holes and nine brake-cooling slots. These look a lot alike, but the centers are not identical. But the two wheels interchange with no problems because 1/2-inch-width difference is not much! Home-market Zs were offered with aluminum-alloy "mags," but no cars exported to North America had anything but plain-vanilla steel rims until the last of the 280Zs.

Restoring wheels involves only stripping and derusting, then refinishing to original specs. I dismount the tire and thoroughly sandblast the wheel, then spot-putty any visible pits. A good coat of primer-surfacer will determine whether further sanding or spot-priming is necessary.

For a really top-notch appearance, I paint the rims *after* mounting the rubber. However, to prevent rust I always paint the *drop center*—section between the flanges that is covered by the tire—with the final finish before mounting the tire. Then the tire can be masked. A quick wet-sanding with

320-grit wet-or-dry paper smoothes any mars from the mounter's tools and cleans up the surface. Wipe with wax and grease remover and mask the rubber. This sounds like a lot of work—and it is. But nothing else will suffice for that really super look a restoration demands.

Datsun may have used the 1600-2000 Roadster wheel on early Zs—the inside is silver and the outside was oversprayed matte black. A bit later they went to gloss black on the inside, with some having a lower gloss on the outside face. Who knows why— and in most instances, who cares? Use an enamel paint on wheels for durability. Have them balanced on the car later using new wheel weights.

Aluminum Wheels

Toward the end of the 280Z model run, Datsun introduced a true aluminum-alloy wheel. The ZX series was introduced midyear in 1978, abbreviating that last year's 280Z model run. The new wheel was of course more heavily identified with that car. It required its own chrome acorn lug nuts with a washer to protect and seat against the aluminum.

These were coated with clear epoxy that suffered yellowing and deterioration from weather and direct sun. Datsun recommended having the clear coat removed by stripping or polishing and respraying with an acrylic clear.

What did everyone do with those early wheel covers? Here are some rare mint-condition originals. Dad's helper is ready to go for a Z-ride.

Wheel Covers

Datsun installed three distinctly different types of wheel covers on Z-cars for North America. All vaguely simulated a "mag" type wheel. The first style was stamped steel with a bright rim and center cone, featuring a textured medallion with the corporate **D** in the center. These are not particularly plentiful in good condition—possibly because they didn't do much to enhance the Z's sporting image. Consequently, dealers and owners cast them aside—along with the narrow wheels—in favor of aftermarket alloy wheels by the hundreds. There must be any number of these covers in mint condition hanging on garage walls or in dealer's attics across the country.

Starting with the 1972 240Z and continuing up through the 1976 280Z was the second-style metal wheel cover. This carried the five-spoke look further with five indented scallops. It featured a center medallion with the Z monogram—perhaps a bit sportier than the first type. Both of these caps followed the "disc" school of design and didn't do more than hint at functionality.

The final 280Z cover was the more attractive simulated "mag" style made of silver plastic with a polished-metal rim. They also had a center cone with the Z logo and featured four holes for access to the chrome acorn-style lug nuts. This necessitated a four-spoke design as opposed to the earlier five-spoke style. Either this design was much more to the liking of buyers or they had absorbed all the California slot-mag rims they wanted. These covers are often seen on 280Z cars.

The first two types can be restored if the plating isn't too far gone. The gray textured area is just paint and is similar, if not identical, to that used on the back-panel finisher, page 173. Medallions can be removed from one cap and swapped to another if good examples can be found.

The 1977—78 style can be repainted as well if the trim ring is removed and the plastic thoroughly cleaned and prepped. Any metallic-silver enamel will do. Ask the counterman for "Corvette Silver" if you want to act knowledgeable. Be careful with the center caps, they break easily.

In addition to the 280Z aluminum wheels, at least two other identifiable aluminum-alloy wheels were produced for the Japanese domestic market. Though one type was offered on European 260Zs, they are seldom if ever seen in North America.

192 How to Restore Your Datsun Z-Car

Author's completed restoration as it appears today (left) and as he envisioned it in 1970 (below).

Z

11 Technical Bulletins, Hi-Lights & Recalls

At the end of each section, Datsun Service Manuals have a "blank" page headed **Service Journal** or **Bulletin Reference**. Dealer service departments use this is page to index various updates and revisions the Nissan Motor Corporation Technical Communications Department distributes to them.

If you have a Service Manual, you may wonder what pertinent information you are missing that is only available to genuine Datsun shop facilities. After all, shouldn't an owner who does his own maintenance and servicing be privy to accurate and complete technical information to do the job right? I have experienced this frustration and suppose many other Z-car owners have. In this section I include a digest of these bulletins, grouped as to the general areas where they apply.

The combined bulletins Nissan supplies to dealers fill several books the size of this one, even omitting items that concern other than Z-cars. So in the interest of reasonable brevity, I selected, condensed and abbreviated where possible. I include some items that concern only *running changes*—made within a model year—that might affect questions of authenticity on a restoration. Although this book does not cover drive-train concerns directly, I include references from the bulletins to these areas in this section for the sake of completeness.

Recalls
Like all auto manufacturers, Datsun has conducted various Recall Campaigns on its products over the years. A number of these involved the Z-car. I include a few significant ones. These inclusions are as complete and accurate as possible based on my research.

The information adapted here is courtesy of Nissan Motor Corporation in the U.S.A. Illustrations from their publications are used with their permission.

Headlight-Bulb Failure
This was due to moisture in rear of sealed-beam plug. Midway through the 240Z run, it was discovered that water, slush and often road salt found their way into the headlight buckets through the wiring opening. This caused some sockets to short out at the sealed-beam-unit plug. Bulb failure was the result in many cases, especially where salt was used on roads in winter.

Datsun supplied a rubber protector to seal the opening. Recommended procedure was to remove the assembly by taking out the four screws from the back and unclipping the wiring group from the fender panel. Then, without disturbing the aiming screws, loosen the three retaining screws and remove the retaining ring, then the headlight.

After unplugging the receptacle from the bulb, thoroughly clean the three male plugs to provide for adequate electrical contact. Push the rubber protector snugly over the three prongs so the crown of the protector rests tightly against its stop. Then reconnect the receptacle after you've made sure it's clean and reassemble the unit. This procedure was also specified for the 510 series.

Fuel-Pump Leaks (some 240Zs and 260Zs)
A possible fire hazard was the result of gasoline leaking from around the top cover of almost 63,000 Z-cars. Fuel-pump covers made of zinc were susceptible to distortion from high underhood temperatures. The top cover, held with five screws, could cease to seal fuel under pressure.

To determine if your car might still have the deficient pump, first check for a daub of red paint on the cover. This is the good one. If none is apparent, it may have been obliterated. So check the part number on the pump. It's on the side facing rearwards.

Part-number 17010 N3601 or 17010 E4104 has a non-distorting aluminum cover. Part-number 17010 N3600 or 17010 E4103 was equipped with the faulty zinc cover, but may have been retrofitted in the original recall. The part number of the aluminum cover is 17016 N3300, but it may not be on the cover.

The manufacturer included a new gasket, part number 17076 21016, in the fix kit and recommended the screws be tightened with a factory tool, torque screwdriver ST25160000. The screws are sequentially torqued in steps of 20, 30 and then 35 in-lb in a crisscross pattern.

Gasoline Seepage
Another fuel-related recall covered almost 32,000 fuel-injected 1975 280Zs, serial numbers HLS30-200001 through -225319 and GLS30-00001 through -007045. These were manufactured between Dec. 1, 1974 and August 31, 1975.

Datsun conducted a thorough retrofix campaign on cars sold and serviced by their dealers at no cost to the owner. Many private shops undoubtedly spotted the defect, but there might be a few Zs without it. For authenticity's sake, the parts involved should be considered original equipment. A decal documenting the fix should have been affixed to the underside of the hood on the upper left corner of the driver's side.

Fuel seeping from swaged metal clamps on the fuel-injection system constituted a potential fire hazard in the engine compartment. The original clamped joints tended to deform on tightening during maintenance according to the recall bulletin, allowing fuel wetting of the hoses near the joints. Datsun recommended changing the injection-system hoses every 25,000 miles, so the recall only hastened the process for those who followed factory recommendations to the letter.

A fuel-hose kit was supplied, which included all hoses, clamps and injector O-rings required to do the job on all injected L28s. Parts numbers are as follows:

1975-to eng. no. L28-024705	16448-N4307
1975-from eng. no. L28-024706	16448-N4306
1976	16448-N4317
1977	16448-N4705
1978	16448-N7616

An additional six clamps were required for the 1975 model up to serial number HLS30-217904 and GLS30-0055400. (Note: Don't confuse these with the engine numbers listed above.) Hose kits were carried under different numbers for the 280ZX and 810 models.

Briefly, the modification involved changing most or all of the underhood fuel-delivery hoses and adding hose clamps. Two types of clamps were specified. Most were the familiar aviation-type clamp, which uses a slotted strap and wormscrew.

On the injector itself, if originally fitted with the swaged-type hose ends, a Bosch-type clamp was specified. Narrower than the aviation variety, it positively secured the hose behind the shoulder of the swaged-type fitting. Injectors using barbed, Christmas-tree-type fittings did not need a clamp at that end.

Hoses that supplied or connected the injectors, fuel pipes, pressure regulator, fuel filter, cold-start valve and fuel-return line were to be removed and replaced. The bulletin recommends injectors be removed from the engine and the swaged-type fitting ground off with a suitable grinding wheel or file. It cautions not to clamp the injector in a vise or let the grinder scratch or overheat the injector itself. The injector should be protected from chip debris and checked carefully for cleanliness before reinstallation. When all connections are finished, the system should be checked for tightness. Any further seepage was to be eliminated by tightening the clamps.

Exhaust Leak

A minor problem on the 1977 Nissan line, which include 61,965 280Zs, was an exhaust fitting on the back-pressure transducer (BPT) valve that loosened. This device is part of the exhaust-gas-recirculation (EGR) system. Serial numbers for this recall include HLS30-350001 through HLS30-410516 and GHLS30-060001 through 102141.

Exhaust back pressure is monitored by the BPT valve. If the weld holding the exhaust fitting fails, the valve will not work. This can keep the car from passing emissions tests. The leak was not considered to be serious even though a small amount of exhaust gas may escape.

A spring clip was deemed sufficient to remedy a loosened fitting as long as the valve body was not damaged by leaking gasses. This clip is part number 14741-H8216 for Z-car applications. All BPT valves in stock were to have the clip installed. Attachment of fittings on later valves were upgraded by the supplier.

For valves on which the fitting is tight, install the clip. Otherwise the valve should be removed for inspection to determine if it should be replaced. A decal applied next to the emission-control-information label indicates the car was retrofitted by a dealer under the recall.

High-Idle Problems

This was due to moisture and blow-by mist in the PCV system. Some 218,930 280Zs may have been affected by accumulation of these contaminants in the air regulator during very cold weather, especially if warm-up time was short. Serial numbers from HLS30-200001 through HLS30-470008 and GHLS30-000001 through GHLS30-124741 are susceptible to this problem as well as other Datsun OHC six-cylinder cars.

The problem involved a sticking throttle-valve shaft in the throttle chamber. The throttle-shaft seal areas were cleaned with STP Carb Spray Cleaner, then tested for sticking by substituting a lower-tension return spring. If following the specified test procedure throttle-shaft action was not free enough to allow a smooth return to the idle position, it was replaced by Datsun.

Some cars required the replacement of the air regulator if they tested defective due to positive crankcase ventilation (PCV) malfunction. No repair procedure was specified for the air regulator.

Modifications to the PCV system included replacing the valve and modifying the air duct between the air-flow meter and throttle chamber. A new hose fitting and hose were used to route blow-by from the cam cover directly to the air duct on 1975, 1976 and 1977 models pre-HLS30-388607 or GHLS30-072195. Cars after these serial numbers used a modified routing instead of retrofitting.

Four separate kits were issued by Datsun, two of which were applicable to Zs. Kit C was spec'd for early 1977 and previous cars; Kit D for late '77 and later applications. A decal indicating the fix was made should be installed on the underside of the hood near the emission label. If your car sports this decal, it should have received all services and modifications specified by the manufacturer.

If you can't find such a decal, the work may still have been done. Or the decal was removed, it was never put on in the first place or the hood was replaced. Check for the modified hose routing which goes from the cam cover to the air duct on the earlier cars.

On later Zs, the PCV valve should be the same as the 1979 280ZX if the recall work was done. The '78 ZX used the earlier-type valve, so don't use it as reference to determine if a correct modification was made. Only the '79-and-up PCV valve is specified. Check the "Engine Fuel" section of your Service Manual for more PCV system illustrations.

The Recall Bulletin noted symptoms were most pronounced in extreme cold weather where very high

Technical Bulletins, Hi-Lights & Recalls

idle speed could be dangerous on snow- or ice-covered roads. All 280Zs were subject to the recall, irrespective of climate zone.

It is possible Zs residing in very warm areas of the country may have escaped modification or, having passed the recall inspection initially, later slipped in performance until the modifications were called for after all. If Datsun and the National Highway Traffic Safety Administration agreed this problem was threatening enough to indicate a recall, you should check on the status of your particular vehicle. This applies to any recall.

Selected Tech Bulletin Summaries:
Engine-Mounting-Insulator Bolts; Dated 8-3-1971.
Beginning with HLS30-13330 (manual transmission) and HLS30-1487 (automatic transmission), higher-strength bolts were used to secure the engine mounts. Part number 11322-E4201, these bolts were installed at a higher torque. Four are used to attach the front engine mounts to the frame pads. Two more secure the transmission mount to the transmission and two attach the crossmember to the body. Torque specs were raised to 23—31 ft-lb. See pages ER-3 and ER-4 in the Service Manual for illustrations.

Clutch Master-Cylinder Valve Case; Dated 7-11-1972.
Beginning with HLS30-064092, a clutch master cylinder was introduced with a redesigned valve case. New part number 30610-E4200 more positively prevented air from entering the cylinder from the bottom of the reservoir. Its internal parts were not interchangeable with former part number 30610-21000. It is interchangeable as an assembly.

Dynamic-Damper Modification Kit for Differential Mounting; Dated 3-25-71.
Datsun supplied this kit to owners of automatic-transmission 240Zs who complained of body vibrations. The problem was caused by coupled vibrations caused by natural body-bending frequencies, torsional movement of the power train and a bouncing and pitching motion of the differential mounting.

A dynamic damper and bracket (part numbers 55490-E8300 and 55491-E8350) is attached to the differential mounting by the rear mount-support studs. Longer studs (part number 08229-22810) were supplied with nuts, bolts and washers to assemble the damper to the bracket. The studs were changed while the differential was supported from below. Then the damper and bracket were attached after the differential was back in its original position. Datsun also added a new washer for the studs, part number 54474-E4100.

Two additional insulators (part number 55478-E8300) were supplied for each side of the rear mount support. Similar in appearance to the existing insulators, these were split to allow installation without removing the mounting bolts. After the nuts were loosened, the castellated rubber insulators could be sandwiched in, castellations mating with the originals. Again, this modification was not installed unless the owner complained of vibration problems. It was not a mandatory recall item, so many 240Zs may have not have them.

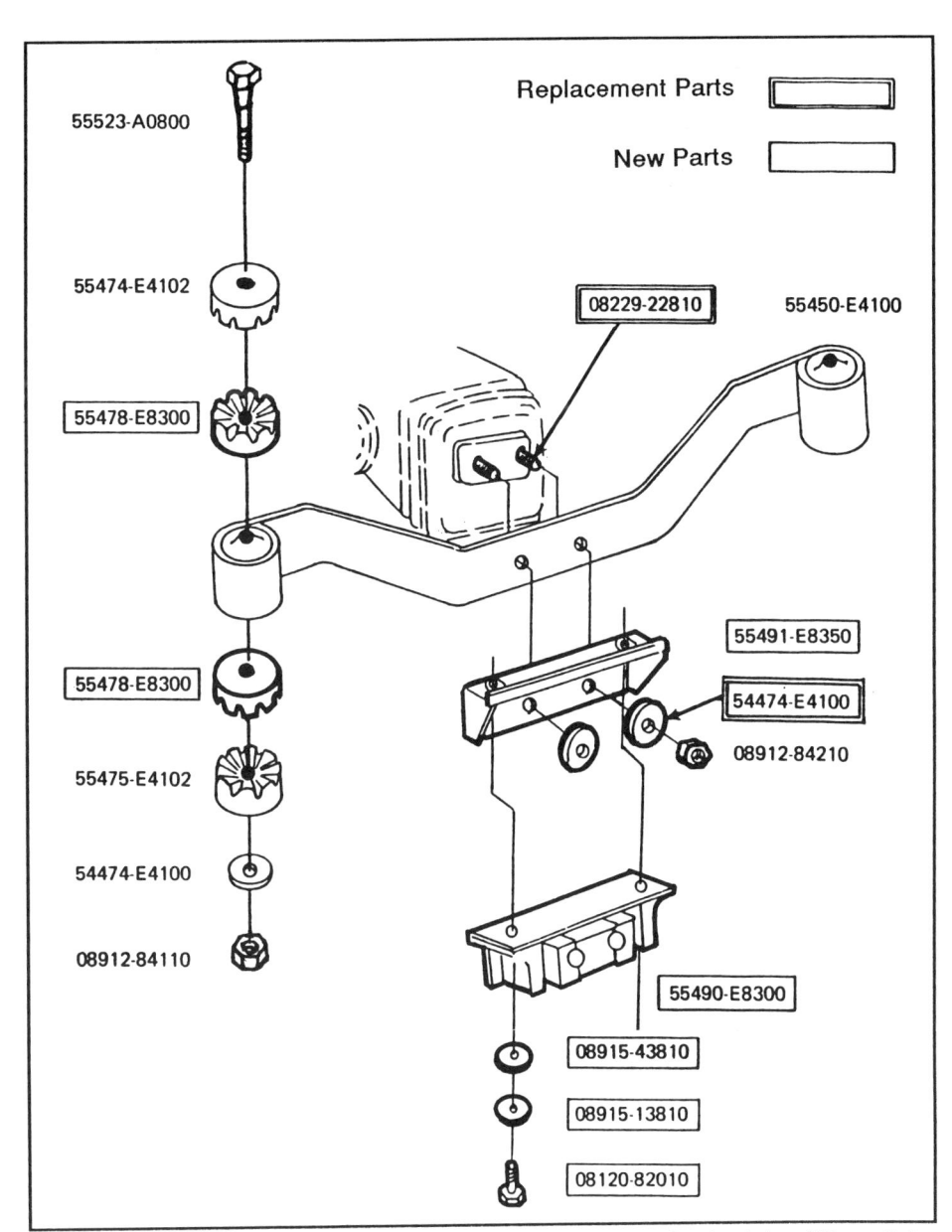

You might find a lead weight hanging from a bracket at the back of the differential housing of your early automatic-equipped Z-car—it is a dealer-installed *fix* for body vibrations. Modification includes larger insulators, which became standard for later Z's. Courtesy Nissan.

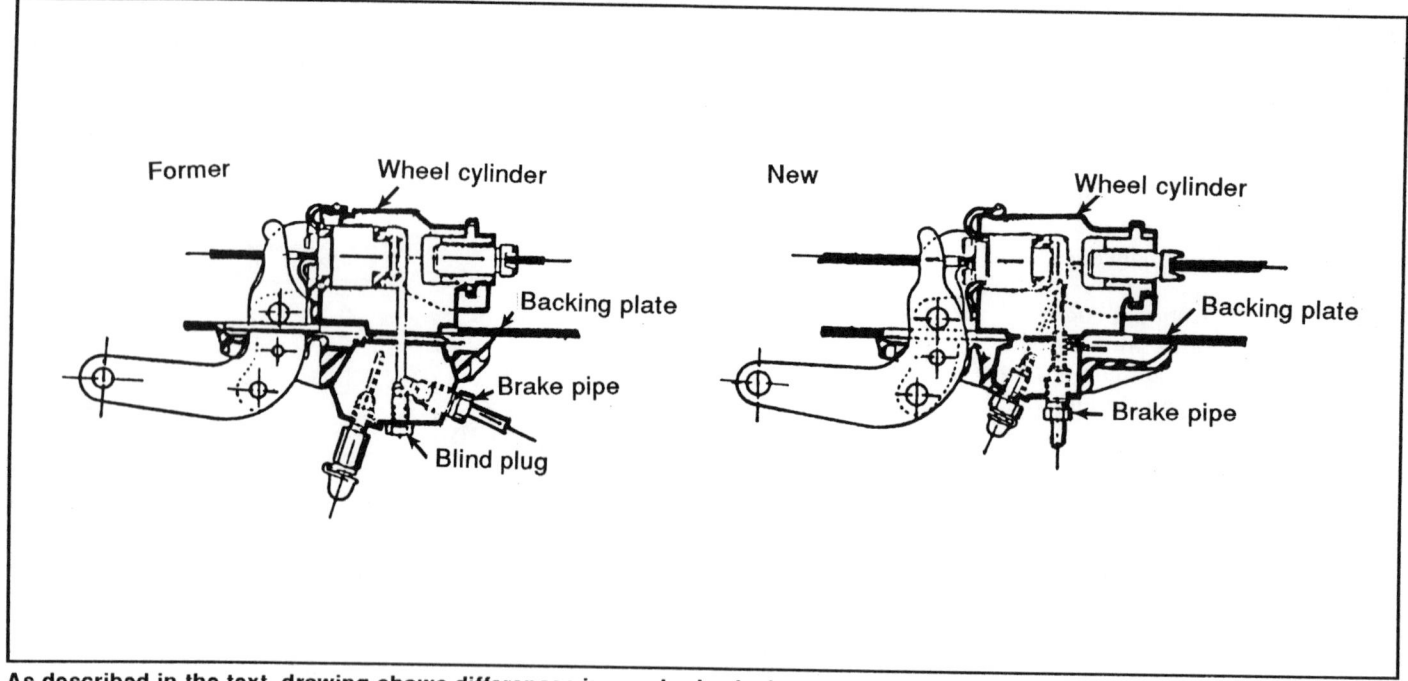

As described in the text, drawing shows differences in rear-brake design that eliminated the sliding wheel cylinder. Newer style adapts to the early hub *if* complete backing plate-and-brake assembly is swapped. Courtesy Nissan.

Noise-Insulating Washer; Dated 1-12-1972.

For rear-axle bearing: Some 240Zs generated undue noise from the rear-axle area. Beginning with HLS30-19584, a phosphor-copper washer, part number 43211-E4100, was installed between the drive-shaft U-joint companion flange and inner bearing. It was necessary to remove the drive shaft, locknut, washer and companion flange to install the washer on earlier cars. Datsun recommended coating both sides with molybdenum-disulphide (moly) grease and torquing companion-flange nut 94—123 ft-lb.

Elimination of Noise-Insulating Washer; Dated 8-3-1974.

By the time the 260Z was introduced, Datsun decided this remedial part was no longer necessary. Starting with RLS30-32966 and GRLS30-002697, the above part was deleted and torque setting reverted to the original figure. No other changes were made to the rear-axle assembly in either instance.

Solid-Wire Choke Cables Specified; Dated 10-1-1970

As of HLS30-01831, the stranded choke cable was replaced with a solid-wire unit, part number 18410-E4502.

Front Carpet Fasteners Increased to Four; Dated 6-13-1972.

Beginning with HLS30-77533, two additional fastening clips were used on the 240Z to keep the carpet in place. No part number was given because clips were placed in the glove compartment and installed by the dealer.

Seat-Belt Holder Added; Dated 7-12-1972.

A loop-type holder that fastened under the console was required to support the automatic-locking retractor belts on the inside of the seats. Beginning number: HLS30-62001.

Rear-Wheel Brakes Changed; Dated 9-29-1972.

As of HLS30-095849, a new-design brake line, wheel cylinder, backing plate, dust shield and parking-brake-lever-guide assembly became standard on the Z. The newer-style wheel cylinder has no blind plug. The brake line enters perpendicular to the backing plate rather than at an angle as before. Only the backing plate is interchangeable without the rest of the parts. See above drawing.

Water-Temperature and Oil-Pressure Gauge Change; Dated 3-27-1972.

Starting with HLS30-06592, the marks in the center of this combination gauge are eliminated! The new part number is 24830-E8301. Gauges interchange.

Defroster-Wire Alignment Changed; Dated 4-11-1972.

Beginning with number HLS30-062001, the rear-window-defroster wires run horizontally rather than vertically. There is no provision for the defroster circuit defroster wiring harness in 240Zs previous to HLS30-01456.

Datsun recommended their accessory relay, part number 25230-E4100, be used with the stock switch, part number 25350-E8200. A 20-amp inline fuse holder and 10- and 18-gauge wires are required. The previous hatch-glass part number is 90301-E4101; the new glass number is 90301-E8800.

Bent Heat-Vent-Door Control Cables

Z owners experienced a lot of cable failures on early cars. Datsun concluded this was due to excess adhesive used to mount the foam-rubber vent-door seal. They recommended a silicone lubricant be sprayed on both sides of the seal and the following repair be made to the cable. I believe the 1972 and later control cable was heavier, however, and thus more serviceable in general use. Many dealer service people substituted better-quality cable assemblies, such as Mercedes-Benz units cut to the correct length. I have successfully used a Z-car choke cable for over 15 years with no problems in my 240Z. Replacing the cable and sheath is much easier than fabricating a new piece from 0.049-inch music wire.

Taillight-Bulb Access Panels.
These are provided in the rear-deck trim panel on the 240Z in October 1970. Beginning numbers are: HLS30-02830 (-03327 California) for black interior. HLS30-03881 (-04364 California) for brown or blue interior.

They attach with four screws per panel.

Change in Oil-Pressure Gauge and Sender; Dated 11-21-1973.
Previous to HLS30-21001, all Z-cars were shipped with an oil-pressure gauge that indicated up to 140 psi. Because the L24 was designed for less than 60 psi, Datsun had received many complaints of low oil pressure from owners, myself included. A gauge that showed a larger proportion of needle sweep for the normal pressure made sense, so a 90-psi gauge was substituted, beginning with late 240Zs.

The lower-reading gauge required a different sender. A 6kg unit supplanted the previous 10kg one. These had to be compatible; a mismatch would give an inaccurate reading so they were only interchangeable as a pair. No change was specified for the water-temperature part of this combination gauge. Parts numbers are:

New Part	Old Part
24830-E8300 or 24830-E8301	24830-E4400
Gauge: 90 psi or 25070-89901	Gauge: 140 psi
25070-89900	25070-89910
Sender switch: 6kg	Sender switch: 10kg

Datsun didn't intend to stock the early 10kg sender after dealer supplies ran out, so if you have to replace yours on an early 240Z, carefully check part numbers. You may need to change your gauge if the 25070-89910 sender switch isn't available. The later gauge is otherwise identical with the original type.

Drive-Shaft U-Joints Provided With Grease Plugs;
Beginning with RLS30-037183, Datsun began fitting Zs with U-joints that could be lubricated. These did not have the popular Alemite-type nipple (zerk) however, but a filler plug that could be removed to add grease. They were interchangeable with previous U-joints on the "drive shaft," often called the *halfshaft*. Don't confuse it with the "propeller shaft," which transmits power from the transmission to the differential. Most aftermarket U-joints come with zerk fittings.

Inner-Fender Protectors; Dated 4-19-74.
To improve corrosion protection, 260Zs from numbers RLS30-18456 and GRLS30-000050 were fitted with inner-fender splash protectors. Parts numbers for these are:

Item	Part Number
Front protector Right/Left	64186/7 N3600
Upper protector Right/Left	64144/5 N3600
Rear protector Right/Left	63830/1 N3600
Front fender Right/Left	63100/1 E4600
Panel, dash Right/Left	66400/1 N3600
Ledge, hood Right only	64100 N3658
Ledge, hood Left only	64101 N365
Reinforcement Right/Left	64150/1 N3400

Z Competition Hood Vent Introduced; Dated 12-13-1974
This hand-laid fiberglass vent was not a factory-installed item, but was released for dealer installation. It had a rather optimistically projected shop time of only one hour! The entire kit, part number 99990-00182, consisted of a black gel-coated hood vent as well as two mounting gaskets and nuts. Also included was a rubber strip to cover the raw edges of the vent hole to be cut into the driver's side of the hood bulge. Three grommets were supplied, two to protect the edges of two holes cut in the rear hood stiffener to provide access to the mounting nuts. The third was for a 1/2-inch hole at the front of the vent for water drainage.

It is interesting to note this was not a hood scoop per se, but a vent. The opening is over the left side of the engine where underhood heat from the exhaust system aggravated the driveability of 240 and 260Zs equipped with the second-series carburetion. Datsun specified the vent could be used as a field fix for vehicles so equipped. As such it can be considered original equipment on Z-cars with the flat-top damper-pot carburetors.

New Rear-Window-Defroster Switch; Dated 3-20-1974.
The quality and assembly of Datsun's electrical-switching parts in early Zs left something to be desired. Perhaps this was a legacy of the company's economy-car past. Starting with HLS30-158735, Z-cars were fitted with an improved rocker switch for the rear defroster. The previously used console-mounted part had not enjoyed a good reputation for reliability. Though visually identical to the old switch, the new ones carry part numbers:

	Fits	Self-Illuminated
25350 E4101	70-71 console	No
25350 E8201	70-71 console	Yes
25350 E8701	72-up console	Yes

Speedometer-Cable Noises in 1974 Models; Dated 7-23-1974.
Some 260Zs were apparently fitted with speedometer-drive cables that were too long. These caused a clicking sound as they bottomed out in the speedometer head. Datsun recommended an additional thrust washer, part number 99990-00181, be added at the transmission end of the cable. The washers have a 0.275-inch OD and a 0.040-inch ID. It is placed next to the original thrust washer on the inner cable after removing it from the housing.

Neutralizing Ignition-Interlock System; Dated 12-12-1974.
For drivers of cars so equipped who wished to be free of the seat belt/ignition interlock and buzzer, the Federal government authorized Datsun to supply technical information for disabling it. Most cars have undoubtedly been modified by now, but you may wish to reactivate the system to restore authenticity. The seat-belt warning light was not included in the legal authorization. Of the three precautions, it is the least offensive.

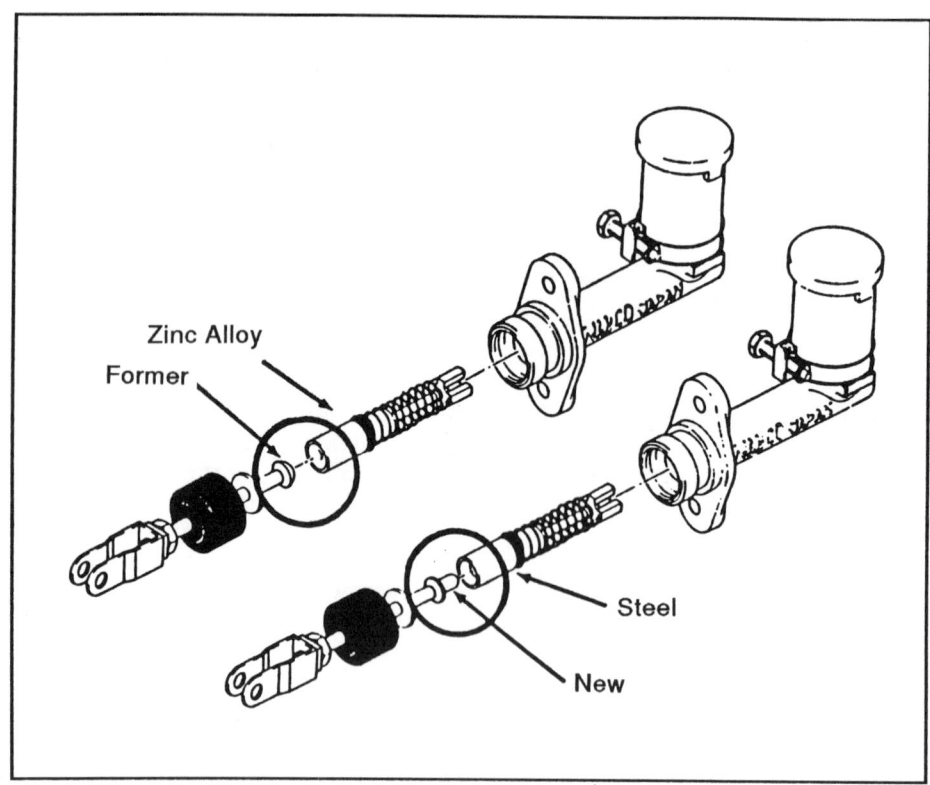

Drawing shows the differences in clutch master cylinders—all internal—dating from 8-31-71. My project Z had the earlier type, which failed after about four years of use. Courtesy Nissan.

The procedure for disabling the ignition interlock, which is behind the relay bracket in the instrument-panel wiring harness, is as follows:
1. Cut both the red/green stripe and red/yellow strip wires about 3 inches from the emergency switch.
2. Join the connector ends of the loose wires.
3. Insulate the connected ends and remaining loose ends on the switch side.

This circumvents the interlock and allows the car to start without the seat belts being connected.

Disabling the buzzer is done is as follows:
1. Locate the unit on its bracket on the back of the speedometer. The pigtail is very short, so Datsun recommends removing the tachometer to provide adequate working space.
2. Cut the blue/red lead on the connector side.
3. Insulate the cut ends with electrical tape.

Alternatively, a switch might be wired into the circuit to allow the buzzer to be used. If you would like to retain the buzzer, but merely want to muffle its sound, simply wrap the unit with electrical tape.

Clutch Master-Cylinder Revision; Dated 2-24-1975.
Beginning with serial numbers RLS30-039512 and GRLS30-004846, a new clutch master-cylinder piston and pushrod were installed to assist clutch disengagement. The parts numbers are as follows:

	Piston Assy.	Pushrod
New	30610-N4200	30631-E4101
Old	30610-E4201	30631-E4100

A longer pedal stroke was found to be necessary for complete clutch disengagement on 260Zs. The piston and pushrod are interchangeable with earlier equipment. See above drawing.

Noise Damper for Differential; Dated 9-5-1975.
A remedy for excessive noise from the early-style or R180 differential was issued by Datsun in 1975. This is not to be confused with the kit used in 1971 to correct high vibration levels of the differential. It is not applicable to the later R200 differential, which has no side-bearing retainers with their five distinctive bolts. Nor is it recommended for 2+2 models due to interference with the rear seat-belt-attachment bolts. The noise was identified as coming from the meshing of the ring-and-pinion gears, then amplified by vibrations in the body. Datsun's solution was to add mass—a 10-pound weight bolted to the differential housing. Also included was a replacement companion flange that included a torsional damper that helped absorb torsional vibration in the drive line. The parts were cataloged under the part number 99991-20000, which included mounting hardware.

The companion flange includes a disc section, much like a crankshaft vibration damper. It is easy to distinguish from the previous part. Installation was the same as that described in the service manual. The mass damper is a solid lead weight that bolts atop the differential pinion-gear housing with two 7/16-inch bolts.

Padded Crash-Pad Repair; Dated 6-20-1975.
Datsun found some Zs, especially 1975 models, coming back for warranty work because of a separation of the metal garnish trim and forward edge of the dash padding. To make the trim piece cover exposed foam edge, a spacer was added under each trim screw to space it rearward approximately 3mm (0.12 inch). Four spacers and longer 10mm screws were supplied for each repair. After removing the original screws and trim piece, Datsun recommended the spacers be glued or taped over the screw holes. If the raw edge had curled up and back, they also recommended using a hair dryer to soften the pad enough to push the material back into position. Then the trim was reinstalled at a more rearward position, hopefully covering and securing the crash-pad edge.

Rear-Suspension Control-Arm Bushing Switching; Dated 4-28-1976.
It was found that front and rear control-arm bushings were commonly being switched in dealer reassembly, causing rear-suspension misalignment and noise from that area. The bushings are similar in appearance, but have slightly different dimen-

sions. The front, part number 55554-E4100, is longer at approximately 2-9/16 inches. The rear, part number 55555-E4100, is shorter—approximately 2-1/8 inches long. Switching bushings moves the control arm about 7/16 inch forward of its correct position, causing a major misalignment problem. Consequences other than noise result if not rectified.

280Z Air-Cleaner-Duct Extension for Wet-Weather Areas; Dated 5-14-1976.

A kit was made available to duct intake air from the engine compartment rather than through the grille area on cars starting with HLS30-281858 and GHLS30-034445. This required disabling the fresh-air vent on the passenger's side of the car by removing the passenger side plastic air-duct elbow just behind the radiator bulkhead, then disconnecting or cutting the vent control on that side of the instrument panel. Then a new duct, part number 62861-N4400, and clamp, part number 62865-N4400, are installed on the existing air-cleaner duct. The extended intake end is fastened to the previous vent-duct opening in the bulkhead with a 6x12mm, 1.0mm-pitch bolt, part number 83-6361626. On 1975 models, a hole must be drilled to correspond with that on the duct. A hole is pre-punched in 1976 and later cars.

Datsun recommended this modification only on cars that suffered from poor engine operation due to water being drawn into the air cleaner. This modification was put into production on all L28-powered Zs.

Modification of Drive Shafts (Halfshafts); Dated 5-4-1977

Beginning with production of February 1977, 280Z, the O-ring, retaining ring and stopper at the end of the halfshaft ball-spline chambers were eliminated. These were replaced with a stopper plug in the tube end and the balls are separated by nylon spacers.

These new components are not applicable to old-style shafts, although the new shafts are interchangeable as complete units. Also, distance between the U-joints centerlines increases from 334mm (13.15 in.) to 344mm (13.54 in.), improving durability.

Engine-Compartment Changes; Dated 5-6-1977

Starting with HLS30-368341 and GHLS 30-065908, several modifications were made to combat excess underhood heat.

1. The rear portion of the 1977 exhaust-manifold heat shield was deleted to increase airflow around the manifold. As a part of this fix, essentially, the 1976 heat shield was reintroduced!
2. A heat-shield plate was added to protect the brake master cylinder and related parts from radiated exhaust heat. This mounts to a bracket on the proportioning valve and another at the inspection-lamp bracket.
3. Insulating tubes on the speedometer cable were extended 100mm (3.94 inches) toward the speedometer side. It still interchanged with the previous cable.

New Clutch and Brake-Pedal Return Spring; Dated 4-15-1977.

Starting with HLS30302611 and GHLS30-039639, a new spring, part number 46582-N4401, is specified. The pedal end of the spring is longer and marked with a daub of white paint. It should be hooked in from the left side of the pedal. The short, unmarked end of the spring attaches to the bracket.

Hand-Brake Clevis Changed; Dated 6-22-1978.

A new cable-and-clevis assembly was phased in on 280Zs to improve serviceability. Instead of attaching the clevis directly to the cable end, a slot on the side permits separation from the little cylindrical end. A longer dust boot was also used. Beginning serial numbers were HLS30-438523 and GHLS30-115881.

The new cable carried part number 36543-N4601; the removable clevis 36544-N4600. The old assembly was part number 36543-N4600. They were interchangeable as an assembly.

Another Front-Fender Splash Protector; Dated 6-15-1978.

Beginning with serial number HLS30-442907 and GHLS30-117214, a lighter and much smaller inner-fender splash protector was instituted on 280Zs sold in California. It is not interchangeable with the older part.

	New	Old
Protector		
Right	63830-N4200	63880-N4200
Left	63831-N4200	63881-N4200
Rubber Mud		
Guard	63835-E4100	None

DATSUN

THE BIG DATSUN DIFFERENCE IS VALUE

240-Z COUPE

SERIAL NO. HL530- 03547   ENGINE NO. L24- 6537

PORT OF ENTRY _____ Houston _____

DEALER'S NAME _____ CALMBACH COMPANY _____

ADDRESS _____ 2719 FREDRICKSBURG _____

CITY _____ SAN ANTONIO, TEX _____

METHOD OF TRANSPORTATION _____

MANUFACTURER'S SUGGESTED RETAIL PRICE $ 3526.00
    REAR WINDOW DEFROSTER
PRICE INCLUDES ALL OF THE FOLLOWING: $ 40.00

                                                                                                                                        $

- 150 H.P., 6 CYL., OVERHEAD CAM ENGINE
- 4-SPEED FULL-SYNCHROMESH TRANSMISSION $
- FRONT DISC BRAKES WITH POWER ASSIST
- FULL INDEPENDENT FRONT AND REAR SUSPENSION
- WINDOWS-UP FRESH AIR SYSTEM $
- APPROVED EXHAUST EMISSION SYSTEM
- UNIT BODY CONSTRUCTION $
- WINDSHIELD WASHERS
- 2-SPEED ELECTRIC WIPERS
- ALTERNATOR -- 45 AMP --12 VOLT
- CARPETS
- ADJUSTABLE BUCKET SEATS
- DELUXE VINYL UPHOLSTERY
- DELUXE WHEEL COVERS
- HEATER & DEFROSTERS
- SAFETY BELTS
- FOAM CUSHION SEATS
- DUAL HORNS
- BACKUP LIGHTS
- OUTSIDE MIRROR
- ALL TRANSISTOR SIGNAL SEEKING AM RADIO
- ELECTRIC POWER ANTENNA
- TACHOMETER
- CIGARETTE LIGHTER
- CONSOLE
- LOCKING STEERING COLUMN
- ELECTRIC CLOCK
- TRIP METER

FACTORY SUGGESTED DEALER D. & H. $ 75.00

LOCAL FREIGHT $ 30.00

TOTAL SUGGESTED RETAIL PRICE $ _____
Plus State, Local taxes and license fees
                                            TINTED GLASS $ 30.00
NISSAN MOTOR CORPORATION IN U.S.A. $ 3671.00 XXXXXXXX
137 EAST ALONDRA BLVD. — GARDENA, CALIFORNIA 90247
400 COUNTY ROAD — SECAUCUS, NEW JERSEY 07094 $ 3,701.00

THIS LABEL IS PREPARED PURSUANT T... 'C LAW 85-506. NISSAN MOTOR CORPORATION IN U.S.A. IS NOT RE-SPONSIBLE FOR DELIVERY TO DEALE... ARRANGING A METHOD OF TRANSPORTATION AND/OR CHARGES.

Here's the window sticker from my car. They gave me a $130 discount for paying cash!

12 Insuring Your Z-car

Is insurance a Sore Subject? Now that your Z is painstakingly restored, how can you protect yourself against some low-life who takes a fancy to it? How about that drunk who ignores the stop sign? A short circuit in the eaves of your garage? Even the nice person parking next to you at the mall?

Perhaps you can't prevent these things from happening, but at least you need to consider protecting your investment. That's what insurance is for—but will your carrier insure your pride and joy? After all, your Z can be no newer than 1978—hardly a late model. What do you need, and what can you afford?

You must have property damage and public liability—or sufficient resources to meet the financial-liability minimums of most states. Additionally, many states require coverage for uninsured motorists. These coverages are not cheap . . . and they don't protect the investment in your car.

Comprehensive coverage reimburses you for all or part of your loss should someone steal your car or parts of it. Collision covers repair or replacement resulting from an accident. You may have to accept a deductible or pay a much higher premium. Most agents discourage insuring for more than the law requires because coverage that actually protects your investment is so expensive versus their adjusted value for the car.

But what is your Z worth to you and, secondarily, to your insurer? Costs and values change, but let's say you have $10,000 tied up in your restoration—car, parts and labor. At least that is what it is worth to you because you like the car and you restored it completely. An insurer, however, looks at the car from a business standpoint. He doesn't care even if it *is* one of three surviving 1969 Nerny S/S with dual-louvered oil pans!

His first reference is the "Blue Book" such as banks use in financing autos. If it isn't in there, he'll probably want you to forget the idea of protecting yourself. If you are lucky, he will be motivated to get or keep your business and will refer to a collectable-car valuation guide, such as the "Gold Book." If your car is listed, you must accept that price range as what you car can be insured for.

So let's say he grants your car might be worth $5000—quite a lot less than your investment—to say nothing of sentimental value! What you want is insurance that reflects increased value or "stated value" in your car. In other words, you declare the car is worth a certain amount and then pay a premium based on that. About the best you can hope for is the insurer will look at the resale value—and allow maybe half that amount more to be added to reflect the total of your restoration investment. For example, $5000 plus $2500 equals $7500 total—absolute ceiling. And that is what you can expect insurers to cover—what they think a car's replacement value should be.

Whether your insurer comes up with something satisfactory is up to you—it will probably be costly in any case. If you drive the car regularly, you may have to accept that offer.

There are insurers offering specialized coverages in cases where their underwriters have decided there is potential in growth and profit.

Collector-Car Insurance

This is different because it has several restrictions that must be complied with, balanced against availability of what is *true* stated-value coverage. If you really don't need to drive your Z-car regularly and it is over 15-years old, you may qualify for bona-fide collector-car coverage. This offers not only the legally required insurance, but also coverage on comprehensive and collision up to any amount within reason—the full $10,000 in our example. You will pay for the stated-value amount based on so much money per each $100 valuation you declare, say $1 per $100 in our case. The annual premium in this case is $1 times 100 (one-hundred $100's is $10,000) equals $100. This, added to whatever the underwriter stipulates for legal liability coverage is what you pay. A few will even waive the deductible, paying for anything you claim.

In return for this protection, you *may* be required to do all or most of the following stipulations:

✓ Certify and sign a statement to the effect that you will use your car only in tours, parades, car shows, club activities and for routine maintenance.

✓ That your car does not have custom graphics or other hard-to-repair paint treatments. This usually doesn't include a simple high-value refinishing that can be duplicated by a competent commercial shop.

✓ That your car has not had the manufacturer's horsepower rating changed nor will you use it in motorsports competition.

✓ That annual mileage will not

exceed a specified amount—typically 2500 miles.
- ✓ That the car be garaged when not in use.
- ✓ That the car be appraised by an accredited antique-car appraiser.
- ✓ That one or more current photographs be submitted.
- ✓ That photocopies of parts and labor receipts be submitted.
- ✓ That all components be marked against resale after dismantling.
- ✓ That an approved burglar alarm be installed and maintained.
- ✓ That no "youthful drivers" be allowed to use car.
- ✓ That applicant be a member of a recognized collector-car enthusiasts' association, for example: Z Club of America, Sports Car Club of America or a regional Z Club or affiliate.

Collector-car insurance usually offers affordable rates simply because the above restrictions focus their clientele into a very low-risk category. If owners were to abuse their agreements on a large scale, this advantage would disappear like the mist—rest assured. Insurance agents and their backers, the underwriters, are business persons first and last. Their interest in your precious collectable Z-car is only incidental.

The Crunch—Of course, most Z-car owners still fall somewhere in between. They have neither a concours-quality restoration nor a completely *roached* everyday "beater." Add to this the fact that many Zs fall between the top "Gold Book" value and bottom end of current "Blue Book." This group will always feel discriminated against. A regularly driven but restored Z—or typically, semi-customized Z—will always be at risk simply because of its vintage. Drivers of all types of specialized vehicles eventually must confront this knotty problem—and learn a lot about the auto-insurance industry as a result. We can always hope conditions will change—but until that time, a good accident and ticket record combined with common-sense care and "risk management" on the driver's part are our major assets.

Shop Around—Get to know the insurance agents in your area and let them know you—your needs, record and your commitment. Remember, the agent and insurer need feel assured they will profit from your relationship.

Following is a list of collector-car insurers. These companies are old hands at insuring true vintage collectables. They have good claims records and will handle most or all applications through the mail. Each have their own stipulations, but one may be just what you need to protect your investment. The author and Fisher Books make nor imply no recommendation as to which insurer to choose.

Auto Collectors Insurance
Attn. Mr. McDougal
P. O. Box 8343
285 N. Kings Hwy.
Cherry Hill, NJ 08034
(800) 257-5758 (New Jersey only)
(609) 779-7212

Condon & Skelly
P. O. Drawer A,
Willingboro, NJ 08046
(800) 257-9496 (New Jersey only)
(800) 624-4699 or (609) 871-1212

J. C. Taylor, Inc.
Attn. Mr. Wallace
320 S. 64th. St.
Upper Darby, PA 19082
(800) 345-8290 (Pennsylvania only)
(800) 552-3535

13 Z-Car Identification & Codes

Identification Plate—On 1970-72 cars, this is on the engine-compartment/passenger's side inner strut tower. On 1973-78 cars, it's on the driver's side hood ledge. This enameled silver plate is attached with four Phillips-head screws.

Vehicle Identification Number (VIN) Plate—It's on the forward edge of the crash pad on the driver's side. This black-enamel metal plate is riveted to the instrument-panel structure. It has the vehicle's full I.D. legend where it can be viewed from the outside at the base of the windshield.

Serial Number—This is stamped on the firewall metal on the driver's side of the hood-latch bracket.

MVSS Plate—This silver plate is riveted to the driver's rear door jamb—where the latch striker mounts. It gives the month and year of manufacture as well as the I.D. legend common to what's provided on other plates.

All Z-cars are S30s to Nissan. This is the official model designation. No matter where it was sold—a 240Z, a 280Z 2+2 or a home-market Fairlady Z432 with DOHC-four and right-hand-drive—is basically an S30.

Building on that code, a letter prefix was added: **H** for L24 or L28-engined cars and an **R** for L26-engined 260Zs. Then comes an **L** for left-hand-drive models, the only kind exported to North America.

All 2+2 models—begun in 1974—added the prefix **G**. After the number on pre-1973 cars comes a dash (-) and then the serial number. Thus, my April-built 1970 project car becomes HLS30-03547—an L24-powered, left-hand-drive Z-car that was number 3547 in serial production.

If your car was originally equipped with an automatic transmission, that number would be followed by the letter **A**; on 280s possibly an **F** for the then-optional 5-speed manual transmission.

On later cars, **U** would designate export to the United States *or* Canada. This might be followed by the letter **N** if destined for Canada or **V** for California. Texans, please don't be envious—this only refers to specific emissions-control equipment required to meet the regulations of those two locations.

Finally, a Z-car equipped by the factory with air conditioning—not dealer-installed, even if Nissan approved—ends with a **C** suffix.

Not too complex—and it was used consistently, which is more than can be said of many collector cars. The principal idiosyncrasy is the use of the same letter prefix for both 2400cc and 2800cc displacement engines—as if that would be a problem in discerning between a serial number below about 136,000 and above 181,000.

Engine Identification—To verify engine numbers, look on the machined pads at the rear of the block on the passenger's side just below the deck. The displacement is indicated behind the **L** and **24**, **26** or **28** stamped on the first pad. The engine number is on the adjacent pad, three digits on 1973 and earlier blocks, four on '74 blocks and six digits on '75 and later blocks.

Transmission Identification—On manual transmissions, this is stamped on the top flange of the bellhousing. On automatics, it is found on the passenger's side of the transmission case.

Paint-Code Label—This is the sticker applied to the top of the radiator-support bulkhead near the hood-support rod. Nissan only coded the in-house paint number.

Various stickers and decals are scattered around the car—engine, engine compartment, underhood, door jambs, glove-box door and so forth. Some were applied at the Hiratsuka, Japan Z-plant and some—especially emissions or recall-related verifications—were left to the dealer to install. These vary greatly and cannot be consistently cataloged.

Parts & Services

Arizona Z Car
2110 W. Devonshire St.
Mesa, AZ 85201
(602) 844-9677
Performance parts, etc. Catalog $2.00

Auto Rust Doctors
2728 Dover Road
Bamber Lake, NJ 08731
(609)693-1631
Kits to replace rusted-out frame rails/floors.

Bob Sharp Racing Parts and Accessories, Inc.
918 Danbury Road
Wilton, CT 06897
(203) 544-8387 Performance parts and accessories, incl. Datsun Comp. hood scoop, headlight covers, *ZG kits.
BSR Datsun Owners Club, $10/yr. for 15% discount.   Catalog $3.00

Classics Unlimited
6 Gerald Ave.
Hicksville, NY 11801
(516) 882-1136
Carpet sets, upholstery kits.

Continental Covers Co.
PO Box 78122
Seattle, WA 95178
(206) 723-7796
Carpet sets.

The Eastwood Company
147 Pennsylvania Ave.
Malvern, PA 19355
(215) 640-1450 (PA)
(800) 345-1178 orders only
Professional quality tools & supplies for restorers. Hi-temp stainless-steel exhaust finish, fuel-tank sloshing compound.   Free catalog

g-Machine Inc. (formerly Kontrolle Automotive Prod. Inc.)
4127 Bay St.
Suite C195
Fremont, CA 94538
(415) 651-0561
Suspension components, heavy-duty and competition.

Impact Parts
Datsun Dept.
Glen Wild, NY 12738
(914) 434-3338
Body, engine, suspension parts.
Free catalog

Imparts Ltd.
9330 Manchester Rd.
St. Louis, MO 63119
(314) 962-0810
Rubber parts, hoses, rebuilt and maintenance parts.

J. C. Whitney & Co.
1917-19 Archer Ave.
P. O. Box 8410
Chicago, IL 60680   Catalog $1.00
(312) 431-6102
Body, mechanical and interior parts and accessories.

Jim Cook Racing
5450 Katella Ave,
Bldg. 107
Los Alamitos, CA 90720
(714) 828-9122 or (213) 431-4605
Body and suspension parts, accessories.   Catalog $3.00

Long Motor Corporation
Box 14991
Lenexa, KS 66215
(913)541-8500
(800) 222-LONG
Z parts and accessories   Free catalog

Northwest Modern Classics
Box 5486
Kent, WA 98064
(800) 854-1751
(206) 631-4144
Interior parts, carpet, upholstery and trim.   Free catalog

Motorsport Auto
1139 W. Collins Ave.
Orange, CA 92667
(800) 633-6331 order
(714) 639-2620 information
Restoration supplies, parts and accessories. Very complete source N.O.S. Datsun parts, some reproduction parts.   Catalog $4.00

Performance World
7450 Ronson Road
San Diego, CA 92111
(619) 571-3811

Premier Products International
7754 Deering Ave. No. 4
Canoga Park, CA 91304
(818) 710-1483   FAX (818) 710-1697
Z Parts and Accessories, stock and modified.

Tabco
30500 Solon Industrial Park Way
Cleveland, OH 44139
(800)782-5226
Steel body repair panels.

Tweeks Ltd.
8148 Woodland Drive
Indianapolis, IN 46278
(800) 428-2200
Restoration, mechanical and performance parts.   Catalog $3.00

Wilco Sales Corp.
Box 1128
Rochester, NY 14603
(800)521-0094
Battery cutoff swithches, exhaust systems, mirrors, steering wheels and wheels.   Catalog $3.00

Year One, Inc.
Atlanta, GA
(404) 493-6568
Original carpet sets.

Z Center
550 Lexington Ave.
Clifton, NJ 07011
(201) 546-9200
"Z Accessory Parts" orig and mod. parts, accessories.
*ZG style, C Production and IMSA GTU style kits.   Catalog $3.00

Z Products
30625 Southwest Boones Ferry
Wilsonville, OR 97070
(503) 682-1267
(800) 331-9027
Aerodynamic body parts, carpet and upholstery kits, performance suspension parts and accessories.
Catalog $2.00

* ZG kit includes fiberglass front end with covered headlights, scoops and bumper.

Parts Illustrations

The following illustrations, pages 205—236, are from the original Datsun 240/260Z Parts Manual. Use these illustrations for referencing 280Z parts, too.

Be aware that original Datsun terminology is retained for illustration titles and parts descriptions. This shouldn't be a problem because you'll have a picture of the parts for clarification.

Z-car Parts Illustrations are here due to the efforts of Eddie Korkes of the Z Club of America and courtesy of Nissan.

For a listing of each illustration and the page it's on, refer to the Index under **Parts Illustrations**.

EXHAUST TUBE & MUFFLER (UP TO JULY 1973)

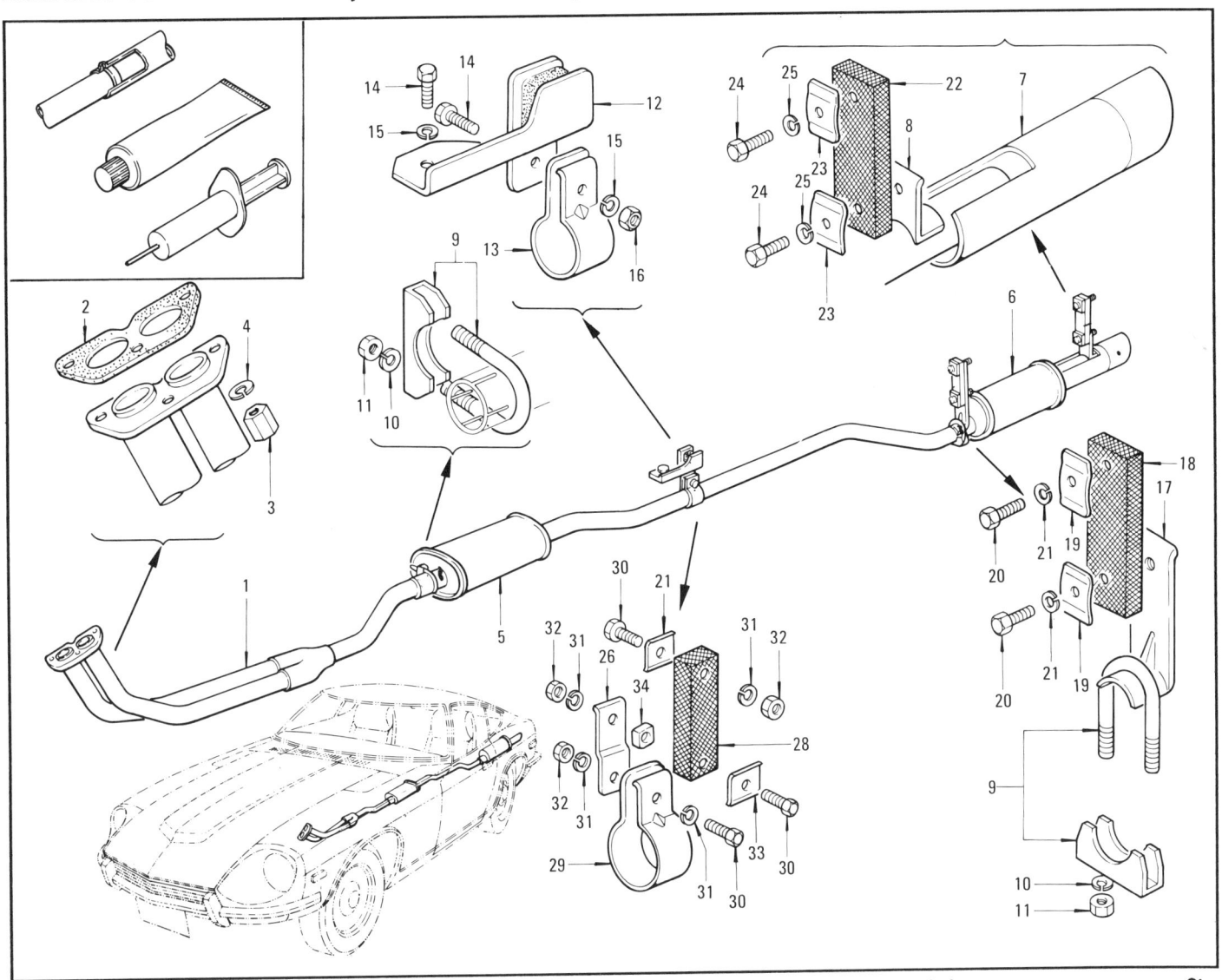

Item	Description	Qty	Item	Description	Qty	Item	Description	Qty
1	Assy-Tube Exhaust Front	1	9	Assy-Clamp U Bolt Exhaust Tube	2	17	Assy-Exhaust Mounting Tube Front	1
2	Gasket-Exhaust	1	10	Washer-Spring	4	18	Strap-Exhaust Hanger	1
3	Nut-Fixing Tube End	3	11	Nut-Hex M8x1.25	4	19	Washer-Plain Exhaust	2
4	Washer-Spring Lock	3	12	Assy-Rubber Comp Exhaust Mounting	1	20	Bolt-Hex M8x1.25	2
5	Assy-Tube Center with Pre Muffler	1	13	Clamp-Exhaust Mounting	1	21	Washer-Spring Lock	2
6	Assy-Muffler with Tail Tube	1	14	Bolt-Hex M10x1.25	1	22	Strap-Exhaust Hanger	1
7	Finisher-Exhaust Tail Tube	1	15	Washer-Spring Lock	2	23	Washer-Plain Exhaust	2
8	Assy-Bracket Exhaust Mounting Tube Rear	1	16	Nut-Hex M10x1.25	1	24	Bolt-Hex M8x1.25	2

205

206 How to Restore Your Datsun Z-car

EMISSION CONTROL DEVICE

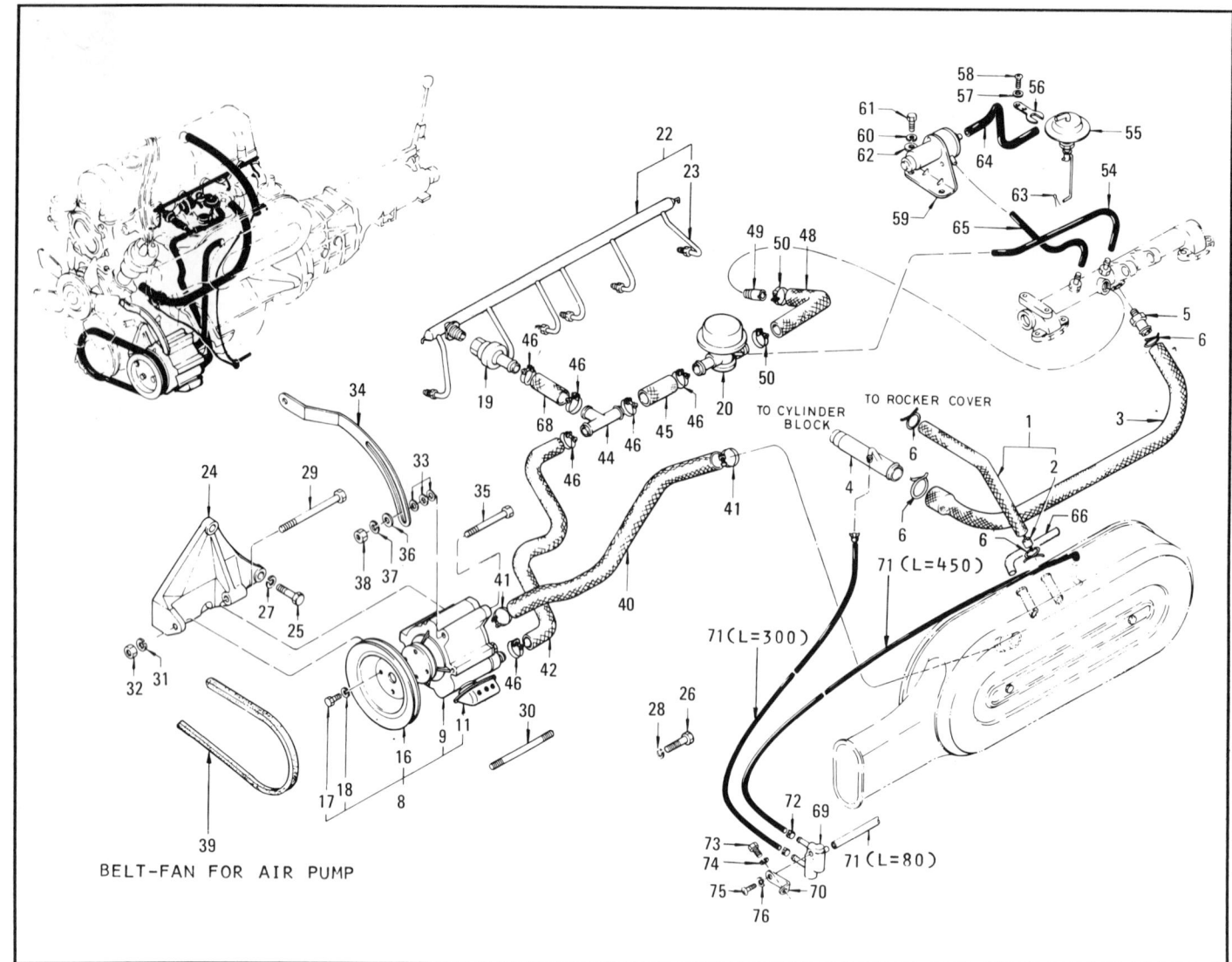

BELT-FAN FOR AIR PUMP

Item	Description	Qty
1	Hose-Rocker Cover to Air Cleaner	1
2	Assy-Flame Arrester	1
3	Hose-Pipe Connector to Control Valve	1
4	Connector-Pipe	1
5	Assy-Control Valve Crank Case Emission	1
7	Clamp-Hose	1
8	Assy-Air Pump with Pulley	1
9	Assy-Air Pump	1
10	Assy-Casing	1
11	Assy-Valve Relief	1
12	Kit-Bearing	1
13	Kit-Vane	1
14	Assy-Bracket	1
15	Assy-Silencer	1
16	Pulley-Air Pump	1
17	Bolt-Air Pump Pulley	4
18	Washer-Spring	4
19	Assy-Valve Check	1
20	Assy-AB Valve	1
21	Orifice-AB Valve	1
22	Assy-Pipe Air Gallery	1
23	Pipe-Air Injection	6
24	Bracket-Air Pump	1
25	Bolt-Hex M10x1.5 Bracket to Cylinder Block	3
26	Bolt-Hex M8x1.25 Bracket to Air Pump	2
27	Washer-Spring Lock Bracket to Cylinder Block	3
28	Washer-Spring Lock Comp to Air Pump	2
29	Bolt-Hex M8x1.25 Bracket to Air Pump	1
30	Stud-Air Pump Fix	1
31	Washer-Spring Lock Bracket to Air Pump	1
32	Nut Hex M8x1.25 Bracket to Air Pump	1
33	Shim-Alternator	*AR
34	Bar-Adjusting Air Pump	1
35	Bolt-Hex M8x1.25 Adjusting Bar to Air Pump	1
36	Washer-Plain Adjusting Bar to Air Pump	1
37	Washer-Spring Lock Adjusting Bar to Air Pump	1
38	Nut-Hex M8x1.25 Adjusting Bar to Air Pump	1
39	Assy-Belt Fan for Air Pump L=856 (33.7")	1
40	Hose-Air Cleaner to Air Pump	1
41	Clamp-Hose	2
42	Hose-Air Pump to Connector	1
43	Clamp-Hose	2
44	Connector Three Way	1
45	Hose-Connector to Air Valve	2
46	Clamp-Hose	6
47	Clamp-Hose	1
48	Hose-AB Valve to Connector	1
49	Connector	1
50	Clamp-Hose	2
51	Tube-AB Valve to 3 Way Connector	1
52	Tube-Manifold to 3 Way Connector	1
53	Connector-3 Way	1
54	Hose-Vacuum Manifold	1
55	Assy-Servo Diaphragm	1
56	Bracket-Servo Diaphragm	1
57	Washer-Tooth	2
58	Screw-Machine	2
59	Assy-Control Valve	1
60	Washer-Spring	2
61	Bolt-Hex M6x40	2
62	Washer-Plain for Servo Diaphragm	2
63	Pin-Cottor Split for Servo Diaphragm	1
64	Tube-Control Valve to Servo Diaphragm	1
65	Tube-Main to Control Valve	1
66	Tube-C/V to Air Cleaner (3.5Dx8.5Dx5000)	1
67	Connector-3Way	1
68	Tube-Manifold to 3 Way Conn	1
69	Assy-Flow Guide Valve	1
70	Bracket-Flow Guide Valve	1
71	Tube-Evapo Control L=80 (3.15")	1
72	Clamp-Hose	4
73	Bolt-Hex M6 Body Fix	1
74	Washer-Spring Body Fix	1
75	Screw-M6x1.0 Bracket Fix	1
76	Washer-Spring Bracket Fix	1
77	Assy-Canister Vapor C625	1
78	Assy-Clamp Canister	1
79	Bolt-Hex	2
80	Washer-Plain	1
81	Screw-Machine Fix Body	4
82	Cap-Rubber	1
83	Tube-Evapo Control L=240 (9.45") Fix Canister to F/Tube	1
84	Tube-Evapo Control Fix Brake Tube to Fuel Tube	1
85	Tube-Evapo Control L=170 (6.70") Fix Canister to V/Vent	1
86	Clamp-Tube Fuel	1
87	Clamp-Hose	6
88	Clamp-Hose	2

*As Required

FUEL TANK

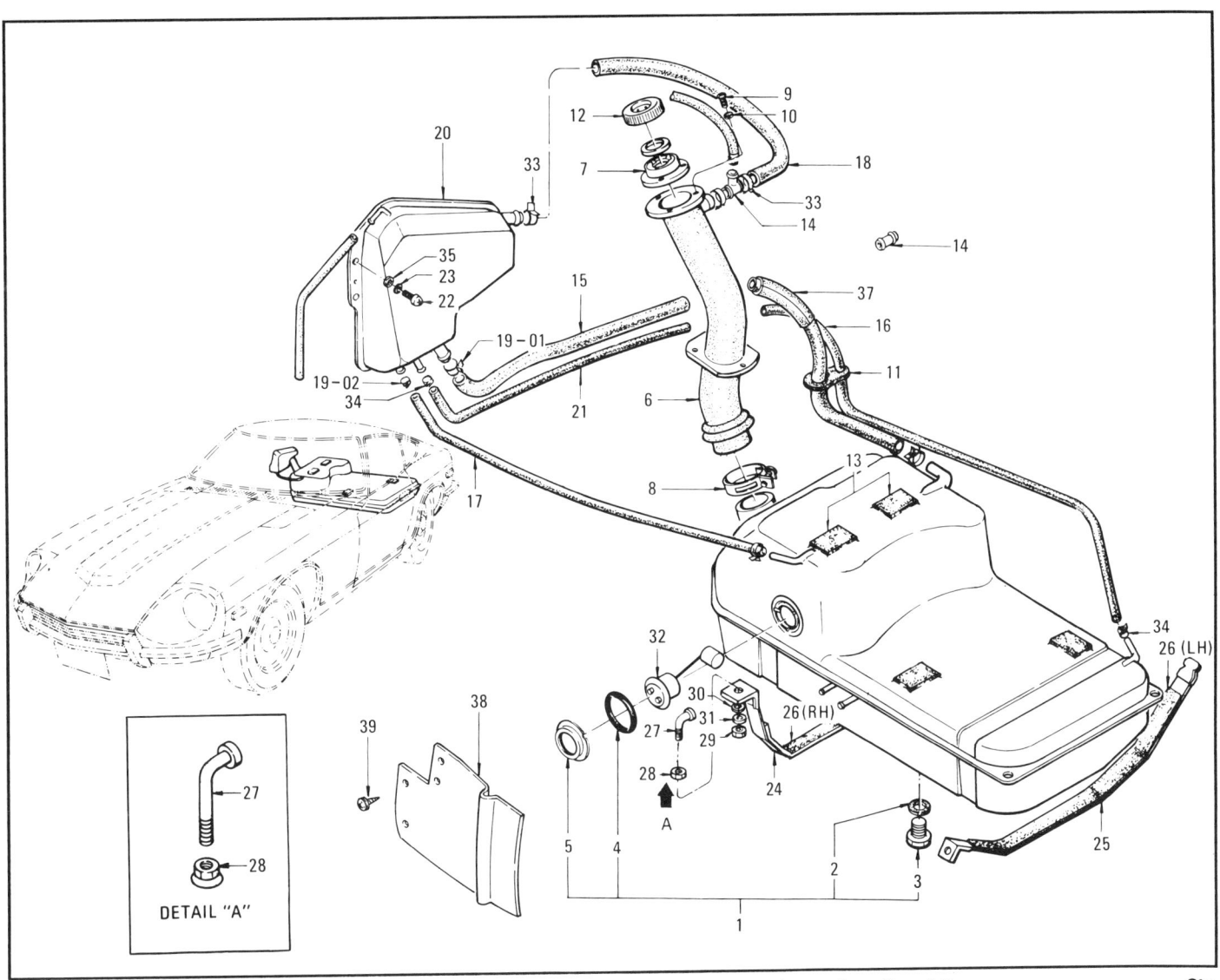

Item	Description	Qty	Item	Description	Qty	Item	Description	Qty
1	Assy-Tank Fuel	1	14	Joint-Tube Breather (3Way)	1	26	Shim-Fuel Tank Mounting RH	1
2	Gasket-Drain Seal	1	15	Hose-Ventilation Tank to Filler Hose	1	27	Bolt-Fuel Tank Mounting Front	2
3	Plug-Drain Gas Tank	1	16	Hose-Ventilation	1	28	Nut-Special	2
4	Ring-"O" Fuel Gauge	1	17	Hose-Ventilation Fuel Tank to Reservoir		29	Nut-Hex	2
5	Plate-Lock	1		Tank FR	1	30	Washer-Plain	2
6	Assy-Hose Filler Fuel Tank	1	18	Hose-Ventilation Reservoir Tank to		31	Washer-Lock	2
7	Neck-Filler for Fuel Tank	1		Filler Tube	1	32	Unit-Gauge Fuel Tank	1
8	Clamp-Hose Fuel Tank	1	19	Clamp-Hose	1	33	Clamp-Hose	2
9	Screw-Machine	3	20	Tank-Reservoir	1	34	Clamp-Hose	2
10	Washer-Spring Lock	3	21	Tube-Reservoir Tank	1	35	Washer-Plain	3
11	Grommet-Rubber	1	22	Screw-Machine	3	36	Washer-Lock	2
12	Assy-Cap Filler Fuel Tank	1	23	Spring-Washer	3	37	Cover-Breather	1
13	Felt-Fuel Tank Mounting B	2	24	Assy-Band Fuel Tank Mounting RH	1	38	Protector-Filler Hose RH	1
			25	Assy-Band Fuel Tank Mounting LH	1	39	Screw-Tapping	4

208 How to Restore Your Datsun Z-car

ENGINE MOUNTING (AUTO ALL, MANUAL UP TO C/# HLS30-46000) (FROM RLS30, GRLS300)

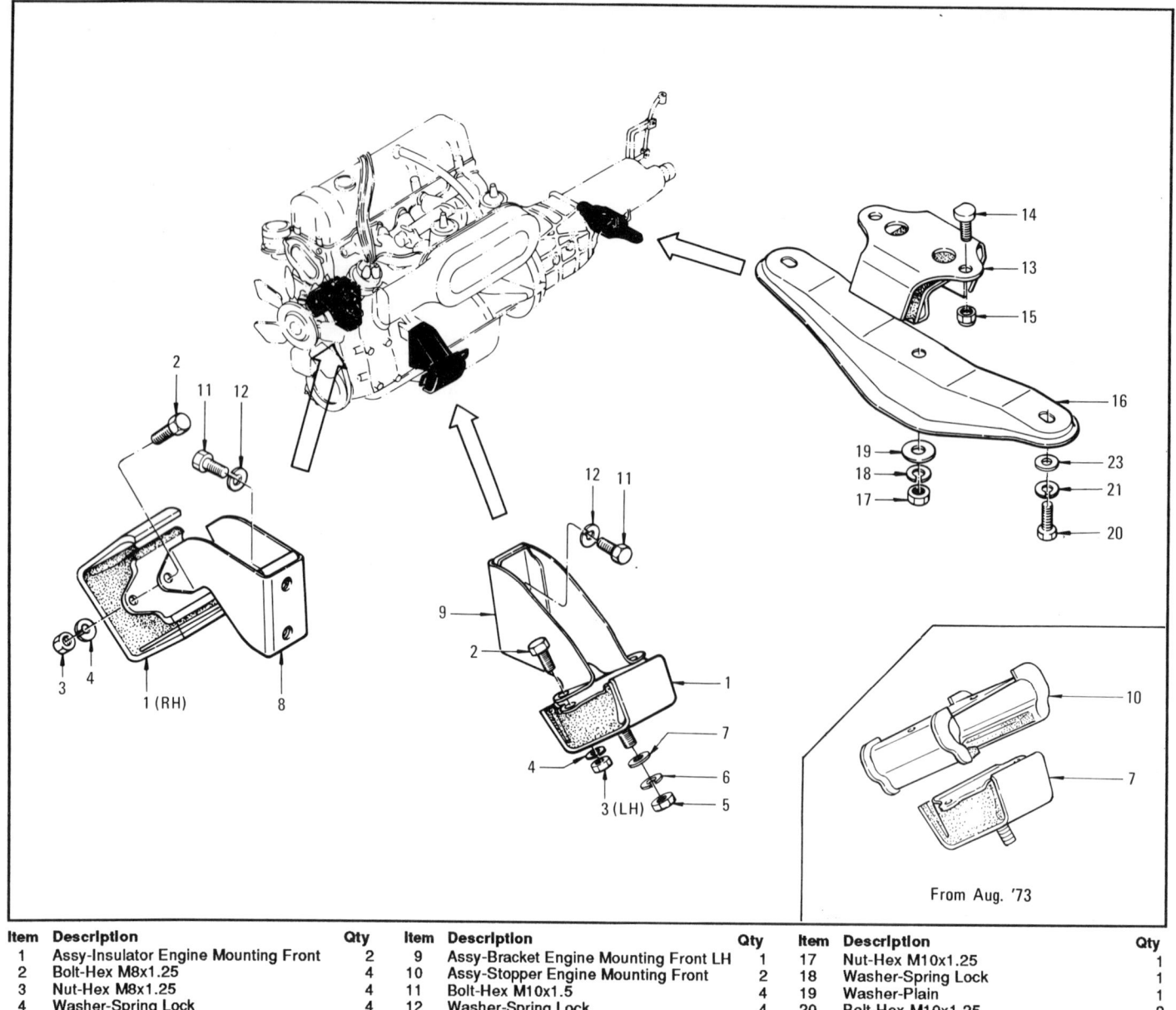

Item	Description	Qty	Item	Description	Qty	Item	Description	Qty
1	Assy-Insulator Engine Mounting Front	2	9	Assy-Bracket Engine Mounting Front LH	1	17	Nut-Hex M10x1.25	1
2	Bolt-Hex M8x1.25	4	10	Assy-Stopper Engine Mounting Front	2	18	Washer-Spring Lock	1
3	Nut-Hex M8x1.25	4	11	Bolt-Hex M10x1.5	4	19	Washer-Plain	1
4	Washer-Spring Lock	4	12	Washer-Spring Lock	4	20	Bolt-Hex M10x1.25	2
5	Nut-Hex M10x1.25	2	13	Assy-Insulator Engine Mounting Rear	1	21	Washer-Spring	2
6	Washer-Spring Lock	2	14	Bolt-Engine Mounting Rear	2	22	Washer-Special	1
7	Washer-Plain	2	15	Nut-Self Locking S	2	23	Washer-Plain	2
8	Assy-Bracket Engine Mounting Front RH	1	16	Assy-Member Engine Mounting Rear	1			

ENGINE MOUNTING (MANUAL FROM C/# HLS30-46001, RLS30, GRLS30)

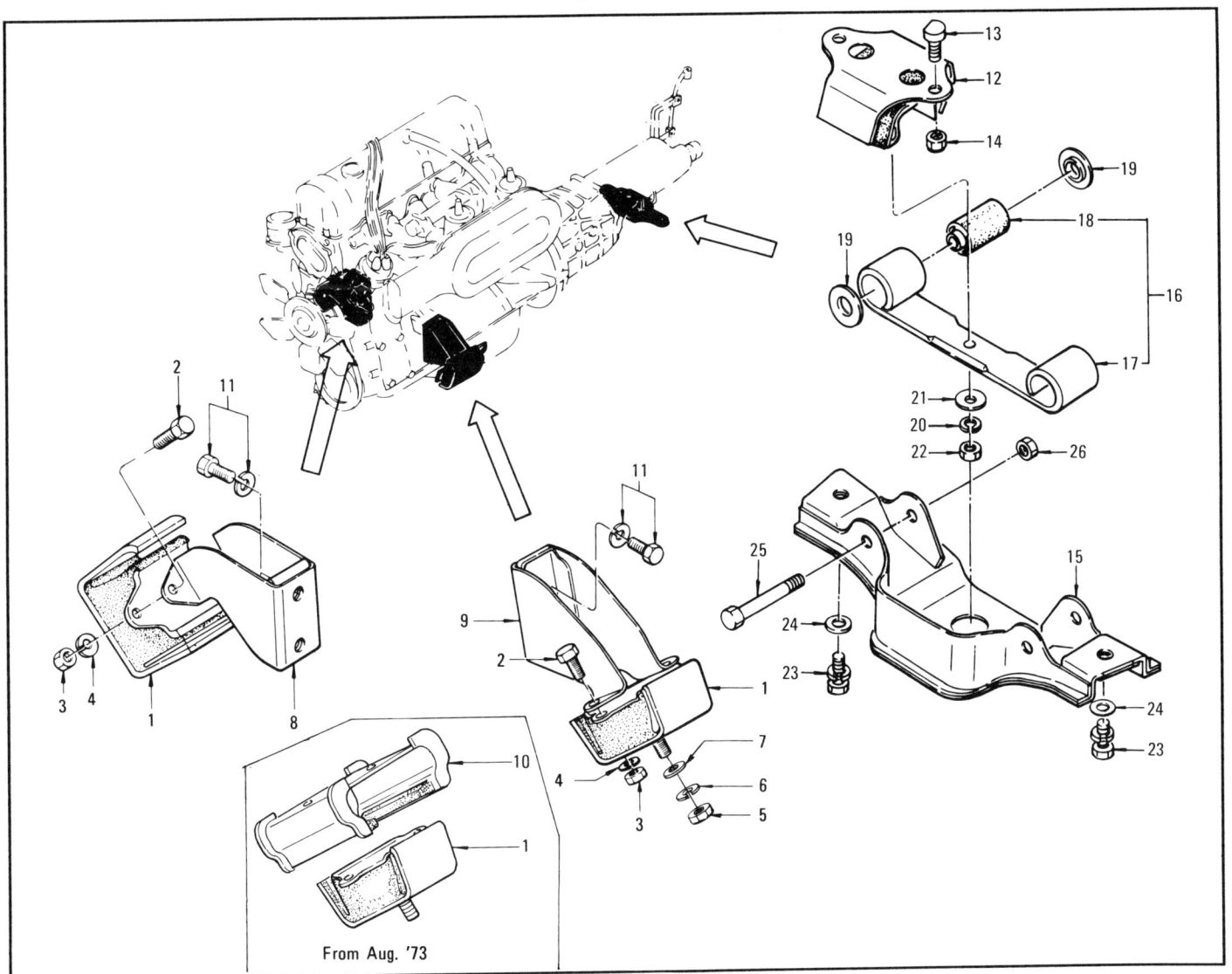

From Aug. '73

Item	Description	Qty	Item	Description	Qty	Item	Description	Qty
1	Assy-Insulator Engine Mounting Front	2	10	Assy-Stopper Engine Mounting Front	2	19	Stopper-Engine Mounting Rear	4
2	Bolt-Hex M8x1.25	4	11	Bolt-Hex with Spring Washer	4	20	Washer-Spring Lock	1
3	Nut-Hex M8x1.25	4	12	Assy-Insulator Engine Mounting Rear	1	21	Washer-Plain	1
4	Washer-Spring Lock	4	13	Bolt-Engine Mounting Rear	2	22	Nut-Hex M10x1.25	1
5	Nut-Hex M10x1.25	2	14	Nut-Self Locking	2	23	Bolt-Hex with Spring Washer	2
6	Washer-Spring Lock	2	15	Assy-Member Engine Mounting Rear	1	24	Washer-Plain (Left Only)	1
7	Washer-Plain	2	16	Assy-Spring Engine Mounting Rear	1	25	Bolt-Hex M12x1.25	2
8	Assy-Bracket Engine Mounting Front RH	1	17	Spring-Engine Mounting Rear	1	26	Nut-Self Locking	2
9	Assy-Bracket Engine Mounting Front LH	1	18	Assy-Bush Engine Mounting	2			

210 How to Restore Your Datsun Z-car

FUEL PIPING

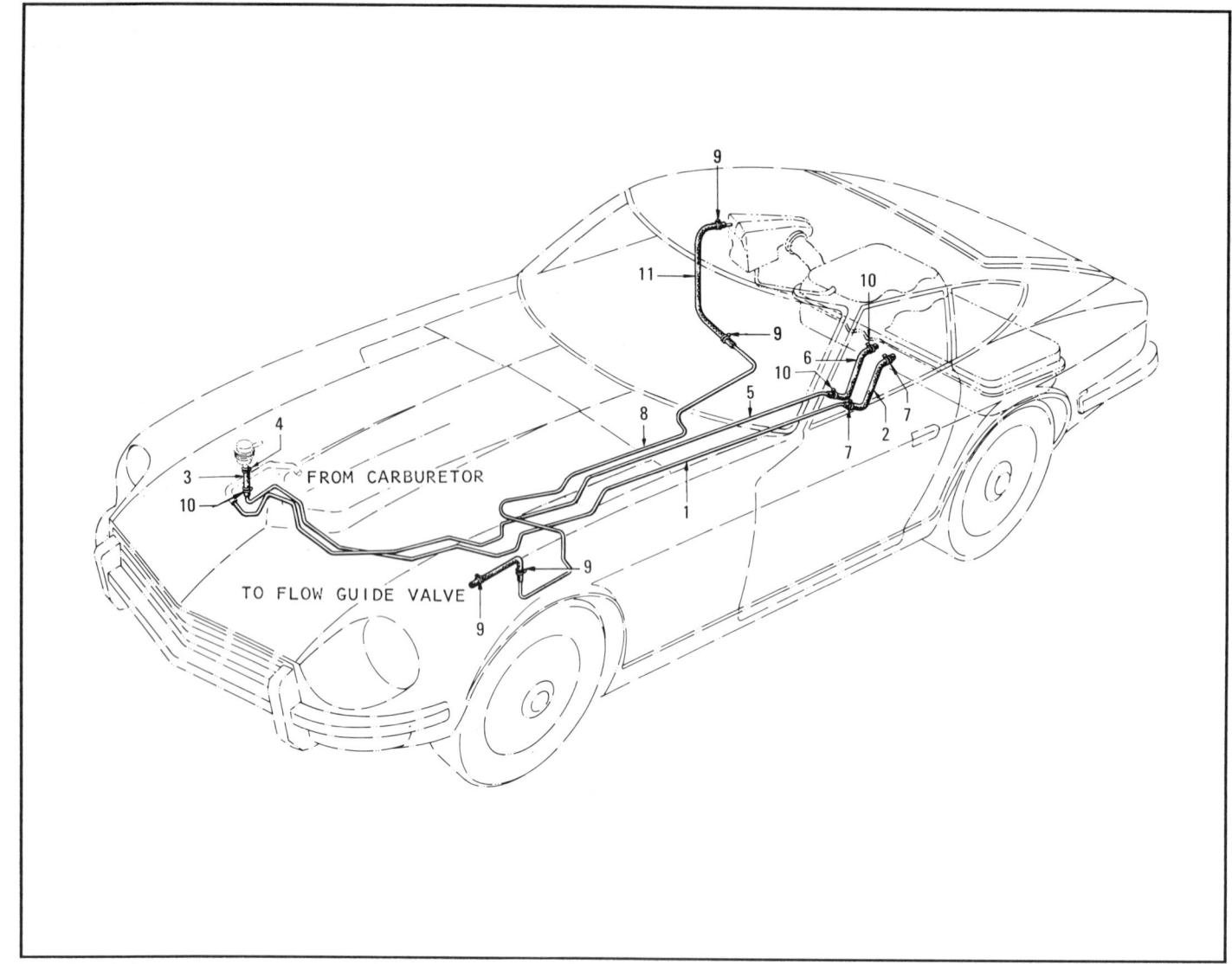

Item	Description	Qty
1	Tube-Fuel Tank To Strainer	1
2	Tube-Flexible Tank to Tube	1
3	Tube-Flexible Tube to Strainer	1
4	Clamp-Hose	2
5	Tube-Fuel Return	1
6	Tube-Flexible Tube to Tank	1
7	Clamp-Hose	4
8	Tube-Air Supplier	1
9	Clamp-Hose	2
10	Clamp-Hose	3
11	Hose-Air Supplier	

Parts Illustrations 211

FRONT SUSPENSION (STRUT & SHOCK ABSORBER)

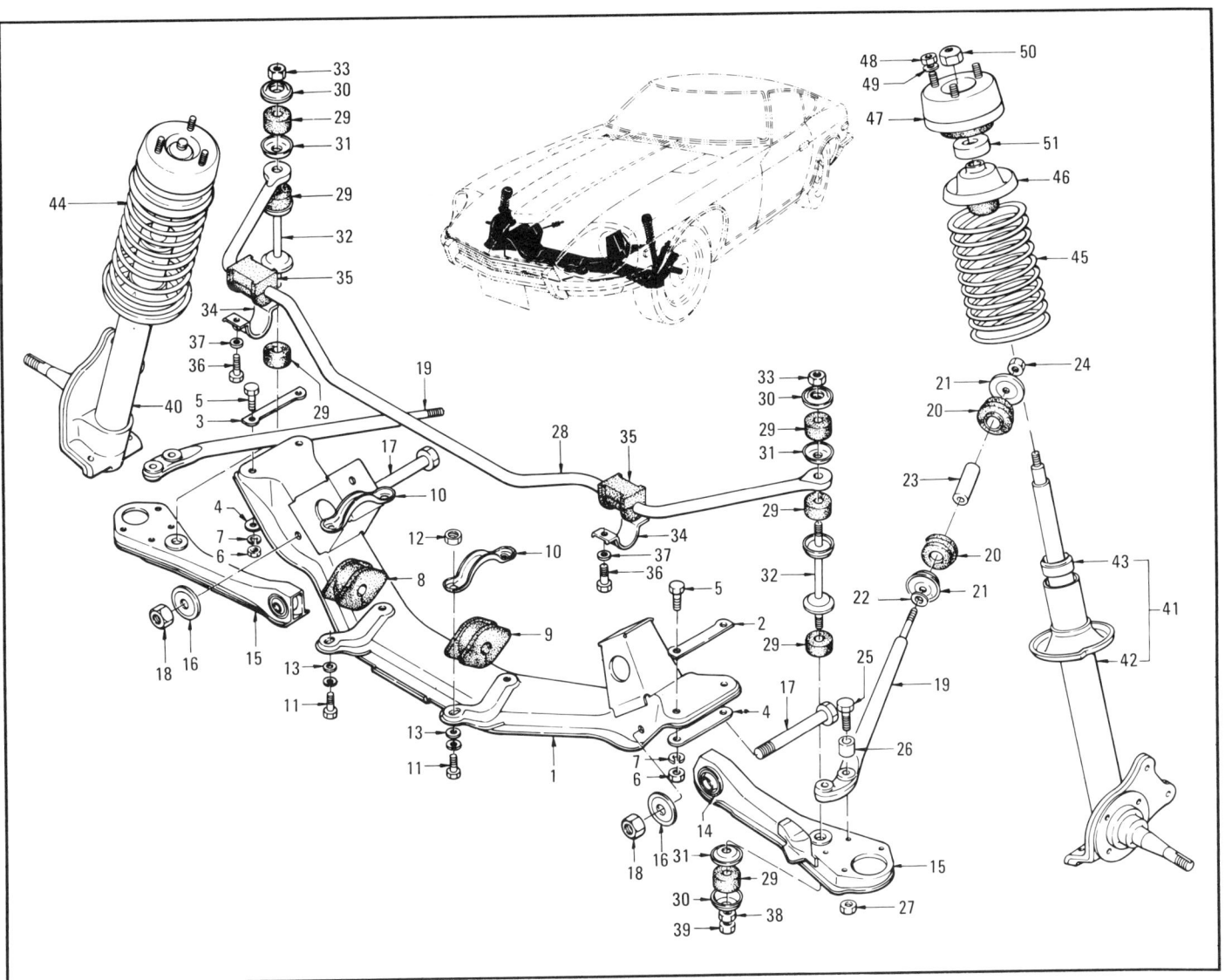

Item	Description	Qty	Item	Description	Qty	Item	Description	Qty
1	Assy-Member Front Suspension	1	18	Nut-Self Locking S	2	35	Bush-Stabilizer Mounting	2
2	Washer-Special	4	19	Rod-Compression Front Suspension	2	36	Bolt-Hex M8x1.25	4
3	Washer-Special	2	20	Bush-Mounting Compression Rod	4	37	Washer-Spring Lock	4
4	Washer-Plain	2	21	Washer-Special Bush Mounting Outer	4	38	Nut-Hex M10x1.25	2
5	Bolt-Hex M10x1.25	4	22	Washer-Plain	2	39	Nut-Hex M10x1.25	2
6	Nut-Hex M10x1.25	4	23	Collar-Bush Tension Rod	2	40	Assy-Strut Front Suspension RH	1
7	Washer-Spring Lock	4	24	Nut-Self Locking S	2	41	Assy-Strut Front Suspension LH	21
8	Insulator-Rack Mounting Steering A	1	25	Bolt-Hex M10x1.25	4	42	Kit-Seal Strut	2
9	Insulator-Rack Mounting Steering B	1	26	Washer-Special	4	43	Assy-Shock Absorber Front	2
10	Assy-Bracket Rack Mounting Upper	2	27	Nut-Self Locking	4	44	Spring-Front RH (Ratio 1.49 KG/MM)	1
11	Bolt-Hex M8x1.25	4	28	Bar-Torsion Front Stabilizer	1	45	Spring-Front LH (Ratio 1.49 KG/MM)	1
12	Nut-Self Locking	4	29	Bush-Rubber Shock Absorber	8	46	Assy-Bumper Bound	2
13	Washer-Plain	4	30	Washer-Special Outer	4	47	Assy-Insulator Strut Mounting	2
14	Assy-Bush Transverse Link	2	31	Washer-Special Inner	2	48	Nut-Hex M10x1.25	6
15	Assy-Link Transverse Front Suspension	2	32	Assy-Rod Connecting Front Stabilizer	2	49	Washer-Spring Lock	6
16	Washer-Special Inner	2	33	Nut-Self Locking S	2	50	Nut-Self Locking S	2
17	Bolt-Transverse Link	2	34	Bracket-Stabilizer Mounting	2	51	Bearing-Strut Mounting	2

212 How to Restore Your Datsun Z-car

REAR SUSPENSION (STRUT, SHOCK ABSORBER & TRANSVERSE LINK)

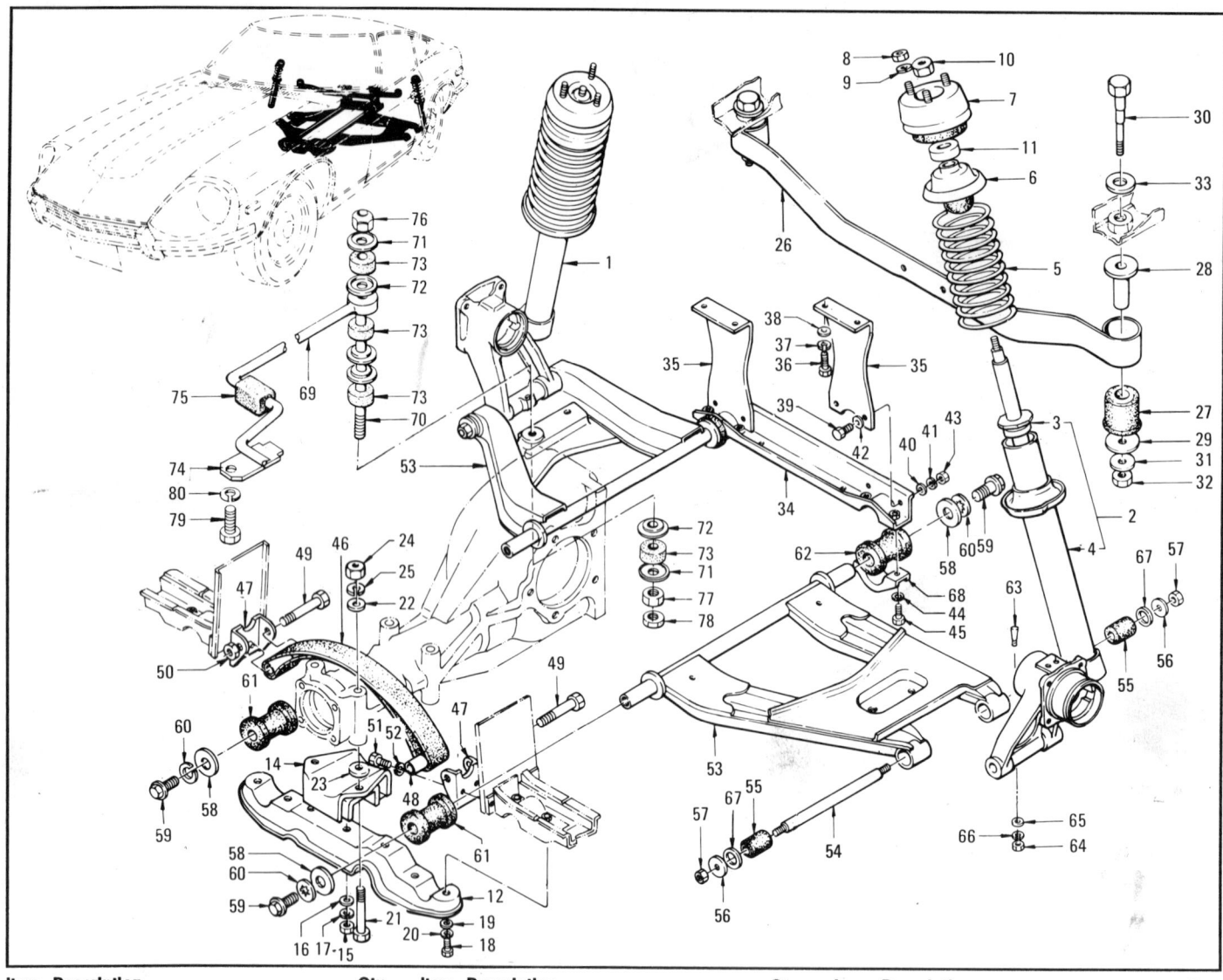

Item	Description	Qty	Item	Description	Qty	Item	Description	Qty
1	Assy-Strut Rear Suspension RH	1	29	Stopper-Differential Mounting Lower	2	56	Washer-Plain M12	4
2	Assy-Strut Rear Suspension LH	1	30	Bolt-Rear Suspension Mounting Rear	2	57	Nut-Self Locking S	4
3	Kit-Seal Strut	2	31	Washer-Plain M12	4	58	Washer-Special B	4
4	Assy-Shock Absorber Rear	2	32	Nut-Self Locking S	4	59	Bolt-Transverse Link MTG Rear Suspension	4
5	Spring-Rear (Ratio 1.80 KG/MM)	2	33	Washer-Plain M18	2	60	Washer-Lock Internal Tooth	4
6	Assy-Bumper Bound	2	34	Assy-Member Transverse Link Mtg Rear Suspension	1	61	Assy-Bush Transverse Link Inner Front	2
7	Assy-Insulator Strut Mounting	2	35	Brace-Transverse Link Mounting	2	62	Assy-Bush Transverse Link Inner Front	2
8	Nut-Hex M10x1.25	6	36	Bolt-Hex M10	4	63	Bolt-Lock Transverse Link Spindle RR Suspension	2
9	Washer-Spring Lock	6	37	Washer-Spring Lock	4	64	Nut-Hex M8	2
10	Nut-Self Locking S	2	38	Washer-Special	4	65	Washer-Plain	2
11	Spacer-Rear Spring	2	39	Bolt-Hex M10	4	66	Washer-Spring Lock	2
12	Assy-Member Differential Mounting Front	1	40	Washer-Plain M10	4	67	Stopper-Rubber Transverse Link	4
13	Washer-Special D	2	41	Washer-Spring Lock	4	68	Bracket-Transverse Link Mounting	2
14	Assy-Insulator Differential Mounting Front	1	42	Washer-Special	4	69	Bar-Torsion Rear Stabilizer	1
15	Nut-Hex M10	1	43	Nut-Hex M10	4	70	Assy-Rod Connecting Stabilizer	2
16	Washer-Plain M10	1	44	Washer-Spring Lock	4	71	Washer-Special Outer	4
17	Washer-Spring Lock	1	45	Bolt-Hex M10	4	72	Washer-Special Inner	4
18	Bolt-Hex M10	4	46	Belt-Arrester Differential Torque	1	73	Bush-Rubber Shock Absorber	8
19	Washer-Plain	4	47	Bracket-Arrester Differential Torque	2	74	Plate-Stabilizer Mounting	2
20	Washer-Spring Lock	4	48	Pipe-Arrester Differential Torque	2	75	Bush-Rubber Stabilizer Mounting	2
21	Bolt-Hex M12	2	49	Bolt-Hex M16	2	76	Nut-Self Locking	2
22	Washer-Plain M12	2	50	Nut-Self Locking S	2	77	Nut-Hex	2
23	Plate-Spacer Differential Mounting	2	51	Bolt-Hex M10	4	78	Nut-Hex	2
24	Nut-Hex M12	2	52	Washer-Spring Lock	4	79	Bolt-Hex	2
25	Washer-Spring Lock	2	53	Assy-Link Transverse Rear Suspension	2	80	Washer-Spring Lock	2
26	Comp-Member Differential Mounting Rear	1	54	Spindle-Transverse Link Rear Suspension	2			
27	Insulator-Differential Mounting	2	55	Assy-Bush Transverse Link Outer	4			
28	Stopper-Differential Mounting Upper	2						

Hand Brake & Hand Brake Cable

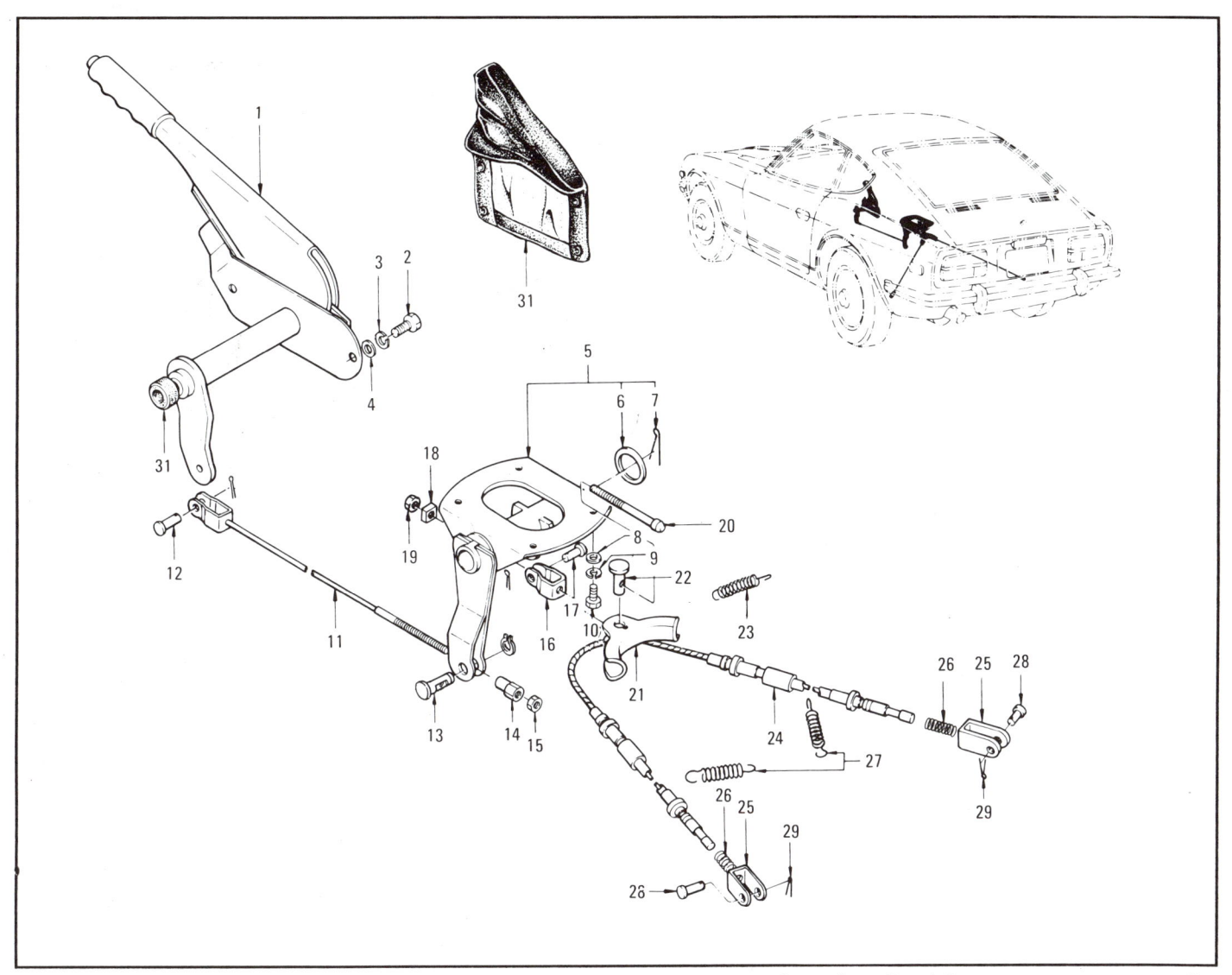

Item	Description	Qty	Item	Description	Qty	Item	Description	Qty
1	Assy-Hand Brake Control	1	12	Pin-Clevis	1	23	Spring-Return	1
2	Bolt-Hex	2	13	Trunnion-Pin Brake Cable	1	24	Assy-Cable Hand Brake Rear	1
3	Washer-Spring	2	14	Nut-Adjust Hand Brake Cable	1	25	Clevis-Hand Brake	2
4	Washer-Plain	2	15	Nut-Hex	1	26	Spring-Return Rear Cable	2
5	Assy-Center Arm Hand Brake	1	16	Assy-Clevis Hand Brake	1	27	Spring-Rear Cable Hanger	2
6	Washer-Hand Brake Shaft	1	17	Pin-Clevis	1	28	Pin-Clevis	2
7	Pin-Cotter	1	18	Nut-Square	1	29	Pin-Cotter	2
8	Washer-Plain	4	19	Nut-Hex	1	30	Retainer-Hand Brake Cable	4
9	Washer-Spring	4	20	Bolt-Hand Brake	1	31	Boot-Hand Brake Lever Shaft	1
10	Bolt-Hex	4	21	Equalizer-Hand Brake	1	32	Cover-Hand Brake Lever	1
11	Assy-Rod Hand Brake Front	1	22	Trunnion-Pin Brake Cable	1			

214 How to Restore Your Datsun Z-car

FRONT BRAKE (DISC BRAKE)

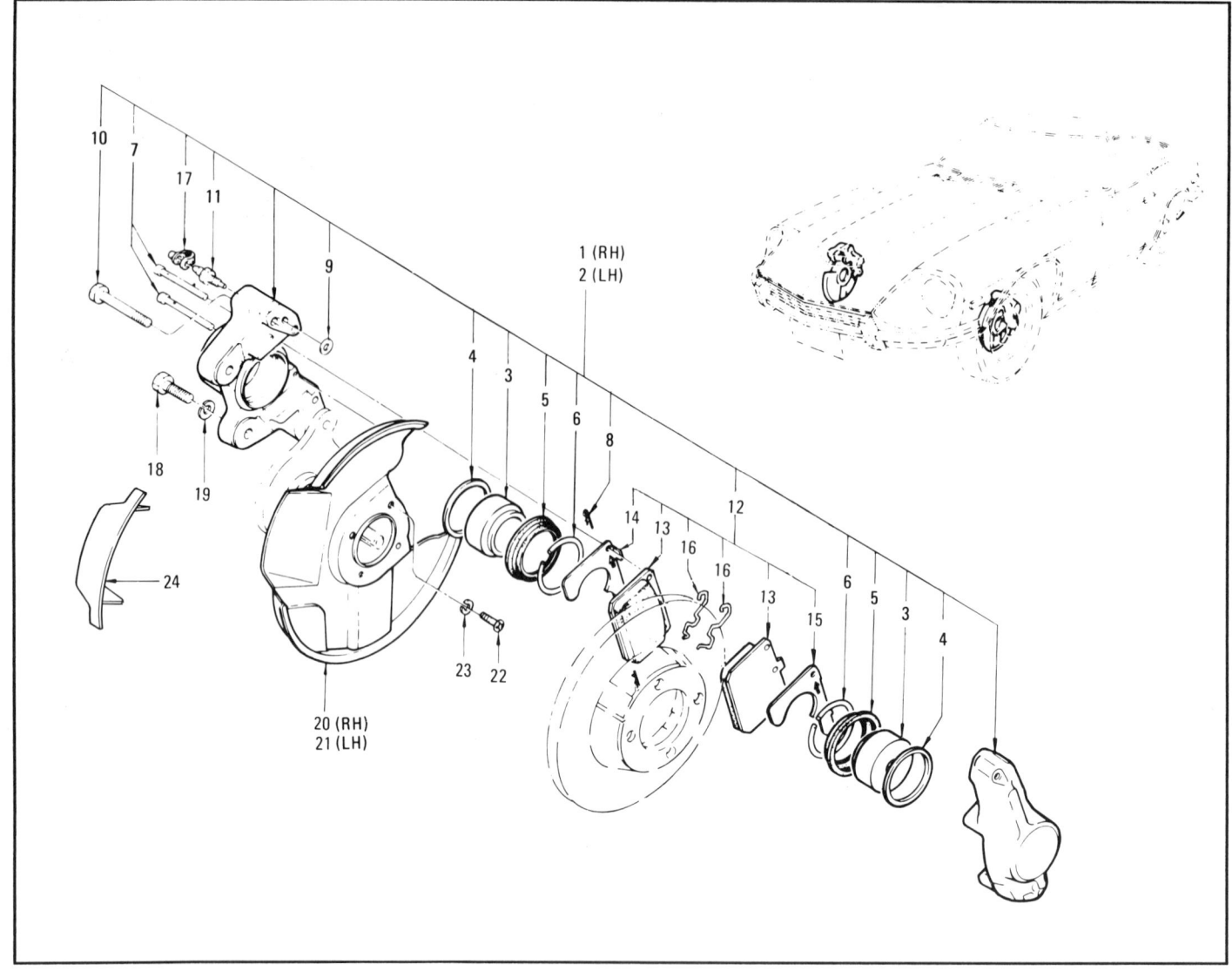

Item	Description	Qty	Item	Description	Qty	Item	Description	Qty
1	Assy-Caliper Front Brake RH	1	9	Seal-Caliper	4	17	Cap	2
2	Assy-Caliper Front Brake LH	1	10	Bolt-Bridge	8	18	Bolt-Fix Caliper	4
3	Piston	4	11	Screw-Breeder	2	19	Washer-Lock M12	4
4	Piston-Seal	4	12	Kit-Pad Disc Brake	1	20	Plate-Baffle Front RH	1
5	Dust-Seal	4	13	Assy-Pad	4	21	Plate-Baffle Front LH	1
6	Retaining Ring	4	14	Shim RH	2	22	Screw-Machine M6x1.0	8
7	Assy-Pin	4	15	Shim LH	2	23	Washer-Lock M6	8
8	Assy-Clip	4	16	Damping-Spring	4	24	Cover-Baffle Plate RH	1

Parts Illustrations 215

REAR BRAKE (DRUM BRAKE)

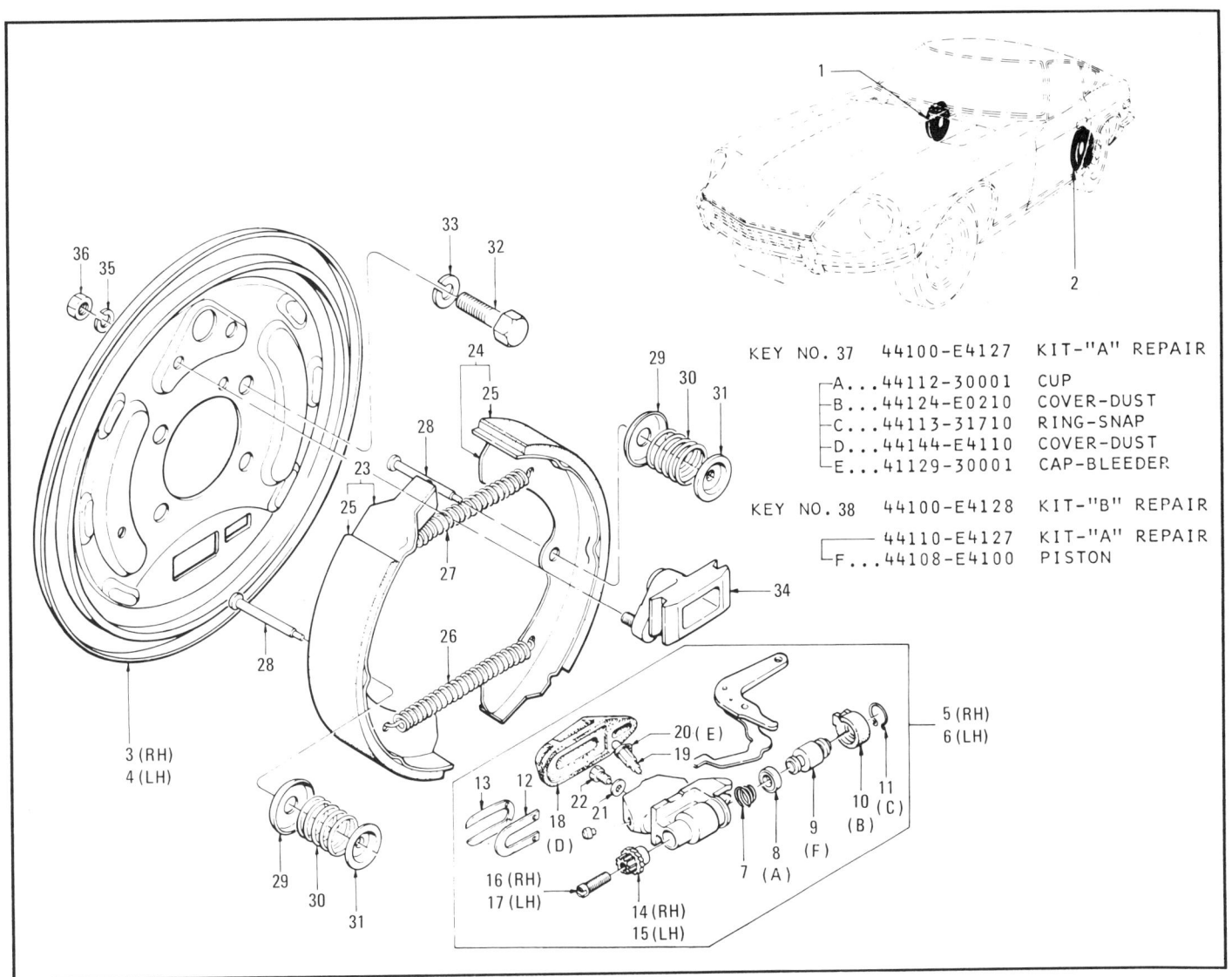

```
KEY NO. 37   44100-E4127   KIT-"A" REPAIR
  A... 44112-30001   CUP
  B... 44124-E0210   COVER-DUST
  C... 44113-31710   RING-SNAP
  D... 44144-E4110   COVER-DUST
  E... 41129-30001   CAP-BLEEDER

KEY NO. 38   44100-E4128   KIT-"B" REPAIR
       44110-E4127   KIT-"A" REPAIR
  F... 44108-E4100   PISTON
```

Item	Description	Qty	Item	Description	Qty	Item	Description	Qty
1	Assy-Brake Rear RH	1	14	Adjuster RH	1	27	Spring-Return Rear Brake Cylinder Side	2
2	Assy-Brake Rear LH	1	15	Adjuster LH	1	28	Pin-Anti Shoe Rattle	4
3	Assy-Disc Rear Brake RH	1	16	Screw-Adjuster RH	1	29	Set-Spring Anti Shoe Rattle	4
4	Assy-Disc Rear Brake LH	1	17	Screw-Adjuster LH	1	30	Spring-Anti Shoe Rattle	4
5	Assy-Cylinder Rear Wheel RH	1	18	Cover-Dust	1	31	Retainer-Spring Anti Shoe Rattle	4
6	Assy-Cylinder Rear Wheel LH	1	19	Screw-Bleeder	1	32	Bolt-Hex M10x1.25	8
7	Spring	1	20	Cap-Bleeder	1	33	Washer-Lock M10	8
8	Cup	1	21	Packing	1	34	Assy-Block Anchor	2
9	Piston	1	22	Stopper	1	35	Washer-Lock M8	4
10	Cover-Dust	1	23	Assy-Shoe Rear Brake, Leading	2	36	Nut-Hex M8x1.25	4
11	Ring-Snap	1	24	Assy-Shoe Rear Brake, Trailing	2	37	Kit-A Repair For Rear Wheel Cylinder	1
12	Plate-Adjuster	1	25	Lining-Brake	4	38	Kit-B Repair For Rear Wheel Cylinder	1
13	Plate-Lock	1	26	Spring-Return Rear Brake Cylinder Side	2			

BRAKE PIPING (UP TO JUNE '72)

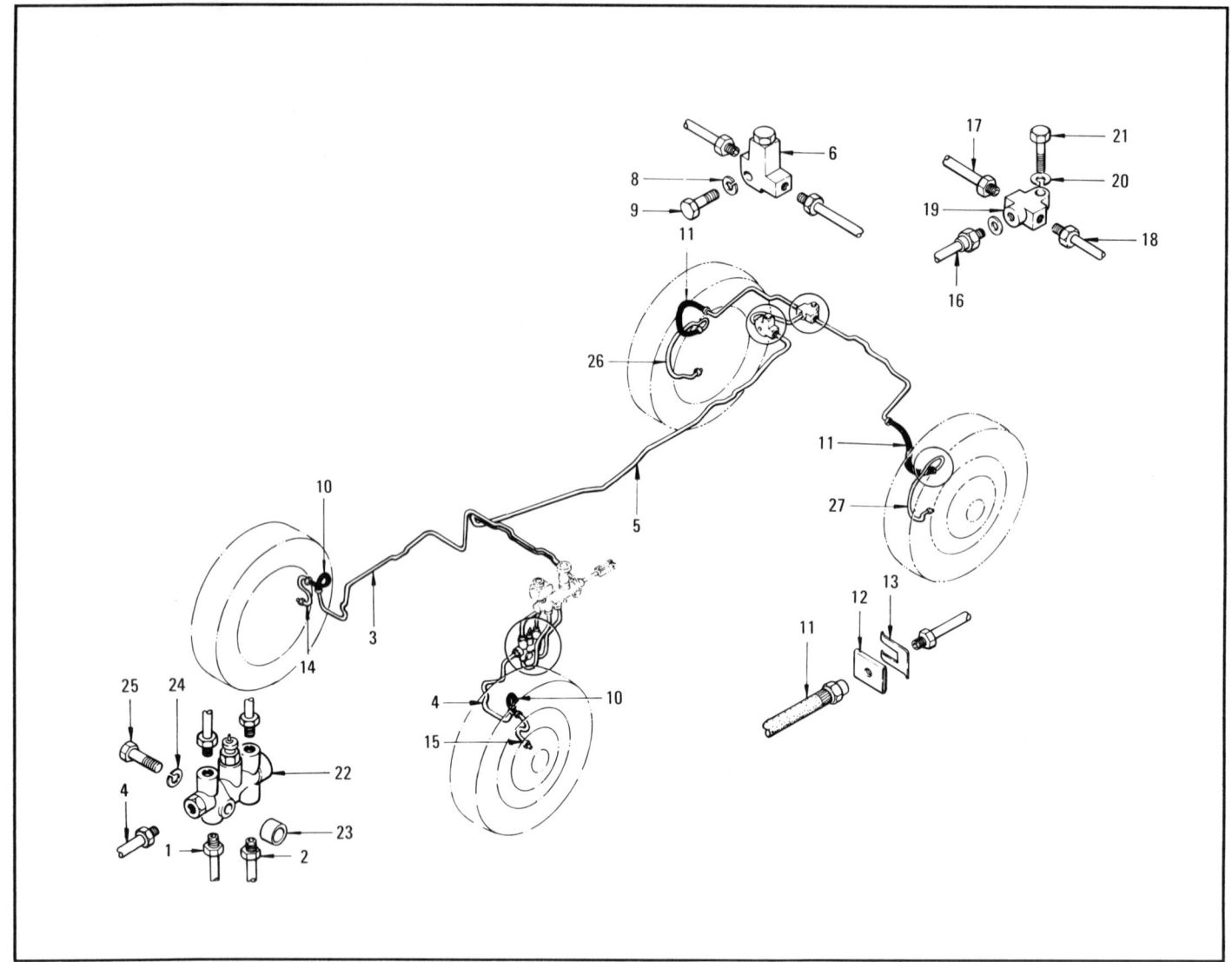

Item	Description	Qty	Item	Description	Qty	Item	Description	Qty
1	Assy-Tube Brake Master Cylinder to F/I Front	1	12	Plate-Lock Brake Hose	8	24	Washer-Lock M6	1
2	Assy-Tube Brake Master Cylinder to F/I Rear	1	13	Spring-Lock Brake Hose	8	25	Bolt-Hex M6x1.0	1
			14	Assy-Tube Bridge Front Brake RH	1	26	Assy-Tube Bridge Rear Brake RH	1
3	Assy-Tube F/I to Front Brake Hose RH	1	15	Assy-Tube Bridge Front Brake LH	1	27	Assy-Tube Bridge Rear Brake LH	1
4	Assy-Tube B/I to Front Brake Hose LH	1	16	Assy-Tube Proportioning Valve to 3 Way Connector	1	28	Assy-Tube F/I to NP Valve Upper	1
5	Assy-Tube F/I to Proportioning Valve	1	17	Assy-Tube 3 Way to Rear Brake Hose RH	1	29	Assy-Tube F/I to NP Valve Lower	1
6	Assy-Proportioning Valve	1	18	Assy-Tube 3 Way to Rear Brake Hose LH	1	30	Rubber-Tube Clamp	2
7	Spacer-Connector Brake Tube	1	19	Connector-3 Way Brake Tube	1	31	Clamp-Tube Upper	2
8	Washer-Lock M6	1	20	Washer-Spring M8	1	32	Screw-Hex with S/Washer	2
9	Bolt-Hex M6x1.0	1	21	Bolt-Hex M8x1.25	1	33	Rubber-Tube Clamp	1
10	Assy-Hose Brake Front L=260 (10.24")	2	22	Assy-Switch Brake Indicator	1	34	Clamp-Tube Upper	1
11	Assy-Hose Brake Rear L=280 (11.02")	2	23	Spacer-Connector Brake Tube	1	35	Screw-Hex with S/Washer	1

BRAKE PIPING (FROM JULY '72)

Item	Description	Qty	Item	Description	Qty	Item	Description	Qty
1	Assy-Tube Brake Master Cylinder to F/I Front	1	12	Plate-Lock Brake Hose	8	24	Washer-Lock M6	1
2	Assy-Tube Brake Master Cylinder to F/I Rear	1	13	Spring-Lock Brake Hose	8	25	Bolt-Hex M6x1.0	1
			14	Assy-Tube Bridge Front Brake RH	1	26	Assy-Tube Bridge Rear Brake RH	1
3	Assy-Tube F/I to Front Brake Hose RH	1	15	Assy-Tube Bridge Front Brake LH	1	27	Assy-Tube Bridge Rear Brake LH	1
4	Assy-Tube B/I to Front Brake Hose LH	1	16	Assy-Tube Proportioning Valve to 3 Way Connector	1	28	Assy-Tube F/I to NP Valve Upper	1
5	Assy-Tube F/I to Proportioning Valve	1	17	Assy-Tube 3 Way to Rear Brake Hose RH	1	29	Assy-Tube F/I to NP Valve Lower	1
6	Assy-Proporting Valve	1	18	Assy-Tube 3 Way to Rear Brake Hose LH	1	30	Rubber-Tube Clamp	2
7	Spacer-Connector Brake Tube	1	19	Connector-3 Way Brake Tube	1	31	Clamp-Tube Upper	2
8	Washer-Lock M6	1	20	Washer-Spring M8	1	32	Screw-Hex with S/Washer	2
9	Bolt-Hex M6x1.0	1	21	Bolt-Hex M8x1.25	1	33	Rubber-Tube Clamp	1
10	Assy-Hose Brake Front L=260 (10.24")	2	22	Assy-Switch Brake Indicator	1	34	Clamp-Tube Upper	1
11	Assy-Hose Brake Rear L=280 (11.02")	2	23	Spacer-Connector Brake Tube	1	35	Screw-Hex with S/Washer	1

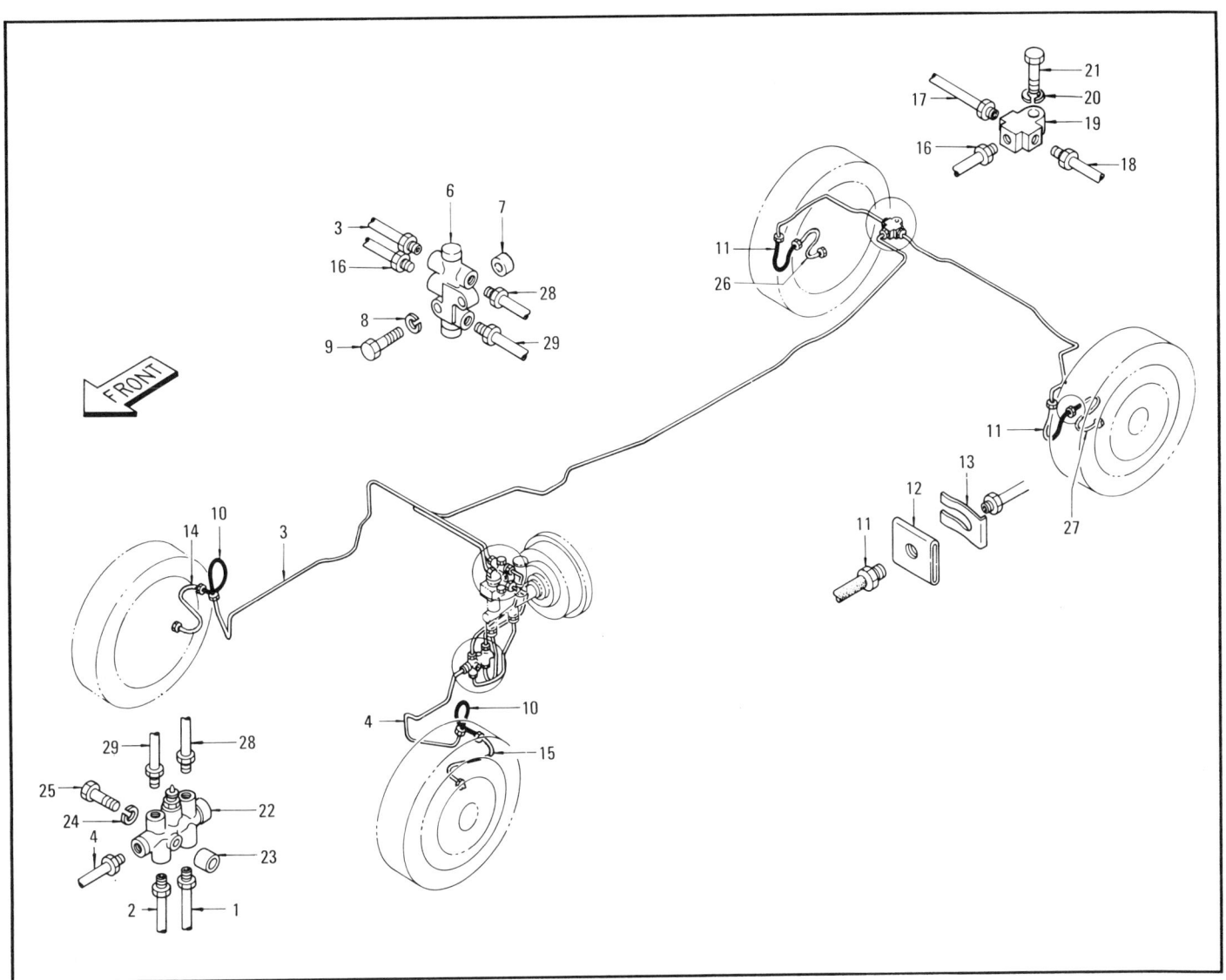

218 How to Restore Your Datsun Z-car

BRAKE & CLUTCH PEDAL

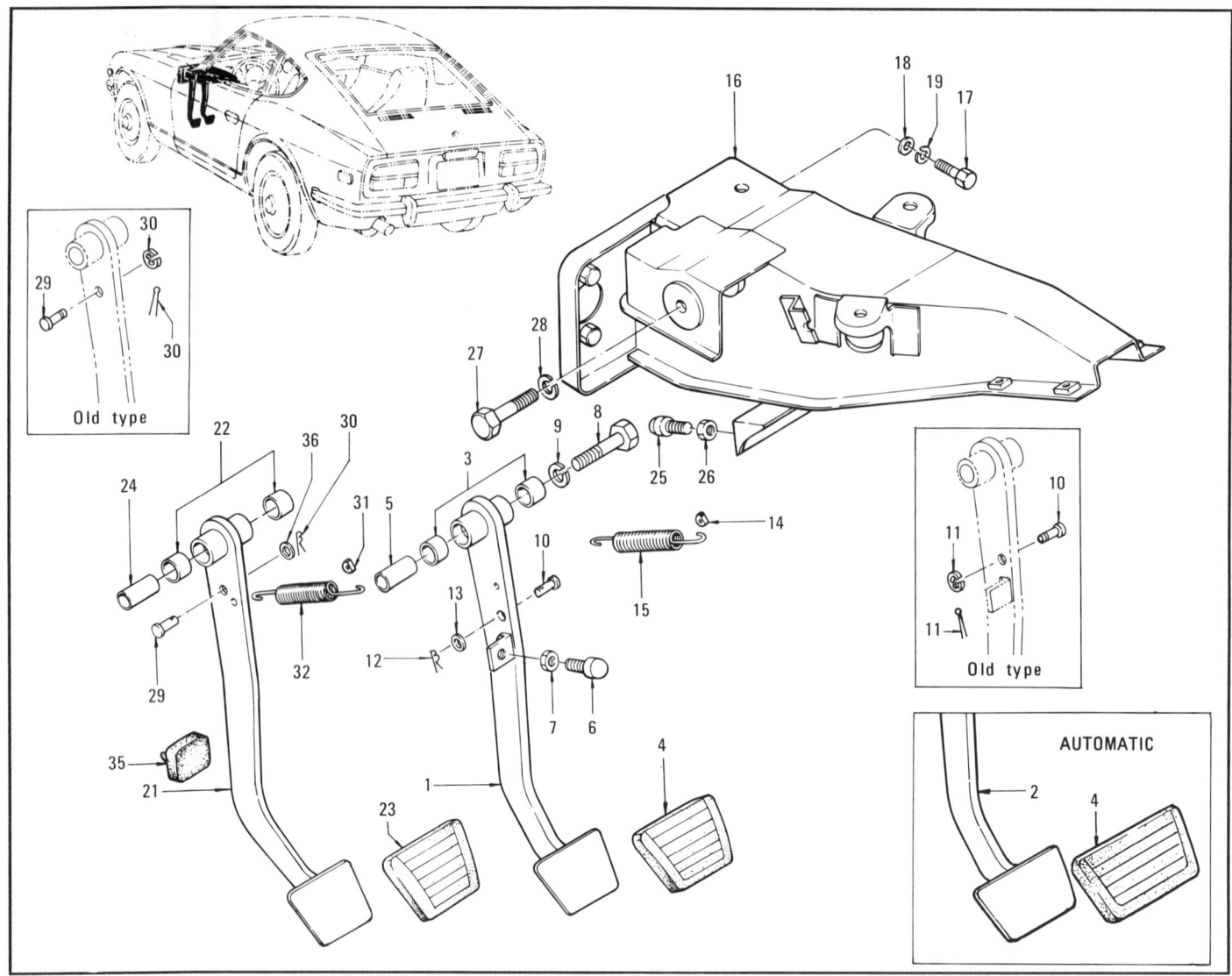

Item	Description	Qty	Item	Description	Qty	Item	Description	Qty
1	Assy-Pedal Brake	1	13	Washer-Plain	1	25	Assy-Stopper Pedal	1
2	Assy-Pedal Brake	1	14	Seat-Return Spring	1	26	Nut-Lock	1
3	Bush-Pedal Brake	2	15	Spring-Return Brake Pedal	1	27	Pin-Fulcrum RH Thread	1
4	Cover-Pedal Pad Brake	1	16	Assy-Bracket Pedal Steering Support	1	28	Washer-Spring M12	1
5	Sleeve-Pedal Shaft	1	17	Bolt-Hex M8	5	29	Pin-Clevis (L 16)	1
6	Assy-Stopper Pedal	1	18	Washer-Plain	5	30	Pin-Cotter	1
7	Nut-Lock	1	19	Washer-Spring	5	31	Seat-Return Spring	1
8	Pin-Fulcurm	1	20	Protector-Flange	1	32	Spring-Return Clutch Pedal	1
9	Washer-Spring	1	21	Assy-Pedal Clutch	1	33	Nut M8x1.25	2
10	Pin-Clevis	1	22	Bush-Pedal Clutch	2	34	Washer-Spring	2
11	Pin-Cotter	1	23	Cover-Pedal Pad Clutch	1	35	Bumper-Clutch Pedal Stopper	1
12	Pin-Snap	1	24	Sleeve-Pedal Shaft	1	36	Washer-Plain	1

MASTER VAC & VAC HOSE

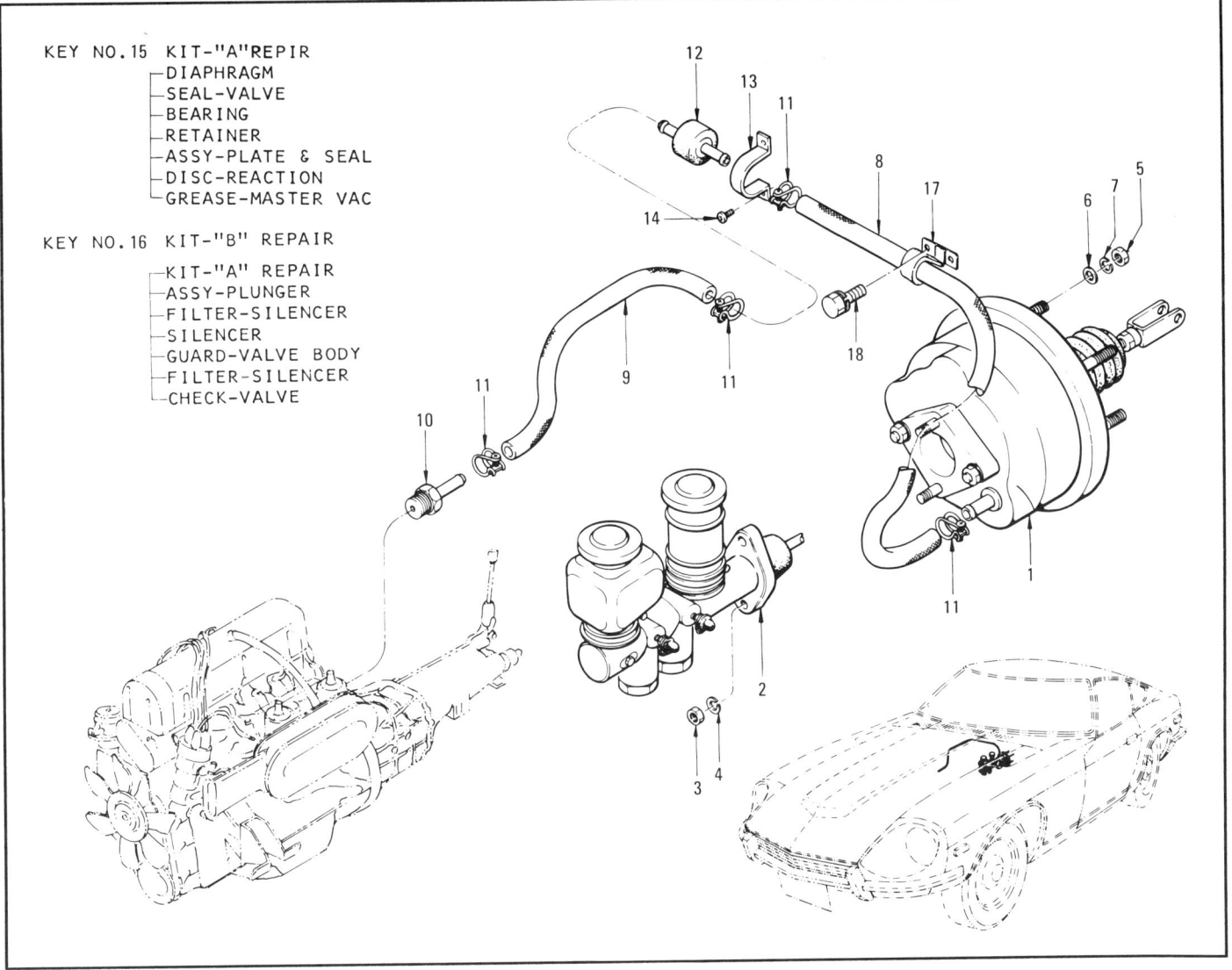

KEY NO. 15 KIT-"A" REPIR
- DIAPHRAGM
- SEAL-VALVE
- BEARING
- RETAINER
- ASSY-PLATE & SEAL
- DISC-REACTION
- GREASE-MASTER VAC

KEY NO. 16 KIT-"B" REPAIR
- KIT-"A" REPAIR
- ASSY-PLUNGER
- FILTER-SILENCER
- SILENCER
- GUARD-VALVE BODY
- FILTER-SILENCER
- CHECK-VALVE

Item	Description	Qty	Item	Description	Qty
1	Assy-Master Vac 6 Inch	1	10	Connector-Vac Hose	1
2	Assy-Cylinder Brake Tandem Master	1	11	Clamp-Hose	4
3	Nut-Hex M8x1.25	2	12	Assy-Valve Check	1
4	Washer-Lock M8	2	13	Clamp-Check Valve	1
5	Nut-Hex M8x1.25	4	14	Screw-Tapping	2
6	Washer-Plain M8	4	15	Kit-A Repair For Master Vac	1
7	Washer-Lock M8x1.25	4	16	Kit-B Repair For Master Vac	1
8	Hose-Master Vac Master Vac Side	1	17	Clamp-Hose Master Vac	1
9	Hose-Master Vac Engine Side	1	18	Screw-Hex With S/Washer	2

FRONT FENDER, HEAD LAMP CASE, HOOD LEDGE & HOOD (UP TO JULY '73)

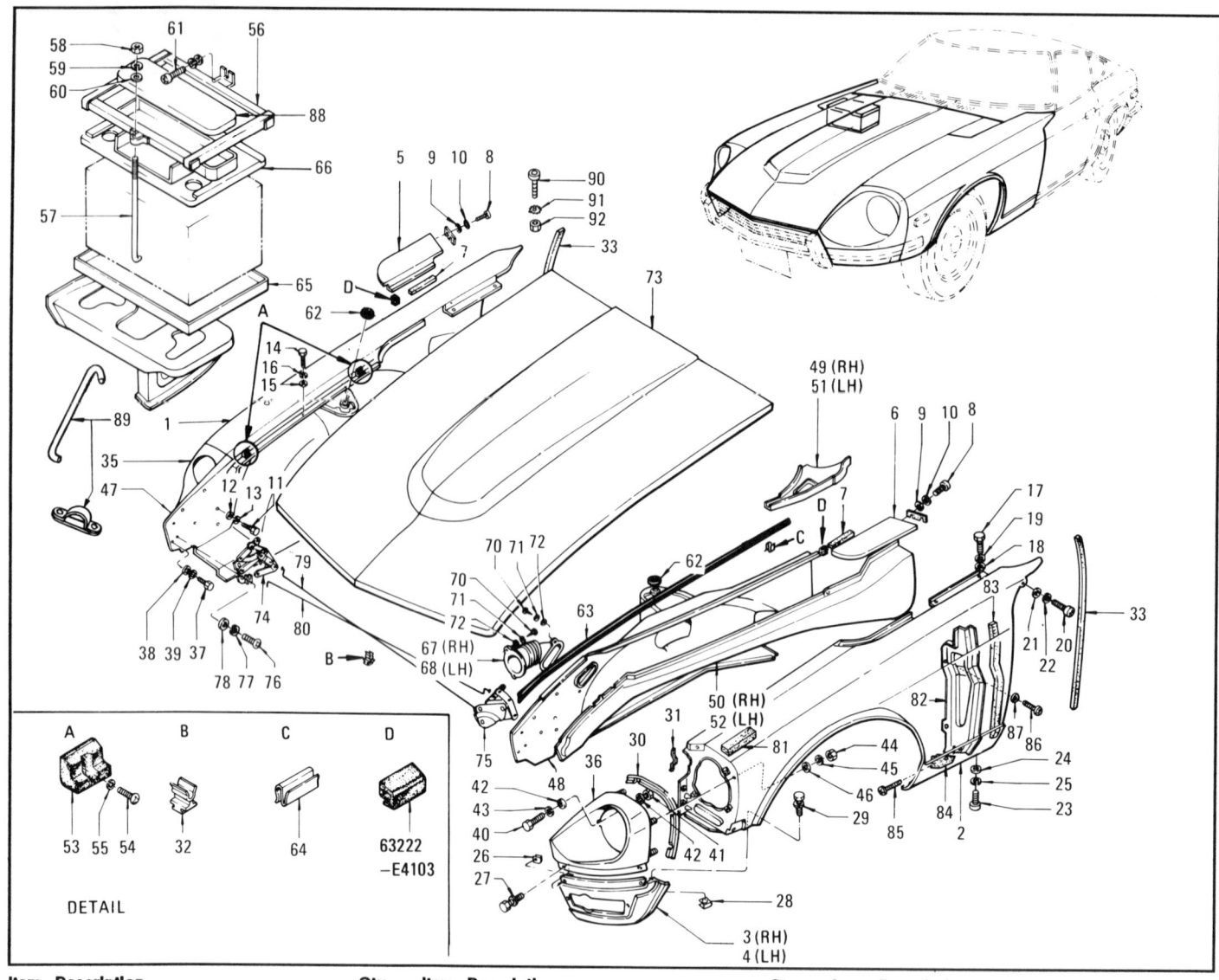

Item	Description	Qty	Item	Description	Qty	Item	Description	Qty
1	Assy-Front Fender RH	1	29	Cam Screw with Washer	4	61	Screw-Machine M6	1
2	Assy-Front Fender LH	1	30	Packing-Front Fender	2	62	Cap-Insulator Front Strut Mounting	2
3	Panel-Front Fender Front RH	1	31	Sealing-Head Lamp Support	2	63	Rubber-Sealing Side	2
4	Panel-Front Fender Front LH	1	32	Lock-Lid Inspection	2	64	Clip-Sealing Rubber	12
5	Assy-Lid Battery Inspection RH (Lock-Put In Type)	1	33	Filler-Baffle Front Fender	2	65	Tray-Battery	1
6	Assy-Lid Battery Inspection LH (Lock-Put In Type)	1	34	Packing-Battery Cover	2	66	Cover-Battery	1
			35	Case-Head Lamp RH (FRP)	1	67	Assy-Guide Air Intake RH	1
7	Rubber-Cushion	2	36	Case-Head Lamp LH (FRP)	1	68	Assy-Guide Air Intake LH	1
8	Screw-Machine M5x0.8	4	37	Bolt-Hex	6	69	Plate-Guide Air Intake	2
9	Washer-Plain	4	38	Washer-Plain	6	70	Screw-Tapping	8
10	Washer-Lock	4	39	Washer-Spring	6	71	Washer-Lock	8
11	Bolt-Hex Head Lamp Support to Hood Ledge	4	40	Bolt-Hex	4	72	Washer-Plain	8
			41	Nut-Hex	4	73	Assy-Hood	1
12	Washer-Plain Head Lamp Support to Hood Ledge	4	42	Washer-Plain	8	74	Assy-Hinge Hood RH	1
			43	Washer-Spring	4	75	Assy-Hinge Hood LH	1
13	Washer-Spring Head Lamp Support to Hood Ledge	4	44	Nut-Hex	6	76	Screw-Machine	10
			45	Washer-Spring	6	77	Washer-Lock	10
14	Bolt-Hex Fender to Hood Ledge	6	46	Washer-Plain	6	78	Washer-Plain	10
15	Washer-Plain Fender to Hood Ledge	6	47	Assy-Hood Ledge RH	1	79	Bar-Torsion Hood Hinge RH	1
17	Bolt-Hex Cowl Top to Fender	4	48	Assy-Hood Ledge LH	1	80	Bar-Torsion Hood Hinge LH	1
18	Washer-Plain Cowl Top to Fender	4	49	Gusset-Hood Ledge Corner Rear RH	1	81	Pack-Front Fender	2
19	Washer-Spring Cowl Top to Fender	4	50	Assy-Reinf Hood Ledge RH	1	82	Mud Guard-Fender RH	1
20	Screw-Machine Fender to Pillar	2	51	Gusset-Hood Ledge Corner Rear LH	1	83	Sealing-Mud Guard	2
21	Washer-Plain Fender to Pillar	2	52	Assy-Reinf Hood Ledge LH	1	84	Rubber-Mud Guard	2
22	Washer-Spring Fender to Pillar	2	53	Bumper-Hood	4	85	Screw	4
23	Screw-Machine Fender to Sill	4	54	Screw-Machine M6	4	86	Screw	6
24	Washer-Plain Fender to Sill	4	55	Washer-Spring M6	4	87	Washer-Plain	6
25	Washer-Spring Fender to Sill	4	56	Assy-Frame Battery Fix	1	88	Cap-Battery Cover	1
26	Nut-Joint Retainer	4	57	Rod-Battery Support	1	89	Assy-Rod Hood Support	1
27	Cam-Screw with Washer	4	58	Nut-Hex M6	1	90	Comp.-Hood Bumper	2
28	Nut-Joint Retainer	4	59	Washer-Spring M6	2	91	Washer-Lock Hood Bumper	2
			60	Washer-Plain M6	1	92	Nut-Hex Hood Bumper	2

FLOOR TRIM, MAT, INSULATOR & REAR WHEEL HOUSE TRIM (UP TO JULY '73)

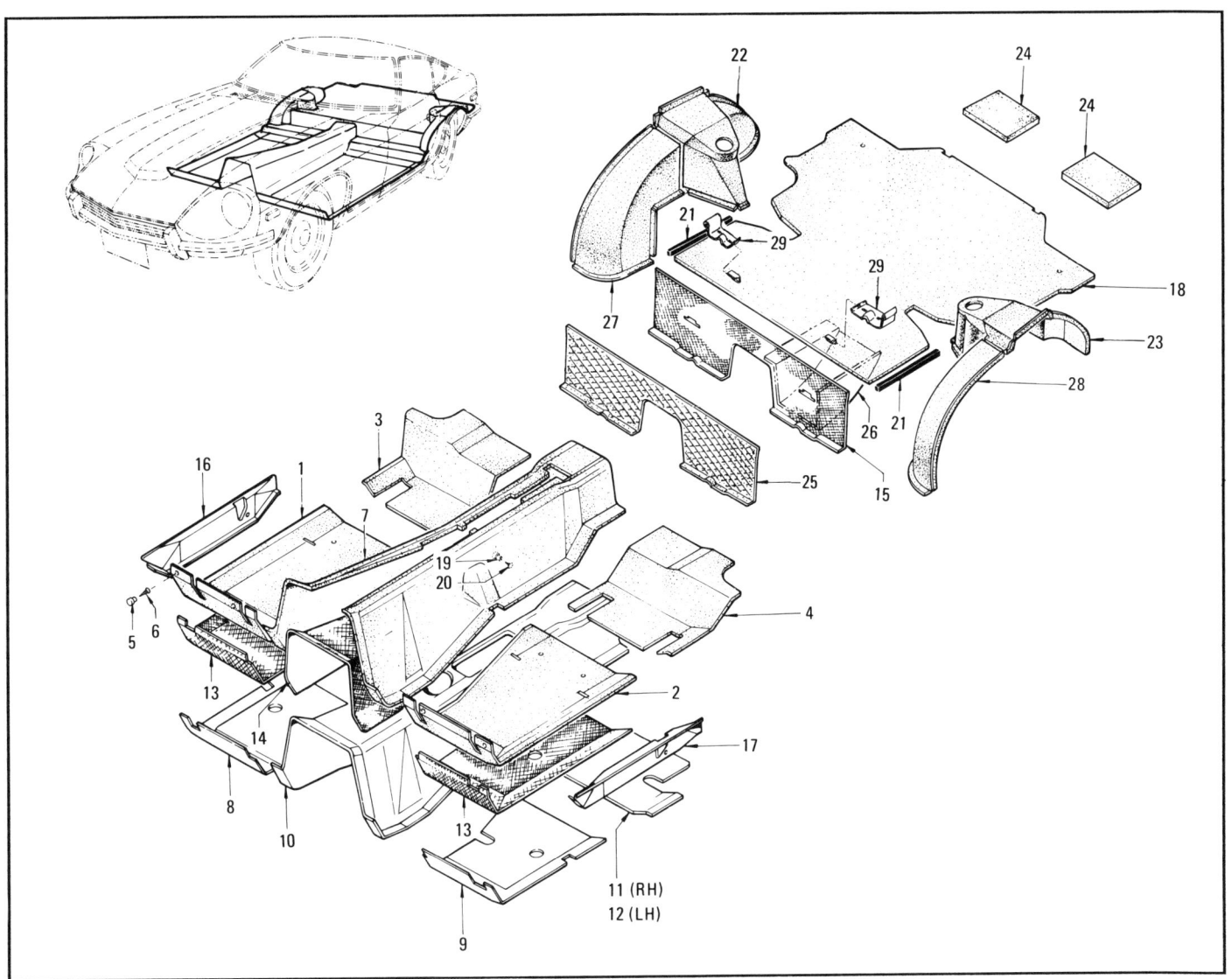

Item	Description	Qty
1	Assy-Trim Front Floor RH Black (Carpet)	1
2	Assy-Trim Front Floor LH Black (Carpet)	1
3	Assy-Trim Rear Floor RH Black (Resin)	1
4	Assy-Trim Rear Floor LH Black (Resin)	1
5	Fastener-Male	14
6	Screw-Tapping M3.5	14
7	Mat-Tunnel Front Floor Black	1
8	Insulator-Front Floor Front RH	1
9	Insulator-Front Floor Front LH	1
10	Insulator-Front Floor Tunnel	1
11	Insulator-Front Floor Rear RH	1
12	Insulator-Front Floor Rear LH	1
13	Jute-Front Floor Front	1
14	Jute-Front Floor Tunnel	1
15	Jute-Front Floor Rear	1
16	Trim-Sill Inner RH Black (Carpet)	1
17	Trim-Sill Inner LH Black (Carpet)	1
18	Assy-Mat Rear Floor Black (Resin)	1
19	Fastener-Male	4
20	Screw-Tapping	4
21	Rubber-Seal Rear Floor	2
22	Trim-Rear Wheel House Inner Rear RH Black	1
23	Trim-Rear Wheel House Inner Rear LH Black	1
24	Assy-Fastener Rear Floor Mat	2
25	Trim-Riser Rear Floor Black (VG-1040)	1
26	Trim-Tool Box, RH	1
27	Trim-Rear Wheel House Inner Front RH, Black	1
28	Trim-Rear Wheel House Inner Front LH, Black	1
29	Clip-Spring Front Floor Trim	4

DOOR LOCK, WINDOW REGULATOR & DOOR HANDLE (UP TO JULY '73)

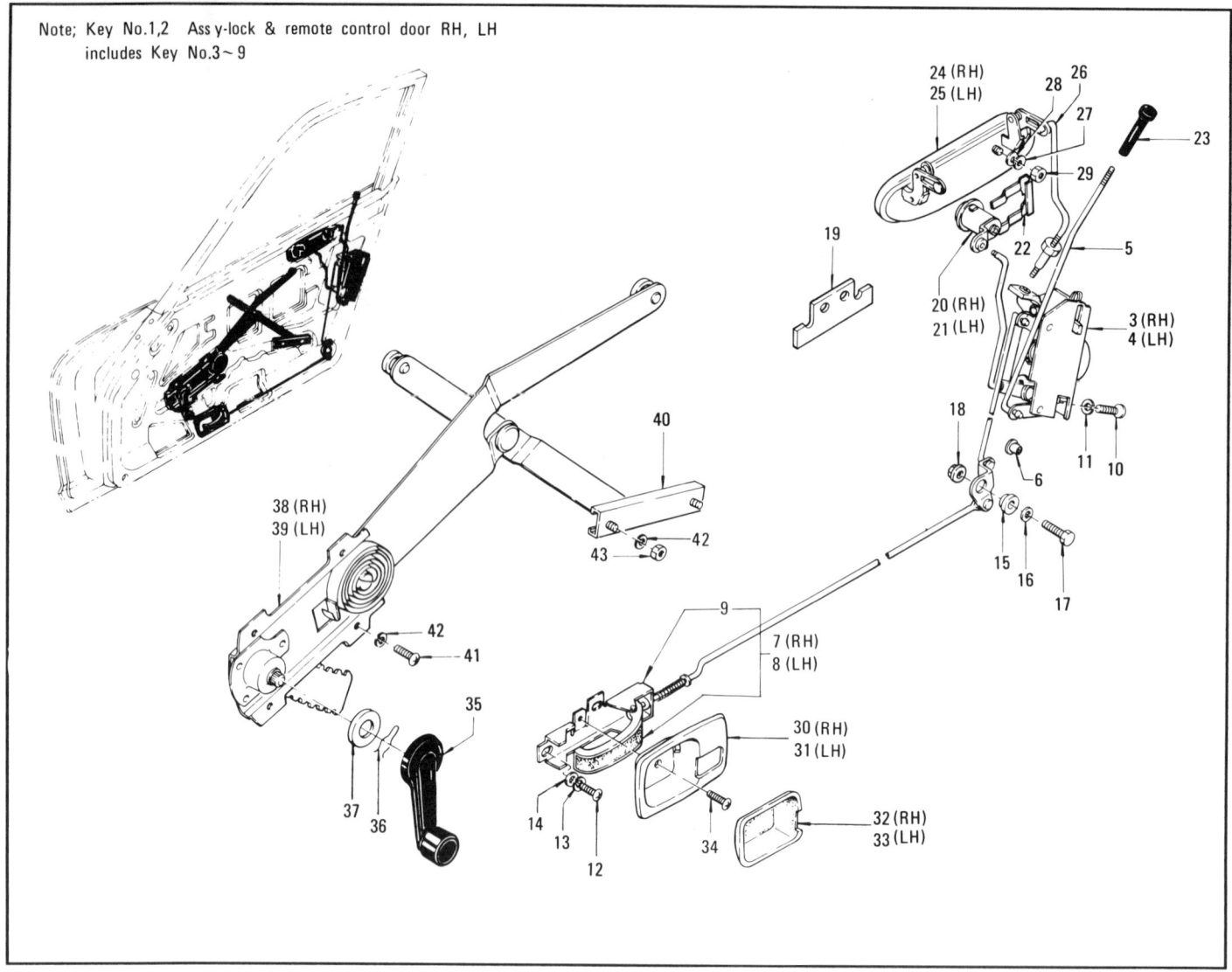

Note; Key No.1,2 Ass y-lock & remote control door RH, LH includes Key No.3~9

Item	Description	Qty	Item	Description	Qty	Item	Description	Qty
1	Assy-Lock & Remote Control Door RH	1	16	Washer-Bell Crank	2	31	Escutcheon-Remote Control LH (with Buffer Rubber)	1
2	Assy-Lock & Remote Control Door LH	1	17	Bolt-Hex Flange Head M6 Fix Bell Crank	2	32	Cover-Escutcheon RH	1
3	Assy-Lock Door RH	1	18	Nut-Flange Bell Crank	2	33	Cover-Escutcheon LH	1
4	Assy-Lock Door LH	1	19	Baffle-Outer Handle	2	34	Screw-Machine	2
5	Rod-Knob Door Lock	1	20	Cylinder-Lock Door RH	1	35	Assy-Handle Door Window Regulator	2
6	Holder-Rod Knob	2	21	Cylinder-Lock Door LH	1	36	Spring-Retaining Handle	2
7	Assy-Remote Control Door RH	1	22	Clip-Retaining Cylinder	2	37	Washer-Seating Handle	2
8	Assy-Remote Control Door LH	1	23	Knob-Door Lock	2	38	Assy-Regulator Door Window RH	1
9	Assy-Inside Handle Door	1	24	Assy-Handle Door Outside RH	1	39	Assy-Regulator Door Window LH	1
10	Screw-Machine M6x1.0 Fix Lock	6	25	Assy-Handle Door Outside LH	1	40	Assy-Guide Door Window Regulator	2
11	Washer-Lock Fix Lock	6	26	Assy-Rod Handle Door Outside RH	1	41	Screw-Machine M6x1.0	8
12	Screw-Machine M6x1.0 Fix Remote Control	4	27	Washer-Spring	4	42	Washer-Spring	12
13	Washer-Spring Fix Remote Control	4	28	Washer-Plain	4	43	Nut-Hex M6x1.0	4
14	Washer-Plain Fix Remote Control	4	29	Nut-Hex	4			
15	Collar-Bell Crank	4	30	Escutcheon-Remote Control RH with Buffer Rubber	1			

Parts Illustrations 223

TAIL GATE PANEL, TRIM, LOCK & REAR BUMPER (UP TO JULY '73)

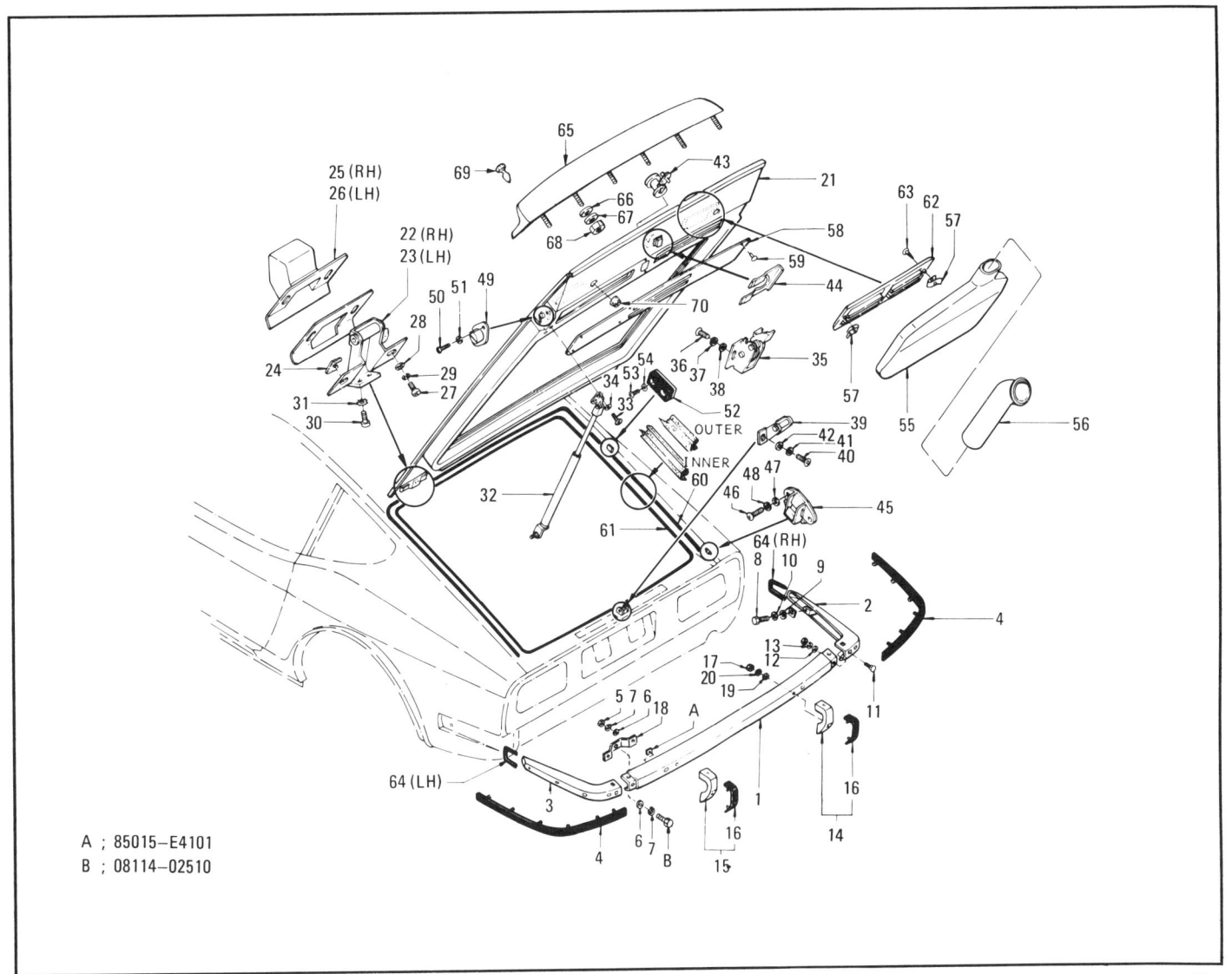

A ; 85015-E4101
B ; 08114-02510

Item	Description	Qty	Item	Description	Qty	Item	Description	Qty
1	Bumper-Rear Center (STD Less Hole)	1	24	Shim-Adjusting Tail Gate Hinge	4	47	Washer-Plain M5	4
2	Bumper-Rear Side RH (Deluxe with Hole)	1	25	Seal-Cover Hinge Tail Gate RH	1	48	Washer-Spring M5	4
3	Bumper-Rear Side LH (Deluxe with Hole)	1	26	Seal-Cover Hinge Tail GAte LH	1	49	Dove Tail-Tail Gate	2
4	Rubber-Rear Bumper Side	2	27	Screw-Machine M8	4	50	Screw-Machine M5	4
5	Nut-Hex	4	28	Washer-Plain M8	4	51	Washer-Spring M5	4
6	Washer-Plain	8	29	Washer-Spring M8	4	52	Bumper-Rubber Tail Gate	2
7	Washer-Lock	8	30	Screw-Machine M8	4	53	Screw-Machine	4
8	Bolt-Hex	2	31	Washer-Tooth M8	4	54	Washer-External Tooth	4
9	Washer-Plain	8	32	Set-Tail Gate Stay (strut)	1	55	Assy-Duct Rear Ventilator Outer	2
10	Washer-Lock	2	33	Screw-Machine	4	56	Tube-Drain	2
11	Bolt-Special	4	34	Washer-Lock Sunk Tooth	4	57	Nut-Push on Spring	4
12	Washer-Plain	4	35	Assy-Tail Gate Lock	1	58	Assy-Trim Tail Gate Black	1
13	Washer-Lock	4	36	Screw-Machine M6	2	59	Rivet-Plastic, Black	10
14	Assy-Over Rider Bumper Rear RH	1	37	Washer-Spring M6	2	60	Weatherstrip-Tail Gate Outer	1
15	Assy-Over Rider Bumper Rear LH	1	38	Washer-Plain M6	2	61	Weatherstrip-Tail Gate inner	1
16	Rubber-Over Rider Bumper Rear	2	39	Assy-Striker Tail Gate Lock	1	62	Grille-Rear Ventilator Outer	2
17	Nut-Hex	2	40	Screw-Machine M6	2	63	Screw-Tapping M4	4
18	Bracket-Rear Bumper "A"	2	41	Washer-Spring M6	2	64	Rubber-Base Bumper RH	1
19	Washer-Plain	2	42	Washer-Plain M6	2	65	Assy-Air Spoiler	1
20	Washer-Lock	2	43	Cylinder-Lock Tail Gate	1	66	Washer-Plain M5 (Air Spoiler)	6
21	Assy-Panel Tail Gate	1	44	Clip-Cylinder	1	67	Washer-Lock M5 (Air Spoiler)	6
22	Assy-Tail Gate Hinge RH	1	45	Assy-Down Stopper Tail Gate	2	68	Nut-Hex M5 (Air Spoiler)	6
23	Assy-Tail Gate Hange LH	1	46	Screw-Machine M5	4	69	Plug-Nylon (Emblem Hole)	5
						70	Grommet	2

224 How to Restore Your Datsun Z-car

SEAT & SLIDE (TYPE 1 ADJUSTER SEAT) (UP TO JULY '73)

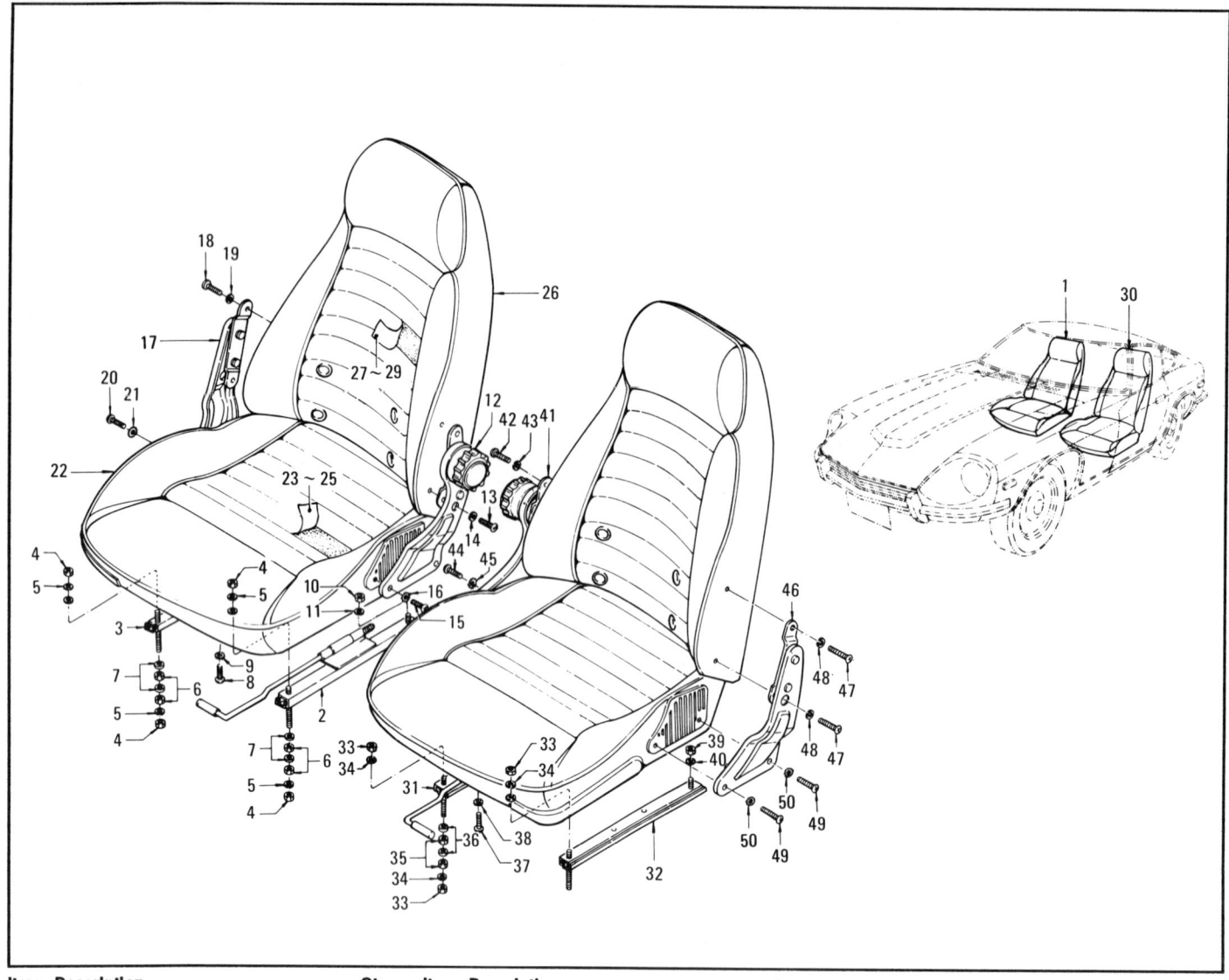

Item	Description	Qty	Item	Description	Qty	Item	Description	Qty
1	Comp-Seat RH Black	1	18	Screw-Machine Fix Bracket	2	35	Spacer-Seat	8
2	Assy-Slide with Lever Seat LH	1	19	Washer-Spring Fix Bracket	2	36	Spacer-Seat	8
3	Assy-Slide less Lever Seat	1	20	Screw-Machine Fix Bracket	2	37	Screw-Machine M8	2
4	Nut-Hex	4	21	Washer-Tooth Lock Fix Bracket	2	38	Washer-Spring	4
5	Washer-Spring	4	22	Assy-Seat Cushion Black	2	39	Nut-hex	2
6	Spacer-Seat	8	23	Trim-Cushion Black	2	40	Washer-Plain	2
7	Spacer-Seat	8	24	Trim-Cushion Brown	2	41	Assy-Adjuster Seat Back RH	1
8	Screw-Machine M8	2	25	Trim-Cushion Blue	2	42	Screw-Machine Fix Adjuster	2
9	Washer-Spring	4	26	Assy-Seat Back Black	2	43	Washer-Spring Fix Adjuster	2
10	Nut-Hex	2	27	Trim-Back Black	2	44	Screw-Machine Fix Adjuster	2
11	Washer-Plain	2	28	Trim-Back Brown	2	45	Washer-Tooth Lock Fix Adjuster	2
12	Assy-Adjuster Seat Black LH	1	29	Trim-Back Blue	2	46	Assy-Bracket Hinge Seat LH	1
13	Screw-Machine Fix Adjuster	2	30	Comp-Seat LH Black	1	47	Screw-Machine Fix Bracket	2
14	Washer-Spring Fix Adjuster	2	31	Assy-Slide with Lever Seat RH	1	48	Washer-Spring Fix Bracket	2
15	Screw-Machine Fix Adjuster	2	32	Assy-Slide less Lever Seat	1	49	Screw-Machine Fix Bracket	2
16	Washer-Tooth Lock Fix Adjuster	2	33	Nut-Hex Fix Slide to Seat	4	50	Washer-Tooth Lock Fix Bracket	2
17	Assy-Bracket Hinge Seat RH	1	34	Washer-Spring Fix Slide to Seat	4			

Parts Illustrations 225

FLOOR CONSOLE, FINISHER & ASH TRAY (UP TO JULY '73)

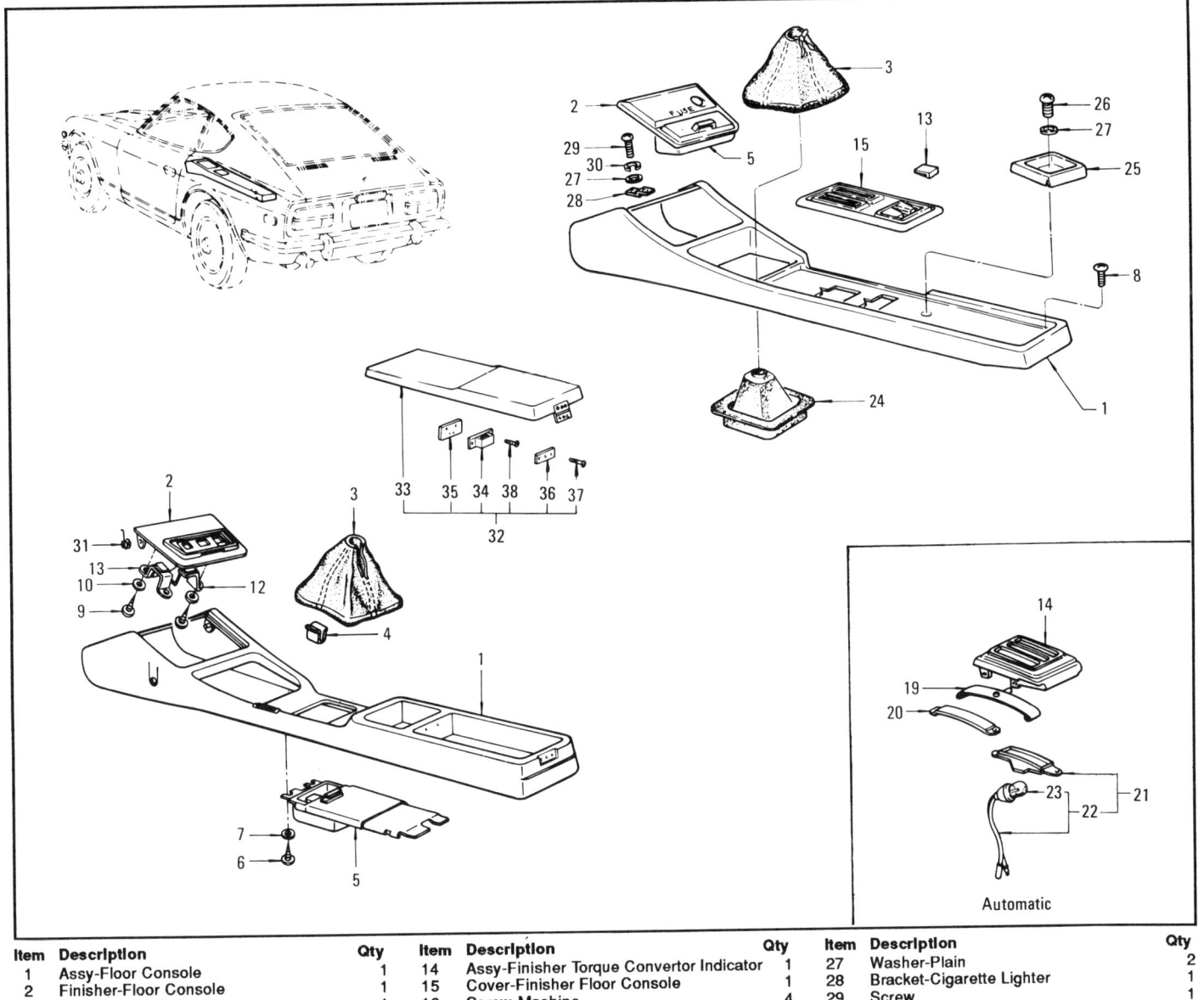

Item	Description	Qty	Item	Description	Qty	Item	Description	Qty
1	Assy-Floor Console	1	14	Assy-Finisher Torque Convertor Indicator	1	27	Washer-Plain	2
2	Finisher-Floor Console	1	15	Cover-Finisher Floor Console	1	28	Bracket-Cigarette Lighter	1
3	Boot-Floor Shift Lever	1	16	Screw-Machine	4	29	Screw	1
4	Clip-Boot Shift Lever	8	17	Washer-Plain	4	30	Washer-Spring	1
5	Assy-Ash Tray	1	18	Washer-Spring	4	31	Spring-Console Lid	1
6	Screw-Self Tapping	4	19	Mask-Shift Lever	1	32	Kit-Lid Glove Box Rear	1
7	Washer-Plain	4	20	Mask-Indicator	1	33	Assy-Lid Glove Box Rear	1
8	Screw-Machine	3	21	Assy-Box Lamp	1	34	Magnet-Console Box	1
9	Screw-Machine	3	22	Assy-Lamp	1	35	Plate-Tapping Front	1
10	Washer-Plain	3	23	Bulb 12V-1.5W	1	36	Plate-Tapping Rear	1
11	Washer-Spring	3	24	Shield-Dust Change Lever	1	37	Screw-Tapping Pan Head	3
12	Grommet-Parking Switch	1	25	Case-Coin	1	38	Screw-Tapping Flat Head	2
13	Grommet-Heat Glass Switch	1	26	Screw	1			

RADIATOR GRILLE, FRONT BUMPER & OVER RIDER (FROM AUGUST '73 2 SEATER)

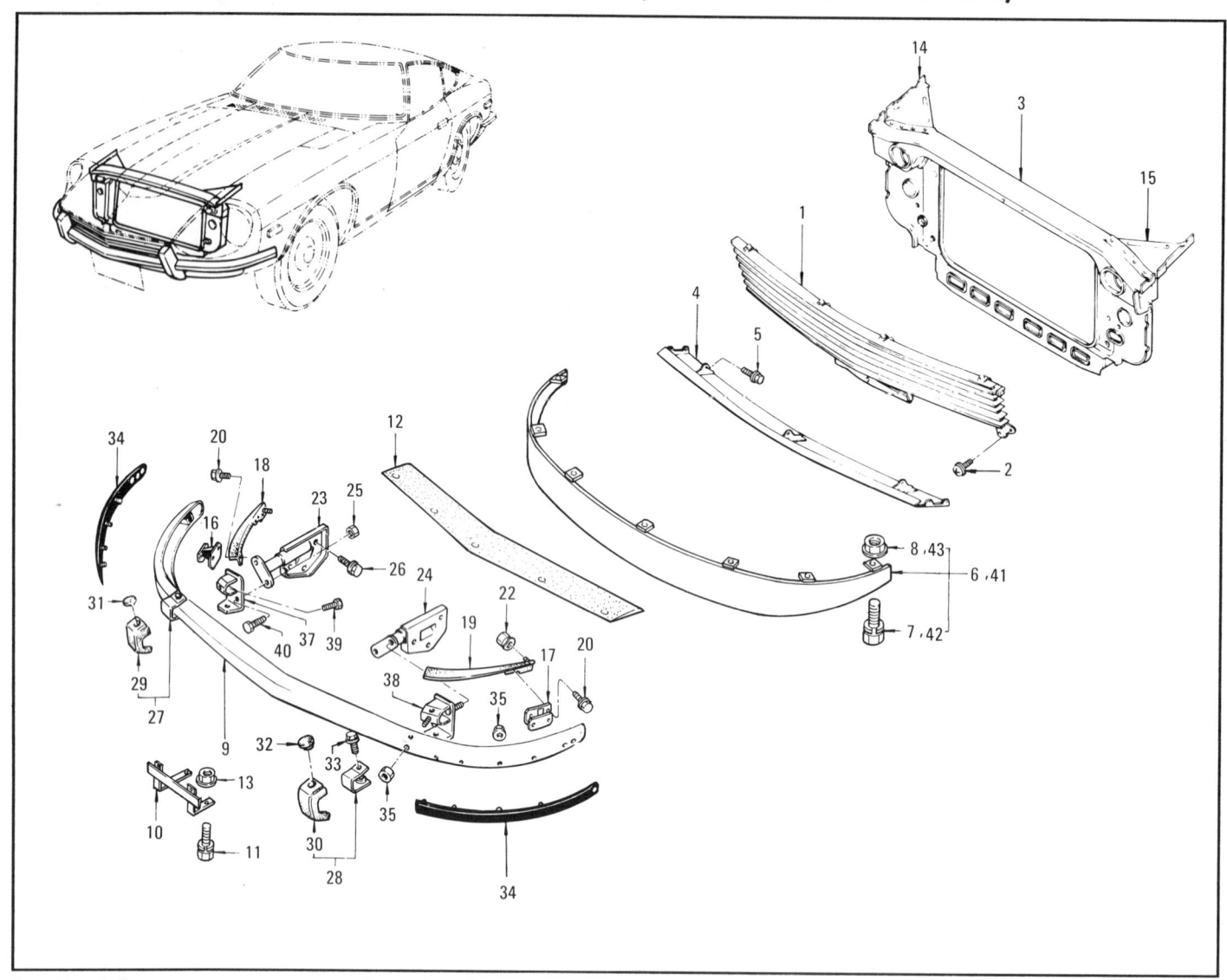

Item	Description	Qty	Item	Description	Qty	Item	Description	Qty
1	Assy-Grille Radiator	1	16	Assy-Mounting, Front Bumper Side RH	1	30	Rubber-Overrider, Front LH	1
2	Screw-Machine	5	17	Assy-Mounting, Front Bumper Side LH	1	31	Plug-Overrider, Front RH	1
3	Assy-Radiator Core Support	1	18	Assy-Packing, Front Bumper TH	1	32	Plug-Overrider, Front LH	1
4	Assy-Panel Front Apron	1	19	Assy-Packing Front Bumper LH	1	33	Bolt-with Washer M8	4
5	Bolt-Hex M6	3	20	Bolt-Hex	2	34	Rubber-Front Bumper	2
6	Assy-Air Spoiler Front	1	21	Washer-Lock	2	35	Nut-Flange M5	8
7	Screw-Machine	7	22	Nut	1	36	Screw-Machine	2
8	Nut-Flange	2	23	Comp-Absorber, Front Bumper RH	1	37	Assy-Joint, Bumper Stay RH	1
9	Assy-Front Bumper	1	24	Comp-Absorber, Front Bumper LH	1	38	Assy-Joint, Bumper Stay LH	1
10	Assy-Bracket, License Plate	1	25	Nut-Hex M8	4	39	Bolt-Hex M8	2
11	Screw	2	26	Bolt-with Washer Fix Absorber to Member	6	40	Bolt-Hex M8	4
12	Assy-Ext. Bumper Front	1	27	Assy-Overrider, Front Bumper RH	1	41	Kit-Spoiler, Air Front	1
13	Nut-Flange M10	2	28	Assy-Overrider, Front Bumper LH	1	42	Screw	7
14	Gusset-Hood Ledge Front RH	1	29	Rubber-Overrider, Front RH	2	43	Nut	2
15	Gusset-Hood Ledge Front LH	1						

FRONT FENDER, HOOD LEDGE & HOOD (FROM AUGUST '73 2 SEATER)

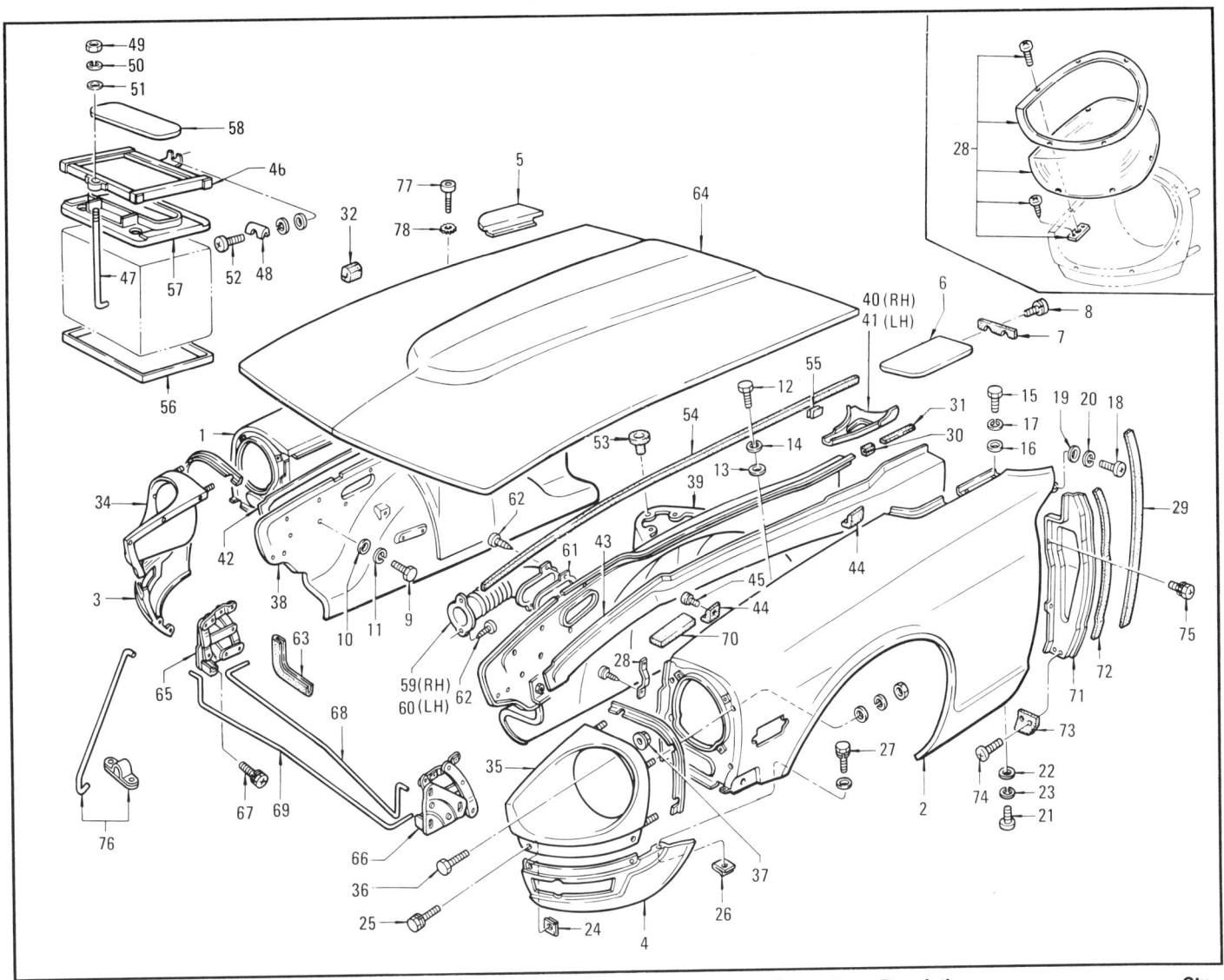

Item	Description	Qty
1	Assy-Front Fender RH	1
2	Assy-Front Fender LH	1
3	Panel-Front Fender Front RH	1
4	Panel-Front Fender Front LH	1
5	Assy-Lid Battery Inspection RH	1
6	Assy-Lid Battery Inspection LH	1
7	Shim-Adjust	2
8	ScrewMachine M5x.08	4
9	Bolt-Hex Head Lamp Support to Hood Ledge	4
10	Washer-Plain Head Lamp Support to Hood Ledge	4
11	Washer-Spring Head Lamp Support to Hood Ledge	4
12	Bolt-Hex Fender to Hood Ledge	6
13	Washer-Plain Fender to Hood Ledge	6
14	Washer-Spring Fender to Hood Ledge	6
15	Screw-Machine Cowl Top to Fender	4
16	Washer-Plain Cowl Top to Fender	4
17	Washer-Spring Cowl Top to Fender	4
18	Screw-Machine Fender to Pillar	2
19	Washer-Plain Fender to Pillar	2
20	Washer-Spring Fender to Pillar	2
21	Screw-Machine Fender to Sill	4
22	Washer-Plain Fender to Sill	4
23	Washer-Spring Fender to Sill	4
24	Nut-Joint Retainer	4
25	Cam-Screw with Washer	4
26	Nut-Joint Retainer	4
27	Cam-Screw with Washer	4
28	Sealing-Head Lamp Support	2
29	Filler-Baffle Front Fender	2
30	Rubber-Cusion	2
31	Packing-Battery Cover	2
32	Bumper-Battery Cover	2
33	Washer-Lock	4
34	Case-Head Lamp RH	1
35	Case-Head Lamp LH	1
36	Screw-Machine	4
37	Nut-Flange	6
38	Assy-Hood Ledge RH	1
39	Assy-Hood Ledge LH	1
40	Gusset-Hood Ledge Corner Rear RH	1
41	Gusset-Hood Ledge Corner Rear LH	1
42	Assy-Reinf Hood Ledge RH	1
43	Assy-Reinf Hood Ledge LH	1
44	Bumper-Hood	4
45	Screw-Machine M6	4
46	Assy-Frame Battery Fix	1
47	Rod-Battery Support	1
48	Cushion-Battery Fix	1
49	Nut-Hex M6	1
50	Washer-Spring M6	1
51	Washer-Plain M6	1
52	Screw-Machine M6	1
53	Cap-Insulator Front Strut Mounting	2
54	Rubber-Sealing Side	2
55	Clip-Sealing Rubber	12
56	Tray-Battery	1
57	Cover-Battery	1
58	Cap-Battery Cover	1
59	Assy-Guide Air Intake RH	1
60	Assy-Guide Air Intake LH	1
61	Plate-Guide Air Intake	2
62	Screw-Tapping	8
63	Rubber-Flange Cover	2
64	Assy-Hood	1
65	Assy-Hinge Hood RH	1
66	Assy-Hinge Hood LH	1
67	Screw-Machine M8	10
68	Bar-Torsion Hood Hinge RH	1
69	Bar-Torsion Hood Hinge LH	1
70	Sealing-Mud Guard	2
73	Rubber-Mud Guard	2
74	Screw-Tapping M5	4
75	Screw-Machine	6
76	Assy-Rod, Hood Support	1
77	Comp-Hood Bumper	2
78	Washer-Lock	2

FLOOR CONSOLE, FINISHER & ASH TRAY (FROM AUGUST '73 2 SEATER)

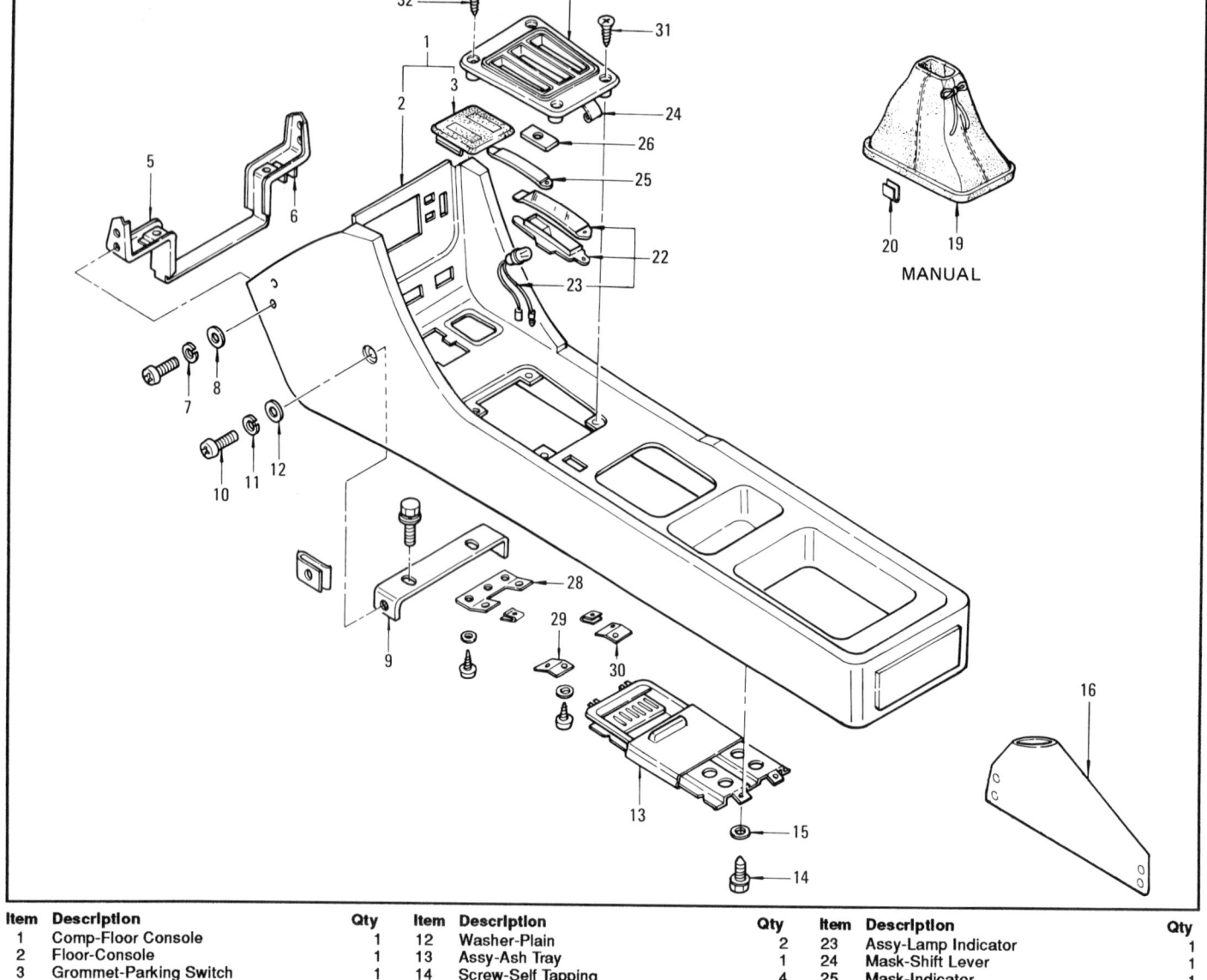

Item	Description	Qty	Item	Description	Qty	Item	Description	Qty
1	Comp-Floor Console	1	12	Washer-Plain	2	23	Assy-Lamp Indicator	1
2	Floor-Console	1	13	Assy-Ash Tray	1	24	Mask-Shift Lever	1
3	Grommet-Parking Switch	1	14	Screw-Self Tapping	4	25	Mask-Indicator	1
4	Grommet-Ash Tray	1	15	Washer-Plain	2	26	Guide-Indicator	1
5	Assy-Bracket, Radio	1	16	Assy-Cover, Hand Brake Lever	1	27	Clip	1
6	Clip	1	17	Fastener-Female	4	28	Assy-Bracket, Torque Convertor Indicator A	1
7	Washer-Lock	4	18	Fastener-Male	4	29	Assy-Bracket, T/Convertor Indicator B LH	1
8	Washer-Plain	4	19	Assy-Boots, Shift Lever	1	30	Assy-Bracket, T/Convertor Indicator B RH	1
9	Assy-Bracket, Floor Console	1	20	Clip-Boots, Shift Lever	1	31	Screw-Tapping	2
10	Screw-Machine	2	21	Finisher-Torque Convertor Indicator	1	32	Screw-Tapping	2
11	Washer-Lock	2	22	Assy-Box Lamp	1			

DOOR LOCK, WINDOW REGULATOR & DOOR HANDLE (FROM AUGUST "73 2 SEATER)

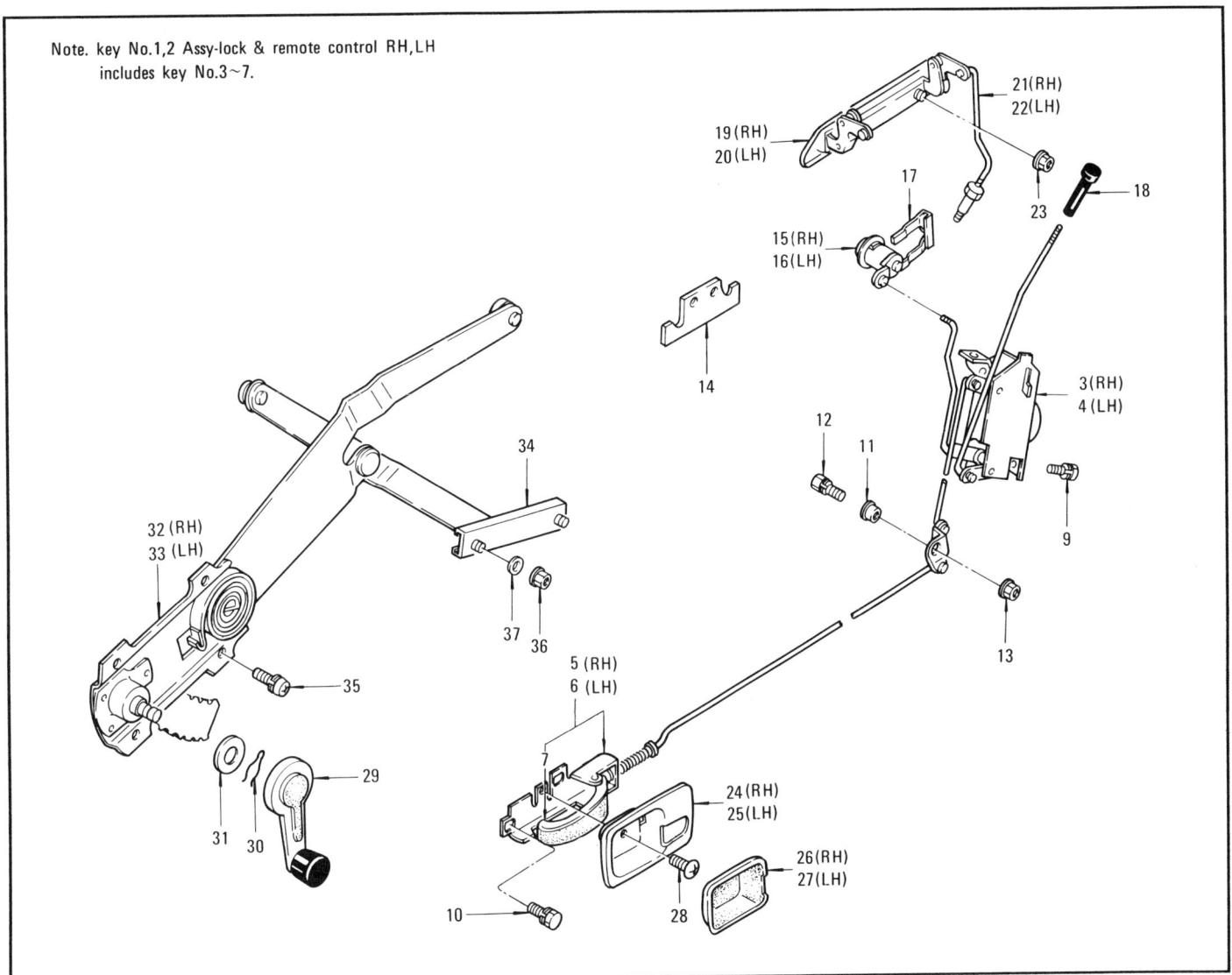

Note. key No.1,2 Assy-lock & remote control RH, LH includes key No.3~7.

Item	Description	Qty	Item	Description	Qty	Item	Description	Qty
1	Assy-Lock & Remote Control Door RH	1	14	Baffle-Outer Handle	2	25	Cover-Escutcheon RH	1
2	Assy-Lock & Remote Control Door LH	1	15	Cylinder-Lock Door RH	1	26	Cover-Escutcheon LH	1
3	Assy-Lock Door RH	1	16	Clip-Retaining Cylinder	2	27	Screw-Machine	2
4	Assy-Lock Door LH	1	17	Knob-Door Lock	2	28	Assy-Handle Door Window Regulator	2
5	Assy-Remote Control Door RH	1	18	Assy-Handle Door Outside RH	1	29	Spring-Retaining Handle	2
6	Assy-Remote Control Door LH	1	19	Assy-Handle Door Outside LH	1	30	Washer-Seating Handle	2
7	Assy-Inside Handle Door	1	20	Assy-Rod Handle Door Outside RH	1	31	Assy-Regulator Door Window	1
8	Dove-Tail Door	2	21	Assy-Rod Handle Door Outside LH	1	32	Assy-Regulator Door Window LH	1
9	Screw-Machine M6x1.0 Fix Lock	6	22	Nut-Flange	4	33	Assy-Guide Door Window Regulator	2
10	Screw-Machine Fix Remote Control	4	23	Escutcheon-Remote Control RH (with Buffer Rubber)	1	34	Screw-Machine M6x1.0	8
11	Collar-Bell Crank	4				35	Nut-Flange	4
12	Bolt-Hex Flange Head M6 Fix Bell Crank	2	24	Escutcheon-Remote Control LH (with Buffer Rubber)	1	36	Washer-Special M8	4
13	Nut-Flange Bell Crank	2						

TAIL GATE PANEL, TRIM, LOCK & REAR BUMPER (FROM AUGUST '73 2 SEATER)

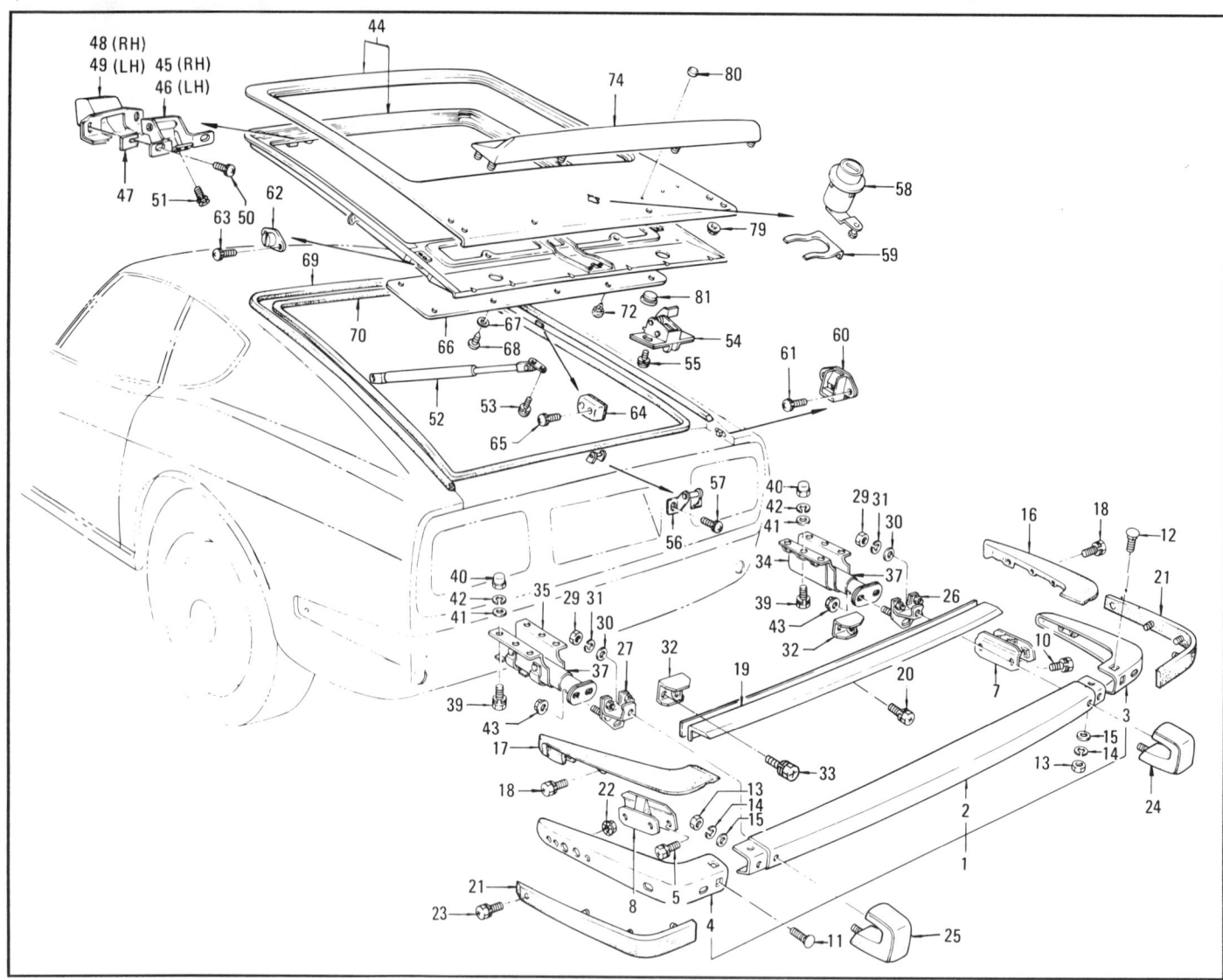

Item	Description	Qty	Item	Description	Qty	Item	Description	Qty
1	Assy-Bumper, Rear	1	29	Nut-Hex	4	54	Assy-Tail Gate Lock	1
2	Assy-Bumper, Rear Center	1	30	Washer-Plain	4	55	Screw-Machine M6	2
3	Assy-Bumper, Rear Side RH	1	31	Washer-Lock	4	56	Assy-Striker Tail Gate Lock	1
4	Assy-Bumper, Rear Side LH	1	32	Assy-Hook, Lashing Rear	2	57	Screw-Machine M6	2
5	Bolt-Hex	4	33	Bolt-Hex	4	58	Cylinder-Lock Tail Gate	1
6	Nut-with Washer	4	34	Assy-Stay, Shock Absorber Rear Bumper RH	1	59	Cllip-Cylinder	1
7	Assy-Insulator Rear Bumper Mounting Side	1	35	Assy-Stay, Shock Absorber Rear Bumper LH	1	60	Assy-Down Stopper Tail Gate	2
8	Assy-Insulator Rear Bumper Mounting Side	1	36	Shim-Joint, Front Bumper	1	61	Screw-Machine M5	4
9	Bracket-Rear Bumper Mounting Side	2	37	Kit-Absorber, Rear Bumper	2	62	Dove Tail-Tail Gate	2
10	Screw-with Washer	8	38	Heat-Shield, Rear Bumper Stay	2	63	Screw-Machine M5	4
11	Bolt-Carriage	2	39	Bolt-with Washer Fix Shock Absorber to S/M	6	64	Bumper-Rubber Tail Gate	2
12	Bolt-Carriage	2	40	Nut-Cup, Fix S/Absorber to Floor	6	65	Screw-Machine	4
13	Nut-Hex	4	41	Washer-Plain, Fix S/Absorber to Floor	6	66	Assy-Trim Tail Gate Black	1
14	Washer-Lock	4	42	Washer-Lock, Fix S/Absorber to Floor	6	67	Washer-Finish	10
15	Washer-Plain	4	43	Nut-Hex, Fix S/Absorber to Joint	4	68	Screw-Tapping	10
16	Assy-Packing Rear Bumper RH	1	44	Assy-Panel Tail Gate Outer with Inner	1	69	Weatherstrip-Tail Gate Outer	1
17	Assy-Packing Rear Bumper LH	1	45	Assy-Tail Gate Hinge RH	1	70	Weatherstrip-Tail Gate Inner	1
18	Bolt-with Washer	6	46	Assy-Tail Gate Hinge LH	1	71	Rubber-Sealing Tail Gate	1
19	Assy-Sight Shield Rear Bumper	1	47	Shim-Adjusting Tail Gate Hinge	4	72	Clip-Trim	8
20	Bolt-with Washer	5	48	Seal-Cover Hinge Tail Gate RH	1	73	Washer-Nylon	4
21	Rubber-Rear Bumper Side	2	49	Seal-Cover Hinge Tail Gate LH	1	74	Assy-Spoiler Air	1
22	Nut-Flange M5	8	50	Screw-Machine M8	4	75	Sealing-Air Spoiler	2
23	Screw	2	51	Screw-Machine M8	4	76	Cushion-Air Spoiler	2
24	Assy-Overrider, Rear Bumper RH	1	52	Set-Stay, Tail Gate RH (strut)	1	77	Nut-Flange	6
25	ASsy-Overrider, Rear Bumper LH	1	53	Screw-Machine	2	78	Plug	6
26	Assy-Joint Rear Bumper Stay "A" RH	1				79	Nut-Flange M6 (Air Spoiler)	6
27	Assy-Joint Rear Bumper Stay "A" LH	1				80	Plug-Nylon (Emblem Hole)	5
28	Assy-Joint Rear Bumper Stay "B"	2				81	Grommet-Heater	2

RADIATOR GRILLE, FRONT BUMPER & OVER RIDER (FROM OCT. '73 2+2 SEATER)

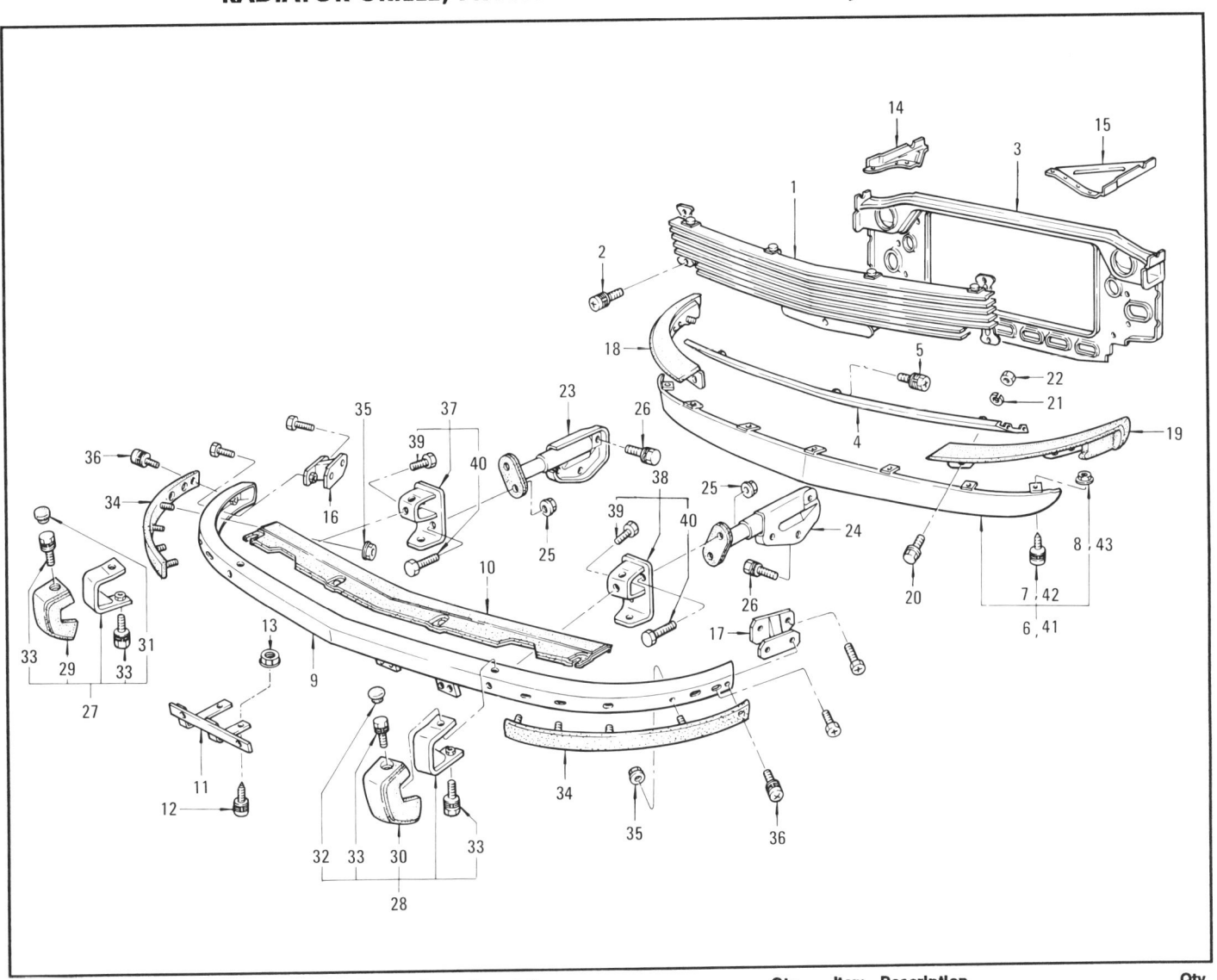

Item	Description	Qty
1	Assy-Grille Radiator	1
2	Screw-Machine	5
3	Assy-Radiator Core Support	1
4	Assy-Panel Front Apron	1
5	Bolt-Hex M6	3
6	Assy-Air Spoiler Front	1
7	Screw-Machine	7
8	Nut-Flange	2
9	Assy-Front Bumper	1
10	Assy-Ext. Bumper Front	1
11	Assy-Brkt. License Plate	1
12	Screw	2
13	Nut-Flange M10	2
14	Gusset-Hood Ledge Front RH	1
15	Gusset-Hood Ledge Front LH	1
16	Assy-Mounting, Front Bumper Side RH	1
17	Assy-Mounting, Front Bumper Side LH	1
18	Assy-Packing, Front Bumper RH	1
19	Assy-Packing, Front Bumper LH	1
20	Bolt-Hex	2
21	Washer-Lock	2
22	Nut	1
23	Comp-Absorber, Front Bumper RH	1
24	Comp-Absorber, Front Bumper LH	1
25	Nut-Hex M8	4
26	Bolt-with Washer Fix Absorber to Member	6
27	Assy-Overrider, Front Bumper RH	1
28	Assy-Overrider, Front Bumper LH	1
29	Rubber-Overrider, Front RH	2
30	Rubber-Overrider, Front LH	1
31	Plug-Overrider, Front RH	1
32	Plug-Overrider, Front LH	1
33	Bolt-with Washer M8	4
34	Rubber-Front Bumper	2
35	Nut-Flange M5	8
36	Screw-Machine	2
37	Assy-Joint, Bumper Stay RH	1
38	Assy-Joint, Bumper Stay LH	1
39	Bolt-Hex M8	2
40	Bolt-Hex M8	4
41	Kit-Spoiler, Air Front	1
42	Screw	7
43	Nut	2

FLOOR CONSOLE, FINISHER & ASH TRAY (FROM OCT. '73 2+2 SEATER)

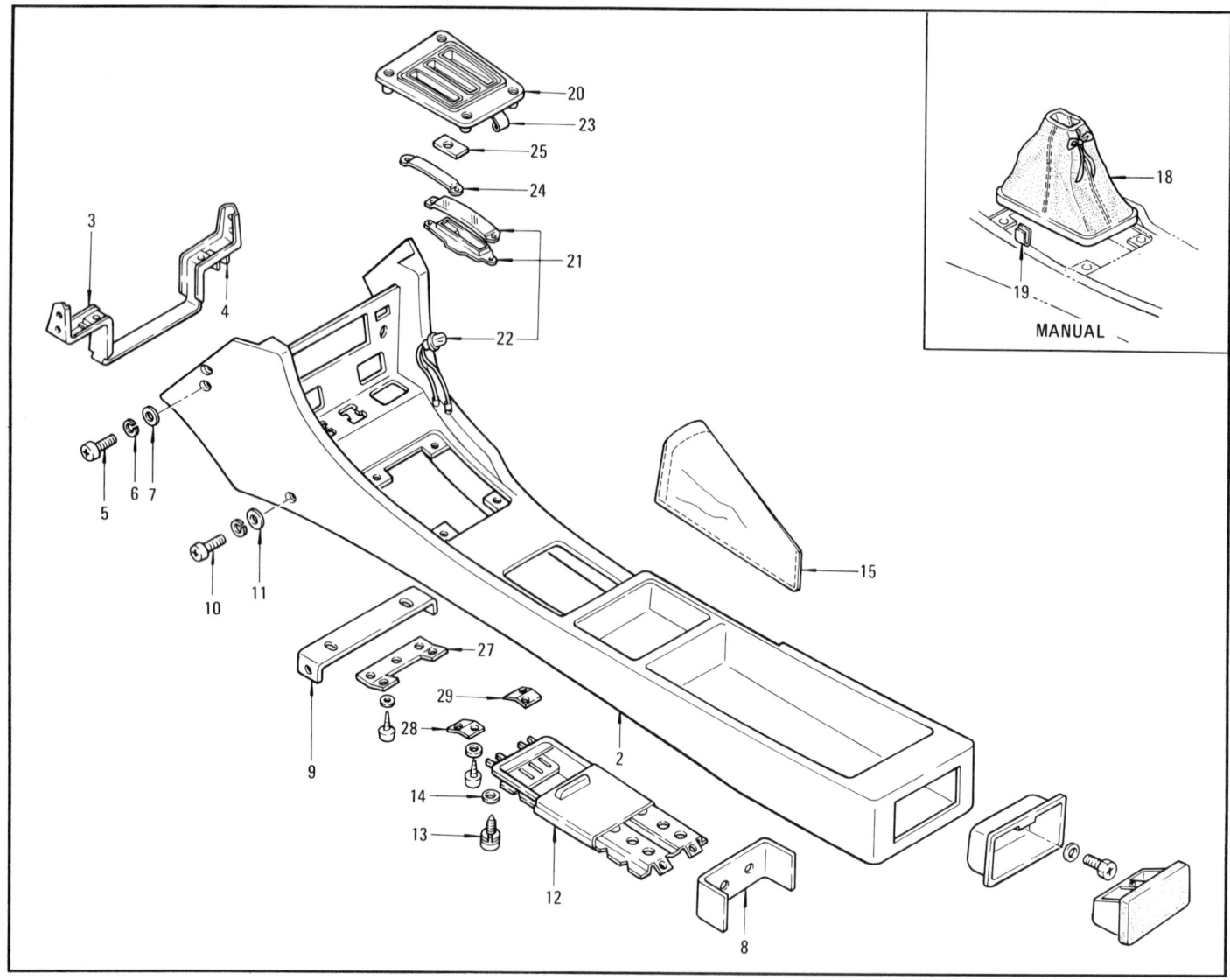

Item	Description	Qty	Item	Description	Qty	Item	Description	Qty
1	Comp-Floor Console	1	11	Washer-Plain	2	21	Assy-Box Lamp	1
2	Floor-Console	1	12	Assy-Ash Tray	1	22	Assy-Lamp Indicator	1
3	Assy-Bracket, Radio	1	13	Screw-Self Tapping	4	23	Mask-Shift Lever	1
4	Clip	1	14	Washer-Plain	2	24	Mask-Indicator	1
5	Screw-Machine	1	15	Assy-Cover, Hand Brake Lever	1	25	Guide-Indicator	1
6	Washer-Lock	4	16	Fastener-Female	4	26	Clip	1
7	Washer-Plain	4	17	Fastener-Male	4	27	Assy-Bracket, Torque Converor IndicatorA	1
8	Assy-Bracket, Ash Tray	1	18	Assy-Boots, Shift Lever	1	28	Assy-Bracket, T/Convertor Indicator B LH	1
9	Assy-Bracket, Floor Console	1	19	Clip-Boots, Shift Lever	8	29	Assy-Bracket, T/Convertor Indicator B RH	1
10	Screw-Machine	2	20	Finisher-Torque Convertor Indicator	1			

FLOOR TRIM, MAT, INSULATOR & REAR WHEEL HOUSE (FROM OCT. '73 2+2 SEATER)

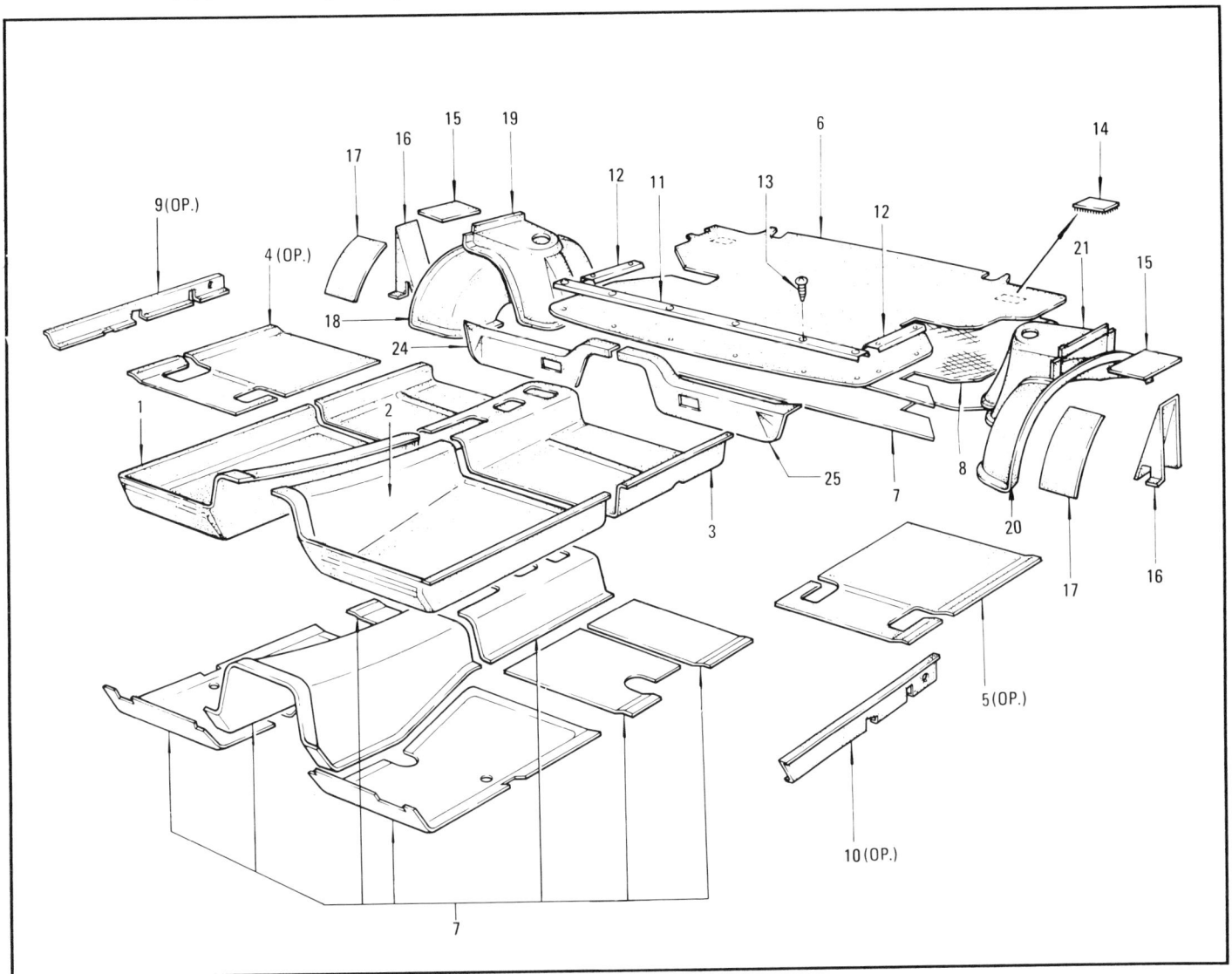

Item	Description	Qty	Item	Description	Qty	Item	Description	Qty
1	Assy-Trim Front Floor RH Carpet Black CG-403	1	9	Plate-Mat Front Floor RH	1	19	Trim-Rear Wheel House Inner Rear RH VG-405 Black	1
2	Assy-Trim Front Floor LH Carpet Black CG-403	1	10	Plate-Mat Front Floor LH	1	20	Trim-Rear Wheel House Inner Front LH VG-405 Black	1
3	Assy-Trim Front Floor Rear CG-403 Black	1	11	Plate-Mat Rear Floor	1	21	Trim-Rear Wheel House Inner Rear LH VG-40Black	1
4	Trim-Front Floor Rear RH VG-101 Black	1	12	Plate-Mat Rear Side	2	22	Cover-Bracket Striker Rear Seat Back RH	1
5	Trim-Front Floor Rear LH VG-101 Black	1	13	Screw	10	23	Cover-Bracket Striker Rear Seat Back LH	1
6	Assy-Mat Rear Floor CG-403 Black	1	14	Assy-Fastener Rear Floor Mat	1	24	Trim-Rear Member RH LG-424 Black	1
7	Set-Insulator Floor (Free Sided)	1	15	Board-Rear Suspension Strut	2	25	Trim-Rear Member LH LG-424 Black	1
8	Jute-Rear Floor	1	16	Protector-Rear Wheel House Trim	2			
			17	Cushion-Rear Wheel House Inner	2			
			18	Trim-Rear Wheel House Inner Front RH VG-405 Black	1			

BODY SIDE TRIM & SIDE WINDOW (FROM OCT. '73 2+2 SEATER)

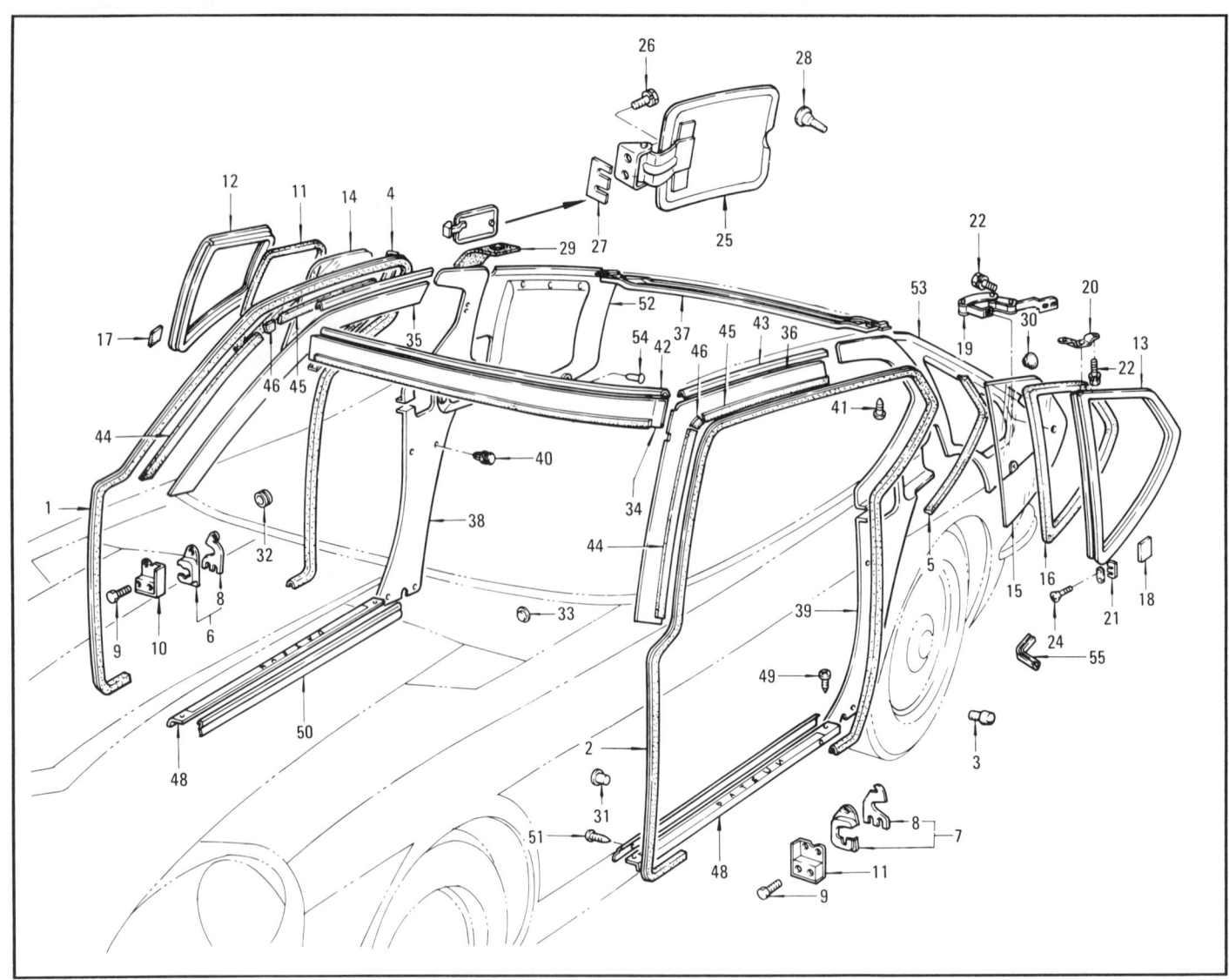

Item	Description	Qty	Item	Description	Qty	Item	Description	Qty
1	Weatherstrip-Door RH	1	19	Assy-Handle, Side Window	2	37	Garnish-Tail Rail Black	1
2	Weatherstrip-Door LH	1	20	Bracket-Side Window Upper	2	38	Garnish-Quarter Panel RH Black	1
3	Rubber-Bumper Door	2	21	Shim-Side Window Lower	4	39	Garnish-Quarter Panel LH Black	1
4	Moulding-Side Window RH	1	22	Screw—Machine, Fix Handle	4	40	River-Plastic	16
5	Moulding-Side Window LH	1	23	Screw-Machine, Fix Bracket	4	41	Screw-Tapping	4
6	Assy-Striker Door RH	1	24	Screw-Machine, Fix Bracket	4	42	Welt-Rail Front	1
7	Assy-Striker Door LH	1	25	Assy-Lid, Gas Filler	1	43	Welt-Rail Side	2
8	Shim-Adjustment T=1.0	3	26	Screw-Machine	2	44	Pad-Piller Front	2
9	Bolt-Special	6	27	Shim-Hinge, Gas Filler Lid	1	45	Pad-Rail Side	2
10	Assy-Down Stopper Door RH	1	28	Bumper-Rubber, Filler LiD	2	46	Pad-Rail Conner	2
11	Assy-Down Stopper Door LH	1	29	Protector-Gas Filler	1	47	Rubber-Grommet 35	2
12	Assy-Sash Side Window RH	1	30	Plug-Rubber	1	48	Plate-Kick Sill Outer	2
13	Assy-Sash Side Window LH	1	31	Plug-Rubber 8	2	49	Screw-Machine	12
14	Glass-Side Window RH	1	32	Grommet-Wiring Fix Inside Front & Rear	3	50	Plate-Scuff	2
15	Glass-Side Windoe LH	1	33	Plug 10 Location Hole Fix Sill Out	4	51	Screw-Tapping Plate Scuff	10
16	Weatherstrip-Side Window Glass	2	34	Leather-Rail Front Black	1	52	Trim-Body Side Rear RH Black	1
17	Rubber-Side Window Lower RH	1	35	Leather-Rail Side RH Black	1	53	Trim-Body Side Rear LH Black	1
18	Rubber-Side Window Lower LH	1	36	Leather-Rail Side LH Black	1	54	Rivet-Plastic Black	12
						55	Protector-Flange	2

DOOR LOCK, WINDOW REGULATOR & DOOR HANDLE (FROM OCT. '73 2+2 SEATER)

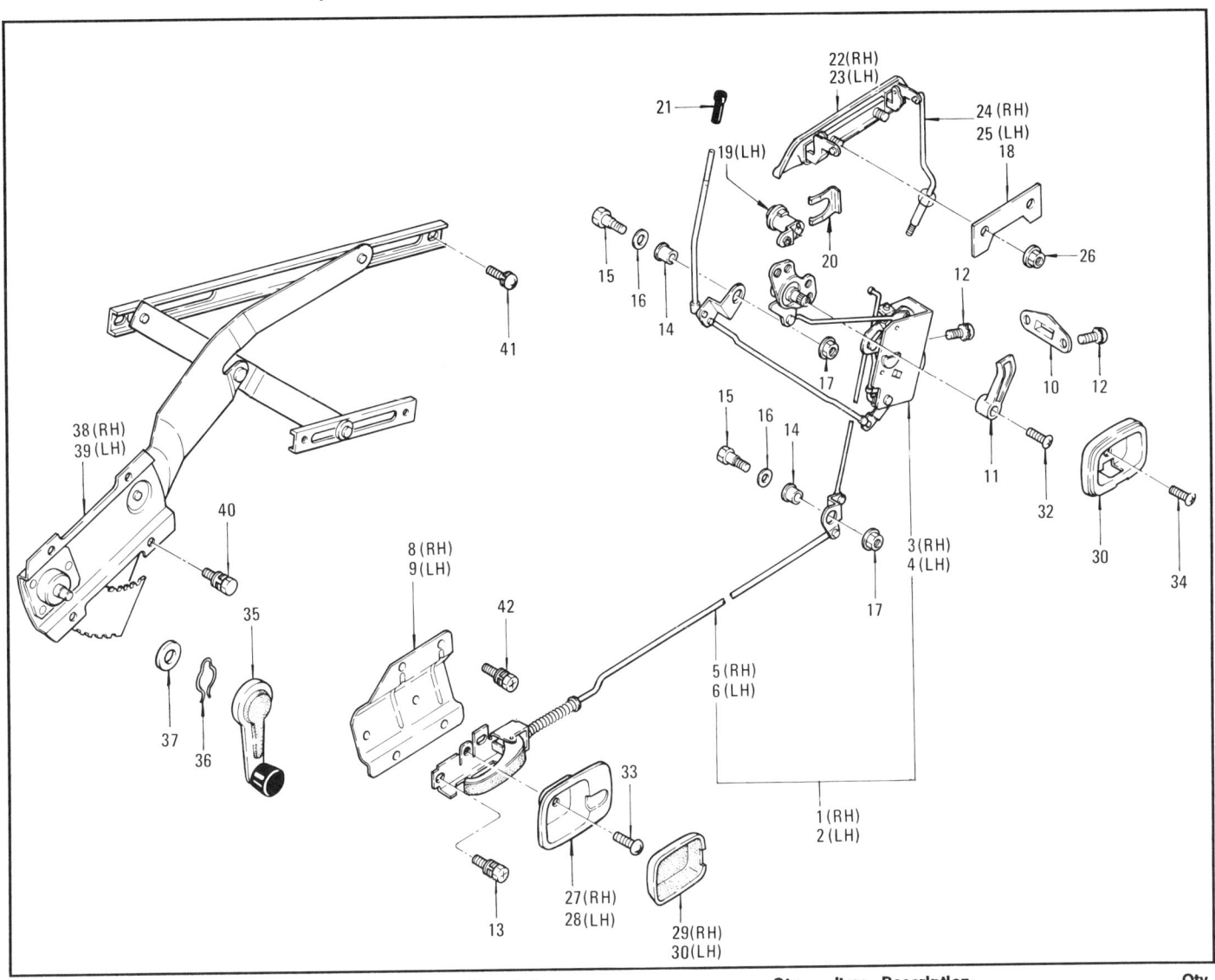

Item	Description	Qty
1	Assy-Lock & Remote Control Door RH	1
2	Assy-Lock & Remote Control Door LH	1
3	Assy-Lock Door RH	1
4	Assy-Lock Door LH	1
5	Assy-Remote Control Door RH	1
6	Assy-Remote Control Door LH	1
7	Assy-Inside Handle Door	1
8	Assy-Bracket, Remote Control RH	1
9	Assy-Bracket, Remote Control LH	1
10	Dove-Tail Door	2
11	Handle Door Inside Rear	2
12	Screw-Machine	6
13	Screw-Pan Head	6
14	Collar-Bell Crank	4
15	Bolt-Special	4
16	Washer-Plain	4
17	Nut-Flange Bell Crank	4
18	Baffle-Outer Handle	2
19	Cylinder-Lock Door LH	1
20	Clip-Retaining Cylinder	2
21	Knob-Door Lock	2
22	Assy-Handle Door Outside RH	1
23	Assy-Handle Door Outside LH	1
24	Assy-Rod Handle Door Outside RH	1
25	Assy-Rod Handle Door Outside LH	1
26	Nut-Flange	4
27	Escutcheon-Remote Control RH (with Buffer Rubber)	1
28	Escutcheon-Remote Control LH (with Buffer Rubber)	1
29	Cover-Escutcheon RH	1
30	Escutcheon-Remote Control Rear	2
31	Cover-Escutcheon LH	1
32	Screw-Machine	2
33	Screw-Machine	2
34	Screw-Machine	2
35	Assy-Handle Door Window Regulator	2
36	Spring-Retaining Handle	2
37	Washer-Seating Handle	2
38	Assy-Regulator Door Window RH	1
39	Assy-Regulator Door Window LH	1
40	Bolt	8
41	Screw-Machine M6x1.0	4
42	Screw-Machine	8

TAIL GATE PANEL, TRIM LOCK & REAR BUMPER (FROM OCT. '73 2+2 SEATER)

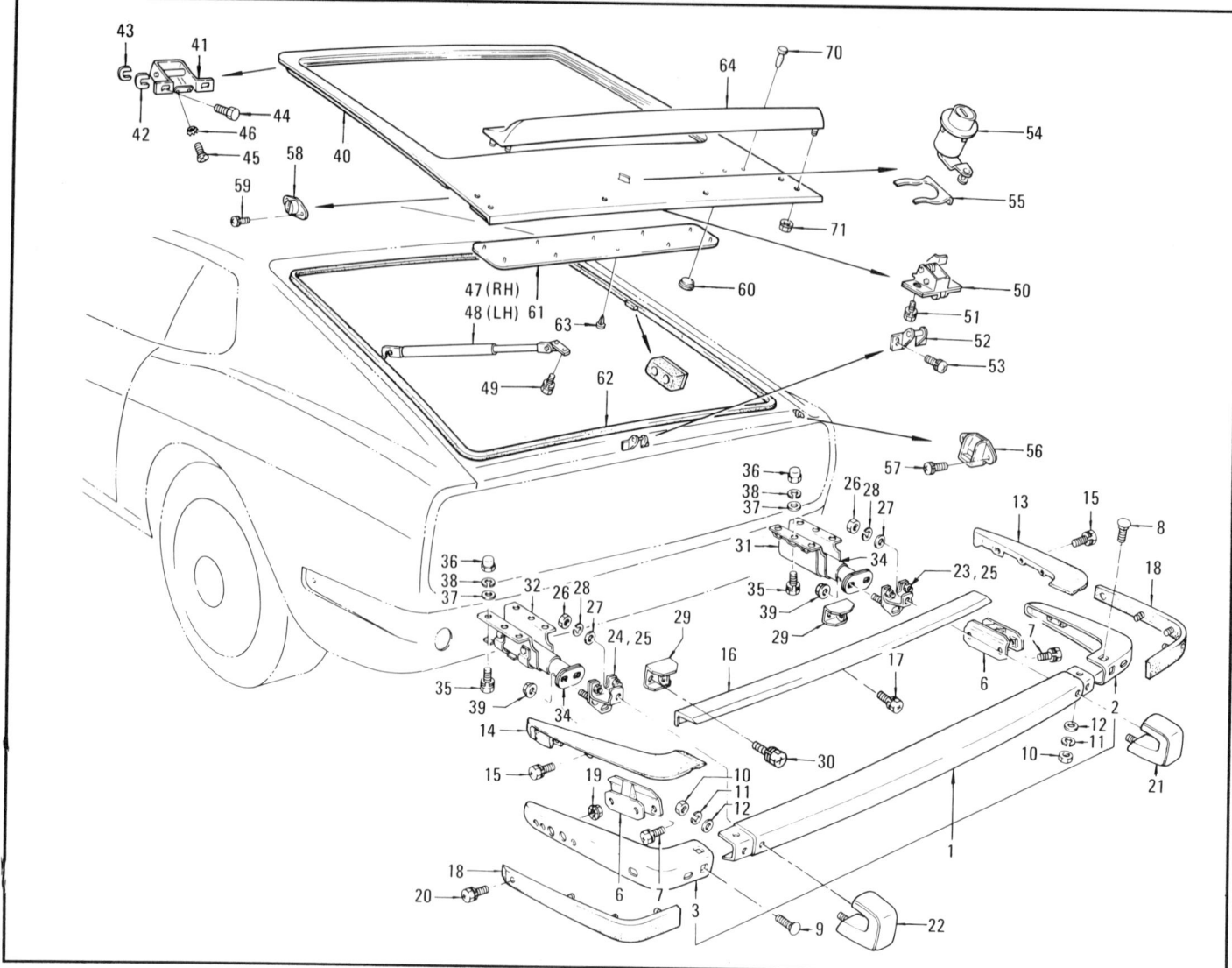

Item	Description	Qty
1	Assy-Bumper, Rear Center	1
2	Assy-Bumper, Rear Side RH	1
3	Assy-Bumper, Rear Side LH	1
4	Assy-Insulator, Rear Bumper Mounting Side RH	1
5	Assy-Insulator, Rear Bumper Mounting Side LH	1
6	Bracket-Rear Bumper Mounting Side	2
7	Screw-with Washer	8
8	Bolt-Carriage	2
9	Bolt-Carriage	2
10	Nut-Hex	4
11	Washer-Lock	4
12	Washer-Plain	4
13	Assy-Packing Rear Bumper RH	1
14	Assy-Packing Rear Bumper LH	1
15	Bolt-with Washer	6
16	Assy-Sight Shield Rear Bumper	1
17	Bolt-with Washer	6
18	Rubber-Rear Bumper Side	2
19	Nut-Flange M5	8
20	Screw	2
21	Assy-Overrider, Rear Bumper RH	1
22	Assy-Overrider, Rear Bumper LH	1
23	Assy-Joint Rear Bumper Stay "A" RH	1
24	Assy-Joint Rear Bumper Stay "A" LH	1
25	Assy-Joint Rear Bumper Stay "B"	2
26	Nut-Hex	4
27	Washer-Plain	4
28	Washer-Lock	4
29	Assy-Hook, Lashting Rear	2
30	Bolt	4
31	Assy-Stay, Shock Absorber Rear Bumper RH	1
32	Assy-Stay, Shock Absorber Rear Bumper LH	1
33	Shim-Joint, Front Bumper	2
34	Kit-Absorber, Rear Bumper	2
35	Bolt-with Washer Fix Shock Absorber to Floor	6
36	Nut-Cup, Fix Shock Absorber to Floor	6
37	Washer-Plain, Fix Shock Absorber to Floor	6
38	Washer-Lock, Fix Shock Absorber to Floor	6
39	Nut-Hex, Fix Shock Absorber to Joint	4
40	Assy-Panel Tail Gate Outer	1
41	Assy-Tail Gate Hinge	2
42	Shim-Adjusting Rail Gate Hinge	4
43	Shim-Adjusting Tail Gate Hinge	4
44	Screw-Machine M8	4
45	Screw-Machine M8	4
46	Washer-Tooth M8	4
47	Set-Stay Tail Gate RH (strut)	1
48	Set-Stay Tail Gate LH (strut)	1
49	Screw-Machine	6
50	Assy-Tail Gate Lock	1
51	Screw-Machine M6	2
52	Assy-Striker Tail Gate Lock	1
53	Screw-Machine M6	2
54	Cylinder-Lock Tail Gate	1
55	Clip-Cylinder	1
56	Assy-Down Stopper Tail Gate	2
57	Screw-Machine M5	4
58	Bumper-Rubber Tail Gate	2
59	Screw-Machine	4
60	Grommet-Heater	2
61	Assy-Trim Tail Gate Black	1
62	Weatherstrip-Tail Gate Inner	1
63	Clip-Trim	10
64	Assy-Air Spoiler	1
65	Washer-Plain	8
66	Sealing-Air Spoiler	2
67	Cushion-Air Spoiler	2
68	Nut-Flange	6
69	Washer	6
70	Plug	6
71	Nut-Flange M6	6
72	Plug-Nylon	5

METRIC CUSTOMARY-UNIT EQUIVALENTS

Multiply	by	to get:	Multiply	by	to get:

LINEAR
inches	X 25.4	= millimeters (mm)	X 0.03937	= inches
miles	X 1.6093	= kilometers (km)	X 0.6214	= miles
inches	X 2.54	= centimeters (cm)	X 0.3937	= inches

AREA
| inches^2 | X 645.16 | = millimeters^2 (mm^2) | X 0.00155 | = inches^2 |
| inches^2 | X 6.452 | = centimeters^2 (cm^2) | X 0.155 | = inches^2 |

VOLUME
| quarts | X 0.94635 | = liters (l) | X 1.0567 | = quarts |
| fluid oz | X 29.57 | = milliliters (ml) | X 0.03381 | = fluid oz |

MASS
pounds (av)	X 0.4536	= kilograms (kg)	X 2.2046	= pounds (av)
tons (2000 lb)	X 907.18	= kilograms (kg)	X 0.001102	= tons (2000 lb)
tons (2000 lb)	X 0.90718	= metric tons (t)	X 1.1023	= tons (2000 lb)

FORCE
| pounds—f (av) | X 4.448 | = newtons (N) | X 0.2248 | = pounds—f (av) |
| kilograms—f | X 9.807 | = newtons (N) | X 0.10197 | = kilograms—f |

TEMPERATURE
Degrees Celsius (C) = 5/9 (F - 32)   Degrees Fahrenheit (F) = 9/5C + 32

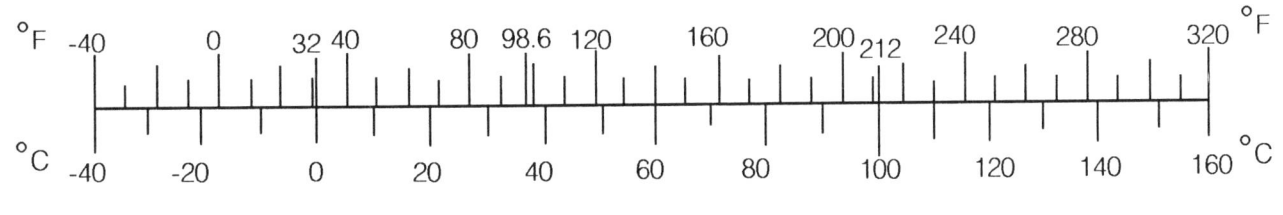

°F -40   0   32 40   80 98.6 120   160   200 212 240   280   320 °F
°C -40 -20   0   20   40   60   80   100   120   140   160 °C

ENERGY OR WORK
| foot-pounds | X 1.3558 | = joules (J) | X 0.7376 | = foot-pounds |

FUEL ECONOMY & FUEL CONSUMPTION
| miles per gal | X 0.42514 | = kilometers/liter (km/l) | X 2.3522 | = miles/gal |

Note:
235.2/(mi/gal) = liters/100km
235.2/(liters/100km) = mi/gal

PRESSURE OR STRESS
inches Hg (60F)	X 3.337	= kilopascals (kPa)	X 0.2961	= inches Hg
pounds/sq in.	X 6.895	= kilopascals (kPa)	X 0.145	= pounds/sq in.
pounds/sq ft	X 47.88	= pascals (Pa)	X 0.02088	= pounds/sq ft

POWER
| horsepower | X 0.746 | = kilowatts (kW) | X 1.34 | = horsepower |

TORQUE
pound-inches	X 0.11298	= newton-meters (N-m)	X 8.851	= pound-inches
pound-feet	X 1.3558	= newton-meters (N-m)	X 0.7376	= pound-feet
pound-inches	X 0.0115	= kilogram-meters (Kg-M)	X 87	= pound-inches
pound-feet	X 0.138	= kilogram-meters (Kg-M)	X 7.25	= pound-feet

VELOCITY
| miles/hour | X 1.6093 | = kilometers/hour (km/h) | X 0.6214 | = miles/hour |

Index

A

A-pillar-trim, remove 70-71
A/C hoses & lines, break loose 24
Accelerator linkage 24, 140
Accident damaged 19
Acme 54
Acrylic enamel 54
Acrylic lacquer 53-54
Air cleaner
  install 184
  remove 24
Air conditioner 74, 140-141
Air-cleaner housing, restore 184
Air-conditioning compressor 24
Air-extractor grilles, install 180
Alkyd enamel 54
Antenna, install 154
Antenna lead 147
Antenna-mast, repair 153-154
Anti-sway bar 82
Arm rests, replace 167
Armor All 38, 50
Armor, Ida Grace 4
Armor, Karen 4
Authorized Service Manual 10
  See also Service Manual
Auto Rust Doctors 41, 43-44
Automatic transmission 27-28
  maintenance 27
  shift mechanism 144
  troubleshooting 22
Auto Upholstery Handbook 11

B

Ball joints 84, 87
Bamper 65
Bathurst, Inc. 120
Battery shut-off switch 119-120
Battery tray 38
Battery
  install 184
  remove 23
Battery-acid corrosion 38
Battery-inspection doors 178
  install 177-178
  remove 29
Bleeder taps 87
Block-sanding 12, 39-40, 53
Bob Sharp Racing 183
Body damage 11-12
Body exterior teardown 29-36
Body parts
  prepping 39
  trial fit 50
Body repair and paint 37
Bondo 40, 47
Bosch L-Jetronic fuel-injection 7
Brake backing plate, remove 105
Brake baffle 92
Brake caliper
  disassemble 85
  install 93
Brake drums 104, 113
  honing 103-104
Brake fluid 31, 113
  DOT 3 38, 113
  silicone-base 113

Brake-hose bracket 104
Brake hose 104
  connect 92
  disconnect 31, 82
Brake master cylinder
  install 138
  remove 31
Brake rotor
  install 91-92
  remove 84
Brake shims and springs 87
Brake shoes 104
  adjust 185
  reassemble 114
Brake system, bleed 185
Brakes 77
  bleed 185
  disassemble 103
  rear 103, 112-114
Brazing 43
Brillo pads 49
Brooke Army Medical Center 5
Brooks, Jerry 4
Buffing 59
Bullen, Anita 4
Bullen, Ross 4
Bumper filler panels, install 177
Bumpers, brackets 49
  cleaning 49
  early-style 48
  federal 49
  install 188-189
  late 260Z & 280Z 50
  reassemble 50
  replate 48-49
  rubber Strips 49

C

C-pillar trim, install 181
Car, jack up 25
Cargo straps 156
Carpet padding, replace 158
Carpets 156
  remove 62
  replace 158
Castano, Mike 4
Cat's Whisker 65, 166
Catalyzed paint 55
  pot life 55
Caulking 42
Chalking 54
Charts
  Metric Customary-Unit Equivalents 237
  Standard Bolt-Torque Specifications 158
Choke cable, install 146-147
Cigarette lighter 122, 125
Clear-coat 55
Clock 124
Clutch 77
  remove 31
Clutch cylinder
  bleed 185
  install 138
  purge 24
Clutch disc, inspect 27
Coil springs, remove 84-85

Coil-spring compressor 85
Coil, remove 30
Collector-car insurance 201-202
Color coat 58
Color-sanding 17, 53-54, 58-59
Compression check 21-22
Concours points 15
Condon & Skelly 202
Console
  install 144, 147
  recondition 144
  remove 79
Control arms 83-84, 99
Control-arm bushings 103, 108-109
Control-arm spindle 102, 109
Coolant 182
Counterfeits 118
Cowl 40
Cowl drains, install 138
Cowl-drain hoses 78
Cowl finisher
  install 179
  remove 34
Crash pad, replace 121
CRC penetrating oil 49

D

Daigh, David 4
Dash bezel, refinish 143
Data plate
  install 190
  remove 63
DAU 82 DelGLo Clear 87
Decals 16
Deck molding 68
Deck-front trim 146
Defroster ducts 122, 126, 141
Degreasing 22
DelGlo Clear Top Coat 55
Deltron 55
DeVilbiss EGA Finger Gun 42
Differential mounting 99
Differential torque arrester 100, 111
Differential transmission, lubricant 184
Differential-limiter strap. See Differential torque arrester.
Differential-mounting members 101-102
Ditzler 330 38, 54
  acrylic-enamel-system 53
  CX-330 Wax and Grease Remover 72
  DPE1202 Ferrochrome Primer-Sealer 46
  DPE1338 Satin Prime 46
  Duracryl DDL 2862 Argent 174
  Epoxy Chromate Primer 40
  Kondar DZ3/7 40
  Low Gloss Black 19 123, 180
  Red-Cap Spot Putty 47
Ditzo wax-and-grease remover 51
Dollying 53
Dome light, install 156
Dome-light wires 119
Donovan, Tim 4
Door-bottom weatherstrip 164
Door Ease 165

Door front sealing rubber 162-163
Door glass 159
Door handle, install 160-161
Door hinges 65, 164
Door jambs, paint 56
Door-jamb finisher 63
Door latch 161
Door-latch assembly, install 161
Door-latch handle 161
Door-latch striker 63, 161
Door-lock cylinder 66, 160
Door moisture barrier 165-166
Door panels 62-63
Door-sill plate, remove 63
Door-sill trimmer, remove 63
Door stainless-steel outer molding 163-164
Door-trim panel
  install 166-167
  remove 62
  restore 166-167
Door weatherstrip
  install 135-136
  remove 65, 72
Door window frame 162
Door-window whisker strip 65, 166
Doors
  adjust 164
  assemble 160
  rear sealing rubber 163
  rehang 164
  remove 64-65
  restore 159
Drip-channel molding, install 163
Drive shafts 101. See also Halfshafts
  disconnect 25
  install 170
  U-joints 170
Drums, install 114
Dry sandpaper 38
Dumdum 42
DuPont
  Acrylic-enamel-system 53
  Duco 53
  Imron 54
Duro Aluminum Jelly 136
DX 330 Cleaner 47
DX 685 Flattening Agent 87
DX-330 123
Dyment Distributing Service 5
DZ40 51

E

Eastwood Hi-Temp Stainless Steel Coating 87
Electric fuel pump 32, 173
Electrical components
  disconnect 24
  replace 118
  suppliers 117
Electrical malfunctions 115
Electrical multi-tester 116
Electrical troubleshooting 116
Electrical wiring 115
Eliminator 51
Emblems, restore 179-180
Enamel paint system 54
Enamel reducer 57

238

Index

Engine
  install 170-171
  rebuild 10
  remove 21, 26-27
  restore 28
Engine compartment
  assembly 181
  detailing 181
  painting 40
  refinishing 38
Engine-compartment harness 79, 119-120
Engine identification 203
Engine mounts 25, 28, 30, 171
Engine-mount brackets, install 170
Engine-mount cushions, replace 29
Epoxy 54
Exhaust leak 194
Exhaust system
  install 183
  remove 26
  rusted-out 28
Exhaust-header pipe 24, 26, 182
Exterior colors 60

F

Fan shroud, install 182
Fan storage 24
Fan 24, 181
Fasteners 96-97
Feather-fill 51
Fender inner gasket, install 175
Fender lower extension, install 177
Fender rust 37
Fender seal, remove 35
Fender splash protectors, remove 35
Fender trim, install 181
Fender, mount 35, 176
Fiber Glass Evercoat Feather Fill 40
Fiberglass body parts 47
Filler 39
Finch, Richard 43
Fire extinguisher 43
Firewall insulator 137
  install 139-140
  remove 77-78
Fittings, grease 186
Five-speed manual transmission 16
Flaming River 120
Flexplate-to-converter bolts 27-28
Floor insulation 138
Floorpan trim 45
Flywheel, check 27
Frame-up restoration 16-17
Frame-rail repair kit 43
Front apron
  install 177
  remove 35
Front bumper 30
Front struts, install 90
Front suspension 81
  install 88, 90
  rebuild 87
Front-suspension crossmember 82
Fuel filler 31, 171
Fuel-filler bib 173
Fuel-filler box, repair 46
Fuel-filler door
  install 173
  remove 32
  restrictor 171
  tube, disconnect 32
Fuel-filler neck 173
Fuel-filter bracket 182
Fuel-gauge sender 171, 173
Fuel lines 170
Fuel pump, leaks 193
Fuel tank
  drain 24
  install 173
  remove 31-32
  slush 172-173
Fuller-O'Brien slushing compound 172

Fusible link 118

G

Gasoline seepage 193-194
Gauges
  install 124-125
  refurbish 123-124
Gearshift knob, install 147
Glass Wax 123
Glass-run channel, new 159
Glazing putty 52
Gloss coat 58
Glove box 121, 141
Glove-box door, remove 74
Goldblatt, Joe 4
Grab handle 62
Grease Relief 61
Grille wiring harness, unplug 30
Grille
  install 188
  remove 30
  restore 187-188
Guide air intake, remove 30
Guide-coat 12, 51-53

H

Halfshafts 112
  R180 type 101
  R200 type 101
  U-joints 101, 112
Hammer-and-dolly work 39
Hatch 71, 169
Hatch air vents, install 168
Hatch dovetails, install 161, 168
Hatch finisher, install 73, 168-169
Hatch glass
  install 132
  remove 72-73
Hatch hinges, install 169
Hatch-jamb hardware, install 169
Hatch latch 168
Hatch struts 71, 72, 169
Hatch trim 73, 181
Hatch ventilation exits 73
Hatch weatherstrip 72, 167-168
Hatch-window defroster leads 72, 119, 170
Hazard-flasher switch 124
Header trim 70-71, 128-129
Headlight bezel 36, 177
Headlight bucket, install 176
Headlight bulb, failure 193
Headlight cover 15
Headlight-mounting hardware, install 177
Headlight wiring, connect 178
Headliner 70-71, 127-128
Heat-shrink tubing 117
Heater 74, 76 140
Heater controls, restore 126
Heater hoses, break loose 24
Hess, Bob 4, 43-44
High-build primer/surfacer 40
High-idle problems 194-195
High-pressure water washer 22
Hitachi/SU carburetors 7
Hofer, Larry 11, 47
Hog rings 148
Hog-ring pliers 150
Honsowetz, Frank 4-5, 11, 183
Hood 23, 186-187
Hood bumpers 30, 34, 186
Hood hinges 30, 186
Hood latch, remove 31
Hood-latch cable, lubricate 145
Hood-support rod 30, 182
Hood-support-rod clip, repair 34
Hood trim, install 180
Hood vent 15
Hood weatherstrip, remove 29
Horns, install 182
Horn cushion 143

Hoses, install 182
How to Modify Your Nissan/Datsun OHC Engine 5, 11, 183
How to Rebuild Your Nissan/Datsun OHC Engine 5-6, 11, 21, 27
Humble, Benita 11
Humble, Brian 4
Humble, Cordy 4
Humble, Holly 4
Humble, Scott 4
Humble, Teri 4
Hydraulic systems, bleed 185

I

Identification plate 203
Ignition switch 75, 142
Inomoto, Yoshihiro 4, 9
Inside door latch, remove 66
Instrument panel 121, 141, 143
Instrument-panel finisher 126
Insulators, restore 137
Insurance 201
Interior colors 60
Interior panels 155
Interior restoration 121, 126
Interior trim 61, 139
Interior-light switches, install 147
Inventory 11
ISO bolt grades 97

J

J.C. Taylor, Inc. 202
J.C. Whitney & Co. 120
Jack stands 25
Jack-stowage lid 156

K

Kick panels 67, 156, 158
Kit cars 18-19
Klix wax-and-grease remover 51
Korkes, Eddie 4, 205

L

Lacquer paint system 53-54
Leiker, Janet 4
License-plate light 175
License-plate-light housing, 32-33, 174-175
Liquid Ebony 180
Listing 148, 150
Lock cylinder, install 168
Loom tape 117
Lower control arms 87
Lucas 120
Luggage tie-down straps 61

M

MacKenzie, Neil 4
MacPherson struts 82, 90
  install 109-110
  rebuild 85
  remove 83
Marker lights, remove 36
Masking 56
MasterVac brake booster 24, 138
Mendivel, Ruben 4
Metric Customary-Units Equivalents 237
Miller, Denis 4
Monroe, Tom 4-5, 11, 13, 43
Motorsport Auto 144, 183
MVSS plate 203

N

Nason 54
Never-Sags 149
Nissan competition parts 11
Nissan Motorsports 183
Nitrocellulose lacquer 53-54
Non-sanding primer 46
Non-sanding sealer 57

O

Odometer-reset knob 125
Oil leaks 22
Oil-pressure gauge and sender 197
Old undercoating 41
Olson, Cameron 4
Open-coat sandpaper 39, 51
Options 16
Orange peel 52-53
Outside door latch, remove 66
Outside mirror, install 160
Over-restoration 14

P

Paint 17
  mix 57
Paint & Body Handbook 11, 47
Paint-code decal 42
Paint-code label 203
Paint preparation 38
Paint system, select 53
Painting 42, 55, 59
Panel-light rheostat 122, 125
Park-and-turn-signal assembly 36
Parking brake 80, 145
Parking-brake cable, install 114
Parking-brake-equalizer bracket and linkage 145
Parking-brake-lever boot 146
Parts & Services 204
Parts books 10
Parts car 18
Parts Illustrations
  Body Side Trim & Side Window 234
  Brake & Clutch Pedal 218
  Brake Piping (From July '72) 217
  Brake Piping (Up to June '72) 216
  Door Lock, Window Regulator & Door Handle 222, 229, 235
  Emission Control Device 206
  Engine Mounting 208-209
  Exhaust Tube & Muffler (Up to July 1973) 205
  Floor Console, Finisher & Ash Tray 227-228, 232
  Floor Trim, Insulator & Rear Wheel House Trim 221, 233
  Front Brake (Disc Brake) 214
  Front Fender & Hood 220, 227
  Front Suspension (Strut & Shock Absorber) 211
  Fuel Piping 210
  Fuel Tank 207
  Hand Brake & Hand Brake Cable 213
  Master Vac & Vac Hose 219
  Radiator Grille, Front Bumper & Over Rider 226, 231
  Rear Brake (Drum Brake) 215
  Rear Suspension 212
  Seat & Slide (Type 1 Adjuster Seat) 224
  Tail Gate Panel, Trim, Lock & Rear Bumper 223, 230, 236
Parts, used 17-18
Pedal, remove 77
Pedal-bracket assembly 136, 138
Photos 10, 12
Pilot bushing, check 27
Pinhole rust 43
Pirelli webbing 149
Plastic interior finishers 67-68
Polyester filler 52

Polyester surfacer 51
Postal, Ray 4
Primer 51
  catalyzed 40
Primer/surfacer 51-52
Priming 42
Project planning 10
Propeller shaft, U-joints 112

Q

Q-PADS 138
Quarter-trim panels 68, 155
Quarter window
  install 134
  remove 69
  restore 133-134
Quarter-window trim 155

R

R-M 54
Rack stopper 89
Radiator
  disconnect 23
  install 181
  refinish 181
  upgrading 181
Radio/stereo tape, remove 121-122, 147
Rear finisher
  install 175
  remove 32-33
  restore 173-174
Rear hub, remove 104-105
Rear-hub bearing, replace 105
Rear-seat attachments, 2+2 157
Rear suspension 99
  assemble 107-108
  refinish 106-107
Rear trim panel, install 156
Rear-window defroster 156
Rearview mirror 132, 69-70
Recalls 193
Repair panels 46-47
Restoration 6, 14, 16
Retaining rings 97
Reusable plastic rivets 32
Richmond, John 4
Rubber plugs, install 189-190
Rust 12, 37, 41

S

S.O.S. pads 49
Salvage yards 18
Salz, Bob 4
Sandblasting bodywork 37
Schlegel Round-up 180
Schlegel Strip 65, 166
Sealing 42
Seats
  assemble 152
  install 158
  disassemble 148
  recover 149
  remove 61
Seat back 150-151
Seat-back cover, install 151
Seat belts 61, 157
Seat-belt warning 149
Seat cushion 148-149
Seat frame 148
Selector-range lever, disconnect 25
Self-control 10
Serial number 203
Service Manual 17, 45, 82, 84, 103, 117, 120

Shift lever, remove 25
Shift-lever boot 144
Shock cartridges, install 110
Shock-tower trim, install 145-146
Shoulder-belt retractors 157
Side-cowl trim panel 64, 155
Side-marker lights, install 179
Side-rail trim 129-130
Silicone-base brake fluid 38
Sill trim 135-136
Sinner, George 4
Small-parts storage 13
Smith, Greg 4
Spare tire 156
Speakers 154
Speedometer 122-124
Speedometer cable, disconnect 75
Spindle bushings, replace 108
Spindle lock bolt 102-103, 109
Splash shield, unbolt 36
Spot putty 39, 51
Spraygun, Binks 69 42
Springs, install 90, 110
Stabilizer bar
  front 91, 112
  rear 99
  remove 81
Stabilizer-bar link 82
Staged restoration 16
Standard transmission 27
Standard-transmission shift lever, install 144
Starter motor, remove 27
Steering arm, remove 83
Steering column 75, 92-93, 141
  assemble 95
Steering column-and-pedal-support bracket 76. See also Pedal-support bracket
Steering-column combination switch 75
Steering-column jacket 74
Steering-column-tube clamp 76
Steering coupler 76, 98
Steering gear 83, 88-89
Steering-shaft U-joints 95
Steering wheel 75
  install 143
  remove 77
  restore 143
Step-plate, remove 63
Storage 9, 12-14, 23
Stowage boxes 68, 156
Strut cartridges, replace 85
Strut mounts 99
Strut rods 90-91
Strut-tower covers, install 146, 157, 182
Stub axle 104
SU carburetor 25
Sunvisors
  install 132
  remove 69-70
Suspension-and-differential assembly 99-100
Suspension crossmember, remove 82-83, 87, 90
Synthetic enamel 54

T

Tachometer 122-124
Tack coat 58
Tack-weld new panels 45
Tacking off 57
Taillight weatherstrip 48
Taillights 152-153
  install 153
  disassemble 47
  remove 33
  restore 46-48

Tarter, Howard 4
Taylor, Don 11, 47, 61
Taylor, Rod 4
Tech Bulletins
  Clutch and Brake-Pedal Return Spring 199
  Clutch Master-Cylinder 198
  Clutch Master-Cylinder Valve 195
  Defroster-Wire Alignment 196
  Drive-shaft U-joints 197
  Dynamic-Damper Modification Kit 195
  Engine-Compartment Changes 199
  Engine-Mounting-Insulator Bolts 195
  Front Carpet Fasteners 196
  Front-Fender Splash Protector 199
  Hand-Brake Clevis 199
  Heat-Vent-Door Control Cables 196
  Ignition-Interlock System 197-198
  Inner-Fender Protectors 197
  Modification of Drive Shafts (halfshafts) 199
  Noise Damper For Differential 198
  Noise-Insulating Washer 196
  Noise-Insulating Washer, Elimination of 196
  Padded Crash-Pad Repair 198
  Rear-Suspension Control-Arm Bushing 199
  Rear-Wheel Brakes 196
  Rear-Window-Defroster Switch 197
  Rear-Suspension Control-Arm Bushing 198
  Seat-belt Holder 196
  Solid-Wire Choke Cables 196
  Speedometer-Cable 1974 Models 197
  Taillight-Bulb Access Panels 197
  280Z Air-Cleaner-Duct Extension 199
  Water-Temperature And Oil-Pressure Gauge 196
  Z Competition Hood Vent 197
Testors 'Namel 123
Thinner 57
3M body caulk 46
3M body shutz 46
3M joint & seam sealer 41
Throttle cable 147
Tierods 89-90
Transmission identification 203
Transmission jack 100, 111
Transmission mount 26, 170
Transmission output-shaft splines 170
Transmission
  drain 25
  install 170-171
  remove 21
  rebuild 27
Transmission-fluid level, check 185
Transmission-tunnel coverings, make 138
Transmission-tunnel jute pad 139
Trim Handbook 61
Trim work 11
Triolo, Joe 4
Trip-odometer reset cable
  install 125
  remove 122
Trouble light 30, 182
Tunnel upholstery, make 138
Turn and park lights, install 177
20 Mule Team Borax 61

U

Undercoating 42
Underpan, paint 100
  rust 41
Unmasking 59
Urethane paint system 54

V

Vapor canister, install 153, 155
Vapor lines 170
Vapor-recovery canister 72, 173
Vehicle identification number 124, 190, 203
Vent elbows, install 182
Video recorder 10
Vinyl fabric 68-69
Vise-Grips 45

W

Wax-and-grease remover 38-39, 40, 51, 56
WD-40 49, 125
Weatherstrip, remove 63
Welder's Handbook 43
Wet look 55
Wet-or-dry paper 38
Wheel bearings, install 91
Wheel covers 191
Wheel cylinders 104, 113
Window-guide channel 160
Wheel-house trim, install 146
Wheels
  aluminum 191
  steel 190-191
Wheels, restore 190-191
Window assembly, install 161-162
Window frame
  install 161-162
  readjust 165
Window guide rails 162
Window regulator
  install 160
  remove 65-66
Window-regulator crank, install 167
Window-regulator handle 62
Window slats 16
Window-stabilizing roller 163
Window washer, install 183
Windshield
  install 130-131
  remove 70-71
Windshield trim 70, 131
Windshield-reservoir, install 182
Windshield-washer hoses, remove 30
Windshield-washer nozzles 182
Windshield-wiper arms, install 183
Windshield-wiper motor
  install 178-179
  remove 34
Windshield-wiper linkage 178
Wiper pivots, remove 34
Wiper-pivot nipples 179
Wire color coding 116-117, 120
Wiring diagrams 116
Wiring harness 115, 124
  install 119
  remove 78
  restore 117
  tracer 117
Wrinkles 151

Z

Z accessory products 183, 204
Z Club of America 202
Z-car history 6